EMPIRES OF LABOR

From the seventeenth century to the First World War, both free and unfree labor were essential for building an empire. This ambitious study examines the relationship between capitalism and coercion across the British, French and Russian empires throughout centuries of economic transformation. Overturning conventional explanations of serfdom, slavery, indentured migration and wage labor, Alessandro Stanziani demonstrates the dominance of aristocratic capitalism across Europe and Eurasia until the end of the nineteenth century. He links the Industrial Revolution, the Great Divergence and the Great Transformation into a single narrative in which the coercion and emancipation of labor are crucial steps. Stanziani argues that if the modern state is now beset with labor inequalities and tensions surrounding mobility, it is not because Western values have been hijacked but because they were built on empire, labor and coercion.

ALESSANDRO STANZIANI is Professor of Global History at the École des hautes études en sciences sociales (EHESS) and Senior Researcher at the CNRS. He is the author of *Earth Capital: The Long History of Capitalism and Its Aftermath*.

EMPIRES OF LABOR

Coercion and the Making of the Modern World

ALESSANDRO STANZIANI

Ecole des Hautes Etudes en Sciences Sociales (EHESS) And CNRS

Shaftesbury Road, Cambridge CB2 8EA, United Kingdom

One Liberty Plaza, 20th Floor, New York, NY 10006, USA

477 Williamstown Road, Port Melbourne, VIC 3207, Australia

314–321, 3rd Floor, Plot 3, Splendor Forum, Jasola District Centre,
New Delhi – 110025, India

103 Penang Road, #05–06/07, Visioncrest Commercial, Singapore 238467

Cambridge University Press is part of Cambridge University Press & Assessment,
a department of the University of Cambridge.

We share the University's mission to contribute to society through the pursuit of
education, learning and research at the highest international levels of excellence.

www.cambridge.org
Information on this title: www.cambridge.org/9781009608572

DOI: 10.1017/9781009608602

© Alessandro Stanziani 2026

This publication is in copyright. Subject to statutory exception and to the provisions
of relevant collective licensing agreements, no reproduction of any part may take
place without the written permission of Cambridge University Press & Assessment.

When citing this work, please include a reference to the DOI 10.1017/9781009608602

First published 2026

Cover image: African American slaves on a sugar cane plantation, woodcut, 1885/ZU_09/
DigitalVision Vectors/Getty Images

A catalogue record for this publication is available from the British Library

*A Cataloging-in-Publication data record for this book is available from the
Library of Congress*

ISBN 978-1-009-60859-6 Hardback
ISBN 978-1-009-60857-2 Paperback

Cambridge University Press & Assessment has no responsibility for the persistence
or accuracy of URLs for external or third-party internet websites referred to in this
publication and does not guarantee that any content on such websites is, or will
remain, accurate or appropriate.

For EU product safety concerns, contact us at Calle de José Abascal, 56, 1°, 28003 Madrid,
Spain, or email eugpsr@cambridge.org

CONTENTS

List of Tables   *page* viii
Acknowledgments   ix

Introduction   1

Scope and Main Argument   1
Book Outline   2
Scales Matter: Global Labor History or Global Microhistory?   10
Empires   15
Categories in Space and Time: Capitalism and Coercion   21
Resistance versus Agency?   25
Law: A Form of Coercion or Resistance?   31

PART I   **Labor Rules and Colonization**

1   The Russian Way: Peasants, Landowners and the Empire   37

Peasant-Soldiers   37
Slaves in Russia   39
Empire-Building and the Demarcation of Serfdom   43
Conclusion: Borderlands and Labor   53

2   The British Empire: Coercion in the Name of Freedom   55

Mainland Labor Rules: Masters, Servants, Apprentices and the Poor   55
British Labor Institutions across the Atlantic   61
Why Slavery?   67
Labor Rules in Eurasia: British India   75
Conclusion: Labor Rules in the British Empire   84

3   The French Touch: Protecting Men in Urban Industry, Excluding Rural People, Women and Colonies   87

Continental Institutions: City versus Country   87
Work Rules in Atlantic France: The Contract of Employment   92
The King's Daughters: Bonded Women across the Atlantic   100
The Rise of Slavery   104
Conclusion Part I: Work Rules and Empire Building   114

PART II The Economics of Bondage

4 The Russian Empire and the Economic Dynamics of Serfdom 121

Economic Growth under Serfdom: The Eighteenth Century 121
The Decline of the Russian Economy, First Half of the Nineteenth Century 126
Reasons for Decline: Serfdom, the Invasion of Ukraine and the Great Divergence 128

5 Labor and the British Industrial Revolution 136

The Role of Labor in the Agriculture and Industrial Revolutions 136
Peasants into Proletarians or Peasant-Workers? 143
Labor Time and Wages 145

6 International Trade, Slavery and the Industrial Revolution 150

The Slave Trade 151
The Sugar Contribution 154
The Triangular Trade and the African Contribution 160
From Sugar to Cotton: Britain and US Industrialization 164
Summary 167

7 With or without You: France and the Empire of Sugar 169

The Role of Slavery 173
Conclusion 181

PART III Labor Empires under Attack: From Abolition to the Great Transformation, 1840–1918

8 Who Is the True Slave? 185

British Utilitarianism 185
French Enlightenment and Abolitionism 190
Abolition and Capitalism in the First Half of the Nineteenth Century 195
British Abolitionism in Practice: The Case of India and the Indian Ocean 203
From Paternalism to 1848: The Long Road of Slavery in the French Empire 209
Conclusion 216

9 The Aristocratic Abolition of Serfdom in Russia 219

Preparing for Abolition 219
After Abolition: Continuities and Changes 221
The Impact of the Abolition of Serfdom on the Empire 227

10 Abolition in the United States and the Great
    Transformation   235
    The Importance of Slavery to American Capitalism   235
    Shifting Borders: Migrants, Employees, Slaves, Apprentices   240

11 Neo-colonialism in the Age of the Welfare State   246
    The Welfare State and the Great Transformation   246
    Occupying Africa: A By-Product of the Great Transformation   253
    Conclusion Part III   269

    General Conclusion and Extrapolations   271

    Bibliography   280
    Index   345

TABLES

5.1 British annual growth rates of output, output per worker and productivity   *page* 149
6.1 Cotton as a percentage of overall British exports   166
7.1 The British and French sugar trades compared, 1775 (000 cwt)   180
9.1 Average annual state income and expenditure by groups of provinces in Russia in 1879–1881 (kopecks per capita)   229

ACKNOWLEDGMENTS

This book took me about twelve years to complete after the first version, which means that I devoted about twenty years to it. During all these long years, many colleagues, friends, archivists and students have helped me. It would be impossible to remember them all, but I would like to mention at least some of them, starting with archivists in Moscow, St Petersburg, Paris, Kew, Aix-en-Provence, Mauritius and Reunion Island, Delhi, Montreal, New York and Brazzaville. Among the colleagues and friends who have helped over the years with suggestions, discussions and critiques, special thanks go to: at Stanford, Richard Roberts and Nancy Kolmann; at New York University, Jane Burbank, Frederik Cooper and Yanni Kotsonis; at Princeton, Ekaterina Pravilova, Jeremy Adelman and Shek Garon; at Chicago, Kenneth Pomeranz; at the European Institute in Florence, Giorgio Riello; at the London School of Economics, Tirthankar Roy; in Delhi, Prabhu Mohapatra, Veena Naregal, Chitra Joshi and Raha Behal; at McGill, Gwyn Campbell; at Toronto, Martin Klein; Boris Kolonitsky in St Petersburg; in Paris, Gilles Postel-Vinay, Mathieu Arnoux, Jerôme Bourdieu, Claude Markovits, Christian Lamouroux, Thomas Piketty, the French Association of Labor History and its steering committee, especially Corine Maitte.

A very special thanks to Michael Watson, my editor in Cambridge, who has always supported me throughout these years, never losing faith in my work during its many versions and then the refereeing process (thanks to the anonymous referees!), patiently tolerating "my" English in the earlier versions.

Introduction

Scope and Main Argument

This book aims to explain the role that labor and laboring people played in the construction of empires and their transmutation between the mid sixteenth century and the First World War.[1] This period saw the emergence of major empires in which labor, and forced labor in particular, shaped political and social hierarchies and determined economic dynamics. Without forgetting African and Asian empires, this book will focus on three empires and their use of labor: French, Anglo-American and Russian. It will be argued that during the period mentioned, the legal and economic tools of coercion, instead of following one another, as in conventional arguments in history, sociology and economics, actually overlapped. In fact, contrary to a view held widely from the nineteenth century up to the present historiography, not only in Russia, but also in Europe, there was no real opposition between pre-modern and capitalist societies, between landowners and slave masters (or serfs), on the one hand, and industrial and merchant capitalists, on the other, but a strong convergence of viewpoints and interests. Aristocratic capitalism determined the absence of rights not only for slaves and serfs, but also for workers. From this point of view, the Western European colonies and the Russian Empire were not the negation of Western values and notions of labor and (un)freedom, but an extreme variation on them. These political and institutional contexts made labor cheap, and explain why, until the Second Industrial Revolution in Western Europe (i.e., after the 1870s), and much later in agriculture and elsewhere in the world, economic growth was labor-intensive and not capital-intensive, contrary to what liberal and Marxist historiographies assert. Coercion was indeed profitable. Colonialism, slavery in the American and Asian colonies and serfdom

---

[1] Linda Colley, "What Is Imperial History?," in David Cannadine, ed., *What Is History Now?* (London: Palgrave MacMillan, 2002): 132–147; John Darwin, *After Tamerlane: The Rise and Fall of Global Empires, 1400–2000* (London: Penguin Book, 2007); Ann Laura Stoler, Carole McGranahan, Peter Perdu, eds., *Imperial Formations* (New York: School for Advanced Research Press, 2007); Jürgen Osterhammel, *Colonialism: A Theoretical Overview* (Princeton: Markus Wiener, 2005); Jane Burbank, Frederick Cooper, *Empires: A World History* (Princeton: Princeton University Press, 2010).

in the Russian Empire all yielded profits, albeit with different products depending on the period (sugar, cotton, wheat). The abolition of slavery and serfdom was therefore not driven by economic imperatives, but by political ones. Abolitionist movements and the defense of workers in Europe contributed to this. These changes drove up labor costs and encouraged the concentration and mechanization of industrial production in Western Europe. At the turn of the nineteenth and twentieth centuries, the alliance between capitalists and agrarians came to an end; stock markets took precedence over agricultural rents, and financial-industrial capitalism over agrarian-commercial capitalism. Against this backdrop, labor standards and practices in Europe and the colonies diverged. While European labor was increasingly protected, in the colonies labor rules remained highly repressive, with legal inequalities between masters and workers, and a capital-poor, labor-intensive economy. Neocolonialism and the scramble for Africa reflected this global transformation. An East–West divide was added: In Russia, the abolition of serfdom gave rise to a society where coercion through labor and the absence of rights for free workers were still in place. The revolution was a reaction against the Second Industrial Revolution and the intensification of capital, but it ultimately gave rise to a regime where large factories coexisted with the persistence of forced labor and empire.

Book Outline

The chapters in Part I cover the main features of labor contracts and institutions in Russia, Great Britain, France and their colonies. In all these cases, it will be shown that legal rules supported coercion and that continental and colonial institutions reinforced each other: the Masters and Servants Acts and other provisions in Britain, indentures and then slavery in its colonies; forms of labor contract in France and, again, indentures and slavery in the colonial world; the multiple forms of colonization, slavery and serfdom in the Russian Empire. Over the decades, the ongoing debate among historians of these regions has focused on the question of whether labor institutions on the continent and in the colonies were linked. Most interpretations of British and French history have argued that increasing freedom on the Continent was opposed to increasing slavery in the colonies.[2] A more recent historiography has focused on the limitations of workers' rights in Britain itself and its links with colonial labor.[3]

---

[2] Among them (many more in later chapters): Jack Greene, ed., *Exclusionary Empire: English Liberty Overseas, 1600–1900* (Cambridge: Cambridge University Press, 2010); Seymour Drescher, *Abolitions: A History of Slavery and Antislavery* (Cambridge: Cambridge University Press, 2009); Seymour Drescher, *Capitalism and Antislavery: British Mobilization in Comparative Perspective* (New York: Oxford University Press, 1987); Olivier Grenouilleau, *Les traites négrières* (Paris: Gallimard, 2004).

[3] Robert Steinfeld, *The Invention of Free Labor: The Employment Relation in English and American Law and Culture, 1350–1870* (Chapel Hill: University of North Carolina

This book will follow this last line of reasoning, demonstrating that the first white migration to the Americas, during the seventeenth century, was based on existing contracts on the continent (master and servant laws for Great Britain, domesticity, rural workers and sailors for France). Coercion was extended and radicalized in the colonies. I will show how the legal and social conditions of indentured migrants and slaves evolved in symbiosis, as one could not be defined without the other.

These relationships prompt us to take a fresh look at Eastern Europe and Russia. As I have already studied the institutions of serfdom elsewhere,[4] here (Part I), I will summarize the main conclusions while developing new concerns, principally the relationship between serfdom and Russian imperial expansion. It will be shown that, on the one hand, Russian serfdom was much further removed from slavery than is generally assumed, while, on the other hand, less harsh conditions were adopted in the Russian colonies than in Central Russia. This solution pitted Russia against the empires of Western Europe, where workers' working conditions were worse in the colonies than on the continent.

Despite these differences, on both sides of the Urals, in Western Europe and Russia, the institutions set up to control peasant mobility sought to link land ownership to labor-intensive economic growth. The unequal distribution of political and legal rights was crucial to achieving this goal. It was this world that Arno Mayer had in mind when he asserted that the collapse of the *ancien régime* did not occur until after the Great War.[5] Coercion favored the coexistence of capitalists, landowners and agricultural elites (sometimes competitors, sometimes allies), very often with the support of the state. Landed aristocrats, peasant-workers and rentier-capitalists dominated the social landscape in Western Europe and Russia. This balance withstood the blows of the revolutions of the late eighteenth century and 1848. The alliance between merchants, capitalists, landowners and the state made coercion even more profitable.

However, institutions and legal provisions did not necessarily serve the purpose of optimizing economic efficiency, as some economists claim;[6] on the contrary, historically, political and social power in the hands of landed and urban aristocrat-capitalists and rentiers gave rise to coercive economic institutions that made labor cheap, while reinforcing inequalities. From the mid

---

Press, 1991); Robert Steinfeld, *Coercion, Contract and Free Labor in the Nineteenth Century* (Cambridge: Cambridge University Press, 2001); Douglas Hay, Paul Craven, *Masters, Servants, and Magistrates in Britain and the Empire* (Chapel Hill: North Carolina University Press, 2005).

[4] Alessandro Stanziani, *Bondage: Labor and Rights in Eurasia, Seventeenth–Twentieth Century* (New York: Berghahn, 2014).

[5] Arno Mayer, *The Persistence of the Old Regime: Europe to the Great War* (London: Pantheon Books, 1981).

[6] For a critique of the law and economics approach: Alessandro Stanziani, *Dictionnaire historique de l'économie droit* (Paris: LGDJ, 2010).

seventeenth to the mid nineteenth century, in the West, and then in other parts of the world in Eurasia and Africa, production increased to meet the growing demand for consumer goods and income. At the time, it was labor, rather than capital or land, that underpinned this process, not only in Africa, Asia and the imperial peripheries of the European powers but also in Europe itself, including Britain.[7] Why was this so? Part II attempts to answer this question. My point of view is consistent with the so-called revisionist approach to the Industrial Revolution, which since the early 1980s has emphasized the role of labor more than that of capital during the Industrial Revolution.[8] According to this approach, proto-industrial and agricultural growth, and even the First Industrial Revolution, required more work, not less. Full-time proletarians, such as self-sufficient peasants, were rare; pluriactivity dominated everywhere: Peasants were also merchants and workers, craftsmen and sailors.[9] The disappearance of peasant economies was still a long way off; the famous privatization of communal land, the prelude to proletarianization, remained partial until the mid nineteenth century.[10] This was true in Great Britain, even more so in France, and above all in Russia and Eastern Europe. A question therefore arises: According to classical economic theories, if economic growth is based on the intensive use of one factor of production – labor – then without technical progress, productivity will decline, and growth with it. Yet empirical data show that this outcome did not actually occur. Why not?

The answer lies in the strength of the empire. Raw sugar and raw cotton produced through slave labor provided the necessary inputs for Britain (and Europe); they added profits, which were otherwise limited in Britain by high rent and labor-intensive production.[11] Sugar and slavery, along with domestic markets, played a major role in financing the First Industrial Revolution.

---

[7] Alessandro Stanziani, "Labour Regime and Labour Mobility from the Seventeenth to the Twentieth Century," in Tirthankar Roy, Giorgio Riello, eds., *Global Economic History* (London: Bloomsbury, 2018): 175–195.

[8] Nicolas Crafts, *British Economy during the Industrial Revolution* (Oxford: Clarendon Press, 1985); Jeffrey Williamson, "Why Was British Growth So Slow during the Industrial Revolution?," *Journal of Economic History*, 44, 3 (1984): 687–712; Charles Knick Harley, "British Industrialization before 1841: Evidence of Slower Growth during the Industrial Revolution," *Journal of Economic History*, 42, 2 (1982): 267–289; Charles Feinstein, Sidney Pollard, eds., *Studies in Capital Formation in the United Kingdom, 1750–1920* (Oxford: Clarendon Press, 1988).

[9] Jan de Vries, *The Industrious Revolution* (Cambridge: Cambridge University Press, 2008); Christine MacLeod, *Inventing the Industrial Revolution* (Cambridge: Cambridge University Press, 1988).

[10] Robert Allen, "Agriculture during the Industrial Revolution," in D. McCloskey, R. Floud, eds., *The Economic History of Britain since 1700*, vol. 1 (Cambridge: Cambridge University Press, 1994): 96–122.

[11] Prasannan Parthasarathi, *Why Europe Grew Rich and Asia Did Not: Global Economic Divergence, 1600–1850* (Cambridge: Cambridge University Press, 2011); Giorgio Riello,

For many years, this point has been the subject of wide-ranging debate. Some authors have insisted on the primacy of the slave trade, then of sugar and cotton production, and finally of the Industrial Revolution in terms of profits, markets and raw materials.[12] Others have taken the opposite view, asserting that the Industrial Revolution rested above all on British capital, markets and technical innovations.[13] I will show that, even if we take the lowest estimate of the net contribution of the slave trade and slavery, they nevertheless played a crucial role in British growth. However, unlike most of the historiography, I do not justify this role by the capitalization of the British economy, as Williams, Beckert and, to some extent, Pomeranz have done, each in their own way.[14] Rather, I argue that the revisionist approach to the Industrial Revolution reveals that its relationship with slavery and the slave trade was fundamental not because capital intensified and peasants were transformed into proletarians, but for the opposite reason: Capital was still expensive and labor highly in demand. Between the mid seventeenth and mid nineteenth centuries, British growth was labor-intensive, requiring additional hectares and labor to cope with an eventual decline in the rate of growth. Markets for manufactured goods were also limited due to the persistence of multiple activities and proto-industrialization; hence the importance of colonial resources and profits.

In this general framework, the timescale is important: As Burnard and Riello have shown,[15] sugar played an important role in the eighteenth century, while American cotton came much later, after the Napoleonic Wars. It didn't help

---

Thirtankar Roy, eds., *How India Clothed the World: The World of South Asian Textiles, 1500–1850* (Leiden: Brill, 2009); Giorgio Riello, *Cotton: The Fabric That Made the Modern World* (Cambridge: Cambridge University Press, 2013).

[12] Among others: Eric Williams, *Capitalism and Slavery* (Chapel Hill. University of North Carolina Press, 1944); Sven Beckert, *Empire of Cotton* (New York: Knopf, 2014). Full discussion in Part II.

[13] Roger Anstey, *The Atlantic Slave Trade and British Abolition* (London: Macmillan, 1975); Stanley Engerman, "The Slave Trade and British Capital Formation in the Eighteenth Century: A Comment on Williams Thesis," *Business History Review*, 46, 4 (1972): 430-443; Patrick O'Brien, "European Economic Development: The Contribution of the Periphery," *Economic History Review*, 35, 1 (1982): 1-18. O'Brien later changed his mind: Patrick O'Brien, Stanley Engerman, "Exports and the Growth of the British Economy from the Glorious Revolution to the Peace of Amiens," in Barbara Solow, ed., *Slavery and the Rise of the Atlantic System* (Cambridge: Cambridge University Press, 1991): 177–209.

[14] Here are a few references on this subject, which will be discussed in detail later: Joseph Inikori, *Africans and the Industrial Revolution in England* (Cambridge: Cambridge University Press, 2002); David Eltis, Stanley Engerman, "The Importance of Slavery and Slave Trade to Industrializing Britain," *Journal of Economic History*, 60, 1 (2000): 123–144; Kenneth Pomeranz, *The Great Divergence* (Princeton: Princeton University Press, 2000).

[15] Trevor Burnard, Giorgio Riello, "Slavery and the New History of Capitalism," *Journal of Global History*, 15, 2 (2020): 225–244.

finance the First Industrial Revolution but contrasted with the slow pace of growth in the first half of the nineteenth century.[16]

France also experienced labor-intensive growth during the eighteenth century, even more so than Great Britain; and for the same reasons, it also relied on colonial profits,[17] which were quite relevant in the eighteenth century and strategically crucial insofar as French domestic markets were less extensive than those of Great Britain.[18] Losing Saint-Domingue, then Mauritius, Louisiana and Pondicherry was an economic catastrophe for France and its empire.[19]

These dynamics interacted with those of Russia, which was not the quasi-periphery of Europe.[20] According to this interpretation, Russian wheat, produced by serfs, supported British and Western European industrialization. The problem with this interpretation is that we now know that Russian economic growth was stronger than generally claimed. It was achieved by following a similar path to that of Western Europe: intensification of labor, coercion, persistence of the peasantry and landed aristocracy, the role of the empire as a source of land and profits.[21] The Russian domestic market was far more developed than Wallerstein asserted; at the same time, Russia supplied wheat to Western Europe and, from this point of view, Russia and its serfdom complemented American slavery and "ghost acres."[22] To this end, Russia invaded the Ukraine and colonized the central Steppes and Siberia. However, the Empire brought Russia far fewer resources and advantages than France and Great Britain: no

---

[16] Robert Allen, *The British Industrial Revolution in Global Perspective* (Cambridge: Cambridge University Press, 2009); Parthasarathi, *Why Europe Grew Rich*; Maxine Berg, Felicia Gottman, Hanna Hodacs and Chris Nierstrasz, eds., *Goods from the East, 1600–1800: Trading Eurasia* (Basingstoke: Palgrave, 2015); Ronald Findlay and Kevin H. O'Rourke, *Power and Plenty: Trade, War, and the World Economy in the Second Millennium* (Princeton: Princeton University Press, 2007). For works including Russia in this perspective: Matthew Romaniello, *Enterprising Empires: Russia and Britain in Eighteenth Century Eurasia* (Cambridge: Cambridge University Press, 2019); Klass Rönnbäck, "New and Old Peripheries: Britain, the Baltic, and the Americas in the Great Divergence," *Journal of Global History*, 5, 3 (2010): 373–394.

[17] Guillaume Daudin, "Profitability of Slavery and Long-Distance Trading in Context: The Case of Eighteenth-Century France," *The Journal of Economic History*, 64, 1 (2004): 144–171. Trevor Burnard, John Garrigus, eds., *The Plantation Machine* (Philadelphia: University of Pennsylvania Press, 2016).

[18] Patrick Villiers, *Le commerce colonial atlantique et la guerre d'indépendance des Etats-Unis d'Amérique, 1778–1783: Essai d'étude quantitative* (New York: Arno Press, 1977); Jean Tarrade, *Le commerce colonial français à la fin de l'ancien régime* (Paris: PUF, 1972).

[19] David Geggus, "Slave Society in the Sugar Plantation Zones of Saint-Domingue and the Revolution of 1791–3," *Slavery and Abolition*, 20, 2 (1999): 31–46.

[20] Immanuel Wallerstein, *The Modern World System: Capitalist Agriculture and the Origins of the European World-Economy in the Sixteenth Century* (New York: Atheneum, 1974).

[21] Alessandro Stanziani, *After Oriental Despotism* (London: Bloomsbury, 2014).

[22] Pomeranz, *The Great Divergence*. "Ghost acres" were lands outside Britain producing sugar, wheat and cotton for Britain.

slaves, no precious metals, no sugar or cotton plantations, but wheat grown by soldier-colonists and by peasants partially or totally emancipated from serfdom. These different trends influenced the historical dynamics of serfdom and slavery. The latter was confronted by the abolitionist movement and the mechanization of production, while the former was gradually transmuted. But how? Resistance from below and reform from above interacted in fairly similar, if different, ways across Eurasia and the Atlantic.

Debates on abolition have essentially focused on two interdependent questions: (1) whether the abolitions of the nineteenth and early twentieth centuries represented a major advance over previous centuries (or even millennia) of human history, during which servitude had been the dominant form of work and the human condition; and (2) whether they were the expression of an action specific to the Western bourgeoisie and liberal civilization. It is true that the number of abolitionist acts and people involved during the extended nineteenth century (1780–1914) has no equivalent in history: thirty million Russian peasants, half a million slaves in Saint-Domingue in 1790, four million slaves in the United States in 1860, another million in the Caribbean (at the time of the abolition of 1832–40), another million in Brazil in 1885 and 250,000 in the Spanish colonies were freed during this period. It is estimated that abolition in Africa at the turn of the century involved around seven million people.[23]

However, this argument has been criticized by those who have argued that abolitionist legal acts take into account neither the high rate of manumission and freedom purchase in Islamic societies, in regions such as Africa, Southeast Asia and the Ottoman Empire,[24] nor the high rate of manumission in Russia and Brazil before general abolition, nor the legal and social constraints on freed slaves and serfs.

This book attempts to provide answers that go beyond the classic oppositions between before and after abolition, on the one hand, and between "the West" and "the rest," on the other. I will focus on the interrelationships in terms of the circulation of ideas and economic and social dynamics between the different spaces: Europe, Russia, Africa, the Indian Ocean and the Americas. From there, I will attempt to identify continuities and changes in the long-term process of emancipation and the interplay between different notions and practices of "freedom." When and why did the golden age of servitude come to an end? Was abolitionism a response to political and/or economic pressure?

---

[23] Drescher, *Abolitions*.
[24] On this debate, see Joseph Calder Millar, *Slavery and Slaving in World History: A Bibliography, 1900–1996* (Armonk, NY: M. E. Sharpe, 1999); Claude Meillassoux, *Anthropologie de l'esclavage* (Paris: PUF, 1986); Moses Finley, *Ancient Slavery and Modern Ideology* (New York: Viking Press, 1980); Orlando Patterson, *Slavery and Social Death* (Cambridge, MA: Harvard University Press, 1985); James Watson, ed., *Asian and African Systems of Slavery* (Berkeley: University of California Press, 1980); William Gervase Clarence-Smith, ed., *The Economics of the Indian Ocean Slave Trade* (London: Frank Cass, 1989).

Part III answers this question. It will be argued that in Russia, the abolition of serfdom was a consequence of both internal tensions and the Great Divergence: The decline of China added to Britain's reorientation towards American corn deprived Russia of most of its foreign markets. Moreover, the diminishing returns of serfdom and proto-industry in the first half of the nineteenth century finally proved the impossibility of reconciling serfdom with long-term economic growth. On the other hand, abolition had a revitalizing effect, although it maintained many of its earlier restrictions, notably on peasant mobility, and pursued the same strategy based on proto-industry and intensive labor that had sustained Western growth almost up to that point. This choice guaranteed a certain degree of social stability and short-term growth, but Russia would soon find itself confronted by the Second Industrial Revolution followed by the First World War, both of which were incompatible with this type of economy. Yet in the French and British empires, profits initially fell after abolition, even as conditions for former slaves and new immigrants improved only slowly. Why was this so?

As with the previous sections, I'll start with the changes in labor institutions (contracts, legal status); according to one interpretation, post-abolition labor resembled forced labor and slavery, and contracts were seen as the expression of a legal fiction.[25] This approach deprives the abolition of slavery of any historical significance,[26] while overlooking all the efforts made by indentured immigrants and former slaves to fight for their own rights.[27] Several historians

---

[25] Hugh Tinker, *A New System of Slavery: The Export of Indian Labour Overseas, 1830–1920* (London: Hansib, 1974); Utsa Patnaik, M. Dingwaney, eds., *Chains of Servitude: Bondage and Slavery in India* (Madras: Sangam Books, 1985); Gyan Prakash, *Bonded Histories: Genealogies of Labour Servitude in Colonial India* (Cambridge: Cambridge University Press, 1990); Sudel Fuma, *De l'Inde du sud à la Réunion* (Port-Louis: Graphica, 1999); Sully-Santa Govindin, *Les engagés indiens* (Saint-Denis la Réunion: Azalées, 1994).

[26] Anna Suranyi, *Indenture Servitude: Unfree Labor and Citizenship in the British Colonies* (Montreal: McGill University Press, 2021); David Northrup, *Indentured Labor in the Age of Imperialism: 1834–1922* (Cambridge: Cambridge University Press, 1995); Marina Carter, *Servants, Sirdars and Settlers: Indians in Mauritius, 1834–1874* (Delhi: Oxford University Press, 1995); Edmond Maestri, *Esclavage et abolition dans l'Océan Indien, 1723–1860* (Paris: L'Harmattan, 2002); Rosemarijn Hoefte, "Indenture in the Long Nineteenth Century," in David Eltis, Stanley Engerman, Seymour Drescher, David Richardson, *The Cambridge World History of Slavery*, vol. 4 (Cambridge: Cambridge University Press): 610–632; Ashutosh Kumar, "Subaltern Mobility and Labor Contract: Indian Indenture in New World History," *Journal of World History*, 32, 1 (2021): 19–28; Mark Harvey, "Slavery, Indenture, and the Development of British Industrial Capitalism," *History Workshop Journal*, 88 (2019): 66–88.

[27] The following bibliographies are useful: Rebecca Scott, Thomas Holt, Frederick Cooper, Aims Mc Guinness, *Societies after Slavery: A Selected Annotated Bibliography of Printed Sources on Cuba, Brazil, British Colonial Africa, South Africa and the British West India* (Pittsburgh: University of Pittsburgh Press, 2004); Seymour Drescher, Stanley Engerman, eds., *A Historical Guide to World Slavery* (New York: Oxford University Press, 1998);

have opposed this viewpoint, demonstrating that the actual conditions of emancipated slaves and new immigrants gradually improved over time.[28] This argument is in line with recent trends in emigration history, which also emphasize the shifting boundary between free and unfree emigration.[29] I will elaborate on this latter view and add a further dimension: Instead of discussing in a vacuum whether former slaves and indentured migrants were "free people" or "slaves in disguise," this book argues that we need to examine in detail and in specific places what workers were forced to do as well as what they were allowed to claim.

The evolution of labor and its rules in the colonies also had an impact on the continent. The final chapters make the link between the abolition of slavery and serfdom, and changes in the rules and practices of work in continental Western Europe (the emergence of the welfare state, the Second Industrial Revolution). Polanyi called the latter process "the Great Transformation," while ignoring the transmutation of colonial empires.[30] I argue that the Great Transformation was a response not only to the rise of social movements and the cost of labor in Europe but also to the abolition of slavery in the colonies and the United States. The abolitions reopened the debate on social and legal labor standards in Europe itself. Social reforms in France and Great Britain accelerated after 1870, in the face of now global competition from Russia, Canada, Australia, the United States, and soon Japan and Germany. The cost of labor rose steadily, and the first forms of welfare state came into being. After 1870, it was no longer possible to pursue the once-dominant strategy of intensive labor in Western Europe and the United States. On the contrary, this strategy found a new lease of life in Russia and the European colonies. Here, workers could not benefit from the growing welfare state, as in Europe. The "national" resident was a new category

---

Pétré-Grenouilleau, *Les traites négrières*; Marcel Dorigny, Bernard Gainot, *Atlas des esclavages* (Paris: Editions Autrement, 2006).

[28] Steinfeld, *The Invention of Free Labor*. On the moving boundary between "free" and "unfree" labor: Stanley L. Engerman, ed., *Terms of Labor: Slavery, Serfdom, and Free Labor* (Stanford University Press, 1999); Michael Bush ed., *Serfdom and Slavery* (New York; London: Longman, 1996); Tom Brass, Marcel van der Linden, eds., *Free and Unfree Labor: The Debate Continues* (Berne: Peter Lang, 1997).

[29] Donna Gabaccia, ed., *The Cambridge History of Global Migration*, 2 volumes (Cambridge: Cambridge University Press, 2023); Jan Lucassen, Leo Lucassen, eds., *Migration, Migration History, History: Old Paradigms and New Perspectives* (Bern: Peter Lang, 1997); David Eltis, *Coerced and Free Migration: Global Perspectives* (Stanford: Stanford University Press, 2002); David Galenson, *White Servitude in Colonial America: An Economic Analysis* (Cambridge: Cambridge University Press, 1981); Farley Grubb, "The Incidence of Servitude in Transatlantic Migration, 1771–1804," *Explorations in Economic History*, 22, 3 (1985): 316–339; Claude Wanquet, *La France et la première abolition de l'esclavage (1794–1802)* (Paris: Karthala, 1998); Christian Schnakenbourg, *Histoire de l'industrie sucrière en Guadeloupe aux XIXe et XXe siècles* (Paris: L'Harmattan, 2007).

[30] Karl Polanyi, *The Great Transformation* (New York: Beacon, 1944).

allowing certain continental workers access to social rights, and excluded women, craftsmen, workers in small units and, above all, colonial workers. This connected history and disconnected social rights between national welfare in the "North" (not for all!) and coercion in the "South" is still with us today.

This book has a long history: About ten years ago, I had already completed a three-volume comparative history of labor, coercion and economic dynamics between the sixteenth and twentieth centuries. I was encouraged to condense it into a single volume; so I put aside the first volume on prisoners of war and the relationship between military and labor markets, and concentrated on the other two volumes. Their revision into a smaller volume took me years. Meanwhile, I went on to produce other articles and books and complementary or partial issues, such as the role of labor institutions in Russia, with a small comparison with Britain; then studies on the Indian Ocean world, and finally an evaluation of the role of law and legal labor institutions from a global perspective. The present book therefore offers a different view: First, it is my first systematic attempt to compare the Anglo-American, French and Russian empires, where the role of the colonial worlds is as important for Russia as that of labor on the mainland. Second, for the first time, I fully develop my discussion of the American continent, the Caribbean and North America. Third, I avoid repeating the analysis of labor institutions (except for the Americas) already present in previous studies, and I put the accent on the economic rationale and performances of labor and coercion. From this perspective, I have tried to connect different historiographies, such as the Great Divergence and the Great Transformation, the history of the Industrial Revolutions, labor, slavery and serfdom. How?

Scales Matter: Global Labor History or Global Microhistory?

Since the start of the new millennium, global labor history has produced a deluge of publications, created associations all over the world and made a major contribution to the renewal not only of the history of labor but of history in general.[31] This field had been in decline since the 1980s–1990s; partly as a consequence of the decline of the "social turn" in history,[32] these difficulties in labor history also reflected those of the activism of many labor historians.[33]

---

[31] Here are a few references from an extremely vast literature: Brass and van der Linden, *Free and Unfree Labor*; Marcel van der Linden, ed., *Workers of the World* (Leiden: Brill, 2008); Alessandro Stanziani, ed., *Labor, Coercion and Economic Growth in Eurasia, Seventeenth–Twentieth Centuries* (Leiden: Brill, 2012); Andreas Eckert, ed., *Global Histories of Work* (Boston: De Gruyter, 2016); Leo Lucassen, "Working Together: New Directions in Global Labour History," *Journal of Global History*, 11, 1 (2016): 66–87; Sabyasachi Bhattacharya, ed., *Towards a New History of Work* (Delhi: Tulika Book, 2014).

[32] William Sewell, *Logics of History: Social Theory and Social Transformation* (Chicago: University of Chicago Press, 2005).

[33] Jacques Bidet, Jacques Textier, eds., *La crise du travail* (Paris: PUF, 1995).

The crisis of the working class and the political and ideological difficulties of the Left thus resulted in a veritable intellectual impasse for most labor historians, not only in France, but also in most other European countries and the United States. Without necessarily resolving these contradictions, the global history of labor took off at the turn of the 1990s–2000s, in the wake of debates on globalization. Labor became topical again from two main angles: the future of Western workers, faced with the decline of the welfare state and offshoring, and the political and social tensions linked to migratory movements.[34] Global histories of slavery have been produced along similar lines: The Cambridge history of slavery, the Palgrave handbook of global slavery and a French world history of slavery have abandoned ancient and Atlantic slavery as a paradigm and instead emphasized the multiplicity of slaveries across the world over the long term.[35] For their part, global histories of migration have constantly shifted their focus and questioned the boundary between free and unfree migration.[36] This effervescence has led to a major shift in the focus of research, from the history of work in the West to a history linking different continents over the long term (usually from the sixteenth century onwards). Never has the history of labor in China, India, the Ottoman Empire, Africa and Latin America attracted so much interest from historians, sociologists and political scientists as in recent decades.[37] One of the great successes of this historiography has been to

---

[34] Prabhu P. Mohapatra, Marcel van der Linden, eds., *Labour Matters: Towards Global Histories: Studies in Honour of Sabyasachi Bhattacharya* (New Delhi: Tulika, 2009); Jan Lucassen, *The Story of Work: A New History of Humankind* (New Haven: Yale University Press, 2022); Marcel van der Linden, *The World Wide Web of Work* (London: UCL Press, 2023); Karin Hofmeester, Marcel van der Linden, eds., *Handbook: Global History of Work* (Oldenburg: De Gruyter, 2018); Christian G. de Vito, Juliane Schiele, Matthias van Rossum, "From Bondage to Precariousness? New Perspectives on Labor and Social History," *The Journal of Social History* 54, 2 (2020): 1–19.

[35] Keith Bradley, Paul Cartledge, David Eltis, eds., *The Cambridge World History of Slavery*, 4 volumes (Cambridge: Cambridge University Press, 2011–2021); Damian Pargas, Julian Schiele, *The Palgrave Handbook of Global Slavery through History* (Basingstoke: Palgrave, 2023); Paulin Ismard, Benedetta Rossi, Cécile Vidal, eds., *Les mondes de l'esclavage. Une histoire comparée* (Paris: Seuil, 2021); Alessandro Stanziani, Gwyn Campbell, eds., *The Palgrave Handbook of Bondage and Human Rights in Africa and Asia*, 2 volumes (New York: Palgrave Macmillan, 2019).

[36] Lucassen, *Migration, Migration History, History*; Eltis, *Coerced and Free Migration*; Gabaccia, *The Cambridge History of Global Migrations*.

[37] Some references: Kate Ekama, Lisa Hellman, Matthias von Rossum, eds., *Slavery and Bondage in Asia, 1550–1850: Towards a Global History of Coerced Labour* (Oldenburg: De Gruyter, 2022); Edward Alpers, *Ivory and Slaves in East Central Africa: Changing Patterns of International Trade to the Later Nineteenth Century* (Berkeley: University of California Press, 1975); Clare Anderson, *Legible Bodies: Race, Criminality and Colonialism in South Asia* (Oxford: Berg Publishers, 2004); Jan Breman, *Labour Bondage in West India* (Oxford: Oxford University Press, 2007); Gwyn Campbell, Alessandro Stanziani, eds., *Bonded Labour and Debt in the Indian Ocean World* (London: Pickering & Chatto, 2013); Gwyn Campbell, ed., *The Structure of Slavery in Indian Ocean Africa and Asia* (London:

overcome the conventional distinction between historians of wage labor and those of slavery, which in turn reflected that between historians of Europe and the United States and those of area studies.[38]

Authors of global labor histories are often accused of superficiality, lack of rigor, unfamiliarity with the regions studied and reliance on secondary literature.[39] However, to attack global labor histories as such is to miss the point: These syntheses are welcome as advanced textbooks; there's no question of depriving ourselves of them, unless we consider that the general public and students are not worthy of attention, or that only national history counts. Nor should these works be criticized for relying essentially on secondary sources (in the case of individual works); why should historical syntheses be acceptable if produced by Hobsbawm (with an emphasis on the English Industrial Revolution and the French Revolution), whereas they should be rejected if produced by Van der Linden or Lucassen?

In fact, the main limitations of these recent syntheses, as well as of the major series published by Anglo-American publishing houses, lie not only in the absence of original sources (which remains a fact), but also in the fact that they pass on almost exclusively from researchers based in American and British centers, and blithely ignore historiographies in languages other than English. It is as if no study in German, Spanish, Portuguese, Italian and of course Arabic, Chinese or Russian deserved attention. The Eurocentrism of sources is no less dangerous than the Eurocentrism of arguments and categories. Global syntheses are almost inevitably still prisoners of this legacy. Would a change in the scale of investigation solve this problem?

Global microhistory,[40] and its first expressions in labor history,[41] aim to restore the role of local contexts and individual lives in global history, accused of producing an exclusive bird's-eye perspective. This is certainly an important goal; the problem is that in this orientation, the micro aspect, described as micro-spatial, actually includes heterogeneous approaches: Italian microhistory, local monographs, biographies, group trajectories and even chapters

---

Frank Cass, 2004); Carter, *Servants, Sirdars and Settlers*; Martin Klein, ed., *Breaking the Chains: Slavery, Bondage and Emancipation in Modern Africa and Asia* (Madison: University of Wisconsin Press, 1993).

[38] Alessandro Stanziani, *Les entrelacements du monde* (Paris: CNRS Éditions, 2018); Alessandro Stanziani, *Eurocentrism and the Politics of Global History* (New York: Palgrave, 2020).

[39] Sebastian Conrad, *What Is Global History* (Princeton: Princeton University Press, 2016).

[40] Emma Rotschild, *The Inner Life of Empires* (Princeton: Princeton University Press, 2011); Natalie Zemon Davis, *The Return of Martin Guerre* (Cambridge: Harvard University Press, 1983). For a broader discussion, see: "Microhistory and Global History," special issue *Annales HSS*, 73, 1 (2018); "Global History and Microhistory," *Past and Present*, 242, supplement 14 (2018).

[41] Christian De Vito, Anne Garritsen, eds., *Micro-Spatial Histories of Global Labour* (London: Palgrave, 2018).

on regional studies. The "local" refers to many different objects, and the same applies to "individuals": A village, a region, even an area can be included in the definition of micro-spatial labor studies. At the same time, the target (i.e., the global), refers only to global syntheses such as those discussed previously and ignores other approaches to global history (connected history and comparative history in particular). This unfortunate mixing of genres is common in historiography, particularly in economic and social history, where regional, urban or company monographs are often confused with micro-history as an analytical approach and epistemological proposition. On the one hand, the original Italian microhistory radically challenged the notion of statistical representativeness, replacing it with the relevance of the case studied to the questions posed. The life of a merchant was not to be "representative" of merchants and trade; this question was irrelevant and openly rejected. On the contrary, an individual life was used to raise broad historiographical questions about, for example, trade and the religious counter-reformation, and to provide new answers. On the other hand, regional monographs and case studies constantly evoke their representativeness.[42] Spatial microhistory, like most Anglo-American microhistory studies, straddles these two approaches. This is why global microhistories of labor still encounter major difficulties in reconciling this micro dimension with the dominant categories (coercion, globalization, capitalism, etc.) needed to link individual cases to structural dynamics. For the moment, micro-studies do not seek to redefine these notions but, on the contrary, to mobilize them to link local studies together. Thus, the broader categories act not as heuristics to raise new questions and provide new answers, but to confirm conventional answers (such as the role of capitalism), while adding "complexity." But what exactly is "complexity"?

We already know, before we begin the historical survey, that every region, every village, every individual is different from another. But so what? This purely descriptive stance confuses the historian's methodological challenges with the survival strategies of working populations. The diversity of their experiences reminds us not only of the epistemological difficulties faced by the investigator, but also of the extremely difficult conditions under which the workers had to operate in order to obtain better living and working conditions. Is gender relevant in this case?

The answer must surely be in the affirmative, as the enormous historiographies on gender in global labor history prove.[43] While studies of women's work

---

[42] Carlo Ginzburg, Carlo Poni, "Il nome e il come. Scambio ineguale e mercato storiografico," *Quaderni storici*, 40, 1 (1979): 181–190.

[43] Some references by way of example: on global labor and labor in Western countries: Laura Levine Frader, "Gender and Labor in World History," in Teresa Meade, Merry Wiesner-Hanks, eds., *A Companion to Global Gender History* (London: Wiley, 2020): https://doi.org/10.1002/9781119535812.ch2. Laura Frader, "Labor History After the Gender Turn,"

in the West emphasize their role in reproduction, precarity, underpayment and lack of rights, in the history of slavery, the focus has again been on women's role in production and reproduction (which in this respect differentiates the United States from other slavery systems).[44] Individual micro-histories were highlighted in this context.[45] Overall, a tension was stressed between production and reproduction: The more women worked, the less they were able to reproduce. A trade-off that could be resolved either by importing more slaves (or workers in Europe) or by mechanizing production. The first solution was profitable as long as the cost of importing was low. The ban on the slave trade partially altered this balance, and even more so, abolitionists' attacks on indentured slavery, seen as a new form of slavery, contributed to the problem. The protection of child and female labor in Europe went hand in hand with this change.[46]

International Labor and Working-Class History, 63 (2003): 21–31. Xavier Vigna, Michelle Zancarini-Fournel, "Intersections between Labour History and Gender History," *Clio*, 38, 2 (2013): 181–208; Ava Baron, "Masculinity, the Embodied Male Worker, and the Historian's Gaze," *International Labor and Working Class History*, 69, spring (2006): 143–160. Laura Lee Downs, *Manufacturing Inequality: Gender Division in the French and British Metalworking Industries 1914–1939* (Ithaca: Cornell University Press, 1995). Alice Kessler-Harris, *Gendering Labor History* (Dekalb: University of Illinois Press, 2007); Sonya Rose, Sean Brady, "Rethinking Gender and Labor History," in John Arnold ed., *History After Hobsbawm, Writing the Past for the 21st Century* (Oxford: Oxford University Press, 2017): 242–258; Amy Dru Stanley, "Histories of Capitalism and Sex Difference," *Journal of the Early Republic*, 36, 2 (2016): 343–350; Merry Wiesner-Hanks, "World History and the History of Women, Gender, and Sexuality," *Journal of World History*, 18, 1 (2007): 53–67.

[44] Diana Paton, "Gender History, Global History, and Atlantic Slavery," *American Historical Review*, 127, 2 (2022): 726–754. Hilary McD Beckles, *Natural Rebels: A Social History of Enslaved Black Women in Barbados* (New Brunswick, NJ: Rutgers University Press, 1989); Barbara Bush, *Slave Women in Caribbean Society 1650–1838* (Bloomington: Indiana University Press, 1990); Elizabeth Fox Genovese, *Within the Plantation Household: Black and White Women of the Old South* (Chapel Hill: North Carolina University Press, 1988); Sonia Maria Giacomini, *Mulher e escrava: Uma introdução histórica ao estudo da mulher negra no Brasil* (Petrópolis: Rio, 1988); Arlette Gautier, *Les sœurs de Solitude: Femmes et esclavage aux Antilles du XVIIe au XIXe siècle* (1985; repr., Rennes: Presses Universitaires de Rennes, 2019). Gwyn Campbell, Suzanne Miers, Joseph C. Miller, eds., *Women and Slavery* (Athens: Ohio University Press, 2008); Silvia Federici, *Caliban and the Witch: Women, the Body, and Primitive Accumulation* (New York: Penguin, 2004).

[45] Sandra Lauderdale Graham, *Caetana Says No: Women's Stories from a Brazilian Slave Society* (Cambridge: Cambridge University Press, 2002); W. Caleb McDaniel, *Sweet Taste of Liberty: A True Story of Slavery and Restitution in America* (New York: Oxford University Press, 2019); Rebecca J. Scott and Jean M. Hébrard, *Freedom Papers: An Atlantic Odyssey in the Age of Emancipation* (Cambridge, MA: Harvard University Press, 2012); Erica Ball, Tatiana Seijas, Terri L. Snyder, eds., *As If She Were Free: A Collective Biography of Women and Emancipation in the Americas* (Cambridge: Cambridge University Press, 2020).

[46] Diane Paton, "Gender History;" Diane Paton, Pamela Scully, eds., *Gender and Slave Emancipation in the Atlantic World* (Durham: Duke University Press, 2005).

This book does not develop gender as such, but systematically brings it to the fore when examining different labor regimes. For example, I will discuss at length the indentured women who crossed the Atlantic in the seventeenth century, particularly in the French colonies. In this case, the lack of migrant families, the violence inflicted on native women and the subsequent importation of marginalized women into France will be interconnected. This solution will be much less easy to apply in post-slavery Mauritius and Réunion, where most of the enlisted people were initially men. These cases and different dynamics will influence the mutual evolution of labor rights in the French and British empires, particularly when, after the 1870s, men's labor rights improve, excluding those of women and colonial workers. The Russian case, as we shall see, was even different: Serfdom was a village and household affair, where patriarchal values met labor hierarchies. In the Russian colonies, there were two main cases: Either peasant-soldiers and fugitives without families, in which case their reproduction was at stake or families on the move, in Siberia, Ukraine and parts of the Steppe. In this case, gender intersects not only with labor, but also with the Russification of the Empire. Moreover, as in the case of slavery, in the case of serfdom, gender strongly influenced the transmission of serf status (matrilineal transmission of legal status). And yet, to return to Western Europe, in the nineteenth century, women were still subject to a different legal status, whether in labor, trade or any other field. In other words, the relevance of legal status goes beyond slavery and serfdom, and concerns "free" work and gender in Europe too.

In summary, this book takes into account the contribution of gender and (global) microhistory, but seeks to develop it from a different perspective: Individual cases, regional investigations and comparative analyses between empires and their regions aim to identify not only the aforementioned tensions between "the local and the global," but also to provide their mutual interaction and co-evolution, and, ultimately, to identify the "local" and the "global" in terms of historical context. For example, on a broader scale, I use the Russian case to reassess the British case. In this broad context, I will not focus on entire empires, but on Russian borderlands and contrast them with the Anglo-American frontier. Regional studies and differences come into play here. Within this box, the individual cases of serfs, indentured servants and slaves will highlight the multiplicity of voices and living courts and their impact on broader trends. These multiple scales interact within a dynamic political and economic configuration that is absolutely central to the period under study: the Empire.

Empires

Of course, this book is not about empires as such.[47] The most impressive *tour de force* on this subject is undoubtedly *Empires: A World History* by Jane

---

[47] Colley, "What Is Imperial History?"; Stoler, McGranahan, Perdu, *Imperial Formations*.

Burbank and Frederick Cooper,[48] which examines a wide range of empires, from antiquity to the present day. Its main focus is on strategies of domination, and therefore on politics and society, rather than economics. Most of the book's arguments are in line with those of Burbank and Cooper, starting with the assertion that the rise of the state in Western Europe is a consequence, not the origin, of Empire. The nation-state was a late and temporary by-product of Empire. A second point on which we agree is that empires cannot be reduced to the opposition between colonizers and colonized, that the latter were never purely passive subjects and that multiple forms of interaction and institutional accommodation were put in place. These solutions have differentiated Empires. More recent works of synthesis have also offered valuable comparisons between several empires, including the Russian Empire.[49] However, unlike Burbank and Cooper, and these other titles too, I do not intend to write a world history of empires from their origins to the present day, focused primarily on political history, but rather a connected and comparative socio-economic history of the relationship between labor and certain empire-building between the seventeenth and early twentieth centuries.[50] The aim here is not to identify imperial repertoires, but rather to grasp the comparative interrelation between labor and empire-building in specific contexts. In this endeavor, one main question arises: Why did so many different forms of empire – in space and time – rely on the coercion of labor? Was this inherent in imperial forms of state and power, or was it a consequence of the market dynamics of which state empires were themselves a by-product?

The answer depends on the empire studied. I will concentrate primarily on three empires: Russian, British and French. This decision does not exclude references to Central and South Asia, China, the Ottoman Empire, Africa and the Americas, for which extensive and valuable historiographies exist.[51] This will

---

[48] Burbank, Cooper, *Empires*.
[49] Krishan Kumar, *Visions of Empire: How Five Imperial Regimes Shaped the World* (Princeton: Princeton University Press, 2017).
[50] From this point of view, my work is also more limited than that of David Abernethy, who seeks to understand the destiny of European empires over the very long term, from the sixteenth century to the present day. David Abernethy, *The Dynamics of Global Dominance: European Overseas Empires, 1415–1980* (New Haven: Yale University Press).
[51] In particular, on the links between labor and Empire in the Dutch kingdom: Ulbe Bosma, *The World of Sugar* (Cambridge, MA: Belknap Press, 2023). On China: Harriet Zurndorfer, *Change and Continuity in Chinese Local History* (Leiden: Brill, 1989); Claude Chevaleyre, "Acting as Master and Bondservant. Considerations on Status, Identities, and the Nature of 'Bondservitude' in Late Ming China," in Alessandro Stanziani ed., *Labour, Coercion and Economic Growth in Eurasia, 17th–20th Centuries* (Leiden: Brill, 2013): 237–272; Claude Chevaleyre, "Insiders by Analogy: Slaves in the Great Ming Code," *Slavery and Abolition*, 43, 3 (2022): 460–481. On the Ottoman Empire: Y. Hakan Erdem, *Slavery in the Ottoman Empire and Its Demise, 1800–1909* (Basingstoke: Palgrave, Macmillan, 1996); Ehud Toledano, *Slavery and Abolition in the Ottoman Middle East* (Seattle: University of

not be an attempt to re-establish a Eurocentric approach to labor and imperial history, but, on the contrary, to reorient Europe itself in a global perspective.[52] The way out of Eurocentrism is not necessarily to study non-European regions (which, incidentally, are themselves subject to Eurocentric or other "centric" approaches), but to study Europe itself without presuming that it is the nucleus of progress and modernity. How does this happen?

From this point of view, the case of Russia offers a particularly clear illustration of the Eurocentrism that continues to guide historical analysis. Over the past few centuries, and still today, Russian, European and Western observers have debated Russia as a "European," "Asian-Mongolian" or ultimately "Eurasian" entity.[53] Even the new approaches to world history, which challenge Chinese "backwardness" and European ethnocentrism, nevertheless regard Russia as the paradigm of unfree labor and the absence of markets. As such, it is either presented in head-on opposition to the Lower Yangtze and Great Britain in the case of Pomeranz, or regarded as an exception in Europe for having put an end to famines and introduced private property and democratic rule in the books of Osterhammel or Darwin.[54] In all these approaches, the "case of Russia" systematically expresses the demarcation line, even the negation, of Western growth and civilization. Russia is on the periphery of global dynamics, both in terms of economic performance and – crucial to any approach to global history – in terms of the decentralization of Europe (or the West). When it comes to Russia, decentralizing perspectives collapse.

Dominic Lieven has given us valuable insights into this comparative perspective of the Russian empire. He accepted the basic arguments used to explain the growth of Western economies (capital, the First Industrial Revolution, the proletarianization of the peasantry, etc.) and channeled them to explain Russian reactions to these same phenomena. Darwin adopted a

---

Washington Press, 1996); Stephan Conermann, Gül Sen eds., *Slave and Slave Agency in the Ottoman Empire* (Bonne: V. and R. University Press, 2019). On Spain: Evelyn Jennings, *Constructing the Spanish Empire in Havana* (Baton Rouge: Louisiana State University Press, 2020). Rebecca Scott, *Slave Emancipation in Cuba, 1860–1899* (Princeton: Princeton University Press, 1985).

[52] Stanziani, *Eurocentrism*.

[53] Stephen Kotkin, "Mongol Commonwealth? Exchange and Governance Across the Post-Mongol Space," *Kritika*, 8, 3 (2007): 487–531; Mark von Hagen, "Empires, Borderlands, and Diasporas: Eurasianism as an Anti-Paradigm for the Post-Soviet Era," *American Historical Review*, 109, 2 (2004): 445–468. Also: Paul Miliukov, "Eurasianism and Europeanism in Russian History," *Festschrift für Th. G. Masaryk zum 80. Geburtstag* (Bonn: F. Cohen, 1930); Nicholas V. Riasanovsky, "The Emergence of Eurasianism," *California Slavic Studies*, 4 (1967): 39–72.

[54] Christopher Bayly, *The Birth of the Modern World, 1780–1914* (London: Blackwell, 2004); Darwin, *After Tamerlane*; Jürgen Osterhammel, *The Transformation of the World: A Global History of the Nineteenth Century* (Princeton: Princeton University Press, 2014); Pomeranz, *The Great Divergence*.

similar approach: He emphasized the Eurasian dimension of modern Western history and the role Russia played in it.[55] He placed Russia within Europe and then sought to give a less Eurocentric picture of the modernization process. In addition, Darwin, like many others, contrasted Western empires with so-called Asian empires: The former excluded and subjugated conquered populations, while the latter were much more inclusive.[56] On the other hand, several other authors contest this allegedly "mild" Russian colonialism.[57] The problem with both approaches is that they are based on more or less idealized images of one of the terms of comparison: Specialists in Russian history portray the West and its empires based on conventional ideas about crucial notions such as the Industrial Revolution, colonization or democracy, while experts on the West start from equally stereotyped images of Russia as a land of serfdom and despotism.[58] Conventional approaches use anhistorical categories of "serfs," "serfdom" and "despotism." This book reorients the identification of serfdom in its relation to the construction of the Russian empire.[59] It will show that serfdom and the Russian empire were not the negation of, but an extreme variation on, the European model of labor and empire.

If so, we are ready to reassess the role of labor in Western empires too. The idea that capitalism, and in particular the English Industrial Revolution, was made possible by institutions that facilitated free contracts and (according to some) a proletarianized peasantry is supported by a long tradition. It goes back at least to the nineteenth century and the classical economists (Smith, Marx), then to Tawney and Polanyi, and most of the historical sociology and economic history of the twentieth century. The world-system approach, while

---

[55] Dominic Lieven, *Empire: The Russian Empire and its Rivals from the Sixteenth Century to the Present* (London: Pimlico, 2003). Darwin, *After Tamerlane*. See also, from a different perspective, the excellent Romaniello, *Enterprising Empires*.

[56] Burbank, Cooper, *Empires*; Greene, *Exclusionary Empire*.

[57] Aleksei Miller, ed., *Rossiiskaia imperiia v sravnitel'noi perspektive: Sbornik statei* (The Russian Empire in Comparative Perspective) (Moscow: Novoe izdatel'stvo, 2004); Alexei Miller, Alfred J. Rieber, eds., *Imperial Rule* (Budapest: Central European University Press, 2004); Kimitaka Matsuzato, *Imperiology: From Empirical Knowledge to Discussing the Russian Empire* (Sapporo: Slavic Research Center, 2007); Geoffrey Hosking, *Russia: People and Empire, 1552–1917* (Cambridge, MA: Harvard University Press, 1997); Andreas Kappeler, *Rußland als Vielvölkerreich: Entstehung, Geschichte, Zerfall* (Munich: C. H. Beck, 1992); Alexander S. Morrison, *Russian Rule in Samarkand, 1868–1910: A Comparison with British India* (Oxford: Oxford University Press, 2008). See also the special issues on this subject, *Kritika*, 7, 3 (2006) and 12, 2 (2012). Thomas Barrett, *At the Edge of Empire: The Terek Cossacks and the North Caucasus Frontier, 1700–1860* (Boulder, CO: Westview Press, 1999); Alexander Etkind, *Internal Colonization: Russia's Imperial Experience* (Cambridge: Polity Press, 2011); Steven Sabol, *The Touch of Civilization: Comparing American and Russian Internal Colonization* (Boulder: University Press of Colorado, 2017).

[58] Jerome Blum, *Lord and Peasants in Russia from the Ninth through the Nineteenth Century* (New York: Atheneum, 1964).

[59] In my previous investigations, I studied serfdom, but without its link to the Empire.

emphasizing the existence of mixed forms of labor and exploitation on the periphery and quasi-periphery, assumed that free wage labor characterized the "core."[60] Acemoglu and other economists before him stressed the relationship between empire and the rise of democracy and private property in Britain: Atlantic trade would have encouraged the Glorious Revolution and the alliance between merchants, capitalists and Parliament at the expense of the Crown and aristocrats.[61] This book follows an important trend in Atlantic and world history[62] and argues that there was indeed a link between England, Europe and the Atlantic, but that it went in the opposite direction of increased freedom: Through slavery and the appropriation of profits, the colonial world helped keep coercive institutions alive in Britain, and the same was true in France. Towards the middle of the seventeenth century, Western Europe experienced a major innovation: not democracy, nor the agrarian and Industrial Revolution, but a new link between labor, coercion and production, both in the European colonies and on the continent. From this perspective, the case of France is equally interesting: France is usually presented not as the land of liberty and revolution, but of absolutism and state intervention. Conventional labor historiography therefore contrasted France with Britain: France was said to have kept alive the peasantry and small units, the putting-out system, small-scale manufacturing and labor-intensive growth paths. Britain was the opposite: capital-intensive, mechanized, proletarianized and industrialized society and economy.[63] The opposition between regulation, free markets and liberalism was also *commonplace* in historiography.[64] This view has been sharply

---

[60] Marc Steinberg, "Capitalist Development, the Labor Process, and the Law," *American Journal of Sociology*, 109, 2 (2003): 445–495.
[61] Daron Acemoglu, Alexander Wolitzky, "The Economics of Labor Coercion," *Econometrica*, 79, 2 (2011): 555–600; Daron Acemoglu, Simon Johnson, James Robinson, "The Rise of Europe: Atlantic Trade, Institutional Change, and Economic Growth," *The American Economic Review*, 95, 3 (June 2005): 546–579.
[62] Beyond the many titles in the New History of Capitalism, see also: the classic Williams, *Capitalism and Slavery*; Inikori, *Africans and the Industrial Revolution*; Robin Blackburn, *The Making of New World Slavery* (London: Verso, 1997); Burnard, Riello, "Slavery and the New History of Capitalism." A full bibliography on this subject can be found in the following chapters.
[63] François Crouzet, *De la supériorité de l'Angleterre sur la France. L'économique et l'imaginaire* (Paris: Perrin, 1985); François Caron, *Histoire économique de la France XIXe-XXe siècle* (Paris: A. Colin, 1996); Nicolas Crafts, "Industrial Revolution in England and France: Some Thoughts on the Question: 'Why Was England First?'" *The Economic History Review*, 30, 3 (1977): 429–441.
[64] Maurice Lévy-Leboyer and J.-C. Casanova, *Entre l'État et le marché. L'économie française des années 1880 à nos jours* (Paris: Gallimard, 1991); Patrick Verley, *L'Échelle du monde. Essai sur l'industrialisation de l'Occident* (Paris: Gallimard, 1997); Dominic Barjot, Olivier Dard, J. Garrigues, D. Musiedlak, É. Anceau eds., *Industrie et politique en Europe occidentale et aux États-Unis (XIXe et XXe siècle)* (Paris: Presses Universitaires de la Sorbonne, 2006).

contrasted: Britain made extensive use of regulation, while conversely, France was more "liberal" and free-market oriented than is generally assumed.[65] In the past, historians have been fond of contrasting the persistence of guilds and the corporatist spirit of French labor law with the Anglo-Saxon free labor market.[66] This is no longer the case, and labor regulation in France is no longer seen as an obstacle to market growth.[67] Moreover, some recent studies have highlighted the fact that the French case encourages a reorientation of the very notion of empire, too often associated with the formal occupation of territories. On the contrary, as the current experience of the United States and the history of post-decolonization confirm, informal empires, which make use of soft power, economic and diplomatic pressure, are just as relevant. Thus, according to this interpretation, nineteenth-century France was a major informal empire with exports of luxury goods such as wine and silk.[68] Despite its virtues, this interpretation nevertheless runs up against several questions, starting with the broad definition of empire (already very broad in Burbank and Cooper's approach): If everything is empire, how can we distinguish this form of governance from others? And why, if informal empire was ultimately less costly than formal empire, have the great imperial powers struggled so hard to maintain or reconstitute their empires (France and England after 1945, Russia after 1917 and today, the Ottomans at the turn of the nineteenth and twentieth centuries)?

Moreover, the informal control of the European powers over the countries of the "South" is quite different from France's exports of wine and silk to European countries and the United States. It is hard to imagine France taking economic control of Great Britain and the United States through its exports of luxury goods to these countries. This approach makes some sense today, but it seems inappropriate to extend it to other historical periods.[69] And yet, we still have to justify the use of the main categories we rely on (labor, coercion, capitalism): How do we reconcile the so-called emic (belonging to the actors and their context) and etic (belonging to today's observer) categories?

---

[65] For a discussion and analysis: Alessandro Stanziani, *Rules of Exchange: French Capitalism in Comparative Perspective, Eighteenth–Twentieth Centuries* (Cambridge: Cambridge University Press, 2012).

[66] Emile Coornaert, *Les corporations en France* (Paris: Gallimard, 1941); Edward P. Thompson, *The Making of the English Working Class* (London: Vintage Books, 1963).

[67] Michael Sonenscher, *Work and Wages* (Cambridge: Cambridge University Press, 1989); Philippe Minard, *La fortune du colbertisme. État et industrie dans la France des Lumières* (Paris: Fayard, 1998).

[68] David Todd, *A Velvet Empire: French Informal Imperialism in the Nineteenth Century* (Princeton: Princeton University Press, 2021).

[69] During the revision of this manuscript, Trevor Burnard published a small methodological work in which he puts his finger on the need to link imperial history and the history of slavery. Trevor Burnard, *Writing the History of Global Empire* (Cambridge: Cambridge University Press, 2023).

Categories in Space and Time: Capitalism and Coercion

It's no coincidence that global labor history is constantly confronted with the same question: What categories are we supposed to use when we move from one era to another, from one space to another? Are labor or slavery adequate categories across the ages and the world? If we refer to the so-called emic categories (used by historical actors), we are confronted with their possible incommensurability between different regions: Can we really translate Chinese, Bengali, Russian, etc. terms as "slave"?

If, on the other hand, we use so-called etic categories, as developed in current social sciences (slaves, wage-earners, etc.), we can circulate in space and time, but we lose specificities. This latter approach, which prioritizes analytical insights over descriptive historicities, is widespread in most global histories informed by sociology, political science and, ultimately, economics. Certainly, there are many ways of breaking this impasse between local and global categories, present and past, without necessarily mastering every language. Let's look first at a few syntheses produced by Dutch authors, as well as an important taxonomy of forms of work developed at the International Institute of Social History (IISG) in Amsterdam. Twenty main labor relations are identified (among them: wage-earners, slaves, servants, serfs), each with sub-types (time-earners, wage-tenants, piece-work wage-earners, domestic, agricultural, sexual slaves, etc.). Each category is associated with a "type of work": reciprocal, market, non-market, tributary-obligatory, etc. The innumerable historical cases are described. Finally, the innumerable historical cases are each placed in one of the boxes of this matrix.[70] Like all taxonomies, it is static and based on categories derived from Marxist thought, opposing the market and the non-market, wage labor and forced labor. These are ideal-types, sometimes useful for asking questions, much less for answering them. For example, in the course of a lifetime, a hired laborer, a slave or even a wage-earner often changes category, even though the market/non-market opposition has been criticized for decades by historians and anthropologists. What is more, this nomenclature doesn't allow us to grasp relationships from one region to another, from one period to another, apart from conflicts of ideal-types and abrupt ruptures. Nomenclatures are useful when they are produced by historical actors; they express benchmarks for understanding their way of thinking and acting. They seem far less useful when used as historians' tools for understanding the worlds of the past.

Another solution is to avoid identifying global history with world history, as Pomeranz argued several years ago.[71] In this case, the question becomes one

---

[70] https://iisg.amsterdam/en/research/projects/global-collaboratory-on-the-history-of-labour-relations-1500-2000.

[71] Pomeranz, *The Great Divergence*.

of selecting specific areas and then comparing them. The relevance of areas never exists in itself, but is dictated by the questions we raise. In Pomeranz's case, the underlying question was why China didn't produce an industrial revolution like Britain did. In many global histories of slavery and abolitionism, the underlying question is why abolitionism only developed in the West. In both cases, these are normative judgments (Why did China behave, or not behave, like Europe? Why was Africa "backward"?) based on comparative approaches. Over the years, several historians have criticized comparative history as inventing artificial comparisons, drawn from economic or social models but not confirmed by original sources. To this approach, they have opposed connected history as the expression of relationships correctly expressed in the sources themselves.[72] However, the same remark about arbitrary choices can be made about archives, both in their original production and in the way historians select and synthesize them.[73] In reality, there is no point in opposing comparative history and connected history, each of which deserves different objectives and leads to different, complementary questions.[74] For example, it is perfectly legitimate to compare the abolition of serfdom in Russia and France, to understand why it took place at such different times. But it is equally legitimate to ask whether French perceptions of Russian serfdom weren't dictated, after all, by the persistent constraints that existed in the French labor market even in the nineteenth century. The Weberian approach, from its founding father through to Tilly, Barrington Moore and Pomeranz, not forgetting a number of Dutch labor historians, takes as its starting point a scheme and categories derived from the social sciences (power, coercion, the state, property, competition, etc.) and then tests their relevance in different historical contexts. A totally different approach, linked to the French historian Marc Bloch, but currently used in more conventional historiographies, predetermines not the questions, but the fields of comparison according to their similarities. For example, Bloch allows a comparison between France and Germany as an expression of European culture, but excludes any comparison between these two countries and Russia as a non-fully European civilization. Bloch gave priority to linguistic skills over social sciences and their patterns, but this did not prevent him from selecting areas on the basis of preconceived assumptions.[75] This means that whatever we do, whether we link or compare, and whether we compare according to one approach or the other, the tensions between

---

[72] Michael Werner, Bénédicte Zimmermann, eds., *De la comparaison à l'histoire croisée* (Paris: Seuil, 2004); Sanjay Subrahamanyam, "Connected Histories. Notes Towards a Reconfiguration of Early Modern Eurasia," *Modern Asian Studies*, 31, 3 (1997): 735–762.
[73] Alessandro Stanziani, *Tensions of Social History* (London: Bloomsbury, 2023).
[74] Heinz-Gerhard Haupt, Jurgen Kocka, eds., *Comparative and Trans-national History* (New York: Berghahn, 2009).
[75] Stanziani, *Les entrelacements du monde*; Marc Bloch, "Pour une histoire comparée des sociétés européennes", *Revue de synthèse historique*, 46 (1928): 15–50.

the emic and etic categories persist. Drawing on my previous methodological (using both comparison and connection)[76] and empirical research,[77] this book will put forward some suggestions for overcoming this impasse.

Firstly, conceptual categories will be used not as tools for preconceived explanations, but as heuristics for raising questions.[78] Secondly, it is possible to adopt emic approaches without losing the comparative and connected story. To explain these points, let me take the two main etic categories guiding this book: coercion and capitalism. As I have already addressed these two categories in previous works, I will simply summarize my main points here. Like Braudel, Sombart and many others,[79] I associate capitalism with finance, monopoly and private property, rather than with the proletarianization of the peasantry and small traders, as argued by Marx, Weber and their many followers.[80] Yet when I began my research into labor many years ago, this point was far from clear to me. I knew the conventional histories of wage labor, slavery and serfdom, and imagined that my regional studies – Russia, Europe, some of the colonies – fitted these patterns perfectly. Over the years, I was disconcerted by the fact that the European colonies and the American South seemed perfectly integrated into the capitalist mechanism; similarly, today, the forced labor practiced by multinationals in the global South with the help of local intermediaries hardly seems to be considered a "deviation" due solely to (bad) local institutions. This means that capitalism is perfectly compatible with forced labor and slavery. From this point of view, this book is close to the New History of Capitalism, which departs from conventional Marxist, Weberian and liberal interpretations associating capitalism with wage labor alone, and which consider slavery, and slave labor in general, to be part of it.[81] However,

---

[76] Stanziani, *Tensions of Social History*; Stanziani, *Eurocentrism*; Stanziani, "Local Bondage in Global Economies. Servants, Wage Earners and Indentured Migrants in Nineteenth Century France, Great Britain and the Mascarene Islands," *Modern Asian Studies*, 47, 4 (2013): 1218–1251; Stanziani, "Serfs, slaves or wage earners? The Legal Status of Labour in Russia in a Comparative Perspective," in Damian Alan Pargas, Felicia Rosu, eds., *Critical Readings on Global Slavery* (Leiden: Brill, 2018): 1044–1068; Stanziani, "Global History, Area Studies and the Idea of Europe," *Cromhos*, 2021, pp. 1–9, DOI: 10.36253/cromohs-12562.

[77] Stanziani, *Rules of Exchange*; Stanziani, *Bondage, Labor and Rights in Eurasia*; Stanziani, *Labor on the Fringes of Empire* (New York: Palgrave, 2018).

[78] Carlo Ginzburg, *Clues, Myths and the Historical Method* (Baltimore: John Hopkins University Press, 2013); Mark Salber Phillips, "Rethinking Historical Distance. From Doctrine to Heuristics," *History and Theory*, 50, 4 (2011): 11–23.

[79] Fernand Braudel, *Civilisation matérielle, économie et capitalisme* (Paris: Colin, 1978); Werner Sombart, *Der Modern Kapitalismus*, 3 volumes (München: Dunker und Humboldt, 1902).

[80] Stanziani, *Rules of Exchange*.

[81] Beckert, *Empire of Cotton*; Edward Baptist, *The Half Has Never Been Told: Slavery and the Making of American Capitalism* (New York: Basic Books, 2014); Sven Beckert, Seth Rockman, eds., *Slavery's Capitalism: A New History of American Economic Development*

this book proposes two main variations on this approach, mainly linked to the periodization of capitalism: It will not focus on the conquest of the Americas or the First Industrial Revolution, but on the long-lasting aristocratic capitalism that stretches from the mid seventeenth century to the First World War. The question is not to explain the political, social and economic revolutions of the turn of the eighteenth and nineteenth centuries, but rather why, despite these turning points, labor and coercion persisted throughout the world.[82]

What is coercion? Anthropologists, sociologists and historians, depending on their disciplines, have highlighted different aspects of labor relations in an attempt to draw the line between "free" and "forced" labor; in particular, slavery. Social status (membership or exclusion from the clan, family, local community), religion, legal status (form of dependence, freedom of movement, hereditary nature of constraints), socio-economic conditions (dependence, non-economic benefits, coercion, etc.), political rights and legal (and procedural) rights were addressed.[83] Researchers identified a number of variables, but were unable to reach a consensus. These issues have been debated with all the more fervor over the last twenty years, as *cultural* and *subaltern studies* have highlighted the relativity of notions of freedom and coercion. As a result, the question is now whether or not a given form of dependence, servitude, etc. observed in a particular society in Africa, Asia, the Indian Ocean or the Americas can be considered "slavery." If the answer is yes, it means that slavery existed before and independently of colonialism; if the answer is no, it means that these forms of dependence and servitude were specific to a particular place and that the "imperialist" and revisionist culture would prefer to call them "slavery" in order to minimize the West's "debt" to the Third World. So, contrary to Marx and Marxist approaches, I don't see the legal and economic aspects of coercion as succeeding one another over time; the former under pre-capitalist modes of production, the latter under capitalism. On the contrary, both coexist under capitalism.[84] By coercion, therefore, I mean forms of unequal labor relations and contracts, in which workers – not only slaves, but also serfs, indentured

---

(Philadelphia: University of Pennsylvania Press, 2016); Walter Johnson, *River of Dark Dreams: Slavery and Empire in the Cotton Kingdom* (Cambridge, MA: Harvard University Press, 2013).

[82] Alessandro Stanziani, *Capital terre*, Paris, Payot, 2021.

[83] Alain Testart, *L'esclave, la dette et le pouvoir* (Paris: Editions errance, 2001); Meillassoux, *Anthropologie de l'esclavage*; Finley, *Ancient Slavery*; Suzanne Miers, Igor Kopytoff, eds., *Slavery in Africa: Historical and Anthropological Perspectives* (Madison, WI: University of Wisconsin Press, 1977); Williams, *Capitalism and Slavery*; Paul Lovejoy, *Transformations in Slavery* (Cambridge: Cambridge University Press, 3rd edition, 2012); Engerman, *Terms of Labor*; Bush, *Serfdom and Slavery*.

[84] Gwyn Campbell, Alessandro Stanziani, eds., *Debt and Slavery in the Ancient and Mediterranean Worlds* (London: Pickering and Chatto, 2013); Stanziani, Campbell, *Bonded Labour and Debt in the Indian Ocean*.

migrants and servants – have a different legal status from their masters, and therefore different rights and obligations.[85] I will not use coercion in its broadest interpretation, as in some sociological interpretations, according to which all forms of dependent labor are an obligation and therefore coercion.[86]

I will use these definitions of capitalism and coercion only to raise questions, not to find answers according to either theory. The way I conceive the global history of labor does not start from a general definition of "free" and "unfree" labor, nor from preconceived taxonomies of labor relations. Rather, my starting point is the way in which historical actors themselves have shifted the boundaries between "free" and "unfree" work. For example, I seek to understand why, at the end of the seventeenth century, in the French and English colonies, slaves were initially called "indentured" and why, a few decades later, a new category (slave) was imposed, wanted by whom and with what consequences. Nevertheless, my intention is not to argue that wage earners were slaves in disguise, but I will try to explain by whom and why this parallel was advanced in the late eighteenth and nineteenth centuries, who opposed it, and with what social and political consequences. This re-examination of historical forms of labor and their definition is not intended to relativize these categories by asserting that "forced labor does not exist" or that it is an "intellectual invention." On the contrary, by placing these elements in appropriate historical contexts, I aim to provide an original explanation of the dynamics of forms of labor. Instead of looking for the emergence of "free labor" and "civilization" or, conversely, stigmatizing the persistence of the "corporate tradition," or even latent forms of slavery, I wish to understand the dynamics of certain historical forms of work by relating them to the tension, also historically situated, between freedom and constraint. To do this, I need to fully unpack the complement of constraint (i.e., resistance).

Resistance versus Agency?

In recent decades, a large number of publications have taken up the letters, songs and testimonies of slaves, workers, migrants and sailors.[87] These documents

---

[85] Steinfeld, *The Invention of Free Labor*; Steinfeld, *Coercion, Contract*; Simon Deakin, Frank Wilkinson, *The Law of the Labor Market: Industrialization, Employment, and Legal Evolution* (Oxford: Oxford University Press, 2005).
[86] Stanziani, *Labor in the Fringes of Empires*.
[87] Jeffrey Brooks, *When Russia Learned to Read* (Princeton: Princeton University Press, 1985); Pier Larson, *Oceans of Letters: Language and Creolization in an Indian Ocean Diaspora* (Cambridge: Cambridge University Press, 2009; Clare Anderson, *Subaltern Lives: Biographies of Colonialism in the Indian Ocean World, 1790–1920* (Cambridge: Cambridge University Press, 2012); Hallam Moorhouse, ed., *Letters of the English Seamen, 1587–1808* (London: Chapman and Hall, 1910); Robert Hay, *Landsman Hay: The Memoirs of Robert Hay, 1789–1847* (London: Rupert Hart-Davis, 1953), William Saunders, "Sailor Songs and

are a powerful testimony to the expression and action of the "subalterns." But what exactly does this posture mean?

One widespread response is to use individual cases to move beyond conventional social histories of labor and slavery that focus on structural dynamics or mass statistics. Flesh-and-blood individuals are reinjected into the historical narrative. This is a valuable yet purely illustrative attempt: It aims at describing how workers and slaves lived. The words "resistance" and "agency" have been mobilized so often that they ultimately seem to include many different forms of action while losing their explanatory power.[88] In E.P. Thompson's original approach, working-class agency sought to emphasize the role of class consciousness and representations as well as structural dynamics in the formation of the working class in Britain.[89] The first generation of subaltern studies reframed this approach in Indian and colonial contexts. These approaches have often been accused of adopting an essentialist stance (anhistorical identification of the subaltern, the poor, etc.), of idealizing the poor.[90] A completely different approach to agency emerged in the 1990s in the work of certain Africanists, and Richard Roberts in particular. The theoretical reference was no longer Gramsci and Marxism, but, significantly, Anthony Giddens. At a time when the existence of a working class in the West was being questioned and the classical welfare state was under attack, Giddens' aim was to restore the role of individual agency in the face of structural social and historical determinism as expressed by Marx and Bourdieu.[91] Roberts took Giddens as a point of reference and then translated his approach into a particular form of agency; namely, the use of law by slaves, former slaves, concubines and wives in colonial West Africa.[92]

Songs of the Sea," *The Musical Quarterly*, 14, 3 (1928): 236; Clare Anderson, *Subaltern Lives*; Marcus Rediker, *Outlaws of the Atlantic: Sailors, Pirates, and the Motley Crews in the Age of Sail* (London: Verso, 2014). As far as slaves are concerned, titles are so few that I cite only a few examples; indeed, slave letters were published as early as the nineteenth century, so much so that, as early as the 1970s, John Blassingame edited *Slave Testimony: Two Centuries of Letters, Speeches, Interviews, and Autobiographies* (Baton Rouge: Louisiana State University, 1977). Sandra Lauderdale Graham, "Writing from the Margins: Brazilian Slaves and Written Culture," *Comparative Studies in Society and History*, 49, 3 (2007): 611–636. Bruce Hall, "How Slaves Use Islam: The Letters of Enslaved Muslims Commercial Agents in the Nineteenth Century Niger Bend and Central Sahara," *The Journal of African History*, 52, 3 (2011): 279–297.

[88] "The Agency Dilemma. A Forum," *American Historical Review*, 128, 2 (2023). See also: Francesca Trivellato, "Is There a Future for the Italian Macrohistory in the Age of Global History?" *California Italian Studies*, 2, 1 (2011): 10.5070/C321009025.

[89] Thompson, *The Making of the English Working Class*.

[90] Sumit Sarkar, *Writing Social History* (Delhi: Oxford University Press, 1997).

[91] Anthony Giddens, *A Contemporary Critique of Historical Materialism* (Berkeley: University of California Press, 1981); Anthony Giddens, *The Constitution of Society* (Berkeley: University of California Press, 1984).

[92] Richard Roberts, "Representation, Structure and Agency: Divorce in the French Soudan during the Early Twentieth Century," *The Journal of African History*, 40, 3 (1999): 389–410.

Two further concepts accompanied Roberts' investigation: On the one hand, power could not be conceived as a monolithic entity; on the contrary, landscapes of power were formed and evolved over time, among other things, in response to the encounter between colonial and local actors and institutions – namely, the law. On the other hand, this complex social and institutional framework, and the fluid interactions between agency and structure, were eager to produce unintended yet powerful consequences in terms of individual and social trajectories. It was a brilliant solution to the problem of historical determinism and the relationship between agency and structure. Unfortunately, over the years, this original inspiration from the political and social sciences and the use of law has gradually been lost or relegated to the background in the vast majority of research that refers to agency as an indefinite form of social action for subaltern social groups. The problem is that, because agency is not an emic concept (internal to the sources) but etic (external to them), it seems difficult to escape a dialogue with the social and political sciences. Which social and political sciences? In this work, as in my previous work, I will not address agency in general, but will refer to a specific form of it, the same as Roberts, namely the use of the law in at least two main ways: Firstly, runaway slaves, serfs, workers, indentured migrants express the main form of resistance as an outlet for people who had only limited access to other forms of expression. Meanwhile, masters and authorities used the law to repress runaways. Secondly, we need to carefully assess the institutional contexts in which workers had some access to the law.

Indeed, the history of slavery is not only that of violence and coercion, but also that of maroons and fugitives. At the heart of the worried accounts of the authorities and planters, then of the rather favorable, but not necessarily enthusiastic, accounts of the abolitionists, maroons are still the subject of studies and novels today.[93] In Jamaica, communities of maroon slaves haunted the

---

[93] Among the enormous number of titles are: Richard Price (ed.), *Maroon Societies* (New York: Anchor Books, 1973; 3rd ed., 1996); Eugene Genovese, *Roll, Jordan, Roll: The World the Slaves Made* (New York: Vintage Books, 1976); Gabriel Debien, "Le marronnage aux Antilles françaises au XVIIIe siècle," *Caribbean Studies*, 6, 3 (1966): 3–43; Marcel Dorigny, ed., *Esclavage, résistances et abolitions* (Paris: CTHS, 1999); Rafael Lucas, "Marronage et marronnages," *Cahiers d'histoire*, 89 (2002): 13–28; Audrey Carotenuto, *Les résistances serviles dans la société coloniale de l'île Bourbon, 1750-1848* (PhD thesis: Aix-Marseille, 2006); Sylviane Diouf, *Slavery's Exiles: The Story of the American Maroons* (New York: NYU University Press, 2014); Alvin Thompson, *Flight to Freedom: African Runaways and Maroons in the Americas* (Kingston: University of the West Indies Press, 2006); William Gervase Clarence-Smith, "Runaway Slaves and Social Bandits in Southern Angola, 1875-1913," *Slavery and Abolition*, 6, 3 (1985): 23–33; Stuart B. Schwartz, "The Mocambo: Slave Resistance in Colonial Bahia," *Journal of Social History*, 3, 4 (1970): 313–333; Stuart B. Schwartz, *Slaves, Peasants, and Rebels: Reconsidering Brazilian Slavery* (Urbana and Chicago: University of Illinois Press, 1992), chapter 4; Anthony McFarlane, "Cimarrones and Palenques: Runaways and Resistance in Colonial Colombia," *Slavery and Abolition*, 6, 3 (1985): 131–151; Richard B. Sheridan, "The Maroons of Jamaica, 1730-1830: Livelihood,

authorities and owners, and were behind the revolts of 1831–1832 that convinced the majority of British parliamentarians to vote for the abolition of slavery. Maroon communities were also numerous, as were their revolts, in Louisiana, Santo Domingo, Cuba, Brazil and the southern states of the United States.[94] The stories of fugitive serfs in Russia are just as significant,[95] confirming the close link between coercion, oppression, escape and the collective imagination. According to folk tales and traditions, the mountains of the North Caucasus were a refuge for bands of runaway peasants. The village of Petrovskoe, on the Kalaus River, is said to have been founded by the fugitive serf Petr Burlak, who took refuge there in 1750 before joining forces with communities in neighboring villages and practicing what the Russian authorities described as banditry. Several thousand fugitive serfs continued to settle in the Caucasus until serfdom was abolished in 1861.[96]

However, it would be a mistake to believe that fugitive stories only concern slave and servile societies; on the contrary, these cases retain their importance

Demography and Health," *Slavery and Abolition*, 6, 3 (1985): 152–172; Richard Allen, *Slaves, Freedmen, and Indentured Laborers in Colonial Mauritius* (New York: Cambridge University Press, 1999); John Hope Franklin and Loren Schweniger, *Runaway Slaves: Rebels on the Plantation* (Oxford: Oxford University Press, 2000); Manolo Florentino and Márcia Amantino, "Runaways and *Quilombolas* in the Americas," in David Eltis, Stanley L. Engerman, Seymour Drescher, David Richardson, eds., *The Cambridge World History of Slavery*, vol. 3, *AD 1420–AD 1804* (New York: Cambridge University Press, 2011): 708–740; Robert Paquette, "Slave Resistance and Social History", *Journal of Social History*, 24, 3 (1991): 681–685; Aline Helg, *Plus jamais esclaves: De l'insoumission à la révolte, le grand récit d'une émancipation (1492–1838)* (Paris: La découverte, 2016); Viola Muller, *Escape to the City: Fugitive Slaves in Antebellum Urban South* (Chapel Hill: The University of North Carolina Press, 2022).

[94] Manuel Barcia, *Seeds of Insurrection: Domination and Resistance on Western Cuban Plantations, 1808–1848* (Baton Rouge: Louisiana State University Press, 2008); Michael Craton, *Testing the Chains: Resistance to Slavery in the British West Indies* (Ithaca: Cornell University Press, 1982); David P. Geggus, *The Impact of the Haitian Revolution in the Atlantic World* (New York: Columbia University Press, 2001); Eugene Genovese, *From Rebellion to Revolution: Afro-American Slave Revolts in the Making of the Modern World* (Baton Rouge: Louisiana State University Press, 1979); Joao José Reis, *Rebellion in Brazil: the Muslim Uprising of 1835 in Bahia* (Baltimore: John Hopkins University Press, 1983).

[95] Elise Kimerling Wirtschafter, *From Serf to Russian Soldier* (Princeton: Princeton University Press, 1990); Steven Hoch, *Serfdom and Social Control* (Chicago: University of Chicago Press, 1986); Richard Hellie, *Enserfment and Military Change in Muscovy* (Chicago: University of Chicago Press, 1971); Roger Bartlett, "Serfdom and State Power in Imperial Russia," *European History Quarterly*, 33, 1 (2003): 29–64; Barrett, *At the Edge of Empire*; Williard Sunderland, "Peasants on the Move: State Peasant Resettlement in Imperial Russia, 1805–1830," *Russian Review*, 52, 4 (1993): 472–485.

[96] A. Tvalchrelidze, *Stavropol'skaia guberniia v statisticheskom, geograficheskom, istoricheskom i sel'sko-khoziaistvennom otnosheniiakh* (The province of Stavropol in statistical, geographical, historical and rural reports) (Stavropol': Tipografiia Koritskogo, 1897); Thomas Barrett, "Lines of Uncertainty: The Frontier of the North Caucasus," *Slavic Review*, 54, 3 (1995): 578–601.

in post-slavery societies. In the British colonies – from the 1840s onwards – in France, after 1848,[97] but also in Russia after the abolition of serfdom in 1861,[98] and in Africa after the abolition of slavery between 1880 and 1914, immigrants, former slaves and workers described as fugitives remain at the heart of the concerns of authorities, landowners and industrialists.[99]

[97] Céline Flory, *De l'esclavage à la liberté forcée. Histoire des travailleurs africains engagés dans la Caraïbe française au XIXe siècle* (Paris: Karthala, 2015); Richard Allen, "A Serious and Alarming Daily Evil: Marronage and its Legacy in Mauritius and the Plantation Colonial World," *Slavery and Abolition*, 25, 2 (2004): 1–17, French version in *Outre-mers, Revue d'histoire*, 89, 336–337 (2002): 131–52; Nigel Bolland, "Systems of Domination after Slavery: The Control of Land and Labor in the British West Indies after 1838," *Comparative Studies in Society and History*, 23, 4 (1981): 591–619; Hay, Craven, *Masters, Servants and Magistrates*; Christopher Tomlins, *Freedom Bound: Law, Labor, and Civic Identity in Colonizing British America, 1580–1865* (Cambridge: Cambridge University Press, 2010).

[98] Boris Gorshkov, "Serfs on the Move: Peasant Seasonal Migration in Pre-Reform Russia, 1800–1861," *Kritika*, 1, 4 (2000): 627–656; John McKay, *Four Russian Serf Narratives* (Madison: Wisconsin University Press, 2009); Daniel Brower, Susan Leyton, "Liberation through Captivity: Nikolai Shipov's Adventures in The Imperial Borderlands," *Kritika* 6, 2 (2005): 259–279; Alexander Nikitenko, *Up From Serfdom: My Childhood and Youth in Russia, 1804–1824*, trans. Helen Saltz Jacobson (New Haven: Yale University Press, 2001); Donald Fanger, "The Peasant in Literature," in Wayne S. Vucinich, ed., *The Peasant in Nineteenth-Century Russia* (Stanford: Stanford University Press, 1968): 231–262; Jeffrey Burds, *Peasant Dreams and Market Politics: Labor Migration and the Russian Village, 1861–1905* (Pittsburgh: University of Pittsburgh Press, 1998); Lewis Siegelbaum, Leslie Page Moch, *Broad is My Native Land: Repertoires and Regimes of Migration in Russia's Twentieth Century* (Ithaca: Cornell University Press, 2014); Daniel Brower, *The Russian City between Tradition and Modernity, 1850–1900* (Berkeley: University of California Press, 1990); Jeffrey Burds, "The Social Control of Peasant Labor in Russia: The Response of Village Communities to Labor Migration in the Central Industrial Region, 1861–1905," in Esther Kingston-Mann, Timothy Mixter eds., *Peasant Economy, Culture, and Politics of European Russia, 1800–1921*, (Princeton: Princeton University Press, 1991): 52–100; Christine D. Worobec, *Peasant Russia: Family and Community in the Post-Emancipation Period* (Princeton: Princeton University Press, 1991); Barbara A. Engel, *Between the Fields and the City: Women, Work, and Family in Russia, 1861–1914* (New York: Cambridge University Press, 1994); Evel G. Economakis, "Patterns of Migration and Settlement in Pre-revolutionary St. Petersburg: Peasants from Yaroslav and Tver Provinces," *Russian Review*, 56, 1 (1997): 8–24; Dale Peterson, *Up from Bondage: The Literature of Russian and African American Soul* (Durham, NC: Duke University Press, 2000); Olga Zolotareva, *Voices of Equality: American Anti-slavery and Russian Anti-serfdom Poetry*, https://ucbcluj.org/voices-of-equality-american-anti-slavery-and-russian-anti-serfdom-poetry/.

[99] Paul Lovejoy, Jan Hogendown, *Slow Death of Slavery: The Course of Abolition in Northern Nigeria, 1897–1936* (Cambridge: Cambridge University Press, 1993); Martin Klein, *Slavery and Colonial Rule in French West Africa* (Cambridge: Cambridge University Press, 1998); Suzanne Miers, Richard Roberts eds., *The End of Slavery in Africa* (Madison: University of Wisconsin Press, 1988); Martin Chanok, *Law Custom and Social Order: The Colonial Experience in Malawi and Zambia* (Cambridge: Cambridge University Press, 1985); Frederick Cooper, *From Slaves to Squatters: Plantation Labor and Agriculture in Zanzibar and Coastal Kenya, 1890–1935* (New Haven and London: Yale University Press, 1980).

Even more troubling, from the seventeenth century to the end of the nineteenth century, in Western Europe, people and workers who were in principle free – domestic servants, agricultural day laborers, apprentices – were described as deserters and fugitives, and condemned as such.[100] This convergence is all the more surprising given that the administrative and legal vocabulary of the time equated these cases with those of soldiers and sailors: Fugitives thus became deserters.[101]

Recent studies have highlighted this global dimension of runaways worldwide.[102] The present study is sympathetic to this synthesis,[103] but I shall depart from it in certain respects, starting with the general association between runaways and capitalism. As I've already mentioned, my own definition of capitalism differs from Marxist-Weberian approaches. It's no coincidence that this mentioned global study on runaways, unlike my approach, doesn't include wage earners, but only slaves, post-slave migrants, serfs, convicts and sailors. In other words, it overlooks the fact that before labor was unionized in the West, it was also subject to harsh conditions and, as I will show, servants were also labeled runaways and deserters. From my point of view, the bifurcation between labor at the core and labor in the peripheries of empires came very late, only with the welfare state in the twentieth century. In order to express this process, in my revised approach to agency and resistance, I will use an interpretation adapted from Hirschman's trilogy of voice, exit and loyalty. In recent books on the "global fugitive," some authors and editors – Van der Linden, Rossum, Lucassen – mention this scheme, and I have done so myself.[104] However, this approach needs to be reassessed. Exit, according to Hirschman, can only be expressed in the market through a negative act of protest (refusing to work, refusing to buy a given product), whereas voice places us squarely in

---

[100] Steinfeld, *The Invention of Free Labor*; Philip Hoffman, *Growth in a Traditional Society: The French Countryside, 1450–1815* (Princeton: Princeton University Press, 1996); Yvonne Crebouw, *Salaires et salariés agricoles en France, des débuts de la révolution aux approches du XXe siècle* (PhD thesis: Paris Sorbonne, 1986); Ronald Hubscher, Jean-Claude Farcy, eds., *La moisson des autres* (Paris: Créaphys édition, 1996).

[101] Matthias von Rossum, Jeannette Kamp, eds., *Desertion in the Early Modern World: A Comparative History* (London: Bloomsbury, 2016); Erik-Jan Zürcher, ed., *Fighting for a Living: A Comparative History of Military Labour, 1500–2000* (Amsterdam: Amsterdam University Press, 2013); Jeremy Black, *A Military Revolution? Military Change and European Society, 1550–1800* (Basingstoke, UK: Macmillan, 1991); Marcus Rediker, *Between the Devil and the Deep Blue Sea: Merchants, Seamen, Pirates, and the Anglo-American Maritime World, 1700–1750* (Cambridge: Cambridge University Press, 1987).

[102] Marcus Rediker, Titas Chakraborty, Matthias van Rossum eds., *A Global History of Runaways: Workers, Mobility, and Capitalism, 1600–1850* (Berkeley: University of California Press, 2019).

[103] Alessandro Stanziani, "Runaways: a Global History," in Matthias von Rossum, Jeannette Kamp, *Desertion in the Early Modern World: A Comparative History* (London: Bloomsbury, 2016): 15–30.

[104] Stanziani, "Runaways."

the realm of politics. The contrast between exit and voice is the same as that between economics and politics; it has enabled a fundamental critique of the perfect competition model, which is why Hirschman's scheme has been so successful in economics, sociology and political science. The problem, as many scholars have observed the problem, lies with loyalty, a residual category that Hirschman barely developed.[105] According to Hirschman, loyalty makes it possible to delay the exit so that the voice and its tensions have more impact: Those who remain can use the exit as Leverage in negotiation. This model works well for consumers and possibly unions, two cases studied by Hirschman and many other authors. Is it also relevant in the case of slavery? Fugitives, maroons, vagabonds and others on the run did not simply express "resistance," as Scott, Petterson and their followers have claimed.[106] If we adopt Hirschman's model (voice, exit and loyalty), fugitives undoubtedly opted for a form of exit where their voice was weak or non-existent, and their loyalty was therefore equally weak.[107] But has exit always been the opposite of voice? Have there been contexts in which they have played complementary roles?

I argue that running away as a form of exit cannot be understood without taking into account the fact that between the seventeenth and early twentieth centuries, workers – slaves or serfs, day laborers or domestic servants, conscripts or convicts – had no voice or only a very limited voice: no political rights, very few civil rights, unequal legal rights, no social rights. They were fugitives because they had no voice and therefore no choice.[108] Work as a service meant that anyone who escaped it was considered a fugitive or a vagabond. Limitations on mobility and people's property titles converged and, in extreme cases, coincided; for example, in the case of slaves, serfs and certain forms of indentured immigrants. The notion of labor as a service led to a normative relationship between the control of time and the control of people.[109]

Law: A Form of Coercion or Resistance?

This explains why the social order is so closely linked to the political order in runaway issues, and in labor issues in general, during the period under study. One of the main aims of the rules governing runaways was to ensure market

---

[105] Jeremy Adelman, *Worldly Philosopher: The Odyssey of Albert O. Hirschman* (Princeton: Princeton University Press, 2014).
[106] James Scott, *Weapons of the Weak: Everyday Forms of Peasant Resistance* (New Haven: Yale University Press, 1985); Patterson, *Slavery and Social Death*.
[107] Albert Hirschman, *Exit, Voice, and Loyalty* (Cambridge, MA: Harvard University Press, 1970).
[108] Frederick Cooper, *Decolonization and African Society* (Cambridge: Cambridge University Press, 1996).
[109] Gary Cross, *A Quest for Time: The Reduction of Work in Britain and France, 1840–1940* (Berkeley: University of California Press, 1989); Gary Cross ed., *Worktime and Industrialization: An International History* (Philadelphia: Temple University Press, 1988).

stability in a well-ordered, hierarchical society. Most rules concerning runaways and fugitives stressed the importance of returning them to their rightful master and/or owner. That is why I'm reframing Hirschman and talking about voice, exit and law.[110] This last variable needs further explanation.

The law offers neither infinite solutions (the position of those who insist on the importance of informal rules) nor a single, predetermined outcome (the Marxist and Foucauldian thesis), but rather a limited set of possibilities. These possibilities derive from a number of factors: the formulation of the rules and, hence, the pressure groups behind them; the country's legal traditions; the intellectual and social framework within which the rules are used and interpreted.[111] There is now a substantial body of literature focusing on the way in which actors appropriate the law, particularly in their labor relations in France, England, Germany, the United States,[112] and Russia.[113] Following this historiography, this study challenges the classical oppositions assumed to exist between ancient regime societies (including Russia and pre-modern France) and modern societies, as different population groups, including peasants, made extensive use of the law not only in Britain, but also in pre-revolutionary France and Russia. In these contexts, law could perpetuate social inequalities, but not necessarily and not in the same way.[114] Studies of colonial law and its use by "colonized" populations have also attracted a great deal of interest over the past twenty years.[115]

[110] Stanziani, *Labor on the Fringes of Empire*.
[111] Stanziani, *Rules of Exchange*.
[112] Some references: Morton Horwitz, *The Transformation of American Law, 1780–1860* (Cambridge, MA: Harvard University Press, 1977); Steinfeld, *Coercion*; Deakin, Wilkinson, *The Law of the Labor Market*; Alain Dewerpe, "En avoir ou pas. A propos du livret ouvrier dans la France du XIXe siècle," in Alessandro Stanziani, ed., *Le travail contraint en Asie et en Europe, XVIIe-XXe siècles* (Paris: MSH éditions, 2010): 217–240; Willibald Steinmetz, ed., *Private Law and Social Inequality in the Industrial Age: Comparing Legal Cultures in Britain, France, Germany, and the United States* (Oxford: Oxford University Press, 2000).
[113] Virginia Martin, *Law and Custom in the Steppe: The Kazakhs of the Middle Horde and Russian Colonialism in the Nineteenth Century* (Richmond, Surrey: Routledge Curzon, 2001); Richard Wortman, *Development of a Russian Legal Consciousness* (Chicago: University of Chicago Press, 1976); William Wagner, *Marriage, Property and Law in Late Imperial Russia* (Oxford: Oxford University Press, 1994); Jane Burbank, *Russian Peasants Go to Court: Legal Culture in the Countryside, 1905–1917* (Bloomington: Indiana University Press, 2004); Peter Solomon, ed. *Reforming Justice in Russia, 1864–1994: Power, Culture, and the Limits of Legal Order* (Armonk, NY: M. E. Sharpe, 1997); Ekaterina A. Pravilova, *Zakonnost' i prava lichnosti: administrativnaia iustitsiia v Rossii, vtoraia polovina XIX v.-oktiabr' 1917* (Legality and Human Rights: Administrative Justice in Russia in the Second Half of the Nineteenth Century to October 1917) (Saint Petersburg: Izd-vo SZAGS, 2000).
[114] Steinmetz, *Private Law and Social Inequality in the Industrial Age*.
[115] Some references in a rapidly expanding field: Hay, Craven, *Masters, Servants, and Magistrates*; Lauren Benton, *Law and Colonial Cultures* (Cambridge: Cambridge University Press, 2002); Richard Roberts, *Litigants and Household: African Disputes and Colonial Courts in the French Soudan, 1895–1912* (Portsmouth: Heinemann, 2005).

The general principle applicable to all these contexts is that law could be a mediating tool, that it could produce inequalities but also reduce them and that the end result never was a foregone conclusion. Nevertheless, the scope of this flexibility should not be overestimated: A legal norm can only be used within precise limits, which depend on its wording, the way it is applied and the relationships between the parties involved. Consequently, it is necessary to determine empirically, in each context, whether and how the concerned actors – serfs, workers, indentured immigrants or former slaves – were able to defend themselves, to what extent and with what success. Lauren Benton and many others have shown that local actors were able to appropriate colonial law by taking advantage of legal pluralism. Legal pluralism in the colonial context reveals that the colonial order was far more complex and institutionally unstable than we usually assume.[116] The coexistence of multiple legal orders enabled different actors to call on different sets of rules.[117] From the point of view of economic and social players, the multiplicity of rules and jurisdictions represented not only a cost but also an opportunity. The possibility of appealing to different rules and jurisdictions was important: Not only did it enable actors to "cheat," it also guaranteed them a certain amount of leeway.

This optimistic vision needs to be reframed, however. If recourse to the law was not an unattainable dream, it was much more accessible to landowners and colonial elites than to workers. The former constantly took the latter to court and won, while the latter constantly faced enormous obstacles. However, despite these difficulties, they continued to use the law, contrary to most interpretations made by observers and researchers on this point. The relevant question, then, is not to set *equality* before the law against *inequality* in the practices of social life. Rather, I would stress that there was considerable inequality both in the text and in the implementation of the law, even in a liberal context. But it is precisely for this reason that the procedures, the burden of proof and the same deserve close scrutiny, which the social actors themselves did at the time. These varieties of "law in action" occurred before, during and after the abolitionist process.

---

[116] R. W. Kostal, *A Jurisprudence of Power: Victorian Empire and the Rule of Law* (Oxford: Oxford University Press, 2005).

[117] M. B. Hooker, *Legal Pluralism: An Introduction to Colonial and Neo-Colonial Laws* (Oxford: Clarendon Press, 1975); Sally Falk Moore, *Social Facts and Fabrications: Customary Law on Kilimanjaro, 1880–1980* (New York: Cambridge University Press, 1980); Brian Tamanaha, Caroline Sage, Michael Woolcock, eds., *Legal Pluralism and Development: Scholars and Practitioners in Dialogue* (Cambridge: Cambridge University Press, 2012).

PART I

Labor Rules and Colonization

While classical liberal economic thought maintains that markets can function on their own without any interference, and Marx and his followers consider that law merely confirms and reinforces the class structure already in place, neo-institutionalist currents have endeavored to prove that law and institutions intervene to ensure the efficient functioning of the market. Many authors (including North)[1] have shown that the rise of capitalism owed much to the introduction of rules protecting private property. In this context, unfree labor can only exist if political institutions intervene and limit the free market; otherwise, the lack of efficiency of unfree labor will tend to exclude it from the market. Neo-institutional economics argues that in places where the market is still "imperfect," it makes sense to have institutions to compensate for this deficiency; economic development will eventually render these institutions obsolete.[2] This model doesn't explain much, however: institutions encompass everything (the state, guilds, organizations, firms, associations, the family, kinship, the village and even the market itself) and are both the source and consequence of market dynamics.[3] If institutions exist, it is because they have an economic raison d'être.[4] The Nobel prize winner Daron Acemoglu and many others[5] have shown that transatlantic trade has encouraged the adoption of rules that are more favorable to trade and manufacturing, as well as more protective of private property and incomes. The Atlantic also altered the political and social balance in Great Britain, where merchants united against the Crown

---

[1] Douglass North, *Structure and Change in Economic History* (New York: W.W. Norton, 1981); Douglass North, Robert Thomas, *The Rise of Western Civilization: A new Economic History* (Cambridge: Cambridge University Press, 1973).
[2] Douglass North, Barry Weingast, "Constitution and Commitment: The Evolution of Institution Governing Public Choice in Seventeenth-Century England," *The Journal of Economic History*, 49, 4 (1989): 803–832.
[3] Stanziani, ed., *Dictionnaire historique de l'économie-droit*; Alessandro Stanziani, "Comment mesurer l'efficacité des institutions?" *Histoire et mesure*, 30 (2015): 3–24.
[4] Sheilagh Ogilvie, "Whatever Is, Is Right? Economic Institutions in Pre-Industrial Europe," *Economic History Review*, 60, 4 (2007): 649–684.
[5] Acemoglu, Johnson, Robinson, "The Rise of Europe."

and supported the Glorious Revolution. All these factors contributed to the economic development of the United Kingdom.[6]

Following a similar line of reasoning, historiography (both Russian and Western) has consistently pointed the finger at Russian institutions – in particular, the absence of representative institutions, the persistence of communal property and the limits of private ownership, and, above all, serfdom – to explain Russia's economic backwardness.[7]

There are several problems with this line of reasoning. Firstly, it is empirically false: slavery and post-slavery coercion have persisted for centuries, and we need to understand why. Secondly, neo-institutionalism takes it for granted that institutions drive history, and links institutional change to economic efficiency: institutions change in response to, and therefore influence, concerns about profit and efficiency. The problem is that institutions also respond to political and social tensions, which are not necessarily in line with profit optimization. In contrast to neo-institutionalism, I argue that the institutions regulating labor (property, labor contracts) are indeed important, but we need to understand the social origin and application of legal and other rules governing labor in the era of plantation and manufacturing capitalism.

---

[6] On this subject, see also Findlay and O Rourke, *Power and Plenty*.

[7] Among many others (see following notes): Jerome Blum, *Lords and Peasants in Russia from the Ninth to the Nineteenth Century* (New York: Atheneum, 1964); Alexander Gerschenkron, *Economic Backwardness in Historical Perspective: A Book of Essays* (Cambridge, MA: Harvard University Press, 1962); Richard Hellie, *Enserfment and Military Change in Muscovy* (Chicago: University of Chicago Press, 1971); Peter Kolchin, *Unfree Labor: American Slavery and Russian Serfdom* (Cambridge, MA: Harvard University Press, 1987). Tracy Dennison, *The Institutional Framework of Russian Serfdom* (Cambridge: Cambridge University Press, 2011).

1

The Russian Way

Peasants, Landowners and the Empire

Peasant-Soldiers

If we want to understand the relationship between empire building and serfdom in Russia, we need to consider three interdependent groups: peasant-soldiers, landowners and the state.

During the seventeenth century, Moscow consolidated its power in the steppe, seizing vast territories in Poland-Lithuania and strengthening its territorial and economic hold while the Crimean Khanate and the Ottoman Empire continued to weaken. In the space of three centuries, Moscow built the world's largest empire with China; together, they shared the whole of Central and Southern Asia. Moscow's expansion was achieved through the systematic displacement and subjugation of the "nomadic" peoples of the steppe.[1] At the same time, this result could not have been achieved without three major ingredients: trade, military and bureaucratic organization, and a special relationship between the state, noble landowners and peasants.[2] Historians have long pointed to Russia's deficits and debts due to military spending. In 1680, Russia spent one million rubles on military operations: half the national budget. At the same time, England and France were borrowing heavily, and their spending far exceeded the budgets allocated to financing their wars. Britain devoted around 70 percent of its national budget to military expenditure between 1689 and 1713. Russia's military spending represented around 50 percent of the country's budget in 1701, but had risen to 70 percent by 1724.[3] Like other European countries, Russia had a large, stable army and comparable budget deficits, despite the per capita tax introduced by Peter the Great. The system was calculated to meet the needs of the army, and peasants and townspeople subject to the tax were

---

[1] Williard Sunderland, *Taming the Wild Field. Colonization and Empire in the Russian Steppe* (Ithaca: Cornell University Press, 2004); Andreas Kappeler, *The Russian Empire. A Multi-ethnic History* (London: Pearson, 2001); Francine Hirsch, *Empire of Nations. Ethnographic Knowledge and the Making of the Soviet Empire* (Ithaca: Cornell University Press, 2005).

[2] Hellie, *Enserfment and Military Change in Muscovy*; Richard Hellie, *Slavery in Russia* (Chicago: University of Chicago Press, 1982).

[3] John Le Donne, *Absolutism and Ruling Class: The Formation of the Russian Political Order, 1700–1825* (Oxford: Oxford University Press, 1991): 276–277, table 15.1.

forced to pay. Alongside the capitation system, indirect taxation developed and was widely detested. At the beginning of the eighteenth century, it covered 50 percent of the budget.[4] In terms of manpower, the armies of the main European countries numbered 40,000 men in the mid-sixteenth century, a figure that gradually rose to around 150,000 by the 1630s. Muscovy began the Thirteen Years' War (1654–1667) against Poland-Lithuania with an army of 40,000 men, and ended it with 100,000. Towards the end of the century, Russia maintained a roughly equivalent regular army of around 100,000 men, which, given its small population at the time (around 15 million), made it one of the countries with the highest percentage of conscripts (1 to 1.5 percent). Finally, in the mid-eighteenth century, Russia and France both had 1.3 percent of their population in uniform, ahead of England (1 percent), but far behind Prussia (4.2 percent).[5]

This is where relations between Russian landowners, peasants and the state come into play. As early as the fifteenth century, the Moscow princes claimed exclusive control over the military services provided by the nobles. The legal definition of the elite was clarified during the reign of Ivan III and Vasily III (between 1459 and 1533): In addition to hereditary estates (*votchina*), the law provided for the granting of land in exchange for military service, known as *pomest'e*. This type of ownership, very similar to the Mongolian and Central Asian Muslim institution known as *iqta*, could only be inherited if the descendant also served the prince. Otherwise, ownership of the land reverted to the state on the death of the officer. The *pomest'e* could not be sold or mortgaged, and could only be exchanged for another *pomest'e*. With this system, the Moscow princes sought to achieve two objectives: to control the elite and to have a relatively stable cavalry.

The problem in the newly conquered regions was the shortage of peasants; Moscow made extensive use of steppe colonization to strengthen its territorial and military power. Moscow authorities allowed peasants who had completed their military service in these regions to pass on their small estates to their descendants. At the same time, members of the lower service class were sometimes salaried and sometimes received a plot of land that was collectively owned.[6] In the second half of the seventeenth century, the state's financial difficulties prevented it from paying salaries and thus reinforced the distribution

---

[4] Evgenii V. Anisimov, "Remarks on the Fiscal Policy of Russian Absolutism During the First Quarter of the Eighteenth Century," *Soviet Studies in History*, 28, 1 (1989): 10–32; Evgenii V. Anisimov, *Podatnaia reforma Petra I: vvedenie podushnoi podati v Rossii 1719–1728 gg* (Tax reform under Peter I: the introduction of per capita taxation in Russia, 1719–1728), (Moscow: Nauka, 1982); Paul Bushkovitch, "Taxation, Tax Farming and Merchants in Sixteenth-Century Russia," *Slavic Review*, 37, 3 (1978): 381–398.

[5] Simon Dixon, *The Modernization of Russia, 1676–1825* (Cambridge: Cambridge University Press, 1999).

[6] RGADA (Russian Archives of Ancient Acts), fond 210 Belgorodskii stb 772.

of land in exchange for service. The annexation of new territories and the colonization of the steppe helped consolidate these prospects. In 1635, a decree authorized local garrison commanders and southern governors to guarantee the residence of fugitive peasants and not return them to their rightful owners. A number of decrees passed between 1710 and 1724 created a new legal category, the *odnodvortsy*: unmarried owners of small estates, identified as landowners by their tax and military systems. At the time, the *odnovortsy* comprised 600,000 Muscovites and their dependents. The *odnodvortsy* was similar to the state peasant: Like the latter, they paid taxes (in money and in kind), but they also had military obligations and enjoyed property rights over the land,[7] which meant that land ownership was no longer a distinguishing feature of the "nobility" in relation to the peasantry. Indeed, along the southern frontier, peasant settlers also benefited from *pomest'e* (non-transferable land ownership).

In short, the distinction between peasants and landowners remained vague in the colonized regions of the Russian Empire. This was because the legal status and social conditions of soldiers and landowners were blurred to support the occupation of new territories. Meanwhile, in central Russia, two other categories of workers emerged, again in connection with imperial expansion and negotiations between state elites and landowners: slaves and serfs. The serfs were expected to be the most numerous; but who were the slaves?

Slaves in Russia

Social status (membership or exclusion from clan, family, local community), religion, legal status (form of dependence, freedom of movement, hereditary nature of constraints), socio-economic conditions (dependence, non-economic benefits, coercion, etc.), political rights and legal (and procedural) rights have all been evoked to define slaves and slavery. The debates often mix two distinct yet related dimensions: The definitions of slavery and forms of dependence given by the historical actors themselves, and those put forward by researchers. These two dimensions were and still are controversial, and historians who defend their attachment to presumed "purely historical" definitions tend to forget that the actors themselves did not share a single definition of slavery. They also underestimate the fact that any conversation between specialists from different periods and fields requires prior discussion of how translations and equivalences of terms can be made. In this book, I always draw on local historical definitions, but I also intend to show that these definitions have always been debated, that they circulated between different spaces and languages and that, as a result, the question of translation and identification of slaves (or serfs) was negotiated and evolved over time. This was not a scholarly

---

[7] Thomas Esper, "The Odnodvortsy and the Russian Nobility," *Slavonic and East European Review*, 45, 104 (1967): 124–135.

issue, but a political and social struggle. It is therefore extremely important to recognize the different forms of extreme dependence in Russia. The category we are concerned with here is *kholopy*. Hellie regarded *kholopy* as slavery. Herbert Leventer objected to the latter translation, pointing out that the status of Russian *kholopy* was not transmitted to their children, that their servitude was temporary and that they could accumulate and transmit property. He therefore believed that *kholop* corresponded more closely to the English word servant.[8] The case of Russia, much less well known than the others, confirms the exceptionality of the Atlantic world, and its definition of slavery, and the need to articulate it with wider historical experience. The first step is to understand who *the kholopy* really were.

Two main sources are generally mentioned in studies of ancient, medieval and modern slavery: debt (largely conceived as a form of individual and/or social obligation) and capture by warring parties or armies. Roughly speaking, the former is seen as something internal to a given society, while the latter is generated by the transgression of territorial boundaries.[9] This taxonomy requires some important clarifications; for example, war captives could be used to obtain ransom, but they could also fall into the category of slaves by being sold; the sale of captives on the domestic market of the victorious war party was quite widespread. However, this movement required the agreement of clan chiefs or the state. In other words, the boundary between a captive of war and a slave was flexible and depended on the relative power of military commanders, political leaders, slave brokers and slave owners who negotiated the disposition of captives of war amongst themselves. In this respect, slaves and captives in ancient Rome or modern Africa evoke quite different phenomena. What about Russia?

Here, *kholopy* had two main origins: captives of war and people in debt.[10] In early modern times, the relationship between captives of war and slavery spread throughout the Mediterranean, Asia and Africa, and, as we shall see, it also penetrated the Atlantic.[11] The legal and social justification for slavery was strictly linked to that of prisoners of war. Indeed, in Russia too, wars with the Crimean Khanate, the Nogays and other tribes, Poland-Lithuania and the Ottoman Empire were frequent. Conflicts generally gave rise to numerous

---

[8] Richard Hellie, "Recent Soviet Historiography on Medieval and Early Modern Russian Slavery," *Russian Review*, 35, 1 (1976): 1–36; Herbert Leventer, "Comments on Richard Hellie's "Recent Soviet …" *Russian Review*, 36, 1 (1977): 64–67; Richard Hellie, "Reply," *Russian Review*, 36, 1 (1977): 68–75.

[9] Alessandro Stanziani, "Slavery and Bondage in Central Asia and Russia: 14th-Nineteenth Centuries," in Christopher Witzenrath, ed., *Eurasian Slavery, Ransom and Abolition in World History, 1200–1860* (Farnham: Ashgate, 2015): 81–104.

[10] Hellie, *Slavery in Russia*.

[11] Stanziani, *After Oriental Despotism*; Linda Colley, *Captives: Britain, Empire, and the World, c.a. 1600–1850* (New York: Anchor, 2004).

captures and exchanges of prisoners of war. In the fourteenth century, Crimean Tatars sold some 2,000 Slavic slaves a year to the Ottomans, a figure that increased in the fifteenth century. The Tatars either bought them on the markets of Central Asia or captured them themselves.[12] Slave incursions into Muscovy reached crisis proportions after 1475, when the Ottomans took over the Black Sea slave trade from the Genoese and the Crimeans began to make the slave trade a major industry, particularly between 1514 and 1654.[13] In 1501, during the Russian campaign in Lithuania, the Crimean Tatars (allied to the Russians on this occasion) seized 50,000 Lithuanian captives. By 1529, half the slaves in Ottoman Crimea had been identified as coming from Ukraine and Muscovy, and between 150,000 and 200,000 Russians were captured in the first half of the seventeenth century.[14] Russia then moved eastwards, extending into Siberia and certain Cossack regions, notably the territory of the Iaik Cossacks.[15] The resulting prisoners of war and ransomed captives fueled a constant slave market.[16] This enormous trade in slaves and war captives fueled the better-known slave trade across the Mediterranean in the Middle Ages and early modern times.[17] This trade found its reservoir not only along the borders between Islam and Christianity, but also in Russia and Central Asia, as confirmed by the words "Tatar" and "Slaves," to designate these slaves.[18]

The *Ulozhenie* (Statute) of 1649 devoted an entire section (number 8) to the question of ransoming Russian captives,[19] and a ransom tax was introduced for this purpose in 1551 and remained in force until 1679. The ransom was set according to the captive's status.[20] Those who did not receive a ransom became

---

[12] Alan Fisher, "Muscovy and the Black Sea Trade," *Canadian-American Slavic Studies*, 6, 4 (1972): 582–593.

[13] Zübeyde Günes-Yagci, "The Black Sea Slave Trade According to the Istanbul Port Customs Register, 1606-7," in Christopher Witzenrath, ed., *Eurasian Slavery, Ransom and Abolition in World History, 1200–1860* (Farnham: Ashgate, 2015): 207–220.

[14] Aleksei A. Novosel'skii, *Bor'ba Moskovskogo gosudarstva s tatarami v pervoi polovine 17 veka* (The struggle of the Muscovite state against the Tatars in the first half of the seventeenth century) (Moscow, Leningrad: Nauka, 1948).

[15] Brian Davis, *State, Power, and Community in Early Modern Russia: The Case of Kozlov, 1635-1649* (Basingstoke, NY: Palgrave, Macmillan, 2004).

[16] Elena N. Shipova, *Slovar' turkizmov v russkom iazyke* (Dictionary of Turkish in the Russian language) (Alma-Ata: Nauka, 1976): 442.

[17] Jacques Heers, *Esclaves et domestiques au Moyen Age dans le monde méditerranéen* (Paris: Hachette, 1996).

[18] Charles Verlinden, "L'origine de sclavus=esclave," *Bulletin du Cange*, XVII (1942): 97–128; Charles Verlinden, *L'esclavage dans l'Europe médiévale* (Bruges: De Tempel, 1955); Steven Epstein, *Speaking of Slavery* (Ithaca: Cornell University Press, 2001).

[19] Richard Hellie, ed. *The Muscovite Law Code (Ulozhenie) of 1649*, part. 1 (Irvine, CA: Charles Schlacks, 1988): 17–18.

[20] Rossiiskaia Akademiia nauk. Arkhiv, fond 1714, op. 1 (A.A. Novosel'skii), delo 66, l. 123; RGADA, fond 123, opis' 3, delo 13.

slaves and were assigned various tasks. In the Crimea, some were employed in agriculture or served as interpreters and guides to lead war troops into Russian territory. Those sold on the slave markets of the Ottoman Empire or the Central Asian Khanates were employed as craftspeople, laborers or domestic servants.[21]

It was mainly during the seventeenth century that the Russians seized prisoners of war and captives for ransom in both Muslim and Catholic regions. Captives were intended to temporarily serve the elite as administrative assistants or servants. They were expected to remain in the elite's service until their master's death. Since the beginning of the seventeenth century, the state attempted to establish a register of military captives, so that central authorities could eventually return them to their country of origin if diplomatic agreement was reached. However, several sources mention the difficulties encountered by the Moscow authorities in ensuring compliance with these standards, and the servitude of war captives persisted. In 1655, Poles, Lithuanians and others, both adults and children, were openly sold on the streets of Moscow.[22] The Nogays, who had joined the Muscovite forces, bought German and Polish prisoners in Moscow.[23] Muslims were frequently captured and sometimes sold, in violation of Islamic law; the Ottoman and Islamic authorities therefore sent injunctions to Moscow to buy them back without compensation.[24]

However, by the end of the eighteenth century, the only slaves and captives held for ransom in the Russian Empire were Tatars or Circassians. It was with the Ottoman Empire that the traffic in slaves and captives was most significant. The Russian Empire maintained relations with Islamic regions where slavery was common and considered the only form of forced labor authorized by Islamic law. The Muslim Tatars of Crimea carried out numerous raids to recruit Russian subjects as well as other Eastern Slavs, Poles and Lithuanians, and exported most of their captives to the Ottomans.

In addition to prisoners of war, there were many other forms of enslaved people in Russia, all referred to as *kholopy*. The meaning of this category is controversial:[25] *kabal'nye kholopy* was the most widespread. Official rules emphasized that *kabal'nye* were not *dolgovye* (indebted) and that *kabal'nye* could only remain obligated for the life of the creditor. The hereditary variety

---

[21] RGADA, fond 123, Krymskie dela 13, l. 53; *Materialy po istorii Uzbeksoi, Tadzhiskoi i Turkmenskoi SSR*, vol. 1 (Leningrad, Moscow: Nauka, 1932): 386–387.

[22] Aleksandr' L. Khoroshkevich, *Russkoe gosudarstvo v sisteme mezhdunarodnykh otnoshenii kontsa XV-nachala XVI v.* (The Russian state in the system of international relations in the late fifteenth and early sixteenth centuries) (Moscow: Nauka, 1980): 30–32.

[23] Michael Khodarkovsky, *Russia's Steppe Frontier* (Bloomington: Indiana University Press, 2004).

[24] RGADA, fond 89, *Turetskie dela*, delo 3.

[25] Of 2,499 documents containing the word *kholop* or *kholopostvo*, 2,116 refer to the *kabal'noe* variety (Hellie, *Slavery*: 33). Examples of contracts can be found in the Saltykov-Shchedrin Library, St. Petersburg, manuscript section, *Obshchee sobranie gramot*, n. 1727, 1937, 1941, 2017, 2019, 2348, 2406, 2635, 2672, 3026, 3081, 3392, 3475, 3486.

(*starinnoe kholopstvo*) comprised almost 10 percent of the entire group and seems to be closest to ancient, transatlantic slavery. It was possible to transfer this *kholopy* by will, as a dowry or gift.²⁶ Available contracts confirm that around 20 percent of *kholopy* were children aged between five and fourteen; parents placed them under one-year, often renewable, service contracts. The city's poorest population groups signed these contracts, and their numbers increased at the turn of the seventeenth century, a period of severe economic crisis. Loans were sometimes the official reason for these contracts, but the conditions of the loans often suggest that they were in fact servants' wages. Temporary servitude fell within the scope of these contracts. Freedom of contract did not preclude the renewal of contracts for up to several decades, or even throughout the life of the "indebted" person.²⁷ In most cases, the status of *kholopy* was not transmissible to descendants; this is essentially what distinguished this system from slavery in Antiquity and the Americas, but related it to the multiple forms of dependence in Africa and Asia. Almost all *kholopy* were domestic servants, and they were rarely assigned to agricultural work. In this way, *kholopy* were similar to the slaves purchased in the Mediterranean region, where domestic service dominated. At the same time, unlike the Mediterranean, there were no early experiments with sugar plantations in Russia, as in Candia, Sicily and the Canary Islands. If *kholopy* were barely present in Russian agriculture, it is because masses of serfs perform these functions. *Kholopy* and serfs therefore seem to have been complementary, and this is one of the dominant features of Russian society at the time.²⁸ In the 1720s, Peter replaced the household tax with the soul tax; this reform made it unacceptable for *kholopy* not to be taxed. At that time, *kholopy* represented 10 percent of the total Russian population. The former *kholopy* became peasants, people of various ranks and city dwellers.

What about the majority of the Russian population, especially in agriculture? They were not *kholopy*, they were not peasant-soldiers like in the colonies. What were they?

Empire-Building and the Demarcation of Serfdom

Nikolai Shipov was born as a serf on a private estate in Nizhny-Novgorod in 1802. In 1813, he accompanied his father, a serf and cattle merchant, and

---

[26] Viktor M. Paneiakh, *Kholopstvo v pervoi polovine XVII veke* (*Kholopstvo* in the first half of the seventeenth century) (Leningrad: Nauka, 1984); Aleksandr' Iakovlev, *Kholopstvo i kholopy v moskovskom gosudarstve XVII v.* (Kholopstvo and kholopy in the Russian state, seventeenth century) (Moscow: Nauka, 1943).
[27] Gyan Prakash, "Terms of Servitude: the Colonial Discourse on Slavery and Bondage in India," in Martin Klein (ed.), *Breaking the Chains: Slavery, Bondage and Emancipation in Modern Africa and Asia* (Madison: University of Wisconsin Press, 1986): 131–149.
[28] Hellie, *Enserfment and Military Change in Muscovy*.

some twenty shepherds to the Orenburg fair in the steppes. Their master, the owner of the estate where they live, knew all about the trip: He was well aware of the profits he could make from enriching his peasants through various trades. Shipov's father paid him a large percentage of sales from each of them. However, while the Shipovs could eventually accumulate some savings, they were also well aware that their master could confiscate them at any time. Legal freedom was no more valuable than economic freedom, both of which depended on the will of the master. In theory, a serf could buy their own freedom, and this is what Nikolai's father proposed several times to the master, always without success. In 1830, Nikolai decided to take a different path, and ran away with 13,000 rubles in his pocket. After a few months, he was told that his father was suffering from a serious illness; he decided to return to the estate. He was then deprived of his "passport" (a domestic document allowing him to leave the estate) but, unlike in the Islamic territories or in the French or British colonies of the time when a slave escaped, he got his papers back a month later. The following year, Shipov fled again, this time with his wife, to Constantinople, where he worked as a merchant, and from there to the Caucasus. Identified in 1837, he was captured by the local police and returned to his original estate. This time, he did not receive his passport back until 1842. He immediately returned to the Caucasus, where he arranged to be taken hostage by a band of pro-independence mountaineers. In fact, under Russian law, payment of his own ransom releases him from any obligation to his master. His merchant associates paid the ransom, and Shipov and his wife were finally released.[29]

Shipov's story raises a number of related issues, starting with the complex relationship between the legal and economic constraints of serfdom: Contrary to common views, a serf was not only obliged to perform corvées, but also to engage in other activities, for which they could eventually earn an income and from which their master took substantial shares. This resembled institutional extortion more than the ideal image of serfdom. Secondly, and even before the official abolition of serfdom, the law accepted multiple forms of emancipation: by the master's will (albeit often ignored by him), by a court, in relation to several situations in which the legal justification for serfdom was deemed non-existent. In order to better understand these outcomes, we need to better grasp the meanings and practices of serfdom. Russian rules never referred to "serfs" but rather aimed to identify those entitled to pass on "immovable" property. In fact, Russian and Western historiography considers *krepostnoe pravo* to be the Russian-language equivalent of the word serfdom, just as *krepostnye liudy* has been translated as serfs. These translations may be correct, but the expression *krepostnoe pravo* didn't

---

[29] Nikolai Shipov, *Istoriia moei zhizni* (Story of my life) (Moscow, Leningrad: Academia, 1933, original 1881); Brower, Leyton, "Liberation Through Captivity."

appear in Russian texts until the late 1830s.[30] If we look at official Russian texts from the sixteenth to the mid-nineteenth century,[31] we don't find the words *krepostnoe pravo*, but only *krepostnye liudy* (people subject to a *krepost'*, an act) and *kret'iane* (a word generally translated as peasant).[32] Unless we believe in a kind of self-censorship of all Russian texts and sources over centuries to avoid using the term, we need to take a closer look at the identification of "serfs." The emergence of serfdom as a category lies at the crossroads of imperial expansion, property relations and the legal status of the population. Throughout the sixteenth and seventeenth centuries, a number of rules were adopted that had the effect of limiting peasant mobility: Until the first half of the seventeenth century, this restriction was considered temporary; in the 1630s, landowners even came to enjoy the right to allow their peasants to move, as evidenced by numerous documents (*otpusknaia gramota*). These documents were signed by the landowners, for example, to allow their peasants to marry on another estate, move to the towns, etc. In exchange for this mobility, the peasants had to pay a fee. The process was not a simple one, as evidenced by the numerous disputes and petitions drawn up by noble families against other landowners claiming the ownership on the same peasants, now living on their estates. However, these rules were hardly enforced, as the various state administrations were unable to cooperate in returning fugitive serfs or punishing landlords whose claims were illegitimate. Landowners (especially the larger ones) continued to hold back displaced peasants, known as "fugitives." Petitions from smallholders and provincial landowners multiplied between 1620 and 1640, and the central government reacted by extending the recovery period for fugitives from five to nine or even fifteen years (decrees of 1637, 1641, 1645, 1648). This is where the famous *Ulozhenie* (statute) of 1649 intervened; according to many interpretations – Russian, Soviet and Western – it marked the definitive adoption of the servile regime in Russia. However, in this case too, as before, the available sources reveal clear attempts by the state to enforce the rules,[33] but, as the

---

[30] *Slovar' russkogo iazika XVIII veka* (Dictionary of the Russian language of the eighteenth century) fasc. 10, ed. (Sorokin: St. Petersburg, 1998), entry *krepostnoi*.

[31] Richard Hellie, *Muscovite Society*, syllabus division (Chicago: University of Chicago Press, 1967); Richard Hellie, "The Law Code of 1649" and "Muscovite-Western Commercial Relations," in *Readings in Russian Civilization*, ed. Thomas Riha, 2nd edition (Chicago: University of Chicago Press, 1969), 154–72.

[32] The term "peasant," so widely used, should be the subject of a thorough semantic and historiographical analysis for Russia and other countries. The word designates completely different people depending on the author, the period concerned, etc. On this point, Stanziani, *Tensions of Social History*.

[33] On peasant mobility, see RGADA, fond 294, opis'2. Emilia I. Indova, "Rol' dvortsovoi derevni pervoi poloviny XVIII v. v formirovanii russkogo kupechestva" (The role of the village court during the first half of the eighteenth century in the formation of a Russian bourgeoisie) *Istoricheskie Zapiski*, 68 (1961): 189–210.

records of disputes between landowners and between urban merchants and landowners clearly show,[34] the legal definition of who had the right to own populated estates remained unclear. As before, large landowners became notorious for luring peasants away from smaller estates. This game became even more complicated when urban elites (for tax reasons) and peripheral authorities (interested in increasing the local population) put pressure on to keep the fugitives in place.[35] In the southern regions, even more than in the heart of the country, the new rules were barely applied.[36] In the eyes of certain tsarist elites, geopolitical considerations took precedence over the political and social defense of estate owners in Russia's central regions. For a few fugitives returned to their rightful owners, millions of other peasants were left behind.[37] The aim was not only to populate empty lands, but also to operate factories.[38] For example, in 1741, Ignatii Kabalysov and his son fled from the Kazan district, stopping off in the Kungur district, three weeks' walk away. There, they worked in a copper factory during the winter. In spring, the father sailed to the town of Laishevo, where he worked as a barge driver. He then sailed to Astrakhan, then to Kazan. He made the return journey to find his wife, only to be caught up again in his home village.[39] These forms of "resistance" need to be properly qualified: it is certain that many serfs sought to move and emigrate. At the same time, they did not necessarily escape serfdom: As we have mentioned, many cases involved serfs moving from one estate to another, often from small estates to large ones where conditions were reputedly better. Alongside these cases, "migrants" were numerous and headed for lands newly occupied by the Russian army. From this point of view, their "voice" was strongly supported by the Russian colonial elites.

---

[34] RGADA, fond 615 (krepostnye knigi mestnyjh uchrezhdenii XVI-XVIII v), opis' 1; fond 294 (Manufaktor-Kontora), *opis-1-3*.

[35] The most comprehensive and recent survey of runaway serfs is Andrey Gornostaev, *Peasants on the Run: State Control, Fugitives, Social and Geographic Mobility in Imperial Russia, 1649-1796* (PhD, Georgetown University, 2020). See also: Aleksandr' A. Novosel'skii, "Otdatochnye knigi beglykh, kak istochnik dlia izucheniia narodnoi kolonizatsii na Rusi v XVII veke" (Fugitive registers as a source for studying colonization in seventeenth-century Russia) *Trudy istoriko-arkhivnogo instituta* 2 (1946): 127–54; Arcadius Kahan, *The Plow, the Hammer, and the Knout* (Chicago: University of Chicago Press, 1985): 76–77. Brian Davies, "The Recovery of Fugitive Peasants from Muscovy's Southern Frontier: The Case of Kozlov, 1636-1640," *Russian History*, 19, 1 (1992): 29–56.

[36] RGIA, fond 379 opis'1; PSZ, sery 1, vol. 40 n 21779; vol. 32 n. 25150.

[37] Gornostaev, *Peasants on the Run*. Also: Evgenii Akelev, Andrey Gornostaev, "Millions of Living Deaths: Fugitives, the Polish Border and Eighteenth Century Russian Society," *Kritika*, 24, 2 (2023): 269–297.

[38] Natalia Kozlova, *Pobegi krest'ian v Rossii v pervoi treti XVIII veka* (Peasants on the run in Russia during the first third of the eighteenth century) (Moscow: Moskovskii universitet, 1983).

[39] RGADA, fond 407, opis'1.

In the end, the definition and identification of "serfs" continued to be in opposition to the categories of "migrants" and "settlers." Colonization could not have worked without accepted emigration and, therefore, a limitation of the power of Central Russian landlords over their peasants.[40] As a result, between 1678 and 1897, peasant settlements in the central forest heartland fell from 69.9 percent to 41.22 percent of total cultivated land, while those in steppe areas rose from 28.78 percent to 41.22 percent. Over the same period, settlement in Siberia rose from 1.32 percent to 7.54 percent. In the southern and eastern settlement areas, one third of the population increase was due to natural growth and two thirds to immigration. In the 1680s, the peasant population of the Ukrainian territories was around half a million; by 1720, it had doubled. By 1678, 3.7 million peasants had emigrated and settled in Siberia, the north-western regions, the Urals, the south-eastern steppe and the Volga.[41] Overall, Russia's population grew from 7 million in 1600 to around 9 million in 1678, 14 million in 1719, 17 million in 1762 and 21 million in 1782.[42] Russian peasant emigrants benefited from access to land, mobility and the rights granted to this category. Most settlements took place on the left bank of the Ukraine (909,651 male souls in 1719) and the Middle Volga (651,405), while the Lower Volga, the southern Urals and the Cossack lands had a total of just 200,000 male souls.[43] At the same time, the Lower Volga also saw the highest concentration of new settlements in the entire empire. In fact, as in other parts of Russia and its borders, in the Volga region too, fleeing peasants from central Russia were numerous among the private landowners of this area.[44]

The definitions of serfdom and the forms of Russian expansion evolved together over time. Russian expansion in the south continued into the nineteenth century, beginning with the annexation of Bessarabia from the Ottoman Empire in 1812 (although the Russian military and colonial presence had been continually reinforced since the 1770s).[45] The administrative reorganization of the entire "steppe" area, stretching from the Lower Danube to the

---

[40] Arkhadii G. Man'kov, *Razvitie krepostnogo prava v Rossii vo vtoroi polovine XVII veka* (The development of serfdom law in Russia in the second half of the seventeenth century) (Moscow and Leningrad: Akademiia nauk SSSR, 1962).
[41] Sunderland, "Peasants on the Move."
[42] David Moon, Russian Peasants and Tsarist Legislation on the Eve of Reform, 1825–1855 (Basingstoke: Macmillan, 1992): 20–21.
[43] Vladimir M. Kabuzan, *Izmeneniia v razmeshchenii naseleniia Rossii v XVIII-pervoi polovine XIX v.* (Changes in the growth rate of the Russian population during the eighteenth and first half of the nineteenth centuries) (Moscow: Nauka, 1971), appendix 2: 59–70.
[44] Serguei N. Abashin, Dimitrii Iu. Arapov, and Nataliia E. Bekmakhanova, eds., *Tsentral'naia Aziia v sostave Rossiiskoi imperii* (Central Asia in the Context of the Russian Empire) (Moscow: Novoe literaturnoe obozrenie, 2008).
[45] George Jewsbury, *The Russian Annexation of Bessarbia, 1774–1828. A Study of Imperial Expansion* (New York: Columbia University Press, 1976).

Urals, followed: It was divided into provinces and regions; all inhabitants were subjects of the Tsar, but unlike the migrant Slav peasants, the Cossacks and nomads had their own recognized rules and institutions. The absence of nobles and serfs, the importance of international trade and legal pluralism set these regions apart from mainland Russia. Unlike the territories beyond the Urals, the steppe was very often considered "Russia," not its colony.[46] Consequently, this "empty space" had to be secured by Russian settlers, military garrisons and possibly new annexations beyond the border line to secure new areas and settlements.[47] Between 1796 and 1835, some 1.7 million new migrants settled in the region, more than three times the total migration of the period 1762–1795. This phenomenon was linked to the growing political importance of the "land shortage" in mainland Russia, as well as to increasing attempts to "Russify" the steppe during the nineteenth century. With the aim of encouraging migration and fostering local development, migrants were classified not only as state peasants, as is generally the case, but also as city dwellers or simply *raznochintsy* (people of various ranks, including small merchants, former peasants, etc.).

Things were different in Poland and the Ukraine. In the last quarter of the eighteenth century, Poland was divided between Russia, Austria and Prussia. In addition, European economic and territorial expansion revealed the weakness of the Ottoman Empire and its former allies, such as the *Khanate* of Crimea, the last survivor of the Golden Horde of Tamerlane and Genghis Khan.[48] Russia took advantage of this instability to expand its territory to the south and west, as access to the Mediterranean had long been an economic and geopolitical objective of the Tsarist elites. This was a pressing objective in the eyes of Catherine II, a follower of mercantilist policies and therefore of the importance of foreign trade. From this point of view, the conquest of Crimea marked a decisive turning point, as the peninsula offered control of the Black Sea and, consequently, access to the Mediterranean. At the time, the rich agricultural lands of the surrounding regions were only partially exploited, due to their isolation from the main trade routes. Catherine's first objective was therefore to strengthen navigation on the Black Sea, as the existing ports (Azov, Taganrog, both located in the Sea of Azov, northeast of the Black Sea to which it is linked by the Kerch Strait) were relatively small. With the construction of overland trade routes linking the various regions of Ukraine to the Black Sea, the port of Taganrog was restructured and expanded.[49] It was a fundamental link with

---

[46] Sunderland, *Taming the Wild Field*, 110.
[47] Iurii M. Tarasov, *Russkaia krest'ianskaia kolonizatsiia iuzhnogo Urala: vtoraia polovina XVIII- pervaia polovina XIX vekoi* (The Russian peasant colonization of south Urals, second half of the eighteenth century, first half of the nineteenth century) (Moscow: Gozizdat, 1984).
[48] Alessandro Stanziani, *Bâtisseurs d'Empire* (Paris: Liber, 2012).
[49] Constantin Ardeleanu, "The Opening and Development of the Black Sea for International Trade and Shipping, 1774–1853," *Euxeinos*, 14 (2014): 30–52.

the agricultural regions of eastern Ukraine. Catherine went even further: In 1778, she founded the town of Kherson, destined to rapidly become a major commercial center linking the Black Sea to the agricultural regions. Sevastopol also benefited from substantial financial support, and its port was improved and enlarged to accommodate the royal navy.[50]

Catherine II encouraged migration (not only of Russians, but also of Poles and Germans) and resettlement to the steppes and Siberia; the "New Russia" (Novorussia, in particular the provinces of Ekaterinoslav and Kherson) explicitly referred to the New World across the Atlantic; here, local populations were classified into three groups: settlers, landowners and military personnel. Peasant-soldiers were encouraged, as Russian settlers were seen as more trustworthy defenders of the frontier than foreign mercenaries or other ethnical groups of the Empire. On the whole, just as in Canada and other northern regions of the Americas, the relative lack of women led the authorities to encourage family migration, household resettlement or simply the transfer of "women of ill repute" from Russian prisons and hospices. Kidnapping was also practiced. In the early nineteenth century, most Russians saw Siberia as a colony where trade was easy and profitable,[51] especially the fur trade.[52] For enlightened reformers, Siberia represented a free land, free of serfdom, and therefore an example to follow; parallels with an idealized and equally free America were frequent. By the 1770s, Siberia was home to around half a million people, but only two-thirds of them were Slavs. One of the regulations of the Siberian reforms of 1822 granted the natives distinct legal protections[53] while recognizing that, unlike the Tatars and other steppe peoples, Siberian nomads could not be transformed into Russians. In the meantime, the Russian authorities were once again promoting the migration of Russian peasants to Siberia. It was still very difficult to find candidates for settlement and only peasants capable of adapting to local life could survive there. Apart from serfs or free peasants, the only possible candidates for Siberian colonization were convicts. Certain Tsarist leaders, such as Mikhail Speranskii, imagined this solution (as well as the transformation of nomads into farmers).[54] After 1822, not only were

---

[50] Evrydiki Sifneos, Oksana Iurkova and Valentina Shandra eds., *Port-Cities of the Northern Shore of the Black Sea: Institutional, Economic and Social Development, Eighteenth–Early Twentieth Centuries* (Rethymnon: Black Sea History Working Papers, 2021).

[51] Mark Bassin, "Inventing Siberia: Visions of the Russian East in the Early Nineteenth Century," *American Historical Review*, 96, 3 (1991): 763–794.

[52] Raymond H. Fisher, *The Russian Fur Trade, 1550–1700* (Berkeley: University of California Press, 1943).

[53] Marc Raeff, *Siberia and the Reforms of 1822* (Seattle: University of Washington Press, 1956); Alberto Masoero, "Autorità e territorio nella colonizzazione siberiana," *Rivista Storica Italiana*, CXV, 2 (2003): 439–486.

[54] Elena Kovalaschina, "The Historical and Cultural Ideals of the Siberian Oblastnichestvo," *Sibirica*, 6, 2 (2007): 87–119.

large numbers of criminals and repeat offenders forcibly transferred to Siberia, but also vagrants, deserters and people banished for misconduct.[55] Between 1807 and 1816, 10,175 people of both sexes (2,035 per year) were transported. In 1824–1826, this figure reached an annual average of 11,116.[56] When they arrived, many fled again: Between 1847 and 1857, this was the case for around a quarter of Nerchinsk's population. Women were often raped during their journey to Siberia and once they reached their destination.

In the same spirit, military colonies, developed in the south since the seventeenth century, were tested in other parts of the empire. From the end of the Napoleonic Wars to the mid-1830s, Russia's top leaders and many economists and agronomists supported the colonies, which they believed would combine order with productivity and freedom with coercion.[57] This economic, political and social experiment involved 750,000 people, but the results were meagre, and the military colonies were abandoned after riots in the early 1830s.[58] The idea of becoming peasant-soldiers, which had enjoyed some success in the seventeenth and eighteenth centuries, no longer seemed a viable option. There were several reasons for this: two centuries earlier, the peasants recruited had first been sent as soldiers, then transformed into farmers in the new territories, where they could benefit from more favorable legal and economic conditions than on the Russian mainland. In the 1820s and 1830s, the situation had changed: Peasants were resettled and subjected to a military regime, with agronomic innovations imposed on them from above, while the legal constraints weighing on private peasants in Russia were gradually relaxed. In this new configuration, it is hardly surprising that the peasants revolted against the military colonies, and even without riots, these institutions always had enormous difficulty in experimenting with new agricultural techniques disconnected from local agrarian and social practices.

In short, serfdom first took the form of compensation for landowners on the Russian mainland in exchange for their support of the central state and colonial expansion, which was costing the nobility dearly as they were obliged to supply soldiers and wheat to the army at the expense of their own income. In exchange, the nobility was granted increasingly strict coercive rules on their

---

[55] *Pol'noe Sobrannye Zakonov Rossiskoi Imperii* (Complete Collection of the Laws of the Russian Empire) (St. Petersburg: Tipografiia II Otdeleniia sobstvennostoi ego Imperatorskogo Velichestva Kantseliarii, 1649–1913), 33 volumes 1st series, no. 29328 (February 23, 1823).

[56] Abby Schrader, "Unruly Felons and Civilizing Wives: Cultivating Marriage in the Siberian Exile System: 1822–1860," *Slavic Review*, 66, 2 (2007): 230–257, esp. 237.

[57] Leonid P. Bogdanov, *Voennye poseleniia v Rossii* (Military colonies in Russia) (Moscow: Nauka 1992).

[58] Richard Pipes, "The Russian Military Colonies," *Journal of Modern History*, 22, 3 (1950): 205–219; Alexander Bitis, Janet Hartley, "The Russian Military Colonies in 1826," *The Slavonic and East European Review*, 78, 2 (2000): 323–330.

peasants. However, the application of these rules was precarious, while the legal and social organization of the new territories undermined serfdom (independent peasant owners). Russian attitudes varied from colony to colony, but in the end a general trend emerged: In the colonized territories, serfdom either did not exist or was much less severe than in the heart of the Empire.

Over time, the colonies even suggested ways to reform serfdom on the continent. The first change was to transfer serfs to the category of state peasants. State peasants had certain obligations only to the state, such as the payment of an annuity, usually in money, sometimes in kind. They were also required to perform work in the public interest, which is generally cited as justification for the existence of forced labor and serfdom in this category. At the same time, state peasants could work in the cities in commerce and industry, provided they had the required documents.[59] Indeed, as the reforms tried out in the western border region proved, landless emancipation led to a marked worsening of the situation of peasants and, consequently, to social and political instability. For these very reasons, several rules were adopted from the early 1840s onwards, to emancipate serfs while providing them with small plots of land. Between 1833 and 1855 alone, 58,225 male peasants (and their families) were emancipated on this basis,[60] a figure that rose to 114,000 male peasants between 1803 and 1855. In the 1840s, further rules were adopted along the same lines, with the result that between 1833 and 1858, the legal status of 343,575 male peasants changed as a result of massive state emancipation: They ceased to be private estate peasants and became state peasants and sometimes *meshchane* (merchants). From this point of view, emancipation was an administrative act that expressed much less the peasants' "resistance" than the Tsarist's ambition to reform the system without abrupt changes.

The influence of annexed territories on serfdom was also expressed through legal disputes. Just as settlers in the colonies challenged the legal status of the serf, so did serfs on the continent. Contrary to conventional historiography, it is now proven that Russian peasants went to court, not only after the abolition of serfdom,[61] but even before. Until the 1770s, there were no special courts in Russia for peasants, who were previously forced to apply to the nobles and their courts for emancipation, a system that greatly reduced attempts to initiate proceedings. The situation changed in 1775 with the introduction of peasant courts, accompanied by a clear legal differentiation between ownership of things and rights over human beings. Throughout the nineteenth century,

---

[59] Nikolai M. Druzhinin, *Gosudarstvennye krest'iane i reforma P.D. Kiseleva* (State peasants and the reform of P.D. Kisele) (Moscow: Nauka, 1958).

[60] Steven Hoch and Wilson Augustine, "The Tax Censuses and the Decline of the Serf Population in Imperial Russia, 1833–1858," *Slavic Review*, 38, 3 (1979): 403–25.

[61] See footnote 113 in the Introduction for a bibliography.

these issues were frequently the subject of court rulings.[62] Thus, between 1827 and 1840, twenty-six peasants belonging to a city-dweller, Ipat Koronvskii, in Vitebsk province, denounced him for illegal serfdom.[63] The case began in 1817, when some peasants denounced Koronovskii for beating them. A local prosecutor opened an investigation and cast doubt on Koronoskii's legally founded possession of serfs.[64] The investigation revealed that Koronovskii's father had bought twenty-six serfs from a noblewoman in 1798. The peasants were legally registered. The following year, Koronovskii's father bought an entire estate and its 265 serfs from the same woman. In 1804, he sold three serfs to a merchant, who freed one (a woman) in 1818, as required by law. Meanwhile, when Koronovskii's daughter married a nobleman, she received a dowry of twenty-nine serfs from her father. In his will, Koronovskii's father granted his daughter full ownership of all his serfs. She was authorized to sell them, thus repaying a debt her father had contracted with her husband. When his brother, Kornovskii junior, replaced his father in the management of the estate, he also sold some of the serfs. A dispute arose as to who was the true owner of the estate, and therefore of the serfs. The court concluded that Kornovskii's son was the true owner. If so, as he was not a noble, he had no rights over the serfs. Thus, in 1827, a Senate decision concluded that, due to the illegal possession of serfs, the estate now belonged to the state. On the other hand, his sister, ennobled by marriage, could keep the serfs she had received as a dowry. As for the serfs who had been sold by Kornovskii, they remained serfs if the buyer was a nobleman, otherwise they were transformed into state peasants (i.e., city dwellers). It was here that twenty-six peasants demanded their freedom in court.

Another serf from the Kazan district, Savelii Nikiforov, sought to retrace his father's steps. Having been abandoned as a child, he discovered where he lived (the village of Sungur), and with the permission of his landlords joined him, only to discover that he had died. He decided to work in Sungur for a while, but stayed there for fourteen years, before leaving as a barge carrier for three years. When he returned to Sungur, he was arrested. However, the Chancellery decided to assign him to Sungur, not to his place of origin. A few years later, his original landlords listed his name among those of his peasants who were to be conscripted. Savelii refused, and the court ruled in his favor.[65]

---

[62] TsIAM, fond 54 (Moskovskoe gubernskoe upravlenie), 1783–1917, opis' 1, e.g., 56, 284, 966, 1509. Several other cases can be found in *Deistviia Nizhegorodskoi gubernskoi uchenoi arkhivnoi komissii* (Proceedings of the Nizhegorod provincial archive commission) (Nizhegorod: provincial publications), several pamphlets, 1890s.

[63] This case was examined by Elise Kimerling Wirtschafter, "Legal Identity and the Possession of Serfs in Imperial Russia," *The Journal of Modern History*, 70, 3 (1998): 561–587.

[64] RGIA, fond 1149, opis' 2, delo 20.

[65] RGADA, fond 407, opis' 1, delo 158.

Lawsuits brought by peasants for illegal serfdom became so numerous that between 1837 and 1840, the Senate even decided to put an end to cases involving serfs still living with their masters.[66] In all, between 1833 and 1858, the Senate registered 15,153 cases of illegal serfdom, while the provincial courts handled 22,000 such cases.[67] In the end, almost half of Russian peasants were released from their obligations to private landlords in the decades leading up to the official abolition of serfdom. These problems were most often the result of administrative decisions imposed from above, or of disputes between landowners' family members. Peasants exploited these lawsuits. The official abolition law of 1861 should therefore be seen in the context of a long and global trend.

Conclusion: Borderlands and Labor

The first conclusion we can draw from the Russian case is that there was no central institution of serfdom, but different rules in each area, where the landowner made their own law. This is an important finding, as it confirms that while the central state was important in fiscal and military terms, the overall rules governing society were left in the hands of local landowners, something that had greatly diminished in Western Europe during this period. In Russia, this was not the case, as landowners and the state had formed an alliance that marginalized peasants and merchants.

This question also helps to explain the regional differentiation of serfdom, and in particular the fact that it was milder in the colonies than on the mainland. In fact, Frederick Jackson Turner's frontier theory cannot adequately explain Russian expansion. First of all, when the frontier was settled in the American West, it corresponded less to the ideal type invented by Turner at the end of the nineteenth century than to a logic of extermination of the natives and immigration of indentured white servants (undoubtedly less free than British servants) and slaves. On the other hand, peasants migrating to the Russian frontier enjoyed more rights than their continental counterparts. The imperial frontier zones were the scene of political and economic experimentation. This result was linked to a special agreement between landowners and the state: The former agreed to relax constraints on recruited peasants and migrants in exchange for greater rights for peasants in central Russia.

The Russian case also eludes the usual comparisons between wage labor, serfdom and slavery, which are based on ideal types rather than historical realities. Thus, slavery and serfdom are defined by the absence of legal rights granted to slaves and serfs, their hereditary status, the master's right of ownership, and the coercive extraction of surplus. The main difference identified is

---

[66] RGIA, fond 1149, opis' 2, delo 90.
[67] Pol'noe Sobrannye Zakonov (PSZ) (II), vol. 20, n. 19283; vol. 22, n. 20825; RGIA, fond 1149, op. 3, delo 125.

that, unlike slaves, serfs are tied to the land.[68] This distinction guided Kolchin's well-known comparison between American slavery and Russian serfdom.[69] Kolchin ignored important differences between American slavery and Russian serfdom such as the fact that Russian serfs did not come from distant lands and did not belong to a different ethnic group. The master-slave relationship had no equivalent in Russia, where the peasant commune and its elders acted as mediators between the estate owner and the peasants. The Russian master was therefore much more obliged to negotiate the services of the peasants than the American slave owner.[70] In fact, the distance between American slavery and Russian serfdom was considerable: Russian peasants and serfs were part of local communities, through the peasant commune, and were not isolated from other contexts like American slaves. On the other hand, Russian peasants were constantly filing lawsuits and developing their own economic activity (they simply had to pay duties to their masters). Above all, the steppe was colonized (with the displacement of a million people) in the seventeenth and eighteenth centuries, and Siberia was colonized in the eighteenth and early nineteenth centuries, before serfdom was officially abolished. It is as if American slaves had colonized the Western frontier before 1865. In short, it is absurd to regard American slavery and Russian serfdom as entirely similar institutions.

The same applies to the *kholopy*: only a small proportion of them could be likened to domestic slaves, while almost all were subjected to multiple forms of dependence, some mild, others extreme. From this point of view, the multiple forms of dependence in Russia seem closer to many other cases, in Asia as in Africa. The Atlantic definition of slavery was the exception, not the rule. If so, how did these differences help explain empire-building and the role of labor in the British realm?

---

[68] For example, Bush, *Serfdom and Slavery*, especially "Introduction" and Stanley Engerman, "Slavery, Serfdom and Other Forms of Coerced Labor: Similarities and Differences": 18–41.
[69] Kolchin, *Unfree Labor*.
[70] Michael Confino, "Servage russe, esclavage américain," *Annales ESC*, 45, 5 (1990): 1119–1141.

2

The British Empire

Coercion in the Name of Freedom

We have just concluded that ideal conceptions of the "serf" did not correspond to historical realities. If so, what about Western social categories of work, such as the wage-earner, the proletarian and the slave?

It is not my intention here to discuss the theories or simply the intellectual history of class definition, of the working class and proletariat in particular.[1] Rather, I wish to reveal how these identifications were made in industrializing British society during the eighteenth and nineteenth centuries; we need to understand the origins and social consequences of these classifications for the actors themselves.

Mainland Labor Rules: Masters, Servants, Apprentices and the Poor

Before the end of the nineteenth century, British workers were not "wage earners" as we know them today, they were not serfs or slaves in disguise, but they were subject to strong legal and economic coercion and were officially "servants." The word "servant" took on different meanings in different eras, and the labor relationship has not consisted of a single, homogeneous legal status. For example, between the fourteenth and sixteenth centuries, contemporaries limited the term "servant" to particular salaried workers who resided with their master, so that laborers and artisans were not included in this category. However, from the sixteenth century onwards, the term "servant" was increasingly used to define all kinds of salaried workers, and thus included journeymen, artificers and other laborers.[2] From the late eighteenth century onwards, court rulings excluded servants from the scope of the Master and Servant Acts, at least in England, where absconding workers, day laborers, domestic servants, farm servants, apprentices and the like were subject to very similar laws under the Workmen's Statute (1351), the Masters and Servants Acts and the Artificers' Statute of 1562.[3] Until then, the

---

[1] For a discussion, Stanziani, *Tensions of Social History*.
[2] Steinfeld, *The Invention of Free Labor*: 17–22.
[3] Ann Kussmaul, *Servants in Husbandry in Early Modern England* (Cambridge: Cambridge University Press, 1981).

statute covered three distinct but related areas: the regulation of contracts, in particular the limitation of departures; the regulation of wages; and the regulation of apprenticeship.[4] The only exception was apprenticeship in husbandry, which was regarded as an entirely separate institution, to be regulated at national level "in the name of the general interest." On the whole, however, despite the existence of a contract, free labor was considered the property of the employer and a resource for the whole community to which the individual belonged.[5] During service, servants' work was legally reserved for their masters.[6] From the second half of the sixteenth century onwards, the tradition of property-based legal control by the master became an important component of the new market society. Workers could be imprisoned until they agreed to return to their employer to complete the agreed service. Any breach of contract on the part of the servant was liable to prosecution. The word "fugitive" was clearly used to refer to apprentices and servants who left their jobs without giving notice. As such, servant labor was considered the rightful property of the master. In fact, resident servants were like wives and children: All were members of the household and all were the legal dependents of its head. This implied, on the one hand, that servants, children and wives had the right to be maintained by the head of the household; on the other hand, they were all supposed to be under his authority, with the head of the household enjoying a higher legal status and more legal rights than his dependents and family. Dependence was a normal part of a differential system of rank and degree in which everyone, adult and child, man and woman, had and knew their place. For women and children, this place was inferior to that of men.

The Glorious Revolution, so celebrated in Whig historiography, wasn't so glorious for everyone: It brought rights to male owners but excluded women and non-owners.[7] According to British legal doctrine of the time, the difference lay in the fact that owning slaves and captives of war meant owning property, whereas labor services meant owning a certain person's time.[8] It was a labor lease in which the borrower had the right to benefit from all the time and capabilities of his labor force. Work as service reflected the strong legacy of the overlap between work and military recruitment, on the one hand, and personal service (domestic and other types of work), on the other.[9] This notion of work

---

[4] Tomlins, *Freedom Bound*: 239.

[5] Steinfeld, *The Invention of Free Labor*, especially chapter 3; Michael Postan, "The Chronology of Labor Services," *Transactions of the Royal Historical Society*, 20 (1937): 169–193.

[6] Steinfeld, *The Invention of Free Labor*: 32.

[7] Robert Zaller, "Representative Governments: How Sure a Thing," in Maija Jansson, ed., *Realities of Representation: State Building in Early Modern Europe and America* (New York: Palgrave, 2007): 215–224.

[8] William Blackstone, *Commentaries on the Laws of England*, 4 volumes (London: Strahan, Woodfall 1793–1795) booklet 2: 402.

[9] On the relationship between work and military recruitment in the Navy, see Alessandro Stanziani, *Les métamorphoses du travail contraint* (Paris: Presses de Sciences-Po, 2020).

as service was adopted by extension in all other forms of labor relations – in agriculture, mining, manufacturing – where master, father and military officer converged into a legal and social actor with full rights over workers. As long as labor leases continue to be understood as transfers of labor ownership, contractual individualism will continue to support unfree labor.[10] The major guilds, city council representatives, local and central authorities all supported these laws.[11]

Why is it important? Because it sheds new light on the historical trajectories of labor under capitalism. In fact, not all these rules were anti-capitalist and anti-industrial, as conventional interpretations – both liberal and Marxist – assert. On the contrary, the proto-industrial and manufacturing development of the eighteenth century gave them new life. The measures of the Masters and Servants Acts became stricter from the 1720s onwards, when penalties against servants who broke their contracts were tightened. Many guilds and industries demanded these provisions. The First Industrial Revolution brought with it stricter constraints than ever on labor mobility. Between 1720 and 1792, ten Acts of Parliament imposed or increased the penalty of imprisonment for abandonment of post or misconduct.[12] Employers strongly supported this legal architecture; as late as 1844, in response to strikes and protests in the mines, attempts were made to extend the provisions of the Masters and Servants Acts to all employment relationships. Extremely strong popular and labor reactions against the bill prevented its passage.[13]

These rules were not an empty shell, but were widely applied by the courts.[14] Some 10,000 people were prosecuted every year for offences committed by masters and servants laws: 7,000 were convicted, 1,700 served time in a house of correction, 2,000 were fined and 3,300 received other types of sanction (reduction in salary and assessment of costs).[15] Overall, 5–8 percent of domestics were prosecuted, but this figure rose to 17 percent in some regions and even 20 percent

---

[10] George Barnsby, *Social Conditions in the Black Country* (Wolverhampton: Integrated Publishing Service, 1980).
[11] Steinfeld, *The Invention of Free Labor*.
[12] Donna C. Woods, "The Operation of the Masters and Servants Act in the Black Country, 1858–1875," *Midland History*, 7 (1982): 93–115; Mark R. Freedland, *The Contract of Employment* (Oxford: Oxford University Press: 1976); David Galenson, "The Rise of Free Labor: Economic Change and the Enforcement of Service Contract in England, 1361–1875," in John James and Mark Thomas, eds. *Capitalism in Context: Essays on Economic Development and Cultural Change in Honor of R.M. Hartwell* (Chicago: University of Chicago Press, 1994): 114–137.
[13] Christopher Frank, "Britain: The Defeat of the 1844 Master and Servants Bill," in Douglas Hay and Paul Craven, eds., Masters, Servants, and Magistrates in Britain and the Empire, 1562–1955 (Chapel Hill: The University of North Carolina Press, 2004): 402–421.
[14] Paul Craven, Douglas Hay, "The Criminalization of Free Labor: Masters and Servants in Comparative Perspective," *Slavery and Abolition*, 15, 2 (1994): 71–101.
[15] *Judicial Statistics, England and Wales, 1857–1875*, 19 volumes (London, Home Office, 1858–1876). See also Steinfeld, *Coercion*: 73–78.

in London in some years. The reaction to changing economic trends and the rate of prosecution were stronger in the countryside than in the city;[16] this was probably due to the major impact of seasonal labor shortages on agriculture, as we shall see in the next chapters. The higher the rate of employment, the higher the rate of worker continuation, suggesting that the allocation of labor between different industries was the key issue. Seasonality therefore played a role: Most prosecutions took place in the summer, during the harvest, while fewer were recorded during the winter months and in October, when most contracts were renewed. The success rate was close to 100 percent for masters and between 20 percent and 70 percent for servants, depending on the county.[17] Why did masters sue servants?

In general, they did not want their workers to be imprisoned, but to return to work, which confirms that master and servant laws were tools to reduce job turnover costs. This is where master–servant laws were linked to poor laws. Polanyi associated Speenhamland's law, the duty to work and the great transformation; in the same line of interpretation, historians of the welfare state have contrasted the latter with the poor law. The former advocated a principle of inclusion and solidarity, while the latter was based on the duty to work. In fact, as many recent studies have convincingly demonstrated, this was not the main difference between the two systems, as social security never abolished the obligation to work.[18]

Work was controlled by the family, the village and the town, and not only by economic activities themselves; this is why public order and economic logic came together. Vagrancy described a state in which an able-bodied person without work or other means of support was liable (in addition to corporal punishment of various kinds) to be sent back to their parish of origin.[19] Since the mid seventeenth century, the Poor Law directly associated relief with workhouses: Anyone without employment or permanent residence was no longer a "pauper," but became a "vagrant" and, as such, was subject to criminal prosecution. Two solutions clashed: one proposed a minimum wage and a prohibition on masters imposing a wage below that level; the other advocated the need to relieve the poor. The latter won out and compulsory labor with it.[20]

However, in the mid eighteenth century, the Poor Laws began to be denigrated as ineffective and expensive. In 1782, Gilbert's Act was passed to allow

---

[16] Sureh Naidu, Noam Yuchtman, "How Green Was my Valley? Coercive Contract Enforcement in Nineteenth Century Britain," *NBUR working papers*, 2009.
[17] For the most complete data, see Hay "England, 1562–1875," table 2.1 in Douglas Hay and Paul Craven, eds., Masters, Servants, and Magistrates in Britain and the Empire, 1562–1955 (Chapel Hill: The University of North Carolina Press, 2004).
[18] Deakin, Wilkinson, *The Law of the Labor Market*: 111.
[19] Deakin, Wilkinson, *The Law of the Labor Market*: 115–116.
[20] K.D.M. Snell, *Annals of the Labouring Poor: Social Change and Agrarian England 1660–1900* (Cambridge: Cambridge University Press, 1985).

neighboring parishes to join together for the purposes of the Poor Law and establish hospices under the aegis of a Board of Trustees. The law separates the incapable from the capable poor, and among the latter, those who do not want to work from those who do but cannot find employment. The reformers drew a clear distinction between the "natural poor" and the indigent (unable to work), and only the latter were allowed to benefit from poor relief. Indeed, a third novelty was introduced, namely the shift from a parish- and county-based system to a national labor market. In rural areas, outside relief for the able-bodied was prohibited, whereas in most urban areas, it could be maintained on condition that it was not cumulated with wages. The obligation to work applied regardless of wage level. The Speenhamland of 1795, at the heart of Polanyi's argument, was originally designed to set a minimum wage. In fact, this solution as such was not accepted; instead, proponents agreed on the notion of a minimum income linked to the price of bread by a sliding scale. In practice, this minimum wage was hardly ever applied; in some counties, magistrates were opposed to this notion, which they considered alien to common law. In fact, the Poor Laws did not regress, but were transformed and even strengthened over the course of the century. Between the adoption of the new Poor Law (1834) and the mid-1870s, there were some 10,000 prosecutions for vagrancy.[21]

The workhouse system completed this institutional architecture. This system cannot be explained by classical Foucauldian arguments; its main aim was not to shift from punishment to surveillance of "deviants," but to put people to work, and it was far from being a marginal phenomenon. It is estimated that in the eighteenth and nineteenth centuries, in times of crisis, around 6.5 percent of the British population was in a workhouse at any one time.[22] A parliamentary inquiry in 1776 revealed the existence of 1,970 workhouses housing a total of 90,000 paupers. In most cases, the work of paupers did not cover the general running costs of a workhouse.[23] In the years following the adoption of the new rules (1834), an increasing number of paupers were interned for criminal offences.[24] The number of internments rose from 940 in 1837 to 2,596 in 1842.[25] Paupers and inmates increasingly resisted the Poor Laws and the workhouse principle, resorting to petitions, sabotage and self-mutilation, particularly among women. Conflicts also broke out within the establishment. Between 1837 and 1842, there were more than 10,500 indictments for breaches

---

[21] Naidu, Yuchtman, "How Green Was my Valley?"
[22] Derek Fraser, *The Evolution of the British Welfare State* (4th ed.), (London: Palgrave Macmillan, 2009): 67.
[23] British Parliamentary Papers (BPP), *House of Commons Committee Reports*, 1st series, IX, 1774–1802: 297–538.
[24] BPP, *Report from the Commissioners for Inquiring into the Administration and Practical Reform of the Poor Laws, 1834*, XXVIII, appendix A.
[25] David Green, "Pauper Protests: Protests and Resistance in Early Nineteenth-Century London Workhouses," *Social History*, 31, 2 (May 2006): 137–159, esp. 141.

of hospice discipline, nearly 2,000 of which came from metropolitan parishes and unions.[26] Most of the offenses committed inside the institution fell into the general category of misconduct, drunkenness and disorder, damage and refusal to work, all of which reflected minor but persistent conflicts between poor people and officials over the running of the institution.[27] The main problems concerned forcing the occasional poor to perform tasks and preventing them from destroying their clothes.[28]

Important individual case histories and stories of life in the workhouses have come to light.[29] Precarious lives of children, apprentices and women emerge. Suffolk-born Ann Candler (b. 1740) married a cottage owner from a neighboring village at the age of 22. A drunkard and repeatedly conscripted, he left Ann six children. She placed four of them in the local hospice, where she also lived and worked.

Charles Shaw, born in 1832 in Tunstall (Staffordshire Potteries), was the sixth of eight children. He began working as an apprentice at the age of seven. In 1842, his father took part in a strike and the whole family was placed in a workhouse in Chell. He wrote about his experiences in the asylum, published in 1903 under the title *When I Was a Child*.[30]

In short, the long-term evolution of labor and labor laws in Great Britain does little to support the traditional argument that early freedom of labor fueled the Industrial Revolution. On the contrary, the Industrial Revolution was accompanied by increasingly strict regulations and criminal sanctions against workers. Labor regulations were a powerful tool in the hands of masters. Workers were neither economic actors freely choosing their activity as entrepreneurs or workers (as in neoclassical and liberal economic theory), nor proletarians in the Marxist sense of the term. Instead, they were legally considered servants, paupers or vagabonds, and were all subject to highly coercive penal rules. As in my scheme of voice, exit and law, servants had few rights

---

[26] BPP, *Return of the number, names, and ages of all persons committed to any prison in England and Wales for any offence in a union workhouse*, 1843, XLV: 343–61.

[27] BPP, *Select Committee on Asiles de district*, 1846, VII: 264, 269.

[28] BPP *Return of the number of persons (inmates and casuals) committed to prison from each union workhouse (England and Wales) for the half year ending on 25 day of March 1874*, 1876 LXII: 393.

[29] Among many others: Peter Higginbotham, *Voices from the Workhouse* (London: The History Press, 2012); Simon Fowler, *The Workhouse. The People, the Places, the Life Behind Doors* (Barnsley: Pen and Sword History 2014); Peter Jones, "Looking Through Different Lens: Microhistory and the Workhouse Experience in Late nineteenth-Century London," *Journal of Social History*, 55, 4 (2022): 925–947; Alannah Tomkins, "Poor Law Institutions Through Working Class Eyes: Autobiography, Emotion, and Family Context, 1834–1914," *Journal of British Studies*, 60, 2 (2021): 285–309. The National Archives now devote a page of their website to letters from the hospice in the Select Committee on District Asylums.

[30] Charles Shaw, *When I Was a Child* (New edition, Churnet: Valley Books, 1998).

and, as such, defended themselves mainly by exit (i.e., by undue seasonal or permanent migration).

We now need to clarify the relationship between labor rules and institutions on the continent and those in the colonies, starting with the American regions. Contrary to the Whig story, my argument will be that labor institutions across the Atlantic pushed toward more coercion, not less. Until the end of the eighteenth century, empire reinforced the idea that coercion was the best possible option for extracting labor.

British Labor Institutions across the Atlantic

The emergence of the concept of the "British Empire" as a political community encompassing England and Wales, Scotland, Protestant Ireland, the Caribbean and the continental colonies of North America did not occur until the late seventeenth century at the earliest.[31] It wasn't until the eighteenth century that "Empire" became an essential part of British political discourse. David Armitage has identified some of the main intellectual underpinnings of this evolution: Britain's Roman heritage, religious debates, political economy and trade. Free trade supported both maritime navigation and territorial penetration against rival powers (European, Asian, etc.) and conflicts with the American colonies.[32] Free trade was associated with liberty, and together they provided the basis for the common interests of the Crown and its colonies in North America from the late seventeenth to the mid-eighteenth century. This principle was gradually transformed into a form of conflict from the early eighteenth century until American independence.[33] In this context, liberty meant opposition to absolutism, protection of private property and free trade under the protection of equitable laws. In this perspective, it aroused the enthusiasm of Arthur Young and Adam Smith, who defended the unique British system of liberty.[34] But this notion did not imply equal rights for all, and that's where coercion at work came in. As early as 1560, in a work on the Elizabethan regime, Sir Thomas Smith asserted that "the necessity and scarcity of slaves induced men to use free men as slaves for all servile services, but in a more liberal and free manner, and with more

---

[31] David Armitage, *The Ideological Origins of the British Empire* (Cambridge: Cambridge University Press, 2010).
[32] Jack Greene, *All Men Are Created Equal: Some Reflections on the Character of the American Revolution* (Oxford: Oxford University Press, 1976).
[33] Armitage, *The Ideological Origins*; Greene, *Exclusionary Empire*.
[34] Arthur Young, *Political Essays Concerning the Present State of the British Empire* (London: Strahan and Cadell, 1772): 50; Adam Smith, *An Inquiry into the Nature and Causes of the Wealth of Nations*, 1776, reprinted in: R.H. Campbell, A. Skinner, *The Glasgow Edition of the Works and Correspondence of Adam Smith*, vol. 2 (Oxford: Oxford University Press, 1976).

equality and moderation than in the days of slaves."[35] The English experience in Ireland marked a turning point. The "Ulster Plantation" offered Scots and English common ground to pursue a joint project of plantation and civilization in a potentially pan-British enterprise.[36] In 1609, English and Scottish settlers were sent to the Ulster plantation to develop Irish lands, along with a thousand Irish enlisted as soldiers in the King's service. The colonization of Ireland and the American colonies both involved the dispossession of indigenous peoples from their lands; both created political entities dependent on England or, after 1707, Great Britain. Profits from the Ulster plantation were scarce, and land leased to Irish Catholic tenants yielded only a low rate of return. Many fortune-seeking English gentry, seeking to subdue Ireland, then embarked on privateering expeditions to the Caribbean.[37] In the sixteenth century, the consolidation of state power was accompanied by the explicit identification of subjects' rights.[38] In the colonies, people not born in Britain were excluded from this notion and practice of freedom.[39] Colonial actors claimed freedom and equality as native Britons and residents of Britain; at the same time, and for the same reason, they were prepared to legitimize slavery as a form of private property. They refused any interference by central government in this area; freedom meant freedom from taxation and freedom to own slaves. Exclusion in the name of freedom was a powerful ideological device in Britain, and even more so in its colonial world; why was it so?

We know that inequality before the law was not merely formal (a legal fiction), it was real. Women, immigrants and workers had few real rights; existing norms reinforced rather than reduced these inequalities. These characteristics must be taken into account when examining indenture and its relationship with slavery. Historians and social scientists have generally compared these categories on the basis of their obligations, duties, rights and social conditions. These comparisons have mainly focused on "colored" servitude after the abolition of slavery, i.e., from the mid-nineteenth century onwards, and we will discuss this in Part III. However, white servitude also existed before and during slavery. For these periods, the relevant comparison, as made by the actors themselves, is between white European indentured migrants, servants and enslaved black people. In fact, Great Britain was exceptional for the mobility of its population. Between 170,000 and 225,000 emigrants left the British Isles for the Americas between 1610 and 1660: 110,000 went to the Caribbean, 50,000 to Virginia and 20,000 to 25,000 to

---

[35] Sir Thomas Smith, *De Republica Anglorum: A Discourse on the Commonwealth of England* (1583, reprinted, edited by L. Alston, Cambridge, 1906): 139.
[36] Armitage, *Ideological Origins*: 58.
[37] Blackburn, *Manufacturing*: 59.
[38] Zaller, "Representative Governments."
[39] Greene, *Exclusionary Empire*.

New England.⁴⁰ Outside the Caribbean, the estimated number of emigrants varied between 472,000 and 510,000 between the years 1630 and 1780; 50,000 of these were convicts and the rest were half indentured and half "voluntary" migrants. Indentured servants accounted for around 60–65 percent in the seventeenth century and 40–42 percent in the following century.⁴¹ Women accounted for around a quarter of the total contingent.

There are many reasons for their departure: the transformation of agriculture in certain regions of Great Britain; the poor, suspected or actual criminals; kidnappings were also rife, to the extent that several rules were enacted to put an end to these acts, without success.⁴² The American colonists spoke of indentured labor in terms of ownership: Runaway servants had to be returned to their rightful owners.⁴³ Prices depended on the age, sex and skill of the indentured immigrant; young, healthy men were rated higher than women, children and the unskilled.

The contract of indenture arose out of the inequalities of labor existing in British practice; namely, rural contracts, particularly servants in husbandry and rural apprenticeships. Clauses of agreement (covenants) detailed duties and conditions. The migrant agreed to work for a specified period, under conditions negotiated with a shipper prior to shipment, in exchange for passage. The shipper recovered transport costs and margins by selling the servant's commitment on arrival. The planter purchased the immigrant's services according to "local custom."⁴⁴ Indentured servitude drew heavily on the rules governing masters and servants and apprentices. Like apprentices, indentured immigrants were subject to a seven-year contract, during which they could be transferred, but were not allowed to move freely without the master's permission.⁴⁵ This means that English migration was built on institutions that specifically aimed to control the service and working hours of all workers, with particular attention to vagrants, the poor and the young.

Now we need to understand how these institutions crossed the Atlantic; in particular, how did the commitment contract evolve when confronted with

---

⁴⁰ Peter Moogk, "Reluctant Exiles: Emigrants from France to Canada before 1760," *The William and Mary Quarterly*, 46, 3 (1989): 463–505.

⁴¹ Farley Grubb, "The Trans-Atlantic Market for British Convict Labor," *The Journal of Economic History*, 60, 1 (2000): 1–29.

⁴² Suranyi, *Indenture Servitude*; Alan Atkinson, "The Free-Born Englishman Transported: Convict Rights as a Measure of Eighteenth-Century Empire," *Past and Present*, 144, 1 (1994): 88–115.

⁴³ Steinfeld, *The Invention of Free Labor*: 89.

⁴⁴ Steven Hindle, *The State and Social Change in Early Modern England, 1550–1640* (New York: Palgrave, 2002).

⁴⁵ Russell R. Menard, *Migrants, Servants and Slaves: Unfree Labor in Colonial British America* (Aldershot: Ashgate, 2001); Richard Dunn, *Sugar and Slaves: The Rise of the Planter Class in the English West Indies, 1624–1713* (New York: Norton, 1973).

American contexts? Were the colonies a land of minor coercion, as in Russia, compared to England, or vice versa?

Indeed, a number of problems had to be resolved before English labor law could be successfully transplanted to the New World, and it is in their resolution that the origins of the indentured servitude system lie.[46] Firstly, credit played a crucial role. Advance payments for passage costs were much higher than salary advances in England and gave rise to a longer period of dependence (five to seven years). Following the model of English law, colonial courts in the seventeenth century assumed that artisans and laborers were legally bound to fulfill their commitments and could be ordered to do so. Secondly, although in principle it was the credit that was transferred, in practice, contracted migrants were regarded as sold. Indentured servants could legally be sold, and regularly were sold; the benchmark, once again, was the ability of English masters to sell their apprentices.[47] American apprentices were no more free to leave their masters than English apprentices. Colonial legislation often contained rules for capturing runaway apprentices and servants. During the term of service, like the masters of English servants, American masters of indentured servants had the right to exercise extensive control over the person of their servants. Initially, the rules were enforced more severely in the colonies than in Great Britain: English law forbids beatings, while many American laws merely prohibit masters from "excessive beating and abuse" of their servants.

Within this general trend, concrete issues and working relationships varied according to location, whether the region of emigration or destination. The links between the local and the global were particularly important during this period due to the weakness of national economies, itself a consequence of the multiplicity of local rules and the fragmentation of markets. From the mid-1620s to the end of the century, between 100,000 and 110,000 English migrants arrived in the Chesapeake region.[48] They came mainly from southeast England, and later from the southwest as a result of agricultural transformations in these regions, particularly the enclosures of the seventeenth century.[49] After the mid-seventeenth century, estates became more

---

[46] David W. Galenson, "The Rise and Fall of Indentured Servitude in the Americas: An Economic Analysis," *The Journal of Economic History*, 44, 1 (March 1984): 1–26.

[47] Russell Menard, "The Africanization of the Workforce in English America," in Gwyn Campbell, Alessandro Stanziani, eds., *Debt and Slavery in the Mediterranean and Atlantic Worlds* (London: Pickering and Chatto, 2013): 93–104.

[48] Russell Menard, "British Migration to the Chesapeake Colonies in the Seventeenth Century," in Lois Green Carr, Philips Morgan, Jean Russo, eds., *Colonial Chesapeake Society* (Chapel Hill: Northern Illinois University Press, 1988): 99–132.

[49] Henry Gemery, "Markets for Migrants: English Indentured Servitude and Emigration in the Seventeenth and Eighteenth Centuries," in Petr C. Emmer, ed., *Colonialism and Migration: Indentured Labor Before and After Slavery* (Dordrecht: Martin Nijhoff 1986): 33–54.

concentrated, smallholders migrated again and large planters relied more heavily on slave labor.[50] This region thus expresses the encounter between smallholders expelled from the rapidly transforming English countryside and the lack of capital in the area of immigration, the latter driving the merger of large estates and a slave capitalist regime.

In an altogether different way, forms of indentured servitude in Virginia[51] owe much to the fact that parish orphans and poor children were explicitly coerced into apprenticeship farming on the continent and to the vagrancy law, obsessed with controlling deviants.[52] In the 1630s, when the number of migrants increased due to the expansion of tobacco plantations, the Assembly decided that laborers and artisans should be forbidden to leave work unfinished. Servitude became a rigorous condition of subordination to a master.[53] This was one of the most precise transpositions of British labor institutions to North America.

Thirdly, in Pennsylvania, small landowners emigrating from northern England joined the considerable number of large landowners based in London and the south-west, who accounted for around 40 percent of all landowners in the region in the 1680s. By the mid eighteenth century, however, more than half of Pennsylvania's population was German, not British. In particular, the Delaware Valley was a territory granted to the duke of York and, as such, was governed by the duke's laws, which remained in force until 1682. These laws expressed a kind of seigneurial justice extended to colonial settlements. Unlike the statutes of the Virginia colony, the measures adopted in Pennsylvania placed greater emphasis on court control of the master–servant relationship and left much less room for the master's discretion. Valley farmers and artisans turned to slavery to cope with labor shortages; convicts and children of German and Irish families also served this purpose.

Forms of resistance were particularly diffuse: Running away and going to court were the most common. Between 5 percent and 10 percent of indentured servants run away.[54] In Maryland and Virginia, the usual punishment was additional time in servitude and whipping.[55] In 1666, a servant, W. Loveridge, who had missed three months, was sentenced to a further

---

[50] Abbott Emerson Smith, *Colonists in Bondage: White Servitude and Convict Labor in America, 1607–1776* (New York: Norton, 1947).

[51] Farley Grubb, "The Market for Indentured Immigrants: Evidence on the Efficiency of Forward-Labor Contracting in Philadelphia, 1745–1773," *The Journal of Economic History*, 45, 4 (1985): 855–868.

[52] Edward M. Riley, ed., *The Journal of John Harrower: An Indentured Servant in the Colony of Virginia, 1773–1776* (New York: Holt, Rinehart & Winston, 1963).

[53] William Waller Hening, *The Statutes at Large; Being a Collection of all Laws of Virginia, from the First Session of the Legislature, in the Year 1619* (New York: Bartow, 1823).

[54] Suranyi, *Indentured Servitude*: 135.

[55] Maryland Archives online, vol. 57, *Provincial court*, several cases.

three years' servitude.[56] The indentured themselves could go to court and denounce violence, illegal contracts and harsh conditions. They were often dismissed while being sued by their masters for perjury, the burden of proof falling entirely on the workers. Over time, however, they won more and more court cases, although this outcome was more common in the mainland colonies[57] than in Jamaica or Barbados, and, on the whole, more for men than for women.

In this context, women were subjected to particularly difficult conditions, given the already strong inequalities existing in British law and society.[58] Thus, the percentage of women kidnapped and transported to the colonies was higher than that of men, and the same was true of fraudulent contracts: most women were promised marriage once they arrived in the colonies, which was not necessarily the case.[59] Convicted women, as well as women placed in workhouses, were also transported to the colonies to serve as domestic servants and eventually as a reproductive force for white settlers.[60] They also performed agricultural tasks, but on the whole received lower fees and dues than men, while being subjected to constant violence and sexual assault.[61]

The condition of girls born out of wedlock was even more difficult. Such was the case of Elizabeth Key Grinstead (c. 1630– c. 1665), born in Virginia to an enslaved African woman and Thomas Key, a former indentured servant (arrived 1619), who became an independent planter, owning several slaves, including Elizabeth's mother. Thomas had an English wife and children. In 1636, he returned to England with his family and signed an indenture for Elizabeth, given to another planter, named Humphreys. Although the contract mentioned nine years of engagement, Elizabeth worked for him for nineteen years. The contract also stipulated that she would be released if Humphreys moved to England. This happened in 1640, but Humphreys retained his rights to Elizabeth, who was transferred to another planter, John Mottrom. Elizabeth worked for him for fifteen years. During this time, Elizabeth had an affair with an indentured servant, William Grenstead, and had two children, only one of

---

[56] Warren Billings, ed., *The Old Dominion in the Seventeenth Century: A Documentary History of Virginia, 1606–1689* (Chapel Hill: University of North Carolina Press, 1975).

[57] Maryland Archives online, Provincial court vol. 49, several cases. Also vols. 65 and 68. On the Chesapeake courts, Suranyi, *Indentured Servitude*.

[58] Susan Amussen, *An Ordered Society: Gender and Class in Early Modern England* (Oxford: Blackwell, 1988); Alan MacFarlane, *Marriage and Love in England, 1300–1840* (Oxford: Blackwell, 1986).

[59] Suranyi, *Indentured Servitude*; Lois Carr, Lorena Walsh, "The Planter's Wife: The Experience of White Women in Seventeenth-Century Maryland," *William and Mary Quarterly*, 34, 4 (1977): 542–571; Lucille Mair, *A Historical Study of Women in Jamaica, 1655–1844* (Barbados: University of West Indies Press, 2006).

[60] Gwenda Morgan, Peter Rushton, *Banishment in the Early Atlantic World: Convicts, Rebels, and Slaves* (London: Bloomsbury 2013).

[61] Menard, *Migrants, Servants and Slaves*.

whom survived. The legal status of Elizabeth and her son remained uncertain until her death. When Mottrom died in 1655, Elizabeth and her son were listed as "negroes" in the inventory.

On the other hand, masters would prosecute migrants for absenteeism, absconding or disrespectful behavior. Hundreds and hundreds of cases are available in the archives.[62] The use of the law revealed a strong influence of unequal rights, as in Great Britain, but with a significantly higher number of prosecutions in the colonies than on the continent.

In short, in the American colonies, as in Russia, local labor rules and forms of dependence were locally rooted and highly differentiated. Unlike Russia, however, labor servitude was more radical in the colonies than in mainland Britain. Indeed, the laws on masters and servants and their transposition to the colonies were the subject of arrangements between landowners, merchants and capitalists, and not between rentiers and the state, as was the case in Russia. Here, slavery disappeared and peasants were transformed into serfs as a result of the alliance between the state and landowners, which led to greater coercion in central Russia and less in the colonies. Conversely, in the British colonies of the Americas, the alliance between landowners and merchants led to the coercion of all workers and the adoption of slavery, which was no longer allowed in mainland Britain. How did this come about?

Why Slavery?

With the rapid development of plantations, African slaves gradually outnumbered indentured servants. Nonetheless, white indentured immigration remained important in North America and Canada at least until the 1830s, responding both to push factors in Europe (industrialization, transformation of the countryside) and pull factors in North America.[63] Why was the immigration of white hired hands accompanied by an increase in the importation of African slaves?

The profitability of white indentured immigrants was limited by the fact that their status was not hereditary: They were not material slaves and could not be bound for life. This was because slavery had disappeared from Northern Europe, and individualism and the protection of individual rights had consolidated in Britain over time. The evolution of the labor market in Great Britain also played a role: The size of the labor force considerably limited emigration and encouraged hostility to it on the part of landowners, industrialists, the state and the army, heads of family, etc., which also helped to keep potential

---

[62] The best analysis is Suranyi, *Indentured Servitude* and Anna Suranyi, "Indentured Servitude, the Right to Counsel and White Citizenship in Seventeenth-Century Chesapeake," *American Journal of Legal History*, 64, 4 (2023): 339–358.
[63] Galenson, *White Servitude in Colonial America*.

emigrants on the continent. Under these conditions, the rate of emigration produced by Great Britain before the rise of the plantation system seems to have been a considerable achievement and could no longer be pushed further.[64]

From the mid seventeenth century onwards, increasing numbers of Africans arrived on American shores. As a result, the number of indentured servants fell from a third of the population in the 1640s to a fifth in 1670 and 12 percent in 1700.[65] Overall, the number of slaves and indentured servants remained stable at about 37 percent of the total population, despite the increase in immigration. This can be explained by the fact that the white non-servant population grew significantly during these years, and rather than simply replacing servants with slaves, this process contributed to the steady growth of the local Creole and white populations.

Thus, the growing influx of slaves at the turn of the eighteenth century was not a response to a labor shortage per se, but to a shortage of forced labor, especially from indentured immigrants. Local masters weren't looking for more labor on the continent by raising wages; they wanted forced labor, so they turned to slaves.

But why and how were African captives defined as "slaves," especially when slavery was outlawed in Britain?

In fact, a dual process took place: First, African captives were referred to as migrants or indentured servants; then, rather quickly, they were transformed into "slaves," while the definition and legal characteristics of white subcontracts also evolved. This is where the differences in labor regimes between the colonies discussed previously become relevant. In Barbados, where indentured servitude was virtually non-existent, planters had three main concerns: first, their land titles were not well established and they wanted official recognition of their ownership; second, English merchants were keen to limit free trade with the Dutch, which ran counter to the interests of planters in Barbados; and third, planters felt overwhelmed by the number of servants and slaves and demanded greater protection.[66] As sugar production increased, monoculture replaced diversified agriculture, and large plantations took precedence over smallholdings. With the arrival of thousands of black people and the departure of white people, destructive demographic patterns took hold; the island began to import food and fuel, and large planters rose to wealth and power. To take advantage of the substantial economies of scale and high profits, sugar was grown most efficiently in large units, greatly increasing the demand for labor.[67] Here, the justification for the legal and institutional rules of slavery was security-oriented: Due to slave

---

[64] Galenson, *White Servitude in Colonial America*.
[65] Terry Anderson, Robert Thomas, "The Growth of Population and Labor Force in the Seventeenth-Century Chesapeake," *Explorations in Economic History*, 15, 3 (1978): 209–312.
[66] TNA, FO, 20/ 636 High Court of Admiralty, Ledgers for Goodes Soulde in ye Barbados, 1636.
[67] Stanley Engerman, "Europeans and the Rise and Fall of Slavery in the Americas: An Interpretation," *American Historical Review*, 98, 5 (1993): 1399–1423.

insurrections, new rules were adopted, and African slaves were gradually given new legal definitions, totally erasing their rights.

Characteristically, by the 1660s, the majority of the continent's small black population was in the Chesapeake region, so it is no coincidence that the first rules on slavery were enacted there.[68] The black population grew from 1,700 in 1600 to 20,000 in the early 1700s and 150,000 in 1750. After 1660, all Restoration landlords, not only in Carolina but throughout the continent, favored the introduction of slavery.[69] The duke of York even dreamed of making New York the main port of entry for slaves. The duke's laws enabled the introduction of slavery in New York, New Jersey and Pennsylvania.[70] This reveals the extreme adaptability of conventional British and even continental European institutions to the Americas. The Maryland law of 1664 *concerning negroes and other slaves* confirmed that "all children born of a negro or other slave shall be slaves as their fathers were."[71]

By contrast, South Carolina held only 6,000 slaves at the end of the seventeenth century.[72] Landholdings and local government were detailed and separated into seigneuries, baronies, colonies and manors, with the aim of transplanting the European agrarian system to this region. Slaveholders in Carolina were granted the same rights as those established in Barbados in 1661,[73] but, at the same time, religion could not be a source of discrimination in the new colonies, and it was precisely for this reason that enslavement and eventual manumission could not refer to it. Thus, English-born freemen were granted absolute rights over their slaves.[74] In 1690, a general law – the Act of the Better Ordering of Slaves – was passed to regulate the mobility of slaves outside family plantations as well as runaways. In 1696, the Act was revised to toughen

---

[68] Philip D. Morgan, *Slave Counterpoint: Black Culture in Eighteenth-Century Chesapeake & Lowcountry* (Chapel Hill: University of North Carolina Press, 1998).

[69] Lorena Walsh, *Motives of Honor, Pleasure & Profit: Plantation Management in the Colonial Chesapeake, 1607–1763* (Chapel Hill: University of North Carolina Press, 2010).

[70] "Duke of York's Book of Law," in George Staughton, Benjamin Nead, Thomas McCamant, eds., *Charters to William Penn, and Laws of the Province of Pennsylvania* (University of Pennsylvania Press, 1986): 1–77; Gloria Lund Main, *Tobacco Colony: Life in Early Maryland, 1650–1720* (Princeton, NJ: Princeton University Press, 1982).

[71] Maryland Archives, vol. 1, *Minutes and Proceedings of the Maryland General Assembly, January 1637/8–September 1664* (Baltimore: Maryland Historical Society 1883): 553–554. Available online: https://msa.maryland.gov/megafile/msa/speccol/sc2900/sc2908/000001/000001/html/am1--533.html.

[72] Robert Weir, "Shaftesbury's Darling: British Settlement in the Carolinas at the Close of the Seventeenth Century," in Nichols Canny, ed., *The Origin of Empire: British Overseas Enterprise to the Close of the Seventeenth Century. Oxford History of the British Empire*, vol. 1 (Oxford: Oxford University Press, 1998): 375–397.

[73] Robert Wells, *The Population of the British Colonies in America Before 1776: A Survey of Census Data* (Princeton: Princeton University Press, 1975).

[74] Peter Wood, *Black Majority: Negroes in Colonial South Carolina from 1670 through the Stono Rebellion* (New York: Knopf, 1974).

penalties and added a new dimension: For the first time, an official definition of a slave was given. Slaves were defined as Negroes, Indians and Mulattoes who had already been sold, bought and held as slaves.

In Virginia, there were only a few hundred black people before the 1630s. Between 1660 and 1680, the black population increased by 2,000, and between 1680 and 1710 by 16,000. The evolution of the legal regime of slavery in Virginia was similar to that of the other colonies: An initial reference was made to the common law of property and inheritance; then laws were passed concerning the order and government of slaves, particularly with regard to fugitives; finally, legal texts concerning racial and legal status were added. However, Virginia's rules on slavery, unlike those of the Carolinas, referred to the laws governing migrant servants in order to clearly distinguish "colored" slaves from white servants.[75] In 1662, it was proclaimed that children would be slave or free depending on the mother's status. Along with New York, this was an exception among the American colonies, all the others having adopted the common law of patrilineal transmission of status. In 1682, the Virginia Assembly defined slaves as

> all servants, with the exception of Turks and Moors ... who, from the publication of this act, shall be brought or imported into this country, by sea or land, whether Negroes, Moors, Mulattoes or Indians, whose parentage and country of origin are not Christian at the time of the first purchase of such servant by a Christian, although subsequently, and before their importation and arrival in this country, they have been converted to the Christian faith.[76]

This act was essential: It enabled the transfer of slaves between colonies, and separated their conversion from their emancipation.[77] It also served to distinguish between indentured servants (who were already Christians) and slaves; a distinction that was lacking, for example, in the Spanish Empire, where white indenture was non-existent.[78] As far as women were concerned, the usual rule was that they and their children belonged to the owner.

The rules were different in Massachusetts where, in 1641, the Body of Liberties confirmed that war captives could be sold. The document refers to Indians, but in 1646, two merchants justified the sale of African slaves on the grounds that they had been captured in war.[79] The text also adds slavery as a

---

[75] Thomas Morris, *Southern Slavery and the Law, 1619–1860* (Chapel Hill: University of North Carolina Press, 1999).
[76] Act to Repeal a Former Law Making Indians and Others Free, Act 1, 1682, in Hening, *The Statutes at Large*, II: 490–492.
[77] Rebecca Anne Goetz, *The Baptism of Early Virginia: How Christianity Created Race* (Baltimore: Johns Hopkins University Press, 2012).
[78] Emmer, *Colonialism and Migration*, introduction; Menard, *Migrants, Servants and Slaves*.
[79] Winthrop Jordan, *White Over Black: American Attitudes Towards the Negro, 1550–1812* (Chapel Hill: The University of North Carolina Press, 2nd edition, 2012): 69–70.

penalty, but this is not for life and cannot be inherited. This was a distinctive feature of the Massachusetts colony, where the incidence of slavery was still low at the time, barely differentiated from servitude and not yet racialized. It wasn't until the eighteenth century that all white immigrants, including indentured servants, became natural-born Englishmen,[80] even though the colony had far fewer slaves than elsewhere and most of them were city dwellers.

In short, as with indenture, definitions of slavery were linked to the particularities of each colony, depending on the social origin of the migrants, the concentration rate of the estates and, of course, the activity. Despite the differences, the identification of slaves and indentured laborers was mutually linked. With the spread and legal definition of slavery, we no longer find statutes forbidding craftsmen and laborers from abandoning their tasks, nor cases where the courts ordered their contract to be enforced.[81] Indentured servitude transmuted into a fully commercialized institution. This happened for at least two different, albeit interrelated, reasons: Firstly, many judges felt that excessive abuse by masters would turn indentured immigrants into slaves, something they were not prepared to accept. Secondly, it was feared that mistreatment and other trials would compromise the colony's reputation in favor of other immigration regions, not only in the eyes of the immigrants themselves, but also of the carriers and, last but not least, of the British colonial authorities eager to increase emigration.[82] If British subjects in the colonies did not enjoy the traditional rights of Englishmen, they were not free men, but slaves.[83] This figurative definition of the term "slave" was intended to distinguish whites (who were not to be treated as slaves) from African slaves. The emancipation of white workers required the identification of "black slaves." The same was partly true for white indentured women, who were increasingly differentiated from enslaved African women, and their rights were better recognized, even if they remained inferior to those of white men. Meanwhile, in the first half of the eighteenth century, the proportion of indentured women crossing the Atlantic fell to less than 10 percent (compared with 20–25 percent in the seventeenth century). This was probably because masters now demanded servants rather than potential wives, as evidenced by the increasing age of migrant women.[84]

This process continued after American independence, when the northern states changed their rules: Without officially abolishing slavery, they

---

[80] Blackburn, *The Making of New World Slavery*: 263–264.
[81] Steinfeld, *The Invention of Free Labor*: 50
[82] Farley Grubb, "Does Bound Labour Have to Be Coerced Labour? The Case of Colonial Immigrant Servitude versus Craft-Apprenticeship and Life-Cycle Servitude in Husbandry," *Itinerario*, 21, 1 (1997): 28–51.
[83] Jack Greene, *Negotiated Authorities: Essays in Colonial Political and Constitutional History* (Charlottesville: University of Virginia Press, 1994).
[84] David Galenson, "Demographic Aspects of White Servitude in Colonial British America," *Annales de démographie historique*, 66, 1 (1980): 239–252.

nevertheless relaxed the rules governing manumission. In 1780, Pennsylvania became the first state to adopt a statute replacing slavery with 25 years' service for all children born into slavery thereafter. Once again, this evolution in the legal rules applicable to slaves had an impact on the legal definition of "servant" and "indentured" migrant. Although the term "servant" was still used in legal proceedings, wage earners often refused to be qualified as such, even though legal documents oppose slavery to the contract of engagement. Many craftsmen and apprentices refused to submit to the traditional rules of masters and servants; wage workers took offense at being called "servants." It was becoming increasingly difficult to reconcile the contractual principle of equality and free will with labor relations in which the legal inequality between master and servant, especially the hired man, was evident from the outset, as was the idea of personal service as property. White workers were no longer called "servants" but "wage earners," with specific rights.[85] By the late 1830s, criminal penalties were no longer imposed to punish breaches of contract by white adult workers.[86]

At the same time, the price of passage from Europe dropped considerably in the 1830s, and few European immigrants needed to resort to indenture to emigrate. This result was also facilitated by the presence of relatives already living in the United States, who paid off the new immigrant's debt. Finally, incentives to migrate from Europe declined between 1815 and 1846, except for the Irish, and did not re-emerge until the agrarian crisis of the last quarter of the nineteenth century.[87]

In short, white indentured immigration was first legally inspired by forms of coercion and inequality already existing in Britain (the Masters and Servants Acts, the Poor Law, and forms of recruitment for the Navy as well as for private companies). Work as a service, obligations and penal rules were common to all these contracts and employment relationships. Unlike Russia, living conditions for migrants in the Americas were worse than in Britain, at least in the seventeenth and early eighteenth centuries. Then, with the arrival of slaves, this situation changed: Gradually, indentured immigrants were assimilated to wage earners rather than servants. White American workers obtained better conditions than their British counterparts, thanks to the existence of slavery in their new homeland. Just as in Russia, the definition of serfdom was in constant interaction with that of the *kholopstvo* and peasant-soldiers, in North America, the identification of indentured migrants evolved in relation to the arrival and definition of slaves. Differences were racialized, and it was here that

---

[85] Steinfeld, *The Invention of Free Labor*: 166–170.
[86] Steinfeld, *Coercion, Contract and Free Labor*: 254.
[87] Farley Grubb, "The End of European Immigrant Servitude in the United States: An Economic Analysis of Market Collapse, 1772-1835," *The Journal of Economic History*, 54, 4 (1994): 794–824.

conditions for white immigrants improved. The categories of wage earner and "free laborer" emerged as the counterparts of racialism in labor relations.[88]

In this context, where slaves had virtually no rights, runaway was their main form of "voice." An enormous bibliography is available on maroons and their societies in the Americas,[89] and there is no need to expand on it here. In Jamaica, for example, maroon society developed from the mid seventeenth century onwards.[90] Over time, two large, distinct communities were formed: one, the Windword maroon, made up of slaves originally imported by the Spanish and claiming land; and the other, the Leeward maroon, grouping slaves imported by the British. The Great Maroonage threatened Jamaica at the turn of the seventeenth and eighteenth centuries. As the maroon societies sought to disrupt the plantation economy while recruiting new members, a first maroon war took place between 1720 and 1740. A treaty signed in 1739 recognized the autonomy of the maroon societies. The maroons gained access to the land, but in exchange were forbidden to recruit new members. In addition, the internal rules governing the maroon societies were declared illegal, and the power of the chiefs was weakened.[91] Within a few decades, land disputes with planters were settled peacefully. Tensions reappeared in the 1780s, and a second maroon war broke out in the 1790s, following the Haitian Revolution.

On the continent, new tools of resistance such as storytelling and spirituals were added to more conventional forms of struggle: degradation of property, refusal to work, etc. Slaves reacted against changes in working or living conditions (particularly in the event of transfer or, on the same plantation, against overseers, especially in the lower Mississippi, where they worked in gangs), against ill-treatment, violence against women and children, etc.[92] At times,

---

[88] Among the immense bibliography on this aspect, a few introductory titles: Justin Roberts, "Race and the Origin of Plantation Slavery," *Oxford Research Encyclopedia of American History*, 2016, https://doi.org/10.1093/acrefore/9780199329175.013.268, accessed April 10, 2022; Michael Guasco, *Slaves and Englishmen: Human Bondage in the Early Modern Atlantic World* (Philadelphia: University of Pennsylvania Press, 2014).

[89] Among the huge number of titles: Price, *Maroon Societies*; Price, "Maroon societies in the Americas," *Oxford Encyclopedia of Africa online*, 2020, https://doi.org/10.1093/acrefore/9780190277734.013.935; Genovese, *Roll, Jordan, Roll*; Genovese, *From Rebellion to Revolution*; Diouf, *Slavery's Exiles*; Thompson, *Flight to Freedom*; Sheridan, "The Maroons of Jamaica, 1730–1830"; Franklin and Schweniger, *Runaway Slaves*; Paquette, Robert. "Slave Resistance and Social History," *Journal of Social History*, 24, 3 (1991): 681–685; Craton, *Testing the Chains*.

[90] Mavis Campbell, *The Maroons of Jamaica 1655–1796* (Trenton: African World Press, 1990).

[91] Helen McKee, "From Violence to Alliance: Maroons and White Settlers in Jamaica, 1739–1795," *Slavery & Abolition*, 39, 1 (2018): 27–52, DOI: 10.1080/0144039X.2017.1341016.

[92] Gabor Borritt, Scott Hancock, eds., *Slavery, Resistance, Freedom* (Oxford: Oxford University Press, 2007); Gerald Horne, *The Counter-Revolution of 1776. Slave Resistance and the origins of the United States of America* (New York: New York University Press, 2014);

slaves sought to organize themselves to cope with or change the rules, giving rise to an enormous fear – sometimes healthy, sometimes not – of "conspiracy" on the part of white planters and society.

Fugitive slaves have also been the subject of passionate accounts since the nineteenth century, and a very substantial historiography has been produced,[93] including biographies of fugitives.[94] Slaves escaped when they were conscripted into the army or sent by their masters to work on another plantation or in an urban activity. Runaways also occurred from plantations near state borders, particularly along the upper Mississippi and Ohio rivers. Alongside the so-called Underground Railroad to the free northern states, many fugitives remained in the southern states, seeking to blend in with the free black population of these states. However, their situation was extremely precarious, and they were in daily danger of being caught and sent back to their homeland. Moses Roper was born in North Carolina in 1815, to a half-white slave and her master. Almost killed at birth by his master's wife, he was sold to another master at the age of twelve. The harsh treatment inflicted by his new master prompted him to run away several times. He was caught and severely punished and tortured. He tried to escape between sixteen and twenty times, after being sold to new masters in Florida and Georgia, from where he reached New York. He then made his way to Massachusetts and Vermont. Almost white, he escaped the fugitive slave hunters and enlisted in the army. He then settled in London, where he began his career as an abolitionist.

However, with the exception of a few cases, when slaves ran away, they were caught and sent back. Repression was brutal, despite the widespread argument that slaves were capital to be preserved. Extreme physical violence, torture and family separation were widespread. Moreover, even in the North, several provisions condemned theft. Numerous judicial decisions, including those of the Supreme Court, confirmed that fugitive slaves had to be returned to their masters, even after a court decision. Planters and authorities also used the law to condemn slave rebellion and conspiracies.[95] On the other hand,

---

Seymour Drescher, Pieter Emmer, eds., *Who Abolished Slavery. Slave Revolt and Abolitionism* (New York: Berghahn, 2010).

[93] Franklin, Schweninger, *Runaway Slaves*; William Loren Katz, *Breaking the Chain* (New York: Atheneum, 1990); Larry Eugene Rivers, *Rebels and Runaways. Slave Resistance in nineteenth Century Florida* (Urbana: University of Illinois, 2012).

[94] Devon Carbado, Donald Weise, *The Long Walk to Freedom. Runaway Slaves Narratives* (Boston: Beacon Press, 2012). Some biographies and autobiographies were already popular before the Civil War: Frederick Douglass, The Frederick Douglass Papers, John Blassingame, ed., 5 volumes (New Haven, Yale University Press, 1991); William Well Brown, *Narrative of William W. Brown, An American Slave* (London: Charles Gilpin, 1949); and Harriet Jacobs, Incidents in the Life of a Slave Girl: Written by Herself (Boston: Maria Child, 1861).

[95] Philip Schwarz, *Twice Condemned. Slaves and the Criminal Laws of Virginia 1705–1865* (New Jersey: The Lawbrook Exchange, 1998).

although extremely difficult, recourse to the law by slaves was not non-existent, as conventional historiography claims.[96] In Louisiana, in particular, slaves sought to exploit legal pluralism – Spanish, French and British-American jurisprudence – to gain their freedom.[97]

In summary, both in the provisions and in the use of the law, between the mid seventeenth and mid nineteenth centuries, in the British colonies and then in the United States, the law progressively differentiated between white workers and servants and black slaves. The former obtained increasing rights, even more so than servants in Great Britain, precisely in response to black slavery and race, rather than as a consequence of the presumed laws of supply and demand on the labor market (lack of arms, and therefore good working conditions and wages for white workers). This issue would play a major role, as we shall see, during and after the Civil War.

We can now ask what happened when the British authorities were confronted not only with "empty spaces" to colonize, but also with other empires, as in India and the Indian Ocean; in this case, how were the rules of labor negotiated with local actors? Was there still a universalist attempt to impose British notions and rules, or, despite initial assertions, were compromises necessary?

Labor Rules in Eurasia: British India

Research is all too often limited to transatlantic interactions, forgetting the role that the Indian Ocean and the Indian subcontinent played in the evolution of labor institutions in the British Empire and in Britain itself. Differentiated local realities had an impact not only on policy, but also on the very notions to which the various British actors resorted when confronted with labor outside mainland Britain. Many cases, such as the case of the Americas just mentioned, and even more so that of India to which I will now turn, reflect a double mutual influence between the continent and specific colonies on labor institutions and

---

[96] Alejandro de la Fuente, Ariela Gross, "Concluding Thoughts. Crossing Borders: Slavery and Freedom, Legality and Illegality, Past and Present," *Journal of Law and History*, 35, 1 (2017): 119–130; Andrew T. Fede, *Roadblocks to Freedom: Slavery and Manumission in the United States South* (New Orleans: Quid Pro Books, 2011); Paul Finkelman, *Slavery in Courtroom. An Annotated Bibliography of American Cases* (New Jersey: The Lawbook Exchange, 1998); Melissa Milewski, "From Slave to Litigant: African Americans in Court in the Postwar South, 1865–1920," *Law & History Review*, 30, 3 (2012): 723–769; Alfred Brophy, "Slaves as Plaintiffs," *Michigan Law Review*, 115, 6 (2017): 895–914.

[97] Vernon Palmer, "The Quest to Implant the Civilian Method in Louisiana: Tracing the Origins of Judicial Methodology," *Louisiana Law Review* 73 (2013): 793–819; John Cairns, "Blackstone in the Bayous: Inscribing Slavery in the Louisiana Digest of 1808," in Wilf Prest ed. *Re-Interpreting Blackstone's Commentaries: A Seminal Text in National and International Contexts* (Oxford: Hart Publishing, 2014): 105–124.

practices. Despite the global circulation of people, ideas and practices, legal and economic models diverged, and the Atlantic and Indian Oceans emerged as distinct regulatory spheres. The Indian Ocean, in particular, was quickly identified as a space where maritime access had to be negotiated with a multitude of coastal powers and traders. Hugo Grotius was one of the founders of modern maritime and international law. When he emphasized natural law as the basis for freedom of navigation, he took into account not only Dutch, British and Latin, but also East Indian conceptions of the sea.[98] The multiplicity of legal orders and contested sovereignty in the Indian Ocean fostered ideas and practices about trade and labor that were quite different from those in the Atlantic. In particular, a flourishing historiography of slavery in the Indian Ocean world (IOW) has emerged, highlighting the specificity of forms of slavery in these regions compared to those in the Atlantic.[99] Indeed, slavery was not introduced into the Indian Ocean by the European colonial powers, but was transformed by them, albeit in a completely different way to the Atlantic. In fact, between 1400 and 1900, 2.5 million slaves were traded by sea along the Indian Ocean coasts, while around 9 million took the trans-Saharan route (3.6 million were exported).[100] Slave exports from East Africa rose from 100,000 in the seventeenth century to 400,000 in the eighteenth and 1,618,000 in the nineteenth, half of them being sent overseas and the other half remaining on the East African coast.[101] More than a million slaves were obtained by the Swahili world alone in the nineteenth century.[102] It is estimated that Europeans traded a minimum of 947,600 to 1,275,200 slaves from East Africa, India, Madagascar and Southeast Asia within and beyond the Indian Ocean basin between 1500 and 1850, with most of this activity concentrated between the 1770s and the early 1830s.[103]

---

[98] Ram Anand, Origins and Development of the Law of the Sea (The Hague: Martin Nijhoff, 1983).

[99] Clarence-Smith, *The Economics of the Indian Ocean Slave Trade*; Abdul Sheriff, *Slaves, Spices and Ivory* (London: J. Currey, 1987); Gwyn Campbell, ed. *Abolition and Its Aftermath in Indian Ocean Africa and Asia* (London: Routledge, 2005); James Francis Warren, *The Sulu Zone, 1768–1898: The Dynamics of External Trade, Slavery, and Ethnicity in the Transformation of a Southeast Asian Maritime State*, 2nd ed. (Singapore University Press, 1981; reprint: National University of Singapore, 2007); Richard Allen, *European Slave Trade in the Indian Ocean, 1500–1850* (Athens: Ohio University Press, 2015).

[100] Ralph Austen, "The Trans-Saharan Slave Trade: a Tentative Census," in Jan S. Hogendorn ed., *The Uncommon Market: Essays in the Economic History of the Atlantic Slave Trade* (New York: Academic Press, 1979): table 2.8: 66; Ralph Austen, "The Nineteenth Century Islamic Slave Trade from East Africa (Swahili and Red Sea Coasts): A Tentative Census," *Slavery and Abolition*, 9 (1988): 21–44.

[101] Paul Lovejoy, *Transformations in Slavery* (Cambridge: Cambridge University Press, 2012): 61–62, 155–158.

[102] Ralph Austin, "The Nineteenth Century Islamic Slave Trade from East Africa (Swahili and Red Sea Coasts): a Tentative Census," in William Gervase Clarence-Smith, ed., *The Economics of the Indian Ocean Slave Trade* (London: Frank Cass 1989): 21–44.

[103] Allen, *European Slave Trade*.

Unlike its transatlantic counterpart, the Indian Ocean slave trade was not controlled by Europeans and was not limited to Africans, but also included Asian slaves. Unlike the Atlantic system, Indian Ocean slaves rarely constituted a special cargo. The Indian Ocean slave trade involved both land and sea routes. It also went far beyond chattel slavery and the plantation economy, which were important in the Mascarenes and along the Swahili coast, but cannot be considered representative of the multiple forms of servitude in the Indian Ocean over the long term. Debt bondage and other forms of servitude were extremely widespread.[104] Debt bondage was sometimes involuntary, while most people submitted to it voluntarily as part of a strategy to secure credit. The main slave export zones from Africa to the Indian Ocean were north-east Africa, east Africa and south-east Africa. North-east Africa drew captives from Ethiopia, Somalia and Sudan and exported them along the Red Sea coast to the Persian Gulf, South Asia and finally Zanzibar. East Central Africa drew from northern Mozambique, Malawi, Zambia and Zimbabwe and supplied the same markets, as well as the Comoros, western Madagascar, the Mascarene Islands and the Seychelles. South-central Africa, extending into the hinterland of southern Mozambique and the Zimbabwe plateau, provided labor for the Cape, western India and the Mascarene Islands. Madagascar was one of the first sources of slaves for the Cape, and one of the main suppliers to the Mascareignes. It is extremely difficult to quantify the Indian Ocean slave trade: Sources are lacking and often far from reliable.[105] Current estimates of the slave trade in the western Indian Ocean (linking East Africa, the Persian Gulf and India) put the number of slaves traded between these regions at around 1,000 per year between 800 and 1700.[106] Data is even more problematic for the eastern Indian Ocean, where Western colonial sources are late and problematic, while sources in vernacular languages are scarce and barely exploited by Western-centric researchers. For Indonesia, for example, some put the figure at 100,000 to 150,000 slaves between 1620 and 1830.[107] Overall, Europeans were directly or indirectly involved in

---

[104] Campbell, "Introduction" in *The Structure of Slavery*: i–xxxii.

[105] Hubert Gerbeau, "The Slave Trade in the Indian Ocean: Problems Facing the Historian and Research to be Undertaken" In: The African Slave Trade from the Fifteenth to the Nineteenth Century (Paris: UNESCO, 1979): 184–207. For a recent study: Richard Allen, "Ending the History of Silence: Reconstructing European Slave Trading in the Indian Ocean," *Tempo*, 23, 2 (2017): 295–313.

[106] Thomas Vernet, ed., *Traites, esclavage et transition vers l'engagisme: Perspectives nouvelles sur les Mascareignes et le sud-ouest de l'océan Indien, 1715-1848* (Réduit: University of Mauritius, 2015); Lovejoy, *Transformations in Slavery*; Titos Chakraborty, Matthias von Rossum, "Slave Trade and Slavery in Asia. New Perspectives," *Journal of Social History*, 54, 1 (2020): 1–14; Ulbe Bosma, "Towards an Indian Ocean and Maritime Asia Slave Database: an Exploration of Concepts, lessons, and Models," *Esclavages et post esclavages*, 3 (2020), https://doi.org/10.4000/slaveries.2946.

[107] Markus Vink, "'The World's Oldest Trade.' Dutch Slavery and Slave Trade in the Indian Ocean in the Seventeenth Century," *Journal of World History*, 14, 2 (2003): 131–177.

the trade of a minimum of 567,900 to 733,200 slaves between 1500 and 1850 in an oceanic world stretching from East Africa and Madagascar to the Persian Gulf, South Asia and the Indonesian and Philippine archipelagos.[108] For the Indian Ocean basin as a whole, Allen estimated the number of slaves traded by Europeans between 1500 and 1850 at around 430,000–560,000.[109] From the last third of the eighteenth century onwards, the slave trade played an important role in the economic history of East Africa. The combined population of the Hijazi cities – Mecca, Medina and their port of Jidda – doubled in the century, while Zanzibar's population rose from 12,000 in 1835 to between 25,000 and 45,000 in 1857.[110]

In many parts of the IOW, slavery has always been legally applied to debtors and their relatives. In Madagascar, for example, creditors could apply the law to enslave a debtor, his wife and children.[111] In this broader context, the case of the Indian subcontinent is particularly striking, despite the fact that the history of slavery in India has not played a role in historiography comparable to that of the Atlantic world;[112] in part, this is due to the fact that most Western experts on slavery do not speak the many vernacular languages of the Indian Ocean, South Asia, Southeast Asia and East Asia. The new approaches have made extensive use of these sources[113] and, on this basis, have emphasized the continuity of forms of dependence in India, as well as the fact that Indian slavery and servitude could not be separated from caste, religion, domestic and military affairs.[114] War and debt were the two most common sources of slavery and servitude in pre-colonial India. Slaves originally came from parts of India, East Africa, Southeast Asia and Central Asia. Military slavery was widespread, and recruitment extended as far as East Africa. The Habshis of the Deccan were of African origin (Ethiopia, Somalia, the Nubian desert and Tanzania) and were imported from the fifteenth to seventeenth centuries. They were

---

[108] Allen, European Slave Trade in the Indian Ocean.

[109] Allen, European Slave Trade in the Indian Ocean; Richard Allen, "Satisfying the Want for Laboring People: European Slave Trading in the Indian Ocean, 1500–1850," *Journal of World History*, 21, 1 (2010): 45–73.

[110] William Ochsenwald, *Religion, Society, and the State in Arabia: the Hijaz under the Ottoman Control* (Columbus: Ohio University Press, 1984).

[111] Gwyn Campbell, *An Economic History of Imperial Madagascar, 1750–1895: The Rise and Fall of an Island Empire* (Cambridge: Cambridge University Press, 2005): 295–296.

[112] Drescher, *Abolitions*; Grenouilleau, *Les traites négrières*; Olivier Grenouilleau, *La révolution abolitionniste* (Paris: Gallimard, 2017); Andrea Major, *Slavery, Abolitionism and Empire in India, 1772–1843* (Liverpool: Liverpool University Press, 2002).

[113] Indrani Chatterjee and Richard Eaton, eds., *Slavery and South Asian History* (Bloomington: Indiana University Press, 2006); Dharma Kumar, "Colonialism, Bondage, and Caste in British India," in Martin Klein, eds., *Breaking the Chains. Slavery, Bondage, and Emancipation in Modern Africa and Asia* (Madison: The University of Wisconsin Press, 1993): 112–130; Prakash, *Bonded histories*.

[114] David Turley, *Slavery* (Malden, MA: Blackwell, 2000).

originally slaves – sometimes mercenaries – but were more often freed and raised to nobility.[115] Slave markets were commonplace in many other parts of India. There were 12,000 slaves at the court of Muhammad bin Tughluq and a further 180,000 under Firuz Shah Tughluq. In the Bahmani empire, there were 60,000 to 70,000 Vijanyanagara captives, mainly women.[116]

The Mughals did not use slave soldiers to conquer India and even tried to limit the extent of slavery. They succeeded in reducing economic slavery; the reason being that, unlike slaves, peasants were taxpayers. At the same time, Mughal merchants were involved in the Central Asian trade and the slave trade. They deported rebels and defaulters and traded them for horses. Domestic slavery also flourished under the Mughals, as it did in the contemporary Rajput and Maratha states of the Indian subcontinent. Under the Marathas, indebtedness (to the state and/or other creditors) often led to enslavement;[117] sexual immorality was also a cause of enslavement.[118] In general, the children of female servants were considered family property.[119]

Debt bondage and other forms of servitude were extremely widespread.[120] In times of disaster, people would often engage in debt bondage or slavery as a survival strategy in exchange for sustenance, either voluntarily, as was the case for many members of the *dvija* caste in India, or driven out by their kinship group. Forms of servitude were also widespread in Gujarat, particularly as a result of marriage advances. A *dubla* (landless laborer) would accept an advance from a higher-caste landowner and become a *hali*, committing himself and his family to work for the master for an entire year. Further advances on grain and reduced periods of activity increased the debt.[121]

Hindu and Muslim families used domestic slaves for household and agricultural work. They were acquired locally, through abduction, debt bondage or marriage to slaves. The men could accompany their masters on military campaigns, while the women provided sexual services. Rajputs and Marathas sold, mortgaged and rented slaves. Slaves were also valuable gifts, circulating as dowries or

---

[115] Shanti Sadiq Ali, *The African Dispersal in the Deccan* (New Delhi: Orient Black Swan, 1996); André Wink, *Al-Hind. The Making of the Indo-Islamic World* (Leiden: Brill, 2004), vol. 3: 146.

[116] Wink, *Al-Hind*, 3: 164.

[117] Ganesh Chimanji Vad, ed., *Selection from the Satara Raja and Peshwas' Diaries* (Pune: Deccan Vernacular Translation Society, 1902–11): in particular, pt 5: 247.

[118] See the case in Vad, *Selection from the Satara Raja*, pt. 8, vol. 3: 252; and BL IOR Mss Mar D 31 fol. 110.

[119] Sumit Guha, "Slavery, Society and the State in Western India, 1700–1800," in Indrani Chatterjee and Richard Eaton, eds., *Slavery and South Asian History* (Bloomington: Indiana University Press, 2006): 162–186.

[120] Gwyn Campbell, "Introduction" to Campbell, *The Structure of Slavery*: i–xxxii; Campbell, Stanziani, eds., *Debt and Bondage in the Indian Ocean Worlds*.

[121] Breman, *Labour Bondage in West India*.

tributes and as part of strategic alliances between families.[122] Dowries contributed to the expansion of the slave trade and slave markets in the Rajput regions.

In Hindu regions, caste origin played a role; slaves retained their caste identity, and masters deliberately identified and publicized their slaves' caste.[123] In fact, ritual and caste influenced the process of enslavement and emancipation.[124] Lower castes were more likely to find themselves in certain forms of extreme dependence and servitude, but not necessarily in slavery.[125] However, while caste identity tended to remain stable over time, this was not the case with slave status.[126] Most slaves did not remain locked into slavery for the rest of their lives. Slaves were integrated into their masters' households. In the Maratha kingdom, slaves could inherit land, while others obtained manumission by buying a slave to be their substitute on the master's property.[127]

These forms of slavery and servitude did not disappear under colonial rule but evolved in conjunction with it. Although India did not suffer from the extreme labor shortage that gave rise to slavery in the New World, it would be wrong to assume that the country enjoyed an abundance of labor. In many activities, the supply of labor was a crucial concern for both the British and local authorities. In the 1790s, the struggle between the East India Company (EIC) and Mysore, for example, considerably reduced production capacity and available manpower in Andhra Pradesh.[128] Indeed, both the British and the local powers resorted to slaves and forced labor and competed for manpower.[129] European colonial regimes facilitated the development of indebtedness by imposing currency taxes, encouraging commercialization and enforcing credit contracts. Thus, the abundance of low-caste workers without land rights did not prevent periodic labor shortages. In southern India, five million slaves were employed in rice cultivation.[130] British reports mention the trafficking of Nepalese workers and children from Assam to Bengal.[131]

---

[122] Ramya Sreenivasan, "Drudges, Dancing Girls, Concubines: Female Slaves in Rajput Polity, 1500–1850," in Indrani Chatterjee and Richard Eaton, eds., *Slavery and South Asian History* (Bloomington: Indiana University Press, 2006): 136–161.

[123] See for example: Vad, *Selection from the Satara Raja*.

[124] Dick Kooiman, "Conversion from Slavery to Plantation Labor: Christian Mission in South India, nineteenth century," *Social Scientist*, 19, 8/9 (1991): 57–71.

[125] Indrani Chatterjee, *Gender, Slavery, and Law in Colonial India* (New Delhi: Oxford University Press, 1999).

[126] Howard Temperley, *British Antislavery, 1833–1870* (London: Longman, 1972).

[127] Vad, *Selection from the Satara Raja*, especially pt. 2, vol. 2.

[128] Kaushik Roy, *War, Culture and Society in Early Modern South Asia, 1740–1849* (Abingdon and New York: Routledge, 2011).

[129] Dirk Kolff, *Naukar, Rajput and Sepoy. The Ethnohistory of the Military Labour Market in Hindustan, 1450–1850* (Cambridge: Cambridge University Press, 1990).

[130] Francis Buchanan, *A Journey from Madras through the Countries of Mysore, Canara and Malabar* (London: Cadell and Davies, 1807).

[131] BL IOR F/4/369 several files, including 9221; also F/4/1034, n. 28499.

This is where British and Indian notions and practices of labor intersected. Colonial authorities distinguished between those in debt bondage and "real" slaves, whose condition they attributed solely to violent capture. As a result, debt bondage and debt slavery developed considerably in the Indian Ocean world, affecting a wide variety of people, from farmers mortgaging their future crops to bridegrooms borrowing the dowry, to small traders living on the credit of larger merchants. The European powers intervened and first sought to engage in the slave trade. In the seventeenth and eighteenth centuries, Europeans exported Indian slaves to their colonies in Southeast Asia, the Mascarene Islands, the Cape and elsewhere. South India saw a very active slave trade, while the coastal regions of Bengal (Arakan in particular) were subject to slave raids by Europeans and their agents. Slave exports from this region rose from 380 in 1626 to 1,046 in 1647 and 1,803 in 1656. Over the same period, slave exports from Coromandel rose from around 2,000 a year in 1622 and 1645 to 8,000–10,000 in 1659–1661.[132] Between 1670 and the end of the eighteenth century, a total of 24,000 Indian slaves were exported to the Mascarenes.[133]

The EIC continued slave raiding until the end of the eighteenth century, when fears of depopulation and a consequent shortage of taxpayers prompted the Company to limit these practices. The Bengal Regulation Act of 1774 prohibited the purchase or sale of persons who were not already in a state of slavery.[134] The holding, sale and purchase of domestic slaves was nevertheless widespread in Bombay, Madras and Calcutta. Domestic slaves were sold openly, as can be seen from articles in the *India Gazette* and other colonial newspapers and documents.[135]

However, unlike their Atlantic counterparts, the British could not simply play their ambivalent slavery game without taking local powers into account. As with Russian power in Central Asia, this was due not only to the continuing strength of these powers, but also to the need for slaves in the colonies. Britain and the EIC were forced to modify their strategy after the abolition of the slave trade (1807): Instead of openly competing with the local powers' demand for slaves, they sought to legally transform the rules of work and property. To meet demand, some British officials reinvented what they called "tradition."

---

[132] Markus Wink, "The World's Oldest Trade. Dutch Slavery and Slave Trade in the Indian Ocean in the Seventeenth Century," *Journal of World History*, 14, 2 (2003): 131–177.

[133] Richard Allen, "The Mascarene Slave-Trade and Labor Migration in the Indian Ocean during the Eighteenth and Nineteenth Centuries," in Gwyn Campbell, ed., The Structure of Slavery in Indian Ocean Africa and Asia (London: Frank Cass, 2004): 35–50.

[134] Richard Allen, "Suppressing a Nefarious Traffic: Britain and the Abolition of Slave-trading in India and the Western Indian Ocean, 1770–1830," *William and Mary Quarterly*, 66, 4 (2009): 873–894.

[135] Michael Fisher, *Counterflows to Colonialism: Indian Travellers and Settlers in Britain, 1600–1857* (Delhi: Permanent Black, 2004).

For example, the term "debt bondage" used by the British encompassed many different relationships, from short-term credit granted to self-employed workers to debt slavery. The British therefore translated debt practices – such as *kamias* in Bihar, *dublas* and *halis* in Gujarat – into their own terms of debt bondage linked to economic transactions. They saw debtors as slaves outside the community, when in fact the opposite was true: Debt relations were a means of including people in the local community.[136] The debate therefore turns on whether or not the debtor entered into servitude voluntarily: In the former case, it was acceptable, whereas in the latter, where violence and lack of free will according to the British legal definition could be proven, it was not. Patronage became an economic relationship.[137] Domestic slavery was clearly opposed to plantation slavery and considered a form of light dependence; as for agricultural slavery, it was linked to the caste system, and therefore to religion.[138] However, British officials and members of the EIC were deeply divided between those who considered these forms of slavery as locally rooted practices and therefore impossible to modify "from above," and those who argued, on the contrary, that British domination consisted precisely in adopting and imposing universal principles. The former approach prevailed during the first decades of British rule, and gave rise to the collection of "local customs" known as the *Code of Gentoo Laws* (1776), an English translation of the ordinances of Hindu law produced with the help of Brahmin *pandits*, and to Charles Hamilton's translation of *The Hedaya, or Guide: A Commentary on the Mussulman Laws*.[139] As in common law, both looked for precedents, but in local ordinances and customary rules.

Similar divergences have arisen with regard to the trafficking of women. On the one hand, there were those who clearly separated prostitution from domestic exploitation, domestic slavery and, for religious reasons, *sati* for Hindus and concubines for Muslims. On the other hand, there were those who considered all these situations to be the expression of a single phenomenon, which should be distinguished as such.[140] The translation of presumed local rules underpinned the EIC's attitudes of legitimizing domestic slavery and concubines as local practices, while admitting prostitution in accordance with contemporary

---

[136] On debt and bondage in India and the Indian Ocean world: Gwyn Campbell, Alessandro Stanziani, eds., *Debt and Slavery in the Indian Ocean World* (London: Pickering and Chatto, 2013).
[137] Breman, *Labor Bondage*.
[138] *British Parliamentary Papers*, "Slavery in India" 1828, section 125.
[139] Major, *Slavery, Abolitionism*: 140.
[140] *British Parliamentary Papers*, 1828, section 125. Also: Samanta Banerjee, *Dangerous Outcast: the Prostitute in Nineteenth Century Bengal* (Calcutta: Seagull Books, 1998); Radhika Singha, "Making the Domestic More Domestic: Criminal Law and the Head of the Household, 1772–1843," *Indian Economic and Social History Review*, 33, 3 (1996): 309–343.

rules and practices in Britain.[141] Sexual exploitation destabilized British ideas of benign domestic slavery. The Bengal Regulation Act of 1774 prohibited the buying or selling of people who were not already in a state of slavery. The Act was also passed in response to growing conflicts between the Crown and the EIC, as well as between Britain and other European powers, such as the French and Portuguese, who were also involved in slavery in India.[142] The holding, sale and purchase of domestic slaves was nevertheless widespread in Bombay, Madras and Calcutta. Domestic slaves were sold openly, as evidenced by articles in the *Gazette de l'Inde* and other colonial newspapers and documents. Historical sources also published advertisements calling for the return of fugitive slaves. Faced with problems enforcing the 1774 regulations, the EIC proclaimed new rules limiting the slave trade and the continuation of slavery in Bengal (1789), Madras (1790) and Bombay (1805). These rules also proved difficult to enforce.[143] The British used violence, kidnapping and deception on a massive scale to enslave people. Sepoys, ordinary migrants and sailors discovered too late that they were not under a temporary "free contract," but in full-fledged slavery. During the same period, Gujarati merchants were heavily involved in the slave trade from Mozambique; slaves were imported via the Portuguese enclaves of Goa, Daman and Dui, then re-exported to the hinterland, to the homes of Hindu or Muslim nobility. These imports represented some 200–300 slaves a year between 1770 and 1834.[144]

Unlike their Atlantic counterparts, Indian powers such as the Marathas in the west, the Nayakas in the south and the Mughals opposed slavery by Europeans, although they still practiced it themselves. The Maratha confederation extended its power in the eighteenth century before succumbing to British expansion in 1818. During this period, various forms of servitude and slavery became widespread in western India. The exaction of forced labor (*veth-beggar*) by the powerful was a common feature of rural life.[145] The movement of British civil servants and armies at the beginning of the colonial era increased the demand for this type of forced labor. Theft, tax arrears and fines were the main sources of enslavement. Internal frontiers, such as those of the Nizam, Mysore and southern Maratha appanages, were the scene of major slave markets. The supply of

---

[141] Singha, "Making the Domestic More Domestic;" Lata Mani, "Contentious Traditions: The Debate on Sati in Colonial India," *Cultural Critique*, 7 (1987): 119–156; Kumkum Sangari, Sudesh Vaid, eds., *Recasting Women: Essays in Colonial History* (New Delhi: Kali for Women, 1989).
[142] Allen, "Suppressing a Nefarious Traffic."
[143] *British Parliamentary Papers*, "Slavery in India," 1828, section 125.
[144] Pedro Machado, "A Forgotten Corner of the Indian Ocean: Gujarati Merchants, Portuguese Indians and the Mozambique Slave Trade, c. 1730–1830," in Gwyn Campbell, ed., The Structure of Slavery in Indian Ocean Africa and Asia (London: Frank Cass, 2004): 17–36.
[145] Guha, "Slavery, Society, and the State."

labor was a key concern for the British and local powers. In the 1790s, the struggle between the EIC and Mysore, for example, considerably reduced production capacity and available manpower in Andhra Pradesh. Thus, the abundance of low-caste workers without land rights did not prevent periodic labor shortages. Francis Buchanan estimated that in South India, five million slaves were employed in rice cultivation.[146] The Mascarene Islands, in particular, were of vital importance; during the Austrian War of Succession, the Seven Years' War and the American War of Independence, they served as a depot and base for French privateers. The Mascareignes depended on sugar production and therefore on slave labor, mainly from Madagascar, Mozambique and the Swahili coast, not forgetting India. Some 21,000 Indian slaves were exported to these islands between 1670 and 1810.[147] Between 1791 and 1807, the British fleet attempted to intercept slaves being transported to the Mascarenes. However, after the acquisition of Mauritius, and despite the Slave Trade Act of 1807, the illegal importation of slaves continued throughout the first half of the nineteenth century. In a century characterized by rising taxes and years of famine, "freedom" for the former marginal slaves, who had been deliberately kept destitute and barred from land ownership, meant the freedom to starve. Some of them became sharecroppers, but with two-thirds of the harvest going to the owner, the risk of failure was high. To survive, many went into debt. In some parts of India, members of the most disadvantaged castes made up the overwhelming majority of those enslaved for debt. The situation was very similar to slavery, in that servitude could be inherited and the vast majority of enslaved people were restricted in their geographical mobility.[148] One of the most common arguments in favor of debt bondage was that crop failure and famine forced peasants to sell their children in order to survive. Although British colonial elites did not invent this link, some of them (not all!) took full advantage of it, and its rhetoric, to perpetuate and justify slavery.[149] Along the borders of the EIC, the Mughal and other Indian states, resistance to slavery by the slaves themselves was difficult to implement: nobody really protected them, other than by claiming ownership. Unlike the Russian steppes and the Americas, no colonial authority seeking to populate "empty lands" offered conditions of freedom.

Conclusion: Labor Rules in the British Empire

The use of coercion developed considerably in Britain and the British Empire between the mid-seventeenth and mid-nineteenth centuries. From a social

---

[146] Buchanan, *A Journey from Madras*.
[147] Allen, "Suppressing a Nefarious Traffic": 888.
[148] Utsa Patnaik, "Introduction" in Patnaik, *Chains of Servitude*: 29–31.
[149] Sudipta Sen, *Distant Sovereignty: National Imperialism and the Origin of British India* (London: Routledge, 2002).

and political point of view, these trends are rooted in the alliance between the British aristocracy and merchants:[150] The Glorious Revolution did not mark the transition from feudalism to capitalism, as conventional Marxist historiography asserts, nor simply reinforce liberal capitalism, as neo-institutionalists and political scientists claim.[151] On the contrary, this alliance gave rise to a particular kind of aristocratic and bourgeois capitalism, based on highly unequal political and civil rights,[152] especially in the labor market.[153] In this area, estate owners, guilds and towns supported rules that severely restricted labor rights. This orientation found its extreme expression in the American colonies, first in the development of indentured immigration, then of slavery. The limitations imposed on labor rights in Britain before and after the Glorious Revolution, and colonial and global slavery, nurtured each other: Apprenticeship, master-servant rules and sailor conscription inspired indenture contracts. In turn, the colonial experience reinforced the conviction of all those in Britain who believed that coercion, rather than higher wages, would yield more labor. This was not because there was a shortage of people (as many economists still believe), but because masters and government identified labor only with coerced labor.

In the Indian Ocean, British power had to negotiate trade and institutions not only with other European powers – the Portuguese in particular – but also with powerful local entities. Imperial sovereignty was therefore not identified with legal and social institutions as it was in the Atlantic world: the idea of "making the world British" could never really be put into practice in the Indian Ocean and Africa. The British relied on local labor and other institutions. In the Atlantic, on the other hand, the British imposed their own notions of labor and coercion.

From this point of view, the situation is exactly symmetrical to that in Russia and its colonies. Here, state power formed an alliance with the peasants with the aim of colonizing the steppes, and against the wishes of mainland landowners and merchants, who were primarily interested in maintaining serfdom. In

---

[150] Ron Harris, *Industrializing English Law: Entrepreneurship and Business Organization, 1720-1844* (Cambridge: Cambridge University Press, 2000); Deakin, Wilkinson, *The Law of the Labour Market*; Robert Allen, *Enclosure and the Yeoman* (Oxford: Clarendon Press, 1992); Patrick O'Brien, Roland Quinault, eds., *The Industrial Revolution and British Society* (New York: Cambridge University Press, 1993); Julian Hoppit, *Britain's Political Economies: Parliament and Economic Life, 1660-1800* (Cambridge: Cambridge University Press, 2017).

[151] North and Weingast, "Constitution and Commitment"; Daron Acemoglu, James Robinson, *Economic Origins of Dictatorship and Democracy* (Cambridge: Cambridge University Press, 2005).

[152] E.P. Thompson, Hobsbawm and recently Thomas Piketty, *Capital and Ideology* (Cambridge: Harvard University Press, 2020); Thomas Piketty, *Capital in the 21st Century* (Cambridge: Harvard University Press, 2014).

[153] Deakin, Wilkinson, *The Law of the Labour Market*.

Britain, the alliance between landowners and merchants strengthened coercion, first on the mainland and then, even more so, in the colonies. Under autocratic agrarian power, the colonies were a place to unleash labor coercion and negotiate empire-building with local authorities; under Western rentier-merchant-industrial capitalism, coercion increased everywhere, including in the colonis where exclusionary policies (of local elites) were adopted. The United States were a notable exception: indentured servants and migrants were transformed into modern wage earners with their own civil and social rights. However, this transition came at a price: As a legal and social category, wage earners (essentially white) emerged in opposition not only to indentured migrants, but also to black slaves.

Between these two opposing cases, the British and the Russian, a third stands before us: that of France. Here, serfdom disappeared later than in Britain, but earlier than in Russia; wage labor was also subject to distinct constraints, different from those in Russia and Britain, and the role of the state was much greater than in Britain and different from that in Russia. Against this backdrop, how did free and unfree work evolve, and what was the role of Empire and state-building in this context?

3

The French Touch

Protecting Men in Urban Industry, Excluding Rural People, Women and Colonies

Continental Institutions: City versus Country

The preceding chapters have shown that in Great Britain, criminal sanctions were extremely widespread in labor relations. Conversely, France appears to have been the first country to abolish lifelong domestic service and penal sanctions in labor disputes.[1] Even in the eighteenth century, France's leading jurists still considered work to be a service.[2] At the same time, French jurisprudence made no clear distinction between hiring out a person for services and "renting" a thing. While the French Revolution abolished lifetime domestic service, it retained the two previous forms of contract: *louage d'ouvrage* and *louage de service*. While the former brought the status of the salaried employee closer to that of the independent craftsman, the latter represents an important legacy of earlier forms of domestic service. These contracts and the general attitude of the industrial tribunals strongly protected workers.[3] As in Britain, the number of cases resolved before the industrial tribunals was correlated with the economic trend: When the economic trend was positive, workers multiplied the number of double jobs, and therefore sought the protection of the industrial tribunals to maintain their double employment without incurring sanctions.[4] The main reason why workers appealed to the *prud'hommes* was that the master failed to pay or withhold wages. Masters generally replied that wages were the only guarantee they had against runaway workers who had already benefited from advances on wages or raw materials.

---

[1] Alain Cottereau, "Droit et bon droit. Un droit des ouvriers instauré, puis évincé par le droit du travail, France, XIXe siècle," *Annales*, 57, 6 (2002): 1521–1557; Deakin and Wilkinson, *The Law of the Labor Market*.

[2] Jean Domat, *Les lois civiles dans leur ordre naturel*, first edition 1697, reproduced in *Œuvres*, Paris, Pierre Aubouin, 1835, t. 1; and Robert-Joseph Pothier, *Traité du contrat de louage* (Paris: Bugnet, 1861).

[3] Cottereau, "Droit et bon droit."

[4] *General Account of the Administration of Civil and Commercial Justice in France and Algeria* corrected by: Ioana Marinescu, *Les prud'hommes sont-ils efficaces?* Master's thesis, under the direction of Thomas Piketty, EHESS, 2002.

As a result, workers accounted for between 75 percent and 90 percent of those bringing claims before the industrial tribunals (the remainder being masters).[5] This is the opposite of the proportion of people using the Masters and Servants Acts in Great Britain (three-quarters being masters). This data is extremely important, as it underlines the crucial role played by the courts in post-Revolutionary France in protecting labor. Does this mean that workers' working conditions were better in France than in Britain?

Indeed, available studies show that *prud'hommes* have protected workers in the textile industry and in certain urban environments.[6] But what about other sectors, particularly agriculture?

Until 1901, rural workers could only appeal to the Justice of the Peace. The latter had exclusive jurisdiction in place of the *conseils de prud'hommes*, which were often absent from rural areas.[7] Unlike the British justice of peace, the French *juge de paix* was a trained lawyer. Thus, even where *conseils de prud'hommes* existed, Justices of the Peace decided all cases involving limited sums of money. Disputes concerning the wages (*gages*)[8] of servants in husbandry and laborers were one of the areas reserved for justices of the peace,[9] notably because masters were taken at their word (until 1868), unlike their dependents, for any question concerning wages, salaries or advances (Article 1781 of the French Civil Code). Cases brought before the justice of the peace were by far the most important in number; most of these cases were resolved before the actual litigation was brought before the court, which meant that the justice of the peace functioned as a conciliation chamber. In the event of a dispute on rural labor, the justice of the peace first of all sought to identify the type of case in question, by trying to determine whether it concerned a day laborer, a servant or a piece-worker, but the distinction was not easy. For example, the wage unit for laborers was a day, which corresponded to a

---

[5] Pierre Delsalle, *La Brouette et la navette: tisserands, paysans et fabricants dans la région de Roubaix et de Tourcoing (Ferrain, Mélantois, Pévèle), 1800–1848* (Lille: Westhoek, 1985).

[6] Jacques Le Goff, *Du silence à la parole. Droit du travail, société, État (1830–1985)* (Quimper: Calligrammes-La Digitale, 1985). Alain Cottereau, "Les prud'hommes au xixe siècle : une expérience originale de pratique du droit," *Justices. Revue de droit processuel*, 8 (1997): 9–21; Françoise Fortunet, "D'une république à l'autre : les conseils de prud'hommes ou l'institution d'une justice de paix de l'industrie," in Jacques Lorgnier, Renée Martinage and Jean-Pierre Royer, eds., *Justice et République(s)* (Lille: Ester Éditions, 1993): 325–335.

[7] Gilles Rouet, *Justice et justiciables au XIXe et XXe siècles* (Paris: Belin, 1999).

[8] In French legal and economic parlance, the wages of servants and domestic servants are known as *gages*, and refer to the monetary element of their remuneration, distinct from food and lodging. This clearly distinguishes *gages* from wages, which were given only for salaried work. It will be interesting to study when and why the English language adopted the word *wages* to designate both configurations, despite the obvious legal, economic and social differences between a servant and a wage-earner.

[9] Jean-Claude Farcy, *Guide des archives judiciaires et pénitentiaires, 1800–1958*, Paris, CNRS éditions, 1992.

unit of work. The length of the working day was the same throughout a given region; it took into account meals, travel time and rest periods, but it differed from season to season, and wages varied according to the length of the working day. Unlike the remuneration of people hired for a specific task, the servant's day's work was paid at an agreed price, regardless of the amount of work done, which encouraged farmers to look for workers on a per-job basis.

In the eighteenth century, servants in husbandry were by far the largest group of wage earners in French agriculture, as well as in Great Britain.[10] Before the Revolution, penalties were imposed on all workers, piece-workers or servants in husbandry who left their jobs before the end of their contract or without the employer's authorization. Various contractual provisions aimed at limiting mobility existed at the time (bonuses for diligent workers, payment by task), as well as general provisions.[11] From the sixteenth to the eighteenth century, farm laborers and servants were free to move and change employers only at certain times of the year (i.e., according to the critical periods of the agricultural calendar).[12] Day laborers, on the other hand, could not leave their master before the end of their contract, and if they did so prematurely, they were liable to heavy penalties and loss of wages.[13] The master could dismiss them at any time. The status of the day laborer was precarious, and he ran the risk of seasonal unemployment, while the employer was faced with a potential labor shortage during peak periods. Finally, rural servants differed from other agricultural employees in the nature of their contract, which was almost always tacit and could only be broken "for the most serious of reasons." Servants were subject to their master's will, which meant that they "owe all their time to the master for any work requested." This subordination to the master's will resulted in making the promised *gages* a lump sum. The master could dismiss the servant without notice or compensation in the event of "dishonesty," "disobedience," "neglect of duties," insults or acts of violence. Servants, meanwhile, complained of poor or insufficient food.[14]

The situation changed in the second half of the nineteenth century, when the number of disputes increased and the demand for agricultural workers

---

[10] Jean-Marc Moriceau, "Les Baccanals ou grèves des moissonneurs en pays de France, seconde moitié du XVIIIe siècle," in Jean Nicolas, ed., *Mouvements populaires et conscience sociale* (Paris: Maloine, 1985): 420–433.

[11] Hoffman, *Growth in a Traditional Society*.

[12] Abbé Rozier, *Cours complet d'agriculture ou Dictionnaire universel d'agriculture*, vol. 8: "Domestique" (Paris: Clouzier 1789): 353.

[13] E. J. T. Collins, "Migrant Labor in British Agriculture in the Nineteenth Century," *Economic History Review*, 29, 1 (1976): 38–59; Gilles Postel-Vinay, "The Dis-integration of Traditional Labor Markets in France: From Agriculture *and* Industry to Agriculture *or* Industry," in George Grantham and Mary MacKinnon, *Labor Market*: 64–83.

[14] *Recueil des usages locaux en vigueur dans le département de la Vienne* (Poitiers: Bertrand, 1865); *Recueil des usages locaux du département d'Indre-et-Loire* (Tours: Guiland Verger, 1863). See also the 1870 parliamentary inquiry in AN C 1157–61.

and domestic servants grew as a result of emigration to the cities. Employers accused justices of the peace of being "on the side of the workers and servants"[15] just as manufacturers, at the same time, accused magistrates on industrial tribunals of being biased against them.

In short, in nineteenth-century France, labor relations were no more governed by criminal sanctions, as this was the case in Britain. However, while here almost all workers fell into the category of servants and, as such, had minor rights compared to those of their masters, in France there was a significant divide between urban and rural workers. The former, especially those working in large units, enjoyed legal protection, while the latter were subject to enormous legal constraints.

Moreover, the absence of penal provisions against workers in France must be qualified; indeed, workers were confronted with penal rules, starting with the interweaving of work and credit. All advances on wages and/or raw materials were very common until the beginning of the twentieth century, and legally constituted a debt in their own right under criminal law. They were therefore recorded in the worker's booklet (*livret ouvrier*). This document was under the control of the master and the local police, and had a dual purpose: to protect the master against "undue leaving" by the worker, and to ensure a form of social order by controlling the mobility of the workforce.[16] To a certain extent, the booklet was also a means for masters to defend themselves against labor poaching by other masters.[17] The passbook recorded all debts contracted by the worker: advances on wages and/or raw materials. Recording debts in the book served as a guarantee that the contract would be respected. In this way, elements of the penal code were integrated into labor relations, because, in addition to indebtedness (which was still covered by the penal code in most), offenses against public order were also mentioned. In practice, however, its use was highly disparate. In the North, where the textile and mining industries predominated, between 20,000 and 25,000 booklets were distributed in 1853, including 4,000 or 5,000 to women. Elsewhere, many observers consider that the booklet gradually fell into disuse, especially from mid-century until it was abolished in 1890. False booklets were widespread among workers. In Roubaix, some had several, obtained when a worker died, was called up for military service or left the industry. In the countryside, it was quite easy to obtain a new passbook by claiming it had been lost or stolen. These practices reflected the resentment of many workers towards the *livret*, which they saw as humiliating and abusive, bringing the worker closer to slavery.[18] In Lyon, workers

---

[15] Cottereau, "Droit et bon droit."
[16] Alain Supiot, *Critique du droit du travail* (Paris: PUF, 2002 [1994]): 46–47.
[17] Norbert Olszak, *Histoire du droit du travail* (Paris: PUF, 1999).
[18] Ministère de l'industrie et du commerce, *Enquête sur les conseils de prud'hommes et les livrets d'ouvriers*, 2 volumes (Paris: Imprimerie impériale, 1869).

felt "a deep aversion to anything that is gratuitously inconvenient, and even more so to anything that can become a cause of wasted time and annoyance."[19] Many owners of small workshops, most of whom could not write, hardly ever recorded the date of entry of their workers, and did not keep their registers up to date. In small towns, the obligation to do so was neglected, so as not to offend a workforce attracted by the higher wages in the big cities.

A second set of criminal provisions concerned workers: rules against vagrancy. The control and repression of vagrancy was undoubtedly a well-established practice under the Ancient Régime, but as France had no system comparable to the Poor Laws, compulsory labor never had the scope and intensity found in Great Britain. Workhouses were also present in France, notably under the Ancient Régime, but were less widespread than in Britain. Turgot abolished beggars' houses in 1776. The Revolution accepted and tolerated indigents, but not the "cunning poor," who fell into the category of vagrants. Nineteenth-century legal texts oscillated between three different terms: indigents, who were genuinely poor and entitled to assistance; vagrants, who deliberately refused to work despite their ability to do so, which was theoretically punishable under the penal code and subject to the supervision of local authorities. Between the two, we find the beggars, a vague category sometimes close to the indigent, sometimes to vagrants, depending on the place and the situation. In the 1830s, liberal paternalists were concerned about poverty, especially in cities; along with Catholics and conservatives, they saw poverty as a sign not only of laziness, but also of structural changes in societies and economies.[20] The solutions they proposed ranged from hospices for the destitute and invalid to Christian morality and charity.[21] This system was flexible enough to move people from one category to another according to economic and political trends. For example, during years of economic growth, when more labor was needed, many poor people became vagrants and, as such, were put to work.

One final point is worth mentioning: trade unions. In France, the outlawing of coalitions severely limited the possibilities of workers' defense: Guilds and unions were banned in 1791 (i.e., during the revolution) as institutions of the Ancient Régime. However, for unions only (and not for master associations), this provision officially lasted until 1864, in fact until 1884. Unions were seen as both an obstacle to competition and a threat to social order. Then the law of 22 Germinal An XI (April 12, 1803) introduced a distinction between employers' coalitions (defined restrictively and punished relatively lightly) and

---

[19] *Enquête sur les conseils de prud'hommes*, vol. 2: 374.
[20] Eugène Buret, *De la misère des classes laborieuses en France et en Angleterre* (Paris: Paulin, 1840); Félicité de Lamennais, *De l'esclavage moderne* (Paris: Pagnerre, 1839).
[21] Baron de Girando, *Traité de bienfaisance publique* (Bruxelles: Société belge de librairie, 1839); Alexis de Tocqueville, *Mémoire sur le paupérisme* (Mémoires de la société académique de Cherbourg, 1835).

workers' coalitions, defined much more broadly and repressed by force under the Restoration and then the July Monarchy (law of April 10, 1834). The French Revolution of 1848 brought short-lived liberalization, immediately followed by further repression. Between 1825 and 1851, nearly 10,000 workers were prosecuted for illegal coalitions, and 6,800 of them were sentenced, 88 of them to more than a year in prison.[22] Between 1846 and 1853, 2,264 workers were convicted, as were 208 employers. The offense of coalition was definitively abolished in 1864, but the right of association was not recognized until 20 years later. During this period, a further 2,700 workers were convicted of unlawful association.[23] Conversely, in Britain, trade unions were not officially banned, unless they were considered to restrict "free competition" and "free will" in contracts, which was almost always the case. The free market with no rights for workers was the British principle, while the regulated market with hierarchical rights, even among workers, was the French attitude.

Now we need to understand how French labor rules met colonial contexts: Was the French case closer to that of Britain (the colonial world as an extension of the metropole) or Russia (the colonial world as an experience of opposition to the metropole)?

Work Rules in Atlantic France: The Contract of Employment

Between the early seventeenth and mid-eighteenth centuries, some 7,000 to 12,000 French emigrated to Canada, compared with 200,000 to the French West Indies, 6,000 to Louisiana and 700,000 to the thirteen British North American colonies.[24] What is more, until the early eighteenth century, two-thirds of French migrants to Canada returned to their country of origin once their service was completed.

In the French West Indies, the last large groups of indentured servants arrived at the turn of the eighteenth century. In Guadeloupe, the percentage of the population born in Europe fell from 80 percent in 1654 to 39 percent 30 years later. In Martinique, the European population fell from 51 percent in 1664 to 29 percent in 1678.[25] Most migrants were recruited in groups and came from Brittany and the Pays de la Loire. Initially, artisans were more in demand than farmers. Over the years, ploughmen and rural day laborers became the dominant categories. They were almost always single. Why do so few French people cross the Atlantic?

---

[22] Le Goff, *Du silence à la parole*: 137.
[23] Gérard Noiriel, *Les ouvriers dans la société française* (Paris: Seuil, 1986); Yves Lequin, *Les ouvriers de la région lyonnaise* (Lyon: PUL, 1974); Alain Supiot, *Les sans-emplois et la loi* (Paris: Calligrammes, 1988).
[24] Cécile Vidal, *Caribbean New Orleans. Empire, Race and the Making of a Slave Society* (Chapel Hill: University of North Carolina Press, 2019).
[25] Fréderic Régent, *La France et ses esclaves* (Paris: Grasset, 2007): 25–26.

Some attribute French attitudes to "cultural" rather than economic forces (pull and push).[26] From this perspective, community traditions, the weakness of the recruitment system and of commercial carriers (French brokers and maritime capital did not find the migrant trade particularly attractive) came into play, as did the comparatively low drawing power of New France,[27] in particular, compared to continental North America. Far more than in Britain, where some pamphleteers supported colonization, the opposite attitude was expressed in France. The royal administration, and Jean-Baptiste Colbert in particular, also feared that France would be weakened militarily and economically by the loss of part of its population. From a strictly economic point of view, depending on the year, migration waves were linked to multiple factors: subsistence crises, political factors (Colbert's support for migration), religious wars (anti-Protestant policies in France). There were also pull factors, such as the development of small farms growing coffee, indigo and tobacco. However, these forces were not enough to drive people across the ocean, as other opportunities were available in mainland France, such as temporary migration to the city or seal hunting.

Recruitment conditions were officially "free." Not all migrants traveled with an enlistment contract – only 20 percent did. The rest were convicts, soldiers or migrants who paid their way. As in the British Empire, in the French colonies, indentured service developed in the seventeenth century. At first, it was intended for white settlers, whose transportation costs were advanced by employers or their intermediaries in exchange for a commitment to work for several years. Indentured laborers (*engagés*) were subject to penal sanctions, and their contracts could be transferred to other masters. Engagements closely resembled laborers and domestic servants (especially under the Ancient Régime), as well as forms of domestic service until the nineteenth century. The *engagement* contract should not be understood in opposition to these other labor relations, but rather as an extension of them in the colonial context. This means that the actors of the time considered the *engagement* contract as a free contract, and that the penalties for breach of contract were quite similar to those applied to workers in metropolitan France. Indeed, the notaries responsible for drawing up the first *engagement* contracts in the seventeenth century explicitly drew on two types of existing contract: the agricultural journeyman contract and the seaman's contract. The agricultural journeyman transferred exclusive ownership of his time and services to his employer; the seaman's

---

[26] Moogk, "Reluctant Exiles."
[27] New France included territories from Louisiana to Newfoundland, as well as present-day Quebec and part of eastern Canada. Most of these territories were lost after the Seven Years' War and transferred to Great Britain in 1763, with the exception of Quebec. Louisiana was divided between the British and the Spanish, before being reconquered by Napoleon in 1800, then sold to the United States three years later.

contract extended the duration of this sale with special clauses relating to travel expenses.[28] It is no coincidence, either, that contracts of *engagement* explicitly mentioned the leasing of services: The indentured servant leased his services (i.e., his entire time) to his master, and terminating a contract was difficult, especially for the indentured servant.[29] Similarly, *engagement* contracts explicitly invoke apprenticeship contracts: The master had the same obligation to take care of the *engagé* as the apprentice, and the same expenses in the event of illness.[30] The *engagement* contract also borrowed from the seaman's contract in that it clearly stipulated the duration and type of service required and, above all, the penalty for desertion.[31]

Once there, the captain could transfer the indentured servant and his debt to a master or share the labor services (or the income they generated) with that master. In the case of partnership, on the other hand, the two *engagés* shared capital and labor; they called each other "my companion," and the partnership usually, but not necessarily, ended when one of the partners married.[32] In general, indentured servants were not allowed to marry without the master's permission, but an indentured servant had the right to redeem his indenture and could force his master to agree to do so.

As in the case of Britain, in the French Empire too, contracts of *engagement* varied according to destination (French West Indies, Canada or Indian Ocean) and historical period. In the seventeenth and eighteenth centuries these contracts mainly concerned white people traveling to the French West Indies and Canada, but also to the Indian Ocean.[33]

In the pages that follow, I will focus mainly on French Canada, where we find a special case: No plantation system and even agriculture took time to develop. This means that the identification of indentured migrants, their rights and obligations took place and evolved without immediate reference to, and ultimately in opposition to, African slaves and the plantation system, as in other French and British colonies. Until the mid-seventeenth century, the French were in principle allied with the Hurons and opposed to the Iroquois, although they preferred to adapt their attitude to avoid any alliance between

---

[28] Gabriel Debien, *Les engagés pour les Antilles 1634–1715* (Paris: Société de l'histoire des colonies françaises, 1952): 45.

[29] Archives Charente Maritime, Minutier Teuleron, 1638–1680. Bibliothèque nationale, section des manuscrits, "Nouvelles acquisitions de France," 9328, which holds copies of documents on immigration to the colonies concerning inhabitants, indentured servants and slaves.

[30] Bibliothèque nationale, section des manuscrits, "Nouvelles acquisitions de France," 9328.

[31] For example, see Archives de Charente Maritime, procès-verbal Ex Moreau, April 19 and 25, 1664.

[32] Régent, *La France et ses esclaves*: 24.

[33] Louise Dechêne, *Habitants et marchands de Montréal au XVIIe siècle* (Paris: Plon, 1974).

the two indigenous tribes.[34] During this period, French strategy was dictated by the urgent need to find local allies against the British, and also for the fur trade. Consequently, they did not seek to push the natives inland, as the British did, but instead encouraged settlements close to their own. Intermarriage was also relatively widespread, at least in the seventeenth century. However, the French colonizing mission improved over time and, with it, greater official resistance to intermarriage.[35] With regard to labor in particular, mutual influences between the French and the Indigenous peoples were significant. The First Nations practiced captivity and forms of serfdom that were never hereditary; those enslaved were most often war captives, and this attitude seemed to become more pronounced after the great diseases brought by Europeans in the late sixteenth and first half of the seventeenth centuries, which decimated the Indigenous population.

For their part, the French resorted to the forced labor of Indigenous people, in principle "free," to clear lands and build infrastructure. They also enslaved native people and imported black slaves. In the second half of the seventeenth century, some 400 Indigenous slaves were recorded, compared with a few dozen African slaves. For the entire period from the early seventeenth to the late eighteenth century, Indigenous slaves numbered around 2,700, while figures for African slaves ranged from 4,200 to several thousand, with no consensus among historians to date.[36] Women were numerous among Indigenous slaves, and were purchased as concubines and domestic slaves.

In the absence of a plantation system, social and political hierarchies were linked to an entirely different economic system, based mainly on the fur and fish trade. The question is to understand how the absence of mass products such as sugar, tobacco or cotton impacted labor relations and the very definition of free and unfree labor. The origins of the migrants, their skills and their assignment once they arrived in Canada also influenced the final outcome. Most migrants came from Normandy and Ile-de-France; rural workers migrated from the central-western regions, while those of urban origin came from Paris, Rouen and La Rochelle. Among the latter, women accounted for almost six to seven out of ten people, while rural migrants were mainly men.

---

[34] Gilles Havard, Cécile Vidal, *Histoire de l'Amérique française* (Paris: Flammarion, 2019).

[35] Ronald Rudin, *Faire de l'histoire au Québec* (Québec: Septentrion, 1998); Éric Bédard and Julien Goyette, eds., *Parole d'historiens. Anthologie des réflexions sur l'histoire au Québec* (Montreal: Les Presses de l'Université de Montréal, 2006); Alain Beaulieu, "L'empire colonial français et les nations amérindiennes," in Serge Joyal, Paul-André Linteau, eds., *France-Canada-Québec* (Montreal: Presses de l'Université de Montréal): 17–38.

[36] Marcel Trudel, *Deux siècles d'esclavage au Québec, suivi du Dictionnaire des esclaves et de leurs propriétaires au Canada français* (Montreal: Hurtubise HMH, 2004); Jean-Pierre Le Glaunec, "Résister à l'esclavage dans l'Atlantique français: aperçu historiographique, hypothèses et pistes de recherche," *Revue d'histoire de l'Amérique française*, 71, 1–2 (2017): 13–33.

Records show that between 1642 and 1653, 250 people, mostly from Angers, were recruited to emigrate to New France by the Société Notre-Dame de Montréal (linked to the Congrégation de Notre-Dame de Paris). Contracts were generally for three years. However, most of these recruits fled once they arrived in Nantes. Many others were recruited by dubious methods in the port itself (around 103).[37] The Société de Notre-Dame invested 300,000 French livres in the immigration of recruits, but soon found itself on the verge of bankruptcy, as New France had little to offer beyond the fur trade. The Société asked the monarchy for help, and the State took over. Recruits were freed upon arrival, but owed the governor a sum of between 300 and 500 livres to cover transportation costs and past and future advances. The term of enlistment was three to five years. The men were aged between 20 and 25, and all but two were single. Nevertheless, two-thirds of the 1653 cohort refused to be emancipated under these conditions, preferring to remain indebted to the Company or local landowners. They considered their initial recruitment and indebtedness onerous but clear enough, whereas transferring these obligations to the State would have subjected their emancipation to rather opaque conditions.[38]

The Compagnie de Saint-Sulpice, which took over from the Société de Notre-Dame in 1659, took charge of recruitment. Many recruits came from the canton of La Flèche. Most of them were from modest social backgrounds, though not destitute, but with great uncertainty about their future, especially given the difficult agricultural situation in the early 1650s. Although some authors have established a link between the agrarian crisis and emigration,[39] it is difficult to confirm.[40] Some other historians have argued that the migrants were mostly city dwellers and not the poor, rather skilled craftsmen.[41] However, detailed surveys of notarial archives prove that most servants were under twenty years of age, and came from extremely poor families in France.[42] Settlers were recruited mainly as laborers to carry out land-clearing work. Consequently, the day laborer contract used in Normandy at the time for this activity served as the main model for these recruitment contracts.[43] Although the contracts

---

[37] Dechêne, *Habitants et marchands*: 56.
[38] Archives publiques du Canada, MG1-G1, 1666 census; MG 17 (church and missionary archives), A 7, 2, 3. See also: Etienne-Michel Faillon, *Histoire de la colonie française du Canada* (Montreal: Bibliothèque paroissiale, 1865–1868): esp. vol. 2: 187–188.
[39] Robert Mandrou, "Vers les Antilles et le Canada au XVIIe siècle," *Annales ESC*, 14, 4 (1959): 667–675.
[40] Peter Moogk, "Emigrants from France in Canada before 1760," *The William and Mary Quarterly*, 46, 3 (1989): 463–505.
[41] Havard, Vidal, Histoire de l'Amérique française.
[42] Arnaud Bessière, "Les domestiques canadiens, ces oublié(e)s de l'histoire de la Nouvelle France," *Canadian Studies*, 82 (2017): 27–45.
[43] Archange Godbout, *Les passagers du Saint-André. La recrue de 1659* (Montreal: Société généalogique canadienne-française, 1964).

distinguish between different trades, the word "*défricheur*" appeared almost systematically, either on its own or in a combined form, such as "*défricheur et paveur*," "*défricheur et cordonnier*" and so on. Of the 123 recruits arriving in 1653 and 1659, fifty-five fell into this mixed category, forty-two others were identified solely as *défricheur* and their wages were lower, twenty-five were tradesmen (carpenters, joiners) and one was a surgeon.[44] Given this link between clearing and recruitment, once the clearing operations were over, recruitment traffic was reduced to almost nothing, as the local workforce was sufficient to meet the demand for servants. Natives were increasingly solicited for these services.

The situation changed again after New France was placed under the control of the Ministry of the Navy (1663) and the French West India Company was created (1664). Colbert wanted to facilitate colonization through state-subsidized immigration. However, the Royal Council was opposed to this, preferring to use recruits. From then on, intermediaries in La Rochelle, Rouen and even Canada took charge of recruitment. These agents were spread throughout the country, as evidenced by the contracts signed before a notary, which indicate the name of the agent and the recruit's village of origin. However, unlike the contracts of previous years, the recruit's original trade was no longer mentioned, only his age and physical stature. The masters of New France were looking for physical strength and the ability to withstand the climate, rather than knowledge, which would be relatively unimportant in these conditions. Recruiters made their selection village by village, and did not limit themselves to physical appearance: Family and village relations showed that there was a relay within villages (174 cases out of 327 between 1663 and 1679).[45]

Crossing the ocean was perilous, and private carriers did not hesitate to sacrifice recruits in the event of difficulties.[46] The use of the French Royal Navy for transport did not improve matters. The death rate during the crossing increased astronomically: Thiry-three passengers out of 200 died during the 1662 recruitment. The following year, out of 300 passengers recruited, sixty died during the voyage and a further twelve shortly after arrival.[47] The authorities decided to turn first to Dutch carriers, then to the West India Company. The mortality rate dropped considerably, although there were discrepancies between the passenger manifest on departure and those recorded in New France. This is

---

[44] Faillon, *Histoire de la colonie française du Canada*: vol. 2: 531–561.
[45] Jacques Mathieu, *La Nouvelle-France. Les français en Amérique du Nord, XVIe-XVIIIe siècle* (Montreal: Presses de l'Université de Laval, 2001): 76.
[46] Charles Bréard, ed., *Journal du corsaire Jean Doublet, de Honfleur* (Paris: Perrin, 1887): 33–37.
[47] The decisions of the Sovereign Council adopted between 1663 and 1760 were collected and published in: *Jugements et délibérations du Conseil Souverain de la Nouvelle-France / Législature de Québec*, 6 volumes (Québec: Imprimerie Coté et Cie, 1885–1891) (henceforth: JDCS), vol. 1, 1885: 201–204.

partly because the Company did not want to be held responsible for losses. The discrepancies can also be explained by the fact that, upon arrival of the cargo, local authorities, notably members of the Sovereign Council, seized the best recruits – at the Crown's expense – without registering them.[48]

The use of intermediaries and recruiting agents in France was a means of limiting direct claims by recruits against their employers, the latter offloading any disputes onto the recruiters. Indeed, half of the workers recruited worked on the lands of the Compagnie de Notre-Dame, then Saint-Sulpice, while the other half worked on private estates.[49] However, recruits were unevenly distributed between the different estates. Very few estates (between three and five in the three counts carried out in 1666, 1667 and 1681) had more than five servants, 452 households out of 563 had no servants, and the rest had only one or two.[50] Migrants were also required to perform public works, corvées as in metropolitan France or Russia (mainly land clearing, roads and fortifications) and served in the local militia. However, many workers rebelled against these obligations, pointing out that in metropolitan France, they would not have been subject to this constraint. This is a central point: Public corvées in France[51] were only introduced in 1738, after they had spread to the colonies. These last suggested new ways for extracting coerced labor. However, local justice in New France argued that these assignments could be justified on two grounds: military defense, for which "*droits*" (rights) could be suspended, and the impossibility for migrants to pay the tax in money. These arguments continued to be used in the French Empire, particularly in Africa, in the twentieth century.

The legal system did much to perpetuate hierarchies and debt bondage. Once in the colony, recruits were subject to penal sanctions and could be sold. Recruits could change master, but not of their own accord. More often than not, a recruit was transferred to a new master along with the land they cleared. The buyer reimbursed the seller for some of the initial expenses, paid the recruit's debts to the first master and, in some cases, deducted them from his salary.[52] The recruit could buy back their contract, but could not force the master to accept this proposal. In this context, there were differences between "non-professional" recruits and those enlisted as doctors, carpenters, etc. The latter signed up for three years instead of five, received a salary and were not subject to the servitude clauses we mentioned for the others.[53]

Recruits could not marry without their master's permission. Of the 250 recruits who left France in 1653 and 1659, only forty-seven married, all after

---

[48] Moogk, "Reluctant Exiles": 478.
[49] ANOM G1, 460, 461, Nouvelle France, recensements de 1659, 1666.
[50] Dechêne, *Habitants et marchands*: 57–58.
[51] Anne Conchon, *La corvée des grands chemins au XVIIIe siècle* (Rennes: PUR, 2016).
[52] Archives de la Marine, Rochefort, série R, 1 R 20, "Colons. Paiement des gages."
[53] Archives de la Marine, Rochefort, série R, 1 R 26, "Actes d'engagement, Canada, 1731–1738."

completing their service.⁵⁴ Nor was a recruit allowed to engage in any economic activity without their master's authorization, including acting as an intermediary in the fur trade, for example. What counts above all was physical strength and working hours. It is no coincidence that, over time, contracts expressed a direct link between wages and strength. The *gages* (essentially dues for hired hands) of adult men considered strong and sturdy were 10 to 20 pounds higher than the usual annual 60 pounds.⁵⁵

In almost all cases, it was the masters who initiated legal conflicts, and they were almost always successful. A few servants tried to sue for unpaid wages, but when the master presented the receipt for advances paid and other evidence that the servant had not fully completed his service, these grievances were weakened.⁵⁶ On the other hand, as in Russia at the same time and in other French colonies, recruits rarely complained of mistreatment or physical violence, the latter being considered quite normal.

Until 1667, only a quarter of households employed indentured servants, and the majority of these had only one. By 1681, most indentured servants were employed by religious communities and wealthy merchants, and worked in bands on large farms.⁵⁷

The legal status of recruits was therefore clearly inferior to that of their masters. It was similar to that of domestic servants, day laborers and sailors in France. The difference with military recruits was therefore minimal: Recruitment methods and penalties for desertion were the same for both groups. It is no coincidence that in Canada, where there were not enough white recruits, soldiers were used to make up the difference. The pseudo-military conscription carried out by the state in 1669 resulted in the recruitment of 300 settlers. Nevertheless, the conditions offered to soldier-colonists were better than those granted to ordinary recruits: three years' service instead of five, nothing to pay back, and on their release, they received 100 livres to settle.⁵⁸ When the recruit completed his service and was debt-free, he could decide to return to France or settle as a colonist. He was entitled to a salary at the end of his five years' service. However, the master deducted transportation costs, drinks, lost or damaged tools, advances paid, linen and medicines. This left the recruit with very little at the end of his service. Ten of the 132 people recruited in 1653 and 1659 remained in service after the end of their contract. In total, of the recruits in 1653 and 1659, thirty-eight died before settling (which is a fairly

---

⁵⁴ Dechène, *Habitants et marchands*: 69.
⁵⁵ Alain Godbout, "Familles venues de La Rochelle," *Rapport aux Archives nationales du Québec*, XLVIII, (1970): 119–126.
⁵⁶ Dechène, *Habitants et marchands*: 71.
⁵⁷ Frédéric Mauro, "French Indentured Servants for America, 1500–1800," Emmer, ed., *Colonialism and Migration*: 105–125.
⁵⁸ ANOM, B3 folio 19, dated February 11, 1671.

high mortality rate), ten remained as domestics after the end of their contract, fifty-four became independent settlers and twenty-two disappeared, either fleeing, disappearing without a trace or returning to France. In subsequent years, according to the censuses of 1666 and 1667, out of 143 recruits, five died during their service, three subsequently became servants, fifty-five settled and eighty left no trace,[59] which means that the percentage of recruits returning to France increased over time rather than decreasing as the French authorities had hoped. Thus, during the first half of the eighteenth century, the rare immigrants were either soldiers, conscripts or those condemned to penal servitude. Between 1721 and 1749, some 720 petty criminals convicted of salt trafficking (*false sauniers*) were exiled to Canada. Like many recruits, they fled to Nova Scotia (Arcadie under the French regime) or tried to return to France on English ships. They often succeeded: France reported the disappearance of a quarter of the recruits, a figure certainly increased by competition with England for the occupation of North America. The violence inflicted on the colonists was coupled with high rates of return to France or disappearance. Even though slaves were relatively rare, their presence in French Canada encouraged white indentured servants to rebel against their treatment. Physical violence and punishment, in particular, were the subject of growing protests, the argument being that "you can't whip Frenchmen like negroes."[60] During the eighteenth century, as in the British colonies, this attitude also spread to French Canada, albeit with a few differences. In particular, public *corvées* were maintained in life, also for the French, precisely because of the absence of a massive slave population. These issues were even more dramatic for women.

The King's Daughters: Bonded Women across the Atlantic

Much more than Britain, France had enormous difficulty convincing people to cross the Atlantic. The use of kidnappings and violence, combined with the recruitment of sailors and prisoners to colonize Canada, made it even less attractive to potential French migrants. As a result, unlike the British colonies, Canada (Nouvelle France, New France) had no migrant families, only men. After the initial military phase, the French monarchy turned its attention to the problem of demographic reproduction. Until the mid-seventeenth century, very few women emigrated to New France. Land-clearers were the most in demand, while servants were recruited either from among former recruits or from the indigenous population. In addition to relatively high transportation costs and modest profits, recruiters had little interest in enlisting women.

Colbert and the King's Council deemed it necessary to make up the shortfall. This was partly to satisfy the sexual needs of the soldier-colonists and to avoid

---

[59] AN G1, 460.
[60] Havard, Vidal, *Histoire de l'Amérique française*: 496.

further incidents with the native peoples, whose women had been raped on several occasions. Over time, however, Colbert's objective shifted to increasing the local population and encouraging permanent colonization.[61] This state-sponsored immigration raised moral questions about the status of women.

The story of the Filles du Roi lies at the crossroads of several histories: the repression of begging and debauchery in France and Europe in the seventeenth century;[62] the exile of prisoners and the "deviant people" to the penal colonies;[63] and the particular role of women in the new social order in Europe and the colonial world.[64] Numerous Quebec and French historians have endeavored to show that, contrary to the arguments of certain contemporary travelers and witnesses, these early immigrant women were not, with very rare exceptions, prostitutes or "wanton" women, but people of modest but virtuous social status.[65]

This debate is surprising. While the stakes in terms of regional identity and historiography seem understandable, by adopting such a moral approach, these studies miss the point, which is not so much to assess the virtue of these early immigrants as to understand how a form of immigration akin to white slavery came to be. The women sent to New France came from French orphanages, hospices and penitentiaries. As in England, women's penitentiaries in France in the seventeenth, eighteenth and nineteenth centuries were fairly widespread, taking in women sentenced to ordinary punishments, prostitutes, beggars, single mothers, but also women deemed "indocile," "possessed" or "insane." The edict of 1632, followed by that of 1657, prohibited begging in Paris and ordered the confinement of beggars in workhouses. In 1657, the Salpêtrière hospice housed 628 women; four years later, the number had risen to 1,460.[66]

---

[61] ANOM, letter from Colbert to Talon, 1671, B 3 folio 23.
[62] Pascal Drouet, Yan Brailowsky, *La bannissement et l'exil en Europe au XVIe et XVIIe siècles* (Rennes: Presses Universitaires de Rennes, 2010).
[63] Odile Krakovitch, "Les archives des bagnes de Cayenne et de Nouvelle-Calédonie: la sous-série colonies H aux archives nationales," *Revue d'histoire du XIXe siècle* 1, 1 (1985): 45–51. DOI: 10.4000/rh19.4
[64] Timothy Coates, *Convicts and Orphans, Forced and State-sponsored colonizers in the Portuguese Empire, 1550-1755* (Stanford: Stanford University Press, 2001); Charles Frostin, "Du peuplement pénal de l'Amérique française aux XVIIe et XVIIIe siècles: hésitations et contradictions du pouvoir royal en matière de déportation," *Annales de Bretagne et des pays de l'Ouest*, 85, 1 (1978): 67–94; Hamisch Maxwell-Stewart, "Convict transportation from Britain and Ireland, 1615–1870," *History Compass*, 8, 11 (2010): 1221–1242; Miranda Frances Spieler, *Empire and Underworld. Captivity in French Guyana* (Boston, MA: Harvard University Press, 2012).
[65] Yves Landry, *Orphelines en France, pionnières au Canada: les Filles du roi au XVIIe siècle* (Montreal: Leméac, 1992): 36; Silvio Dumas, *Les Filles du roi en Nouvelle-France. Étude historique avec répertoire biographique* (Québec: Société historique de Québec, 1972).
[66] Jean-Pierre Carrez, *Femmes opprimées à la Salpêtrière de Paris (1656–1791)* (Paris: Éditions Connaissances et Savoirs, 2005).

Once women were confined to these institutions, hope of escaping was virtually non-existent. One of the few possibilities, introduced in the mid-1660s, was to become a *"Fille du Roi"* (King's Daughter), which meant severing all legal ties with one's family and assuming orphan status. This is why we need to be very careful when studying contemporary documents that refer to immigration to Canada as "orphans raised at the King's expense." These were not necessarily orphans per se, nor young girls, but adolescents and young women who had been confined in hospices, orphanages and penitentiaries. These women left France with a contract of enlistment.[67] The thirty-one women who arrived with the 1653 and 1659 recruits were all married within the year. Between 1663 and 1673, a further 770 *Filles du Roi* arrived, most of them from the Salpêtrière hospice in Paris or the diocese of Rouen, where the Compagnie de Saint-Sulpice had connections. To encourage their marriage, the State provided them with a dowry of 50 livres.[68] On the other hand, "debauched" women (i.e., those who had been raped during the crossing and had the misfortune to become pregnant) were sent back or, in some cases, mutilated or reported missing.[69] By sending them back, the disgruntled Governor Argenson wrote that he hoped to prevent "the French from sending them such beasts."[70]

Other women, who managed to avoid being impregnated during the voyage, were not much luckier. For example, Marie-Major, who had been interned at the Salpêtrière by her own family to prevent her from claiming an inheritance, was sent to New France in 1668, at the age of 31. Like the other girls and women, she was given in marriage to a soldier. But sixteen years later, her husband was murdered by the husband of a woman with whom he was having an affair. Marie-Major was blamed for her husband's downfall (she had not "honored" him enough, leading him to seek satisfaction in the arms of another woman). Her two children were taken away from her, along with her late husband's property. She ended up as a prostitute, and no trace of her was found until her death in 1689 at the Hôtel-Dieu in Quebec City. She was recently the subject of a novel, *L'histoire romancée d'une fille de roi*, now in its seventh edition.[71]

---

[67] David Gilles, "La condition juridique de la femme en Nouvelle-France: essai sur l'application de la Coutume de Paris dans un contexte colonial," *Cahiers aixois d'histoire des droits de l'outre-mer français*, Aix-en-Provence, 1, 1 (2002): 77–125; David Gilles, "Les filles du roi en Nouvelle-France: administrer une politique de peuplement colonial sous l'Ancien régime," in Eric Gasparini and Patrick Charlot, eds., *La femme dans l'histoire du droit et des idées politiques* (Dijon: Éditions universitaires de Dijon, 2008): 29–59.

[68] ANOM, C 11A5 folio 54 and folio 165; also folio 106.

[69] Faillon, *Histoire de la colonie française*, X: 136.

[70] Dumas, *Les Filles du roi*: 76

[71] René Forget, *Eugénie, fille du Roy*, 3 volumes (Québec: Michel Brulé, 2006–2012); Sergine Desjardin, *Marie Major* (Montréal: Guy Saint-Jean Éditeur, 2002).

Most of the time, the girls were placed in a special house (Maison Saint-Gabriel) under the supervision of nuns. Suitors would visit them and choose the one they liked. Some witnesses of the time compare this procedure to the purchase of cattle. A large number of marriage proposals were cancelled, as some settlers were only interested in approaching the girls rather than marrying them, and illegitimate children were born.[72] These children and their mothers disappeared from archival records, and it was difficult to keep track of them, with the exception of those who had been locked up in prisons or orphanages as "dishonorable" or "potentially dangerous." Women who were able to marry did not do so under the best of conditions. Often, the King's dowry was not mentioned in marriage contracts, as the husband or the religious order that took them in seized it before the wedding. Sometimes, their husbands hid the fact that they were already married in France (as in the case of Marie Dallon); more often, very young women aged 15 (such as Elisabeth Pépin) were forced to marry an older widow. Nicole Souillard discovered after her marriage that her husband was saddled with debts; he forced her to work to help pay them off.

Of the 770 Filles du Roi landed in 1663 and 1673, seventy-six were aged between twelve and fifteen, half of them from the Salpêtrière hospice. The rest were aged between sixteen and thirty (247 between sixteen and twenty, 204 between twenty-one and twenty-five).[73] Only 4 percent were unmarried. Most of the others (80%) married within six months. However, of the 700 or so cases identified, 104 marriages were annulled. Marriage certificates also confirm that between 75 percent and 80 percent of spouses were unable to sign their names.[74] Archival documents show that many daughters had dowries in excess of the King's 50 livres: between 200 and 500 livres. In this case, their marriages were a little more fortunate, as they were less often married to soldiers from the regiment than to local residents – immigrants who had already completed their contracts – or even to craftsmen from France.

In all, immigration between 1650 and 1760 was made up of soldiers and recruits (60 percent); captives, prisoners and slaves (16 percent); merchants, officers and clergy (15 percent); single women (4 percent); married women and children (6 percent).[75] On the occasion of the 350th anniversary (in 2013) of the arrival of the first contingent of *Filles du roi*, the former Maison Saint-Gabriel became an attraction and a place of historical interest for all of Quebec.

---

[72] The Société d'histoire des Filles du Roy has produced excellent biographies, such as *Les filles du Roy pionnières de Montréal* (Québec: Éditions du septentrion, 2017); and *Les filles du Roy pionnières de la Côte Sud* (Québec: Éditions du septentrion, 2022).

[73] Dumas, *Les Filles du roi*: 67.

[74] Yves Landry, "Les filles du Roi émigrées au Canada au XVIIe siècle, ou un exemple de choix du conjoint en situation de déséquilibre des sexes," *Histoire, économie et société*, 11, 2 (1992): 197–216.

[75] Robert Larin, *Brève histoire du peuplement européen en Nouvelle-France* (Québec: Éditions du septentrion, 2000): 92.

The King's Daughters are now considered the mothers of Quebec, and the smiling girl who appears on the site defies historical sensibility.

The colonization of Canada can be considered forced insofar as, alongside convicts, the immigrants were mainly soldiers, soldier-colons, recruits and women in servitude. The de facto and de jure inequalities that existed in France at the time between men and women, adults and children, masters and servants, became even more pronounced in New France. Canada was very different from Louisiana and the West Indies, where white recruits worked mainly on plantations.[76] The massive arrival of African slaves from the second half of the seventeenth century onwards initially had a negative effect on white migrants' living condition. As in the British colonies in North America, initially the living conditions of slaves and white indentured were close, and diverged only in time. This was not the case in Canada, where, in addition to the low level of African slave immigration, conditions for white immigrants improved slowly but surely from the mid-eighteenth century onwards.

The Rise of Slavery

Unlike Britain, where the need to add African slaves to white indentured servants was social and economic (need for unfree labor), in the French colonies, geopolitical reasons dominated. The French colonies faced hostility from the British in Canada and the Spanish (and then again the British) in the West Indies. Conflicts abounded between the colonial powers of Spain, Portugal, France, the Netherlands and England in the seventeenth and mid-eighteenth centuries. Throughout this period, these conflicts took place in Europe, America and Asia. Islands and colonies often changed hands. French colonial policy was shaped by competition with Spain, then with the Netherlands and England, which had a strong influence on relations between the colonists and metropolitan France. From 1670 onwards, the colonists of Saint-Domingue repeatedly rebelled against the Crown, demanding free trade with the Dutch and lower taxes on their trade and profits. While Great Britain moved from monopoly to differentiated tariffs for its colonies, France retained the old system, provoking further protests from the colonists. Peace and the Treaty of Utrecht in 1713 led the French monarchy to increase pressure on its colonies. Opposition intensified in Martinique and Saint-Domingue.

These conflicts took the form of skirmishes and sometimes larger clashes between royal ships and pirates or privateers, often financed by the same countries.[77] Pirates had different attitudes towards slaves: They sometimes

---

[76] Vidal, *Caribbean New Orleans*.
[77] Richard Blakemore, "The Politics of Piracy in the British Atlantic, 1640–1649," *International Journal of Maritime History*, 25, 2 (2013): 159–172; Angus Konstam, *Buccaneers, 1620–1700* (Oxford: Osprey Publishing, 2000); Angus Konstam, *Privateers and Pirates,*

freed slaves, as Rediker has shown; others, on the other hand, emphasize the involvement of pirates and privateers in the traffic and sale of slaves.[78]

Blackburn asserted that demand for plantation products developed more slowly in France than in Britain because peasants were stronger and agriculture less commercial. He added that, for this reason, French colonization depended more on the state and less on civil society.[79] However, French agriculture was highly monetized and integrated into the market, whereas the state played a role in British colonization. The difference with France lay less in the respective roles of the state and civil society than in the forms taken by state intervention and the interactions between the two. In particular, the French fully developed the Atlantic slave trade at roughly the same time as the British (i.e., around the middle of the seventeenth century). The reasons were the same: Indentured labor was too expensive and unprofitable, especially with the growth of sugar plantations. Initially, the cost of a slave exceeded that of transporting an indentured man, but this cost could be amortized over time, especially as the duration of indentures was gradually reduced from seven years to five, then to three, and finally to eighteen months. From the 1630s onwards, Richelieu sought to develop the slave trade by supporting the activities of companies such as the Compagnie de Saint-Christophe, which enjoyed a ten-year monopoly on trading in Senegal, Cape Verde and the Guinean coast.[80] The Compagnie Rozée, also known as the Compagnie Cap Vert or Compagnie Normande, was an association of merchants from Dieppe and Rouen. In 1658, it was bought out by the Compagnie du Cap-Vert et du Sénégal. The following year, the Saint-Louis trading post was fortified. In 1664, the French West India Company obtained exclusive rights to the slave trade. However, as it was unable to meet the growing demand for slaves, other private companies were also authorized. They received the same support and encouragement from the state. In 1673, the Compagnie de Sénégambie took over and established itself in Senegambia. In 1716, after the failure of all these companies, the King opened the slave trade to merchants from Le Havre, La Rochelle, Nantes and Bordeaux. In 1718, the Compagnie du Sénégal and the Compagnie d'Occident merged. As a matter of fact, the Compagnie française

---

1730–1830 (Oxford: Osprey, 2001); Angus Konstam, *The Pirate Ship, 1660–1730* (Oxford: Osprey, 2003); Margarette Lincoln, *British Pirates and Society, 1680–1730* (London: Routledge, 2014); Michèle Battisti, ed., *La piraterie au fil de l'histoire, un défi pour l'État* (Paris: Presses de la Sorbonne, 2014); Stefan Eklöf, Leos Müller, eds., *Persistent Piracy: Maritime Violence and State Formation in Global Historical Perspective* (Houndsmill, Palgrave Macmillan, 2014); Alejandro Colas, Bryan Mabee, eds., *Mercenaries, Pirates, Bandits and Empires. Private Violence in Historical Context* (London: Hurst, 2011).

[78] Gilbert Buti, Philippe Hrodej, *Histoire des pirates et des corsaires. De l'antiquité à nos jours* (Paris: CNRS éditions 2016): 216–217.
[79] Blackburn, *The Making of New World Slavery*: 279.
[80] Abdoulaye Ly, *La Compagnie du Sénégal* (Paris: Karthala, 1993).

des Indes orientales had been created in 1664, then suppressed and restored several times until the Crown took control in 1701.

However, this state-owned company was unable to cope with the bulk of the trade, which developed on the initiative of private companies.[81] Between 1640 and 1820, 4,220 slave trade expeditions were financed by private capital. Nantes supplied 43 percent of the ships, followed by La Rochelle (12.9 percent), Le Havre (12 percent) and Bordeaux (11.8 percent). At the same time, the Compagnie française des Indes orientales supplied the Mascareignes. Here again, Nantes was by far the leading port. In any case, French-flagged ships were unable to keep up with demand, which was also met by Portuguese, English and a few Dutch vessels.

In Louisiana, after France conceded its colony to John Law's company in 1717, over a thousand European criminals and indentured laborers arrived. Most of them died of disease or starvation; the remaining population in 1721 consisted of 178 indentured laborers working for 853 French colonists.[82] The governor and the main colonial elites asked for slaves; after an initial refusal (and the colonists' recourse to pirates to buy slaves), the French authorities granted the request. In 1719, 2,000 slaves disembarked, but a year later only 680 had survived. By this time, colonists were ready to move their settlement from the arid Gulf coast to the fertile Mississippi River valley, and the new Compagnie des Indes was distributing land grants. Initially, most of the slaves were used to make New Orleans a livable city; they built dikes and drainage ditches and cleared the forest. Within a year, black slaves were also planting and preparing corn, beans and rice for subsistence. Then, new concessions began planting tobacco. Some 7,000 Africans arrived in Louisiana between 1718 and 1735. However, the black population in 1735 was only 3,400. During the 1720s, most slaves performed agricultural work between New Orleans and Natchez. Meanwhile, Company and private slaves were apprenticed to brickmakers, carpenters, blacksmiths, locksmiths, sculptors, wheelwrights, saddlers, masons and carpenters. Slaves were also employed in public works. Indigo, tobacco and sugar plantations were the main destinations. As planting and slavery developed later in Louisiana than in the West Indies, access to the slave trade was more difficult from the 1720s onwards. This had certain consequences: Slaves were immediately put to work, whereas in the West Indies they benefited from a few months of "soft labor" to make them stronger after the middle passage and thus avoid losing capital. Moreover, slave reproduction was much more encouraged in Louisiana than in the West Indies, confirming the trend observed in certain nearby British colonies.

---

[81] Jean Mettas, *Répertoire des expéditions négrières françaises au XVIIIe siècle*, 2 volumes (Paris: Société française d'histoire d'outre mer, 1978).

[82] Daniel Usner, "From African Captivity to American Slavery: The Introduction of Black Laborers to Colonial Louisiana," *The Journal of Louisiana Historical Association*, 20, 1 (1979): 25–48; Vidal, *Caribbean New Orleans*.

In 1700, the French Caribbean colonies held around 30,000 slaves – 6,700 in Guadeloupe, 14,200 in Martinique and 9,000 in Saint-Domingue – compared with 100,000 in the British colonies. However, by 1713, Saint-Domingue already counted 24,146 slaves. In all, between the sixteenth and early nineteenth centuries, some 850,000 slaves were taken to Saint-Domingue, 366,000 to Martinique and 291,000 to Guadeloupe. The most recent estimates indicate that around 2.3 million slaves were taken to the French colonies between 1625 and 1848. According to the database, the French themselves traded around 1.4 million slaves across the Atlantic.

The origin of the slaves was clear: At the beginning of the eighteenth century, between 1715 and 1728, Guinea, Sierra Leone, Liberia and Côte d'Ivoire supplied most of the slaves (42%), followed by the Bight of Benin (29%), Senegambia (19%) and Central Africa (10%). A century later, after the Napoleonic Wars, an illicit trade developed mainly from Biafra (29%) and the region of Guinea, Sierra Leone, Liberia and Côte d'Ivoire (28%), while Senegambia (15%) and Central Africa (14%) supplied the remainder.[83]

In the Indian Ocean, the French transported between 165,000 and 205,000 slaves from India, East Africa and Madagascar to the Mascarenes between 1700 and 1807. Between 1807 and 1848, a further 120,000 to 130,000 slaves were transported illegally to the same destination.[84] Like the British, the French relied unofficially on Gujarati and Portuguese slave traders. Gujarati merchants were heavily involved in the slave trade from Mozambique; slaves were imported via the Portuguese enclaves of Goa, Daman and Dui, then re-exported to the hinterland, to the houses of the Hindu or Muslim nobility. Between 1770 and 1834, these imports represented some 200–300 slaves a year.[85] In the Mascarenes, 45 percent of slaves (then 36 percent) came from Madagascar or via East Africa (40 percent and 43 percent, respectively). At the beginning of the eighteenth century, India still supplied 13 percent of slaves; a century later, it no longer supplied any, replaced by West Africa (15 percent).[86] The vast majority of slaves destined for the French colonies were men, the most sought-after being tall and aged between 12 and 16. How were slaves legally identified?

We have seen that in the British colonies, this was a long and locally rooted process, and that ultimately, the legal characteristics of slaves were defined in resonance with the simultaneous evolution of the status of white indentured migrants. In the French colonies (with the exception of Canada), the

---

[83] Serge Daget, *La traite des Noirs* (Editions Ouest-France, 1990); Régent, *La France et ses esclaves*: 45.
[84] Edward Alpers, "The French Slave Trade in East Africa 1721–1810," *Cahiers d'études africaines*, 10, 37 (1970): 80–124; Jean-Marie Filliot, *La traite des esclaves vers les Mascaraignes au XVIIIe siècle* (Paris: Orstom 1974): 96; Shérif, *Slaves, Spices and Ivory*.
[85] Machado, "A Forgotten Corner."
[86] Filliot, *The slave trade*: 318–319. Musleem Jummer, *Les affranchis et les Indiens libres à l'ile de France au XVIIIe siècle, 1721–1803* (Ph.D., University of Poitiers, 1984).

institutional shift from indentured labor to slavery is often associated with the "Code Noir," which is said to be the expression of the centralized authority of the king. This history contrasts with the progressive local evolution of indentured labor and slavery in the British colonies, confirming the centralization of the French empire and its rules. Indeed, recent detailed analyses show that a similar decentralized process (to that of Britain) was also at work in the French colonies. Local rules were adopted, adapted and transformed in the various colonies, and the central Code Noir was merely a later synthesis. In 1670, the duration of an engagement was officially reduced to 18 months, but engagements still lasted around three years.[87] Two years earlier, the monarchy had openly mentioned slavery and its development as an objective and a means of developing sugar plantations.

It is no coincidence that French authors often used the words *serf* and *esclave* interchangeably. The difference we recognize today – the slave can be sold without land, while the serf is tied to it – is a political and historiographical construct that developed over the course of the nineteenth century. At the end of the eighteenth century, philosophers and economists overlapped the two phenomena, mainly to contrast them with free labor (wage labor). This perception actually emerged in response to a particular intellectual and political context, namely the question of the status of labor in France and in its colonies. The Code Noir (1685) sought to condense local rules and codes into a single set of laws. The Code also justified slavery by Christian (Jesuit) values. In the wake of the Edict of Nantes, the Code extended religious intolerance to the colonies.[88] It aimed at maintaining the discipline of the Catholic Church and justifing slavery, while seeking to synthesize existing police regulations concerning slaves.[89] The text clearly enumerated the limits of masters' power over their slaves, and identified the conditions of transmission of the slave's legal status (generally matrilineal). Although slaves were movable property, they also had rights, particularly if they were baptized. The 1685 edict applied first to Martinique and Guadeloupe, then two years later to Saint-Domingue. The edict (in fact letters patent) adopted on Réunion Island and Mauritius (Ile de France) in 1723 was a transposition of the Saint-Domingue code. No legal definition of a slave was given, so race was hardly an identifying factor: A black person was not necessarily a slave. Rather, it was a declaration of condition. However, even if slaves were movable property, they were not dehumanized, insofar as they were recognized as having certain legal capacities, as well as economic management skills. The amalgam between these versions and the

---

[87] Debien, *Les engagés pour les Antilles 1634–1715*: 64.
[88] Several versions of this edict were promulgated, and the term "Code Noir" was not adopted until the eighteenth century.
[89] Jean-François Niort, *Le Code Noir. Idées reçues sur un texte symbolique* (Paris: Le cavalier bleu, 2015).

use of the expression "Code Noir" in the 1720s emphasizes the "free people of color" and thus enshrines the racial aspect.

Then, the new Code Noir of 1767 combined the original edict of 1685 (thirty-eight pages) with 408 additional pages made up of several other decrees and codes adopted between 1685 and 1767 in different colonies. Each colony had its own version and its own rules on slavery. Some were royal rules, others were adopted by local governors, still others by local courts. Some rules were common to all: the legal status of slave was transmitted to children (via the mother); slaves were chattel with no civil rights; masters were obliged to provide food, lodging and clothing.[90] Again, no clear definition of slavery was provided.

It was only in the 1825 Louisiana Civil Code that an explicit definition of a slave was given: "A slave is one who is under the power of a master and who belongs to him; so that the master can sell him and dispose of his person, his industry and his labor, without him being able to do anything, have anything, or acquire anything that does not belong to his master" (Article 35).

In all cases, unions between whites and non-whites were the crux of the problem. These unions were relatively tolerated in the early seventeenth century, then increasingly forbidden in the various colonies, notably Réunion. As for children, mulattoes, considered free until the 1660s, were then considered slaves through matrilineal descent. The number of mulatto slaves in the West Indies continued to rise, from around 150 to 850 in 1687. In Guadeloupe, while only 1 percent of slaves had European ancestry in 1671, this figure had risen to 13–14 percent by 1770. As a result, the "free people of color" were now counted separately. In addition to the mulattoes, there were slaves freed by their masters and slave soldiers who had served in the Seven Years' War; in Mauritius, thirty years of military service were required to be freed. On the eve of the Revolution, the number of freedmen of color was estimated at around 3,000 in Guadeloupe and 5,700 in Martinique, representing 18 percent and 33 percent of the free population, respectively. Half of the freedmen in Saint-Domingue were of mixed race. However, these free people of color did not enjoy all the rights of whites, and were subject to numerous measures of exclusion and repression, especially in the West Indies and even more so in the Indian Ocean.

The tension between, on the one hand, property and slavery and, on the other, slaves as legal and economic persons, persisted not only in texts, but also in practices, where repression and incitement, exclusion and inclusion coexisted, albeit unevenly depending on the context. Indeed, most repression took place on the estate itself: Masters had authority over their own jurisdiction, and relatively few proceedings against slaves were brought before the

---

[90] The sources collected at this time are as follows: Médéric Elie Louis Moreau de Saint-Méry, *Lois et constitutions des colonies française de l'Amérique sous le vent de 1550 à 1685*, 6 volumes (Paris: Delabarre de Nanteuil).

courts. The local police carried out most of the repression, except in the case of major crimes, in which case the official courts took charge. Masters had certain obligations towards their slaves (food, clothing), while slaves had few if any rights.

Resistance was strong, but varied from colony to colony and from period to period. There were fewer slave revolts in Saint-Domingue than in Jamaica. Yet the slaves' living conditions were no better. High mortality and low fertility were strikingly similar. French slave imports were particularly concentrated and important in the 1770s and 1780s.[91] Absenteeism and sabotage were commonly cited. Masters also accused slaves of poisoning them, practicing voodoo and so on.[92] Marronage was also significant. Depending on the year and location, maroons represented between 0.4 percent and 6.6 percent of the slave population between 1735 and 1847.[93] As usual, these figures must take into account the variable distinction between absenteeism (*petit marronage*) and running away (*grand marronage*). In principle, there were rules of distinction based on the length of absence, but in practice this boundary was flexible and depended on the relationship between master and slave, the attitude of magistrates and the general context. Small marronage was often accepted for "good slaves."

The authorities intervened in various ways. Repression was most severe when public order was threatened by bands of maroons. But, in general, very few fugitives were recovered: because many fugitive slaves found another domain and their new master had no interest in handing them over to the authorities or to their original master. Some maroons were captured and sold openly, even at a very good price, as notarial archives testify. The illegality of these sales did not prevent the practice: If the original owner failed to show up, the buyer retained his rights and notaries confirmed that the transaction took place at the buyer's own risk, with the only recourse being against the seller.[94]

However, unlike the British colonies, in the French colonies, the gradual evolution of slavery rules did little to improve those concerning white indentured servants, at least initially. In fact, contractual and actual conditions for indentured laborers even deteriorated in the 1660s, when they were often working in the fields alongside the first slaves. Over the following decades, new rules prohibited the introduction of children as indentured servants, but it wasn't until the turn of the century that local conflicts and royal rules led to an emphasis on the racial difference between slaves and indentured servants and, consequently, to demands for better conditions for the latter. Yet the purpose of this

---

[91] Debien, *Slaves in the West Indies*: 345–346.
[92] Régent, Les esclaves aux Antilles françaises, XVIIe-XVIIIe siècles: 157–159.
[93] ANOM G1 497, Population census; Jean Fouchard, *Les marrons de la liberté* (Paris: Deschamps, 1988).
[94] ANOM, Noariat Valeau Saint-Fi, minute of December 28, 1791.

rule was partially ignored by the growing number of French convicts sent to the West Indies in the first half of the eighteenth century.[95]

This question had an impact on the identification of slaves in France itself. We will discuss British jurisprudence and its role in the abolitionist process in Part III. Instead, it is worth noting the interaction between the legal identification of slaves in the colonies and in France. In 1738, slaves were allowed to testify in court, except against their masters (but they served as witnesses against other whites).[96] Over the years, penalties for violence and abuse of slaves by masters increased, especially from 1780 onwards. Strictly speaking, slaves had no rights, but masters were obliged to feed and clothe them. Great Britain relied on jurisprudence and common law; the Somerset ruling was adopted in this context. In France, on the other hand, from the beginning of the eighteenth century, the French provincial courts demanded legislation that would unambiguously resolve the problem of slaves.[97] According to Seymour Drescher, this demand arose from the fact that, unlike Great Britain, the French monarchy did not have to consult an elected body to adopt new rules.[98] While this interpretation seems plausible, it does not explain all. French slaves had recourse to the courts in cases of illegitimate slavery – in France, for example – or because their masters failed to meet their obligations in terms of food and health. Sue Peabody, and recently Miranda Spieler, have carefully analyzed the lawsuits brought by slaves arriving in France.[99] According to the Edict of 1716, slaves could only be brought to France to receive religious instruction or a trade. In all other cases, special authorization had to be obtained, failing which slaves were freed on arrival in France. As in Britain, the question of the arrival of slaves in the French Hexagon arose. But unlike Britain, where there was no positive legislation on the subject, and cases were resolved by case law alone, France introduced special legislation. In response to the growing demands of the provincial courts, the royal edict of 1716 stipulated that colonial owners and military officers could bring their slaves to France without losing their ownership. However, the edict required that authorization be given by the colonial governor and that a register be kept by the Admiralty on arrival in France, failing which the slave would be set free. The Parliament of Paris (similar to a supreme court) did not ratify this ordinance, however, and different decisions were still taken. As a result, and also because the number of slaves traveling to France was increasing in parallel with their numbers in the colonies, a

---

[95] Gérard Lafleur, "Le peuplement des Antilles françaises au XVIIe siècle," *Actes des Congrès nationaux historiques et scientifiques*, 133, 6 (2012): 53–69.
[96] ANOM, F3 236: 708, Ordinance of July 15, 1738.
[97] Sue Peabody, *There Are No Slaves in France* (New York: Oxford University Press, 1996): 6.
[98] Drescher, *Abolitions*.
[99] Peabody, *There Are No Slaves*; Miranda Spieler, *Slaves in Paris: Hidden Lives and Fugitive Histories* (Cambridge, Mass: Harvard University Press, 2025).

new rule (*Déclaration pour la police des noirs*) was adopted in 1777 to prohibit all "blacks, mulattoes and other colored people" from entering France. Race became a tool for preserving freedom, not limiting it. In principle, a slave in France becomes a domestic servant and is expected to receive food, clothing and lodging. However, this process was extremely complicated. The Court of Admiralty in Paris was responsible for fugitive slaves in France and for those who submit petitions. As for fugitive slaves, a master could only recover them if he has complied with all the rules laid down by law. In practice, courts took different decisions. For example, the case of Catherine Morgan, presented to the Nantes Admiralty (and discussed by Sue Peabody),[100] confirms not only the plurality of legal rulings and rules, but also the way slaves could possibly exploit them to gain their freedom. She claimed that a lawyer took her from her master in Saint-Domingue, promising to free her once in France. During the voyage, however, the captain impregnated her. After disembarking in Nantes, she met a lawyer, named Terrier, and gave him a sum of money to investigate her case. Unfortunately, the lawyer did not act as promised and employed Catherine as a servant. Catherine then went to the Admiralty and presented her case. Terrier proposed a completely different version, according to which Catherine went to Nantes with her master and their small child. Once in Nantes, the master began mistreating and beating Catherine, who met with Terrier's benevolence and sought to induce the master to cease his actions. Catherine was returned to him. After further violence, Catherine went into hiding with Terrier, who sought to win her case by placing her in a convent. At the hearing, it transpired that Catherine's master has been condemned in Saint-Domingue for violence against slaves, and that he was ruined. The Admiralty condemned Catherine to be confiscated from Morgan, given to the King, then sent back to Saint-Domingue. It is at this point that the captain sent the court the letter with which this story had begun, a fraud, signing in Catherine's place.[101]

However, some of the positive aspects described in Peabody's work contrast with the much more nuanced cases Spieler had examined in detail. Strong differences emerged between Nantes, Paris and other places where trials were settled, as well as between judges' decisions.

On the whole, the Nantes Admiralty ruled in favor of the masters, while the Paris Admiralty freed 247 slaves between 1730 and 1790: 154 following a trial for freedom and ninety-three following an act of freedom.[102] In these cases, the slaves became servants and were fed, clothed and housed. This is where the line between freedom and unfreedom becomes blurred. Servants were not always paid a wage, and could be punished and beaten. In the colonies, too, the legal status of reformed slaves was close to that of servants. The absolute number and

---

[100] Peabody, *There Are No Slaves*, chapter 3.
[101] Archives Nationales, Marine, B3 455, folios 62 to 136.
[102] AN Z1D (Admiralty of France), minutes of judgments, 126–137, quoted in Peabody, *There Are No Slaves*: 55.

percentage of *free people of color* increased over the course of the eighteenth century, particularly in Guadeloupe and Martinique, where they represented 18 percent and 31 percent of the population, respectively, in 1788.[103] Faced with this trend, French and local authorities decided in the 1720s and 1730s to introduce new taxes on manumission and impose stricter conditions for its granting. New rules also limited the rights of freed slaves.

At the end of the eighteenth century, the free colored population of the French colonies represented almost 5 percent of the total population, compared with 2.5 percent for the British Isles. In 1775, there were 6,897 free people of color in Saint-Domingue, compared with 3,700 in Jamaica, representing 2.4 percent and 1.7 percent of the total population, respectively. In 1789, there were 54,000 whites in the French West Indian colonies, including many *small whites*, compared with 36,000 free people of color and no fewer than 675,000 slaves.[104] In 1788, free people of color represented 18 percent of the free population in Guadeloupe, 31 percent in Martinique, 44 percent in Saint-Domingue, 36 percent in Mauritius and 11 percent in Réunion Island.[105]

In Saint-Domingue, freed slaves and free *"gens de couleur"* were much more numerous in town than in the countryside. In 1804, almost half the population of Point-à-Pitre was free. Freedmen living in towns worked mainly in construction (35–40 percent depending on the town), textile manufacturing (30–50 percent), services and domestic service (3–8 percent).[106] Freed slaves were recruited to work with slaves on infrastructure, ports, roads and bridges.

Master emancipation was possible, but increasingly restricted over time. In fact, the number of mixed marriages and concubines freed by their masters was considered excessive, as was the fact that slaves accumulated money to buy their freedom, which was considered contrary to good social order and an incitement to theft.[107] Increasing taxes for emancipation were imposed on masters, while "self-purchase" was forbidden, except in certain special cases such as sailors and artisans. Emancipation was completed and definitively sanctioned by Christian baptism.

After the Seven Years' War, the administrative emancipation of slave soldiers by the colonial government was accepted. However, freed slaves did not enjoy the same rights as free whites. They still had to "respect" (submit to) their former masters. In the event of theft, they were punished as before (as slaves) and were not allowed to assemble. After 1765, this prohibition was extended to marriage and festivities. Manumitted slaves (i.e., freed by their owners) were still forbidden to bear arms and, after the 1770s, they could no longer bear the name of their former master.

---

[103] Régent, *La France et ses esclaves*: 183.
[104] Blackburn, *The Making of New World Slavery*: 440.
[105] Régent, *La France et ses esclaves*, table 22: 183.
[106] Régent, *La France et ses esclaves*: 125.
[107] ANOM F 3 222, Code de la Guadeloupe.

Conclusion Part I: Work Rules and Empire Building

Russian, French and British historical sources never justify serfdom or slavery as a simple response to labor shortages, as nowadays economic theory pretends to be, so the "law" of supply and demand doesn't apply. Nor does the argument of "imperfect markets" seem to justify the existence of coercion: Masters and authorities were not looking for free labor, but explicitly wanted forced labor. On the contrary, they refused to raise wages or allow labor to circulate freely. They applied rules to keep workers in place, and refused any wage increases as a substitute for coercion. Why was this so?

In the case of Russia, serfdom was institutionalized in response to colonial expansion and the tsar's need to reconcile military recruitment and peasant settlement, with the demands of noble estate owners to keep their peasants in place. It was a political compromise between elites and within the imperial dynamic, achieved on the shoulders of peasants and the colonized. In the case of France and Great Britain, in the seventeenth and early eighteenth centuries, strict labor regulations in the metropole were the answer to the growing demand for forced labor in a context where the new capitalists and old rentiers agreed to shift the burden of growth onto the shoulders of the workers. It was a social and political orientation, not a response to the "labor shortage" per se. Slavery and indenture thus developed as complementary, rather than substitutive, forms of labor.

Everywhere, labor rules in metropolitan France and the colonies were linked; there was no opposition between "free" labor in metropolitan France and "unfree" labor in the colonies. As part of this common trend, in the case of France and Great Britain, labor rules in the colonies were a strict extension of those in force in metropolitan France. Conversely, in Russia, this relationship was reversed, and some colonies became the land of less coercion than serfdom in central Russia. This happened for several interrelated reasons: In the Russian Empire, there was no sea between the metropolis and its colonies; coercion was extreme in the metropolis, and the attempt to control its evolution from above led Tsarist rulers to adopt more flexible attitudes in the new colonies. Another factor was that few Russians lived on the steppe and had to be moved from the mainland. This solution weakened the legal status of landowners and admitted temporary property by peasants and soldiers; consequently, the only way to keep both serfdom and colonization alive was to partially relax it in the peripheries.

Exactly the opposite was true in the French and British colonies, where labor institutions evolved from indenture to slavery, and where both were more severe in the colonies than on the continent. This is because, firstly, the transition from indentured migration to slavery and its institutional definition were not seen as opposing markets, as dominant economic theories now assert. On the contrary, forced labor and the development of international markets went hand in hand. What is more, coercion increased despite population growth, confirming that in the eyes of the British and French elites, the problem was not the lack of labor, but that of forced labor. The French and British exported the labor institutions of the metropole to their colonies, progressively racialized and radicalized them, and the level of coercion was undoubtedly much higher in the colonial worlds than in the metropole. There were also reciprocal effects: The consolidation and persistence of servitude in the colonies helped to maintain discrimination and coercion at work on the continent too. However, in the case of Britain, white indentured workers were gradually transformed into wage earners, as opposed to black slaves. It was by openly opposing blacks that better conditions for whites were achieved. In France and its colonies, race certainly played a role, but at the same time it masked a persistent opposition between the urban and rural (including colonial) worlds, with the former increasingly protected, not the latter. As we shall see, these differences influenced the path of abolitions.

Ultimately, these different issues in the three empires were linked to the political and social relations between the state and the various social groups. Landed aristocracies played a central role in all three cases, even where capitalism developed (Britain), and of course more so in France and Russia, where the capitalist classes were weaker. In Russia, landed aristocrats were not independent of the tsar, while merchants were much less autonomous in Russia than in France and Britain. In Russia, it was the tension, then agreement, between landowners and the state in the context of imperial expansion that led to the extension and intensification of serfdom. From this perspective, coercion was a response to territorial expansion and the political and social hierarchies between the state, landowners and the peasantry.

In Britain, the alliance between merchants, capitalists and landowners, so enthusiastically presented in Whig historiography as the origin of democracy and modernity, in fact led to a strengthening of coercion on the Continent, and even more so in the colonies. All workers were affected. The relative marginalization of the crown and the inclusion of merchants and capitalists in the political configuration were huge differences with Russia, and led to a generalization of coercion. "Progress" was achieved on the shoulders of all workers.

In France, unlike in Britain, the monarchy retained a leading role, on which aristocratic capitalism developed. The owners of rural estates were also granted greater political and social power than in Britain. In this context, the initial subordination of all workers, both in metropolitan France and in the colonies, gave way, after the Revolution, to an enormous gulf between urban workers, on the one hand, and agricultural workers, slaves and indentured migrants, on the other.

We now need to understand the impact of these institutional, legal and political factors on economic dynamics: Was coercion profitable? To whom?

PART II

The Economics of Bondage

In the preceding chapters, the political, social and legal foundations of coercion were delineated. However, the economic rationale behind the utilization of coercion remains to be elucidated. A significant number of economists and economic historians adhere to Domar's model, which was strongly influenced by H. J. Nieboer, a Dutch ethnographer who lived during the late nineteenth and early twentieth centuries.[1] This model posits that labor coercion is likely to emerge when there is a shortage of labor relative to land. The concept has been largely informed by the historical precedent of Russian and medieval European serfdom, and has been applied to a range of contexts, including in Russia, Africa, Asia, Britain and the United States. Theories of this nature are of considerable interest, not so much for the explanations they provide, but for the doubts they raise. Domar's model posits that slavery and serfdom were established when labor was scarce. In contrast, H. J. Habakkuk, Michael Postan, Douglass North and Robert Thomas emphasize that in Western Europe, the scarcity of labor was not the primary factor that led to the decline of serfdom and the subsequent intensification of capital.[2] In the first case, the scarcity of labor resulted in the use of coercive measures. In the second, it led to an increase in wages, which in turn prompted the adoption of capital-intensive production methods.[3]

Similarly, divergent interpretations of Domar's model (often lacking substantial empirical evidence) emerged in the context of the colonial world. The cases of Australia and Canada demonstrate that the colonization of new

---

[1] Nieboer, *Slavery as an Industrial System*; Domar "The Causes of Slavery or Serfdom; Domar, Machina, "On the Profitability of Russian Serfdom." For more recent discussions: Acemoglu, Wolitzky, "The Economics of Labor Coercion."

[2] Michael M. Postan, *Cambridge Economic History of Europe: Expanding Europe in the Sixteenth and Seventeenth Centuries* (Cambridge: Cambridge University Press, 1973); Douglass North, Robert Thomas, "The Rise and Fall of the Manorial System: A Theoretical Model," *Journal of Economic History*, 31 (1971): 777–803.

[3] Hrothgar John Habakkuk, "The Economic History of Modern Britain," *Journal of Economic History*, 18, 4 (1958): 486–501; Hrothgar John Habakkuk, *American and British Technology in the Nineteenth Century* (Cambridge: Cambridge University Press, 1962); Allen, *The British Industrial Revolution in Global Perspective*.

territories did not inevitably result in significant slave imports, as observed in the United States.[4] In Russia, the scarcity of labor never was a prominent feature in historical sources. Additionally, the abolition of slavery in the British Atlantic colonies was not primarily driven by demographic trends. As Seymour Drescher observed, there was no significant alteration in demographic trends in the tropical regions beyond Europe during the pivotal period between 1760 and 1790. Wrigley and Schofield demonstrated that Britain established its overseas slave system during the very decades when the net emigration rate reached a tercentennial peak (1641–1661). Conversely, British abolitionism reached its zenith precisely when the net emigration rate reached its lowest point in three centuries (1771–1791).[5]

A similar pattern was observed in other regions. Prior to the eighteenth century, Asia had the largest population of any continent. However, while Europe's population more than doubled from 190 million to 423 million in the nineteenth century, the population of Asia only reached 970 million in 1900, after nearly 200 years. Of course, the rate of growth varied considerably from region to region.[6] However, there was no direct correlation between population density and coercion: Forced labor was sometimes commonplace in highly populated areas and periods of demographic growth, and conversely, was relaxed in relatively highly populated areas.[7]

Similar debates have taken place concerning Africa. Economic historians of Africa have frequently cited Nieboer and the imbalance between scarce labor and abundant land as key factors perpetuating slavery and coercion on the continent.[8] They believe that the lack of capital and the predatory nature of the states discouraged investment and large-scale operations, but enhanced coercion and labor intensification. Demographic stagnation in Africa was the result of instability, petty warfare, and, above all, the slave trade.[9] Austin, the scholar

---

[4] Engerman, Terms of Labor.
[5] Edward Anthony Wrigley, Roger Schofield, *The Population History of England: A Reconstruction* (Cambridge: Cambridge University Press, 1982): 218–221.
[6] Cuirong Liu, Ts'ui-jung Liu, James Lee, David Sven Reher, Osamu Saito, Wang Feng, eds., *Asian Population History* (Oxford: Oxford University Press, 2001).
[7] Thirtankar Roy, *Rethinking Economic Change in India. Labour and Livelihood* (London: Routledge, 2005); Thirtankar Roy, "Labour Intensity and Industrialization in Colonial India," in Gareth Austin, Kaoru Sugihara, eds., *Labour-Intensive Industrialization in Global History* (London: Routledge, 2012): 107–121.
[8] Anthony Hopkins, *An Economic History of West Africa* (New York: Columbia University Press, 1973); Gareth Austin, "Factor Markets in Nieboer Conditions: Pre-Colonial West Africa, c.1500–c.1900," *Continuity and Change*, 24, 1 (2009): 23–53.
[9] Patrick Manning, "The Slave Trade: The Formal Demography of a Global System," *Social Science History*, 14, 2 (1990): 255–279; Patrick Manning, *Slavery and African Life: Occidental, Oriental and African Slave Trades* (Cambridge: Cambridge University Press, 1990); Martin Klein, "Simulating the African Slave Trade," *Canadian Journal of African Studies*, 28, 2 (1994): 296–299.

most convinced of the validity of Nieboer's model for Africa, asserts that wage labor was not an economic option because there was no wage rate that would have been mutually advantageous for an employer to offer or a worker to accept, due to the possibility of access to land.[10] Other authors are adamant that people made a conscious decision to own people rather than land, which played a significant role in incorporating outsiders into African societies.[11]

Several other economic historians of Africa disagree with Nieboer and his followers. They argue that in the colonial context, highly populated countries – not Africa – encouraged labor-intensive processes under coercion and discouraged capital innovation. In their view, Africa contradicts the Harrod–Nieboer model.[12]

In short, economic models based on simple labor demand and supply yield extremely divergent interpretations of the origin and primary causes of coercion in labor markets. But they have been unable to find adequate empirical validation for them. The central argument of this study is that explanations of labor coercion based on supply and demand must be overcome. During the majority of the period under investigation, institutions discussed in Part I, as well as societies and markets, converged, rendering coercion socially and institutionally binding and economically profitable.

---

[10] Gareth Austin, "Slavery in Africa, 1804–1936," in David Eltis, Stanley Engerman, Seymour Drescher, David Richardson, *The Cambridge World History of Slavery, Vol. 4 AD 1804–AD 2016* (Cambridge: Cambridge University Press, 2017): 174–196.

[11] Lovejoy, *Transformations in Slavery*; Meillassoux, *Anthropologie de l'esclavage*; Miers and Kopytoff, *Slavery in Africa*.

[12] Daron Acemoglu, Simon Johnson, and James Robinson, "Reversal of Fortune: Geography and Institutions in the Making of the Modern World Income Distribution," *Quarterly Journal of Economics*, 117, 4 (2002): 1231–1294; Acemoglu, Wolitzky, "The Economics of Labour Coercion"; Domar "The Causes of Slavery or Serfdom"; Domar "On the Profitability of Russian Serfdom."

4

The Russian Empire and the Economic Dynamics of Serfdom

Economic Growth under Serfdom: The Eighteenth Century

In Russia, landlords had the right to demand quit-rent or labor services (corvées) from peasants. Western, Russian and Soviet historiography has long held the view that quit-rent encouraged trade and economic growth, while labor service had the opposite effect.[1] This argument has been forcefully reiterated by historians of serfdom in both Western and Eastern Europe.[2] The question at the heart of this debate is crucial: Was serfdom incompatible with markets?[3]

It is clear that quit-rent increased in the first half of the eighteenth century, while labor services flourished in the second half. In the first half of the nineteenth century, quit-rent regained its prominence, although to a lesser degree than previously. Regional differences were significant; corvées were more widespread in the "Black Earth" (the central, most fertile regions of European Russia), whereas the quit-rent system was more widely practiced near industrial areas.[4] Overall, agricultural prices climbed during much of the eighteenth century, making service labor more profitable than the quit-rent.[5] The revival of corvées was accompanied by an increasing integration of the demesne in

---

[1] Blum, *Lord and Peasant*.
[2] Robert Brenner, "Agrarian Class Structure and Economic Development in Pre-industrial Europe," *Past and Present*, 70, 1 (1976): 30–74; Trevor Aston, Charles Philpin, eds., *The Brenner Debate: Agrarian Class Structure and Economic Development in Pre-industrial Europe* (Cambridge: Cambridge University Press, 1985); William Hagen, *Ordinary Prussians: Brandenburg Junkers and Villagers, 1500–1840* (Cambridge: Cambridge University Press, 2002).
[3] For a more detailed presentation of these issues, see Stanziani, *Bondage*.
[4] Vasilii I. Semevskii, *Krest'ianskii vopros v Rossii v XVIII i pervoi polovine XIX veka* (The peasant question in Russia in the eighteenth to the first half of the nineteenth century), 2 volumes (Saint Petersburg: Obshchestevennaia pol'za, 1888); Vasilii I. Semevskii, *Krest'iane v tsarstvovanie Imperatritsy Ekateriny II* (The peasantry under the reign of Catherine II), 2 volumes (Sankt-Peterburg: tipografiia F. S. Sushchinskago 1901); Ivan D. Koval'chenko, *Russkoe krepostnoe krest'ianstvo v pervoi polovine XIX v.* (Russian serf peasantry during the first half of the nineteenth century) (Moscow: Nauka 1967).
[5] Boris Mironov, *The Social History of the Russian Empire*, 2 volumes (Boulder, CO: Westview 1999).

proto-industrial activity and in local and national markets for agriculture and manufactures.[6] In 1760, nobles' estates were the sites of 413 out of 1,143 rural fairs (36 percent). By 1800, this number had risen to 1,615 out of 3,180 (51 percent). This means that landlords and their peasants alike decisively entered the rural agrarian markets. Peasant activity in rural markets even surpassed that of merchants and small urban traders.[7] Therefore, contrary to traditional arguments, trade in estate production increased with *barshchina* (corvées). This was compatible with exportation and long distances, as well as with the rise of local and national markets.[8] Local markets were widespread and offered a wide range of products, including agricultural produce and proto-industrial goods. Since the mid eighteenth century, peasants had been purchasing significant quantities of proto-industrial products while enjoying rising incomes.[9] Noble landowners took control of these market by reclaiming the sale of products from their estates and entering into urban trade circuits with determination.[10] Proto-industry became ruralized.[11] The percentage of private factories owned by nobles rose from 5 percent in the 1720s to 20 percent by 1773. In 1725, 78 percent of industrial activity was located in cities. By 1775–1778, that number had dropped to 60 percent, and by 1803, it had fallen to 58 percent.[12] The second half of the eighteenth century saw a drastic increase in landlords entering the proto-industrial sector. This was not a symptom of demesne autarchy; it was the opposite. It testified to the demesne's increasing commercialization. Many serf-entrepreneurs registered businesses or even proto-industrial

---

[6] Dennison, *The Institutional Framework of Russian Serfdom*; Peter Czap, "The Perennial Multiple-Family Household, Mishino, Russia, 1782–1858," *Journal of Family History*, 7, 1 (Spring 1982): 5–26; Carol Leonard, *Agrarian Reforms in Russia* (Cambridge: Cambridge University Press, 2011).

[7] Boris Mironov, *Vnutrennyi rynok Rossii vo vtoroi polovine XVIII – pervoi polovine XIX v* (The domestic market in Russia during the second half of the eighteenth century-first half of the nineteenth century) (Leningrad: Nauka 1981): 153–154.

[8] Koval'chenko, *Russkoe krepostnoe*.

[9] Klaus Gestwa, *Proto-industrialisierung in Russland* (Göttingen: Vandenhoeck and Ruprecht 1999); Ksenia N. Serbina, *Krest'ianskaia zhelezodelatel'naia promyshlennost' tsentral'noi Rossii XVI-pervoi poloviny XIXe vekoi* (The peasant metallurgic home industry in Central Russia from the sixteenth to the first half of the nineteenth century) (Leningrad: Nauka, 1978).

[10] Tatiana F. Izmes'eva, *Rossiia v sisteme evropeiskogo rynka. Konets XIXe-nachalo XX v.* (Russia in the system of the European market, end of the nineteenth to the early twentieth century) (Moscow: Nauka, 1991).

[11] RGADA, fond 199 (G. F. Miller); Emilia I. Indova, "O rossiskikh manufakturakh vtoroi poloviny XVIII v." (On the Russian manufactures during the second half of the eighteenth century), *Istoricheskaia geografiia Rossii: XIX-nachalo XX v.* (Moscow: Nauka 1975): 248–345; Emilia I. Indova, *Dvortsovoe khoziaistvo v Rossii* (The palace economy in Russia) (Moscow: Nauka 1964).

[12] Mironov, Boris. "Consequences of the Price Revolution in Eighteenth-century Russia." *The Economic History Review*, 45, 3 (1992): 457–478.

and industrial activities – sometimes on behalf of the landowner and sometimes quite independently[13] – and they often employed workers in their proto-industrial activity.[14]

Landlords were determined to keep the best master peasants, who trained other artisans. Litigations on runaways and estate records confirm that many estate owners did not send their peasants to work in town, but kept them on the estate:[15] They were determined to take over the proto-industrial and manufacturing sector, which had previously been dominated by merchants.[16] Landlords were keenly invested in cultivating a form of "protectionist" politics that would prove advantageous to the estate's peasants and craftsmen.[17] Peasants and landlords made arrangements to shape markets and competition rules to their advantage and to exclude urban merchants and producers. The output of both agricultural produce and proto-industrial products increased throughout the eighteenth and early nineteenth centuries. This sustained the demand for manufactured goods, which was mostly satisfied by local proto-industrial activity that utilized labor-intensive technology.[18] The coexistence of corvées and quit-rent on the same estate enabled the peasant economy and that of the noble landowners to withstand economic fluctuations.[19]

Therefore, the peasant economy under "serfdom" did not align with the Chayanovian model of a peasant who satisfies his family's needs and enters the market only when necessary.[20] It also did not fit Kula's model of peasants who were forced to produce by landlords who took all the products and sold them on the market.[21] Peasants were already integrated into market activity, and proto-industry was not necessarily residual. The integration of peasants and nobles into the market does not confirm the link between labor as compulsory

---

[13] On serfs-entrepreneurs, see: RGADA, fond 294, opis' 2 and 3; fond 1287, opis' 3. TsIAM, opis' 2, dela 31, 40, 82, 124, 146; RGADA, fond 210: razriadnyi prikaz; fond 1287 (Sheremetev), opis' 5 and 6; RGIA, fond 1088 (Sheremetev, opis' 3, 5, 10). Also: Robert Rudolph, "Agricultural Structure and Proto-industrialization in Russia: Economic Development with Unfree Labor," *The Journal of Economic History*, 45, 1 (1985): 47–69; Iurii A. Tikhonov, *Pomeshchic'i krest'iane v Rossii: feodal'naia renta v XVII-nachale XVIII v* (The private estates' peasants in Russia: The feudal rent in the seventeenth to early eighteenth century) (Moscow: Nauka, 1974).
[14] Serbina, *Krest'ianskaia*, 37.
[15] Dennison, *The Institutional Framework of Russian Serfdom*.
[16] Edgar Melton, "Proto-industrialization, Serf Agriculture, and Agrarian Social Structure: Two Estates in Nineteenth-century Russia." *Past and Present*, 115, 1 (1987): 73–81.
[17] RGIA, fond 1088, opis' 10, dela 611, 616 and 618.
[18] Domar, Machina, "On the Profitability of Russian Serfdom."
[19] Tracy Dennison, Steven Nafzinger, "Living Standards in Nineteenth Century Russia," *Journal of Interdisciplinary History*, 43, 3 (2013): 397–441.
[20] On Chayanov and his application in Russian studies: Alessandro Stanziani, *L'économie en revolution. Le cas russe, 1870–1914* (Paris: Albin Michel, 1998).
[21] Witold Kula, *An Economic Theory of the Feudal System* (London: New Left Books, 1976).

service and poor market development. Peasants' and landlords' participation in markets helps us understand their alliance with the tsarist authorities, both opposing the urban merchants and manufacturers. It is wrong to interpret this as "hostility to market": Peasants and landlords opposed other merchants and industrialists because they were interested in trade and proto-industrialization. It was a fight to occupy markets, not to contrast them.

Wallerstein's argument that "backward" Russia increased serfdom and wheat exports to "advanced" Europe is unfounded.[22] Serfdom, as we have seen, was linked to imperial expansion, while there is little doubt that exports increased and that Russian markets became increasingly integrated into international and European markets. Moreover, the growth of exports did not take place at the expense of local and national markets. In fact, by 1760 the demand for grain in the heartland created a rise in grain prices and Russian local markets became more integrated into a national market.[23] Russia engaged in international trade, supporting this domestic trend by trading with Europe and Asia. Russian grain exports expanded significantly through the Baltic Sea during the second half of the eighteenth century. At the time, Russian overseas trade with Britain grew in volume and value, and Russia consistently enjoyed a favorable balance of trade.[24] Russia was the leading continental European exporter to the British Isles throughout this period, with Russian commodities comprising about 8 percent of British imports in pounds sterling.[25] Russia's main exports passed through Kronstadt and Riga, which accounted for 70 percent and 18 percent, respectively, of all trade from Russian ports.[26] During this period, Russian merchants and ships gained an increasing share of the import trade (mostly articles of clothing and colonial luxury items such as sugar) via these ports.[27]

Trade through the Black Sea only developed after the Russian conquest in the 1780s. The primary reason for this was the Napoleonic Wars and the

[22] Wallerstein, *The Modern World-System*; for critics escaping this Eurocentric perspective: Alessandro Stanziani, "Russia Economic History in Global Perspective," in Matthias Middell, ed., *The Perspective of Global History* (London: Bloomsbury, 2019): 115–137; Alessandro Stanziani, "Russian Capitalism. Exceptionalism versus Global Labour-Intensive Path, 1700–1914," in Kaveh Yazdani, Dilip Menon, eds., *Capitalisms. Towards a Global History* (Oxford: Oxford University Press, 2020): 95–127.

[23] Boris Mironov and Carol S. Leonard, "In Search of the Hidden Information: Some Issues in the Socio-Economic History of Russia in the Eighteenth and Nineteenth Centuries," *Social Science History*, 9, 4 (Autumn 1985): 339–359; Mironov, *Vnytrennii rynok*.

[24] Herbert Kaplan, "Russia's Impact on the Industrial Revolution in Great Britain during the Second Half of the Eighteenth Century," *Forschungen zur Osteuropäischen Geschichte*, 29 (1981): 7–59.

[25] Herbert Kaplan, "Observations on the Value of Russia's Overseas Trade with Great Britain during the Second Half of the Eighteenth Century," *Slavic Review*, 45, 1 (1986): 85–94.

[26] TNA (The National Archives, Kew), FO (Foreign Office), 65/6; 97/340, 341; BT (Board of Trade) 6/141.

[27] TNA, FO 65/6.

blockade. By 1802, grain (essentially wheat) made up 17.5 percent of its total exports. The development of the Baltic ports undoubtedly enhanced Russian exports to Europe. However, as late as the 1790s, grain represented only 6.9 percent of its total exports. Other crops, hemp, flax, livestock products and even industrial goods played a far greater role in Russian trade, accounting for 43 percent, 20.2 percent, 12.6 percent, 12.1 percent and 22.2 percent, respectively.[28] By the end of the eighteenth century, England (without Ireland and Scotland) was already responsible for between three-quarters and four-fifths of Saint Petersburg's flax and hemp exports and about half of Riga's. English imports of Russian iron bars also increased dramatically, from 13 tons in 1714 to 8,000 tons in the 1750s, and then to 25,000 tons per year during the last quarter of the eighteenth century. Russian exports of iron to England exceeded those of Sweden (between 16,000 and 18,000 in those years) during this period. At the turn of the century, flax and hemp still made up 30.3 percent of Russian exports to Europe, while tallow accounted for 15.8 percent and grain 17.5 percent.

Russian trade with Inner Asia was a major part of the Russian economy. The strong ties between Turkestan and South Asia were undoubtedly damaged by the tsarist movement into the region. Tensions and rivalries between and within these political entities allowed Russia to advance in the north and the European powers to advance in the south.[29] This process occurred concurrently with the gradual fragmentation of the Muslim world, which consisted of Central Asia and the Ottoman, Mughal and Safavid empires. The Ottoman Empire's progressive withdrawal from Asia and its general decentralization undoubtedly contributed to this regional reconfiguration. Archives show that the Russian administration actively encouraged Asian merchants to shift their trade from the Iran-Caspian-Astrakhan line to overland routes through Central Asia to Orenburg. Asian merchants began to favor Orenburg, Omsk and Ufa, which brought about changes in the relative importance of various areas in Central Asia. By the middle of the eighteenth century, one-third of the total Persian silk production was being directed to Moscow, rather than exclusively to market towns in Germany and the Low Countries.[30] The Russians also showed a growing interest in the Khanate of Kokand (Uzbekistan) due to the pivotal role of Kokandi merchants in trade between Orenburg and Tien Shan, Yarkand and other Xinjiang cities. The Khanate gained further prominence when cotton crops were developed in the Fergana Valley. Tashkent's role was strengthened, as was the role of Russian textile production in the colonies as a substitute for imports from Iran and India.

---

[28] Kahan, *The Plow, the Hammer and the Knout*: table 4.2:160.
[29] Marshall Hodgson, *Rethinking World History* (Cambridge: Cambridge University Press 1993); Christopher Bayly, *The Imperial Meridian* (London: Longman, Pearson Education, 1989).
[30] Jos Gommans, *Mughal Warfare* (London: Routledge, 2002).

As a result, Russian aggregate national income increased five-fold between 1718 and 1788, raising per capita income by 85 percent. After 1788, the annexation of rich southern provinces intensified this growth.[31] Demographic data confirm this positive trend; recent analyses have accounted for the overall underestimation of birth rates in eighteenth- and nineteenth-century censuses, as well as the annexation of new territories and the resettlement (legal and illegal) of the peasantry. Once these biases were corrected, the natural rate of population growth was considerable: On peasant estates, it was about 0.70 percent between 1678 and 1719, 0.62 percent between 1719 and 1744, 0.97 percent between 1744 and 1762 and 0.96 percent during the next twenty years. It fell to 0.60 percent between 1782 and 1795, rose again to 0.86 percent between 1795 and 1811, and then collapsed during the Napoleonic Wars to −0.42 percent. From this point on, the Russian economy and serfdom in particular struggled to keep up with domestic and international trends. We must understand why.

The Decline of the Russian Economy, First Half of the Nineteenth Century

The natural rate of growth of Russia's peasant population increased during the first half of the nineteenth century. It reached 0.94 percent in 1815–1833, 0.59 percent between 1833 and 1850 and 0.54 percent between 1850 and 1857.[32] These general figures mask significant variations between localities and stark social inequalities.[33]

The high birth rate undoubtedly corresponded to an equally high rate of death, particularly among children. This trend is often seen as proof of Russia's backwardness and poverty. However, high child mortality was not primarily caused by famine. Rather, it was due to diseases linked to poor hygiene, particularly regarding water, as well as epidemics and wars.[34] Nevertheless, the overall population growth was slower than in previous decades.[35] This is a clear

---

[31] For a full discussion, see Blanchard, *Russia's Age of Silver*, chapter 5 and appendix 2, revised in Ian Blanchard, "Le développement économique en perspective historique: l'avenir de la Russie à la lumière de son évolution à l'époque moderne (1700–1914)" in Michèle Merger and Dominique Barjot, eds., *Les entreprises et leurs réseaux: hommes, capitaux, techniques et pouvoirs xixe-xxe siècles. Mèlanges en l'honneur de François Caron* (Paris: Presse de l'Université de Paris-Sorbonne, 1998): 381–392.

[32] Moon, *The Russian Peasantry*: 27.

[33] Koval'chenko, *Russkoe*; Dennison, *The Institutional Framework of Russian Serfdom*.

[34] Kabuzan, *Izmeneniia v razmeshchenii naseleniia Rossii*; Alain Blum, Irina Troitskaia, "La mortalité en Russie au XVIIIe et XIXe siècles. Estimations locales à partir des Revizii, *Population*, 51 (1996): 303–328; Steven Hoch, "Famine, Disease, and Mortality Patterns in the Parish of Borshevka, 1830–1912," *Population Studies*, 52, 3 (1998): 357–368.

[35] Moon, *The Russian Peasantry*: 27.

indication that the rate of growth of the country's economy, which was still high in the last quarter of the eighteenth century, declined during the first half of the nineteenth century. By 1842, per capita income had plummeted to an all-time low. It was lower than at the end of Peter I's reign (1725) and far below that of Britain, its rival.[36]

These negative trends were reflected in a huge concentration of noble properties. The number of small estates declined, while large properties became the rule. In 1857, noble estates with less than twenty-one peasants accounted for barely 3.2 percent of all estates. Those with between twenty-one and 100 peasants made up 15.9 percent. The great majority of estates had between 100 and 500 peasants (37.2 percent), 500 and 1,000 peasants (14.9 percent) or even more than 1,000 peasants (28.7 percent).[37] This trend was undoubtedly linked to the increasing indebtedness of the estate owners and the limited capital markets available to them. The growing institutional pressure of a tsarist state favoring peasants' emancipation and merchants' development also contributed to the concentration of estates.

Meanwhile, other indicators point to a growing dynamism in the Russian economy. Regional specialization increased; central and other industrial and proto-industrial areas specialized, while agricultural areas lost non-agrarian activities. Factories shut down and proto-industrial activity declined in the Steppe and central Black Earth areas, whereas the surface area of cultivated land expanded in the territory as a whole and inside the main estates.[38] During the first half of the nineteenth century, grain prices in Russia showed a clear tendency toward homogenization and correlation on the national level.[39]

In the central industrial regions, the main difference from the previous century was that noble landowners no longer restricted peasant movements between the city and country. In part, more volatile prices prompted some landlords to diversify their economic strategies. The main issue was the intensified use of *obrok* (quit-rent) and the increased movement of peasants in the city and neighboring estates.[40] Noble landlords also began renting out peasants and

---

[36] Blanchard, "Le développement économique."
[37] Aleksandr' Troinitskii, *Krepostnoe naselenie v Rossii po 10 narodnoi perepisi* (The Russian serf population according to the tenth census) (Saint Petersburg: Wulf, 1861): 45.
[38] Irina V. Ledovskaia, "Biudzhet russkogo pomeshchika v 40-60kh godakh XIX vekoi" (Estate owners' budgets in the 1840s–'60s), in Akademiia Nauk SSSR, *Materialy po istorii sel'skogo khoziaistva i krest'ianstva SSSR*, vol. 8, (Moscow: Nauka 1974): 240–245.
[39] Mironov and Leonard, "In Search of the Hidden Information": 339–359; Ivan D. Koval'nchenko, L.V. Milov, *Vserossiskii agrarnyi rynok XVIII-nachala XXv.* (The all-Russian agrarian market, eighteenth century to the early twentieth century) (Moscow: Nauka, 1974).
[40] Koval'chenko, *Russkoe krepost'noe*: 394; Boris Gorshkov, "Serfs on the Move: Peasant Seasonal Migration in Pre-reform Russia, 1800–1860," *Kritika: Explorations in Russian history* 1, 4 (2000): 627–56.

craftsmen to non-noble merchants and manufacturers.[41] In rural and proto-industrial areas close to industrial districts, social differentiation between peasants was more pronounced. However, these regions offered higher incomes per capita than agricultural regions. Their diversified economies provided protection against both crop failure and market downturns. In these areas, the return to proto-industry from the countryside to the town was not a decline of the putting-out system;[42] cotton-printing firms had no incentive to spend capital on centralized weaving establishments because they had a flexible network of knowledgeable peasant weavers. In Vladimir province, in the early 1850s, 18,000 factory looms merely supplemented the 80,000 peasant looms filling factory orders. The majority of Russian weaving was carried out in peasant homes across the central industrial region. It was done either as an independent *kustar'* (craftsmen) activity, on commission from printing factories, or on commission from independent middlemen who distributed yarn and then sold the finished cloth to printing factories.[43]

In short, markets and market relationships developed during the first half of the nineteenth century, estates concentrated and peasants won relative "freedom," moving to town. In a neoclassical economic model, these shifts should have pushed the economy up. The opposite was true. The rate of growth declined, and even the population increase slowed down. Why was it so?

Reasons for Decline: Serfdom, the Invasion of Ukraine and the Great Divergence

Ideal development models exist only in textbooks; in reality, political negotiations and social constraints intervene. In the Russian case, some markets and social reforms (relaxing serfdom without abolishing it) did not reach the intended goal. This was due to the persisting institutional constraints on the economy, despite their relative relaxing. Peasants still lacked full access to property and control over the income from their secondary activities, while merchants and industrialists were still burdened by tax and other institutional restrictions. Russia was left more vulnerable to market shocks due to a lack of essential infrastructure, including roads, trains, financial resources and credit. Furthermore, market development intensified social conflicts. These included disputes between landowners and peasants who were moving to town, between

---

[41] RGADA, fond 342, opis' 3, delo 749. Also: RGADA, fond 1287 (Sheremetev), opis' 3, chast' 1, delo 107, 117, 1745.

[42] Dave Pretty, *Neither Peasant nor Proletarian: The Workers of the Ivanovo-Voznesensk Region, 1885–1905* (Ph.D. dissertation, Brown University, 1997).

[43] Olga Crisp, "Labor and Industrialization in Russia," in Peter Mathias and Michael Postan, eds., *The Cambridge Economic History of Europe*, vol. 7, pt. 2 (Cambridge: Cambridge University Press, 1978): 308–415.

merchants, peasants and landlords regarding production conditions and remuneration, and between peasant-masters and their workers.[44] Peasant migration was negotiated at three levels: within the family; between the family and the village assembly; and between the village and the landlord. Households and landlords were united in their pursuit of a single objective: Ensuring a consistently high level of labor capacity during the peak season. This system was based on short-term, intensive labor and strong seasonal differences in the intensity of agricultural labor.

Peasants were sometimes forced by their village commune to work in the factory to pay off their debts. At other times, they entered freely into the agreement for the same purpose. As the putting-out system expanded in the early 1800s, many independent domestic weavers found themselves increasingly dependent on factories or particular putting-out middlemen. This was because they had accepted loans or advances to buy yarn or more advanced looms. Workers were required to remain at their places of work until the expiration of their contracts.[45] The result was a system that was much less effective than in previous decades. This was because markets grew stronger while patriarchal and landlord authorities weakened. It was a transitional period, and it was difficult to find new equilibriums.

In fact, beyond the contradictions between legal and political variables and economic dynamics inside Russia, the empire itself became a source of stagnation rather than of economic growth. This is a long-standing debate in historiography, and it requires a thorough investigation, starting with Central Asia.[46] It is clear that before the mid-nineteenth century, there were relatively few Russian settlers in Central Asia. At the same time, Russian merchants and policymakers sought to achieve a monopoly or at least priority in local and inter-regional trade. Trade was a central aspect of the colonies. In Siberia, it involved furs. In the Steppe and the East, it centered on textiles, horses, tea and proto-industrial products. In the South and Southwest, it focused on textiles, wheat and other goods. However, the revenues from these activities were far below the cost of maintaining the empire's military presence, infrastructure and administration.

It is evident that the Russian state invested significantly more funds in the colonial provinces than it received in return, particularly in Siberia and Central

---

[44] For the Sheremetevs' estates in Pavlovo and Vors'mo: RGIA fond 1088; opis' 3, delo 626, 974, 440, 370, 417.
[45] RGIA fond 18, opis' 2, delo 1927, ll. 1, 3, 212–13; TsIAM fond 14, opis' 1, delo 3266, ll. 2–38 and TsIAM, fond 2354, opis' 1, delo 41, ll. 197a–99, 228.
[46] Eli Weinerman, "The Polemics Between Moscow and Central Asians on the Decline of Central Asia and Tsarist Russia's Role in the History of the Region," *The Slavonic and East European Review*, 71, 3 (1993): 428–481; Morrison, *Russian Rule in Samarkand*; Marco Buttino, *Samarcanda* (Roma: Viella, 2015); Sunderland, *Taming the Wild Field*; Jeff Sahadeo, *Russian Colonial Society in Tashkent, 1865–1923* (Bloomington: Indiana University Press, 2007); Martin, *Law and Custom in the Steppe*.

Asia, but also in Bessarabia and the Caucasus. Poland was also unable to provide resources due to the high military expenditures required to control the independentist and nationalist forces.[47] Military expenditures were considerable in most colonies, while taxes were difficult to collect, either because the nobility was exempt or because there was an inadequate administrative apparatus on the mainland, especially in the newly acquired territories.[48]

The Russian empire simply did not offer the same abundance of easily accessible resources as the British and, to a lesser extent, the French empires. The Russian colonies produced no sugar or cotton (except in some areas in Central Asia, where it developed after the mid-nineteenth century).[49] Fur, timber, iron, hemp and flax were the main export items. Other commodities and resources could not compensate for the military and administrative burden of the empire. What about wheat, the main export?

Russian wheat was the main export item, accounting for 39.7 percent of the total between 1826 and 1830, 48 percent between 1831 and 1835, and 36.2 percent between 1836 and 1840. At this moment, grain was and remained mainly exported through the Black Sea ports, with no grain via the Baltic. In fact, grain was destined for Italy, France and the Ottoman Empire.

The British repeal of the Corn Laws in 1842 and 1846 did little to help Russia, as Britain immediately began importing larger quantities of grain from Canada and the United States. The robust growth of the Atlantic economy during this period strengthened ties between Western Europe, particularly Britain, and the Americas, while weakening those with central and eastern Europe. Russian grain exports to Britain plummeted after 1846.[50]

Facing difficulties in the Baltic area, Russia's "window to the West," it sought to develop its exports through the Black Sea. The invasion of Ukraine, which led to the partition of Poland and the war against the Ottoman Empire, was initially geopolitical. However, it soon became an economic affair. Ukraine's wheat was crucial for Russia in competing with the new American cereals. From this standpoint, the Black Sea and wheat were central to the Great Divergence. They sought to respond to the Atlantic connection while preserving Russia's role on the international chessboard. Wheat was the main contribution of new colonial lands across the Volga and in Ukraine. Russia's occupation of Ukraine and the subsequent expansion of wheat production in the area were the primary drivers

---

[47] Ekaterina Pravilova, *Finansy Imperi. Dengi i vlasti v politiki Rossii na nationaln'nykh okraninakh, 1801–1917* (Imperial finance. Money and power in the politics of Russia in the national borderlands) (Moscow: Novoe Izdatelstvo, 2006).

[48] Ekaterina Pravilova, "Tsena Imperii: Tsentr' i Okrainy v rossiiskom biudzhete XIX-nachala XX vv." (Price of the Empire: center and periphery in the Russian budget, nineteenth-early twentieth centuries), *Ab Imperio*, 4 (2002): 115–144.

[49] Artur Atman, "The Russian Market in World Trade, 1500–1860," *Scandinavian Economic History Review*, 29, 3 (1981): 177–202.

[50] Izmes'eva, *Rossiia v sisteme evropeiskogo rynka*.

of the geopolitics of grain production. The Tsarist empire divided Ukraine into three regions. To the south was the new Russia, taken from the Crimean Khanate in 1783. To the west (right bank) of the Dnieper river were regions annexed in 1793. To the east (left bank) were regions taken from Poland in 1667.[51]

The Napoleonic Wars placed the Black Sea at the center of the strategic and geopolitical chessboard. France and the United Kingdom were determined to gain access to the Dardanelles Strait and the Black Sea. They sought favor with the Ottomans and Russians to advance their geopolitical influence over the Ottoman Empire and Russia, as well as their commercial interests.[52] With the continental blockade and grain shortages in the Mediterranean and Western Europe, Russian wheat was essential for maintaining social peace and economic stability in the belligerent countries. This explains the astounding export figures achieved in 1815.[53]

Russia was determined to maintain this level of exports after the wars ended, despite the recovery of grain production and trade in Europe.[54] Tensions around the Black Sea resurfaced in the 1830s when Russia seized the opportunity to take advantage once again of the Ottoman Empire's decline. This worried the other European powers, above all the United Kingdom, which was anxious to prolong the status quo. The British saw the Black Sea as a route to Persia and India, which they controlled. Silk, carpets, tea and spices were the main items traded. The British were also determined to develop another route, via the Caucasus, in collaboration with Armenian merchants in the region. This would link Leipzig to the Caucasus and from there to Persia. However, the British were not willing to let the Russians have the more northerly route via the Black Sea, linking the Mediterranean with Persia and Central Asia.[55] Tensions between the two countries reached a boiling point when the Russians attempted to restrict work on the Danube and its western Black Sea access by the Austrians. The British could not tolerate this attitude. The Crimean War (1853–1856) was one of the causes of the Russian defeat, and it was one of the reasons for the abolition of serfdom in 1861. However, Russia launched a new war with the Ottoman Empire and seized Bessarabia in 1877.

---

[51] Alan Fisher, *The Russian Annexation of the Crimea, 1772–1783* (Cambridge: Cambridge University Press, 1970); Matthew Smith Anderson, "The Great Powers and the Russian Annexation of the Crimea, 1783–1784," *The Slavonic and East European Review*, 37, 88 (1958): 17–41.
[52] Edhem Eldem and Sophia Laiou, eds., *Istanbul and the Black Sea Coast: Shipping and Trade, 1770–1920* (Istanbul: The ISIS Press, 2018).
[53] Luigi Mascilli Miglorini, Mirella Mafrici, eds., *Mediterraneo e Mar Nero. Due mari tra età moderna e contemporanea* (Naples: ESI, 2012).
[54] Charles King, *The Black Sea. A History* (Oxford: Oxford University Press, 2015).
[55] Constantin Ardeleanu, "Russian British Rivalry Regarding Danube Navigation and the Origins of the Crimean War (1846–1853)," *Journal of Mediterranean Studies*, XIX, 2 (2010): 165–186.

These aggressive strategies towards other powers and repressive ones towards the subjugated populations are unmistakably evident in Ukraine. Russia annexed the western part of nowadays Ukraine towards the end of the eighteenth century, but the Polish landed elites and Polish and Jewish merchants remained. The peasants were Lithuanian, Belarusian, Ukrainian, Catholic, Orthodox or even Uniate. As for the Jews, who had enjoyed considerable autonomy within Poland-Lithuania, Catherine II classified them among the urban groups and merchants. However, as early as 1804, the Russians assigned them a special status, barring them from many areas and regions, schools, land ownership and certain commercial activities.[56] The Russians knew full well that western Ukraine was far richer and could bring in more taxes than its eastern counterpart. They therefore sought to divide and control its elites. They alternated between policies of inclusion and repression towards the Polish nobility, especially as the latter tried on several occasions (1830–1831, 1863–1864) to propagate a nationalist independence movement.[57] Many Polish nobles were stripped of their titles and lands. After the 1831 revolt, 340,000 nobles were affected. Only 70,000 kept their titles, but in 90 percent of cases, they owned neither land nor serfs. The Russians also supported the Ukrainian peasants, who encouraged them to oppose or even revolt against their Polish landlords. However, this strategy was ineffective for two reasons. First, the convictions of Polish landlords accused of mistreating their serfs were often short-lived. Second, the peasants were more tied to their masters than to the new Russian power. The Russians then encouraged Russian peasants to settle in Ukraine, provoking violent clashes between them and Ukrainian peasants.[58] In 1847–1848, the Russian government announced a new reform of local serfdom, designed to weaken the power of Polish landlords vis-à-vis their peasants. The peasants were assigned plots of land. However, the plots were so small and of such poor quality that there was widespread dissatisfaction among both the peasants and their former Polish masters. Polish landowners demonstrated their loyalty to Russian rule during the Crimean War by willingly responding to Russian army requisitions. The Tsarist authorities promptly abolished serfdom at the end of the conflict (1861), just as a new Polish revolt was brewing in Warsaw. Conflicts in Ukraine were the result of several interconnected phenomena concerning land management and grain production. In the eastern regions, it was the subjugation of "nomads" and expropriation of their land.

---

[56] Daniel Beauvois, *La bataille de la terre en Ukraine* (Lille: Presses Universitaires de Lille, 1993).

[57] Timothy Snyder, "Ukrainians and Poles," in Dominic Lieven, ed., *The Cambridge History of Russia*, vol. 2 (Cambridge: Cambridge University Press, 2006): 165–183.

[58] Przemyslaw Milewicz, "National Identification in Pre-Industrial Communities: Peasant Participation in the November Uprising in the Kingdom of Poland, 1830–1831," *Jahrbücher für Geschichte Osteuropas*, 58, 3 (2010): 321–352.

Repression of non-Russian landowners intervened in all Ukrainian areas. In western Ukraine, control of the peasantry and nobility, divided on ethnic and religious grounds, was also a significant factor. These events, from the 1770s to the First World War, reflected the reconfiguration of European and Eurasian empires, with the decadence of the Ottoman and, in part, Austrian empires. Trade through the Black Sea underwent considerable fluctuations throughout the period. This could not offset the losses in international trade via the north to Western Europe.[59]

It is important to recognize that these challenging economic circumstances, which are influenced by global dynamics and Russia's management of its vast empire, also have some positive outcomes. The evolution of the legal status of peasants in peripheral regions significantly impacted the legal status of the entire peasantry in mainland Russia. In 1847–1848, a reform was initiated in Right-Bank Ukraine, where estate owners were primarily Catholic Poles, while the latter were Orthodox Ukrainians. The Tsar and his Governor-General in the region, Dmitrii Bibikov, came to the conclusion that reforming local serfdom might be a way of weakening the Polish elite. The reform ensured that serfs could continue to use their allotments on a permanent basis and set out detailed regulations regarding their obligations to their landlords. However, it should be acknowledged that the reforms did not provide sufficient land for peasants, which led to some discontent on both sides, among the Polish elites and the Ukrainian peasants. The tsarist authorities nevertheless sought to provide Ukrainian peasants with some protection against their Polish masters. In 1838–1840, Governor-General Bibikov took the initiative to conduct a comprehensive inquiry into the mistreatment of peasants. The investigation indicated that the estate intendants may have been involved in some of the excesses. On May 26, 1847, Bibikov put forth the suggestion of conducting an inventory of the private estates in Right-Bank Ukraine. This was to be the first significant institutional change in the empire prior to the 1861 reform. The Inventories Law sought to define a sort of ideal of serfdom, outlining all the corvées and service obligations and establishing the amount of land allotted to each peasant community. The peasant commune never played the same role in these provinces as it did in Russia. It was more marginal and outstripped by the individual possessions attributed to peasant households by the feudal lords themselves. It is worth noting that the reform was also used by landlords to reduce the allotments granted to the peasants. In the context of the 1848 revolutions in Western Europe, the Tsar found himself in a position where he was compelled to reconsider his strategy regarding the Polish landlords in Ukraine. These landlords were seeking a different approach to the management of serfdom.

[59] Ardeleanu, "The Opening and Development of the Black Sea"; Jean-Louis van Regermorter, *La Russie méridionale, la Mer Noire et le commerce international, 1774–1861* (PhD dissertation: Paris IV, 1984).

During the conflict in Crimea, landowners were keen to demonstrate their loyalty by accepting the requisitions of the Russian army, thereby continuing to utilize and potentially abuse the corvée system without interference. When a new Polish insurrection began to emerge in Warsaw, the imperial authorities proclaimed the abolition of serfdom.[60]

In short, the Black Sea and Ukraine were designed to contrast the growth of the Atlantic economy and the competition for American wheat. This attempt was only partially successful. Russia occupied Ukraine, and this, combined with the limits of serfdom and the rise of nationalism and social tensions, led to a significant shift in the region.

This is where the "Great Divergence" intervened. Pomeranz asserts that Britain's turn to North America, which enhanced its markets and economic development, was a turning point.[61] China, on the other hand, could not benefit from similar colonial resources. What Pomerantz and all the other participants in the debate failed to notice is that Britain's reorientation toward the Atlantic and China's decline have had a significant impact on the Russian economy. Russian international trade with Britain was eroded and trade with China also suffered. In fact, during the first half of the nineteenth century, exports from Baltic ports, particularly grain, were sent to Britain. In 1845, a full 75 percent of shipped wheat was directed to Britain.[62] However, wheat of Russian origin fluctuated between 13 and 18 percent, while American wheat began to increase. Moreover, the amount of Russian intermediate goods exported to Britain declined, while Russia imported increasing quantities of British textiles, unlike the previous period. Russia's balance of trade with Britain therefore turned red, reversing the favorable trend that had held until the end of the eighteenth century. In the face of Britain's growing strength and unwavering economic growth after the Napoleonic Wars, Russia's economic advantages – supplying wheat and intermediate goods as well as tea – became liabilities as Britain purchased those items elsewhere.

Russia also suffered from the decline of China, which began at the turn of the eighteenth to the nineteenth century, as a result of the Great Divergence. For almost a hundred years, from the mid-eighteenth to mid-nineteenth centuries, the bulk of Sino-Russian trade took place in Kyakhta-Maimachin. Trade in Kyakhta exploded, growing by 1,550 percent (from 837,000 to 13.8 million rubles). This growth was concentrated entirely in the years between 1750 and 1820, and then stagnated. Inland trade was not affected by competition from maritime trade during the first period. However, in the second period, European – mainly British – maritime trade took the lead. The Treaty

---

[60] Beauvois, *La bataille de la terre*.
[61] Pomeranz, *The Great Divergence*.
[62] Fredrik Andersson, Jonas Ljungberg, "Grain Market Integration in the Baltic Sea Region in the Nineteenth Century," *The Journal of Economic History*, 75, 3 (2015): 749–790.

of Nanking in 1842 finally brought China's foreign trade under British control. This resulted in a continuous decline in Russian exports to China during the first half of the nineteenth century. While previously Russia had exported furs to China and imported textiles, this dynamic shifted. Russia now sold its own textiles and other manufactured products in exchange for tea – making up 90 percent of its imports by value.[63] Russia imported increasing amounts of silver at Bukhtarma, another trading post on China's western border, until 1830. In 1827, it imported 60,000 silver rubles, and in 1828, it imported 148,000.[64] Then, the trade collapsed. In fact, China suffered from its silver standard and its depreciation and the worldwide fluctuations caused by Britain; China lost its silver and the monetary autonomy it had enjoyed in previous centuries.[65] This impacted Russian dynamics, severely reducing trade with China while contributing to the outflow and contemporaneous devaluation of silver on the international scene.

In conclusion, the Chinese decline and Britain's reorientation to the Atlantic had a profound impact on Russia. Domestic markets declined significantly during the first half of the nineteenth century, particularly in proto-industry and grain. Estates were concentrated, and despite its relative flexibility, serfdom proved inadequate in the face of this new trend. The persisting institutional constraints on the economy left no room for serfdom to adapt and compensate for losses related to the Great Divergence. The decline of the Ottoman Empire and growing geopolitical instability in the Balkans proved to be a decisive blow for Russia and the fate of serfdom. With these aspects in mind, we can now compare the Russian economic dynamic with the empires of Britain and France. It is clear that while serfdom and empire enabled growth in Russia, they did not support an industrial revolution. So, what did support the latter in Britain? Its domestic production and markets or its empire? Capital, wage labor or slavery?

---

[63] Mikhail Iosifovich Sladkovskii, *History of Economic Relations between Russia and China* (New Brunswick and London: Transaction Publishers 2008, original 1966): 70–75.
[64] Sladkovskii, *History of Economic Relations*: 65.
[65] Man-Houng Lin, *China Upside Down: Currency, Society and Ideologies, 1808–1956* (Cambridge, MA: Harvard University Press, 2006).

5

Labor and the British Industrial Revolution

To understand slavery, we must consider not only the labor system in mainland Britain, as discussed in previous chapters, but also the unique structure of Britain's labor markets. This chapter asserts that previously studied institutions made labor cheap. However, this solution also had a consequence: British growth was labor-intensive, which meant that labor was scarce, not only in the American colonies, but in Britain itself. Furthermore, the slow growth in mainland Britain, tied to this labor-intensive path, demanded extra support from its colonies in the form of natural resources, markets, and labor (slavery). In other words, both the argument that slavery was linked to capital intensification and the role of slavery in British industrialization need to be reassessed. How?

The Role of Labor in the Agriculture and Industrial Revolutions

Conventional approaches to the role of labor in the Industrial Revolution seem to ignore crucial points in terms of both logic and empirical evidence. The liberal Whig approach considered that the transition from pre-industrial constraints to industrial free markets was beneficial for workers. This approach also emphasized the importance of innovation and capital intensification under the Industrial Revolution. This view is problematic because it defends both increasing wages and capital intensification at the same time. The evidence shows that real wages remained constant until the last quarter of the nineteenth century. This raises the question of whether the labor market operated according to the theory of supply and demand, as the liberal approach maintains. If, as Marxists and socialists claim, machines replaces workers, there should have been increasing unemployment and therefore falling wages.

In fact, the labor market was not operating according to the law of supply and demand: There was no capital-intensive path, but a labor-intensive path. However, despite this pressure on labor, there were no increasing wages. Why was it so?

According to Marx and his followers, the Industrial Revolution was based on primitive accumulation: First, peasants' lands were expropriated; then, workers were paid subsistence-level wages. This interpretation presents a significant logical dilemma: If workers were so abundant after the privatization of the commons and wages were at the subsistence level, it is unclear why capitalists invested in costly machines. This is nonsense.

This book challenges the conventional wisdom that the British Industrial Revolution was based on proletarization, capitalization and free wage labor. The central role of labor in the Industrial Revolution is indisputable, as evidenced by the so-called "revisionist" approach.[1] The ideas of proto-industry and the industrious revolution are fully compatible with the labor-intensive path. The data confirm that proletarization was limited, but wages were kept at a subsistence level so long as labor was the main input. This was achieved through repressive legal actions. We will see that the rate of capital formation in Britain remained relatively slow until the mid-nineteenth century. At the same time, the ratio of labor to capital increased. This tendency was not reversed until the 1870s.[2]

I will start with demographic data, which is crucial for understanding the availability of arms during the Industrial Revolution. The population in Britain and the rest of Europe grew before the Industrial Revolution. This growth was linked to the consumer revolution, proto-industry and trade.[3] The demographic regime of England remained unchanged between the sixteenth and mid-nineteenth centuries. However, there were significant differences in birth rates between the wealthy and the poor. The former had more children than the latter. Towns and rural areas had higher death rates, as did the poor.

The data do not support Wrigley and Schofield's assertion that increased wages and well-being led to higher rates of marriage and fertility. Wages, especially real wages, did not rise in the eighteenth century. They did not precede demographic changes; they followed them.[4] In particular, areas that underwent more rapid growth, such as Lancashire and Yorkshire, undoubtedly

---

[1] Crafts, *British Economy during the Industrial Revolution*; Feinstein and Pollard, *Studies in Capital Formation*; Allen, *The British Industrial Revolution in Global Perspective*; Findlay, O'Rourke, *Power and Plenty*.
[2] Crafts, *British Economy*; Williamson, "Why Was British Growth So Slow"; Harley, "British Industrialization before 1841"; Phyllis Deane, W. A. Coale, *British Economic Growth, 1688-1959* (Cambridge: Cambridge University Press, 1962); Stephen Broadberry, Bruce Campbell, Alexander Klein, Mark Overton, Bas van Leeuwen, *British Economic Growth, 1270-1870* (Cambridge: Cambridge University Press, 2015). For a reply: Nicholas Crafts, "Understanding Productivity Growth in the Industrial Revolution," *Economic History Review*, 74, 2 (2021): 309–338.
[3] Edward Anthony Wrigley, Robert Davies, Jim Oeppen, Roger S. Schofield, *English Population History from Family Reconstitution, 1580-1837* (Cambridge: Cambridge University Press, 1997).
[4] Pat Hudson, ed., *Regions and Industries: A Perspective on the Industrial Revolution in Britain* (Cambridge: Cambridge University Press, 1989).

experienced a faster rate of population growth.[5] Fertility increased across Britain, not just in areas with industrial employment opportunities.[6]

This leads us to a curious conundrum. If we consider that population was increasing and that the Industrial Revolution required more capital and less labor, then it would seem that labor should be in excess, as Marx argued. If this is the case, it would be interesting to understand why labor rules studied in Part I were so keen on putting as many people as possible at work, as if labor was scarce. Why were there so many legal constraints?

The main reason is that capital did not play quite the same role during the Industrial Revolution as we might have expected, while labor remained the most important factor of production. With regard to monetary capital, the initial industrial revolution necessitated relatively modest capital outlays while the advent of business banks was still some way off. Family and commercial credit were the most widespread sources, while the stock exchange and most complex forms of incorporation began to emerge during the second half of the nineteenth century and mostly in the twentieth century.[7] This scarcity of monetary capital helps us to gain a deeper understanding of the main forms and limitations of physical capital. It would be remiss not to mention that land was undoubtedly one of the most pervasive and influential forms of capital during this period. It is often thought that the privatization of the commons and the consequent proletarization of peasants were necessary preconditions for the emergence of capitalism. This view is held by many, including those with liberal, Marxist and current neo-institutionalist perspectives. However, it would be inaccurate to assume that the privatization of the commons was a strictly eighteenth-century phenomenon as these authors argue. In fact, it began in the early sixteenth century, but remained limited to such an extent that in 1750, 24 percent of English arable lands were still held in common.[8] It is also important to note that private property and large estates were relatively rare in the early nineteenth century, when family settlements and strong legal limitations on the sale of land were in place.[9]

Moreover, the role of enclosures has been the subject of much reflection and reconsideration. Robert Allen and Donald McCloskey have presented

---

[5] Inikori, *Africans and the Industrial Revolution*: 69–73.

[6] Marie B. Rowlands, "Continuity and Change in an Industrializing Society: The Case of the West Midlands Industries," in Pat Hudson, ed., *Regions and Industries: A Perspective on the Industrial Revolution in Britain* (Cambridge: Cambridge University Press, 1989): 103–131.

[7] Harris, *Industrializing English Law*; Philip Hoffman, Gilles Postel-Vinay, Jean-Laurent Rosenthal, *Priceless Markets* (Chicago: University of Chicago Press, 2000); Stanziani, *Rules of Exchange*; Timothy Guinnane, Ron Harris, Noemi Lamoreaux, Jean-Laurent Rosenthal, "Pouvoir et propriété dans l'entreprise," *Annales HSS*, 63, 1 (2008): 73–110.

[8] Allen, *Enclosure and the Yeoman*.

[9] Frances Michael Thompson, *English Landed Society in the Nineteenth Century* (London: Routledge, 1963).

evidence suggesting that, in Britain, output and productivity may have increased prior to the enclosure movement, which is thought to have begun in the sixteenth century. This perspective suggests that common lands may not have been entirely misguided in a context where productive risk was high and market development was limited.[10] Therefore, private ownership of land may not have been the sole driving force behind the agrarian revolution. Data indicates that open-field farmers were involved in a British agricultural revolution that took place before 1740.[11] Common fields were as efficient as, or perhaps even more efficient than, private land. The existence and survival of common fields was not the issue. It is therefore somewhat perplexing why common fields were converted into private property. If not for efficiency, then why?

Enclosure led to a significant increase in rents, with figures reaching 90 percent in Warwickshire, 150 percent in Leicester and 74 percent in Northamptonshire. In Oxford, the gains were even more significant, ranging from 100 to 400 percent.[12] On the whole, enclosures raised rents by around 40 percent. It is also worth noting that the interest cost of the capital expenditures required to move land from the common field to the private state was in the order of 25 to 35 percent of the rental value of common land circa 1800. Thus, privatization made only a modest contribution to the growth of agricultural productivity. Output and productivity rose before enclosures, since the sixteenth century and then again in the nineteenth century, and then only to a limited extent in the period 1650–1820 and even less between 1740 and 1800.[13] Ultimately, the net efficiency gain after the costs of conversion reached its maximum at approximately 3 or 4 percent.[14] If we consider that privatization did not account for agrarian growth, it would be interesting to understand what factors did.

It would be remiss of us not to give special attention to livestock, which plays a unique role in agrarian forms of capital. The abundance of livestock has often been considered a defining feature of the "West," particularly Britain, in comparison to other continents. Similarly, Britain's advancement in agricultural development within Europe has often been attributed to its livestock.[15]

---

[10] Allen, *Enclosure and the Yeoman*; Robert Allen, "Tracking the Agricultural Revolution in England," *Economic History Review*, LII, 2 (1999): 209–235; Donald McCloskey, "The Enclosure of Open Fields: Preface to a Study of Its Impact on the Efficiency of English Agriculture in the Eighteenth Century," *The Journal of Economic History*, 31, 1 (1972): 15–35.
[11] Allen, "Tracking the Agricultural Revolution."
[12] Arthur Young, *General Report on Enclosures* (London: British Library, 1808).
[13] Gregory Clark, "Agriculture and the Industrial Revolution,1750–1850," in Joel Mokyr, ed., *The British Industrial Revolution: An Economic Perspective* (Boulder: Westview Press, 1993): 227–266; Gregory Clark, "Commons Sense: Common Property Rights, Efficiency, and Institutional Change," *Journal of Economic History*, 58, 1 (1998): 73–102.
[14] Clark, "Commons Sense": 77.
[15] Broadberry and others, *British Economic Growth*; Michael Overton, *Agricultural Revolution in England* (Cambridge: Cambridge University Press, 1996).

Asian and African economic backwardness is explained, among other crucial variables, by the lack of livestock. Indeed, recent empirical analyses have shown that livestock densities in many parts of England were stable throughout the modern period up through the mid-nineteenth century.[16] The rise in livestock numbers in Britain does not fully account for the rise in yields that occurred before 1800.[17]

If not land or livestock, it would be interesting to consider other forms of capital; in particular, agrarian techniques and machines. A conventional interpretation underlines that technical change played a pivotal role in the British agrarian revolution of the eighteenth and nineteenth centuries.[18] The notion that high wages were essential to spur technological innovation, as espoused by Habakkuk and numerous others,[19] is predicated on a fallacious premise: Technical progress was essentially a matter of weighing equivalent options and that these decisions hinged on prices.[20] In fact, there is no evidence whatsoever that technical progress emerged as labor-saving in the eighteenth and early nineteenth centuries. First, the primary objective of innovation was to improve product quality or reduce capital expenditure, not labor.[21] Recent analyses confirm this conclusion: Labor and labor intensity are identified as the main source of agricultural growth before 1850, with physical capital playing a secondary role.[22] In Britain, technical progress accounted for only 15 percent of the increase in agricultural worker output between the mid-eighteenth and mid-nineteenth centuries. The rest was due to reduced leisure time and more intense work.[23] Until the machine age, the rise in productivity and growth in output depended more on the intensive use of known technology than on novel methods. The so-called new husbandry was not new at all.[24] In fact, it required more labor, not less.[25] Labor and labor intensity were the main source of agricultural growth before 1850, with physical capital playing a secondary role. Labor intensity in agriculture grew during the eighteenth century and its last quarter, as well as during the entire first half of the nineteenth century. Long after steam became the dominant form of power in manufacturing, farmers

---

[16] Allen, *Enclosure and the Yeoman*.
[17] Allen, "Tracking the Agricultural Revolution": 226.
[18] Eric Jones, *Agriculture and Industrial Revolution* (Oxford: Oxford University Press, 1974); Overton, *Agricultural Revolution*.
[19] Habakkuk, *American and British Technology*.
[20] Joel Mokyr, *The Lever of Riches* (Oxford: Oxford University Press, 1990): 165.
[21] MacLeod, *Inventing the Industrial Revolution*.
[22] George Grantham, "Agricultural Supply during the Industrial Revolution: French Evidence and European Implications," *Journal of Economic History*, 49, 1 (1989): 43–72; Giovanni Federico, *Feeding the World: An Economic History of Agriculture, 1800–2000* (Princeton, NJ: Princeton University Press, 2005).
[23] Grantham, "Agricultural Supply".
[24] Federico, *Feeding the World*.
[25] Grantham, "Agricultural Supply"; Allen, *Enclosure and the Yeoman*.

continued to rely on human, animal, wind and water power.[26] Labor-intensive techniques linked to the dissemination of knowledge and attractive markets (with increasing crop prices) remained dominant. This trend was not reversed until the last quarter of the nineteenth century, when agricultural prices fell and wages rose.[27]

Regional variations were considerable. Starting in the seventeenth century, the so-called pastoral belts, (i.e., Britain's south-western and western counties), became new areas for corn.[28] Over the course of the century, the western areas became the center of arable agriculture. A similar process took place in East Anglia. The major problem for most people involved in agriculture during this period was to extend the area cultivated and raise yields per acre. Labor per unit of output was not the primary concern, not only in Britain, but throughout Europe and the United States. Polish peasants in the Middle Ages required as much labor per bushel for these operations as American farmers in the early nineteenth century. The majority of the discrepancy between countries was not due to different techniques but rather to more intense labor (i.e., the greatest amount of work performed per day).[29]

If we accept that labor remained the main factor of production in agriculture, we must also consider its role in industry. Machines undoubtedly played a new role here, as conventionally argued. And yet, since the late 1970s, several analyses have shown that the rate of capital intensification in British industry was relatively limited until the mid-nineteenth century,[30] casting doubt on traditional views based on neoclassical models.[31] Feinstein asserts that the labor force grew by just under 1 percent annually from 1760 to 1800 and by slightly more than 1.5 percent from 1800 to 1860. It is clear that capital and labor grew at a similar rate from 1760 to 1830. There was no effective change in the capital/labor ratio during this period. The ratio did rise over the last three decades as capital per worker increased at a rate of about

---

[26] Patrick O' Brien, "Agriculture and the Industrial Revolution," *Economic History Review* 30, 1 (1977): 166–181; Gregory Clark, "Productivity Growth without Technical Change in European Agriculture before 1850," *The Journal of Economic History*, 47, 2 (June 1987): 419–432.

[27] Frances Michael Thompson, "The Second Agricultural Revolution, 1815–1880," *Economic History Review*, 21, 1 (1968): 62–77.

[28] Ann Kussmaul, *A General View of the Rural Economy of England, 1538–1840* (Cambridge: Cambridge University Press, 1990).

[29] Clark, "Productivity Growth." Against this, Grantham considers that differences were due to market power and not to labor intensity.

[30] Deane, Coale, *British Economic Growth*; Peter Temin, "Labor Scarcity and the Problem of American Industrial Efficiency in the 1850s," *Journal of Economic History*, 26, 3 (1966): 277–298.

[31] Kenneth Arrow, Henri Chenery, B. Minhas, and Robert Solow, "Capital-labor Substitution and Economic Efficiency," *Review of Economics and Statistics*, 43, 1 (1961): 225–250.

0.5 percent per year.[32] It was the annual household earnings, not the daily wages of individuals, that became the key variable. The participation of wives and children was crucial.[33]

De Vries' notion of an "industrious revolution" is the perfect explanation for this trend. The participation of all household members in the labor market produced rising incomes despite declining nominal (and sometimes real) individual hourly and daily wages. This, in turn, justified increased household spending, greater work effort and sustained high demand for labor before, during and after the First Industrial Revolution.[34] Despite severe criticism,[35] the evidence seems to support the thesis of the industrious revolution, and this is consistent with the fact that the rate of capital formation in Britain was relatively slow until the mid-nineteenth century. Up to this time, the rate of labor/capital increased, and this tendency was reversed no earlier than the mid-century for industry, even later in agriculture.[36]

Total Factor Productivity (TFP) data confirm that the difference between the rate of growth in output and aggregate inputs was real.[37] A number of scholars have made use of this measure; however, the conclusions they have reached vary significantly. For example, for the period 1700–1800, the rate of change in TFP in England has been estimated at 0.2 by Phyllis Deane and W. A. Cole and Nicholas Crafts, 0.6 by Allen and 0.0 by Gregory Clark. These same authors confidently estimate the TFP for the years 1800–1850 at 1.4, 0.50 and 0.60, respectively.[38] However, notwithstanding these discrepancies, there is one point of consensus among the scholars: Labor contributed to growth to an equivalent or greater extent than capital, at least until the 1830s (or the 1850s, according to the authors).[39] This prompts a conundrum: If labor was the

---

[32] Charles Feinstein, "Capital Formation in Great Britain," in Peter Mathias and Michael Postan, eds., *The Cambridge Economic History of Europe*, vol. VII: *The Industrial Economies: Capital, Labor and Enterprise*, (Cambridge: Cambridge University Press, 1978): 28–94.

[33] Jane Humphries, *Childhood and Child Labour in the British Industrial Revolution* (Cambridge: Cambridge University Press, 2011).

[34] de Vries, *The Industrious Revolution*.

[35] Robert Allen, J. L. Weisdorf, "Was There an Industrious Revolution Before the Industrial Revolution? An Empirical Exercise for England, 1300–1830," *Economic History Review*, 64, 3 (2011): 715–729. Broadberry and others, *British Economic Growth*.

[36] Crafts, *British Economy*; Williamson, "Why Was British Growth So Slow?"; Feinstein, Pollard, *Studies in Capital Formation*.

[37] The TFP analyses assume: prefect competition, constant returns to scale and constant factor shares – Cobb-Douglas production function.

[38] Allen, "Agriculture During the Industrial Revolution"; Gregory Clark, "Agriculture and the Industrial Revolution, 1750–1850," in Joel Mokyr, ed., *The British Industrial Revolution: An Economic Perspective* (Boulder: Westview Press, 1993): 227–266.

[39] On this topic we need to be careful. Labor intensification has been differently defined according to the authors: an increase in labor productivity; a growth of labor time; a growth of labor supply as compared to capital.

predominant factor of production in all sectors, including industry, services and agriculture, how was it distributed?

Peasants into Proletarians or Peasant-Workers?

Economic models supposing that economic actors have to choose between mutually exclusive forms of employment[40] are inadequate for understanding the period under investigation. In this period, pluri-activity was the norm. Before 1914, only Great Britain, Belgium and France saw a decline in agricultural employment; the decline did not start in the Great Britain until after 1850, or according to Clark, after 1869. In France and Belgium, it began after 1870. In the rest of Western Europe, it began only after 1918. The decline was not perceptible in the rest of Europe until after the Second World War.[41] The picture is quite different when expressed in relative terms. In this case, the percentage of agricultural employment declined in Britain in the sixteenth century, even though men already made up 55 percent of agricultural workers. However, it did not decline any further until the last quarter of the eighteenth century.[42]

The absolute number of workers employed in agriculture remained roughly constant between 1701 and 1831, and then increased until the 1870s. The number even rose slightly between 1801 and 1851 as new techniques in husbandry demanded more labor, not less.[43] Despite the percentage of the population employed in agriculture falling from 60 percent to 30 percent, agriculture did not retain more than a small portion of the increase in total labor supply that became available as a result of population growth in the countryside.[44] These figures do not reflect the reality of pluri-activity and continuous seasonal mobility between the town and the countryside. The statistical margins of error for large occupational groups such as agriculture, commerce and manufacturing trades in mid-nineteenth century censuses are probably within the range of 40 percent to 66 percent.[45]

This was so because, due to the persistent need for labor in agriculture, dual employment (rural and urban) was the rule until the mid-nineteenth century. Most people still found it convenient to maintain dual residency in order to

---

[40] Broadberry and others, *British Economic Growth*: chapter 8.3. Jan Lucassen, ed., *Wage and Currency* (Bern: Peter Lang, 2008). Lucassen, *The Story of Work*.
[41] Federico, *Feeding the World*: 57.
[42] Clark, *Agriculture and the Industrial Revolution*, table 3.
[43] Charles Timmer, "The Turnip, the New Husbandry, and the English Agricultural Revolution," *Quarterly Journal of Economics*, LXXXIII, 3 (1969): 375–395.
[44] O'Brien, "Agriculture and the Industrial Revolution".
[45] Peter Lindert and Jeffrey Williamson, "Revising England's Social Tables, 1688–1867," *Explorations in Economic History*, 19, 4 (1982): 385–408; Peter Lindert and Jeffrey Williamson, "English Workers' Living Standards During the Industrial Revolution: A New Look," *Economic History Review*, 36, 1 (1983): 1–25.

move seasonally between the countryside and the town.[46] The critical factor affecting the proportion of families assigned to agriculture was the degree of seasonality of labor requirements. Seasonal workers were necessary, but only for short intervals of time. Male employment in agriculture peaked in the summer and reached a low point in winter throughout the eighteenth and well into the mid-nineteenth century. In contrast, women moved from a seasonal work situation similar to that of men to increasingly taking part in spring farming activities associated with livestock.[47] The lack of labor in town was also caused by the persistence of proto-industrial activities in the countryside. Rural workers were often involved in proto-industry when they were not in the fields. This was not only common practice in skilled industries such as pottery but also in textiles.[48] Cottage industries could and did compete with technically more efficient manufactories because they were more effective at harnessing a part-time or off-peak workforce whose opportunity cost was low. This trend was unquestionably stronger in textiles than in other industries such as metallurgy, where stable workforces and increasing mechanization had existed since the early nineteenth century.

In sum, the leading industries of the First Industrial Revolution were, in fact, much more labor-intensive than is usually assumed. The Second Industrial Revolution saw a further acceleration in mechanization and the advent of new, highly capital-intensive industries. This helps explain the main features of labor contracts previously discussed. Masters and authorities sought to retain workers from moving back and forth between the countryside and the town. The requirement of advanced notice was designed to ensure that employers had sufficient time to replace departing workers and avoid sudden stoppages. However, the frequency of departures, mostly in connection with the harvest, also proves that the law had little impact on workers' behavior. Masters therefore sought alternative solutions, such as allowing workers to sublet looms and tools and find a substitute.[49] This solution was particularly widespread in textile mills, where family members who received a family wage usually worked small spinning mules.[50] While some firms in Lancashire had developed alternative

---

[46] Kenneth L. Sokoloff and David Dollar, "Agricultural Seasonality and the Organization of Manufacturing in Early Industrial Economies: The Contrast Between England and the United States," *The Journal of Economic History*, 57, 2 (1997): 288–321.

[47] K. D. M. Snell, "Agricultural Seasonal Unemployment, the Standard of Living, and Women's Work in the South and East, 1690–1860," *The Economic History Review*, 34, 3 (1981): 407–437; Sara Horrell and Jane Humphries, "Women's Labour Force Participation and the Transition to the Male-Breadwinner Family, 1790–1865," *The Economic History Review*, 48, 1 (1995): 89–117.

[48] Charles Sabel, Jonathan Zeitlin, eds., *World of Possibilities* (Cambridge: Cambridge University Press, 1997).

[49] Richard Biernacki, *The Fabrication of Labor* (Berkeley: University of California Press, 1995).

[50] Michael Huberman, *Escape from the Market: Negotiating Work in Lancashire* (Cambridge: Cambridge University Press, 1996).

strategies of "fair wages" since the mid-nineteenth century, they were a tiny minority. Most masters and employers openly defied wage laws, even resorting to criminal punishment to obtain the required amount of labor.

The problem was that rural employers made use of similar arguments: They sought to obtain a one-year contract from servants in husbandry, and the yearly fairs in the fall – just before ploughing – were an important moment of signature, during which mobility was allowed. Another moment was just before the great summer works. The choice of these periods also gave the master a great bargaining power over the servants: By starting the contract at the end of this slack period, the servant was the party that paid first, and the master was the party that paid last (providing food and shelter through the slack months). Yet this proved to be insufficient and many working people left during the slack periods to go to town, or even in the peak periods to work for masters who offered higher wages. This problem could be solved: During the First Industrial Revolution, many firms shut in the summer; some found substitute workers that the servants provided themselves to replace them at the loom. But, in other seasons, in principle, there would be enough labor. This was not always the case, and masters were highly concerned by poaching (other masters stealing their workers) as judicial archives and new legislation adopted during this period testify. This is where labor time became relevant.

Labor Time and Wages

The work of E. P. Thompson and the literature of the 1960s and 1970s posited that workers engaged in longer and more arduous workdays following the Industrial Revolution than they did prior to this period.[51] However, since the 1980s, quantitative methodologies have challenged this assertion, demonstrating the absence of empirical evidence to substantiate it, given the lack of direct data on working time until the 1850s.[52] In more recent times, a number of studies have revisited Thompson's argument by examining data from earlier periods. De Vries has put forth the argument that working hours must have been increasing rapidly in early modern Europe, as neither a rise in real wages nor capital-intensive innovations can account for the increased standards of consumption.[53] This argument aligns with the slow increase of capital and large-scale participation of labor in explaining British growth during the Industrial Revolution. Further confirmation can be found in judicial archives, which indicate that the length

---

[51] Edward P. Thompson, "Time, Work-discipline and Industrial Capitalism," *Past and Present*, 38, 1 (1967): 56–97.

[52] Joel Mokyr, ed., *The Economics of the Industrial Revolution* (Totowa: Rowman and Allanheld, 1985).

[53] De Vries, *The Industrious Revolution*; Douglas Reid, "The Decline of Saint Monday," *Past & Present*, 71, 1 (1976): 76–101; Douglas Reid, "Weddings, Weekdays, Work and Leisure in Urban England, 1791–1991," *Past & Present*, 153, 1 (1996): 135–163.

of the workday increased significantly during the eighteenth century and the first half of the nineteenth century.[54]

Rather than focusing on the daily wages of individuals, the analysis shifted to annual household earnings, which became the key variable. The labor of wives and children played a crucial role in this context. De Vries' concept of an "industrious revolution" provides a comprehensive explanation for this trend. It posits that all members of the household engaged in labor market activities, thereby enhancing the household's income, despite a decline in nominal (and in some cases, real) individual hourly and daily wages. The contribution of industrious family members thus accounts for the observed increases in budget expenditures, the growth in labor effort, and the persistent high demand for labor before, during, and after the First Industrial Revolution.[55]

Masters often had an incentive to extend the workday during periods of high demand in order to expedite the production and distribution of goods. Conversely, during periods of low demand, masters would often lay off workers or reduce their hours. As the pace of mechanization was in fact slower than is commonly portrayed in textbooks, the number of working hours increased, particularly in the textile mills.[56]

Consequently, until the middle of the nineteenth century in industry, and throughout most of this century in agriculture, the supply of labor increased, both in terms of the number of individuals and the amount of time devoted to work, up to a certain point in terms of productivity. Nevertheless, the average real income of wage earners remained stable until the late 1870s.[57] It is important to emphasize that this phenomenon was not limited to the industrial sector, but permeated the entire economic landscape,[58] particularly in agriculture and in domestic service.[59] The remuneration paid to domestic servants in rural England exhibited a modest increase between 1700 and 1860. However, this growth occurred at disparate rates, contingent upon the geographical region and the specific occupation of the servant in question. By 1851, the national census indicated that at least 24.5 percent of women over the age of 20 in

---

[54] Hans-Joachim Voth, "Time and Work in Eighteenth Century London," *Journal of Economic History*, 58, 1 (1998): 29–58; Hans-Joachim Voth, *Time and Work in England 1750–1830* (Oxford: Oxford University Press, 2000).

[55] De Vries, *The Industrious Revolution*.

[56] Eric Hopkins, "Working Hours and Conditions During the Industrial Revolution, a Reappraisal," *Economic History Review*, 35, 1 (1982): 52–67.

[57] Robert Allen, "Pessimism Preserved. Real Wages in the British Industrial Revolution," *Oxford University Department of Economics Working Paper* 314, 2007.

[58] Gregory Clark, "Farm Wages and Living Standards in the Industrial Revolution: England, 1670–1869," *Economic History Review*, 54, 3 (2001): 477–505; Gregory Clark, "The Long March of History: Farm Wages, Population, and Economic Growth, England 1209–186," *Economic History Review*, 60, 1 (2007): 97–135.

[59] Jacob Field, "Domestic Service, Gender, and Wages in Rural England, 1700–1860," *Economic History Review*, 66, 1 (2013): 249–272.

employment were engaged in domestic service, compared with 1.5 percent of men. The majority of servants, particularly those employed as maids, did not experience a notable increase in their wages.

Globally, between 1778 and 1857, the increase in real weekly earnings, allowing for unemployment and short-time work, was less than 30 percent.[60] In general, the average real income of wage earners remained relatively stagnant for approximately 50 years, until the early 1830s. While there was some incremental improvement during this period, earnings subsequently declined during the cyclical depression of 1838–1842. Subsequently, by the mid-1840s, wages commenced an ascent; however, more substantial gains were not achieved until the 1860s. It was only after the post-1873 downturn in prices that average real earnings finally accelerated.[61] A detailed quantitative investigation into the fields of agriculture and services yielded comparable results, particularly with regard to the experiences of women.[62] Therefore, real wages did not benefit from economic growth. What factors can be identified as responsible for this phenomenon?

A conventional answer accepted the basic explanation in terms of supply and demand; namely, that labor was inexpensive because it was abundant. However, our findings challenge this argument, at least in its general terms. Labor was, in fact, scarce and in high demand, although the specific tasks and skills required of workers and the nature of the activities counted. It seems more appropriate to focus on the role of institutions as discussed in Part I. As has been demonstrated, there was no clear break in coercive labor rules and practices between the eighteenth and nineteenth centuries. The evidence presented here challenges the conventional interpretation of coercion, which is shared by Adam Smith and liberal thinkers as well as Marx and socialists. According to them, physical and legal coercion preceded monetary sanctions; it was typical of pre modern areas. They were wrong; indeed, pecuniary and non-pecuniary pressures were not mutually exclusive, but rather complementary tools over a long period of time (the last quarter of the nineteenth century in Western Europe and much later in other parts of the world).[63] Those in positions of authority, including masters, heads of households, parishes and traders-manufacturers also had a vested interest in maintaining control over the laboring population. Rules provided masters with a means of ensuring the

---

[60] Charles H. Feinstein, "Pessimism Perpetuated: Real Wages and the Standard of Living in Britain during and after the Industrial Revolution," *The Journal of Economic History*, 58, 3 (1998): 625–658.
[61] Allen, "Pessimism Preserved".
[62] Field, "Domestic Service".
[63] Richard Rudolph, ed., *The European Peasant, Family, and Society: Historical Studies* (Liverpool: Liverpool University. Press, 1995); Gay Gullickson, "Agriculture and Cottage Industry: Redefining the Causes of Proto-Industrialization," *The Journal of Economic History*, 43, 4 (1983): 831–850.

desired labor force, particularly during periods of labor market volatility. It was not fortuitous that criminal penalties were most frequently enforced in regions and sectors where mobility was greater and during periods of economic growth. From this perspective, contract enforcement served as a substitute for higher wages, with masters utilizing it as a means of securing labor as long as they were able to do so.

However, this system also exhibited inherent limitations. While coercion did enhance labor effort, production and overall profits, it simultaneously constrained labor productivity. The use of coercion and the labor-intensive path proved to be a profitable strategy, yet it permitted only a relatively slow rate of growth.[64]

Recent estimates aimed at demonstrating the long-term impressive growth of the British economy contest the revisionist approach to it. However, even these estimates show that the annual rate of growth of agricultural output was far from impressive. For the period 1750–1800, the rate was 0.93 percent; for 1750–1800: 0.93 percent; 1800–1830: 0.77 percent; and 1830–1860: 0.85 percent.[65] Between 1740 and 1800, agricultural output increased by only 10 percent. Food consumption per person did increase in the second quarter of the nineteenth century, but it did not exceed sixteenth-century levels until the very end of the period.[66] This indicates that the expansion of agriculture was a gradual process that spanned several centuries and remained relatively limited until the 1830s.

A comparable trend was observed in industrial output. According to a highly optimistic calculation, the total output of the industrial sector (1700 = 100) reached 132 in the 1750s, 271 in 1800 and then exhibited minimal growth until the end of the 1820s, before experiencing a significant surge to 1,163 in the 1850s.[67] If we disaggregate these large spans of time, the yearly rate of growth of the British industrial output can be calculated as follows: 1700–1761: 0.71; 1760–1780: 1.96; 1801–1830: 2.78; 1831–1870: 3.06 (see Table 5.1).[68]

When we consider the entire economy, we find that the rate of growth of the GDP (percent per year) was: 0.3 between 1700 and 1760; 0.17 between 1760 and 1800; 0.52 between 1800 and 1830; and 1.98 between 1830 and 1870.[69]

In summary, despite the discrepancies between the various statistical evaluations, the evidence suggests that agricultural, industrial and economic progress was relatively slow during the eighteenth century and until the 1830s. This is

---

[64] Crafts, *British Economy*; Jeffrey Williamson, "Why Was British Growth"; Feinstein and Pollard, *Studies in Capital Formation*.
[65] Broadberry and others, *British Economic Growth*, table 3.16.
[66] Allen, "Tracking the Agrarian Revolution".
[67] Broadberry and others, *British Economic Growth*, table 4.03.
[68] Crafts, *British Economy*; Harley, "British Industrialization".
[69] Crafts, *British Economy*.

Table 5.1 *British annual growth rates of output, output per worker and productivity*

Period	Productivity	Net output (percent)	Net output per worker (percent)
1525–1605	−0.06	0.31	−0.32
1605–1745	0.15	0.24	0.11
1745–1795	−0.12	−0.08	−0.21
1795–1865	0.44	0.73	0.30
1865–1905	0.39	0.26	0.67

Sources: Elaboration from B. R. Mitchell, *British Historical Statistics* (Cambridge: Cambridge University Press, 1988); Clark, *The Agricultural Revolution*: 22.

evident from the analysis of key indicators such as labor productivity, yields, GDP and GDP per capita. These values are consistent with the qualitative indicators and descriptions from historical sources, which indicate that progress was gradual, labor remained the primary factor of production and its intensification increased. This process was accompanied by an improved division of labor (Smithian growth) and the introduction of minor yet significant innovations in tools. This resulted in the labor-intensive path of growth that we had previously outlined. There was an increase in labor productivity during the seventeenth and eighteenth centuries; however, the rate of growth declined at the turn of the eighteenth and nineteenth centuries and at least until the 1830s.[70] This assessment is consistent with the thesis of the Industrious Revolution and with classical political economy, which posits that the rate of growth will diminish due to a lack of capital-intensive technical progress (Malthus), a lack of land, high rents (Malthus, Ricardo) and protectionism.

Nevertheless, this trajectory may have precipitated a collapse in British living standards (Malthus, Ricardo) and even the collapse of the entire economy (Marx). However, this was not the case. The rate of growth was relatively modest up to the 1830s, yet it did not decline. What, then, were the reasons for this? The answer can be found in the impact of international trade on the one hand and the role of slavery, American resources and markets on the other. These factors all contributed to the enhancement of British growth.

---

[70] Broadberry and others, *British Economic Growth*. See also Robert Allen, "The High Wage Economy and the Industrial Revolution: A Restatement," *Economic History Review*, 68, 1 (2015): 1–22.

6

International Trade, Slavery and the Industrial Revolution

The British Industrial Revolution was supported by international trade, innovation and the domestic market.¹ But it is also important to acknowledge the role of slavery in this context.² The proportion of British GDP accounted for by exports was 8.4 percent in 1700, 14.6 percent in 1760, 9.4 percent in 1780, 15.7 percent in 1801, 14.3 percent in 1831 and 19.6 percent in 1851. The proportion of industrial exports in the total export market was 18 percent in 1760, 25 percent in 1780, 40 percent in 1801 and 49 percent in 1831. The growth in exports was responsible for 21 percent of the overall increase in GDP between 1780 and 1801.³ It is against this background that the role of colonial products and slavery must be considered.⁴ In 1944, Eric Williams advanced the thesis that slavery financed the Industrial Revolution and that its abolition contributed directly to the transformation of capitalism.⁵ Subsequently, numerous scholars have engaged in this discourse. One interpretation posits that the ascendance of the Atlantic and the slave trade were a consequence of, rather than a cause of, British economic growth.⁶ In a recent publication, McCloskey presents a compelling argument challenging the conventional wisdom regarding the role of slavery and the slave trade in the Atlantic economy. She posits that the fundamental driver of Britain's Industrial Revolution was not cotton, but rather the broader context of democratic governance, innovation and

---

[1] David Richardson, "The Slave Trade, Sugar, and British Economic Growth, 1748–1776," *Explorations in Economic History*, 17, 4 (1987): 739–769; Eltis, Engerman, "The Importance of Slavery and Slave Trade to Industrializing Britain."

[2] Among the most recent approaches seeking to conciliate all these variables: Findlay and O'Rourke, *Power and Plenty*; Nuala Zahedieh, *Capital and the Colonies: London and the Atlantic Economy, 1600–1700* (Cambridge: Cambridge University Press, 2010); Burnard, Riello, "Slavery and the New History of Capitalism"; Maxine Berg and Pat Hudson, *Slavery, Capitalism, and the Industrial Revolution* (Cambridge: Polity Press, 2023).

[3] Crafts, *British Economy*: 131.

[4] Findlay, O' Rourke, *Power and Plenty*: 334.

[5] Eric Williams, *Capitalism and Slavery* (Chapel Hill: University of North Carolina Press, 1944).

[6] Knick Harley, "Slavery, the British Atlantic Economic and the Industrial Revolution," University of Oxford Discussion Papers in Economic History 113, 2013, www.nuff.ox.ac.uk/economics/history/paper113/harley113.pdf

domestic markets.⁷ Some other scholars posited that Britain would have found uncultivated land and resources outside of the Americas by other means, even in the absence of slavery.⁸

Klas Rönnbäck, however, argued that the impact of slavery and the slave trade on British economic growth was significant and increased over the eighteenth and nineteenth centuries.⁹ In a recent contribution to the debate, Berg and Hudson suggested that slavery contributed to innovation in industrial organization, labor performance, consumption style, etc.¹⁰ Burnard and Riello advanced an intermediate orientation, proposing that slave cotton expanded only after the Industrial Revolution had taken place.¹¹ To fully assess the veracity of this proposition, it is essential to conduct a comprehensive examination of the relevant arguments. These include an analysis of the number of slaves, the profitability of the slave trade and of the plantations, the role of slaves in capital accumulation in Britain and the United States, and finally, the role of cotton in the Industrial Revolution.

The Slave Trade

There is room for debate on a number of topics, including the profitability of slavery and its role in the Industrial Revolution. However, there is no doubt that the slave trade expanded significantly between the sixteenth and nineteenth centuries, and that Britain played a crucial role in it.¹² In total, more than twelve million individuals were enslaved and transported across the Atlantic Ocean between the sixteenth and nineteenth centuries. As late as 1650, the total number of Africans in English America was only 17,000, representing a mere 2.5 percent of the total population. The majority of Africans

---

⁷ Deidre McCloskey, *Bourgeois Dignity. Why Economics Can't Explain the Modern World* (Chicago: The University of Chicago Press, 2011).
⁸ Gregory Clark, Kevin H. O'Rourke, and Alan M. Taylor, "Made in America? The New World, the Old, and the Industrial Revolution," *American Economic Review*, 98, 2 (2008): 523–528; C. Nick Harley, "Slavery, the British Atlantic Economy, and the Industrial Revolution," in Adrian Leonard and David Pretel, eds., *The Caribbean and the Atlantic World Economy: Circuits of Trade, Money and Knowledge, 1650–1914* (Basingstoke: Palgrave Macmillan, 2015): 161–83; David Eltis, Pieter C. Emmer and Frank D. Lewis, "More than Profits? The Contribution of the Slave Trade to the Dutch Economy: Assessing Fatah-Black and Van Rossum," *Slavery & Abolition*, 37, 4 (2016): 724–735.
⁹ Klass Rönnbäck, "On the Economic Importance of the Slave Plantation Complex to the British Economy During the Eighteenth Century: A Value-Added Approach," *Journal of Global History*, 13, 3 (2018): 308–327.
¹⁰ Berg, Hudson, *Slavery, Capitalism, and the Industrial Revolution*.
¹¹ Burnard, Riello, "Slavery and the New History of Capitalism."
¹² www.slavevoyages.org/tast/assessment/estimates.faces; David Eltis, Stephen D. Behrendt, David Richardson and Herbert S. Klein, *The Trans-Atlantic Slave Trade: A Database on CD-ROM* (Cambridge and New York: Cambridge University Press, 1999)

resided on the Caribbean islands. In 1650, the number of Africans residing on the mainland was approximately 2,000. The number of Africans enslaved and exported across the Atlantic Ocean increased steadily throughout the sixteenth century, reaching 328,000, and then again in the seventeenth century, reaching 1.3 million. This figure reached a peak of 6 million in the eighteenth century, before declining to 3.6 million in the nineteenth century, which marked the end of the Atlantic slave trade.[13] In the eighteenth century, the British were responsible for transporting approximately 40.5 percent of enslaved individuals, followed by the Portuguese (31 percent), the French (18.1 percent), the Dutch (5.7 percent) and North Americans (3.4 percent). In the period between Britain's prohibition of the Atlantic slave trade in 1807 and Brazil's final abolition of slavery in 1888, the Portuguese maintained a dominant position in the Atlantic slave trade. The primary regions from which slaves were exported were Angola and Congo, followed by the Bight of Benin, the Gold Coast, the Bight of Biafra and Senegambia. It is important to note that these figures do not include slaves embarked in the Indian Ocean and shipped to the Americas (see hereafter). Moreover, given the extensive existing literature on the subject, there is no need to provide a detailed account of the history of slavery and transatlantic slavery. Instead, an evaluation of the profitability of this trade is required.

The evaluation of profits derived from the slave trade is a challenging undertaking for a number of reasons. Primarily, it is necessary to ascertain the number of slaves embarked on each vessel, the price per slave and the associated costs. To obtain a more accurate picture of the profitability of the slave trade, it is necessary to supplement the ship ledgers with traders' accounting books, including details of insurance costs, freight and so on. It has been estimated that an error of approximately 5 percent in the evaluation of sales (quantity and prices) results in an error of approximately 55 percent. In addition to the typical 5 percent margin of error in cost estimation (slaves, ships, insurance, freight), net profits are likely to have been underestimated or overestimated by a factor of 100 percent.[14] Finally, profitability was contingent upon the return voyage or, more problematically, the triangular trade, which involved at least two additional voyages by the same vessel. In order to assess the profitability of the triangular trade, it is necessary to have data regarding the costs and revenues associated with each voyage.

---

[13] David Eltis and David Richardson, *Extending the Frontiers: Essays on the New Transatlantic Slave Trade Database* (New Haven, CT: Yale University Press, 2008); Eltis et al., *The Trans-Atlantic Slave Trade*.

[14] Daudin, "Profitability of Slavery and Long-Distance Trading in Context"; Guillaume Daudin, *Commerce et prospérité: la France au XVIIIe siècle* (Paris: PUPS, 2005); Guillaume Daudin, "Empires et économie," http://spire.sciencespo.fr/hdl:/2441/5l6uh8o gmqildh09h4dqk0kai/resources/empireseteconomieversionpreliminaire.pdf; Guillaume Daudin, "Comment calculer les profits de la traite?" *Outre-mer*, 89, 336–7 (2002): 43–62.

These uncertainties help to explain why each of the many historians involved in this debate over decades has produced their own weighting and correction of the data, resulting in a multitude of disparate results. For instance, in his writings on the slave trade, Williams occasionally discussed individual ships and their voyages with enslaved people, yet at other times, he drew general conclusions about the profitability of the slave trade.[15] His data were subjected to criticism by several parties, who argued that he had underestimated costs. Richardson posited that the rate of profit in the slave trade was 4 percent to 5 percent. From this figure, he deducted the contribution of the slave trade to British capital formation, which he attributed primarily to domestic demand.

Stanley Engerman adopted a macroeconomic approach, recognizing that it was not feasible to evaluate the profits from each individual voyage, let alone the reinvestment of those profits in industrial activities. Accordingly, the pertinent inquiry was: What percentage of British profits were derived from the slave trade?[16]

It is worth noting that this question does not include the Keynesian multiplier effect of the slave trade, which is challenging to evaluate. However, it is essential to consider this effect in any analysis of the economic impact of the slave trade. This implies that the cascade effects on disparate areas, industries, activities and the consumption of the entire economy were not incorporated into the assessments of slavery and the associated discourse. In light of these constraints, we may examine Engerman's solution. He multiplied the number of enslaved individuals transported to obtain their average price, then deducted the cost of the voyage and insurance. He concluded that the rate of profit in this trade was not significantly different from that observed in other trades. In 1770, the profits derived from the slave trade constituted 0.54 percent of the British national income, 7.8 percent of the total investment and 38.9 percent of the total commercial and industrial investment. The contribution of the slave trade to capital formation in Britain between the years 1688 and 1800 was found to be between 2.4 percent and 10.8 percent. This conclusion supported Williams' thesis and was further corroborated by the works of Inikori, Barbara Solow,[17] and William Darity, who posited that the rate of profit in the slave trade was as high as 17 percent.[18] This indicates that the slave trade between the 1660s and the end of the eighteenth century constituted a pivotal element in the

---

[15] Williams, *Capitalism and Slavery*.
[16] Engerman, "The Slave Trade."
[17] Joseph Inikori, "Market Structures and the Profits of the British African Trade in the Late Eighteenth Century," *Journal of Economic History*, 41, 4 (1981): 745–776; Barbara Solow, "Caribbean Slavery and British Growth: The Eric Williams Hypothesis," *Journal of Development Economics*, 17, 4 (1985): 99–115.
[18] William Darity, "The Number Game and the Profitability of the British Trade in Slaves," *Journal of Economic History*, 45, 3 (1985): 693–703; William Darity, "Profitability of the British Trade in Slaves Once Again," *Explorations in Economic History*, 26, 3 (1989): 380–384.

financing of the English and later British economy. Nevertheless, before corroborating this conclusion, it is imperative to incorporate not only the profits derived from the slave trade but also those derived from slave labor into our analysis. It is therefore necessary to construct a clear timeline in order to distinguish between the different forms of slavery, namely that of the sugar plantations and that of the cotton plantations.

The Sugar Contribution

The global economy of Caribbean sugar was a complex system in which Asia provided the original sugar cane and a portion of the supply, Africa supplied labor and other food crops were indigenous to the islands.[19] North America contributed fish, grain, building materials and livestock, while Europe provided managers, capital, technology and manufactured goods.[20] Nevertheless, despite the global nature of the chain, the technological possibilities available at the time of the sugar boom were relatively limited. The basic unit of heavy equipment on the plantation remained the crude cane-crushing mill, which was powered by animals, wind or water. The utilization of steam and mechanical energy was not widespread until the latter part of the nineteenth century. The distribution of rainfall had a greater impact on the annual production routine than any other factor.[21] The planting of cuttings from the tops of canes was accomplished through two primary methods: trenching and hoeing. Trenching entailed the excavation of lengthy trenches and the interment of a double row of cane cuttings, which were subsequently covered with soil. By the early eighteenth century, a new system had been introduced, consisting of excavating holes five or six inches deep and five feet square. This method was designed with the objective of conserving topsoil. The practice of hoe-farming was persistently critiqued by agronomists and abolitionists. However, those who sought to introduce plows were typically disappointed. Local cattle were unable to effectively pull plows through heavy soil or on hilly terrain. Additionally, plowing proved to be less efficient than hoeing in preparing the seed bed and distributing fertilizer.[22]

[19] For a recent synthesis: Bosma, *The World of Sugar*; Ulbe Bosma, Juan Giusti-Cordero, Roger Knights, eds., *Sugarland Revisited, Sugar Colonialism in Asia and the Americas, 1800–1940* (New York: Berghahn, 2007).

[20] Sidney Mintz, *Sweetness and Power: The Place of Sugar in Modern History* (New York: Penguin Books, 1986).

[21] Michael Craton, James Walvin, *A Jamaican Plantation: the History of Worthy Park, 1670–1970* (Toronto: University of Toronto Press, 1970); James Walvin, *Searching for the Invisible Man: Slaves and Plantation Life in Jamaica* (Cambridge, Mass: Harvard University Press, 1978).

[22] Ira Berlin, Philip Morgan, eds., *Cultivation and Culture: Labor and the Shaping of Slave Life in the Americas* (Charlottesville: University Press of Virginia, 1993).

6 SLAVERY AND THE INDUSTRIAL REVOLUTION

With the growing recognition of the comparative advantage of cane sugar, there was a shift towards monoculture production. This trend was accompanied by a reorganization of labor, whereby enslaved individuals armed with machetes harvested the ripened canes. The canes were initially cut close to the root and stripped of leaves, then cut into shorter pieces. They were subsequently gathered into bundles, tied with cane tops and transported to the mill. The capacity of the mill was the determining factor in the quantity of canes that could be harvested at any given time.[23] Subsequently, the cane juice was boiled and clarified. The slave who oversaw these operations was known as "the boiler," and his expertise and decision-making abilities often determined whether the venture would be profitable or not.[24] Cane crops could be harvested for up to ten to fifteen years before new planting was required. However, over time, the soil lost its fertility, necessitating the use of fertilizers.

In light of the gradual evolution of techniques and the necessity for control of labor, it is evident that the initial use of white indentured labor was a strategic decision. As sugar production increased, the reliance on African slaves became a significant factor in the labor force. In Barbados during the 1620s, the population was comprised of 2,000 individuals who had entered into indentured servitude and 200 enslaved people.[25] In the 1650s, the number of slaves had reached approximately 20,000, compared to 8,000 indentured immigrants. The number of slaves rose to 50,000 in 1666, primarily imported by Dutch merchants, and by 1770, there were 75,334.[26] However, the mortality rate was significant, reaching approximately 5 percent on the island (not including the Middle Passage) during the early eighteenth century. It subsequently declined, partly due to planters' gradual shift in perspective, whereby they recognized that providing better nourishment and reproductive support to existing slaves was more profitable than purchasing new slaves.[27]

In 1661, the population of Jamaica was comprised of approximately 3,000 white immigrants and 514 enslaved individuals. In 1673, despite the establishment of the Royal African Company for the purpose of trading slaves, the census recorded a total of 7,768 whites and 9,504 Africans.[28] From 1673 to 1708,

---

[23] Roderick A. McDonald ed., *Caribbean Accounts: Essays on the British West Indies and the Atlantic Economy* (Kingston: University of the West Indies, 1996).
[24] Eric Williams, *Capitalism and Slavery* (Chapel Hill: University of North Carolina Press, 1944): 115.
[25] Gary Puckrein, *Little England: Plantation Society and Anglo-Barbadian Politics, 1626–1700* (New York: New York University Press, 1984): 31.
[26] *British Parliamentary Papers*, 1790, 29: 697–8.
[27] TNA CO 1/43, n. 37. J. Harry Bennett, *Bondsmen and Bishops, Slavery and Apprenticeship on the Codrington Plantation of Barbados, 1710–1838* (Berkeley: University of California Press, 1958).
[28] Bryan Edwards, *The History, Civil and Commercial of the British Colonies in the West Indies* (Edinburgh: Mundell, 1798), vol. 1: 232.

an additional 1,467 slaves were imported to Jamaica (33,184 in Barbados).[29] Similarly, as in Barbados, the escalation in the price of slaves in the British West Indies throughout the eighteenth century (from 10–14 pounds sterling at the turn of the century to 30–40 by the mid-eighteenth century)[30] prompted planters to improve the treatment of their slaves.[31]

Despite its small size, Barbados exhibited the profitability of sugar plantations. It benefited from a favorable environment but suffered from competition between its major English owners, namely the Earl of Pembroke and the Earl of Carlisle.[32] The expansion of the Barbados sugar plantations continued unabated despite the civil war in England. In 1655, approximately 7,787 tons of sugar were exported to England, with an estimated value of approximately 380,000 pounds.[33] In 1643, the Assembly of Barbados enacted a resolution declaring that henceforth, no rent would be paid to plantation owners in England. Additionally, planters were opposed to Britain's monopoly on trade and sought to maintain their trade relations with the Dutch. In order to achieve this objective, the Barbados planters formed an alliance with those in Britain who supported the Parliamentary cause against the Crown.[34] The Restoration resulted in the expulsion of planters who had supported the Parliamentary cause. In addition, the Embargo Act of 1650 and the Navigation Act of the following year re-established England's monopoly on trade, a status that was subsequently confirmed by further legislation in 1660 and 1663. In consequence, English manufacturers were accorded preferential treatment, Crown revenues increased, and the profits of English middlemen and shippers were also enhanced. At the time, this situation was particularly challenging for Barbados planters to accept, given that England re-exported two-thirds of the sugar.

The initial settlers lacked substantial financial resources. The transition to cane sugar production necessitated the consolidation of estates, as a consistent level of fixed capital was indispensable. This resulted in a corresponding increase in the importation of slaves. Up through the mid-seventeenth century, when sugar production was diversified and extensive, the majority of planters were heavily indebted to merchants. Sources from the period offer insights into the financial aspects of plantation life, including assessments of the costs, profits and debts of the planters. In Barbados at the conclusion of

---

[29] BL IOR Cal.S.P.Col., 1669–1674; TNA CO 140/2, 1673 census in Jamaica; the Barbados census of 1676 is summarized in TNA CO 318/2/115.
[30] *British Parliamentary Papers*, 1789, 36, n. 646a part 4.
[31] BPP 1789, 36, 646 part 4, Barbados. Also: Hector McNeill, *Observations on the Treatment of Negroes in the Island of Jamaica* (London: G.G.J. and J. Robinson, No. 25, Pater-Noster-Row, and J. Gore, 1788).
[32] See for instance: TNA CO 152/14; 152/13.
[33] Dunn, *Sugar and Slaves*: 87.
[34] Robert Brenner, *Merchants and Revolution: Commercial Change, Political Conflicts and London's Oversea Traders, 1550–1653* (London: Verso, 1983).

the seventeenth century, the cost of slaves constituted between one-third and two-thirds of the total expenditure. Depreciation costs were considerable, particularly when the mortality rate of slaves was approximately 5 percent per year, in addition to the corrosion of metals (hoes) in tropical conditions. It was challenging to reduce these costs, and medical care was also costly. Overall, profits were highly unstable and fluctuated in accordance with the size of the estate. Consequently, it was unsurprising that Barbados plantations became highly concentrated at the turn of the seventeenth to the eighteenth century. As the number of small planters declined, disparities between the few remaining white planters and their enslaved labor force intensified. In 1680, planters with sixty or more slaves constituted 6.9 percent of the total number and owned 54.3 percent of the slaves. Over time, these figures continued to increase in favor of the larger planters. The practice of monoculture and estate consolidation increased significantly during the 1670s and 1680s. In 1673, fifteen of the seventy-four proprietors held less than 300 acres, twenty-four held between 300 and 399 acres, and only two held more than 900 acres. By 1780, 112 proprietors were cultivating estates of the same size, thirty-eight proprietors were cultivating estates of a similar size, and no one was cultivating estates of the same size.[35] By 1750, seventy-four proprietors, representing one-third of the families owning a sugar plantation, had acquired three or more estates, collectively controlling 56.9 percent of the total land. The same percentage of families were in possession of 52.5 percent of the mills.[36]

In Jamaica, the degree of estate concentration was even more pronounced. From 1670 to 1754, the number of landowners increased from 724 to 1,599. However, the number of landowners holding less than 100 acres decreased from 384 to 263, while the number of landowners holding more than 1,000 acres increased from forty-seven to 467. Within this latter group, the number of estates covering between 5,000 and 9,000 acres increased from two to fifty-two, and the number of estates between 10,000 and 23,000 acres increased from 0 to 9.[37] In 1754, there were 467 large planters, each owning more than 1,000 acres. Collectively, their plantations accounted for 77.8 percent of the land available for cultivation.[38] However, this process was not accompanied by an increase in capital but rather by a labor intensification. Indeed, the larger the estate, the greater the ratio of labor to capital.[39] This was because established planters had access to a skilled workforce, which was managed directly by

---

[35] TNA, CO 1/44, ff. 142–379. Richard Dunn, "The Barbados Census of 1680: Profile of the Richest Colony in English America," *William and Mary Quarterly*, 3rd series, 26, 1 (1969): 3–30.
[36] Williams, *Capitalism and Slavery*: 145.
[37] TNA CO 142/31, "A List of Landholders in the Island of Jamaica," December 31, 1754.
[38] Blackburn, *The Making of New World Slavery*: 406.
[39] Williams, *Capitalism and Slavery*, tables 10.3 and 10.4: 230–1.

overseers. Also, the skilled labor force was unable to unionize, thereby negating the necessity for mechanization.[40] Additionally, the enslaved population cultivated their own food, produced garments from the cloth they were given and manufactured their own household utensils. However, due to soil depletion, the planter faced the risk of having an excess of slaves and experiencing a significant decline in the value of the estate within the first two decades. This meant that high profits, which ranged from 8 percent to 10 percent depending on the year,[41] had to be balanced against a strong dependence on the merchants who were responsible for supplying the plantation and selling its products.

It is notable that the personal property inventories of the median Jamaican sugar estate, from 1771 to 1775, indicate the following values: The total value of slaves was 7,641 pounds sterling, livestock were valued at 1,380 and utensils at 340, resulting in a total value of 9,361 pounds for the estate. In contrast, the total value of the inventory of a medium-sized sugar plantation was 19,027 pounds sterling. The total value of the slaves, utensils and livestock was identical to that of the median estate (approximately 9,000 pounds). The discrepancy was in the value of the cultivated acres, which was 9,963.[42]

These dynamics were directly related to the island's ties with the British mainland. Caribbean planters exhibited considerable animosity towards prominent British landowners, whom they accused of exerting control over land ownership and political equilibrium in the colonial world. Additionally, Caribbean planters had highly contentious relationships with merchants, who exercised control over the trade of slaves, cotton and other commodities. Furthermore, the influence of merchants was undoubtedly a significant factor in the consolidation of estates in the Caribbean. During the initial six decades of the eighteenth century, planters and commission merchants endeavored to establish an accord. Such sentiments were espoused by elected parliamentarians and formal trade organizations.[43] These groups sought to reduce taxes on sugar and to secure free trade for their islands. They achieved some success in passing legislative acts in the 1730s and 1740s that were designed to enhance profits in the islands. It is therefore pertinent to inquire whether they in fact achieved their aim.

In 1740, the British and French Caribbean accounted for 70 percent of all sugar entering the North Atlantic market, rising to 80 percent by 1787. Together with Brazil, the Americas supplied the majority of Europe's sugar imports, with modest quantities arriving from Java, Ile Bourbon (Réunion Island) and the Atlantic islands.[44] Over time, there was an increase in the proportion of British

---

[40] Blackburn, *The Making of New World Slavery*: 415.
[41] James R. Ward, "The Profitability of Sugar Planting in the British West Indies, 1650–1834," *Economic History Review*, 31, 2 (1978): 197–213.
[42] Williams, *Capitalism and Slavery*, tables 10.3 and 10.4.
[43] TNA CO 137/32.
[44] Blackburn, *The Making of New World Slavery*: 403.

sugar imports retained for domestic consumption. This rose from 59.6 percent in 1775 to 85.2 percent in 1799, despite the fact that total imports almost doubled during this period.[45] In contrast, in 1775, France imported a lesser quantity of sugar (1,601 compared with 2,000 thousand cwt), yet retained only 37.4 percent.[46] This discrepancy can be partially attributed to the interconnection between tea and sugar consumption, which was significantly more prevalent in Britain than in France. Additionally, there were fewer disparities in real income in Britain, and its residents had greater access to sugar and colonial products. In the colonies, planters and merchants initially competed with one another but subsequently formed coalitions against Britain and its taxes. British sugar planters also benefited from an expanded and protected home market that was superior to the foreign market.[47] This is why the domestic market became increasingly important, whereas in France re-export was more profitable than direct import due to the country's limited domestic markets and heavy fiscal policies. In 1776, the ten British colonies exported 80,285 tons of sugar annually, while the three French colonies exported 77,923 tons. Saint-Domingue was the primary exporter, with a total of 61,247 tons, followed by Jamaica (36,021), Antigua and Cuba (approximately 10,000 each), Martinique and Guadeloupe (approximately 8,500 each) and Barbados (approximately 7,819).[48]

In Britain, the consumption of sugar and tea became so pervasive during the eighteenth century that by 1780, they had both attained the status of mass-consumption goods. At that juncture, Britain was importing 108,000 tons of sugar per annum, in comparison to 30,000 tons during the period between 1711 and 1720. Between the mid-1750s and the mid-1770s, the rate of consumption in England and Wales increased twenty-fold, while the population increased only from 4.5 to 7.5 million. During this same period, the percentage of re-exported sugar declined from approximately 40 percent to 10 percent of the total imports.[49] It is imperative to consider the phenomenon of re-exportation when analyzing the profitability of the sugar economy in the Caribbean. This phenomenon can be attributed, in part, to a relaxation of trade policies and a decline in the influence of merchants relative to that of planters. The merchants had endorsed the Navigation Acts and the monopoly, whereas the planters had argued in favor of free trade. During the initial period, the discrepancy between British prices and the international price of sugar facilitated fraud and illicit trade. However, as time progressed, the political influence of planters grew, leading to their acquisition of the right to trade colonies.

---

[45] BL add Mss 36/ 785; TNA CO 318/1.
[46] David MacPherson, *Annals of Commerce* (Edinburgh: Nichols, 1805), vol. 3: 583.
[47] Arthur L. Sinchcombe, *Sugar Island Slavery in the Age of Enlightenment. The Political Economy of the Caribbean World* (Princeton, NJ: Princeton University Press, 1995).
[48] Williams, *Capitalism and Slavery*, tables 6.1 and 6.2: 100–1.
[49] TNA, CO 318/1 (customs); Williams, *Capitalism and Slavery*, table 2.1: 22.

Consequently, re-export was reduced. Additionally, the combination of rising income levels, evolving consumer preferences and the impact of military conflicts and trade restrictions (such as the War of 1739–1748 and the Seven Years' War of 1756–1763) that limited the potential for re-export also contributed to this outcome.

The sugar islands in the Caribbean continued to feature large estates[50] with considerable profits until the abolition of slavery.[51] Beginning in 1726–1728, the annual average value of commodity exports from the British West Indies was £1,594, while the annual average value of imports was £1,023. In the subsequent period, from 1748–1750, the annual average value of exports was £2,068, while the annual average value of imports was £1,417. Finally, in the period from 1773–1774, the annual average value of exports was £5,197, while the annual average value of imports was £3,151. The primary destinations for exports were Britain, the North American colonies and Africa, while imports originated from these same regions. Before reaching a conclusion regarding the profitability of the slave trade and slavery and their contribution to British growth, it is necessary to include Africa and the so-called triangular trade in the analysis.

The Triangular Trade and the African Contribution

The phenomenon of the triangular trade and the role of Africa in this context have been subjects of intense scrutiny over the past few decades. Gareth Austin is one of the leading scholars in this field, having produced one of the most comprehensive studies on African economic dynamics from a global perspective.[52] He has put forth a compelling argument that local institutions and factor endowments are the key determinants of Africa's historical trajectory. The scarcity of labor relative to land rendered Nieboer's argument applicable to Africa. Coercion was a response to the lack of labor, but also to the exclusion of free labor markets due to the prevailing institutional hierarchies. Together, these factors encouraged the institution of slavery when local and international demand increased. However, Austin did not neglect to consider the significance of local markets for products in Africa. The lack of capital and labor intensification,[53] potentially under coercion, diminished the overall impact of these markets. Consequently, Austin aligns with the prevailing perspective on the

---

[50] BL Add. Mss 38, 714, f. 37; 8133 c f 237; TNA CO 137/19; 152/14, R 101; 318/1, 13; 390/6: 31–2.
[51] Ward, "The Profitability of Sugar"; Keith Aufhauser, "The Profitability of Slavery in the British Caribbean," *Journal of Interdisciplinary History*, 5, 1 (1974): 45–46.
[52] Gareth Austin. "Reciprocal Comparison and African History: Tackling Conceptual Eurocentrism in the Study of Africa's Economic Past", *African Studies Review*, 50, 3 (2007): 1–28.
[53] Gareth Austin, Kaory Sugihara, *Labour-Intensive Industrialization in Global History* (London: Routledge, 2012).

Industrial Revolution, positing that innovation and British markets, rather than African exploitation, were the primary drivers of this historical transformation.

Conversely, numerous scholars, including Wallerstein and Inikori, have posited that the purchase of British and European textiles and other goods by Africans since the seventeenth century financed Europe and Britain in particular.[54] They further contend that the export of African labor through slavery not only accelerated the Industrial Revolution but also precipitated a population decline and economic stagnation in Africa. After the abolition of the slave trade, European powers sought to expand legitimate trade in Africa, which provided the West with essential products while perpetuating slavery in Africa itself.[55]

Nunn has articulated a comparable perspective, underscoring the influence of extractive policies on the African continent with regard to raw materials, the slave trade and slave raids. However, these attitudes contributed to the reinforcement of inefficient institutions and the lack of resources and labor force, which resulted in further constraints and corruption in Africa and contributed to its long-term poverty and underdevelopment.[56]

Nevertheless, it can be argued that even more than products, capital, credit and money were central to the question of assessing the contribution of Africa, slavery and the slave trade to the "rise of the West." Joseph Miller, arguably the foremost expert on the role of credit in the history of slavery and the slave trade, has made a significant contribution to this field of study.[57] He posited that the strategies employed by Europeans to invest in the Atlantic economy, as well as in purchases from highly productive Asian economies in the Indian Ocean, were all predicated on credit. Commercial debtors borrowed cash, or liquidity, which they repaid by reducing cash expenditures and maximizing cash returns, or returns in nearly equivalent liquid form, on their investments. When feasible, they acquired resources or production factors – such as land, labor and raw materials – from external sources, namely domestic communities with less familiarity with cash transactions. The availability of capital in Europe was relatively limited, particularly given its already significant mobilization for trade, manufacturing and agriculture. This scarcity of capital explains why European powers developed their colonies on credit.[58] The acquisition of financial credit was a consequence of the pursuit of specie that underpinned the

---

[54] Immanuel Wallerstein, *The Modern World-System: Capitalist Agriculture and the Origins of the European World-Economy in the Sixteenth Century* (New York: Atheneum, 1974).
[55] Inikori, *Africans and the Industrial Revolution*.
[56] Nathan Nunn, "The Long-term Effect of Africa's Slave Trades," *Quarterly Journal of Economics*, 123, 1 (2008): 139–176.
[57] Joseph Millar, *The Problem of Slavery as History* (New Haven: Yale University Press, 2016).
[58] Joseph Millar, "Credit, Captives, Collateral and Currencies: Debt, Slavery and the Financing of the Atlantic World," in Gwyn Campbell, Alessandro Stanziani, eds., *Debt and Slavery in the Mediterranean and the Atlantic World* (London: Pickering and Chatto, 2013): 105–122.

seventeenth-century expansion of the Atlantic. The Royal African Company was granted a charter in 1672, thereby establishing an English commercial presence on Africa's Gold Coast. The Royal African Company was established with the specific objective of acquiring gold in Africa. Consequently, up until the conclusion of the seventeenth century, Europeans financed their primary Atlantic endeavors through the utilization of the islands situated off the coast of western Africa, extending to the Caribbean and the northern and southern regions of continental North America, with a comparatively minimal investment of financial capital.[59]

In the eighteenth century, a substantial inflow of Brazilian gold reinforced monetary reforms and the advancement of the City of London as well as banknotes backed by the Bank of England.[60] The British-led commercial capacity that financed the rapid growth of indebted productive sectors of the American economies in the eighteenth century also contributed to the expansion of the African economy. In this context, suppliers and buyers alike engaged in excessive investment in the slave trade, a pattern that was later repeated in legitimate trade. The provision of commercial credit, in conjunction with the sale of assorted goods on a trust basis, served to stimulate the slave trade and the commercial sectors of African economies.[61]

It can be argued that violent foreclosure on debts became as important a source of captives as systematic militarization. The practice of plundering, or in the African case, capturing people to sell as slaves, rapidly reached a point of diminishing returns as the targeted communities constructed defensive structures or retreated to inaccessible locations.[62] This financial dynamic, whereby initial successes are followed by rising costs based on borrowing, has been described as a moving frontier of slaving violence.[63] As Toby Green stressed, the growth of the export of slaves also meant the emergence of a balance of payments deficit. This was due to the fact that enslaved persons had become the ultimate unit of account in many African areas. As the volume of exported captives increased massively in the eighteenth century, this deficit had a tendency to increase. As a consequence of the sourcing of credit lines from Europe, Africa

---

[59] William A. Pettigrew, *Freedom's Debt: Politics and the Escalation of American Slavery, 1688-1752* (Chapel Hill: University of North Carolina Press, 2012).

[60] H. E. Stephan Fisher, *The Portugal Trade: A Study of Anglo-Portuguese Commerce, 1700-1770* (London: Methuen, 1971).

[61] Rebecca Shumway, *The Fante and the Transatlantic Slave Trade* (Rochester NY: University of Rochester Press, 2011).

[62] Charles Piot, *Remotely Global: Village Modernity in West Africa* (Chicago: University of Chicago Press, 1999); Robert Martin Baum, *Shrines of the Slave Trade: Diola Religion and Society in Precolonial Senegambia* (New York: Oxford University Press, 1999).

[63] John Thornton, *Warfare in Atlantic Africa, 1500-1800* (London: Routledge, 2000). See also Richard J. Reid, *Warfare in African History (New Approaches to African History)* (New York: Cambridge University Press, 2012).

became increasingly economically dependent on European economies. This resulted in a series of economic shocks that significantly weakened the continent over the following decades and centuries. Concurrently, the European demand for captives elevated the African demand for currencies in circulation, consequently increasing the cost of purchase for European traders.[64]

In light of the triangular trade and the African contribution, we may construct the following picture, as previously proposed by Robin Blackburn. It is important to note that this evaluation is limited to the year 1770.

Thomas/Ward, plantation profits: £1,307,000
Anstey, slave trade profits: £115,000
West Indian trade: £1,075,000
African Trade: £300,000
Total: £2,797,000[65]

Blackburn determined that the aggregate profits generated by the Atlantic system amounted to nearly three million pounds. His upper estimate was £4,336,000. Furthermore, he noted that a considerable proportion of these profits were reinvested, amounting to between 30 percent and 50 percent. This indicates that profits from the Atlantic system could account for approximately one-half to four-fifths of the gross fixed capital required to finance a significant industrial undertaking such as canal construction. Blackburn references Davis's data on export destinations, noting that exports to the Atlantic colonies constituted 43 percent of the total from 1784 to 1786 and 57 percent from 1806 to 1808. To further reinforce his argument, he references Crafts' most recent data, which indicates that the growth in exports accounted for 56.3 percent of the overall increase in industrial output between 1700 and 1760, and 46.2 percent between 1780 and 1800. It is important to note that this does not imply that domestic markets were unimportant; only, as Findlay and O'Rourke had previously emphasized, international markets and the Atlantic, including slavery, also played a role. Rönnbäck's assessments have also corroborated that the American plantation system and associated industries increased from an annual value-added of 3.5 percent of the GDP in the 1700s to 11 percent a century later.[66] To evaluate the significance of this contribution, it is sufficient to note that, in 2022, according to official statistics, the quarterly sector (finance) as a whole accounts for approximately 5.6–7.3 percent of the GDP of Britain.[67]

When these points are considered, an intriguing conclusion emerges. The confluence of conquest, slavery, sugar, international trade, the Industrious

---

[64] Toby Green, *A Fistful of Shells* (London: Penguin, 2018): 294–5.
[65] Blackburn, *The Making of New World Slavery*: 541.
[66] Rönnbäck, "On the Economic Importance."
[67] www.ons.gov.uk/economy/nationalaccounts/uksectoraccounts#:~:text=The%20percent20UK%E2%80%99s.

Revolution, demand and the labor-intensive path, which relied heavily on coercive labor, all contributed to the Industrial Revolution. During the eighteenth century, the rate of growth of Britain was the result of increasing labor intensification, additional acres and forced labor across the Atlantic, and expanding markets, both domestic and international. The coexistence of slavery in the colonies, peasants-workers and aristocratic capitalism on the mainland was mutually sustaining: Labor coercion in Britain and its colonies influenced each other in terms of labor rules and institutions and their economic rationale. The intensification of labor and its scarcity led to an increase in coercion, at least as long as labor remained cheap and capital expensive. At the same time, this process responded to increasing demand and expanding markets, both in Britain and internationally, which also contributed to growth.

We may now inquire as to how this depiction altered during the initial six decades of the nineteenth century, when coercion and the labor-intensive path demonstrated an increasing inability to sustain growth. Cotton played a pivotal role in this context; unlike sugar, it did not contribute to the British "primitive accumulation," which refers to the accumulation before and during the initial stages of the Industrial Revolution, between 1650 and 1750. Instead, after the Napoleonic Wars, American cotton helped to maintain the rate of growth, despite the continued reliance on a labor-intensive and coercive path.

From Sugar to Cotton: Britain and US Industrialization

With regard to the relationship between cotton (and textiles more generally), slavery and British economic growth, two distinct yet interrelated areas of inquiry have emerged. On the one hand, some scholars have emphasized the relationship between British textiles and India. On the other hand, other scholars have underscored the interconnection between American cotton, slavery and the Industrial Revolution. In the first group, Prasannan Parthasarathi built upon the historiography discussed previously, drawing parallels with the arguments put forth by Paul Mantoux, Paul Bairoch and Wallerstein.[68] He posited that Britain's technical superiority was not the sole factor responsible for the decline of Indian cotton; rather, it was the country's monopolistic commercial policies towards India that played a pivotal role.[69] During the initial phase, spanning from the late seventeenth to the early eighteenth century, Britain engaged in a significant importation of Indian

---

[68] Paul Mantoux, *The Industrial Revolution in the Eighteenth Century: an Outline of the Beginning of the Modern Factory System in England* (New York: Harper, 1928, French original 1906); Bairoch, Paul, "L'économie française dans le contexte européen à la fin du XVIIIe siècle," *Revue économique*, 40, 6 (1989): 939–964; Paul Bairoch, *Economics and World History: Myths and Paradoxes* (Chicago: University of Chicago Press, 1993).

[69] Parthasarathi, *Why Europe Grew Rich*; Berg and others, *Goods from the East, 1600–1800*.

6 SLAVERY AND THE INDUSTRIAL REVOLUTION

textiles, simultaneously establishing connections with local producers. The argument then proceeds to suggest that Britain subsequently adopted a policy of "import substitution," which involved replacing Indian textiles with British textiles. This was initially done in Britain and then in India itself through the implementation of aggressive commercial policies that made Indian cotton more expensive. The advent of technical progress and massive production ultimately led to the same outcome. In summary, the success of the British in the textile industry in India was due to the combination of state power and commercial policies, which were backed by military force. This line of reasoning directly challenges the Eurocentric perspective that justifies British global leadership in textiles and economic power based on creativity, innovation and culture (as proposed by Eric Jones, David Landes and Marxists such as Robert Brenner).[70]

Similarly, Giorgio Riello has demonstrated that Europe, and particularly Britain, initially imitated Asian textiles, adopting their innovative techniques before subsequently transforming them.[71] As in the case of Africa, the role of money and credit in this outcome cannot be overlooked. Chaudhuri and Om Prakash made significant contributions to the study of the arrival of silver and gold in India and its subsequent impact on prices.[72] During the final decades of the seventeenth century and the early decades of the eighteenth century, at least one-fifth of the global production of silver entered India, along with copper imported from Japan and destined for local trade. Consequently, India became increasingly reliant on Western silver and gold, which paved the way for a growing economic dependence. These characteristics are now widely accepted, despite some attempts by liberal historians to demonstrate that India and its production were already in decline prior to the arrival of the British.[73] The question thus arises as to whether these import substitution policies were

---

[70] David Landes, *The Unbound Prometheus. Technological Change and Industrial Development in Western Europe since 1750 to the Present* (Cambridge: Cambridge University Press, 2003); Eric Jones, *The European Miracle* (Cambridge: Cambridge University Press, 1981).

[71] Riello, Roy, *How India Clothed the World*; Riello, *Cotton*; Allen, *The British Industrial Revolution in Global Perspective*.

[72] Kirti N. Chaudhuri, *The Trading World of India and the English East India Company, 1660–1760*, (Cambridge: Cambridge University Press, 1978); Prakash, Om, *The Dutch East India Company and the Economy of Bengal, 1630–1720* (Princeton: Princeton University Press, 1985).

[73] Stephen Broadberry and Bishnupriya Gupta, "The Early Modern Great Divergence: Wages, Prices and Economic Development in Europe and Asia, 1500–1800," *Economic History Review*, 59, 1 (2006): 2–31; Patrick O'Brien, "Review of Ten Years of Debate on the Origin of the Great Divergence," *Reviews in History* (2010): www.history.ac.uk/reviews/review/1008; Robert Allen, Jean-Pascal Bassino, Debin Ma, Christine Moll-Murata and Jan Luiten van Zanden, "Wages, Prices, and Living Standards in China, Japan, and Europe, 1738–1925," *Economic History Review*, 64, 1 (2011): 8–38.

Table 6.1 *Cotton as a percentage of overall British exports*

Year	Cotton in percent of British exports
1784–6	6
1794–6	15.6
1804–6	42.3
1814–16	42.1
1824–6	47.8
1834–6	48.5
1844–6	44.2
1854–6	34.1

Source: Ralph Davis, *The Industrial Revolution and British Overseas Trade* (London: Leicester University Press, 1979): table 2: 15.

able to sustain the Industrial Revolution. This will require a shift from imports from India to manufacturing in Great Britain and its main sources of supply.

In this case, as in that of sugar, it is essential to distinguish between cotton as a raw material and its role, the profits at the estate level, the international cotton trade, capital circulation and accumulation. It seems quite challenging to refute the assertion that the exponential growth of the English textile industry would not have been possible without American cotton as a raw material. Cotton imports to Britain increased from £16 million in the 1784–1786 period to 803 million pounds in the 1854–1856 period. At the outset of this period, the West Indies constituted the primary supplier of cotton. The United States had become the source of 75 percent of all cotton imports in terms of quantity.[74] In this latter case, cotton was transformed in Britain and then exported as a finished product, as shown in Table 6.1.

Cotton exports were insignificant until the end of the eighteenth century. Then, they increased dramatically in the first half of the nineteenth century. This period saw a surge in American raw cotton production, followed by a decline in the mid-century, when American cotton exports faced challenges due to the abolition of the slave trade and the Civil War. This means that American cotton and cotton export played a limited role in financing the

---

[74] Seymour Drescher, *Econocide. British Slavery in the Era of Abolition* (Pittsburgh: University of Pittsburgh Press, 1977; new edition: University of North Carolina Press, 2010): 57, 84–5.

First Industrial Revolution. Instead, they contributed to sustaining the rate of growth of Britain between the Napoleonic wars and the Second Industrial Revolution, roughly between the 1810s and the end of the 1840s. During that period, the Corn Laws, the burden of war and the labor-intensive path all contributed to limiting the rate of growth of Britain. Cotton played a role in counterbalancing this trend, along with the expansion of domestic markets during the same period.[75]

Summary

Proponents of British and Western exceptionalism contend that British economic growth was not contingent on slavery or exploitation of African and Asian populations. Instead, they assert that it was driven by British creativity, institutional framework and local market expansion. According to this view, the profitability of slavery and the slave trade is a matter of debate, while trade with Africa and India did not yield significant profits. In the sixteenth century, these regions already exhibited lower incomes and a lower standard of living than Western Europe.

Conversely, numerous scholars have emphasized the pivotal role of slavery and the slave trade in Britain's economic and social development. This line of reasoning neglects the role of domestic markets in Britain, as well as the intensification of labor.

Previous pages advanced an intermediate orientation: The agrarian revolution, the consumer revolution, the Industrious Revolution and the First Industrial Revolution were all long-term and labor-intensive processes. Therefore, the demand for labor exceeded the supply in mainland Britain, thereby precluding the possibility of significant free migration to the colonies. Forms of coerced migration, including seamen-peasants, indentured migrants and slaves replaced free migration. Certainly, the availability of African slaves was influenced by the existence of African institutions and the capacity of the slave supply to adapt to changing demand. At the same time, the importation of slaves also found a rationale in the connection between plantations and the labor-intensive path in Britain.

In this configuration, profits were generated in Britain by maintaining wages at a subsistence level while increasing the intensity of labor, despite a high seasonal turnover of the workforce. As Ricardo correctly observed, the remainder of income was appropriated by rents and aristocratic capitalism. However, this situation constrained the rate of growth in Britain itself. This was the price to be paid in order to reconcile economic growth and modernization, while preserving the existence of peasant-workers and land aristocracies alongside those of proletarians and capitalists. In a certain sense, the scheme advanced

[75] Findlay, O'Rourke, *Power and Plenty*.

here is compatible with the classical model in political economy (subsistence wages), to which it must be added the role of demand and the industrious revolution, international markets, colonies and slavery. In this configuration, the New World offered the potential for elastic supplies of land, while Africa implied an elastic supply of labor. The net effect was an elastic supply of raw materials, which benefited the Industrial Revolution by providing lower prices for raw materials than would have been available in a closed economy without slavery. The slave trade and slave production were lucrative enterprises that provided the financial resources necessary to fuel the Industrial Revolution in Britain; the "ghost acres" of America reduced the cost of production of raw materials in Britain. Slavery served to reduce the cost of labor in two distinct ways. Primarily, it contributed to the retention of a larger proportion of the population within Britain, thereby limiting the extent of wage growth. Secondly, it played a pivotal role in the sustenance of coercive institutions, largely through the influence of the colonial realms on labor rules in Britain itself. However, this was the case in the eighteenth century to a much greater extent than it was in subsequent periods. During the initial four decades of the nineteenth century, the rate of growth stagnated. Britain addressed this setback by initially relying on slave cotton, followed by embracing free trade and the Second Industrial Revolution.

However, if the great divergence may be related to the American markets and resources, British "ghost acres" were not limited to the Atlantic region but also extended across the Urals, reflecting a global dynamic. Cereals were a crucial component in feeding labor; Britain initially sourced a significant portion of its wheat from Russia, before transitioning, around the mid-nineteenth century, towards the United States and Canada. Therefore, Russia and its serfdom also contributed to sustain the British growth.

Before drawing broader conclusions, it is necessary to focus on a final example: France. In this case, we observe the persistence of the ancient régime, but the absence of serfs, as in Russia, and the absence of criminal penalties for workers, as in Britain. In addition, the French Empire relied on a labor force of slaves, indentured servants, and sugar production, but not on cotton as the Anglo-Americans did. What was the logic of this system?

7

With or without You

France and the Empire of Sugar

Conventional history claims that economic growth in France stagnated throughout the eighteenth century.[1] In recent decades, new works have challenged this view and shown that there was considerable dynamism during the century, especially in agriculture.[2] As shown in Part I, criminal sanctions were abolished at the end of the eighteenth century, while the use of the law was a powerful tool in the hands of working people, at least in the cities. We now need to integrate these views with the functioning of labor markets.

In the eighteenth century, agricultural servants were by far the largest group of wage earners in French agriculture.[3] In the nineteenth century, official statistics show that day laborers were common in the southern Mediterranean, Alsace-Lorraine, Île-de-France and Picard.

It is estimated that in 1862 about half of the 4 million agricultural wage earners were day laborers; thirty years later, that number had dropped to 1.2 million. Much of this trend was related to a sudden decline in the number of small landowners between 1862 and 1892; in contrast, servants in husbandry made up an increasingly large proportion of the agricultural workforce.[4]

On the eve of the Revolution, France had a rate of urbanization roughly equal to that of the major European countries, including England, but with a larger population. Market segmentation remained the rule in France until about the end of the nineteenth century, and as a result there was no uniformity in prices, wages or skills. With few exceptions, pluriactivity was the norm.[5]

---

[1] Patrick O'Brien, Caglar Keydar, "Les voies de passage vers la société industrielle en Grande-Bretagne et en France," *Annales ESC* 34, 1 (1979): 1284–1303; Michel Morineau, *Les faux-semblants d'un démarrage économique: agriculture et démographie en France au XVIIIe siècle* (Paris: Colin 1971).

[2] George W. Grantham "Divisions of Labour: Agricultural Productivity and Occupational Specialization in Pre-Industrial France," *The Economic History Review*, 46, 3 (1993): 478–502.

[3] Hoffman, *Growth in a Traditional Society*.

[4] Jean-Luc Mayaud, "Salariés agricoles et petite propriété dans la France du XIXe siècle," in Jean-Claude Farcy and Ronald Hubscher, eds., *La moisson des autres* (Nice: Créaphys édition, 1996): 29–56.

[5] Gérard Gayot, *De la pluralité des mondes industriels. La manufacture royale des draps de Sedan, 1646–1870* (Paris: EHESS, 1995).

In the nineteenth century, the rural population in France declined more slowly than in Britain, but more rapidly than in any other European country.

George Grantham evaluated the labor input for the major agricultural operations in several French regions over a long period of time – roughly the eighteenth and nineteenth centuries – and concluded that labor productivity increased throughout the country during this period, particularly in intensive farming and more in tillage than in harvesting. In some areas, notably the Paris Basin, labor productivity was almost equal to that of the best agricultural areas in Britain at the time. As late as 1851, however, only 27.6 percent of the working population was employed in industry (16 percent in 1815; 21 percent at the end of the 1830s). In 1855–1864, cottage production was still 1.6 times higher than industrial production.[6]

Labor intensification in agriculture increased, and output and yields were much higher in Britain than in France for an equal increase in the number and length of working days. The organization of labor and capital may explain these differences. The contribution of labor dominated French growth at least until the 1870s, if not after, and it played an even greater role than in Britain.[7] Wheat output (in kilograms per hectare) was lower in France than in Britain, the Netherlands and Belgium. The same was true of the overall productivity of its agricultural labor force.[8]

In industry, as in Britain, the working day in France was extended in every sector during the eighteenth century and much of the nineteenth century.[9] Louis-René Villermée's graph shows this dynamic in several sectors, especially in textiles,[10] where the cottage industry's workday grew longer than in any other sector.[11] The 1848 survey of working conditions in France confirms this graph: The average length of the working day was 12–13 hours, but there were considerable seasonal variations. The number of hours of daylight was also a factor, as was the travel of workers to and from work, which required those who stayed to work longer days. Working conditions and the length of the working day varied from place to place, often within a short distance of each other. In the Isère department, miners in the canton of Avellard reportedly

---

[6] Grantham, "Divisions of Labour": table 3, p. 486.
[7] Federico, *Feeding the World*.
[8] Paul Bairoch, "L'économie française dans le contexte européen à la fin du XVIIIe siècle," *Revue économique*, 40, 6 (1989): 939–964.
[9] Patrick Fridenson, Bénédicte Reynaud, eds., *La France et le temps de travail, 1814–2004* (Paris: Odile Jacob, 2005); Claude Thelot, Olivier Marchand, *Deux siècles de travail en France* (Paris: Nathan, 1997); Gary Cross, *A Quest for Time. The Reduction of Work in Britain and France, 1840–1940* (Berkeley: University of California Press, 1989).
[10] Louis-René Villermé, *Tableau de l'état physique et moral des ouvriers employés dans les manufactures de coton, de laine et de soie* (Paris: Jule Renouard, 1840).
[11] François Jarrige, Bénédicte Reynaud, "La durée du travail. La norme et ses usages en 1848," *Genèse*, 85, 4 (2011): 70–92.

worked eight hours a day, while night crews in Bourg-d'Oisans worked 12 hours a day. The differences depended on the activity, local customs, the place of work and the workers' ability to defend their interests.[12] In general, seasonal work was more intense during the periods that workers spent in the cities, and even more so for peasant workers in the countryside. The seasonal nature of agricultural work led to a considerable degree of regional mobility, which was already considerable in the seventeenth century and remained high until around the end of the nineteenth century. In the mid-nineteenth century, about 25 percent of the industrial labor force moved from one sector to another during the summer.[13] These trends in different rural areas corresponded to those in different industrial activities; here, closures were less frequent in highly capital-intensive firms. Indeed, a national market was still lacking in nineteenth-century France (at least until after the 1880s), and peasants argued on the basis of a comparison between local wages in agriculture and industry. This explains why in *départements* where industrial wages were high, agricultural wages followed suit, and vice versa: Workers compared and eventually equalized the imbalance between the two. For the same reason, summer shutdowns were more common in companies that paid their workers less than the summer wage for agricultural work.

Where possible, employers could try to compensate for the loss of men by employing women, adolescents and children. Although agricultural wages were lower than industrial wages for most of the year, the situation was reversed during the peak season, especially for women. Their wages were systematically lower than those of men, but they recovered the difference in both agriculture and industry during the summer. It was as if agriculture offered a high wage for a short period each year in order to attract workers who were normally employed in industrial production.[14]

This general behavior was particularly well suited to highly labor-intensive crop areas. When labor was required at different intervals, as in flax, hemp, and vegetable and oilseed crops, workers did not look to distant markets for compensation. In these cases, their wages would not be compensated by going to distant markets.

In wine-producing regions, on the other hand, workers did respond to higher wages in distant markets, and to an even greater extent did workers in pastoral counties. Those in the pastoral counties – in northern France, the Vosges and parts of Normandy and Brittany – left industry in the summer to

---

[12] AN, F12 4476.
[13] *Source. Industrial Census 1860* in Thierry Magnac, Gilles Postel-Vinay, "Wage Competition between Agriculture and Industry in Mid-Nineteenth Century France," *Explorations in Economic History*, 34, 1 (1997): 1–26.
[14] Jean-Pierre Bompard, Thierry Magnac, Gilles Postel-Vinay, "Migrations saisonnières de main-d'oeuvre: Le cas de la France en 1860," *Annales d'Économie et de Statistique*, 19 (1990): 97–129.

work in neighboring grain-producing regions with excess demand, in Picardy, Champagne, Lorraine and the Paris basin.[15]

This situation disappeared almost entirely after 1875, when seasonal migration declined sharply. Between 1860 and 1890, the earlier practice of combining agricultural and industrial employment largely disappeared. In 1860, at least 500,000 and probably as many as 800,000 workers left their jobs during the summer. By 1890, only 100,000 were still doing so.[16]

In short, more than in Britain and less than in Russia, labor in France was the main support of growth for much of the nineteenth century, especially in agriculture but also in most industries. Moreover, as in Britain, the distribution of national income in France favored capital, not labor, during the first three quarters of the nineteenth century; this trend was reversed only since the 1880s, with the growing power of the unions and the new equilibria on the labor market. Since then, and even more so with the First World War, rents also decreased.[17]

Along with labor, international trade was the mainstay of the French economy. By the end of the 1780s, France was the largest trading power in Europe, far ahead of Britain.[18] International trade generated per capita GDP 10–14 percent higher than the rest of continental Europe. The rate of GDP growth in volume was about +1.67 percent between 1821 and 1841, +1.78 percent between 1841 and 1866, and +1.16 percent in 1866–1891. During this period, population growth explains about one third of this growth, while labor productivity accounts for 63.9 percent in 1821–1841, 71.3 percent in 1841–1866 and 73.5 percent in 1866–1891, only after it was largely abandoned and replaced by technical progress.[19] Textiles and food dominated manufacturing, while wheat and wine dominated agriculture: All were labor-intensive activities, including textiles, where mechanization of cotton plants was much more limited than in Britain, especially in the first half of the nineteenth century. Domestic markets grew, but while they only partially explain the Industrial Revolution in Britain, they played a relatively limited role in France, at least until the 1860s, when they recovered rapidly. Wine and luxury goods made up the bulk of French exports, especially in the first half of the century; thereafter, wine retained its leading position until the phylloxera plague, but manufactured goods became more diversified. The returns on French foreign trade were higher than those on public debt and domestic commercial investment.[20] Profits were between 33

---

[15] Alessandro Stanziani, *Histoire de la qualité alimentaire* (Paris: Seuil, 2005).
[16] Postel-Vinay, "The Dis-integration ".
[17] Thomas Piketty, *Le capital au XXIe siècle* (Paris: Seuil, 2013): 317; 356–357.
[18] Daudin, "Profitability."
[19] Maurice Lévy-Leboyer, François Bourguignon, *L'économie française au XIXe siècle. Analyse macroéconomique* (Paris: Economica, 1985); Patrick Verley, *Nouvelle histoire économique de la France contemporaine*, vol. 2 (Paris: La découverte, 1995): 9.
[20] Daudin, "Profitability"; François R., Velde, and David R. Weir, "The Financial Market and Government Debt Policy in France, 1746–1793," *The Journal of Economic History*, 52, 1 (1992): 1–39.

percent and 70 percent higher than the internal rate of return on a land portfolio and 20 percent higher than the internal rate of return on private rents. They were also higher than the most secure foreign government bonds. It was only after the Seven Years' War that Britain took markets and profits away from France, and French profits from international trade fell dramatically.[21] With these features in mind, we can now turn to the role of slavery.

The Role of Slavery

The question is whether the slave trade and colonial products played a role in French growth comparable to that of Britain. Unfortunately, compared to Britain, we have few quantitative studies of the role of the slave trade and slavery in the French economy. We do know that in the seventeenth and eighteenth centuries in the Atlantic, indentured immigration was mainly related to tobacco; many indentured immigrants and first slaves were also employed in domestic activities. In the Indian Ocean, the French traded between 334,000 and 384,000 slaves to the Mascarene Islands between 1500 and 1850.[22] In the eighteenth and nineteenth centuries, about 200,000 slaves were imported to Réunion Island for sugar production, mostly from Madagascar and East Africa.[23] Indians were also present: In 1708, the total number of adult slaves was 268 (197 men and 71 women); 20 percent of the men and 36 percent of the women were Indians.[24] A century later, they made up about 3 percent of the 54,000 slaves.

Between 1640 and 1840, French merchants undertook at least 4,220 slave expeditions; about 1.3 million slaves reached the French colonies in the Americas. The development of the French Atlantic slave trade peaked between 1783 and 1792, with more than 100 expeditions per year. Three-quarters of the slaves in the French colonies were transported by French ships. Nantes was responsible for 43 percent of this traffic (in terms of expeditions), followed by La Rochelle, Le Havre and Bordeaux (11 percent each).[25]

Up to the middle of the eighteenth century, 42 percent to 47 percent of the slaves came from Guinea, Sierra Leone, Liberia and the Ivory Coast, after which

---

[21] Patrick Villiers, *Marine royale, corsaires et trafic dans l'Atlantique de Louis XIV et Louis XVI* (Lille: Société dunkerquoise d'histoire et d'archéologie Septentrion, 1991); Villiers, *Le commerce colonial atlantique*.

[22] Allen, *European Slave Trade*; Jean-Marie Filliot, *La traite des esclaves vers les Mascareignes au XVIIIe siècle* (Paris: Orstrom, 1974); Hubert Gerbeau, "Les esclaves asiatiques des Mascareignes: Enquêtes et hypothèses," *Annuaire des pays de l'Océan Indien*, 7 (1980): 169–197; Marina Carter, "Indian Slaves in Mauritius (1729–1834)," *Indian Historical Review*, 15, 1–2 (1988–1989): 233–247.

[23] ADR (archives départementales de la Réunion), série C*1272 (traite 1746–1753) and C 1273 (traite 1758–1765).

[24] Filliot, *La traite des esclaves*.

[25] Mettas, *Répertoire des expéditions*.

Central Africa and Biafra became the main sources.[26] This change was related to French networks in Africa, the British embargo after 1807 and the destination of the slaves. In 1796–1817, coffee plantations in Saint-Domingue purchased slaves mainly in Central Africa (37 percent to 38 percent) and the Bight of Benin (30 percent). In Guadeloupe and Martinique, more than 50 percent came from Biafra in 1789–1794.

Between the mid-seventeenth century and the mid-nineteenth century, Martinique imported 366,000 slaves, Guadeloupe 291 and Saint-Domingue 864,000 until its independence.[27] Between 1713 and 1789, 78.2 percent of French expeditions went to Saint-Domingue, 15.8 percent to Martinique and 3.3 percent to Guadeloupe. Most were men (54 percent in Martinique between 1714 and 1721).[28]

Although most slaves were imported to the French islands by French ships, the percentage changed over the years: 87 percent before 1740, 45 percent between 1740 and 1760, and 85 percent thereafter. The remainder of the slaves sent to the French islands were transported and sold by British, then Spanish and Portuguese ships. About 23 percent of the slaves that arrived in Jamaica were re-exported. Thus, France had a deficit in the slave trade and imported some of them from other colonial powers. The reasons for this were Britain's superiority in buying slaves in Africa and the lower cost of importing them. France operated through the system of privilege and monopoly much more than the British, which drove up costs. French merchants seldom specialized in the slave trade, preferring to arrange the trade of several items at once. There were also numerous intermediaries to finance the slave trade: Shipowners put up little capital and tended to rely on either credit or the captain's responsibility for the rest. Once in the colonies, it was estimated that five to six return cargoes were needed to offset the arrival of one slave cargo. Because planters were in debt to purchase slaves, capital rotation was slower than in Britain. British cargoes had greater and earlier access to banks. In France, this was only the case for the Protestants in Nantes. France also had few posts in Africa, while Britain multiplied its warehouses. Most importantly, British traders exported first Indian and then British textiles to Africa, further linking the slave trade to the textile industry.[29] The French, on the other hand, exported mainly *pacotilles* (cheap goods).[30]

---

[26] Serge Daget, *La répression de la traite des noirs au XIXe siècle* (Paris: Karthala, 1997).
[27] Philip Curtin, *The Atlantic Slave Trade* (Madison: University of Wisconsin Press, 1969): 88.
[28] Mettas, *Repertoire des expéditions*.
[29] On all these points: Daudin, *Commerce et prospérité*; Daudin, "Profitability." Also David Eltis, "The Slave Economies of the Caribbean: Structure, Performance, Evolution and Significance," in F. Knight, ed., *The UNESCO General History of the Caribbean* (London: Macmillan, 1997): 104–137.
[30] Eugenie Margoline-Plot, *Les pacottilles d'indiennes, la boutique et la mer* (PhD, University of Lorient, 2014); Philippe Haudrière, *La compagnie française des Indes* (Paris: Les Indes savantes, 2005).

Finally, the British were more efficient at transportation; their ships carried almost 50 percent more slaves per ton than the French.[31] David Eltis attributes this difference to the fact that French ships were larger and had more crew, because French slave traders were also warships, which was related to the concentration of French colonies in the Americas and French outposts in Africa. Britain, on the other hand, operated in a more decentralized manner in Africa and the Americas, using smaller ships but with more slaves on board. Finally, the mortality rate among slaves during the Middle Passage was higher on French than on British ships. In the end, and despite these limitations, profits from the slave trade were around 4 percent to 6 percent for the French, while they ranged between 5 percent and 10 percent for the British, depending on the year.[32]

What about slave production? Was it profitable? As in the British Isles, the process of enslavement coincided with a concentration of estates. In fact, slavery required a higher initial investment than indentured servitude, but it was more profitable in the long run. In 1660, 10 percent of Martinique's plantations were managed by family members only; the average additional labor for each was 0.8 white *engageés* and 3.7 slaves;[33] 45 percent had no slaves at all, and a third had between one and five slaves. By 1680, indentured whites accounted for 27 percent of the labor force and slaves for 41.8 percent. The figures for Guadeloupe were about the same. By the mid-eighteenth century, when the process of estate concentration was well underway, there were an average of 112 slaves per sugar plantation and far fewer for coffee (fifty-two in Saint-Domingue and thirty-one in Guadeloupe). French plantations produced all the sugar, coffee and indigo needed on the mainland and held a dominant position in these products on the continental European markets. The organization of labor on French and British plantations was similar: Slaves worked in gangs under constant supervision, using hoes rather than plows; night work was done in the sugar mills.[34] The overseer managed the plantation, while the owner often lived on the mainland, especially on large estates. Skilled slaves were responsible for manufacturing and tools, as well as supervising field crews. Women were mainly assigned to field work.

A microeconomic approach complements these observations: Consider Paul Cheney's study of the Cul de Sac estate in Saint-Domingue,[35] a relatively large estate that owned between 200 and 300 slaves, depending on the period. Its owner belonged to one of the aristocratic families (the Ferronays) in the wealthiest 13 percent of the kingdom. This was a typical example of the kind of aristocratic capitalism found throughout Europe and some of its colonies

---

[31] Eltis, *The Trans-Atlantic Slave Trade*.
[32] Eltis, *The Trans-Atlantic Slave Trade*.
[33] BN NAF 93227, *Recensement de la population de la Martinique en 1660*.
[34] Geggus, "Slave Society."
[35] Paul Cheney, *Cul de Sac* (Chicago: University of Chicago Press, 2017).

during the period under study. With land and rent as their main resources in France, the family decided to diversify their investments by moving to Santo Domingo in the 1760s. Like most other landowners, the Ferronays decided to hire a steward. They chose one who had already managed their properties in France. Through a strategic marriage, this steward accumulated a good fortune and invested heavily in the property, earning about 10 percent of the profits. The latter, however, depended on many variables, starting with the dynamics of international trade and relations with French merchants.

Like other large slaveholders, the Ferronays were torn between the need to make the most of their plantations and slaves in the short term and the need to maintain the profitability of their land and slaves in the long term. They enjoyed the advantages of size, number of slaves, access to their market and relative power in relation to merchants, but undoubtedly greater than that of small landowners. As a result, like other large landowners, they were more inclined, but also more advantaged, to adopt medium- and long-term strategies. This is a situation we found in Russia, France and its colonies, but also in the British colonies: Large landowners adopted strategies less based on immediate exploitation of the land and their slaves or workers, who were often better treated than on small estates.[36]

While it seems difficult to prove that this attitude was related to their "benevolence" toward slaves or their "economic rationality," it is certain that economies of scale favored such attitudes. This observation in no way excludes the use of coercion and violence on the plantation; it simply was not considered the only attitude to adopt toward slaves. It should also be remembered that the strategy of the Ferroneys, like that of other large landowners, was less to invest in land capital, such as infrastructure, than to intensify slave labor through better organization of the work itself and the introduction of agronomic innovations.[37]

In other words, as elsewhere, the intensification of labor went hand in hand with an increase in the size of plantations. Many historians have noted the similarity, even the anticipation, of the plantation to the factory. This is a valid argument: The plantation was the inspiration for Smith's and then Marx's famous enlarged factory, not the integrated factory of the twentieth century, which is completely different in terms of both the organization of work and the relationship between labor and capital.

This fragile equilibrium was linked to the dynamics of international trade, which in turn depended heavily on conflict. The Seven Years' War (1756–1763), followed by the American War of Independence with its naval blockade led to a decline in the sugar market and a drop in profits, all the more so as the price of

---

[36] For a further development of this point, see: Stanziani, *Bondage*; Stanziani, *Labor on the Fringes of Empire*.
[37] Cul de Sac archives in Archives Nationales T 210/2.

slaves rose. Slaves' diets suffered all the more because the area devoted to these crops had been reduced in favor of sugar cane in previous years. Sickness and death among the slaves increased dramatically, as did the number of revolts, both in Saint-Domingue and in Jamaica and Barbados. In the French case, the solution found by the planters consisted of agreements with the slaves, who were given more time and resources for their food crops, and with the monarchy, which eased the planters' profits, which had previously been heavily confiscated by the tax authorities.

Available estimates show that the overall performance of French plantations in the eighteenth century was superior to that of the British. The lower profitability of British plantations was related to natural endowments and social institutions:[38] For example, Saint-Domingue and Martinique benefited from water resources and the support of the colonial state in infrastructure investments. In the British islands, residents were more dependent on imported food and more vulnerable to maritime connections, while the French islands produced comparatively more food and imported the rest from nearby Spanish America. Until the mid-eighteenth century, the French had less to fear from the other Bourbon kingdom, Spain, in their trade with the Americas than did the British. Martinique also had a refining industry – and the privileged status that went with it – and supplied 90 percent of France's white sugar, while Saint-Domingue supplied 98 percent of its raw sugar. Despite these limitations, Saint-Domingue produced 87,000 tons of sugar in 1787, compared to 49,000 tons for Jamaica.[39]

This is partly explained by the fact that the French brought new varieties of sugar cane to the Caribbean; inventories of estates in Saint-Domingue show that the improved cane land could be worth as much as the sugar mill and slave labor combined.[40] In the 1780s, British planters in Jamaica compared their 3–4 percent profits to the 8–12 percent in Saint-Domingue.[41] But this seemed to underestimate costs such as the price of acquisition, epidemics, old slaves and interest.[42] French estates borrowed more heavily than their British counterparts, and substantial amounts of profits went into the hands of merchant creditors. For example, Romberg, Bapts et Cie of Bordeaux owned sixteen sugar refineries. On the eve of the Revolution, the larger estates were owned by the

---

[38] Debien, *Plantations et esclaves*; Sheridan, *Sugar and Slavery*.
[39] Burnard, Garrigus, *The Plantation Machine*.
[40] James McClennan III, *Colonialism and Science. Saint-Domingue in the Old Regime* (Chicago: The University of Chicago Press, 2010, orig. 1992).
[41] Blackburn, *The Making of New World Slavery*: 435.
[42] Debien, *Plantations et esclaves à Saint-Domingue*; Gabriel Debien, *Les esclaves aux Antilles françaises, XVIIe-XVIIIe siècles* (Basse-Terre, Société d'histoire de la Guadeloupe: Guadeloupe, 1974); David Geggus, "Sugar and Coffee Cultivation in Saint-Domingue," in Ira Berlin and Philip Morgan, eds., *Cultivation and Culture* (Charlottesville: University of Virginia Press, 1993): 73–98.

families of merchants or high officials.[43] Small French planters, in turn, diversified their products and were less inclined than the British to switch to a sugar monoculture. Secondary crops in the French colonies grew as rapidly as sugar plantations. The number of indigo estates[44] in Saint-Domingue rose from 1,182 in 1713 to 3,445 in 1739.[45] Overall, sugar plantations were highly profitable compared to other activities in France at the end of the eighteenth century; Saint-Domingue was the true core of French sugar production. In 1788, there were 793 sugar refineries in Saint-Domingue, 324 in Martinique and 362 in Guadeloupe. In the same year, Saint-Domingue produced 86,000 tons of sugar.

Other cultures also contributed to this production. From about the middle of the century, Saint-Domingue began to produce increasing quantities of coffee at a lower price than Martinique. Coffee plantations were smaller than sugar plantations, and slaves were organized into gangs. After the tobacco crisis, the small planters, unable to invest in sugar, turned to cotton. Cotton developed in Martinique after 1730 and in Guadeloupe from 1760, but again Saint-Domingue took the lead with 789 cotton plantations in 1788 (660 in Guadeloupe and 233 in Martinique).[46] In 1790, the so-called secondary products – coffee, cotton, cocoa – accounted for 45 percent of Martinique's exports. At that time, Saint-Domingue exported 3,040 tons of cotton, 68,993 tons of sugar and 33,255 tons of coffee.

If the rate of profit was higher on French than on British plantations in the Caribbean, who did benefit the most? While the British planters in the West Indies were gradually gaining a monopoly on trade in Britain – though sometimes in conflict with the British merchants (as mentioned previously) – the French planters were still under the power of the merchants of Bordeaux and Nantes, who appropriated a greater share of colonial profits than the British merchants. The commissioners who administered the colonial towns were mostly from French city ports; by the 1720s, all the major merchant families from Bordeaux and Nantes had representatives (usually family members) in the Antilles.[47] They acted as intermediaries between the mainland merchants and the planters, providing loans and crop advances to the latter and negotiating prices for the former. If debts were not repaid, these intermediaries and sometimes metropolitan merchants would seize the property and become planters themselves. Merchants sold European products in the colonies, imported slaves and exported colonial products. When the merchant acquired the plantation,

---

[43] Alexandre-Stanislas de Wimpffen, *Haiti au XVIIIe siècle* (Paris: Pluchon, 1993).
[44] John Garrigus, "Blue and Brown: Contraband Indigo and the Rise of a Free Colored Planter Class in French Saint-Domingue," *The Americas*, 50, 2 (1993): 233–263.
[45] Blackburn, *The Making of New World Slavery*: 433.
[46] Régent, *La France et ses esclaves*: 98.
[47] Lucien Abenon, Jacques Cauna, Liliane Chauleau, *Antilles 1789. La révolution aux Caraïbes* (Paris: Nathan, 2019).

production and commercial risk shifted. As we have seen, in the British Isles the risk was borne by the planter, while on the French side it was borne by the merchant. Planters and merchants were constantly at odds in the French islands, while this hostility was overcome over the years among their British counterparts. French merchants extended credit to planters, but they had few mechanisms to compel repayment. On the contrary, British commissioners and merchants received most of their profits and remitted them to Britain; this was rarely the case on the French side.

Profits and their distribution were also the result of commercial policy. French colonial trade was conducted under the so-called exclusive system: The colonies could only sell their products to the mainland; they were not allowed to transform raw products into manufactured goods; the mainland had a monopoly on trade with the colonies; and French ships had a monopoly on trade. Thus, a double monopoly of trade and manufacturing was established. In practice, however, the French colonies traded with Spain and, to a lesser extent, with British America. This illegal trade was supported by all the colonial milieus. The trade monopoly was abolished in 1789 and only partially restored after 1815.

As a result, some minimize the importance of colonial profits,[48] while François Crouzet noted that French foreign trade grew faster than English trade between 1715 and 1784.[49] In 1716, colonial products accounted for 17.7 percent of total French exports; France's exports were valued at 50 million livres, with imports of about the same amount. In that year, imports from the Antilles were about 4.5 million livres and exports to the Antilles were only 2.1 million. In 1784 and 1790, the average annual value of French colonial imports was 203.3 million livres.[50] In 1786–1790, imports from the Antilles in millions of pounds sterling were worth 3.5 in Britain and 9.1 in France.[51]

The colonies were also important importers: In 1789, 19 percent of all French exports went to the colonies; together with the African trade, the plantation component of French trade was close to 25 percent. In 1788, 37.6 percent of French exports to the colonies were textiles or other manufactured goods (23.6 percent). By this time, war and independence had raised costs for American planters.

---

[48] Paul Bairoch, *Economics and World History: Myths and Paradoxes* (Chicago: University of Chicago Press, 1993); Jacques Marseille, *Empire colonial et capitalisme français. Histoire d'un divorce* (Paris: Albin Michel, 1984); Daudin, *Commerce et prospérité*; Guillaume Daudin, "Empires et économie," working paper, http://spire.sciencespo.fr/hdl:/2441/5l6 uh8ogmqildh09h4dqk0kai/resources/empireseteconomieversionpreliminaire.pdf.
[49] François Crouzet, ed., *Britain Ascendant: Comparative Studies in Franco-British Economic History* (Cambridge: Cambridge University Press, 1990).
[50] Tarrade, *Le commerce colonial français*.
[51] François Crouzet, *La guerre économique franco-anglaise au XVIIIe siècle* (Paris: Fayard, 2008): 114.

Table 7.1 *The British and French sugar trades compared, 1775 (000 cwt)*

	Imports	Re-exports	Retained imports	Percentage retained
Great Britain	2,002.2	418.4	1,587.4	79.3
France	1,601.2	1,002.0	599.2	37.4

Source: Sheridan, *Sugar and Slavery*: 25

The American colonies produced about 15 percent of all French exports in 1754 and 17 percent in 1787. They accounted for about 16 percent of all French imports in 1716, 34 percent in 1754 and 32 percent in 1787.[52] Textiles accounted for 45 percent of the Antilles' imports. After Spain, the Antilles were the second most important place for French exports. Martinique and Saint-Domingue re-exported French colonial and domestic products to the Spanish colonies. In France, Atlantic trade fueled the development of Nantes and Bordeaux.

However, while the British Antilles could purchase goods, especially timber, from the Thirteen Colonies, this was not the case for the French Antilles, which received very little timber from Canada. This lack of energy increased the final cost of local production, but was partially offset by other technical solutions. In Martinique and Saint-Domingue, planters used coulter pressure in plowing and produced semi-refined sugar. This required more initial capital than muscovado sugar, as in Brazil, but also more than genuine raw sugar. It was cheaper to transport because the volumes were smaller. Jamaica also practiced this solution, but not the other British islands. The added value was therefore higher on the French side.[53] But what was the relationship between colonial trade and the French mainland economy?

First, there was much more re-export of sugar on the French side than on the British side, as seen in Table 7.1.

Contemporary observers believed that French sugar consumption lagged behind that of Great Britain because of lower incomes and considerable inequalities on the continent, but less sugar consumption with tea in France also contributed. In the rest of France, the price of sugar was double the price in Bordeaux due to internal taxes. This reduced the diffusion of sugar compared to Britain, but improved the country's export market, which was still the main target of French merchants. In 1788, the average per capita consumption of sugar in France was ten times less than in Britain, but France exported about 70 percent of its sugar. This means that there was a relationship between France's

---

[52] Paul Butel, *L'économie française au XVIIIe siècle* (Paris: Sedes, 1993): 87.
[53] Crouzet, *La guerre*.

colonies and its export markets, not between its colonies and its domestic markets as in Britain. A major consequence of this was that any loss of colonies would have a major impact on foreign trade and the entire French economy, which could not compensate for the loss with domestic production and markets. This will be the case with the loss of Saint-Domingue, with its devastating impact on the entire French economy.

The hierarchical relationships between planters, merchants and the French monarchy also contributed to this outcome. Even when profits were made and remitted to France, they were divided between the king and the large merchants; the latter reinvested in the slave trade and re-exportation, while the crown had to repay the public debt. In Britain, domestic taxes were lower, while profits were shared among planters, merchants and manufacturers in Britain. In short, as most observers pointed out, the colonies and colonial trade and production did not contribute directly to France's industrial development. Instead, the French colonies promoted the diffusion of a variety of products and supported a general market and capitalist esprit. In France, the power of the monarchy was not constrained as it was in Britain, and its colonial expansion was based on luxury goods, unlike Britain and "democratic" sugar, followed by cotton.

Weak fiscal resources and increasing wars did not help either and contributed to the erosion of the profits generated by slavery. France and Britain fought no less than sixty-four years of war between 1689 and 1815. In particular, the Seven Years' War (1756–1763) had a decisive impact on France: It lost colonies and influence, incurred heavy debts and saw its supremacy wrested from Britain. France lost another part of Quebec as well as Pondicherry. Historians explain France's defeat by Britain's more efficient taxation compared to France's. Despite its larger population and higher GDP, France collected barely half of Britain's tax revenue. As a result, Britain cut France off from India and trade with North America, severely limiting its influence in the Caribbean. Then France lost both Louisiana and Saint-Domingue; the impact of these losses on the entire French economy was enormous, adding to the economic impact of the Revolution. By 1815, the French economy was much smaller than it had been in the mid-eighteenth century.

Conclusion

If we now compare the economies of coerced labor in our three empires, we find that between the mid-seventeenth century and the mid-nineteenth century, various forms of slavery, serfdom and servitude, as well as wage labor with many restrictions but no rights, clearly dominated and drove production. In the empire's mainland, coercion persisted, and the demand for labor far exceeded the supply, especially during periods of growth and agricultural work. Pluriactivity remained the rule. With a small amount of credit and capital available, the main resource was labor; hence the strengths and limitations of this system: increasing labor intensity, mostly due to coercion, and, after some decades of growth, stagnating and sometimes declining labor productivity. Hence the importance of occupying more land and increasing colonial profits. The latter were relatively limited in Russia and decreased even more with the Great Divergence, which limited Russian exports to Britain and China. Serfdom proved capable of steady growth during the eighteenth century, until the Great Divergence radically changed the international economy and Russia's role in it.

France made important gains in the Caribbean, but it destroyed them in ruinous wars that added to a weak fiscal state. The loss of Louisiana and Saint-Domingue added to limited domestic markets and the effects of the Revolution. Britain increased its profits through the slave trade and slavery, but domestic markets also contributed to its growth. Slavery and its profits contributed much less to "primitive accumulation" than to bringing some profits in the eighteenth century, mostly related to sugar, and to partially offset the slow path of growth after the Napoleonic wars and as a result of the labor-intensive path between the 1820s and 1840s. The colonies made it possible to postpone the decline in the rate of growth on the mainland by increasing the number of ghost acres and, above all, by slavery and coercion. The absence of labor rights on the mainland helped to keep alive the world of intensive labor, landed aristocracies and small capitalists.

Since the mid-nineteenth century, however, several forces have closed off this world. The use and profitability of coercion have gradually declined: in part because of declining labor productivity; in part because of increasing political pressure (the abolitionist movement, trade unions on the continent); and in part as a result of growing political and economic competition between empires. The next chapters will describe this process in detail.

PART III

Labor Empires under Attack

From Abolition to the Great Transformation, 1840–1918

Why were slavery and serfdom abolished? One of the answers, inherited from Smith, partly from Marx, and reaching as far as liberals and neo-Marxists (Williams, Inikori), is that forced labor was no longer profitable and therefore wage labor was introduced to increase profits. However, as we have seen, forced labor and slavery were profitable, albeit at a declining rate. Consequently, their abolition must be also linked to other variables; namely, religion (i.e., Quakerism), political and social dynamics (slave resistance, workers' mobilization, etc.) I will refer to these debates, but because a vast historiography is already available, I will include them in a broader perspective; namely, the transformation of the capitalist worlds during the long nineteenth century. I will argue that, as in slavery and serfdom, and in their aftermath, the identification of the rights and duties of emancipated people was closely linked to those of 'free' wage-earners. As we have seen in previous chapters, aristocratic capitalism dominated France, Britain and Russia during the eighteenth and most of the nineteenth centuries. This alliance between the new capitalists and the old rentiers implied the subjugation of workers, both urban and rural, in Europe and its colonies. Slavery compensated for the relatively slow growth of labor-intensive economies. We also know that this system faced increasing difficulties after the Napoleonic Wars: technical constraints (falling yields and productivity), but also social and political constraints. From the 1830s, labor resistance and the abolitionist movement gained momentum. These movements were linked, but not always as one might think: Labor movements were sometimes supportive of anti-slavery but sometimes hostile. We need to understand why.

8

Who Is the True Slave?

I will not enter into debates comparing French and British or Anglo-American and Russian abolitionism in order to discuss, as most historiography does, the importance of popular participation and civil society in the Anglo-American cases, its weakness in France and its total absence in Russia. Ideal types of "civil society," divorced from their historical meanings, are used to compare these realities, forgetting that Civil and political rights in the United States and Britain did not include everyone, certainly not slaves, nor women and many workers (prohibition of trade unionism). Again, this is not to suggest a flat equivalence between Russia, the United States, Britain and France, but rather to problematize the meaning of abolitionism in each context, beyond the facile celebration of Western freedom. To this end, I will focus on a constant red line, easily identifiable in historical sources and strangely absent from most historiography: the close relationship between the identification and emancipation of slaves (or serfs) and wage-earners. I will show that the way this relationship was recognized and discussed strongly influenced the direction of abolitionism and the actual conditions of workers and former slaves and serfs after abolition. The issue was not civil rights in the abstract, but their implementation in everyday life and their transformation into social rights, the latter too often missing from abolitionist celebrations.

British Utilitarianism

The genesis of the anti-slavery movement in England was concomitant with the Somerset ruling of 1772, which sanctioned the institution of slavery in the British colonies while prohibiting its practice on the British mainland. Consequently, any individual who was a slave and entered England was automatically emancipated. This decision was met with staunch support from the English and American anti-slavery movements. Notably, in a seminal ruling, the judge presiding over the case declared that a black man named James Somerset could not be considered a slave within British territory. This decision defied the wishes of his master, who had bought him in Virginia and brought him to England.[1]

---

[1] Samuel Estwick, *Considerations on the Negroe Cause, Commonly So Called, Addressed to the Right Honourable Lord Mansfield, Lord Chief Justice of the Court of King's Bench* (London: J. Dodslay, 1773, second edition).

This decision immediately raised the issue of slaves moving between the colonies and Great Britain. The legal discourse of the era was characterized by profound divisions among jurists concerning the question of the unity of English and colonial law. Consequently, the jurists' discourse was characterized by a dichotomy, with some advocating for the unification of the two legal systems as a single body of law, while others upheld the de jure and de facto distinctions between England and its colonies.[2] The former concluded that slavery was permissible everywhere, while the latter saw the colonies as an exception to the rule, which applied not only to North America, but also to India, where local forms of dependence could not be considered slavery. In practice, in the early 1770s, the population of black people residing in Great Britain was estimated to be between 10,000 and 15,000, which was approximately twice the number residing in France during the same period.[3] The Somerset ruling provoked a contentious debate surrounding the status of enslaved individuals in the British context. Critics denounced the ruling as a violation of private property rights and challenged the fundamental principle of manumission for Black individuals within British territory. In response, proponents of the ruling invoked the prevailing fundamental freedoms in Great Britain, such as those enshrined in the Bill of Rights, to substantiate their position. However, it was also noted that a favorable ruling for the slaveholders would likely encourage English masters to import slaves into Great Britain, which would have a negative impact on British servants. This endeavor to establish continuities and discontinuities in space (between English and colonial law) and time (precedents extending to the Middle Ages) was not merely an academic exercise, as major political and social issues were at stake.[4] Abolitionists pointed out that serfdom (*villeinage*) was abolished because the English language was evolving and increasingly defending individual rights and freedoms. Defenders of slavery, on the other hand, saw serfdom as a legal precedent that legitimized slavery.[5] It is interesting to note that, contrary to what we might imagine today, or even what most nineteenth-century actors emphasized, abolitionists added racial considerations to the historical argument: Race was an argument for abolition. The blood ties between English serfs, who were necessarily white, were not the same in slavery practiced on other races or individuals, often unrelated. For this reason, slavery was different from serfdom (*villeinage*) and therefore had to be abolished, even in the absence of a legal precedent. As a result, slaves residing on British soil were increasingly freed: By 1807, only

---

[2] Granville Sharp, *A Representation of the Injustice and Dangerous Tendency of Tolerating Slavery, or of Admitting the Least Claim of Private Property in the Persons of Men*, in England (London: Legaret Street, 2023, original London: 1769): 10-40.
[3] Drescher, *Abolitions*: 99.
[4] Blackstone, *Commentaries on the Laws of England*: 92.
[5] Helene T. Catterall, ed., *Judicial Cases Concerning American Slavery and the Negro*, 5 volumes (Washington: Carnegie Institution, 1926-37).

fifteen of the 4,000 individuals identified as people of color were still formally enslaved; all others had been freed either voluntarily by their masters upon arrival in Great Britain or by the courts.[6] How did legal decisions come into play in public debates?

In contemporary historiographical debates concerning the evolution of the abolitionist movement, Eric Williams' arguments have exerted a profound influence, prompting a concentrated focus on the question of whether capitalists were in favor of abolition.[7] The historiography on this question is divided: Brion Davis argues that the abolitionist movement diverted public attention from the tensions surrounding British wage earners;[8] David Eltis, on the other hand, perceives abolitionism as part of the industrialization process, in which it played a useful role. In his view, the laissez-faire approach inspired Britain's policies on slavery and labor.[9] Seymour Drescher and Richard Huzzey have adopted a more nuanced position, emphasizing that the relationship between capitalism and slavery, at least rhetorically, depends on the period and the groups involved.[10]

It is important to distinguish between the first abolitionist movement (1770 to 1807) and the second (1820 to 1840). During the initial period, economic arguments seldom permeated the discourse surrounding slavery, particularly within public debates. This is notable because Adam Smith's critique of slavery as an unproductive system had minimal influence during this time. Jeremy Bentham argued that the difference between a servant and a slave was that the slave's master had unlimited power and the slave had no rights. According to him, slavery is defined as unlimited and compulsory labor. Bentham contended that the condition of the enslaved individual could be ameliorated, drawing parallels between various forms of bondage, including ancient slavery, Russian serfdom and American slavery, which he regarded as the most onerous and extreme manifestation of dependency.[11] Bentham ultimately concluded that the conditions of wage labor could be worse than those of slavery, even if the two could not be confused. In summary, Bentham's position was that wage earners were not enslaved, but rather, they were legally bound servants. Consequently, Bentham proposed that the abolition of slavery must explicitly differentiate

---

[6] Kathy Charter, "Black People in England, 1660–1807," in Stephen Farrell, Melanie Unwin, James Walvin, eds., *The British Slave Trade: Abolition, Parliament and People* (Edinburgh: Edinburgh University Press, 2007).
[7] Williams, *Capitalism and Slavery*.
[8] David Brion Davis, *The Problem of Slavery in the Age of Emancipation* (Ithaca: Cornell University Press, 1988).
[9] David Eltis, *Economic Growth and the End of the Transatlantic Slave Trade* (New York: Oxford University Press, 1987).
[10] Richard Huzzey, *Freedom Burning: Anti-Slavery and Empire in Victorian Britain* (Ithaca and London: Cornell University Press, 2012).
[11] Jeremy Bentham, *Principles of Morals and Legislation*, chapter 2, "On slavery," par. 3310, in John Bowring, ed., *The Works of Jeremy Bentham*, 11 volumes (Edinburgh: William Tait, 1838–1843) v. 1.

between these aspects, and, in accordance with utilitarian theory, consider both its utility and its disadvantages for the community. Bentham's analysis thus established a novel link between criticism of slavery, the obligation to assist the poor and the limitation of the wages of free laborers. This link was justified on the basis of a comparison between utility and pain.

Similar connections between servants, the poor and slaves could be found in the thought of Thomas Malthus, William Pitt and Edmund Burke.[12] Debates on the Poor Laws and the conditions of workers in Britain took place at the same time and in the same forum, and sometimes even in the same books, as those on the abolition of slavery. This convergence of elements is what best describes British abolitionism at the time: Criticism of slavery did not imply that free people could be allowed to work whenever and however they pleased; on the contrary, it meant that subsistence wages, supervision and a healthy dose of coercion were necessary.

In opposition to these views, some authors associated slavery with wage labor, insisting that wage laborers were the true slaves. In 1768, Dr. Daniel Burton, former Chancellor of the Diocese of Oxford, wrote that it was impossible to dissociate slavery from the Masters and Servants Acts, as both deprived man of his freedom.[13] On the face of it, this was a universalist position, but as we shall see, it could quickly be transformed into a means of protecting domestic workers from the "invasion" of former slaves.

The tension between these two attitudes is corroborated by the link between abolitionism and free trade. The parliamentary commission set up in 1787 came out solely in favor of eradicating the slave trade.[14] However, several parliamentarians objected that this measure would only reinforce planters' dependence on slave traders, without effectively reducing the trade itself.[15] Immediately afterwards, several merchants' associations declared that any measure banning the trade or slavery would weaken their position in relation to merchants from other countries.

Of course, these attitudes depended on the product in question. In the 1780s, the abolitionist debate focused on sugar. Several associations proposed boycotting sugar from slave plantations. The East India Company supported the abolitionist movement by contrasting "free" sugar, which it imported from Asia, with American sugar produced by slaves: American chattel slavery was considered reprehensible compared with forms of family dependence in India.[16]

---

[12] Edmund Burke, *The Works of the Right Honourable Edmunde Burke* (London: Bell, 1889): V, p. 84.
[13] Prince Hoare, *Memoirs of Granville Sharp, Esq.* (London: Colburn, 1828): 262.
[14] *Proceeding of the Committee for the Abolition of the Slave Trade*, 1787–1819, vol. 1, pp. 14–18, BL Additional Manuscripts 21254–21256.
[15] Ibid.
[16] *British Parliamentary Papers*, 1828, 125.

It was against this backdrop that a conflict arose over trade tariffs in trade with Asia and the Americas. Several British industrialists attacked the favorable tariffs granted to the East India Company and a protectionist policy on sugar, while the Company itself and groups wishing to trade with Asia denounced the preferential tariffs on Atlantic products. Slavery was used as an argument in this tariff war. Merchants with trade links to India, fervent abolitionists and those who presented themselves as "specialists" on India were all firmly convinced that "true slavery" was not practiced on the subcontinent; they also disputed the superiority of free labor over slave labor, pointing out that protective tariffs were necessary to maintain the supply of American sugar. They advocated the adoption of a free-trade policy to force American sugar to compete on the market, which, they argued, would eventually lower prices and thus profits on both sides of the Atlantic.[17] The debate remains open, however, with the British Parliament unable to impose an unambiguous policy towards India.

When production shifted from sugar to cotton, these attitudes changed again; the textile regions most opposed to economic liberalism were also those where the first anti-slavery leagues were founded.[18] These early abolitionist groups, made up partly of small producers and partly of workers, saw the danger of large-scale production based on American cotton. In the 1780s, hostility to slavery went hand in hand with hostility to mechanization in England. Workers needed to be protected from machines just as slaves needed to be freed.[19] That is why tariffs on slave sugar went hand in hand with criticism of mechanization. Free trade and machines were the same target. Quakers and early abolitionist movements attacked materialism and utilitarianism and criticized African slavery on this basis. The growing European demand for sugar was one of the sources of slavery, hence the Quakers' criticism of profit-seeking and consumerism. However, not all entrepreneurs and workers agreed: Some saw anti-slavery protectionism and boycotts as a potential source of higher prices and lower wages. They therefore supported free trade, which at the time was not synonymous with abolitionism.[20]

It therefore seems difficult to identify a "capitalist" support or hostility to slavery (as in Williams' debate), as trades and society were deeply fragmented on this point. However, despite the differences, common trends emerged: The issue of slavery was strongly linked to the defense of property; human rights were a selective and ambiguous notion, heterogeneous in terms of race

---

[17] David Brion Davis, *Slavery and Human Progress* (New York: Oxford University Press, 1984): 181–4.
[18] Thomas Cooper, *Supplement to Mr Cooper's Letters on the Slave Trade* (Manchester: Wheeler, 1787).
[19] *The Morning Chronicle*, June 24, 1788; *The Bristol Gazette*, January 24, 1788.
[20] *Proceeding of the Committee for the Abolition of the Slave Trade*, 1787–1819, vol. 1, pp. 14–18, BL Additional Manuscripts 21254–21256.

and social status (e.g., workers) depending on the speaker; whatever the attitude, the fates of slaves and workers were constantly linked, either in association or in opposition to each other. Was this attitude purely British or shared in France?

French Enlightenment and Abolitionism

The Enlightenment and later forms of French liberalism gave rise to approaches analogous to, but in part different from, those adopted on the subject by the British.[21] Rousseau, Voltaire, Raynal and Diderot criticized slavery as a means of attacking the monarchy.[22] In this way, a common reflection developed around the status of labor: A group of authors from diverse backgrounds examined slavery in the colonies, serfdom in Russia and guild labor in France in order to prove that freedom was a natural right and, for some, that non-free forms of labor were unprofitable.[23] In these works, the serfdom of absolutist and medieval Europe was contrasted with the free labor of Enlightenment Europe; at the same time, and for the same reasons, slavery was synonymous with all forms of heavy dependence. It was, above all, a metaphor rather than a specific reality.[24] As such, slavery included not only dependence on labor, but also all forms of civil and political deprivation. This broad definition of slavery expressed both the strength and the main limitations of the Enlightenment. As Abbé Baudeau pointed out, peasants who were still slaves and Africans were both slaves and for the same reason.[25] It was the link between these debates that caused the definition of labor – and the distinction between free and forced labor – to take on certain characteristics and not others. In the eighteenth century, the work of slaves, serfs and apprentices was considered not only from an ethical point of view, but also increasingly from the standpoint of efficiency. From this perspective, much more than in Great Britain where, as we have seen, Smith's considerations were partially ignored, in France, economic calculations were at the heart of the debates. This was mainly because there was no mass, popular

---

[21] Grenouilleau, *Les traites négrières*; Dorigny, Gainot, *Atlas des esclavages*; Cooper, *Decolonization and African Society*.

[22] Charles Secondat, baron de Montesquieu, *Esprit des lois* (Paris: Garnier, 1967, orig. 1748), chapter XV; Michèle Duchet, *Anthropologie et histoire au siècle des lumières* (Paris, Albin Michel, 1971).

[23] Steven L. Kaplan, *La fin des corporations* (Paris: Fayard, 2001); Minard, *La fortune du colbertisme*; Gilbert Faccarello and Philippe Steiner, *La pensée économique pendant la révolution française* (Grenoble: Presses universitaires de Grenoble, 1990).

[24] Alessandro Stanziani, "Free Labor-Forced Labor: An Uncertain Boundary? The Circulation of Economic Ideas between Russia and Western Europe from the eighteenth to the mid-nineteenth century," *Kritika, Explorations in Russian and Eurasian History*, 9, 1 (2008): 27–52.

[25] Abbé Baudeau, "De l'éducation nationale," *Éphémérides du citoyen*, 2, 11 (1767): 165–85.

abolitionist movement in France, only discussions within the intellectual and political elites. Interest and calculation, rather than morality, were proposed as the basis for abolitionism.[26] In 1774, long before Adam Smith, Baron de Bessner stressed the need to condemn slavery on economic grounds.[27] He criticized Montesquieu not for his ideas, but for his abstraction and failure to take practical constraints into account. In the same vein, Condorcet declared that, although slavery was profitable for an individual master, it was pernicious for the colony and the kingdom. As a form of monopoly, slavery limits competition and therefore production.[28] Civil liberties and the freedom to trade were the main solutions he advocated. The uncertainty of the abolitionists themselves about the profitability of slavery and how to calculate it was immediately echoed in the arguments of the anti-abolitionists. The welfare of slaves would be greater than if they had remained in Africa; profits were relatively limited, but abolition would only lead to the collapse of the colonies and the impoverishment of former slaves.[29]

Thus, for most of the eighteenth century, the attitudes of French philosophers, economists and travelers toward forced labor (serfdom and slavery) were nuanced by both economic (forced labor is advantageous in certain situations) and political (reforms must be gradual, and both owners and slaves must be educated before the system is abolished) considerations. The 1780s saw a radicalization of philosophers' positions towards the French monarchy, Russia and, ultimately, slavery. Rather than trusting the reforms implemented by monarchs, now considered despots, it was now preferable to trust popular movements. France first abolished slavery in 1794. Then, following Napoleon's reinstatement of slavery in 1802, it abolished it again in 1848.[30] Most histories of French abolitionism separate the two events, confining the story within national borders.[31] More recently, France's (re)discovery of the Haitian revolution has shifted the focus of discussion to the tensions of empire and those between the Enlightenment and slavery.[32] Historians have widely debated the restoration of slavery under Napoleon and the weakness of the

---

[26] Caroline Oudin-Bastide, Philippe Steiner, *Calcul et Morale. Coûts de l'esclavage et valeur de l'émancipation, XVIIIe-XIXe siècles* (Paris: Albin Michel, 2015).
[27] Baron de Bessner, "De l'esclavage des nègres," *Archives Nationales* FM C/14/42.
[28] Condorcet (under the name Schwartz), *Réflexions sur l'esclavage des nègres* (Neufchâtel: Société typographique, 1781).
[29] Oudin-Bastide, Steiner, *Calcul et Morale*, especially chapter 3.
[30] A vast collection of abolitionist documents was published in twelve volumes: *La révolution française et l'abolition de l'esclavage* (Paris: Edhis, 1968).
[31] Marcel Dorigny, ed., *Les abolitions de l'esclavage* (Saint-Denis: Presses Universitaires de Vincennes, 1995); Wanquet, *La France et la première abolition de l'esclavage*.
[32] Laurent Dubois, *Avengers of the New World* (Cambridge, MA: Belknap Press, 2004); Alyssa Goldstein Sepinwall, *Haitian History: New Perspectives* (New York: Routledge, 2013).

French abolitionist movement compared to its British counterpart.[33] The absence of industrialization or of groups like the Quakers in France, as well as the absence of pressure from the American colonies, have been invoked to explain these differences.[34]

Other works attribute the abolition of 1794 and the reinstatement of 1802 to contingent events and external pressures, notably war.[35] According to some authors, the emergence of human rights in a political context specific to France produced this result: nationalism,[36] and the role of the state,[37] have also been cited to explain the phenomenon. More radically, other authors attribute these results to the main characteristics and limitations of the French Enlightenment itself.[38] In fact, the scales of investigation are crucial to grasping the significance of the first French abolition. On the one hand, the French Revolution responded to global and imperial upheavals: the emergence of global economies and their impact on Ancient Régime France,[39] the dislocation of empires in Asia and the transformation of polities in Europe, as well as the decline of the Mediterranean and the development of Atlantic economies.[40] On the other hand, the views of specific colonies were also fundamental. Initially, the implementation of the revolution ran up against serious problems in the colonies, where free people of color demanded their full integration in terms of rights, while whites – not only masters and elites, but also those from other countries whose rights had just been recognized – opposed it. The result differed according to location: Civil rights were granted to freedmen in Mauritius, but not in Réunion Island, where they were not granted political rights until 1793.[41] A similar distinction was observed in the French West Indies, where freed people of color were granted the right to vote in Saint-Domingue, but not in Guadeloupe. However, even in these cases, the

---

[33] Drescher, *Capitalism and Antislavery*.
[34] Drescher, *Abolitions*.
[35] Lynn Hunt, *Inventing Human Rights: A History* (New York: Norton, 2007); Jeremy Popkin, *You Are All Free: The Haitian Revolution and the Abolition of Slavery* (Cambridge: Cambridge University Press, 2010).
[36] Hunt, *Inventing Human Rights*.
[37] Samuel Moyn, *The Last Utopia: Human Rights in History* (Cambridge: Belknap, 2010).
[38] Yves Benot, *La révolution française et la fin des colonies* (Paris: La Découverte, 2004); Nelly Schmidt, *Abolitionnistes de l'esclavage et réformateurs des colonies, 1820–1851. Analyses et documents* (Paris: Karthala, 2000); Drescher, *Capitalism and Antislavery*; Robin Blackburn, *The Overthrow of Colonial Slavery, 1776–1848* (London: Verso, 1988); Davis, *The Problem of Slavery*; Grenouilleau, *Les traites négrières*.
[39] Suzanne Desan, Lynn Hunt, William Maw Nelson, *The French Revolution in Global Perspective* (Ithaca and London: Cornell University Press, 2013).
[40] David Armitage, Sanjay Subrahamanyam, *The Age of Revolution in Global Context* (New York: Palgrave, 2010).
[41] Claude Wanquet, *Histoire d'une Révolution, la Réunion, 1789–1803* (Paris: Editions Laffitte, 1980–1984).

central government in Paris and the island's elites repealed the law. Slave insurrections altered this outcome: Freed people of color formed alliances with whites and won their rights.[42]

The abolition of 1794 was a radical and revolutionary act, responding in part to earlier debates on liberty and in part to the changing political situation in France, Europe and the colonies. Universal rights and extended citizenship were both ideals and a practical tactical necessity at a time when the British occupied several French colonies.[43]

However, the actual implementation of abolition was not immediate, as resistance remained strong. In 1796, under the Directoire, discussions continued on the desirability and modalities of abolition in the Isle de France (Mauritius).[44] The British threat and the risk of economic crisis linked to the emancipation of slaves were systematically evoked and put the brakes on abolitionist ardor. Even where slavery was formally abolished, as in Saint-Domingue and Guadeloupe, numerous measures introduced forms of "administrative work." In Guadeloupe, as soon as the reconquest of 1794, Victor Hugues, at the head of the Republican military expedition, paid tribute to the valor of the black soldiers, but expressed skepticism about immediate abolition and its compatibility with the protection of private property. In the months that followed, he adopted several ordinances governing working hours and days, as well as compulsory labor.[45]

In Paris, the difficulties encountered in the colonies favored the convergence of a priori different objectives: defense of the colonies, defense of the nation and restoration of order. With a few exceptions, the link between the revolution and the end of colonialism was never really asserted, and the implementation of abolitionist provisions was de facto delayed in the name of national security.[46] The events in Saint-Domingue encouraged this trend.[47] At the beginning of 1801, Napoleon was still hesitating between two options: To consolidate the regime set up by Toussaint Louverture, or to

---

[42] Marcel Dorigny, Bernard Gainot, *La société des amis des Noirs. Contribution à l'histoire de l'abolition de l'esclavage* (Paris: Unesco, 1998); Laurent Dubois, *Les esclaves de la République. L'histoire oubliée de la première émancipation 1789-1794* (Paris: Calman-Levy, 1998).

[43] Hunt, "The French Revolution in Global Context," in Armitage, Subrahamanyam, *The Age of Revolution in Global Context*: 20-36.

[44] ANOM, FM, C 4 1720-1750.

[45] ANOM, C 7A 47, Victor Hugues au Comité de salut public, 4 thermidor an II (July 22, 1794).

[46] Benot, *La révolution française*.

[47] Laurent Dubois, *A Colony of Citizen: Revolution and Slave Emancipation in the French Caribbean, 1787-1804* (Chapel Hill: University of North Carolina Press, 2004); David Geggus, *Slavery, War, and Revolution: The British Occupation of Saint-Domingue, 1793-1798* (Oxford: Clarendon Press, 1982); Popkin, *You Are All Free*; Scott, Hebrard, *Freedom Papers*.

send a fleet and re-establish white supremacy. At the time, the first solution seemed more attractive: better to produce less sugar but have allies against the British and Americans than risk losing the island and ending the Revolution's influence in the Caribbean.[48] His final decision was linked to several major events on the international scene. In Russia, the assassination of Tsar Paul I dashed any hopes of Russian intervention in the British Indies and compromised the attack on Jamaica. Shortly afterwards, Great Britain showed the first signs of a truce. Napoleon prepared for the reconquest of the colony, declaring that the principles of fundamental liberties would not be called into question.[49]

The revolution in Saint-Domingue played a decisive role: in Paris and throughout the colonial world, planters, merchants and supporters of independence from Great Britain were concerned about the weakness of France and its colonies,[50] and numerous petitions were sent to the capital.[51] Finally, the Peace of Amiens came just before the law of May 20, 1802, which recognized slavery in territories that had not applied the abolitionist law (Martinique and Réunion), reintroduced the slave trade in these colonies and announced future decisions for colonies where slavery had been abolished (Saint-Domingue and Guadeloupe).[52] Shortly afterwards, several decrees were issued against free people of color in mainland France.[53]

Although, in principle, only slaves freed before 1789 were guaranteed their freedom in Saint-Domingue, in practice most slaves emancipated since that date have not returned to slavery, as Napoleon legitimized the resumption of the slave trade.[54] He consolidated certain revolutionary principles, but not universal freedom; he sought to reconcile the citizenship of some slaves in metropolitan France with slavery and the empire.[55]

Napoleon's decision breathed new life into the British abolitionist movement. It was now possible to preach the abolition of the slave trade, and even slavery, without sounding like a Jacobin. While Great Britain was taking over

---

[48] Jean-Baptiste Vaillant ed., *Correspondance de Napoléon I*^{er} *publiée par ordre de l'empereur Napoléon III*, 32 volumes (Paris: Imprimerie impériale, 1858), vol. 7: 44–45.
[49] ANOM, FM, F/3/202, Napoléon Bonaparte, "Proclamation du Consul à tous les habitants de Saint-Domingue" (17 brumaire an X [November 8, 1802]).
[50] François-Richard de Tussac, *Cri des colons contre un ouvrage de M. l'évêque et sénateur Grégoire, ayant pour titre de la littérature des nègres* (Paris: Les Marchands de nouveautés, 1810).
[51] AN, CC 9A/27; CC 9 A/30; CC 9C/1.
[52] Yves Benot and Marcel Dorigny, eds., *Rétablissement de l'esclavage dans les colonies françaises* (Paris: Maisonnove et Larose, 2003); Wanquet, *La France et la première abolition*.
[53] YEAR CC9; YEAR B24.
[54] Thierry Lentz and Pierre Branda, *Napoléon, l'esclavage et les colonies* (Paris: Fayard, 2006).
[55] Régent, *La France et ses esclaves*: 275.

the French, Spanish and Dutch colonies, Napoleon's unsuccessful attempt to restore the old order in Haiti convinced Pitt and several other top British leaders of the need to avoid such a situation for the British Empire, particularly in Jamaica, where slave insurrections were multiplying.[56] With the continental blockade extended to colonial products and slaves, the abolition of the slave trade was voted on February 23, 1807. While parliamentary debates prior to the abolition of the slave trade had returned to the link between slavery and wage labor, in the aftermath of the abolition of the slave trade, several members of parliament proposed adopting a relatively liberal stance on the labor market in Great Britain: To avoid insurrections, the free market was seen as the best solution, hence the limitation of corporate rules and the reform of apprenticeship in 1812. This complex outcome of the French Revolution would shape the forms of abolitionism during the first half of the nineteenth century.

Abolition and Capitalism in the First Half of the Nineteenth Century

In Great Britain, women formed their own associations within the movement from 1825 onwards.[57] An abolitionist petition signed by 187,000 women was delivered to Parliament in May 1833. Of the 1.3 million people who signed the petitions produced that year, 30 percent were women.[58] The new wave of abolitionists was even more deeply rooted in religious movements, particularly Baptists and Methodists, the latter accounting for 18 percent of signatories in 1833.[59] This religious component facilitated links with the United States and, through missionaries, with the colonial world. Again, the question of abolition intersected with that of trade policy.[60] As at the end of the eighteenth century, between the 1820s and 1840s, the relationship between trade policy and abolitionism depended on the groups and products concerned.[61] During the 1830s, Manchester industrialists called for the development of cotton in India, partly because demand was still rising, and partly because criticism of the

---

[56] *Proceedings of the Committee for the Abolition of the Slave Trade, 1787–1819*, vol. 1: 14–18, British Library, Additional Manuscripts 21254–21256.

[57] Linda Colley, *Britons: Forging the Nation 1707–1837* (New Haven: Yale University Press, 1992); Kathryn Kish Sklar, James Brewer Stewart, eds., *Sisterhood and Slavery* (New Haven: Yale University Press, 2006); Claire Midgley, *Women Against Slavery* (London: Routledge, 1992).

[58] Elizabeth Clapp, Julie Roy Jeffrey, eds., *Women, Dissent and Anti-Slavery in Britain and America, 1790–1865* (New York: Oxford University Press, 2011).

[59] Drescher, *Abolitions*: 252.

[60] Robert Fogel, *Without Consent or Contract* (New York: Norton, 1994), vol. 1: 203–204.

[61] Richard Huzzey, "Free Trade, Free Labor, and Slave Sugar in Victorian Britain," *Historical Journal*, 53, 2 (2010): 359–379. Huzzey, *Freedom Burning*.

United States was growing within the abolitionist movement.[62] Some members of the abolitionist movement believed that free trade would encourage slave production in America, and therefore recommended protectionism and boycotts as anti-slavery measures. At the time, these abolitionists saw any agreement with free traders as a capitulation.[63]

In this context, the link between wage labor and slavery also resurfaced. The limits of abolitionism and its practices were not only a consequence of the ambiguities of liberalism(s), in particular the relationship between freedom and private property, and the idea that workers themselves should have limited rights. Workers' associations also maintained ambiguities about the distinctions and relationships between wage-earners and slaves. The question of "who is the real slave?" was not merely rhetorical but had a lasting influence on the universality of freedom from the workers' point of view. It spanned religious, ethical, economic and political divides. Not only in England, but also in France, Russia and Germany, there was a revival of interest in two questions, partly inherited from the previous period, which were to become increasingly prominent throughout the nineteenth century, particularly in the second half: "Should wage labor and industrialization be seen as factors of progress? Should wage labor and industrialization be regarded as progress and freedom, or as a new form of slavery?"

The responses of liberal economists did not always coincide with those of the labor movement. The debate on labor (the rapid development of wage labor, the status of workers) was at the heart of a reflection on the values of bourgeois capitalist society; criticism of wage labor as a new form of slavery pervaded political and intellectual circles in Europe. The subject was taken up by socialists such as Fourier, Owen and Saint-Simon, whom Marx and Engels (especially the latter) described as "utopians," as well as by French Christian socialists and ultra-Catholics. Marx also fell victim to the same rhetoric, despite his criticism of economists who associated wage labor with slavery. He compared servants to the domestic slaves of antiquity,[64] described child labor in factories as real slaves, and saw slavery as thinly disguised capitalism. In short, for Marx, the main difference between slavery and wage labor lay in the way surplus value was extracted: by law and physical coercion before capitalism, by economic coercion under capitalism.

The main liberal and utilitarian currents were equally ambiguous on the subject. After condemning slavery on moral grounds, Jean-Baptiste Say explained that the master's right of ownership over the slave protected both master and slave: Say believed that slavery could reinforce both the division of labor

---

[62] *Hansard Parliamentary Debates*, 3rd series, XVI (March 1833), 18: 729–730.
[63] Seymour Drescher, *The Mighty Experiment: Free Labor versus Slavery in British Emancipation* (Oxford: Oxford University Press, 2002).
[64] Karl Marx, *Das kapital* (Italian translation, Roma, Einaudi, 1972), vol. I: 491–492.

and efficiency.[65] Herman Merivale added that in the colonial context, wage labor was less productive than slave labor.[66]

The labor movement, which agitated Lancashire between 1830 and 1833, revealed the contradictory positions of abolitionists on the fate of British wage earners. Radical and Yorkshire abolitionists emphasized the link between slavery and wage labor, and called for reforms of both.[67] By 1832, it was impossible to find an abolitionist petition, meeting or pamphlet that did not associate the fate of slaves with that of child laborers in Britain.[68] Among the working classes and in Protestant circles, no distinction was made between wage-earners and slaves.

On the other hand, moderate abolitionists saw the condition of slaves as a reason to impose stricter standards on free labor in Great Britain. For Frederick Douglass, there was no question of "industrial slavery": wage earners were not slaves; nor were apprentices in Britain or the colonies.[69] Yet, in his view, both groups needed coercion to function properly.

The success of the abolitionist position reinforced the latter attitude.[70] It was no coincidence that, when slavery was abolished in the colonies (1833), British wage-earners lost all traditional forms of assistance: the new Poor Law, passed in 1834, forced paupers to choose between work and the house of correction. Debates in Parliament highlighted the clear link between the eradication of slavery and changes in the continent's labor institutions.[71] The introduction of apprenticeships in the colonies encouraged debate on the practice in Britain and helped promote Poor Law reforms. The assimilation of quasi-slaves to child laborers and apprentices was highlighted in parliamentary debates.[72] A transitional period of six to twelve years, referred to as an "apprenticeship," was imposed on slaves; this was no coincidence, as the period of individual emancipation for slaves was identical to the duration of the apprenticeship contract in England. Slaves thus became apprentices, with a contract similar to apprenticeship contracts in Great Britain. Like miners in mainland France, quasi-emancipated slaves had to go through a transition period before their

---

[65] Jean-Baptiste Say, *Cours d'économie politique* (Brussels: Meline, Cans et Compagnie, 1843): 522.
[66] Herman Merivale, *Lectures on Colonization and Colonies* (London: Orme, Brown, Green and Longmans, 1841).
[67] *The Poor Man's Guardian*, November 17, 1832; *Manchester Guardian*, September 8, 1832.
[68] Drescher, *Abolitions*: 260.
[69] Alan Rice, Martin Crawford, eds., *Liberating Sojourn: Frederick Douglass and Transatlantic Reform* (Athens: Ohio University Press, 1999).
[70] BL MSS Brit. Emp. S 2o, E2/4 (Anti-Slavery Papers, minute book of the committee of the Anti-Slavery Society).
[71] Charles R. Dod, *Electoral Facts 1832–1853 Impartially Stated*, ed. H. J. Hanham (London: Harvester Press, 1972); *Hansard Parliamentary Papers*, second series, April 15, 1831 III: 1425–1445.
[72] Brion Davis, *The Problem of Slavery*.

final emancipation.⁷³ Slaves and children were not recognized as legal subjects in their own right and were therefore submitted to their masters or fathers. In the 1830s, the exploitation of child labor in Great Britain and of former slaves in its colonies went hand in hand.

During the transitional years, slaves were therefore referred to as apprentices; they were not expected to learn a trade, but to behave like free people.⁷⁴ Under the new laws, "apprentices" were required to work forty-five hours a week for their master in exchange for their freedom; any unjustified absence or failure to meet standards (determined by the master) was punished by an extension of the apprenticeship period and the length of the working day. Corporal punishment, theoretically prohibited for slaves in the 1820s, was reintroduced for apprentices. Not surprisingly, abuses multiplied.⁷⁵

Although the former slave owners received about twenty million pounds sterling in compensation from the British Crown, most of them tried to increase their income by claiming as much of the labor of their (almost) former slaves as possible. Of course, the final outcome depended on the colony, the conditions of access to land, the forms of coercion used, the types of activities, the new rules governing labor and, last but not least, the credit system in place. In Barbados, for example, the planters took over almost all the land, which they then leased to their former slaves, who often remained in their former workplace. In Jamaica, Trinidad and British Guiana, although former slaves were officially entitled to own land, most of them were so indebted to their masters that they returned to work on their former plantations.⁷⁶ This didn't prevent them from resisting by working irregular hours or even running away. The decline of sugar production in Jamaica is one of the main signs of this resistance.

The choice of transitional apprenticeship as a solution to abolition was based on the assumption that there was no "natural" economic incentive for black people, an argument that revived the Poor Laws debate in Great Britain.⁷⁷ In both cases, the same hypothesis was invoked: Workers, like former slaves, were not spontaneously inclined to maximize their work effort;⁷⁸ it was therefore necessary to pay them minimum wages and resort to more or less legal methods of coercion to overcome their "indolence."⁷⁹ The new Poor Law

---

[73] The National Archives (TNA), Kew, CO (Colonial Office), 318/116.
[74] House of Commons, *Papers in Explanation of the Condition of the Slave Population*, November 5, 1831, *Parliamentary Papers*, 1830–1, 230, 16.1: 59–88.
[75] James R. Ward, *British West India Slavery, 1750–1834: The Process of Amelioration* (Oxford: Oxford University Press, 1988).
[76] Thomas Holt, *The Problem of Freedom. Race, Labor and Politics in Jamaica and Britain, 1832–1938* (Baltimore and London: Johns Hopkins University Press, 1992).
[77] Eltis, *Economic Growth*.
[78] *Hansard Parliamentary Papers* 1833, vol. 19: c. 1252–72. 1834, vol. 22: c 938; vol. 25: 435–56.
[79] *Hansard Parliamentary Papers* 1833, vol. 18: 1378, 976; vol. 19: 2549.

therefore reduced assistance to the poor and forced vagrants into workhouses. This was the argument originally put forward by Bentham, whose name was invoked to justify these measures: the old Poor Laws were too costly, while being of no use either to society or to the workers themselves; it was therefore necessary to replace assistance by putting the poor to work. The same principle applied to British wage-earners and former slaves.[80]

In the 1840s, as before, sugar linked the living conditions of British workers to slavery. For some, sugar was a necessity for the worker and the protectionist tariff didn't deserve it. But, on the other hand, free trade would improve the standard of living of the British working class while reinforcing slavery.[81] Here again, the connections and disconnections between British India and the British Atlantic come into play. In March 1808, Joint Magistrate J. Richardson denounced the persistent tolerance of slavery in India.[82] No official action was taken, apart from the keeping of a register of slaves.[83] Mediation between these positions is hampered by the problematic relationship between the British government of India and the princely states. For the EIC, the main concern was not the abolition of slavery, but political stability and the cross-border trade. On the ground, interaction was complicated by the multiplicity of agreements and rules binding Great Britain and these states. In this context, the lack of control was a source of concern for a number of British officials. In 1811, when the Bengal government adopted Regulation X prohibiting the sale of slaves and their entry into British territories, the question arose as to how this regulation could be applied to the Mughal state's neighbors in Delhi. Debates continued over the relevance of local customs to British law, particularly with regard to slavery. In fact, opinions diverged in Bengal, Madras and Bombay, depending on the views of local colonial elites. James Mill's reflections on slavery and India are part of this shifting context.[84] As an officer in the EIC, he was directly concerned with the problem of slavery in India and, consequently, with the related questions of the imperial administration, the form of domination (direct or indirect) and therefore the role of local courts and local knowledge.[85]

---

[80] Tom Franzmann, "Antislavery and Political Economy in the Early Victorian House of Commons: A Research Note on 'Capitalist Hegemony'," *Journal of Social History*, 27, 3 (1994): 579–593.
[81] *Hansard Parliamentary Papers*, third series: 1840, lviii; 1841, lviii; 1846, lxxxviii.
[82] BL IOR, Bengal Judicial Consultations, P/132/21.
[83] BL IOR, Bengal Judicial Consultations, P/132/57.
[84] Allison Dube, "The Tree of Utility in India: Panace or Weed?," in Marin Moir, Douglas Peers, Lynn Zastoupil, eds., *J.S. Mill's Encounter with India* (Toronto: University of Toronto Press, 1999): 34–52; Karuna Mantena, *Alibis of Empire: Henri Maine and the Ends of Liberal Imperialism* (Princeton: Princeton University Press, 2010).
[85] James Mill, "Colony," in *Supplement to the Encyclopedia Britannica* (London, 1820): 31–33, reprinted in G.W. Smith, ed., *John Stuart Mill's Social and Political Thought: Critical Assessments* (London: Routledge 1998), vol. III, Politics and Government: 498.

Mill believed that Mughal feudal law should be replaced by British law[86] and was convinced that poverty and ignorance could be cured by making the right laws. From this point of view, India was a tabula rasa that could be shaped by utilitarianism. Mill claimed that the indolent, superstitious character of the natives was the product of despotism and religious tyranny. Contrary to Mill, in the eyes of most British elites in India, efficiency had less to do with the abstract principles of utilitarianism than with the application of the law.[87] In the event of a conflict between abstract justice and practical sovereignty, priority must be given to the latter. This means that Islamic law must be preserved – even if it runs counter to certain principles of British justice – as long as it guarantees compliance. James Mill criticized this solution, believing it failed to provide the strong centralization needed for military purposes.[88] In 1837, a commission was set up to study the labor standards to be applied after the abolition of slavery, but it was divided: some members felt that the colonial Masters and Servants Acts should be applied in a version specifically adapted to India; other members, including Thomas Macaulay, wanted the new labor relations to be governed by civil law provisions. The majority of commission members opted for the first plan, and the draft code therefore introduced penal sanctions in the event of breach of contract. Workers were described as servants and assimilated to beggars. The British Masters and Servants Acts served as a model for regulating free labor in India.

In June 1840, the First World Anti-Slavery Convention in London adopted a series of resolutions condemning slavery in India. Universal evangelical values were added to the growing criticism of the power of the EIC. Abolitionism in India goes hand in hand with the end of the EIC's political powers. John Stuart Mill repeated his attacks on the Company.[89] However, like many other criticisms of slavery since the eighteenth century, this critique was not accompanied by the granting of political rights to the freed. According to Mill, slaves, children and barbarians had limited capacities to exercise reason. Reason and restrictions on political inclusion went hand in hand.[90] Slavery was thus officially abolished in India; however, no one, including British officials, knew exactly who this reform was aimed at, or what concrete policy to adopt. Slavery was abolished in 1843; however, uncertainty persisted over "who were the real slaves in India." Instead of putting an end to the slavery question, this result raised new ones, starting with Britain's relations with the Indian states.

---

[86] James Mill, *The History of British India* (London: James Madden, 1858, first edition: 1817).

[87] C.E. Grey and E. Ryan, "Some Observations on a Suggestion of a Code of Law," submitted to the Governor General in Council on September 13, 1830. Bentick to Grey and Ryan, October 9, 1831, British Parliamentary Papers, 1831, VI: 140.

[88] *British Parliamentary Papers*, 1831–2, February 16, 1832: 14

[89] BL, IOR, Political dispatch to India, February 13, 1838, E/4/753: 909–912.

[90] Uday Mehta, *Liberalism and Empire* (Chicago: University of Chicago Press, 1999).

Local governors and elites took very different views depending on their own definition of slavery. For example, debt bondage was systematically excluded from this category and therefore tolerated.[91] We'll look at the real significance of the end of slavery in India in a moment.

International debates evolved after the mid-1840s. Abolitions were adopted in Sweden, Denmark and France; in this context, advocates of an Atlantic free-trade economy found increasing success. Abolitionist-protectionists now found it hard to justify their orientation in the face of rising sugar prices following abolitions; "free economies" now produced cheaper sugar. In 1846, Great Britain lowered customs duties on wheat and colonial sugar.[92]

At the time, mutual influences on slavery were shaping debates on both sides of the Atlantic. *Uncle Tom's Cabin* (1852) was a huge success in Britain, where ten different editions were published in a matter of weeks and 1.5 million copies were sold in less than a year.[93] Hundreds of spin-off books appeared in the years that followed, while the rise of Victorian newspapers and the periodical press accelerated the trend. Some commentators came to believe that the British public was exerting a growing influence on American slaveholders.

However, public debate in Britain was divided over whether immediate emancipation of American slaves was desirable; the gradualists supported their viewpoint, arguing that it was strategic to convince slave owners. They also feared the rise of radicalism and advocated slave insurrection to oppose abolition from above, as in Britain. There was also the problem of secession: Even pro-Union thinkers like Mill believed that an independent South would emancipate slaves more quickly.[94] In addition, unlike the British campaigns, it was difficult to raise funds to support American antislavery: It was not clear to whom the money should be sent; moreover, some of the extremism of American antislavery societies was not worth seeing in Britain.

In this context, the question of whether or not industrial labor was slavery took on a new dimension. Some saw them as totally distinct, and as such, emancipation was the removal of an unjust institution. This view saw slavery as a deprivation of freedom and a denial of rights, while some others sustained a voluntary orientation emphasizing positive rights.[95] Frederick Douglass supported the first attitude.[96]

---

[91] Campbell, Stanziani, *Bonded Labour and Debt in the Indian Ocean World*.
[92] Anthony Howe, *Free Trade and Liberal England, 1846–1946*, (Oxford: Oxford University Press, 1997); Paul A. Pickering and Alex Tyrrell, *The People's Bread: A History of the Anti-Corn Law League* (London and New York: Continuum, 2000).
[93] Huzzey, *Freedom Burning*: 21.
[94] John Stuart Mill, "Review of John Elliot Cairnes, The Slave Power," *Westminster Review*, (July 1862): 489–510.
[95] On these debates, see Eltis, *Economic Growth*, Steinfeld, *Coercion*.
[96] Frederick Douglass, *The Frederick Douglass Papers*, John Blassingame editor, 5 volumes (New Haven: Yale University Press) 1: 343

Conversely, others argued that social conditions were identical and that wage labor and slavery could therefore be placed on an equal footing. Cobden's *White Slaves of England* is an important example of this attitude[97] and Dickens also suggested that the evils of American slavery and British industry needed to be considered together.[98] Carlyle also criticized abolitionism on paper while ignoring the suffering of slaves; he advocated a paternalistic order opposed to wage labor.[99] Chartrists also stigmatized "the hypocrisy of abolitionism."[100]

These conflicting attitudes influenced the economic and political policies to be adopted. A new generation of Quakers and a transatlantic network of abolitionists proposed using boycotts rather than tariffs to combat slavery. Some abolitionists favored free trade and restrictions on immigration to the Caribbean, arguing that emancipated slaves should not suffer from the arrival of new immigrants. Conversely, others believed that new immigration would help former slaves find new jobs in urban activities. As we shall see, local planters were mostly in favor of limited mobility for former slaves and new immigrants to compensate for their "losses" and/or investments. In the end, all parties agreed that new immigration would contribute to lower wages, but this was inevitable because the former slaves and new immigrants had only basic needs and were encouraged to work for low wages.

In short, British abolitionism cannot be reduced to iconic representations of Williams and his opponents. It presents continuities and changes over several decades, between the 1770s and the mid nineteenth century. Ethical arguments prevailed over economic logic, until the abolition of slavery. Abolitionists were also anti-consumerist and ultimately protectionist for decades and only became full-fledged supporters of free trade in the 1840s. Inhabitants of the colonies were supposed to be free, but with a high compensation to the former owner and without real economic, social and political rights. Abolition confirmed the alliance between landowners, aristocratic capitalism and the state. This led to peaceful abolition, without revolution as in Saint-Domingue or civil war as in the United States. However, the convergence of British elites, rural and urban aristocrats and the middle classes came at the expense of former slaves and the working class, who paid for the bulk of emancipation through taxation and compulsory labor (in the colonies). Finally, the unresolved conceptual and political tensions between workers and slaves spilled over into concrete policies and political movements across the political spectrum.

---

[97] John Cobden, *The White Slaves of England: Compiled from Official Documents* (New York: Saxton, 1860).
[98] Charles Dickens, *All The Year Round*, June 15, 1867: 585.
[99] Thomas Carlyle, *Occasional Discourse on the Negro Question* (first published in *Fraser's Magazine for Town and Country*, 1849 vol XL, 1849, then London, 1853).
[100] Malcom Chase, *Chartism. A New History* (Manchester: Manchester University Press, 2007).

British Abolitionism in Practice: The Case of India and the Indian Ocean

These uncertainties affected the conditions of former slaves and new indentured immigrants in the British Empire. For example, between the official abolition of slavery in 1834 and 1910, 450,000 indentured servants arrived in Mauritius, mostly from India but also from Madagascar. Two-thirds stayed, allowing the Indian population to grow steadily from 35 percent in 1846 to 66 percent in 1871.[101] Many observers have pointed out the inhumane living conditions of these immigrants.[102] To these figures must be added the other indentured servants from South Asia and Africa: 30,000 in 1851 and double that number ten years later. Both forms of immigration to Mauritius provoked protests from English landowners and industries such as the railroads in India and East Africa, who complained of unfair competition from the Mauritians, aided by the French, who had contributed to this human traffic before and after 1848.[103] Women's immigration to Mauritius remained secondary, at least initially, and had to be controlled by the state.[104] It did not develop rapidly until the mid nineteenth century, after the abolition of slavery, with the arrival of new indentured servants and their families and the considerable demand for domestic and urban labor, as well as more traditional labor on the sugar plantations.[105]

Indian immigrants arrived from three ports: Bombay, Calcutta and Madras. Between 1834 and 1912, of the two million Indian emigrants bound for other parts of the British Empire, 95 percent came from Bengal. Initially recruited from the coastal regions, the recruiters' radius of action then extended inland. Between 1834 and 1842, 15,042 male immigrants came from Calcutta, 9,524 from Madras and 264 from Bombay. Of the 50,000 Indian immigrants who landed in Mauritius in 1858–1859, the majority came from the north-western regions. The Calcutta recruits often belonged to the untouchables or came from the tribal areas of the interior. In all, these tribal immigrants numbered 50,000 between 1834 and 1870.[106]

In Mauritius, abuses by estate owners and, even more so, by their stewards and overseers, were noted in British parliamentary reports,[107] and confirmed by estate inspectors.[108] Yet the workers' cause was rarely won in the courts.[109]

---

[101] Auguste Toussaint, *Histoire de l'île Maurice* (Paris: PUF, 1974).
[102] Colonie of Mauritius, annual report, 1854, British Parliamentary Papers 1854, 52 (2050).
[103] British Parliamentary Papers 1841, 45: 16, Petition from the inhabitants of Calcutta.
[104] Carter, *Servants, Sirdars and Settlers*: 3.
[105] Stanziani, *Labor on the Fringes of Empire*.
[106] MNA B1B, First Immigration, Arrivals of Indian Immigrants.
[107] British Parliamentary Papers 1842, 30: 26
[108] MNA RA 1955, Immigration, Protectors of slaves, police; TNA (The National Archives, Kew), CO (Colonial Office) 167/263, Mauritius Island; British Parliamentary Papers, 1847 (325) 39.
[109] TNA CO 167/213, 202, 266. Colony of Mauritius, annual reports, 1860–1890.

The number of lawsuits filed by indentured servants against their masters, which was low in the 1850s, rose sharply thereafter. In the 1860s and 1870s, about 10 percent of indentured servants took legal action against their masters, and more than 70 percent of them won.[110] The disputes mainly concerned the payment of wages, which masters delayed for months or even years. Between 1860 and 1895, non-payment of wages accounted for 76 percent to 87 percent of complaints, followed by complaints about insufficient or poor food. At the "Providence" estate in the Flacq district, which employed 410 people, workers were paid every four months, which, according to the owner of the estate, encouraged them to save. Of course, the workers claimed otherwise and demanded their wages.[111] Almost all the testimonies from the estates were split down the middle between the estate owners and what they claimed were the workers' wishes, and the workers' point of view.

An important exception seems to have been the "La Grande Baie" estate in the Rivière du Rempart district, with 380 acres and 180 workers, almost all from Calcutta. In 1873, the owner of the estate lodged an astonishing complaint: he claimed that, although he wanted to pay his laborers every month as required by law, he was met with protests from the laborers, who stopped working and demanded to be paid every two months. The estate owner said that these virtuous workers had told him they wanted to save money for their families back in India. As a result, they stopped working, and the estate owner had been forced to impose substantial penalties on them, taking back a large part of their wages. Moral of the story: a bad law had ended up penalizing the workers. The immigrants gave a radically different version: they *wanted to* be paid every month and, faced with the estate owner's refusal, had stopped working.[112]

Wage disparities and living conditions were also the source of complaints. This was the case at "La Providence," a 250-acre estate in Flacq, where 410 laborers were employed, 195 of whom had embarked from Calcutta, 192 from Madras, twenty-one from Bombay and two from an unspecified origin. The Bombay immigrants came from Chiplun, in the southern Konkan region. They refused to be mixed with immigrants from other regions: Mahrattas, Muhajirs and Chummars. According to reports and testimonies by the owners, tensions also arose among immigrants when people of different castes were placed in the same dormitory. According to the owners, these complaints had a negative impact on productivity and caused unrest on the plantations. As a result, most estates preferred to recruit immigrants who were more homogeneous in terms of caste and regional origin. In Pamplemousse, the 200-hectare "Mon

---

[110] British Parliamentary Papers, 1875, 704: 34 and appendices A and B. Colony of Mauritius, 1860–1885. For a full development of case studies on law in Mauritius: Stanziani, *Labor on the Fringes of Empire*.
[111] ANOM Gen c149 d1248.
[112] Ibid.

Choix" estate employed 110 recruits, 104 of them from Calcutta. This solution had certain advantages: it reduced tensions between workers and broadened the planters' relationships with intermediaries from the same region of India. It also had certain disadvantages: the *sirdars* more easily sided with the workers and, according to some owners, they encouraged rebellion.[113]

Denunciations of physical violence were much rarer, partly because of pressure from judges and colonial authorities, who emphasized their exceptional nature, and partly because of the attitude of the immigrants themselves, who often declared that they could bear physical violence if necessary, but not the loss of their wages.[114]

In addition to the use of the law, other forms of resistance were put in place. Absenteeism and absconding were among the most common, so much so that between 1860 and 1870, planters filed 70,000 legal complaints on these grounds.[115]

By 1845, an estimated 35,000 Indians had deserted the colony (6 percent of the workforce), while 11 percent were absent and 8 percent were sick.[116] Thanks to new regulations adopted in the 1860s, landowners increased the number of complaints to about 6,000 a year; by this time, between 8 percent and 10 percent of the colony's workforce had absentee status; in addition, 8 percent of workers were arrested each year as vagrants. Most of these complaints were dismissed because the workers were never found, either because they were in town and difficult to identify, or because they were picked up by other planters who promised them better conditions.[117]

If we examine the information by estate in detail, we discover that there was a strong correlation between the number of abuses committed by the planter (violence, withholding of wages, etc.) and acts of resistance by workers. In the Pamplemousse district, for example, the Mont Choisy estate, with its 724 hectares and 276 workers, caused a scandal in 1871, after numerous worker complaints and an administrative investigation revealed frequent wage deductions, insufficient food and working days of up to twenty hours, against the twelve hours stipulated by law. These conditions led to a high turnover rate (208 over the year, out of 276 workers), as well as enormous absenteeism, denounced by the boss and confirmed by the books. This led to extreme monetary penalties: Of the £11,200 in wages due over the year, only £8,400 were actually paid to the workers.[118] In other words, faced with worker

---

[113] ANOM Gen c149 d1248.
[114] ANOM FM/ SG REU c380/d228; Gen c149 d1248; MNA RA 1955, 2205.
[115] MNA RA 1955, Immigration, Police, 2205, Immigration; Colony of Mauritius, *Protector of Immigrants*.
[116] ANOM Gen c149 d1248.
[117] TNA CO 167/252; MNA H66, Planters' petitions.
[118] ANOM Gen c149 d1248.

resistance, the planters reacted by increasing penalties and withholding a large proportion of wages, while adding days and days of unpaid work to compensate for the workers' initial debt in terms of transportation, food advances, etc. In 1874, out of one million pounds of wages, the masters deducted £229,225 for absenteeism and £91,000 for sickness; the following year, these deductions rose to £254,193 and £103,756, respectively, for sickness. The owners deducted one day's wages for each day of illness, and double for each day of imprisonment or unjustified absence.[119] In sum, freedom for planters meant, above all, freedom to abuse workers, whether they were former slaves or new indentured immigrants.

In India itself, the abolition of slavery took on multiple meanings, depending on the British officials, masters and estate stewards in the various regions of the subcontinent.[120] The abolition of slavery immediately raised the question of the rules that would govern the labor market. There were multiple labor markets in India: the agricultural labor market, migration abroad, internal migration to plantations, recruitment for public works, labor for handicrafts and small-scale industries, employment in large-scale industries, railways and mines, urban labor, including prostitution, domestic service and municipal work.[121] The relationship between debt and the obligation to work was common to all sectors: recruiters made considerable use of debt to secure workers, just as the colonial administration appealed to taxpayers. The production of indigo in Bengal and tea in Assam were paradigmatic cases.[122]

The continuities between precolonial and colonial indigo production and the persistence of Indian producers and traders alongside the British during the colonial period are significant.[123] Most indigo was grown by small tenants of British planters or Indian landowners. The latter advanced money to the peasants and then made repayment of the debt as difficult as possible, imposing fines for poor

---

[119] ANOM, FM/SG REU 380/3228, minute 7.
[120] For a full analysis, see Stanziani, *Labor on the Fringes of Empire*, chapter 3, and "Slavery in India," in Eltis and others, *The Cambridge World History of Slavery*, vol. 4.
[121] Michael Anderson, "India 1858–1930: The Illusion of Free Labor," in Douglas Hay, Paul Craven, *Masters, Servants, and Magistrates in Britain and the Empire, 1562–1955* (Chapel Hill: The University of North Carolina Press, 2004): 422–454.
[122] Sugata Bose, *Peasant Labour and Colonial Capital: Rural Bengal since 1770* (Cambridge: Cambridge University Press, 1993); Prabhat Kumar Shukla, *Indigo and the Raj: Peasant Protests in Bihar, 1780–1917* (Delhi: Pragati Publication, 1993); Benoy Chowdhury, *Growth of Commercial Agriculture in Bengal, 1757–1900* (Calcutta: R K Mitra, 1964); Jacques Pouchepadass, *Planteurs et paysans dans l'Inde coloniale. L'indigo du Bihar et le mouvement gandhien du Champaran (1917-8)* (Paris: L'Harmattan, 1986), English translation: *Champaran and Gandhi: Planters, Peasants and Gandhian Politics* (New Delhi: Oxford University Press, 1999); Prakash Kumar, *Indigo Plantation and Science in Colonial India* (New York: Cambridge University Press, 2012).
[123] Ghulam Nadri, *The Political Economy of Indigo in India, 1580–1930. A Global Perspective* (Leiden: Brill, 2016).

performance, absenteeism and so on.[124] The regulations of 1830 made breach of contract by indigo growers an offence punishable summarily by magistrates with a month's imprisonment. Until the 1840s, the rising price of indigo on the world market prompted planters to demand increasingly stringent rules to control workers and tenants. By the 1840s, prices continued to fall, as did production. The "tenants" (*raiyats*) refused to plant indigo. Incidents involving planter brutality towards *raiyats* became commonplace, with planters forcing peasants to produce. After the Sepoy mutiny, the planters demanded and obtained (in 1859) stiffer penal sanctions for breach of contract.[125] As Prabhu Mohapatra has shown, these attitudes were expressed under the aegis of the contractors.[126] In the spring of 1860, peasants refused to sow and planter-manufacturers brought a large number of lawsuits before the magistrates' courts, claiming breach of contract.[127] In the years that followed, indigo exports fell sharply as they were rapidly replaced by synthetic dyes on the world market.

Unlike Bengal, the system in Assam did not comprise a number of planters and *raiyats*, but rather a large corporation made up of plantations employing a type of "wage laborer"; in effect, indentured immigrants. In the late 1830s, an Assam Company was created, derived from the EIC. Between 1840 and 1850, when the area under cultivation and tea production barely increased, the government had little involvement in the recruitment and employment of workers. The Company therefore insisted on the need to import "coolies." Company agents operated in Bengal, exploiting the labor market for farm laborers, seasonal migrants and the emerging market for indentured laborers for overseas colonies. By the 1850s, the Company was emphasizing the urgent need to reduce recruitment and labor costs and increase productivity through effective supervision and legal coercion.[128] Production and labor immigration increased in the 1850s, but the Company complained about the continued desertion of coolies, their absenteeism and lack of motivation.[129] Planters also raised racial concerns, claiming that Kachari immigrants were unreliable and lazy.[130] In the

---

[124] BL IOR V 3244.
[125] *British Parliamentary Papers* 1861, 72 include *Papers Relating to Indigo Production in Bengal, Preliminary to the Appointment of the Commission, 1854–1860. Papers Relating to the Passing of Act X of 1859 (an Act to Amend the Law Relating to the Recovery of Rent in the Presidency of Fort William in Bengal)* (Calcutta: Office of the Superintendent of Government Printing, 1883).
[126] Prabhu Mohapatra, "From Contract to Status or How Law Shaped Labour Relations in Colonial India, 1780–1880," in Jan Breman, Isabelle Guerin, Aseem Prakash, eds., *India's Unfree Workforce: Of Bondage Old and New* (New Delhi, 2009): 96–125.
[127] *British Parliamentary Papers*, Papers Relating to Indigo Cultivation in Bengal, 44, 1861.
[128] Nitin Varma, *Coolies of Capitalism: Assam Tea and the Making of Coolie Labour* (Oldenburg: de Gruyter, 2016).
[129] Jayeeta Sharma, *Empire's Garden: Assam and the Making of India* (Durham: Duke University Press, 2011).
[130] BL IOR/V/23/101, No. 37, Papers Related to Tea Cultivation in Assam, 1859–1860.

early 1860s, government policies caused land prices to fall and the price of tea to rise. Recruiters began enlisting workers in the East Indian regions; immigrants were first housed in warehouses and then transported across the Brahmaputra River to Assam. The mortality rate of indentured migrants, which was 1.5 to 5 percent on journeys to Mauritius and the Réunion Islands, climbed to 20 percent and even 50 percent for migrants to Assam.[131] A commission was set up to investigate the causes of this high mortality rate. It concluded by blaming local contractors and middlemen. Nevertheless, between 1863 and 1866, half of the 85,000 migrants were declared dead or deserters.[132] Thus, breach of contract and desertion, as set out in a new law of 1865, became the central problem facing planters and the colonial state.

Planters sought to recruit and retain workers without increasing their wages. For over seventy years, until 1915, nominal wages on Assam's plantations remained fixed at five rupees per month. This was considered a minimum wage that could not be increased for fear of encouraging "laziness" and desertion. Low wages led to more illness and higher mortality rates (4–5 percent per year), which greatly reduced labor productivity. They also encouraged desertion, with the added cost of recovering fugitives, and discouraged the arrival of new emigrants by again increasing the remuneration of recruiters instead of increasing the wages of workers.[133] Violence and abuse against the workers continued throughout the period studied.[134] In just three years – between 1863 and 1866 – 32,000 of the 84,000 workers brought to Assam died.[135] Their European masters were systematically acquitted, even in cases where the evidence against them was more than convincing.[136] Paradoxically, planters continued to complain that they were at the mercy of their servants.[137] During this period, masters rarely used the law to prosecute workers (only 5–6 percent of workers per year, and almost always for desertion). Under the Breach of Contract Act, 595 violations were reported in 1879–82, followed by 534 convictions. Planters made extensive use of their legal power to coerce workers. In fact, planters had their own militias to control workers and recover fugitives

---

[131] *British Parliamentary Papers*, 1863, 41: 271 "Statement Exhibiting the Moral and Material Progress and Condition of India."

[132] *Reports on the Tea and Tobacco Industries in India* (London: Stationary Office, 1974): 38–40.

[133] Prabhu Mohapatra, "Assam and the West Indies, 1860–1920: Immobilizing Plantation Labor," in Douglas Hay and Paul Craven, *Masters, Servants, and Magistrates in Britain and the Empire, 1562–1955* (Chapel Hill and London: The University of North Carolina Press, 2004): 455–480.

[134] *British Parliamentary Papers*, 1894, 58, "Chief Commissioner to the Government of India, May 4, 1894."

[135] Elizabeth Kolsky, *Colonial Justice in British India* (Cambridge: Cambridge University Press, 2009): 155.

[136] Examples in BL IOR L/R/5/11.

[137] BL IOR L/PJ/6/635.

and did not necessarily need to resort to the law to achieve their ends. Injustice and abuse were not limited to labor relations. Sexual abuse by British masters was common, as was the persistent use of violence. Assam was a lawless frontier, as some British officers acknowledged.[138]

From Paternalism to 1848: The Long Road of Slavery in the French Empire

In the 1820s, as well as under the July Monarchy, two opposing trends emerged: while in most of the French colonies, the emancipation and social conditions of freed slaves improved (in Martinique, freed slaves owned slaves and worked in trades),[139] the illegal slave trade to the French West Indies and Réunion Island increased, partly in reaction to this trend and to the growing difficulties of French colonial production. Between 1817 and 1835, an estimated 450,000 illegal slaves were imported into Réunion.[140]

In France itself, attention to slavery began to change. Under the Restoration, the abolitionist movement was extremely weak; a few authors called for the abolition of the slave trade. The ambivalence of French abolitionists was reflected in the political and economic thought of the time. Jean-Baptiste Say, a disciple of Smith and Jeremy Bentham, was initially radically opposed to slavery on the basis of Smith's arguments, but gradually changed his mind. In the mid 1820s, he morally condemned slavery but added that the slave's right to property imposed constraints on both master and slave, notably against the master's encroachments and against any infringement of the slave's capacity to work. He also considers slavery beneficial to the division of labor and productivity.[141]

It was in this context that France began its occupation of Algeria in 1830, with a mixture of improvisation and the desire to restore French grandeur. Initially a military enterprise, the conquest of Algeria was gradually transformed into a form of colonization, first exploiting the mines (after the 1860s), then the land expropriated from the local population to grow wine and wheat (after the 1870s). Once again, the debates on colonialism and slavery intersected. In 1833, Sismondi, a renowned defender of peasant agriculture, lamented the absence of a genuine anti-abolitionist movement in France. At the same time, he opposed the British approach to abolition, which freed slaves without giving them land. In his view, apprenticeship was a form of

---

[138] BL IOR L/PJ/6/376.
[139] Fréderic Régent, *Esclavage métissage, liberté* (Paris: Grasset, 2004); Dale Tomic, *Prelude to Emancipation: Sugar and Slavery in Martinique, 1830–1848* (Madison: University of Wisconsin Press, 1978).
[140] Monica Schuler, "The Recruitment of African *Indentured* Laborers for European Colonies in the nineteenth Century," in Petr Emmer, *Colonialism and Migration: Indentured Labour Before and After Slavery* (Dordrecht: Martinus Nijhoff, 1986): 125–161.
[141] Say, *Cours d'économie politique*: 522.

slavery in disguise, while the compensation paid to planters was insufficient to continue production on a new basis. He proposed a system similar to sharecropping, which in the colonial context would produce the best results for all concerned. Four years later, he added that, unlike Britain, which had turned slaves into proletarians, France should turn them into peasants.[142] Thus, conservatives sought to limit proletarianization and avert the danger of socialism, while socialists focused on the condition of the working-class in France. For both, slaves in the colonies were a secondary concern. Both expressed protectionist tendencies: national labor must be defended against the free market and free immigration. As a result, abolitionist and free-trade concerns never converged as they had in Britain.[143]

In 1842, Victor Schoelcher presented a detailed plan for abolition, in which he gave a central role to the "principle of association," which allowed groups of freed slaves to associate with their former masters and share the benefits.[144] In 1844–45, he won the support of labor organizations, which sent several massive petitions to the government demanding the immediate abolition of slavery.[145] A timid law was therefore passed in 1845, encouraging manumission and the gradual purchase of freedom by the slaves themselves. Slaves were granted legal capacity and could therefore own movable and immovable property. But this approach soon came up against the changing situation in the colonies and in France. In 1846–47, several thousand slaves escaped from the French West Indies to the British Isles (5,000 from French Guiana to Trinidad, of whom 2,000 reached their destination) and 1,000 from Guadeloupe to Dominica.[146] In response, the slave owners of Saint-Martin (a small island shared by the Dutch and the French) sent a petition to the Chamber of Deputies calling for the immediate manumission of their slaves to prevent them from fleeing to the neighboring British Isles.[147] Increased sugar production in Mauritius and the rapid development of sugar beet production in France, combined with falling sugar prices, exacerbated the situation.

Social tensions also rose in France, where artisans complained of increasing hardship and urban workers protested low wages, long hours and job

---

[142] Simon de Sismondi, *Études sur l'économie politique* (Brussels: Société typographique belge, 1837).

[143] Frank Trentmann, *Free Trade Nation: Commerce, Consumption and Civil Society in Modern Britain* (Oxford: Oxford University Press, 2008); Pierre Rosanvallon, *La société des égaux* (Paris: Seuil, 2011).

[144] Victor Schoelcher, *Des colonies françaises. Abolition immédiate de l'esclavage* (Paris, 1842, republished by CTHS, 1998).

[145] Schmidt, *Abolitionists*.

[146] Régent, *La france et ses esclaves*: 286.

[147] *Pétition des habitants de l'ile de Saint-Martin à la chambre des députés* (Petition of the inhabitants of the French part of the island of Saint-Martin to the Chamber of Deputies), July 8, 1846, Archives Nationales (AN), C 2222.

8 WHO IS THE TRUE SLAVE?

insecurity. Strikes intensified in Paris and throughout France in 1847. In August of that year, Victor Schoelcher and the French Society for the Abolition of Slavery sent out a new petition calling for immediate abolition.[148] Slave and labor unrest were intertwined. Tensions between masters and slaves grew in the French West Indies and Réunion Island; in Martinique and Guadeloupe, several cases of slave riots and fires were added to the growing number of lawsuits filed by slaves against their masters for violence and abuse.[149] This link between slaves and workers has been largely underestimated, even though it was at the heart of the revolutionary regime's concerns in 1848, when commissions were set up to abolish slavery. Under Schoelcher's leadership, a parliamentary commission proposed a bill for the immediate abolition of slavery and the granting of French citizenship to all slaves. Discussions focused on compensation for slave owners and the possibility of a period of apprenticeship; the majority of the commission favored both measures. Freedom was considered a natural right, and all emancipated slaves were declared French citizens.[150] Freedom was considered a natural right, and all emancipated slaves were declared French citizens.

However, very similar problems were discussed by the parliamentary labor commissions in metropolitan France: the organization of judicial tribunals to deal with labor disputes, pensions for the infirm and elderly, national workshops, the control and punishment of vagrancy, the length of the working day, etc. Thus, in February 1848, the working day in France was limited to ten hours,[151] following a similar rule adopted in Great Britain in 1847 (on child labor) and the French law of 1841 limiting child labor.[152] The new decree provoked much debate among workers, entrepreneurs, chambers of commerce and other institutions, as well as numerous discussions in Parliament and the Labor Commission.[153] In May, the provisional government decided to set up a labor commission to determine working conditions and the length of the working day in different activities and regions.[154] Finally, in early September, the March decree was repealed and the twelve-hour working day was reinstated.[155]

---

[148] AN C 2225.
[149] ANOM SG Martinique C 33 d 289.
[150] ANOM Généralités 162 d. 1326, Comptes rendus des séances de la Commission d'abolition de l'esclavage.
[151] Fridenson, Reynaud, La France et le temps de travail.
[152] Maurice Agulhon, 1848 ou l'apprentissage de la République (1848–1852) (Paris: Seuil, 1992).
[153] Thomas Bouchet, Un jeudi à l'Assemblée. Politique du discours et droit au travail dans la France de 1848, (Québec: Editions Nota bene, 2007).
[154] AN C 944 to 963, Enquête sur le travail agricole et industriel prescrite par le décret du 25 mai 1848.
[155] Émile Carrey, Recueil complet des actes du Gouvernement provisoire (février, mars, avril, mai 1848) (Paris: A. Durand, 1848).

This issue had a major impact on debates about working conditions in the colonies. Initially, the British Abolitionist Commission imposed a rule on freed slaves and new immigrants that was very similar to that in force in metropolitan France (i.e., a ten-hour workday) except in special circumstances such as the sugar harvest. However, the repeal of the law in France encouraged local colonial elites to ignore any rules regarding the length of the work day, as we'll see in the case of Réunion Island.

A second mutual influence between labor reform in France and slavery in the colonies concerned the national workshops. Discussed at the time of the 1789 Revolution, they came to the fore again in the 1830s when Louis Blanc proposed his idea of collective workshops. Schoelcher saw it as an advantageous solution for emancipated slaves who found themselves without work. In France, in the particular context of 1848, these workshops were a response to the unemployment of the previous years. The "right to work" was supported by various socialist currents, but after lengthy debates within the Labor Commission, it was decided not to include it in the Constitution of 1848. Pierre-Joseph Proudhon, the socialist movement and the republicans developed the idea in different directions. The right to work was variously associated with socialist equality or solidarity, republican assistance and possibly charity, or liberal paternalism and philanthropy.[156] Tocqueville and Catholic thinkers such as Baron de Girando believed that the Poor Laws in Britain had been reformed in 1834 precisely because they had the perverse effect of making people less willing to work.[157] Similarly, Adolphe Thiers argued that social protection and social rights could not, strictly speaking, be "rights" because they depended on the situation of each individual, whereas rights, by definition, are universal.[158] In the continental context, the right to work was primarily a response to economic crisis and early unemployment,[159] but it is also a form of labor law, in particular the right to a wage. From this point of view, the slavery of the working class and the slavery of the colonies are sometimes seen as synonymous, sometimes as an expression of competition between the two.[160] The Workers' Commission discussed forms of pensions and mutual insurance for workers, an important issue since the Revolution of 1789: social aid was mentioned several times, but in the end individual solutions, family networks and public assistance for the

---

[156] Buret, *De la misère*; Albin de Villeneuve-Bargemont, *Traité d'économie politique chrétienne ou recherches sur les paupérisme* (Paris: Paulin 1834).
[157] de Girando, *Traité de bienfaisance publique*; Tocqueville, *Mémoire sur le paupérisme*.
[158] Pierre Rosanvallon, *L'État en France de 1789 à nos jours* (Paris: Seuil, 1990).
[159] Philippe Lefebvre, *L'invention de la grande entreprise. Travail, hiérarchie, marché. France, fin XVIIIe-début XXe siècle* (Paris: Presses universitaires de France, 2003).
[160] Robert Castel, *Les métamorphoses de la question sociale* (Paris: Fayard, 1995); François Vatin, "Romantisme économique et philosophie de la misère en France dans les années 1820–1840," *Romantisme*, 133, 3 (2006): 35–47.

poor were the main solutions.[161] In 1848, however, support for public insurance and state aid was expressed only by a few socialist groups.

This helps explain why the right to work, proclaimed in February 1848,[162] failed to live up to abolitionist ideals. In the colonies, the national workshop became a kind of workhouse, and the right to work turned into an obligation to work.[163] This attitude was already evident in 1848, in the way colonial elites interpreted the emancipation decrees; work became compulsory in 1852, when vagrancy was again criminalized and the workman's book was introduced in the colonies. In fact, the repression of vagrancy, although severely criticized in France, was introduced in the colonies after emancipation and justified by the "natural indolence" of former slaves and new immigrants, as well as by the need to maintain order in post-abolition society. Another argument used to justify the obligation to work rather than the right to work in the colonies was that the new citizens could hardly be expected to pay taxes while enjoying the support of the French state. As for the elderly and invalids, one of the decrees of 1848 stipulated that they could remain on the plantation or in the workshop if the other former slaves agreed to support them. Schoelcher also failed in his attempts to include in the decrees his proposals for the payment of damages to slaves (and not just their masters), the compulsory cession of a small amount of land and the priority of European workers to replace slaves. In France, as in the colonies, pensions were not yet on the agenda.

Finally, the reform of the *prud'hommes* in France also had an impact on labor law reform in the colonies. We have shown that in metropolitan France, *prud'hommes* (labor courts) were located primarily in urban areas. In rural areas, justices of the peace were empowered to adjudicate labor disputes.[164] In accordance with metropolitan legislation, the colonies were therefore supposed to have justices of the peace, not *prud'hommes*. After 1848, cantonal juries (the equivalent of justices of the peace) were established in the colonies. These regional juries were designed to resolve disputes between former masters and slaves, as well as within each group, on a wide range of issues such as housing, land, wages, work, etc.[165] In 1849, former slaves immediately began

---

[161] Catherine Duprat, *Usages et pratiques de la philanthropie. Pauvreté, action sociale et lien social, à Paris, au cours du premier XIXe siècle* (Paris: Comité d'histoire de la Sécurité sociale, 1996).

[162] Francis Demier, "Droit au travail et organisation du travail en 1848," in Jean-Luc Mayaud, ed., *1848: Actes du 150ème anniversaire* (Paris: Créaphys, 2002): 159–184.

[163] Oruno D. Lara, *La liberté assassinée. Guadeloupe, Guyane, Martinique et La Réunion, 1848–1856* (Paris: Editions L'Harmattan, 2005).

[164] Jean-Claude Farcy, "Les archives méconnues de la justice civile," in Frédéric Chauvaud, Jacques-Guy Petit, eds., *Histoire et archives. L'histoire contemporaine et les usages des archives judiciaires (1800–1939)* (Paris: Champion, 1998): 397–408.

[165] Myriam Cottias, "Droit, justice et dépendance dans les Antilles françaises, 1848–1852," *Annales HSS*, 59, 3 (2004): 547–567.

taking their cases to these courts, but it was very difficult for them to prove their arguments, especially in cases against their former or current masters.[166] I will discuss these problems in more detail in a moment.

Overall, these developments produced different results in different colonies. On Réunion Island, where there were no indigenous courts, French law governed labor relations and post-slavery dynamics without taking into account the condition of immigrants and former slaves. On the contrary, the experiences of Algeria and Senegal were to have a considerable influence on French legal and labor policies in sub-Saharan Africa after 1880, as we will see in the next chapter. At the end of 1848, the conservative parties led by Louis Napoléon won the elections; their success reflected the fears of the rural and financial elites about the emergence of the peasantry and socialist proletarians. These fears were confirmed in May 1849, when the new tendencies became dominant, especially in the countryside. The Second Empire tried to reintegrate the peasantry among its supporters. The social legislation passed in 1848, which had been relatively favorable to workers, was largely repealed.

In concrete terms, these rules translated into a new form of extreme dependence at work in the colonies. For example, the elites of Réunion Island got together to prepare a petition and a series of documents designed to demonstrate the need to delay abolition in order to preserve the island's economy and stability. Otherwise, the entire population, including the slaves, would suffer from the sudden collapse of sugar production.[167] The importation of slaves continued until 1848, when the practice was definitively abolished. Under these conditions, it was difficult to distinguish between slaves and indentured servants; the fragile boundary was perceptible on arrival and departure. In 1847, there were 6,508 indentured servants, including Indians, Chinese, Africans and Creoles. The shortage of available labor prompted several owners to request the importation of additional indentured laborers, this time from Africa, especially as France was moving towards the abolition of slavery. Indeed, as in the British Empire in the 1830s and 1840s, the abolition of slavery in the French colonies in 1848 was followed by a revival of the *engagés* system. The supply routes for indentured laborers and immigrants partly replicated those of the slave trade and the commercial networks already in place. Indian workers were brought to the island through Arab and Indian middlemen, who often competed with each other.[168] Long-term contracts were required by law, so planters offered this type of contract, but in reality they employed short-term workers, as seasonal fluctuations confirmed.[169] As in Mauritius, the indentured workers in La Réunion had the right to go to court to denounce cases of mistreatment and abuse.

[166] On legal proceedings in Mauritius and Réunion, see Stanziani, *Labor on the Fringes of Empire*.
[167] *Feuille hebdomadaire de l'Ile Bourbon*, August 30, 1848 and October 11, 1848.
[168] TNA FO 84/174.
[169] ADR 10M9 statistiques du travail (labor statistics).

But when immigrants went to court to denounce abuses, they were often sent back to their employer, who at best punished them for insubordination and reduced their wages; at worst, the employer sued them for breach of contract and defamation. In 1864, for example, an Indian laborer knocked on the door of the Court of Appeal in Saint-Denis la Réunion with a chain around his neck. He explained that for several years he and other workers on the same plantation had been regularly whipped, while their wages had been confiscated by the master. He said that he had gone to the Union for the Protection of Immigrants on several occasions, but that this association, which was set up by the Réunion authorities to protect immigrants, had refused to take legal action against the planter in question. Faced with this attitude and after an escalation of mistreatment, the worker fled. Caught by the police, he was sentenced to 100 days of hard labor in a workhouse for desertion before being returned to his master. The master had him flogged. The Indian laborer ran away again, but was caught, sentenced to hard labor and returned to the planter. This time, after whipping him in the presence of the local priest – who was supposed to help the Indian make amends – the planter put a ring around his neck and chained him up. Twelve days later, the Indian escaped and went to the Court of Appeal. This time, an investigation was launched and the facts were confirmed. Unfortunately, the case did not come to trial until several years later, and the planter was eventually given a one-month suspended jail sentence.[170]

This case, described as exceptional by the Réunionese authorities, was in fact far from exceptional. Faced with these difficulties, workers sometimes unite to denounce illegal practices, but they risk being sentenced by the judge and the police to two months of hard labor in a workhouse for illegal association and disturbing the peace.[171] Renewal of contracts, payment of wages and corporal punishment were the most common issues raised by indentured servants in lawsuits. Unlike slaves, indentured servants had the right to return home; the terms were negotiated in the contract, which was supposed to respect the general provisions of the law. In practice, however, repatriation was difficult. In the 1850s and 1860s, one-third of all indentured immigrants (mostly Indians) returned home. This percentage was close to that of Mauritius, the Caribbean, Surinam and Jamaica at the time, but far from the 70 percent repatriation rates of Thailand, Malaysia and Melanesia. Distance and transportation costs were only two of the variables influencing repatriation; policies and concrete forms of integration were also important factors.[172] On the island of Réunion, conditions were harsh: the authorities and the planters confiscated the immigrants' wages and bank accounts and, if possible, imposed heavy penalties ("laziness" and failure to complete assigned tasks on time are the most common arguments

---

[170] ANOM FM SM SG/Reu c 382 d.3323.
[171] ANOM FM SM/Reu c 379 d 3211 and c 383 d 3323.
[172] Northrup, *Indentured Labor*: 129–32.

for the imposition of penalties). In this way, the worker's "debt" was never repaid and the contract was extended. The standards and targets for daily work were gradually raised, so that few workers were able to meet them; they were therefore subjected to heavy penalties while working eighteen to twenty hours a day instead of the ten hours mentioned in the contracts and official rules.[173] And as if all this wasn't enough, employers didn't hesitate to use physical violence to force workers to renew their contracts. Over time, the use of coercion became increasingly indispensable in public works such as the construction and repair of roads, bridges and harbors. Forced labor as a disciplinary measure and workhouses existed in the days of slavery to punish slaves under the jurisdiction of public authorities; slaves were therefore assigned to workhouses or public works rather than to their masters to atone for their punishments.

Conclusion

Unlike sociological surveys, I have not attempted to define the boundaries between slaves and wage earners. Instead, I have insisted that this distinction was constantly debated in the historical contexts presented here. In its most abstract form, this debate concerned the relationship between the social order and the legal order of societies. Those who emphasized law clearly separated slaves from wage earners, while those who criticized this separation emphasized social conditions and questioned the impact of abolition. This was not just a philosophical or theoretical issue, however, but one with major political implications. In both France and Britain, the identification of slaves and wage-earners led to the adoption of closely related policies: for example, as shown in Part I, it was the mutual identification of white indentured migrants and African slaves that gradually led to the narrowing of the definition of "slave" and the reorientation of indentured workers toward the status of wage-earners. This latter recognition would not have been possible without the former identification. Then, at the time of abolition, the near-freedom of slaves, now called apprentices, led to a redefinition of servants, apprentices and wage-earners in Britain. In France, where the categories of workers and freed slaves evolved in tandem with the revolution of 1848, the same blurring occurred. The clear opposition between free and unfree people gave way to a hierarchy of rights and duties for former slaves, new immigrants to the colonies and French workers.

Taken together, concrete British and French abolitionist policies show that the main European emancipatory approaches to labor and freedom (British utilitarianism, French egalitarianism), for different reasons, were unable to provide an adequate response to the question of reconciling civil and social rights. The French Revolution abolished domestic servitude for life, while the

[173] ANOM FM SG/Reu c 379 d 3211.

nineteenth century saw the gradual abolition of slavery, first in the British colonies, then in France. However, this process did not go hand in hand with the emergence of a free labor market among legally equal actors. In Britain, France and their colonies, indentured servants and immigrants were not slaves in disguise (as much nineteenth-century literature claimed), but they had an inferior legal status and far fewer rights than their masters. From this point of view, the colonies were not only territories of slavery, but above all, forms of forced labor inspired by status inequalities rooted in Europe. The inequalities of status in France and Great Britain served as a model for those in the colonies, but the *engageés*, bonded laborers, servants and wage earners were the expression of a free contract. The *engageé* was not a slave but was subject to forms of servitude that are not formally or necessarily hereditary, although the resulting debts were often passed on to descendants. However, unlike the traditional slave status, the legal status of the *engageé* was not automatically transferred to descendants, which made all the difference in the development of post-slavery forms of labor in the twentieth century.

This observation forces us to reconsider our view of the comparative evolution of economic and legal labor systems. From an economic point of view, forced labor is traditionally associated with pre-industrial economies and colonies. The history we have just traced challenges these divisions. It would be wrong to associate forced labor and slavery in the colonies with the plantation economy, and to conclude that pre-plantation migration consisted of colonization by white settlers, and that later, with the advent of mechanized plantation labor, the use of slavery no longer made sense.

Paradoxically, labor protections came later in Britain than in France, but the anti-slavery movement in the British colonies was much more closely allied with the pro-labor movement in Britain than was its counterpart in the French colonies for greater labor protections in France. French subjects were not French citizens, but that was also the case in the British Empire. In both cases, colonial subjects were granted some rights, but not all. But this lack of universality was also found in nineteenth-century Europe, where women and the lower classes had few political and social rights. In this respect, the colonies were a continuation of continental ideas and institutions rather than the opposite. In France and Britain, labor was managed under unequal legal and contractual conditions, and their respective colonies were merely a radical development of this general attitude.

This brings us to the relationship between imperial rule and freedom. From this perspective, the question is not so much whether the Enlightenment was for or against freedom and equality. As in the case of utilitarianism, multiple attitudes were possible under a common philosophical umbrella. Utilitarianism and various forms of liberalism strongly influenced the architecture and functioning of the British Empire. But the reverse is also true: imperial constraints also influenced the development of British liberalism. Bentham and

Mill sought to export their ideas to India; the reverse influence was equally important. The French Enlightenment, and the liberalism that followed, had a more complicated relationship with empire; despite Smith, the efficacy of slavery played a greater role in France than in Britain, where the moral argument of the Quakers was crucial. In France, the economic argument prevailed, along with forms of philanthropy and Catholic charity more often associated with Restoration ambitions than with the ethics of a market society (feeding the poor in France and starving immigrants in Réunion). Thus, in France, as opposed to Britain, the argument of liberty and rights was linked either to libertarian and revolutionary thinking or to a religious and aristocratic perspective. In both cases, freedom was intended for a world to come and appealed to immediate exclusion as the basis for future inclusion.

If this is the case, we now need to understand how notions and practices of "abolition" were transformed into contexts in which totally unfree labor was widespread not only in the colonies, but also on the continent itself. In this case, how did the divide between "freedom" and "unfreedom" evolve in the face of the transformation of global markets and its impact on local social hierarchies?

To answer this question, we need to look at two other cases: Russia and the United States. To a certain extent, these were extreme situations compared to the previous ones, although for different reasons: serfdom for the whole population, slavery only for the "colored" part of it, added to a territorial unity very different from the distant sovereignty that France and Great Britain expressed in their colonies. With what consequences for work, rights and social identities?

9

The Aristocratic Abolition of Serfdom in Russia

Preparing for Abolition

According to some historians, the defeat in the Crimean War was at the root of the great reforms,[1] while many others have pointed out that this point was barely mentioned in the debates.[2] We have shown that Russia's economic decadence in the first half of the nineteenth century was linked not only to serfdom, but also to its responses to the Great Divergence and Russia's consequent loss of British, European and Asian markets. If this is the case, the question is to understand how the forms taken by abolition were able to cope with these new challenges of the international economy.

The Russian intelligentsia was deeply divided on the question of serfdom. Radical intellectuals and supporters of Westernization in general saw reform as a means of abolishing serfdom and bringing Russia closer to Europe. Their opponents often shared the tendency of certain Western authors (planter lobbies) to relativize the opposition between free and forced labor; proletarians were considered the true slaves, while serfs enjoyed quite reasonable living and working conditions. In the end, the nobility feared not so much the emancipation of the peasants as their proletarianization; they therefore gradually accepted the abolition of serfdom on condition that peasants did not become proletarians, for political reasons (fear of socialism) but also for economic reasons (need for manpower in the countryside). The debate on serfdom therefore intersected with that on the peasant commune.[3] Most of the nobility and populist radicals defended the commune as an institution that would help modernize Russia without capitalism and the massive proletarianization of the peasantry.

---

[1] Donald Field, *The End of Serfdom: Nobility and Bureaucracy in Russia, 1855–1861* (Cambridge: Harvard University Press, 1976).
[2] Moon, *Russian Peasants and Tsarist Legislation*.
[3] Andrzej Walicki is one of many authors who have analyzed the debate between Slavophiles and Westernists at this time. See A. Walicki, *The Slavophile Controversy: History of a Conservative Utopia in Nineteenth-century Russia* (New York: Oxford University Press, 1975). For a review of economic debates on this subject, see Esther Kingston-Mann, *In Search of the True West* (Princeton: Princeton University Press, 1999), and my *L'économie en révolution*.

The commune was seen as a defense of the social status quo for another reason: Until then, the nobility had had a legal monopoly on inhabited land. With general emancipation, there was a risk that the "bourgeois" merchants and the new urban rich would claim rights to the land, while the commune could oppose them.[4] In short, the nobility was in favor of abolition as long as the existing aristocratic-renter-merchant system was maintained.

The Tsar decided to set up local commissions to identify regional specificities and determine local criteria for abolition. The provincial nobility took an active part in these commissions[5] and won some concessions; in particular, the amount of land to be given to emancipated peasants was reduced to a minimum. The provincial nobility also succeeded in ensuring that the state would not financially support the emancipated peasants in running their farms. In their view, if the peasants lacked resources, they would need help from their former landlords and would therefore remain dependent on them. Faced with a major financial crisis in 1859 and a growing public debt, central government reformers eventually accepted this solution.[6]

The official abolition of serfdom, on February 19, 1861, was the subject of a long and complex text, accompanied by several other decrees detailing the main points.[7] The process of emancipation was divided into three stages: The first stage was a two-year transitional period to implement the basic rules of emancipation and define the main criteria to be applied in the second stage (e.g., the size of individual allotments, the total amount of land to be given to peasants in different areas, etc.); then came the second stage, an indefinite period during which peasants had to work for the landlord and the state to redeem their freedom and land allotment; the third and final stage was full redemption, which was supposed to complete the whole process within forty-nine years.[8] In practice, the size of the land allotted to

---

[4] Terence Emmons, *The Russian Landed Gentry and the Peasant Emancipation of 1861* (Berkeley: University of California Press, 1968); Lidia G. Zakharova and John Bushnell, eds., *The Great Reforms in Russia* (Bloomington: Indiana University Press, 1994); and Boris N. Chicherin, *Sobstvennost' i gosudarstvo* (Property and the state), 2 volumes (Moscow, 1882-83; new edition, St. Petersburg: Izdatel'stvo Russkoi Khristianskoi gumanitarnoi akademii, 2005).

[5] Daniel Saunders, *Russia in the Age of Reaction and Reform, 1801-1881* (London: Longman, 1992).

[6] Steven Hoch, "The Banking Crisis, Peasant Reforms, and Economic Development in Russia, 1857-1861," *American Historical Review*, 96, 3 (1991): 795-820.

[7] Igor Khristoforov, *Sud'ba reformy: Russkoe krest'ianstvo v pravitel'stvennoi politike do i posle otmeny krepostnogo prava (1830-1890-e gg.)* (The fate of reforms: the Russian peasantry and the government policies before and after the abolition of serfdom, 1830-1890) (Moscow: Sobranie, 2011). See also: Mikhail Dolbilov, *Zemel'naya sobstvennost' i ozvobozhdenie krestian'* (Land ownership and peasant freedom) (Moscow: Rosspen, 2002).

[8] Lidia Zakharova ed., *Velikie reformy v Rossii, 1856-1874* (The Great Reforms in Russia, 1856-1874) (Moscow: Nauka, 1992).

peasants in local statutes varied considerably according to soil fertility, population density and farming practices. Land allotments in the Steppe and outside the Black Earth belt were larger than those in the Black Earth localities, where the land was more fertile and population pressure greater. In fact, instead of a fixed amount of land per inhabitant (or per family or per commune), each statute identified a range of possible allocation sizes within which the final amount of land was to be determined. The local statutes also specified the amount of labor or fees that the peasants had to provide during phase 2. The amount of work was set at forty days per year for men and thirty for women, to be performed mainly during the summer and other periods of heavy agricultural work.[9] There was a complex system that varied the amount of work depending on the region, the fertility of the land, the size of the plot, and so on. The rules for cash payments were even more complicated: They depended on the distance from St. Petersburg, the main cities and markets, and the size of the farm. Because peasants were considered indebted until they fulfilled their obligation to repay, the state and landowners retained the right to restrict mobility and require formal permission for all market transactions (selling, offering labor, etc.). What were the economic and social consequences of this policy?

After Abolition: Continuities and Changes

In many places the landlords abused their position and imposed unfair conditions on the peasants; the landlords often gave away their worst land and the peasants had to buy it back at the highest price.[10] Does this mean that the peasants' living conditions worsened after abolition and that the Abolition Law did not bring about any real change?[11]

It is important to distinguish between the impact of the reform on political and civil rights, on the one hand; and on the economy, on the other. From the first point of view, the abolition of serfdom was not accompanied by the dissolution of the traditional inheritance order of the old regime (the *Soslovie* system in Russia). The population and its rights were divided into a few main groups (peasants, landowners, priests, merchants) and innumerable sub-groups, each subject to its own legal rules and social status.[12] The nobles continued to enjoy

---

[9] Khristoforov, *Sud'ba reformy*.
[10] Boris Litvak, *Russkaia derevniia v reforme 1861 goda: Chernozemnyi tsentr 1861–1895 gg* (The Russian campaign in the reform of 1861: Central Black Earth, 1861–1895) (Moscow: Nauka, 1972); Serguei Kashchenko, *Reforma 19 Fevralia 1861 goda na severo-zapade Rossii* (The reform of 1861 in the north-west of Russia), (Moscow: Mosgosarakhiv, 1995).
[11] Corinne Gaudin, *Ruling Peasants. Village and State in Late Imperial Russia* (Dekalb: Northern Illinois University Press, 2007).
[12] Gregory Freeze, "The Soslovie (Estate) Paradigm in Russian Social History," *American Historical Review*, 91, 1 (1986): 11–36.

special rules and privileges, while the peasants, despite their growing legal rights,[13] still had few political rights. Merchants and urban groups enjoyed some rights at the local level, but very few at the national level until the 1905 revolution forced the tsar to adopt a constitution. In particular, the reforms of 1861–1864 introduced local governments (*zemstvos*), which could levy local taxes and adopt public policies on health, welfare, education and the local economy. The *zemstvos* played an important role in the development of Russian political, social, intellectual and economic life until the Revolution.[14]

Conventional historiography emphasized the limits of the reforms, the growing poverty of the peasantry and the persistent backwardness of Russia.[15] Critics of the reforms, many Soviet historians and later Gerschenkron and all those who espoused the impoverishment thesis (the bad conditions of the peasants after and because of the reforms) emphasized the fact that the peasants were so poor that they were unable to buy back their land. More recent historiography has painted a very different picture. Russia underwent significant social change and economic growth between 1861 and 1914; revised demographic trends show that mortality and birth rates were lower than previously thought.[16] The impoverishment of the peasantry and the number and severity of major famines decreased.[17] The period between 1861 and 1914 was marked by a steady improvement in agricultural production and living standards.[18] Rather than limiting growth and social welfare, communal land ownership helped to improve them: The communal land allocation system was relatively efficient in adjusting land ownership and, more generally, in compensating for market

---

[13] Burbank, *Russian Peasants go to Court*.
[14] Terence Emmons, Wayne Vucinich, *The Zemstvos in Russia: An Experiment in Local Self-Government* (New York: Cambridge University Press, 1992).
[15] Geroid T. Robinson, *Rural Russia Under the Old Regime* (New York: Longmans, 1932); Alexander Gerschenkron, *Economic Backwardness in Historical Perspective* (Cambridge, MA: Harvard University Press, 1962).
[16] Hoch, "Famine, Disease and Mortality Patterns; Steven Hoch, "On Good Numbers and Bad: Malthus, Population Trend and Peasant Standard of Living in Late Imperial Russia," *Slavic Review*, 53, 1 (1994): 41–75; Steven Hoch, "Serfs in Imperial Russia: Demographic Insights," *The Journal of Interdisciplinary History*, 13, 2 (1982): 221–246.
[17] Stephen Wheatcroft, "Crisis and Condition of the Peasantry in Late Imperial Russia," in Esther Kingston-Mann, Timothy Mixter, eds., *Peasant Economy, Culture and Politics of European Russia, 1800–1921* (Princeton, 1991): 101–127.
[18] Elvira M. Wilbur, "Was Russian Peasant Agriculture Really That Impoverished? New Evidence from a Case Study from the 'Impoverished Center' at the End of the Nineteenth Century," *Journal of Economic History*, 43, 1 (1983): 137–144; Esther Kingston-Mann, "Marxism and Russian Rural Development: Problems of Evidence, Experience and Culture," *American Historical Review*, 86, 4 (1981): 731–752; James Y. Simms, Jr, "The Crisis in Russian Agriculture at the End of the Nineteenth Century: A Different View," *Slavic Review*, 36, 3 (1977): 377–398; James Simms Jr, "The Crop Failure of 1891: Soil Exhaustion, Technological Backwardness, and Russia's Agrarian Crisis," *Slavic Review*, 41, 2 (1982): 236–250.

imperfections, especially on labor markets.[19] Peasant land ownership more than doubled between the 1870s and the First World War, and acquisitions were made not only by land communes but also, increasingly, by individual households. Between 1863 and 1872, Russian peasants bought land to supplement their communal lands. More than three-quarters of peasant acquisitions on the open market were made by private individuals. This trend accelerated with the creation of the State Peasant Bank, which was designed to encourage loans to peasants who wanted to buy land. Peasant land ownership doubled between 1877 and 1905. In 80 percent of the cases, the transactions were carried out by the peasant commune or peasant associations. In the following years, between 1906 and 1914, the state sold 1.5 million *desiatina* (1 *desiatina* = 1.10 hectares) to peasants; landowners sold them one-fifth of their land (i.e., 10.2 million out of 49.7 *desiatina*). Two-thirds of the purchases were made by peasant associations and communes, and one-third by individual households. Cossack and peasant property increased by 9.5 million *desiatina* to a total of 170.4 million.[20]

This means that farmers were buying up more and more land. At the same time, *zemleustroistva* (land consolidation) operations were an important factor in strengthening the peasant economy while preserving the commune. They were carried out as part of the Stolypin reforms (1906–1911). These reforms have generally been associated with the "privatization" of communal land, partly due to Tsarist propaganda, partly due to interpretations by the intelligentsia. The reality, however, was much more complex.[21] Peasants could ask to leave the commune and have their land privatized, but they could also simply ask to have their land (which, as we've seen, was scattered in several strips) regrouped without leaving the commune. These practices had been in place since the 1880s.[22] Land redistribution was limited in most peasant communes, which adopted an intermediate solution between classical communal ownership and private property. This attitude was maintained under Stolypin where, despite official propaganda and the efforts of senior officials, almost all peasant requests concerned the latter form of consolidation, achieved through the division of large villages, whereas the division of common land – the real equivalent of English enclosures – rarely took place.[23] The cooperation of local officials and lower-ranking officials in charge of these operations made this possible. In

---

[19] Steven Nafzinger, "Land Commune and Factor Market Imperfections: Micro Evidence from Late Nineteenth Century Russia," *Explorations in Economic History*, vol. 47, 4 (2010): 381–402.
[20] *Ezhegodnik GUZiZ* (Yearbook of the Land Colonization Commission) (St. Petersburg: Ministerstvo zemledeliia, 1908–1916).
[21] Judith Pallot, *Land Reforms in Russian 1906–1917* (Oxford, 1999); George Yaney, *The Urge to Mobilize. Agrarian Reform in Russia, 1861–1930* (Urbana: Illinois University Press, 1982).
[22] Pallot, *Land Reforms*: 87–88.
[23] Steven Nafzinger, "Communal Property Rights and Land Redistribution in Late Imperial Russia," *The Economic History Review*, 69, 3 (2016): 773–800.

other words, the "privatization" of agriculture announced by Tsarist officials did not play a major role in the pre-war Russian countryside. Overall, between 1906 and 1914, about 11 percent of peasant land in European Russia underwent some form of colonization.[24] Comparatively speaking, land colonization was demanded and practiced more in industrial and proto-industrial areas than in rural regions.[25] Economic growth was underpinned by the evolution of Russia's main social institutions, such as the peasant commune. It is no coincidence that, over the past twenty years, as the history of enclosures in Britain and agriculture in Europe has been re-examined,[26] the image of the Russian commune has also been called into question.[27] Recent estimates for Russia confirm that there is no correlation between land redistribution practices and economic productivity.[28] Periodic redistributions have had far less impact on productivity than endogenous investment decisions. When redistributing plots, communes often took into account soil quality and improvements made by the previous tenant. Redistributions allowed land communes to respond to sudden and unexpected changes in their size due to epidemics or migration, to reshape open fields and to bring order to field strips by reducing their number.[29]

Between 1861 and 1914, Russia underwent significant social transformation and economic growth; revised demographic trends show that mortality and birth rates were lower than previously thought.[30] Pauperization of the peasantry decreased, and famines were less frequent and less severe.[31] The period from 1861 to 1914 was marked by a steady improvement in agricultural production and living standards.[32]

The rate of growth and commercialization of Russian agriculture also accelerated.[33] Between the 1880s and 1900s, thanks to the grain trade, capitalism

[24] Ministerstvo sel'skogo khoziaistva, *Obzor dejatel'nosti za...* (Report on the Activity of the Ministry, 1908-1914) (St. Petersburg: Ministerstvo sel'skogo khoziaistva, 1909-1916); Pavel Pershin, *Zemelonoe ustroistvo dorevoliutsionnoi dereveni* (Moscow: Gozizdat, 1928).
[25] Pavel Zyrianov, *Krest'ianskaia Obshchina Evropeiskoi Rossii 1907-1914 gg* (The peasant commune in European Russia) (Moscow: Nauka, 1992).
[26] McCloskey, "The Enclosure of Open Fields".
[27] Esther Kingston-Mann, "Peasant Communes and Economic Innovation: A Preliminary Inquiry," in Kingston-Mann and Mixter, eds. *Peasant Economy, Culture, and Politics of European Russia, 1800–1921* (Princeton: Princeton University Press, 1991): 23–51; Zyrianov, *Krest'ianskaia obshchina Evropeiskoi Rossii.*
[28] Nafzinger, "Communal Property Rights".
[29] Pallot, *Land Reforms*: 81.
[30] Hoch, "Famine, Disease and Mortality"; Hoch, "On Good Numbers and Bad"; Hoch, "Serfs in Imperial Russia".
[31] Stephen Wheatcroft, "Crisis and Condition of the Peasantry".
[32] Kingston-Mann, "Marxism and Russian Rural Development"; Simms, "The Crisis in Russian Agriculture"; Simms, "The Crop Failure".
[33] Paul Gregory, *Russian National Income 1885-1913* (Cambridge: Cambridge University Press, 1982); Peter Gatrell, *The Tsarist Economy, 1850–1917* (New York: St Martin's Press, 1986).

spread to the remotest corners of the empire,[34] and the Russian wheat market became fully integrated into world markets.[35] Agriculture's contribution to national income grew at a rapid pace, comparable to that of contemporary Western European economies. Russia experienced growth rates similar to those of Germany, France, America, Japan, Norway, Canada and Great Britain: 1.35 percent average annual growth in agricultural productivity between 1883–1887 and 1909–1913, three-quarters of the rate of growth in industrial productivity and almost as much as the 1.5 percent rate for the economy as a whole.[36]

Net grain production increased by 3.1 percent per year between 1885 and 1913; Russia produced more grain than any other country in 1861 and was ahead of the United States by 1913.[37] The average annual growth rate of wholesale grain and potato production in European Russia between 1870 and 1913 was 2.5 percent: 1.6 percent in the first thirty years and 4.4 percent after the turn of the century. Gregory estimated the rate of economic growth in the Russian Empire as a whole, including the border regions, from 1883–1887 to 1909–1913 at 2.8 percent, with some fluctuations in between.[38] The value of labor increased by 42.6 percent between 1861 and 1913, an average annual rate of 1.7 percent.

This revised vision of Russian agriculture corresponds to new assessments of Russia's industrialization. According to recent estimates, between 1881 and 1913, industry's share of national income rose from 25 percent to 32 percent. Labor productivity was 28 percent higher than in agriculture.[39] The rate of urbanization was considerable,[40] largely attributable to the influx of peasant migrants who accounted for 93 percent of all factory workers in Moscow in 1902,[41] most of them in the textile industry. Industry remained geographically concentrated in the central provinces of Moscow and Vladimir and in and around the imperial capital. This means that despite increasing urbanization and regional specialization, the peasant worker remained the figurehead of the Russian economy.[42] The relatively small number of industrial workers was not due to internal passports or legal restrictions on mobility,[43] but to the strength of agriculture, its profitability, and people's interest in staying in rural areas

---

[34] Koval'chenko, Milov, *Vserossiiskii agrarnyi rynok*.
[35] Barry K. Goodwin, Thomas J. Grennes, "Tsarist Russia and the World Wheat Market," *Explorations in Economic History*, 35, 4 (1998): 405–430.
[36] Gregory, *Russian National Income*: 126–130; 168–194.
[37] Robert Allen, *Farm to Factory: A Reinterpretation of the Soviet Industrial Revolution* (Princeton: Princeton University Press, 2003).
[38] Gregory, *Russian National Income*: table 6.3.
[39] Gregory, *Russian National Income*: 132.
[40] Gatrell, *The Tsarist Economy*.
[41] Pretty, *Neither Peasant nor Proletarian*.
[42] Burds, *Peasant Dreams and Market Politics*.
[43] Leonid Borodkin, Brigitte Granville and Carol Scott Leonard, "The Rural/Urban Wage Gap in the Industrialisation of Russia, 1884–1910," *European Review of Economic History*, 12, 1 (2008): 67–95.

and leaving only for seasonal employment in the city.[44] At the same time, areas where serfdom was stronger and more persistent before 1861 were also areas where coercion in the labor market was reproduced after that date. Landowners exerted all sorts of pressures on agricultural workers that contributed greatly to limiting the growth of wages and welfare in these regions.[45]

Mobility, on the one hand, and land acquisition, on the other, have weakened household unity and the overall economic and social equilibrium associated with it. Because of the social status of the head of the family in peasant communities, young male peasants tended to leave their father's home at an early age.[46] Young children and women who work and live in town for several months a year were generally reluctant to give their entire income to the head of the family, and were also sensitive to urban fashions, which encouraged them to increase their individual spending.[47] Local courts also recorded an increasing number of disputes over these issues between 1870 and the First World War.[48] The number of households rose from 8,450,782 in 1877 to 12,019,255 in 1905. In fifteen provinces of European Russia, the rate of new household formation was between 30 percent and 60 percent for the period 1861–1882. This rate was two to four times higher than the population growth rate in these same regions. As a result, despite the increase in land purchases and emigration to Siberia, the amount of cultivated land per family fell from 13.2 to 10.2 *desiatina* between 1877 and 1905. In other words, social and economic changes gradually deprived people of the social framework of the extended family and the commune. The First World War put an end to the previous economic dynamic and exacerbated social tensions within the village and between peasants and landowners.

Thus, unlike in Great Britain and, to some extent, France, the abolition of serfdom in Russia was not the result of a social movement; it was essentially a top-down process. At the same time, as in the Western colonies, legal and social continuities were important in Russia too: Former serfs, like former slaves, were subject to strong legal inequalities. The difference was that emancipated Russian peasants retained their land, which was a major difference from emancipated slaves in the Americas. Partly because of the persistence of

---

[44] Leonard, *Agrarian Reforms*.
[45] Johannes Buggle and Steven Nafzinger, "The Slow Road From Serfdom: Labor Coercion and Long-Run Development in the Former Russian Empire," *Bofit (Bank of Finland) Discussion Paper*, 22, 2018.
[46] Alessandro Stanziani, "The First World War and the Disintegration of Economic Spaces in Russia," in Judith Pallot, ed., *Transforming Peasants. Society, State, and the Peasantry, 1861–1930*, (London: MacMillan 1998): 174–194.
[47] Details of conflicts in Vladimir province, near Moscow, in REM (Rossiiskoi etnograficheskii musei), fond 7, opis' 1.
[48] REM, fonds 7, opis' 1; TsSK (Tsentral'nyi Statisticheskii Komitet), *Statisticheskiya dannyya o razvodakh i nedeistvitel'nykh brakakh za 1867–1886* (Statistical data on marriages and separations, 1867–1886) (St. Petersburg: MVD, 1893): 16–21.

coercion, the European colonies had great difficulty recovering from the abolition of slavery, while Russia experienced economic growth based mainly on the pluriactivity of peasants and a labor-intensive process. Nevertheless, the emancipation of slavery affected the European colonies, while the abolition of serfdom mainly affected Central Russia. What about the Russian colonies?

The Impact of the Abolition of Serfdom on the Empire

Abolitionism transformed the Western empire, both institutionally (direct vs. indirect rule) and economically (globalization of trade), while leaving colonial workers in a state of extreme dependency. What about the Russian Empire?

The process of migration began at the end of the seventeenth century and continued throughout the next century, throughout the nineteenth century, before and after the abolition of serfdom. In the 1860s, 31,000 migrants settled in Orenburg, 102,000 in Novorussia and 73,000 in the North Caucasus. In the eyes of local political and social elites, these numbers were insufficient, and they feared that emancipation would significantly reduce migration.[49]

The central authorities, for their part, supported migration but wanted to channel it in the right direction; they financed mass migration from regions where land pressure was greatest. Most tsarist leaders were convinced that social and political stability required continued migration to the frontier regions. From the 1880s, the state also subsidized railroads and new infrastructure to facilitate migration. This led to the implementation of the Great Siberian Migration Plan, while the south and the Steppes were no longer the main, indeed almost exclusive, destinations. Between 1871 and 1896, these regions received half of the settlers of the Russian Empire: about two million people.[50] As before, migrants to the south and east came mainly from the provinces of central Russia, Ukraine and the Volga region. Many of them traveled without the required documents, namely a certificate of release issued by their commune of origin, which made it extremely difficult to obtain land. Without credit or additional resources, they had little choice but to register in existing villages and pay for registration documents.[51] The authorities were ambivalent about ethnicity and nationality: On the one hand, in order to encourage migration, they tried to avoid any official discrimination; in practice, however, such attitudes were widespread, and non-Russian Jews and migrants were ostracized by local authorities and the population alike.[52]

---

[49] RGIA, fond 1291, opis 53, delo 280.
[50] Viktor M. Kabuzan, *Naselenie Severnogo Kavkaza v XIX-XX vekakh: etnostatisticheskoe issledovanie* (The population of the North Caucasus in the nineteenth and twentieth centuries: an ethnostatistical study) (St. Petersburg: BLITs, 1996).
[51] RGIA fond 1291, opis 53, delo 8.
[52] Martin, *Law and Custom in the Steppe*.

In the colonies, as in the rest of Russia, agronomic techniques and knowledge were used to increase agricultural productivity. The writings and activities of Vasilii Vasil'evich Dokuchaev were particularly useful in the Steppe. As head of the Soil Research Bureau of the Ministry of Agriculture, Dokuchaev organized expeditions and studies in several regions and drew up a detailed map of the different qualities and compositions of soils.[53] His work on soil studies contrasted with the generic vision of the "Steppe" that had prevailed among tsarist administrators up to that point.[54] However, at the turn of the nineteenth and twentieth centuries, this approach was not synonymous with the recognition of local techniques, but, on the contrary, with the need to bring scientific knowledge to nomadic peoples. In the same vein, ethnographic studies of indigenous populations reflected the idea of a civilizing mission on the part of the Russians.

On the whole, and despite the reforms and the end of serfdom, the Russian Empire still did not contribute significantly to state revenues. The Russian state spent far more money than it received from the colonial frontier regions: Poland cost the empire dearly because of its persistent military burden, as did Finland; the southern provinces were developing trade and agricultural production, but Central Asia, the Caucasus and Transcaucasia were still unprofitable (Table 9.1).

In Poland, the three south-western provinces were administered separately. Russia's goal was to transplant the mir (local peasant community) to new territories to encourage the migration of Russian peasants. Tsarist leaders also imagined that, as in Russia, the mir would guarantee social stability in Poland. Thus, peasants were allotted plots of land, which they would buy back with their labor. The statutes were drawn up by district commissions headed by a mediator, a landowner appointed by the nobility (i.e., a Pole). The mediator surrounded himself with other Polish landowners who, as in the case of the estate inventories of 1847, tried to use the law to their advantage. The supposedly emancipated peasants responded by rioting. When the Polish landlords reduced the land allotted to the peasants by another 10 percent, the peasants responded by refusing to perform the compulsory labor. Finally, the landlords' delay in implementing the promised reforms (the deadline was postponed from 1861 to 1863) led to a further refusal by the peasants to pay their taxes and sign the statutes.

During the Polish nationalist uprising of 1863, Polish rebels vowed to give all the land to the peasants. The Russian government responded by crushing the uprising and granting more favorable terms to peasants in some regions than in others. Local rules for the abolition of serfdom required peasants to buy back their land, or it would be transferred to new Russian owners. In the end, Ukrainian peasants received 18 percent more land than the average Russian

---

[53] David Moon, *The Plough that Broke the Steppe* (Oxford: Oxford University Press, 2013).
[54] Vasily Dokuchaev, *Sochinenia* (Collected works) (Moscow: Gozizdat, 1961).

Table 9.1 *Average annual state income and expenditure by groups of provinces in Russia in 1879-1881 (kopecks per capita)*

Province groups	Treasury receipts	Cash expenses	Rate of return, in percent
Capital cities	28.58	82.25	−65
North	4.33	3.27	32
Eastern Europe	3.92	2.20	78
Centrale-Industrielle	5.16	2.91	77
Central Black Earth	5.20	5.13	1
Little Russian	4.90	4.04	21
Baltic	10.85	3.52	208
Northwest	4.00	5.67	−29
Southwest	6.48	3.52	84
South	7.74	6.71	15
North Caucasus	3.42	4.77	−28
Transcaucasia	2.39	11.36	−79
Polish	6.78	6.71	1
Siberian	4.62	4.97	−7
Turkestan	1.55	4.36	−64

Source: Pravilova, "Tsena Imperii".

peasant. Land was also allocated to the significant number of landless peasants. In addition, the peasants were guaranteed privileged access to the landowners' meadows, pastures, forests and water sources. In right-bank Ukraine, the peasants' redemption payments – and thus the nobles' compensation – were reduced by 48 percent. As for land prices, while in Russia and left-bank Ukraine the freed peasants were overtaxed by 47 percent, in western Ukraine they paid the market price.

In addition, as a result of the revolt, Polish nobles were forced to pay an additional 10 percent tax on the annual income from their estates.[55] Between 1866 and 1893, the total area of Russian-owned land doubled from 24 percent to 50 percent of all Ukrainian arable land.[56] Two conflicts ensued: one between Russians and Poles, the other between Poles and Ukrainians. The first conflict, which arose after the 1863 uprising, was encouraged by the tsarist authorities,

---

[55] Beauvois, *La bataille de la terre*: 24. Serhii Plokhy and Frank E. Sysyn, *Religion and Nation in Modern Ukraine* (Edmonton: Canadian Institute of Ukrainian Studies Press, 2003).

[56] Alexej Miller *"Ukrainskij vopros" v politike vlastej v russkom obchtchestvennom mnenii (vtoraja pol. XIX v.)* (The Ukrainian question in the politics of power in Russian social thought) (St. Petersburg: Aleteia, 2000).

who took measures such as prohibiting Poles from acquiring new land (1865),[57] imposing highly unfavorable taxes and restricting credit. Russian buyers were also unable to obtain the expected financing from the state or land banks and faced political opposition from the Polish elite. Finally, after an assassination attempt on the Tsar in 1866, Russian state policy changed: The Tsar decided to encourage land ownership by nobles of all nationalities to combat social disorder. In 1873, the Poles who had participated in the 1863 uprising and had been exiled to Siberia were granted amnesty and allowed to return. At the same time, the indebtedness of the Russian and Polish nobility increased during this period, as did the sale of estates. The tsarist state helped by providing financial resources to Russian and, to a lesser extent, Polish landowners. Between 1866 and 1896, 2.4 million *desiatina* passed into the hands of Russian owners in the three provinces of Kiev, Podolia and Volhynia.[58]

There were also conflicts between Poles and Ukrainians. After the riots of 1863, a law was passed authorizing the creation of peasant militias to hunt down insurgents in exchange for a promise to transfer land confiscated from Polish landowners to the peasants.[59] The *Ukase* (decree) of 1863 put forth an alternative solution: In contrast to the Russian plan, which imposed a temporary obligation on freed peasants to work for their masters until they had repaid their debts, Ukrainian peasants were required to purchase their plots outright, but at a 20 percent discount. The Russian state had evidently anticipated these expenses, which led to a rapid increase in the number of buy-back certifications between 1863 and 1871. Concurrently, Polish elites perceived these policies as a strategy to erode their influence. Consequently, the area of land owned by peasants increased from three to four million *desiatina*, often on infertile land. The peasants' demands for easements over woods and forests encountered opposition from both the Russian and Polish landowners. The absence of a comprehensive land registry, coupled with the peasants' animosity towards surveyors tasked with measuring properties and delineating their boundaries, impeded the attainment of a consensus. This dynamic gave rise to several confrontations. The Russian authorities' capacity to execute these operations was constrained, and the process continued until nearly the close of the nineteenth century.

Concurrently, wheat production exhibited a marked increase in Ukraine, where the net yield for the Russian budget was the highest; second only to that

---

[57] *Pol'noe Sobrannoe zakonov*, 2nd series, vol. XL, no. 42759.
[58] Beauvois, *La bataille*: 70. Andreas Kappeler, Zenon E. Kohut, Frank E. Sysyn and Mark von Hagen, eds., *Culture, Nation, and Identity: The Ukrainian–Russian Encounter, 1600–1945* (Edmonton: Canadian Institute of Ukrainian Studies Press, 2003).
[59] Andreas Kappeler, *"Great-Russians" and "Little-Russians": Russian-Ukrainian Relations and Perceptions in Historical Perspective* (Seattle: University of Washington Press, 2003); Andreas Kappeler, *Der schwierige Weg zur Nation: Beiträge zur neueren Geschichte der Ukraine* (The difficult path to nationhood: Contributions to the history of modern Ukraine) (Vienna: Böhlau, 2003).

of the Baltic regions. While 28.9 million acres of wheat were cultivated in the fifty provinces of European Russia in 1881, this figure increased to 50.8 million acres in 1900 (sixty-four provinces) and 62.7 million acres in 1910. A particularly noteworthy increase in wheat production was observed in Ukraine, where the province of Ekaterinoslav experienced a surge from 1.2 million *pud* (1 *pud* equaling 16.38 kilograms) per year between 1896 and 1900, to 2.3 million ten years later. In Kursk province, wheat production rose from 1 to 1.2 million *pud* over the same period, and in Kharkiv from 0.9 to 1.2 and 1.7 in 1911–13.[60] Between 1864 and 1913, the hinterland of the Crimean ports experienced a 69 percent increase in grain production, while the North Caucasus witnessed a 562 percent surge, the Siberian region a 279 percent rise, the southern Steppes a 269 percent growth, Ukraine a slight decrease of 168 percent and the southern Black Lands a notable 168 percent increase.

A detailed breakdown of the figures by crop type reveals that rye and oats continued to dominate in the Black Lands. In contrast, in southern Russia and Ukraine, wheat accounted for 44.7 percent of the crop, followed by barley (29 percent), rye (17.1 percent) and oats (9.1 percent).[61] This increase in production was no longer based solely on the intensification of work, as in the past – even if this remained the main factor of progress – but was accompanied by technical improvements, albeit unevenly distributed across the regions. Crop mechanization was predominant in Ukraine and southern Russia (82.8 percent of total Russian agriculture), while its adoption was less widespread elsewhere (12 percent in the central regions, 4.8 percent in the western provinces and 0.4 percent in the north).[62]

Turkestan merits significant consideration as well. Following the abolition of slavery in the United States, it emerged as a leading candidate to supply Europe with cotton, prompting significant investment from the tsarist elites in this endeavor.[63] However, the initial outcomes were modest, and the Russian authorities were unable to implement the ambitious economic strategies they had envisioned for Turkestan. While cotton production increased, marketing the cotton on the global market proved challenging due to the market's preference for a specific type of cotton. Consequently, several entrepreneurs initiated the introduction of US cotton to the region. Initially, the dissemination of US cotton seeds was undertaken by Konstantin Petrovich von Kaufman, the first Governor General of Turkestan. However, it was not until the 1870s and 1880s that a substantial "cotton boom" emerged, driven by private Russian and

---

[60] Aleksandr' V. Ostrovskii, *Zernovoe proizvodtsvo Evropeiskoi Rossii v kontse XIX-nachala XX v.* (The production of wheat in the European Russia during the nineteenth-early twentieth centuries) (St. Petersburg: Poltorak, 2013).
[61] V. Ostrovskii, *Zernovoe proizvodtsvo*: 219–221.
[62] Goodwin and Grennes, "Tsarist Russia".
[63] Beatrice Penati, "The Cotton Boom and the Land Tax in Russian Turkestan, 1880s–1915," *Kritika*, 14, 4 (2013): 741–774.

Muslim entrepreneurs, including numerous textile companies from Moscow and Łódź. The scarcity of adequate irrigation systems hindered the expansion of cotton cultivation, and by 1914, only 3.6 percent of the total cotton area in Turkestan, excluding the Transcaspian region, was under irrigation (not all of which was dedicated to cotton cultivation).[64] It is acknowledged that advancements in transportation, innovations such as mechanical cleaning and sowing, and the utilization of fertilizers, in addition to transformations and changes in the local credit system and property rights, contributed to this development.[65] Despite the desire of the Russian rulers for cotton expansion, it was in fact achieved through a small-scale, well-organized process carried out mainly by local Muslim actors using conventional agronomic methods. This economic activity reveals the difficulties faced by the Tsarist authorities in effectively monitoring and controlling the players in Turkestan. The Russian endeavor in Turkestan was not only characterized by colonialism, exclusion and violence, but also by a conspicuous absence of effective coordination from above. Local governors and military authorities primarily assumed responsibility for implementing policies, perceiving them as a means of political and military control rather than as a catalyst for economic growth.[66] Land taxation constituted a primary instrument of cotton production. Until 1887, the authorities demanded a tenth of the harvest. Thereafter, the amount to be paid by each fiscal unit (or "rural community") depended on a sampling of local yields, multiplied by the average market prices of production over the previous five years.[67] The objective of this initiative was to encourage "abundant harvests," thereby increasing the value of domestic production and enhancing the fiscal viability of Turkestan. However, the disparities in yields between districts, compounded by the challenges in stabilizing American cotton production, prompted the Tsarist rulers to allocate subsidies in the early 1890s. However, these measures yielded only modest results. In 1898, a special commission was established in Turkestan, which determined that yields were declining both quantitatively and qualitatively due to the absence of crop rotation. The commission also identified that the price structure was becoming unsustainable. The wages were high and increasingly incompatible with falling yields and declining cotton prices on the Moscow wholesale market.

This state of affairs persisted until 1908, when the Russian treasury realized its first profit since 1868, with a modest surplus exceeding expenditures by

---

[64] Muriel Joffe, "Autocracy, Capitalism, Empire: The Politics of Irrigation," *Russian Review*, 54, 3 (1995): 365–388.

[65] Stuart Thompstone, "Russian Imperialism and the Commercialization of the Central Asian Cotton Trade," *Textile History*, 26, 2 (1995): 233–257.

[66] Paolo Sartori, ed., *Explorations in the Social History of Modern Central Asia (Nineteenth–Early Twentieth Century)* (Leiden: Brill, 2013).

[67] Pravilova, *Finansy imperii*: 288–290.

1.6 percent. This surplus can be interpreted as a dividend on the state's investment in Turkestan. From 1908 to 1911, the rate of profit increased significantly (to 14.8 percent), before falling back to 7.7 percent in 1912; from 1913, the regional budget was again in deficit.

Nevertheless, excluding military expenditure, many regions had been profitable since the 1880s;[68] more importantly, the official calculation did not include the profits and earnings from private activities, particularly commerce, which undoubtedly brought in growing revenues during this period.[69] An in-depth survey conducted by the Ministry of Finance in 1901 substantiated that growth rates and per capita incomes in the "peripheral" provinces were comparable to those in metropolitan France.[70] In summary, the colonial zones were a source of profits that served almost exclusively to cover military and administrative expenses, reflecting Russia's geopolitical concerns as well as the vision of the Tsarist elites who saw the "peripheral" provinces as zones of Russification and control.

In summary, throughout the nineteenth century and up to the First World War, Russia experienced greater economic growth than is generally acknowledged. This economic growth was primarily driven by the country's prior development and the capacity of Russian economic institutions, particularly the commune, to meet escalating demands. While this approach has facilitated the attainment of comparable growth rates to those observed in major Western countries, it has not yet achieved parity. Moreover, it has not adequately addressed the persistent tensions between economic advancement and social and political inequality. The abolition of serfdom was unable to overcome the limitations of domestic growth and social reform, or the burden of empire, which was primarily conceived in geopolitical terms as a tool for Russification. While race was not entirely absent from this process, nationalism played a more significant role in the abolitionist movement than in the Americas and, at least until the late 1800s, in India.[71] This approach contributed to the challenges

---

[68] Iurii P. Bokarev, *Ekonomicheskie posledstviia raspada rossiiskoi imperii v rezul'tate pervoi mirovoi voiny* (The economic consequences of the collapse of the Russian empire because of WWI) (Ekaterinburg and Moscow, Moscow: UMT, 2009).

[69] Izmes'eva, *Rossia v sisteme evropeiskogo rynka*.

[70] *Materialy vysochaishe uchrezhdennoi 16 noiabria 1901 g. Komissii po issledovaniiu voprosa o dvizhenii s 1861 g. po 1901 g. blagosostoianiia sel'skogo naseleniia sredne-zemledel'cheskikh gubernii sravnitel'no s drugimi mestnostiami Evropeiskoi Rossii: V 3 chastiakh* (Materials collected by the 1901 Commission on the study of economic development from 1861 to 1901, comparison between the central agrarian provinces and other regions of European Russia) (Saint Petersburg: Ministry of Agriculture, 1903).

[71] David Rainbow, ed., *Ideologies of Race. Imperial Russia and the Soviet Union in Global Context* (Montreal: Mac Gill-Queen University Press, 2019); Marina Mogilner, *Homo Imperii: A History of Physical Anthropology in Russia* (Lincoln: University of Nebraska Press, 2013); Eugene Avrutin, Stephen Norris, eds., *Racism in Russia: from the Romanovs to Putin* (London: Bloomsbury, 2022).

associated with resource extraction in Central Asia and Siberia, and significantly constrained the economic dynamism of the empire as a whole in comparison to the experiences of the French and British empires. In these regions, the transition from slavery to new forms of labor was accompanied by two significant developments. The colonies experienced a shift towards concentrated and mechanized production, facilitated by the emergence of new forms of labor that were not directly subject to abolition. This transition was accompanied by a second industrial revolution on the European continent, which contributed to economic growth despite the increasing cost of labor. In Russia, the colonies remained unprofitable, while economic growth on the continent was predicated on the fragile compromise between the landed aristocracy and the transforming peasantry, with some uneven improvement in urban economies still confronted by the dualism between small and large units. Noteworthy exceptions to this pattern included the Baltic regions, which continued to benefit from trade between Russia and Europe, and Ukraine, which relied on the Black Sea for substantial profits from wheat and trade. The continued viability of the Russian economy, as well as its expansionist endeavors, were contingent upon the export of wheat and other agricultural products to European markets. As in preceding periods, this outcome rendered Russia's economic and social trajectory contingent on the progression of international markets. From this perspective, the abolitionist movement in the United States offers a comparable yet symmetrical scenario to that of Russia, with international markets supporting slavery in the Southern states and domestic markets and slavery favoring industrialization in the Northern states.

10

Abolition in the United States and the Great Transformation

The purpose of this chapter is not to offer a new interpretation of the abolition of slavery in the United States, which is beyond the scope of this book. Rather, I intend to pose the following question: How did the abolition of slavery in the United States affect the fate of labor in the three empires examined here? It will be argued that the abolition of slavery in the United States led to a fundamental change in global capitalism. This change occurred not only in the terms already studied by Beckert (new supplies of cotton and forced labor around the world), but also in a new relationship between capitalism, labor and the state. I will argue that the Second Industrial Revolution and the Great Transformation, as Polanyi called it, were the main outcomes of this process, although most historiographies of these topics have never linked these dynamics to the American convulsions.

The Importance of Slavery to American Capitalism

Despite important constraints, Russian serfs were better integrated into society than black American slaves, and the same was true after their emancipation. Russian peasants were not indentured slaves and did not face racial exclusion. On the other hand, they weren't farmers either, and they didn't ally themselves with merchants and industrialists against the landlords, as they did in the northern United States. If the Russian peasants were in favor of the market, they wanted to keep it in check. They also remained highly suspicious of the land market, adhering, like the tsarist elites and landowners, to a policy of restricting access to it and, like them, viewing with suspicion any encroachment by the "bourgeois" and urban capitalists in this area. Pacts like those in the United States between northern farmers and capitalists against southern slaveholders would simply be unthinkable in Russia. Why and how did such a common front emerge in the United States?

Although barely mentioned in the vast bibliography on American slavery and the Civil War, the history of indentured labor that we developed in Parts I and II needs to be reintroduced here. The first reason is that, from a legal and institutional point of view, the very identification of slaves, post-slaves (emancipated) and migrants depended entirely on this history. In particular, as we have shown, the legal rights of indentured migrants gradually converged with racialized categories, without which the complementary alternative definition of "wage earner" would not have been possible. Because indentured laborers moved from the status of servants to that of wage earners, and because the latter were essentially white, they could be clearly distinguished from emancipated slaves and the new "coolies" (also of color) in the postbellum United States. The ambiguities of freedom for the emancipated and enslaved after 1865 were thus rooted in the ways in which free and unfree labor had been intertwined in the United States over the preceding decades and centuries.

The voluminous evidence of runaway life stories in the antebellum South attests to these ambiguities.[1] Runaways could certainly rely on the black urban population to help them escape and eventually work, to the extent that their stories can be interpreted less as individual cases of resistance than as social forms of migration.[2] This means that the choice between fleeing to the city and staying in the countryside was not as obvious as is often assumed. Certainly, in the city they could blend in with the local population and find better opportunities. At the same time, many runaways fled to the countryside, often to other plantations where living and working conditions were perceived to be better.[3]

These links between people and forms of labor were also reinforced by the way slave and non-slave economies interacted before and after the Civil War. Indeed, the Civil War was not only linked to the issue of slavery: Tariffs (protectionism *versus* liberalism), the structure of the economy (priority to industry or agriculture), monetary (inflation or stability) and fiscal policies (forms of taxation, rates of progressivity, etc.), the federal organization and the political and economic structure of the United States were also affected. Federal organization and criteria for representation in Congress,[4] and in particular the orientation of new states in the South and West, such as Texas,[5] were other sources of conflict.

---

[1] Blassingame, *Slave Testimony;* Charles Mitchell, Jean Baker, eds., *The Civil War in Maryland Reconsidered* (Baton Rouge: Louisiana State University Press, 2021); Frederick Douglass, *Narrative of the Life of Frederick Douglass, an American Slave. Written by Himself* (Boston: Anti-Slavery Office, 1845); Harriet Jacob, *Incidents in the Life of a Slave Girl: Written by Herself* (Boston: The Author, 1861); Seth Rockman, *Scraping by: Wage Labor, Slavery, and Survival in Early Baltimore* (Baltimore: Johns Hopkins University Press, 2009); Sylviane Diouf, *Slavery's Exiles: the Story of the American Maroons* (New York: New York University Press, 2014).

[2] Muller, *Escape to the City.*

[3] Johnson, *River of Dark Dreams.*

[4] William C. Davis, *Look Away! A History of the Confederate States of America* (New York, NY: Free Press, 2002); George C. Rable, *The Confederate Republic: A Revolution Against Politics* (Chapel Hill, N. C.: The University of North Carolina Press, 1994).

[5] Eric Foner, *Free Soil, Free Labor, Free Men: The Ideology of the Republican Party before the Civil War* (Oxford: Oxford University Press, 1995).

If these antagonisms crystallized around slavery,[6] the underlying question was that of the political balance of the United States.[7] From the 1850s onwards, the dynamics of international trade, with the adoption of free trade in Great Britain, then in France and most European countries,[8] reignited tensions between Southern cotton growers (free traders), Midwestern grain farmers and certain Northern industrialists, who wanted to be protected from British competition.[9] The trade policies adopted had to be supported by coherent monetary policies: The creditor North supported a stable currency, while the indebted exporter South favored a weak dollar.[10] In this context, Southern property owners did not hesitate to invoke the exorbitant cost of abolition and its incompatibility with the defense of private property.[11] On this point, the debate, which had already inflamed France and Great Britain, took a particular turn in the United States, where several local and federal judges sanctioned in their decisions the idea that the abolition of slavery clashed with the principle of the inviolability of property. The argument also fueled the debate on American sovereignty: In the face of British criticism, several anti-abolitionist political representatives denounced Great Britain's presumption of treating the United States as if it were still one of its colonies.[12] This accusation had all the more impact on American public opinion because British ships did not hesitate to requisition vessels carrying slaves to the United States, not only between Africa and America,[13] but also between American states, as in the case of *La Créole* in 1841, sailing between Virginia and Louisiana,[14] whose interception after a revolt by slaves on board provoked a major diplomatic crisis in 1842.

---

[6] Michael A. Morrison, *Slavery and the American West: The Eclipse of Manifest Destiny and the Coming of the Civil War* (Chapel Hill: University of North Carolina Press, 1997); Baptist, *The Half Has Never Been Told*.

[7] Maris A. Vinovskis, ed., *Toward a Social History of the American Civil War: Explanatory Essays* (Cambridge: Cambridge University Press, 1990); Gabor S. Boritt, ed., *Why the Civil War Came* (Oxford: Oxford University Press, 1996).

[8] Findlay, O'Rourke, *Power and Plenty*.

[9] James Scott and David Lake, "The Second Face of Hegemony: Britain's Repeal of the Corn Laws and the American Walker's Tariff of 1846," *International Organization*, 43, 1 (1989): 1–29.

[10] Nicolas Barreyre, *Gold and Freedom: A Spatial History of the United States after the Civil War* (Charlottesville: University of North Carolina Press, 2015); Howard Bodenhorn, *A History of Banking in Antebellum America: Financial Markets and Economic Development in an Era of Nation-Building* (Cambridge: Cambridge University Press, 2000). On divisions in taxation, Roman Huret, *American Tax Resisters* (Cambridge, MA: Harvard University Press, 2014).

[11] Eugene D. Genovese, *The Slaveholders' Dilemma: Freedom and Progress in Southern Conservative Thought, 1820–1860* (Columbia: University of South Carolina Press, 1992); Gavin Wright, *Slavery and American Economic Development* (Baton Rouge: Louisiana State University Press, 2003).

[12] Huzzey, *Freedom Burning*.

[13] Eltis and Richardson, *Extending the Frontiers*.

[14] Fogel, *Without Consent or Contract*.

In turn, international markets interacted strongly with American business and domestic markets, and both strongly influenced the profitability of slave plantations in the USA. This was a controversial topic then and still is today.[15] *Time on the Cross*,[16] published in 1974, did much to reopen this debate. It showed that, contrary to all arguments since Adam Smith and the abolitionists, plantations were indeed profitable and that abolition was adopted for essentially moral and political reasons. The thesis, along with empirical observations limited to a few large plantations, was immediately criticized. The authors went on to produce detailed analyses by region and even by plantation,[17] which were again challenged. The main objection was one of perspective: It consisted in showing that the profitability of plantations, even if it could be admitted that it was positive, at least for the large units, on the eve of the Civil War, was bound to decline over time due to the demotivation of slaves, changes in the international economy and the efficiency of other economies.[18]

In the end, it was the economic calculation of the planters that was emphasized, which was very different from the one determined by our current criteria. The latter mistakenly believed that they were making a profit from slavery and that the transition to wage labor required money and labor, both of which were in short supply in the southern states. In practice, according to this interpretation, they underestimated costs (which did not take into account non-monetary costs and therefore artificially inflated profits), as did Fogel and Engerman.[19]

We could certainly go on debating in a vacuum whether planters and investors would have made higher profits in a truly competitive "free" wage labor market. But the fact is that American plantations made profits, as did most Caribbean plantations until the abolition of slavery, and Russian units until the abolition of serfdom. The question is rather one of understanding the role of slave production in relation to other production for export and to Northern industries and markets. Did slavery contribute to the industrialization of the United States?

Sven Beckert, Edward Baptist and proponents of the New History of Capitalism (NHC) took up the earlier work of Williams and Inikori and

---

[15] Alfred H. Conrad and John R. Meyer, "The Economics of Slavery in the Antebellum South," *The Journal of Political Economy*, 66, 2 (1958): 95–130; Claudia Dale Goldin, *Urban Slavery in the American South, 1820–1860: A Quantitative History* (Chicago: University of Chicago Press, 1976).

[16] Robert W. Fogel and Stanley L. Engerman, *Time on the Cross: The Economics of American Negro Slavery* (New York: Norton, 1974).

[17] Fogel, *Without Consent or Contract*.

[18] Gavin Wright, "Slavery and the Cotton Boom," *Explorations in Economic History*, 12, 4 (1975): 439–451.

[19] Paul David, Herbert Gutman, Richard Sutch, Peter Temin, Gavin Wright, eds., *Reckoning with Slavery: A Critical Study in the Quantitative History of American Negro Slavery* (Oxford: Oxford University Press, 1977).

highlighted the contribution of slavery to the industrialization and growth of the United States.[20]

Gavin Wright, Alan Olmestead and Paul Rhode have challenged the data used by the NHC and thus one of its main arguments; namely, the contribution of slavery to American capitalism. According to these critics, US domestic markets and local endowments contributed far more to financing the Industrial Revolution than slavery, while slavery contributed very little; cotton accounted for a very small percentage of US exports, far behind corn.[21] This argument bears a striking resemblance to those that were previously advanced in regard to the role of slavery in the British Industrial Revolution. In the context of the United States, it is noteworthy that by the mid nineteenth century, the northern United States had already established itself as the vanguard of the capitalist economy, far outpacing Britain and preceding the Second Industrial Revolution, which led to the widespread adoption of a high ratio of capital to labor. This assertion was initially put forward in the 1960s by H.J. Habakkuk, who contended that the scarcity of labor in the United States led to an increase in wages, thereby fostering the adoption of mechanization.[22] A substantial improvement in real wages and working conditions for whites was documented in the northern states prior to the Civil War.[23] It seems reasonable to conclude, then, that in terms of industrial inputs, the North needed Southern cotton; in terms of profits, the South was still reaping the rewards in the 1850s: It was an excellent market for British and now American manufactured goods, as well as for corn. Cotton exports partly financed the American economy, while Northern capital was increasingly present in the South and contributed significantly to the development of its industry. It is true, as Gavin Wright has pointed out, that slave production could not be sustained in the long run, and that without an increase in the area devoted to cotton or sugar, productivity would have declined. But this does not mean that mechanization and wage labor (and thus the abolition of slavery) were the only possible solutions to this problem, as this argument implies. The United States was not a closed economy, far from it. Another way to continue producing cotton with forced labor was to globalize it (i.e., to move it from the United States to other parts of the world); indeed, this is what the United States and Western capitalism more broadly did after the abolition of slavery in the United States. The outsourcing of forced labor in the face of the abolition of slavery in

---

[20] Cathy Mason, ed., *The Economy of Early America: Historical Perspectives & New Directions* (University Park: Pennsylvania State University Press, 2006); Johnson, *River of Dark Dreams*; Baptist, *The Half Has Never Been Told*; Beckert, *Empire of Cotton*; Calvin Schermerhorn, *The Business of Slavery and the Rise of American Capitalism, 1815–1860* (New Haven: Yale University Press, 2015); Beckert and Rockman, *Slavery's Capitalism*.

[21] Alan Olmstead, Paul Rhode, "Cotton, Slavery and the New History of Capitalism," *Explorations in Economic History*, 67, January (2018): 1–17.

[22] Habakkuk, *American and British Technology in the Nineteenth Century*.

[23] Sokoloff and Dollar, "Agricultural Seasonality".

the United States confirms the importance of servitude for capitalism in general and for American capitalism in particular, as NHC argues. As we will see in the next chapter, global capitalism and intensive forced labor in the "peripheries" coexisted with the intensification of capital in the center. Before considering the global implications of American abolition, it is worth examining the transformation of labor in the United States in some detail.

Shifting Borders: Migrants, Employees, Slaves, Apprentices

Unlike Britain, the American North quickly turned to full-time workers, capital intensification and heavy industry, which contributed greatly to growth and to national and international markets. With this outcome in mind, we need to understand how multiple labor worlds and sets of actors came into play in the United States: It wasn't just a confrontation between white wage earners and black slaves; massive new white immigration and access to land also played a central role. How did this happen?

According to anti-abolitionists, Judge Mansfield's famous decision in Somerset would not apply across the Atlantic because the United States was a sovereign state, but also because, unlike piracy, slavery did not violate international law.[24] Consequently, slavery could only be criminalized by state laws.[25] On the basis of these assumptions, the Southern states again called for the reintroduction of the slave trade in the mid-1850s, but their request to Congress was rejected.

The question of the legitimacy of free labor became all the more acute in the United States in the 1840s, when two other related issues arose: access to land for new immigrants massively arriving from Europe, especially Ireland, and the redefinition of labor relations in the northern states.[26] Although the term "servant" was still widely used, its legal and economic meaning had gradually shifted away from its English meaning by the end of the eighteenth century. American urban workers came to associate it with English rule and European corporations, and refused to have the term imposed on them, along with the penal standards based on the Masters and Servants Acts. Their opinions were in line with court rulings, which emphasized the need to avoid any difference in status between *masters* and *servants*, and therefore opposed penalizing the latter for breach of contract, in the name of contractual equality and the free will of the parties.[27]

---

[24] Larry E. Tise, *Proslavery: A History of the Defense of Slavery in America, 1701–1840* (Athens: University of Georgia Press, 1987).

[25] William W. Freehling, *The Reintegration of American History: Slavery and the Civil War* (Oxford: Oxford University Press, 1994).

[26] Jeffrey R. Hummel, *Emancipating Slaves, Enslaving Free Men: A History of the American Civil War* (Chicago, Ill.: Open Court, 2014).

[27] Robert J. Steinfeld, *Coercion, Contract, and Free Labor*.

Wage earners also criticized indentured servitude, which by the 1820s was quickly considered unfree by white workers and many judges.[28] Established workers, especially those born in the United States, were anxious to distinguish themselves from new immigrants, who were always hired under this form of contract. But even for the latter, short-term contracts gradually became the norm.[29] This development did not reflect a preference on the part of the employers; on the contrary, they were opposed to it. The need for labor and the resistance of the workers eventually forced them to accept shorter contracts and better working conditions, especially since the action of co-villagers and family members already settled in the United States enabled the new immigrants to pay off the indenture debt very quickly, thus eliminating any possibility of employers keeping them under their control. As a result, instead of a continuum of dependency, the American labor world became polarized between free and wage labor on the one hand and slavery on the other.

The strong bargaining power of workers in the northern states had other consequences: The rural-urban mobility that was so widespread in Europe at the time rapidly declined in the northern United States. Seasonality was lower than in Britain because agriculture was more diversified and less tied to wheat than to corn, which required fixed periods of major farm labor.[30] Although the seasonal nature of the work was reduced, it was still badly appreciated by employers, who from the 1820s tried to impose annual contracts with payment of a large proportion of the wages on the due date. This solution was in contrast to the practice of advance payments, which had become widespread in France and partly in Great Britain, and which put workers in debt and forced them to stay on. In the United States, judges were reluctant to criminalize the relationship created by advances. In addition, a growing number of masters and employers relied on innovation to alleviate labor shortages. The northern states were characterized by early concentration and mechanization.[31] The world of labor was not subject to the same legal constraints as in Europe and often benefited from relatively higher wages than on the other side of the Atlantic. What about the South?

While neoclassical economists emphasized the beneficial role of markets and thus the overall improvement in living conditions (for all workers), some neo-institutionalists emphasized the market distortions caused by racism, especially by raising the cost of credit and money. Indeed, between 1860 and 1880, per capita output in the US South fell by about 23 percent, while it rose by about 35 percent in the North.[32] The most reasonable explanation for this

---

[28] Robert J. Steinfeld, *The Invention of Free Labor*: 166–170.
[29] Grubb, "The End of European Immigrant Servitude in the United States".
[30] Sokoloff and Dollar, "Agricultural Seasonality".
[31] Habakkuk, *American and British Technology*.
[32] Stanley Engerman, "The Economic Impact of the Civil War," *Explorations in Entrepreneurial History*, 3, 3 (1966): 176–199.

decline is not the migration of black labor, which was relatively limited at the time, at least in the more agriculturally oriented states,[33] but the efficiency of production units, particularly the shift from large plantations and a system of banded labor to small units.[34] There were also the costs and effects of the war itself and, of course, the decline in international demand for American cotton.[35] Foner's work influenced the orientation of a generation by suggesting that, despite poverty and many social and political limitations, the postwar reconstruction of the South was successful.[36] Like their British and French counterparts before them, American anti-abolitionists initially focused on the "miserable" lives of wage earners. But this argument was quickly disproved by the net increase in wages and improvement in working conditions in the northern states. It would be a mistake, however, to conclude that emancipation was an unqualified success, for the abolition of slavery revealed the limits of abolitionist rhetoric. The irreconcilable opposition between free labor and slavery on which it was based gave way to the acceptance of a black-white fault line:[37] Although all workers were free in principle, some were less so than others, depending on their race and slave past.

Criminal sanctions in the labor market, which disappeared for whites in the 1830s, reappeared after the Civil War for former slaves,[38] as well as new indentured migrants of color, mainly Chinese and Indian coolies.[39] New anti-vagrancy laws were passed in most southern states, as well as elsewhere, such as Massachusetts.[40] Each year, thousands of workers, most of them black, were prosecuted for vagrancy and imprisoned in workhouses. A small number of judges objected to this trend and ruled that these actions were unlawful.[41]

---

[33] Jay Mandle, "The Plantation States as a Sub-Region of the Post-bellum South," *The Journal of Economic History*, 34, 3 (1974): 732–738.

[34] James Irwin, "Explaining the Decline in Southern per Capita Output After Emancipation," *Explorations in Economic History*, 31, 3 (1994): 336–356.

[35] Gavin Wright, *Old South, New South* (Baton Rouge: Lousiana State University Press, 1997); Paul Temin, "The Post-Bellum Recovery of the South and the Cost of Civil War," *The Journal of Economic History*, 36, 4 (1976): 898–907.

[36] Eric Foner, *Reconstruction: America's Unfinished Revolution, 1863–1867* (New York: Harper 2002, first edition 1988); Eric Foner, *Nothing but Freedom: Emancipation and Its Legacy* (Baton Rouge: Louisiana University Press, 1983).

[37] David R. Roediger, *Towards the Abolition of Whiteness: Essays on Race, Politics, and Working Class History* (London: Verso, 1994); Bruce Baker, Brian Kelly, eds., *After Slavery: Race, Labor, and Citizenship in the Reconstruction South* (Gainesville: University Press of Florida, 2013).

[38] Ralph Shlomovitz, "Bound or Free? Black Labor in Cotton and Sugar Cane Farming, 1865–1880," *Journal of Southern History*, 50, 4 (1984): 569–596.

[39] Steinfeld, *Coercion, Contract*: 29–38

[40] Amy Dru Stanley, *From Bondage to Contract: Wage Labor, Marriage and the Market in the Age of Slave Emancipation* (New York: Cambridge University Press, 1999); Davis, *Slavery and Human Progress*.

[41] *Portland v. Bangor*, 65 Maine, 120.

In 1897, the Supreme Court ruled that the forced apprenticeship of black people was a form of involuntary servitude and therefore violated the Thirteenth Amendment.[42] However, these were very few convictions compared to the enormous mass of prosecutions of black workers. In fact, the notion and practice of "free labor" that emerged after the Civil War was less an expression of the success of liberal ideas of coercion than of the tensions within the American liberal and abolitionist movements between freedom of contract and personal freedom. Workers, especially black workers, won the former, but not the latter.[43] Anti-vagrancy laws, with criminal penalties for breach of contract, were consistently enforced against black workers;[44] lower wages and persistent coercion accompanied this attitude,[45] which also affected black sharecroppers.[46] Bound by year-round contracts, sharecroppers paid for slightly greater control over production by giving up their right to move. White planters attempted to compensate for the lack of capital through coercion, as they had before abolition.[47] Meanwhile, white people also experienced new social trajectories: In the five main cotton-producing states, 40 percent of single-family tenant farms were operated by whites in 1880.[48] In Georgia, the number of white sharecroppers and tenants exceeded the number of black sharecroppers and tenants in 1910.[49] Yet sharecropping, about which so much has been written,[50] was long seen as one of the causes of southern economic

---

[42] *Robertson v. Baldwin*, 165 US 275 (1896): 280–281.
[43] Robert Steinfeld, "Changing Legal Conceptions of Free Labor" in Stanley Engerman, ed., *Terms of Labor: Slavery, Serfdom, and Free Labor* (Stanford: Stanford University Press, 1999): 137–167.
[44] Lee Alston, Joseph Ferrie, *Southern Paternalism and the American Welfare State: Economics, Politics, and Institutions in the South, 1865–1965* (Cambridge: Cambridge University Press, 1999).
[45] Suresh Naidu, "Recruitment Restrictions and Labor Markets: Evidence from the Post-Bellum US South," *Journal of Labor Economics*, 28, 2 (2010): 413–445.
[46] Roger Ransom, Richard Sutch, *One Kind of Freedom: The Economic Consequences of Emancipation* (New York: Cambridge University Press, 1977).
[47] William Cohen, *At Freedom's Edge: Black Mobility and the Southern White Quest for Racial Control, 1861–1915* (Baton Rouge: Louisiana State University Press, 1991).
[48] Roger Ransom, Richard Sutch, "Capitalists without Capital: The Burden of Slavery and the Impact of Emancipation," *Agricultural History*, 62, 3 (1988): 133–160.
[49] Lee Alston, Kyle D. Kaffman, "Competition and the Compensation of Sharecroppers by Race: A View from Plantations in the Early twentieth Century," *Explorations in Economic History*, 38, 1 (2001): 181–194.
[50] Among others: David Davis, *Driven to the Field: Sharecropping and Southern Literature* (Charlottesville: University of Virginia Press, 2023); Joseph Reid, "White Land, Black Labor, and Agricultural Stagnation. The Causes and Effects of Sharecropping in the Post-bellum South," *Explorations in Economic History*, 16, 1 (1979): 31–55; Harold Woodman, "Sequel to Slavery. The New History Views the Post-bellum South," *The Journal of Southern History*, 43, 4 (1977): 523–554; Suresh Naidu, "Suffrage, Schooling, and Sorting in Post-Bellum South," *NBER working paper* 18129 (2012), www.nber.org/system/files/working_papers/w18129/w18129.pdf.

"backwardness" and racial discrimination until new approaches emphasized its role in minimizing production and business risks when the market (especially the credit market) is weak and imperfect.[51] Beyond the theory, we also know that sharecropping differed from region to region (different percentages of the harvest to be allocated to the tenant and the landlord, or the number of days to be worked for him, etc.).

For this reason, it would be difficult to speak of the South in general; the general trends mentioned took on different solutions in different regions. In the areas of the unplanted belt, small white and African farmers faced enormous changes: new leases, new international and national markets, shortage of credit and capital. Rice production also changed, with the decline of labor-intensive paddy farming along the Atlantic coast and the emergence of new rice production in the south-west. In the cotton regions, renting quickly became the optimal solution for estate owners faced with cash shortages and the mobility of former slaves.[52] In sugar states like Louisiana, planters preferred to employ gangs of workers under the control of a foreman. After the war, Louisiana became relatively marginal in the international sugar market, and the industry survived thanks to tariff protection. Then, beginning in the mid-1870s, as sugar prices plummeted, planters resorted to increasing legal pressure on workers. This increased the mobility of the workforce, leading to further legal action.[53] Mechanization came later, between the two world wars.[54] In this context, former slaves were marginalized in their access to education, property rights and equal conditions in the labor market. There were also striking differences between the cotton-growing regions themselves (Tennessee, Virginia, Georgia, etc.),[55] not to mention the importance of farmers' secondary occupations. Pluriactivity was the rule, and with it the interconnectedness of rural and urban areas. This examination has led a growing body of historiography to focus on the evolution of gender relations in the postbellum South. Many women retreated from the fields, creating new relationships with other agricultural activities and with urban industries.[56]

In contrast to post-emancipation Russia, demographic trends in the postbellum South were similar to those in many colonial regions of the West Indies and elsewhere: While infant mortality declined modestly over the decades, the

---

[51] Frederick Allen, "On the Fixed Nature of Sharecropping Contracts," *The Economic Journal*, 95 (1985): 30–48; Pranab Bardhan, *The Political Economy of Development in India* (New Delhi: Oxford University Press, 1984).
[52] Wright, *Old South, New South*.
[53] Naidu, "Recruitment Restrictions."
[54] Rebecca Scott, "Defining the Boundaries of Freedom in the World of Cane: Cuba, Brazil, and Louisiana after Emancipation," *The American Historical Review*, 99, 1 (1994): 70–102.
[55] Robert Tracy McKenzie, *One South or Many? Plantation Belt and Upcountry in Civil War Era Tennessee* (New York: Cambridge University Press, 1994).
[56] Ransom Sutch, *One Kind of Freedom*; Wright, *Old South, New South*.

birth rate among former slaves declined while the death rate actually increased. Life expectancy remained stable or declined until the 1880s, then increased at the turn of the century.[57] Black mortality rates were particularly high in cities. In short, the abolition of slavery in the United States was accompanied by a profound transformation of labor markets in which white wage earners were increasingly favored over newcomers, such as former slaves and new coolies and other immigrants of color. As in Britain and France, the emancipation of slaves and workers created a deep divide between them. The rise of the welfare state will further consolidate this new divide in the context of a new global economy.

---

[57] Robert Higgs, *Competition and Coercion: Blacks in the American Economy, 1865–1914* (Cambridge: Cambridge University Press, 1977): 18–22.

11

Neo-colonialism in the Age of the Welfare State

In the second half of the nineteenth century, related transformations took place in the worlds of labor and empires; the American War drove up the price of cotton while stimulating the creation of new cotton plantations around the world, much of it based on forced labor, if not slavery. At the same time, political transformations in Europe gave workers greater rights, and the first welfare states contributed greatly to this outcome. But this process also had two side effects: On the one hand, small units collapsed and capital concentrated in the West; on the other, new opportunities were sought outside Europe, especially where labor was unprotected. The result was neo-imperialism in Asia and in Africa. Thus, the world of work became deeply fragmented, with protected white (male) workers on one side and women, colonial and "colored" workers on the other, who enjoyed no social protection and were still subject to strong coercion.

The Welfare State and the Great Transformation

Polanyi reproduced Weber and Marx's analysis of the first industrial revolution (self-regulating markets, mass expulsion of peasants from the countryside, transformation into proletarians, mechanization). According to what we have shown in Parts I and II, this analysis was wrong, because the nineteenth century was by no means self-regulating: Liberal capitalism was highly regulated in all Western countries; at the same time, the privatization of land and the mass proletarianization of peasants did not take place until the second industrial revolution. In fact, the "Great Transformation" took place between 1870 and the Second World War (and this is in fact the original meaning Polanyi gave it), with the collapse of the peasant-workers, peasant, landed aristocracies and small manufacturers, and the emergence of the full-time proletariat, the final privatization of the commons, the rise of the welfare state and the success of large-scale, capital-intensive industries. These changes date from the turn of the nineteenth century to the early twentieth century, or even later, and certainly not from the eighteenth and early nineteenth centuries. This collapse of previous systems in the West was linked to a dual process: On the one hand, increasing mechanization and falling prices for food, colonial products and wheat; and on the other hand, increased resistance by workers. It was precisely because of the previously mentioned debates about "who is the real slave" that abolitionism in Britain and France, followed by the Civil War in the United States, strengthened workers' movements in Europe to demand better conditions. This political turnaround raised the cost of labor and prompted capitalists to invest in machinery. In other words, the second industrial revolution, the welfare state, the emergence of the masses on the political scene and the decline of labor-intensive processes led to a disjunction between profitable production and coercion, at least in Europe.

The period between the 1870s and the First World War saw the emergence of what we now call the employment contract. These new legal institutions marked a break with the labor institutions that had underpinned economic growth and social change in Europe between the seventeenth and mid nineteenth centuries. In Britain in the early 1870s, most industrial enterprises were still independent family businesses employing fewer than a hundred workers. Mass production was developing slowly and was still rare in 1870.[1] The mid nineteenth century saw a decisive shift to an industrialized economy in which sustained increases in per capita production supported a growing population, which in a virtuous cycle provided a source of increased demand.[2] From the mid-1880s, large corporate combinations began to emerge, particularly in the textile, coal and engineering sectors. This process was accompanied by changes in the nature of internal company organization: Management functions developed, while technological change influenced the contract system. Internal contracts were often linked to traditional methods of craft control, which were under pressure from increasing mechanization. Vertical integration, the welfare state and the evolution of labor institutions went hand in hand. Vertical integration required a stable workforce and large units; the peasant worker, the traditional poor and the poor laws hardly fit into this process. For Sidney and Beatrice Webb, the emergence of a fully developed and stable form of trade union organization in the last decades of the nineteenth century was linked to the establishment of wage labor as the dominant form of employment.[3] Previously, the Journeymen's Association had been no more than a subdivision of the Masters' Guild under the status of craftsmen and apprentices. Picketing was a criminal offense, and under the Masters and Servants Acts, individual workers who participated in strikes could be prosecuted. The Trade Union Act and the Criminal Amendment Act of 1871, as well as the Conspiracy and Protection of Property Act and the Employers and

---

[1] Joel Mokyr, *The Lever of Riches* (Oxford: Oxford University Press, 1990): 114.
[2] Edward Wrigley, *Continuity, Chance and Change: The Character of the Industrial Revolution in England* (Cambridge: Cambridge University Press, 1988).
[3] Sidney Webb and Beatrice Webb, *The History of Trade Unionism*, 2nd edition (London: Longmans, 1911).

Workmen Act, both of 1875, provided a basis for the development of trade unions. Union membership grew steadily after 1870; by 1914 it was twice as high as in 1905.[4] These changes meant that the Poor Law remained in place, but only to deal with residual cases outside the statutory social insurance system.[5] The development of state-sponsored collective bargaining contributed to the same process. Before 1870, the reduced legal status of trade unions limited collective bargaining. After 1875, with the abolition of criminal sanctions for labor contracts and union activities, collective agreements began to emerge.[6] However, despite these advances, seasonal and casual workers were excluded from these provisions and were referred to as independent contractors.[7] The definition of "self-employment" therefore became a source of contention, as employers sought to avoid responsibility for the social risks associated with sickness, accident and unemployment.

By analogy, in France, the law of March 21, 1884 legalized trade unions and the notion of an employment contract emerged. The term "*contrat de travail*" was not widely used in France until the mid-1880s. However, once the term became established, it was used in the turn-of-the-century legislation on (mainly industrial) accidents at work (law of 1898),[8] which introduced the objective liability of the employer in the event of an accident. This paved the way for social insurance, which developed around this time.[9]

The overall economic development of the period strongly supported this trend. Until then, seasonal workers had been well suited to task work, which allowed them to return to the countryside during the summer and other periods of intense rural activity. Even in the countryside, harvests and other important work were paid on a piece-rate basis; it was only between 1860 and 1890 that the earlier practice of combining agricultural and industrial employment largely disappeared. In the summer of 1860, at least 500,000 and probably as many as 800,000 workers walked off the job. By 1890, that number had fallen to 100,000.[10] Despite significant regional and sectoral differences, the agrarian crisis and the second industrial revolution attracted more stable, mostly unskilled workers to cities and factories.

---

[4] Hugh Armstrong Clegg, Alan Fox and Alvin Thompson, *A History of British Trade Unions since 1889*, vol. 1 (Oxford: Clarendon Press, 1964).
[5] Gilbert Bentley, *The Evolution of National Insurance in Great Britain: The Origins of the Welfare State* (London: Joseph, 1966); Jose Harris, *Unemployment and Politics: A Study in English Social Policy, 1886–1914* (Oxford: Clarendon Press, 1972).
[6] Deakin and Wilkinson, *The Law of the Labor Market*: 206.
[7] Quoted in Deakin and Wilkinson, *The Law of the Labor Market*: 93.
[8] Bruno Veneziani, "The Evolution of the Contract of Employment," in Bob Hepple, ed., *The Making of the Labor Law in Europe* (London: Mansell, 1986): 31–72.
[9] Simon Deakin, "Contrat de travail," in Alessandro Stanziani, ed., *Dictionnaire historique de l'économie-droit, XVIIIe-XXe siècles* (Paris: LGDJ, 2007): 289–98.
[10] Postel-Vinay, "The Dis-integration."

11 NEO-COLONIALISM IN THE AGE OF THE WELFARE STATE   249

Public order and competition also pushed for a new labor regime. In 1890, the *"livret ouvrier"* was abolished, and in 1900, the judiciary was asked to impose a private law solution where public law solutions had become anachronistic.

But rather than reducing legal, social and economic inequalities among workers, the new labor law widened them. It excluded large categories such as small entrepreneurs, artisans and peasants.[11] All of these groups were marginalized as "independent" workers.[12] They were not required to fulfill the many obligations that other workers had to their employers, but they could not enjoy the same social security benefits as other workers.

Against this backdrop, a new role for the state emerged.[13] As we have argued, the conventional opposition between "liberal" nineteenth century and self-regulating markets, followed by a period of regulation during the long twentieth century, does not stand up to historical scrutiny. Markets have always been regulated, the big difference being that regulation in the nineteenth century was designed to increase inequalities, whereas afterwards it helped to reduce them.[14] For much of the nineteenth century, the state in Britain, the United States and France intervened to control capital speculation, restrict labor rights, protect property, police vagrants, levy indirect taxes and finance military and colonial expansion. Intervention promoted social inequalities and preserved the rentiers and the landed and industrial aristocracies. Since the 1870s, this situation has changed; a new liberal social order has emerged, and with it a new role for the state. The dominance of the landed aristocracy declined and gradually disappeared in favor of new industrial and urban elites. Trade unions, strikes and other forms of civic expression were permitted, and women and children were given greater legal rights. But this new world did not stop at the borders of Europe or the United States. In the colonial worlds and the US South, human servitude and violence were still part of everyday life. Parallel to the great transformation of Western economies – the crisis of small units and the search for expanded markets for larger units – this political and economic mix pushed toward a new wave of colonialism. This is the price that millions of people around the world have paid for improved working conditions for workers in the North.

Global migration intensified: Between 1840 and 1940, 55 to 58 million Europeans and 2.5 million Africans and Asians reached the Americas; during

---

[11] Robert Salais, Nicolas Bavarez and Bénédicte Reynaud, *L'invention du chômage* (Paris, PUF, 1986).
[12] Marta Torre-Schaub, *Essai sur la construction juridique de la catégorie de marché* (Paris: LGDJ, 2002); Stanziani, *Rules of Exchange*.
[13] Steinmetz, *Private Law*; John Commons, *Legal Foundations of Capitalism* (London: MacMillan, 1924, new edition New Brunswick and London: Transaction Publishers, 1995); William Novak, *The People's Welfare: Law and Regulation in Nineteenth Century America* (Chapel Hill: University of North Carolina Press, 1996).
[14] On this subject: Stanziani, *Rules of Exchange*.

the same period, 29 million Indians, 19 million Chinese and 4 million Africans and Europeans settled in Southeast Asia, the Pacific Islands and the Indian Ocean rim. Finally, 46 to 51 million people from north-east Asia and Russia moved (or were forced to move) to Siberia, Manchuria and Central Asia.[15]

Economic factors played an important role, but they were not the only ones that provoked this phenomenon. Strongly stimulated by the transportation revolution (the definitive success of steamboats and railroads), global migration brought about a major shift in the distribution of the world's population. The three destinations mentioned previously experienced enormous demographic growth, multiplying by a factor of 4 to 5.5 between 1850 and 1950. Growth rates in these regions were more than double those of the world population as a whole, and about 60 percent higher than in Africa, a region with low net immigration. By comparison, growth rates in emigration regions were lower than world population growth and less than half those in immigration regions. Together, the three major destination regions accounted for 10 percent of the world's population in 1850 and 24 percent in 1950.[16]

While movement within a single empire was significant (especially in the Russian and British empires), so too were trans-imperial, intra-continental, regional and local migrations, demonstrating the inadequacy of the Eurocentric paradigm that explains migration in terms of Western expansion.[17]

In fact, migration was widespread and involved almost every region of the world. Nearly 4 million Indians went to Malaysia, over 8 million to Ceylon, over 15 million to Burma and about 1 million to Africa, other parts of Southeast Asia and islands in the Indian and Pacific Oceans. Up to 11 million Chinese (mostly from the southern provinces) traveled from China to the Straits, although more than a third transited to the Dutch East Indies, Borneo, Burma and further west. Nearly 4 million traveled directly from China to Thailand; between 2 and 3 million to French Indochina; more than a million to the Dutch East Indies (for a total of over 4 million, including trans-shipments from Singapore); and just under a million to the Philippines. At the same time, the construction of railroads and the relative easing of borders between Russia and China also caused 28 to 33 million northern Chinese to migrate to Siberia and Manchuria.[18]

---

[15] Adam McKeown, "Global Migration, 1846–1940," *Journal of World History*, 15, 2 (2004) 155–189; Donald Treadgold, *The Great Siberian Migration: Government and Peasant in Resettlement from Emancipation to the First World War* (Princeton, NJ: Princeton University Press, 1957): 33–35; Thomas Gottschang and Diana Lary, *Swallows and Settlers: The Great Migration from North China to Manchuria* (Ann Arbor: University of Michigan, Center for Chinese Studies, 2000): 171.

[16] McKeown, "Global Migration."

[17] Kevin O'Rourke and Jeffrey Williamson, *Globalization and History: The Evolution of a Nineteenth-century Atlantic Economy* (Cambridge, MA: MIT Press, 1996).

[18] Robert H. G. Lee, *The Manchurian Frontier in Ch'ing History* (Cambridge, MA: Harvard University Press, 1970).

Migration within each region increased and interacted with long-distance emigration. Irish migrants went to England to work, while others left Eastern and Southern Europe for the industrial regions of Northern Europe, particularly France and Germany. In Russia, migrants settled in fast-growing cities and agricultural regions in the south. In India, they settled in the tea plantations of the south and north-east, in the mining and textile regions of Bengal and in newly irrigated land and urban areas throughout the sub-continent.[19]

It would therefore be reductive to explain the emigration of the late nineteenth and early twentieth centuries as a simple "expansion of the West," as the triumph of work and free emigration over slavery. It is true that a whole series of laws were passed around the world to defend "freedom." Free migration developed with the increasing restriction of indentured servitude and its final abolition in 1920. In the United States, the Anti-Peonage Act of 1867 extended the prohibition of servitude (voluntary or involuntary) to all states of the Union. The Indian government first restricted and then banned Indian indentured labor in 1916, while an 1874 agreement between the Chinese and Portuguese governments ended the export of Chinese indentured labor from Macau. Chinese authorities investigated the conditions of Chinese migrants in Cuba, Peru and the United States, leading to the suspension of most of these contracts.

At the same time, the formal rules of emigration were not always accompanied by genuine legal rights for immigrants once they reached their destination. More importantly, various forms of servitude and indebtedness survived into the twentieth century. Chinese, Indian and, to some extent, even European emigrants were still subject to disguised forms of indenture and servitude.[20]

Thus, local bondage coexisted with the intercontinental flow of free and less free people; laws and reciprocal, multilateral agreements between the powers hindered and regulated the flow. This opened the door to extreme forms of local servitude, albeit directly linked to global dynamics.

As Beckert shows,[21] the shortage of cotton on international markets led to increased production in other regions, such as Egypt, Russian Turkestan, India and Brazil. The long-term impact on local labor patterns and economic growth, however, depended on the recovery of US production as well as local dynamics. By the end of Reconstruction in 1877, US production was about 25 percent higher than in 1860, and exports had nearly reached the level of the 1860 total. Between 1877 and 1900, exports more than doubled. At the same time, Russian imperialism in Central Asia and the development of cotton fields in the Fergana

---

[19] Arjan de Haan, "Migration on the Border of Free and Unfree Labor: Workers in Calcutta's Jute Industry, 1900–1990," in Jan Lucassen and Leo Lucassen, eds., *Migration, Migration History: Paradigms and New Perspectives* (Bern: Peter Lang, 1997): 197–222.
[20] McKeown, "Global Migration."
[21] Sven Beckert, "Emancipation and Empire: Reconstructing the Worldwide Web of Cotton Production in the Age of the American Civil War," *The American Historical Review*, 109, 5 (2004): 1405–1438.

Valley were not only a response to the American Civil War, but also a response to Russia's longstanding (since the seventeenth century) efforts to stabilize its southeastern frontier while threatening British India.[22] Attention to cotton certainly increased in the 1860s, but it didn't really take off until twenty years later, under the combined effect of Russian tariff policy and railroad construction.[23]

Egypt was the second major region affected by the collapse of American cotton production. Higher production levels were achieved largely through increased imports of slaves: some Circassians from Russia and Central Eurasia, some from Africa. Imports from Africa fell from about 5,000 per year in the 1840s and 1850s to about 3,000 per year in the 1870s, when they began to decline again due to the recovery in the United States.[24]

India was the third region where abolition in the United States had a major impact. Immediately after the outbreak of the American Civil War, British producers increased their pressure on the Indian cotton-growing regions, where the rules regarding masters and servants were much stricter. At the same time, rising cotton prices encouraged Indian producers to increase their own production. The British thus competed with the French for the most cotton while trying to divert it from the Indian domestic market. In millions of pounds, Indian cotton exports rose from about 346 in 1860 to 806 in 1866. This was no temporary boom, for contrary to the conventional story of India's deindustrialization, recent work shows that India demand sustained local production throughout the nineteenth century and from the 1870s onwards.[25]

In Brazil, slave imports increased during the nineteenth century, especially after the abolition of the slave trade by the British and Americans. The peak was reached in the 1830s, when the number of slaves in Brazil was around 2.5 million. A more active policy was not adopted until 1850, when the importation of slaves declined significantly. Due to high mortality, the lack of women and the high rate of emancipation, the number of slaves fell to 1.5 million in the 1850s and to 750,000 on the eve of abolition in 1886. Brazilian slave society was also peculiar in that many men and women, although of African descent, shed their slave status. At the beginning of the nineteenth century, they represented 12.5 percent of the Brazilian population, a figure similar to that of Spanish America at the time, but very different from that of the southern United States, where it was barely 4.5 percent. In Brazil, the sugar industry did not rely as heavily on large plantations as in the Caribbean, and mining and urban slavery also played important roles (unlike in the United States). Thus, slave ownership rested on a very broad

---

[22] Seymour Becker, *Russia's Protectorate in Central Asia, Bukhara and Khiva, 1865-1924* (London: Routledge 2004).

[23] Maria Rozhkova, *Ekonomicheskie sviazi Rossii so Srednei Aziei: 40-60gg XIX veka* (Economic ties between Russia and Central Asia in the 40s to 60s of the nineteenth century) (Moscow: Nauka, 1963).

[24] Lovejoy, *Transformations*: 149.

[25] Thirtankar Roy, *Traditional Industry in the Economy of Colonial India* (Cambridge: Cambridge University Press, 1999).

social base, and the abolition of the slave trade did not put an end to the domestic market: Between 1850 and 1880, a dynamic domestic market for slaves was maintained.[26] In the 1860s, an abolitionist movement emerged that mirrored the policies of the United States. However, as in the other cases mentioned previously the continuity of social conditions was as important as official abolition. By the 1870s, many slaves had already signed official contracts for work, sale, etc., while after 1888, criminal sanctions and harsh treatment of now-freed slaves were commonplace.[27] The scramble for Africa was part of this global trend.

Occupying Africa: A By-Product of the Great Transformation

The so-called "scramble for Africa" has been the subject of a number of pertinent interpretations, one of which emphasizes geopolitical factors. The European powers were engaged in global competition, and from this perspective, when one of them moved in a new direction, the others immediately reacted by doing the same or stopping it. In particular, the new rise of the German Empire and then Belgium, both in search of new lands to occupy, threatened the French and British empires. What is more, in the 1870s, the acceleration of transportation and technological innovation led most European powers to move into one of the world's few undeveloped regions, supposedly rich in minerals and timber. The completion of the Suez Canal in 1869 also radically altered international trade and networks, placing Africa at the center of the connections between Europe and Asia. The decline of the Ottoman Empire contributed to heightened tensions in Europe and throughout the Mediterranean, with Egypt falling into a dangerous decadence and eventually passing from Ottoman to British rule. This eventuality increased geopolitical instability and heightened tensions between European powers throughout Eurasia, from the Balkans to Turkey and Egypt. Finally, the great transformation and radical changes in European economies and societies also contributed to the interest in Africa.[28] The decline of the rentier and the rising role of finance in Europe led both to seek new frontiers for their investments. Africa seemed the most appropriate place for these interests to converge. This interest found strong support in the past and present development of trade in and around Africa.[29]

---

[26] Robert Conrad, *The Destruction of Brazilian Slavery, 1850–1888* (Berkeley: University of California Press, 1972).

[27] Katia de Queirós Mattoso, *To be a Slave in Brazil, 1550–1888* (New Brunswick, N.J.: Rutgers University Press, 1987).

[28] Denis Cogneau, "Histoire économique de l'Afrique: renaissance ou trompe l'œil?," *Annales HSS*, 71, 4 (2016): 879–896; J. Forbes Munro, *Africa and the International Economy* (London: Rowman and Littlefield, 1976); M. E. Chamberlain, *The Scramble for Africa* (London: Routledge, 2010).

[29] Ewout H. P. Frankema, Jeffrey G. Williamson, and Pieter J. Woltjer, "An Economic Rationale for the West African Scramble? The Commercial Transition and the Commodity Price Boom of 1835–1885," *The Journal of Economic History*, 78, 1 (2018): 231–267.

However, at least in the early decades, these multiple interests took two main forms: military occupation and control of labor. Here, too, the European powers drew on conventional arguments about slavery to justify their intervention. The abolition of slavery in the French and British empires underpinned the great transformation, the growth of welfare and the Second Industrial Revolution in Western countries. This process also had a collateral effect on the occupation of Africa: The globalization of the notion of abolition became an argument used by European elites to justify the occupation of new territories as partial compensation for the opportunity costs of the welfare state. Abolition was not an indigenous African concept: Masters could free slaves through manumission, and slaves could sometimes redeem themselves.[30] Each European power therefore exported its own idea(s) of what abolition and freedom meant. The British began by fighting the slave trade, as they had done in the Atlantic world nearly a century earlier. They concentrated their efforts on the trans-Saharan and Red Sea trade, but gradually extended their reach to the Gold Coast and other western regions of Africa, and then to the Cape Coast. Colonial methods, competition between colonial states and the weight of humanitarian motivations over political and economic objectives were the underlying issues.

In this context, the Indian experience strongly influenced British rule in Africa.[31] In fact, after the creation of the Raj and the end of the EIC regime in India in 1858, Henri Sumner Maine encouraged a two-fold change: On the one hand, he promoted the construction of the Indian penal code, especially in matters of labor (see Part II), and on the other, he declared that henceforth "local customs" and forms of authority, known as indirect rule, would replace the old "direct rule". In other words, in certain areas, Indians could govern themselves under the control and patronage of British authority. This solution, according to Maine, would ensure better control of the subcontinent and avoid traumatic events such as the Sepoy Rebellion that led to the new regime.[32] In the same vein, and with overt reference to India, British officials sought to avoid confrontation with Islamic authorities, especially with regard to the practice of concubinage, which was left untouched; Islamic customary law was invoked to justify its legitimacy. Some British colonial elites believed that control of the colonies should be achieved through agreements with local chiefs, while the abrupt abolition of any form of dependency qualified as slavery risked the collapse of local economies and societies, and thus of imperial authority.[33]

---

[30] Miers, Roberts, *The End of Slavery in Africa*.
[31] Thomas Metcalf, *Imperial Connections* (Berkeley: University of California Press, 2007); Sugata Bose, *A Hundred Horizons* (Cambridge, Mass: Harvard University Press, 2006); Sujit Sivasundaram, *Waves Across the South* (Chicago: University of Chicago Press, 2021).
[32] Mantena, *Alibis of Empire*.
[33] Martin Klein, *Slavery and Colonial Rule*; Miers, Roberts, *The End of Slavery in Africa*; Lovejoy, Hogendown, *Slow Death of Slavery*.

The transfer of Indian rules to Africa also applied to labor. When it came to slavery – and not just the slave trade – British rulers explicitly looked to India as a model from the very beginning. In Africa, as in India, sovereignty, colonial rule and slavery were intertwined. In 1866, Zanzibar became a part of Her Majesty's Indian Empire for the purpose of the administration of justice to British subjects.[34] The subsequent extension of Indian law to the African mainland was the result of the extension of British power from Zanzibar.[35] A subsequent Foreign Office Order in Council confirmed this orientation, and some twenty Indian laws were introduced in various parts of British Africa. These Indian laws and procedures coexisted with "native customs" and Islamic law. Thus, the protectorate court in Mombasa, which could appeal to Zanzibar and its subordinate courts, exercised jurisdiction over all protected British and non-British subjects, as well as foreign nationals. Native courts, whether presided over by tribal chiefs, rulers or British officials, were supposed to enforce native customs. As in India, the adoption of legal codes in Africa was based on the principle of indirect rule. In India, indirect rule first appeared in the late eighteenth and early nineteenth centuries, then again in response to the Sepoy Mutiny. The British adopted the same principle in Africa, where Henry Maine's approach found an ardent supporter in Frederick Lugard.[36] During this period, local forms of slavery were considered "mild" compared to "real" (chattel) slavery, as they had been in India almost a century earlier, and were often described as domestic servitude. Lugard himself insisted on the difference between domestic slavery and chattel slavery (the former prevents idleness). On his arrival in Buganda in December 1890, he declared that direct interference in the breeding and disposal of slaves (a source of chaos) should be avoided.[37] In his opinion, slaves should only be emancipated in areas under direct protectorate, such as Zanzibar.

These views evolved gradually: In the Gold Coast, an ordinance banning the holding of slaves was issued in 1874, while in several other regions this attitude was not accepted until the 1880s. Tolerance of local slavery practices was challenged for two main reasons: they had been adopted for the pragmatic purpose of cooperating with local chiefs in administering the colonies and recruiting labor. Neither goal was achieved, as the cooperation was limited and the chiefs failed to provide the necessary manpower (both to the colonial state and to private companies) while continuing their slave trade. Change came as the British abolitionist movement intensified its campaign against African practices and

---

[34] Henry Frances Morris, James Read, *Indirect Rule and the Search for Justice: Essays on East African Legal History* (Oxford: Clarendon Press, 1972): 112–3.
[35] Metcalf, *Imperial Connections*.
[36] Mantena, *Alibis of Empire*.
[37] Rhode House Library, Oxford, Lugard Papers, Mss. British Empire, 30–99; printed version of Lugard's diary: Margery Perham, Mary Bull, eds., *The Diaries of Lord Lugard* (Evanston: Northwestern University Press, 1959), 4 volumes, in particular, vol. 1: 171–173.

British tolerance.[38] The Protestant movement in Britain and missionaries in Africa intensified their actions. As in earlier cases of abolition, humanitarian goals, religion, moral values and economic interests converged to support the radical abolition of slavery itself, not just the slave trade. Evangelical philanthropy joined forces with "Burkean" colonial abolitionism to eradicate all forms of slavery in Africa. But it was the abuse and murder of enslaved people, not the desire to abolish slavery itself, that spurred them to action. They were supported by a third movement that asserted "the elementary rights of humanity". This movement included trade unions, the Aborigines' Protection Society and groups of British merchants who advocated direct trade with the "natives" without the colonial state acting as an intermediary. From this perspective, free trade and freedom of labor came together, just as trade unions combined anti-colonialism with local workers' rights.

This political reorientation posed a dilemma for colonial officials: How to reconcile the maintenance of law and order with the political need to defend humanitarianism. Reactions and timing varied from colony to colony, but a general trend emerged. Supported by British antislavery movements, colonial administrators and public opinion blamed the "barbaric and backward" attitudes of Africans accused of enslaving their countrymen. This argument was used to justify the "civilizing mission" of this or that European country and served as the basis for discussions between Great Britain, France, Germany and Belgium at the Brussels Conference of 1889 to define the criteria for the partition of Africa. All participants strongly advocated the introduction of free labor, order and discipline.[39] This process was to take place in two stages: First the emancipation of the slaves, then the establishment of a real labor market. However, the Brussels Act of 1890 left the procedures against slavery to the discretion of each imperial power. Great Britain took an extreme position on these two stages: It pushed much harder than the other powers for the abolition of the slave trade; it adopted a much more cautious attitude toward the abolition of slavery, using the "Indian case" as an example; and at the same time, it kept its Masters and Servants Acts alive as the basis and expression of "free" labor in its new African acquisitions much longer than the other colonial powers. It was therefore up to the colonial state to determine the most appropriate measures to facilitate the transition to a free labor market while guaranteeing the maintenance of order. The introduction of anti-vagrancy laws and masters and servants laws in Africa was their response to this dilemma. This helps to explain the attention that European authorities paid to labor regulations after

---

[38] Cooper, *From Slaves to Squatters*; Millar, *The Problem of Slavery as History*; Dennis D. Cordell and Joel W. Gregory, eds., *African Population and Capitalism: Historical Perspectives* (Boulder: Westview Press, 1987); Denis Cogneau, *L'Afrique des inégalités. Où conduit l'histoire* (Paris: Éditions de la rue d'Ulm, 2006); Cogneau, *Un empire bon marché* (Paris: Point, 2024).

[39] Frederick Cooper, "From Free Labor to Family Allowances: Labor and African Society in Colonial Discourse," *American Ethnologist*, 16, 4 (1989): 745–765.

emancipation. Europeans, especially the British, needed workers for their companies and businesses, the infrastructure and public works of the colonial state, as well as military recruits and domestic servants. Despite the denunciation of the new colonial forms of slavery by critical missionaries,[40] in many British and French regions (Oubangui-Chari, Coastal Guinea, Sudan, Somalia, Northern Nigeria), fugitive slaves, "vagabonds" (i.e., slaves freed without a formal work contract) and "disguised slaves" freed by the colonial authorities were still captured and eventually re-slaved.[41] Several measures were adopted to increase the supply of labor and direct it towards colonial rather than local players: increasing the amount of taxes to be paid in labor; economic policies unfavorable to local economies, such as the obligation to obtain low prices for harvests, the requirement to have specific crop etc.[42] Passes restricted the free mobility of labor, while access to better-paid jobs was limited for Africans. Indeed, colonial officials firmly believed that the African continent could only be developed if Africans learned that they were not free to choose where, when and how to work. A campaign was launched against vagrancy, theft, alcoholism and interpersonal violence; the aim was not only to control African labor, but also to promote labor discipline for the benefit of black elites.[43] Within these broad approaches, which were more or less common to different regions of Africa, specific policies varied from place to place within each empire (British policies differed in Zanzibar, Kenya, the Cape and the Gold Coast) and between empires, although trans-imperial commonalities also emerged. Kenya and Southern Rhodesia, like Portuguese Angola and French Algeria, prioritized cheap labor, direct forms of taxation and pre-emptive rights to land granted to white settlers.

Here we see a major shift from earlier periods in the relationship between labor institutions in Britain and its colonies.[44] Until the last quarter of the nineteenth century, colonial free-labor practices and institutions had been an

---

[40] Kevin Grant, *A Civilized Savagery: Britain and the New Slaveries in Africa, 1884–1926* (New York: Routledge, 2006).
[41] Lovejoy, *Transformations in Slavery*.
[42] Babacar Fall, *Le travail forcé en AOF* (Paris: Karthala, 1993).
[43] TNA, CO 533/16, W. D. Ellis minute, October 12, 1906; Protectorate of East Africa, no. 8, 1906.
[44] Cooper, *From Slaves to Squatters*; Cooper, *Decolonization and African Society*; Andreas Eckert, "Regulating the Social: Social Security Social Welfare, and the State in Late Colonial Tanzania," *The Journal of African History*, 45, 3 (2004): 467–489; Mary Dewhurst Lewis, *The Boundaries of the Republic: Migrants Rights and the Limits of Universalism in France, 1918–1940* (Stanford: Stanford University Press, 2007); Pierre Rosanvallon, *La société des égaux* (Paris: Seuil 2011); Paul-André Rosental, "Le BIT et la politique mondiale des migrations dans l'entre-deux-guerres," *Annales HSS*, 61, 1 (2006): 99–134; Caroline Douki, David Feldman, Paul-André-Rosental, "Pour une histoire relationnelle du ministère du Travail en France, en Italie et au Royaume-Uni dans l'entre-deux-guerres: le transnational, le bilatéral et l'interministériel en matière de politique migratoire," In Alain Chatriot, Odile Join-Lambert, Vincent Viet, eds., *Les Politiques du Travail (1906–2006). Acteurs, institutions, réseaux* (Rennes: Presses Universitaires de Rennes): 143–159.

extension of continental institutions, in particular the Masters and Servants Acts, apprenticeship rules and vagrancy. In the colonies, these were extreme variants of those in Britain, with even greater statutory and procedural inequalities between masters and servants (or indentured immigrants). Henceforth, the creation of Masters and Servants Acts in Africa no longer meant the transplantation and local adaptation of British rules, but a deliberate decision to impose specific legislation considered outdated in the country of origin. The new Masters and Servants Acts were adopted in Africa at precisely the same time as they were repealed in Great Britain (1875). In this case, the civilizing mission was based on two judgments: Africans needed to be educated (and the law served this purpose), but at the same time, they were lagging behind in their development and, consequently, the old British rules were more appropriate to the African context than the contemporary ones.[45] As a result, in contrast to the earlier colonial period, the repeal of the Masters and Servants Acts in Britain and the emergence of the welfare state, the path to work and freedom in the colonies (especially in Africa) diverged from that on the British mainland. While British workers enjoyed greater protection and welfare, workers in the colonies were still subject to unequal legal and labor regimes. From this perspective, the welfare state and its national orientation intensified rather than reduced inequalities within the Empire and especially among workers.[46]

The same was true in French Africa, both in Sudan, Senegal and Guinea, as well as in AOF (French West Africa)[47] and AEF (French Equatorial Africa).[48]

---

[45] G. St. J. Orde Brown, *The African Labourer* (London, 1933, reprinted by Frank Cass, 1967).

[46] Cooper, *Decolonization and African Society*; Cooper, *From Slaves to Squatters*.

[47] In 1895, the colonial government decided to federate its West African colonies. Senegal, French Sudan, Guinea and Côte d'Ivoire formed a new administrative entity called French West Africa. In practice, the AFO government was not established until 1904–1905. Dahomey was added in 1899, Niger and Mauritania in 1904 and Upper Volta in 1919. Klein, *Slavery and Colonial Rule in French West Africa*; Richard Roberts, *Two Worlds of Cotton: Colonialism and Regional Economy in the French Soudan, 1800–1946* (Stanford: Stanford University Press, 1996); Fall, *Le travail forcé en AOF*; Boubacar Barry, *La Sénégambie du XVe au XIXe siècle; traite négrière, Islam, conquête coloniale* (Paris: L'Harmattan, 1988); Denise Bouche, *Les villages de liberté en Afrique noire française, 1887–1910* (The Hague: Mouton, 1968); Martin Klein, *Islam et impérialisme au Sénégal: Sine-Saloum 1847–1914* (Stanford: Stanford University Press, 1968); Patrick Manning, *Slavery, Colonialism and Economic Growth in Dahomey, 1640–1960* (Cambridge: Cambridge University Press, 1982); François Renault, *Libération d'esclaves et nouvelle servitude: les rachats de captifs africains pour le compte des colonies françaises après l'abolition de l'esclavage* (Abidjan: ANSOM, 1976); Richard Roberts, *Warriors, Merchants and Slaves: the State and the Economy in the Middle Niger Valley, 1700–1914* (Stanford: Stanford University Press, 1987); Henri Brunschwig, *Noirs et blancs dans l'Afrique noire française ou comment le colonisé devient colonisateur (1870–1914)* (Paris: Flammarion, 1983).

[48] AEF is the French acronym for French Equatorial Africa. The General Government of AEF was officially conceived in 1910. According to the 1910 borders, French Equatorial Africa comprised Moyen-Congo, Gabon, Oubangui-Chari and Chad. Prior to this date,

As noted previously France occupied Algeria between 1830 and 1848, after which it tightened its control, particularly in the mining sector, and only later (after the 1870s) in the agricultural sector (especially wine and wheat). The Maghreb colonies supplied 10 percent of France's wheat imports in the 1880s, rising to 20 percent in the following decade. Grain production in Algeria was made possible by the expropriation of land from the local population.[49] As in the case of other Western empires, the legal fiction consisted in classifying as "non-property" the multiple statuses of land tenure scattered throughout the conquered territory, which could therefore be attributed as such to the French power. At the beginning of the twentieth century, the surface of Algerian territory devoted to cereals amounted to about 2.8 million hectares, with total production (durum wheat, barley, millet) varying between 14 and 25 million quintals, depending on the year, between 1900 and 1914.[50] France played an active role in international wheat speculation and demanded wheat even after several bad harvests, as in the Maghreb in the 1870s and in Mali at the beginning of the century. As a result, famine hit these regions hard.[51]

In Senegal, too, France began its colonial enterprise under Napoleon III in the 1850s, when it had two island bases: Saint-Louis and Gorée. Slaves, rubber and millet were traded. The abolition of slavery in 1848 was followed by the gradual establishment of freedom villages, where runaway slaves could be rounded up and eventually sold as "free migrants" to French planters on Réunion Island. Meanwhile, local chiefs and elites could still own slaves.[52]

There were contradictions between France's revolutionary principles and the forms of labor in its colonies. The economic interests that underpinned French colonization in Africa played a role,[53] but broader geopolitical considerations were also at play.[54] In fact, far from being mere window dressing for repressive policies, liberal ideals actually set limits on the degree of coercion that colonial administrators could use.[55] The Third Republic and its gradual move toward universal suffrage saw no contradiction between the extension of democracy in metropolitan France and colonialism. In 1885,

---

in 1898, Gabon, Congo and the interior regions had been grouped together to form a huge colony known as French Congo. Catherine Coquery-Vidrovitch, *Le Congo au temps des grandes compagnies concessionnaires* (Paris: EHESS, 2001).
[49] Ismet Touati, *Le Commerce du blé entre l'Algérie et la France, xvie-xixe siècles* (Saint-Denis: Bouchêne, 2018).
[50] Stanziani, *Les guerres du blé*.
[51] Charles-Robert Ageron, *Les Algériens musulmans et la France, (1871–1919)* (Paris: PUF, 1968); Laurent Heyberger, *Les Corps en colonie. Faim, maladies, guerres et crises démographiques en Algérie au XIXe siècle* (Toulouse: PUM, 2019).
[52] Klein, *Slavery and Colonial Rule in French West Africa*.
[53] Coquery-Vidrovitch, *Le Congo*.
[54] Marseille, *Empire colonial et capitalisme*.
[55] Alice Conklin, *A Mission to Civilize* (Stanford: Stanford University Press, 1996).

Jules Ferry declared that "the superior races have a right over the inferior races."[56] Economic recession and growing stagnation undoubtedly influenced these attitudes.[57] Various groups supported colonialism: commercial lobbies interested in African raw materials, military elites and certain Catholic circles hoping to expand their missionary activity in Africa.[58] In the years that followed, the Radicals promoted colonialism even more fervently than the Republicans.[59] They were enthusiastic proponents of colonization, stressing the importance of Africa to French big business, which in turn needed it to compete in a dynamic economy with British, German and American big business.[60] However, they had to temper their enthusiasm in the face of the skepticism of many other political representatives and the limited revenues of the French state.[61] The anti-colonial movement, for its part, seems to have been very uncertain about its objectives. Paul Leroy Beaulieu and Victor Schoelcher were quick to associate the protection of the "natives" with colonialism, the fight against slavery and France's civilizing mission. Anti-colonialism was a relatively secondary concern for socialists until 1895, and the movement did not really take off until 1905.[62] Some socialists, including Jaurès, did not criticize colonialism as such, but only its harshness, even though they believed in France's civilizing mission. They believed that Africa needed a period of transition from slavery to freedom, during which the colonizers would help spread the ideas and practices of freedom.[63] As the years went by, Jaurès's position evolved and, on the eve of the First World War, he came closer to radical anti-colonialism.[64]

In Senegal, Louis Faidherbe had initially defended the assimilationist principle, according to which French citizenship could be granted to those who adhered to French political and "civilizing" principles. Support for this

---

[56] Charles Robert Ageron, *France coloniale ou parti colonial* (Paris: PUF, 1978).
[57] Raymond Betts, *Assimilation and Association in French Colonial Theory, 1890–1914* (New York: Columbia University Press, 1961); Urban Yerri, *L'Indigène dans le droit colonial français* (Paris: fondation Varenne, 2010).
[58] Jean Meyer, *Histoire de la France coloniale, I. Des origines à 1914* (Paris: Colin, 1991); Jean-Marie Mayeur, *Les débuts de la IIIe République, 1871–1898* (Paris: Seuil, 1973).
[59] Madeleine Rebérieux, *La République radicale? 1898–1914* (Paris: Seuil, 1975).
[60] André Masson, "L'opinion française et les problèmes coloniaux à la fin du Second Empire," *Revue française d'histoire d'outre-mer*, 51, 3–4 (1962): 366–455.
[61] Hubert Deschamps, *Les méthodes et les doctrines coloniales de la France du XVIe siècle à nos jours* (Paris: Colin, 1953).
[62] André Lebon, *La politique de la France en Afrique, 1896–1898* (Paris: Plon, 1901).
[63] René Gallissot, "Socialisme colonial, socialisme national des pays dominés," *L'homme et la société*, 4, n. 174 (2009): 75–96.
[64] Gilles Manceron, *Jean Jaurès vers l'anticolonialisme. Du colonialisme à l'universalisme* (Paris: Les petits matins, 2015); Jacqueline Lalouette, *Jean Jaurès. L'assassinat, la gloire, le souvenir* (Paris: Éditions Perrin, 2014); Daniel Lefeuvre, *Pour en finir avec la repentance coloniale* (Paris: Flammarion, 2006).

approach gradually waned in the 1880s and 1890s, when Pierre Savorgnan de Brazza, among others, advocated the principle of association based on his experiences in equatorial Africa. According to this position, the main objective was to establish extensive sovereignty and develop trade relations. Finally, following the example of its neighbor, the Belgian Congo, at the turn of the century the French Congo adopted the principle of incorporation based on concessionary companies. In this case, French companies took control of the land and also had rights over the labor force. Thus, although the Third Republic overcame earlier attitudes toward Africans as "barbarians," it sought only to legitimize the presence of its subjects within the republic, not to grant them full rights. Indeed, the rejection of assimilation was tantamount to saying that Africans were not yet capable of understanding the meaning of freedom.[65]

What is more, at the turn of the century, balancing the budget and reducing spending were two priorities on the political agenda. Such a balance seemed difficult to achieve, as the metropolitan state was increasing its social intervention during the same period. Given the low level of political support for the occupation of Africa, the resources available to implement colonial policy were extremely limited. The French state imagined making up for this shortfall by allowing French companies to establish their own military and legal order in Africa, using forced labor instead of taxes. To this end, the French took advantage of the widespread practice of slavery in the region, forming alliances with local chiefs to share labor.[66] When the French began to penetrate the region, they encountered enormous difficulties in establishing posts and an organized administration. In this context, they were wary of adopting an aggressive policy toward slavery that would complicate an already fragile situation. The elimination of slavery was not essential for economic development or depopulation.[67] The lack of military forces encouraged military elites to use local slaves for their operations, and many civilian colonial officers had no problem with slavery.[68] In reality, this loose definition of "true slavery" was used to negotiate the availability of labor with local chiefs. At times when maintaining an alliance with clan chiefs was a top priority, African workers were called "servants". On the other hand, when the labor needs of the colonial companies became critical, or when the colonial authorities wanted to play elbow with the local chiefs, these same workers were called "slaves" and thus "freed" to be more or less reclaimed by the companies and the French authorities.[69] Officially, French policy had three aims: to abolish slavery, to gradually introduce new labor rules and to create

---

[65] Martin Klein, "The End of Slavery in French West Africa," in Hideaki Suzuki, ed., *Abolitions as a Global Experience* (Singapore: NUS Press, 2016): 199–227.
[66] Conklin, *A Mission*; Cooper and Stoler, *Tensions of Empire*.
[67] Patrick Manning, *Francophone Sub-Saharan Africa* (Cambridge: Cambridge University Press, 1998).
[68] ANOM FM SG GCOG/XIV 1 and 2 recruitment of Kroumen workers.
[69] On this ambivalence in FWA: Klein, *Slavery and Colonial Rule*.

a genuine labor market. It never occurred to anyone that the new rules could be the same as those in force in France. Forced labor was integrated to meet the demands of colonial authorities and private companies;[70] it was considered necessary to improve the "barbaric Africans"[71] and cope with labor shortages.[72]

French policy changed, however, with the rise of the anti-colonial movement in France and the Brussels Conference of 1899 (where the British attempted to force the other colonial powers to adopt their anti-slavery policy). Between 1903 and 1905, slavery was declared illegal, first in French West Africa (FWA) and then in French Equatorial Africa (FEA). In 1905, official French statistics, based on an unidentified method of calculation, showed 2 million slaves in the FWA out of a population of 8 million.[73] According to the new strategy, slavery had to be eradicated to break the resistance of local chiefs and put an end to their "disloyalty."[74] Colonialist rhetoric and the "civilizing mission" were revived, as was the rhetoric about the "vestiges of feudalism." The civilizing and colonizing mission was seen as a new chapter in the French revolution.[75] Civilization was associated with private property, a free labor market and social stability. The French colonial elites were disappointed by the attitude of the Africans who, despite the "revolution" and the contribution of civilization, continued to "cheat" (i.e., they didn't behave as the colonial authorities had hoped). Instead of "independent peasants" and urban workers, the French found themselves confronted with populations that migrated from one empire to another, often at the whim of the seasons.[76] In 1905, slaves began a mass exodus throughout French Sudan, despite French attempts to reconcile masters and slaves.[77] Refugee communities in Sudan pose a threat to the demographic stability of eastern Ubangi-Chari.[78] It was difficult to distinguish

---

[70] Fall, *Le travail forcé*; François Renault, "L'abolition de l'esclavage au Sénégal. L'attitude de l'administration française 1848–1905." *Revue française d'histoire d'outre-mer*, 58, 1 (1971): 5–80.

[71] ANOM Afrique équatoriale, gouvernement, G 1 AEF 2H/8, From the Governor of Cameroon to the Minister of Colonies, September 14, 1917.

[72] ANOM, G 1 AEF 2H/8, From the Governor of Cameroon to the Minister of Colonies, September 14, 1917.

[73] Jean-Louis Boutillier, "Les captifs en AOF (1903–1905)," *Bulletin de l'IFAN*, 30, série B, 2 (1968): 520.

[74] ANOM, GGAEF, 4(1) D2. N'Djolé, Rapport du capitaine Curault, administrateur de la région de l'Ogooué sur le groupement hostile de Mikongo et la nécessité d'une répression immédiate contre le chef Ngoua-Midoumbi et ses partisans, Années 1906 [Report by Captain Curault, administrator of the region of Ogooué, about the hostile coalition by Mikongo and the necessity to repress it and to take action against Ngoua-Midoumbi and his supporters, 1906].

[75] ANOM Afrique équatoriale, gouvernement, G 1 AEF 2H/8.

[76] Renault, "L'abolition de l'esclavage au Sénégal."

[77] Klein, *Slavery and Colonial Rule*. Marie Rodet, *Les migrantes ignorées du Haut-Sénégal, 1900–1946* (Paris: Karthala, 2009).

[78] Cordell, "The Delicate Balance."

refugees from slaves,[79] while incidents between the French and the local population increased.[80] The regular army and the concessionary militias intervened in joint acts of violence.[81]

To counteract these trends, the French authorities, following the British example, instituted a highly repressive labor discipline. Former slaves were not expected to work where and when they pleased; if they did not have a proper work contract, they could be convicted of vagrancy; if they left before completing their task, they could be convicted of desertion. These measures proved ineffective, however, because the various colonial authorities were reluctant to cooperate: The French, British, Belgians, Germans and Portuguese competed for labor and were always ready to recapture fugitives.[82] Coercive measures were also weakened by competition within the French empire itself, between different regions and between companies and authorities.

In 1902, the value of FEA exports in current dollars was US$1.6 million, compared to US$13.1 million for FWA. In 1913, FWA exports reached UA$29.2 million, while FEA exports stagnated.[83] The colonial powers, especially France and Belgium, became interested in the Congo and Gabon only with the advent of steam navigation, when it became possible to use the Congo River to transport goods and connect with the various European empires in Africa. It should also be noted that the French government was generally reluctant to finance its colonies, preferring to concentrate its limited resources on the FWA.[84] During this period (1900–1920), France adopted the concession system, granting operating monopolies to private companies. In this respect, colonial policy in the AEF differed markedly from that of the neighboring AEF, where concessions were rare and private companies dominated. Despite these advantages, few companies invested in the AEF before the First World War, and almost none before 1900. French capitalists preferred Turkey, Russia and Indochina to Africa, especially equatorial Africa, which was considered too difficult to exploit profitably. By 1903, only one-third of the companies created in the previous decade were still in business; in the years that followed, they merged until, by 1909, only six companies controlled all French activities in equatorial Africa. Until the 1920s, these companies operated a predatory economy, seeking to extract maximum resources with minimum investment and maximum coercion. Both the companies and the colonial government sought to eliminate any form of profit from indigenous agriculture in order to create a larger available labor force for

[79] ANOM AEF GGAEF 3D/3. Mission Fillon.
[80] ANOM FM 2 AFFPOL/19 Incidents at Bas M'Bomou.
[81] ANOM, GGAEF 8Q58.
[82] ANOM, G 1 AEF 2H/8.
[83] David Fieldhouse, "The Economic Exploitation of Africa: Some British and French Comparisons" in Prosser Gifford and William Roger Louis, eds., *France and Britain in Africa: Imperial Rivalry and Colonial Rule* (New Haven: Yale University Press, 1971): 659–60.
[84] Coquery-Vidrovitch, *Le Congo*.

their own activities. These maneuvers impoverished the regions concerned, but did not contribute to the development of the colonial enterprise.[85] The French army, the concessionary companies and the colonial state constantly accused Africans of indolence and laziness.[86] This argument proved useful to the concession companies in suggesting the need for coercion.[87] In the absence of explicit government authorization in this regard, concession companies could recruit workers either directly or through tribal chiefs. However, the authority of local chiefs was often limited to their own villages, and they rarely provided all the workers needed.[88] Companies usually paid in kind, arguing that local workers did not understand the value of money.[89] Forced labor led to resistance and desertion.[90] The French military authorities resorted to various forms of forced conscription: Women were held hostage until the men came forward.[91] Wages were very low or non-existent, given the extremely arduous nature of the work; recruiters conducted manhunts in deserted villages, particularly in the Cercle de Gribingui region.[92] The French League for Human Rights denounced these abuses,[93] but little concrete action took place to put an end to these practices. In short, the concession system raised questions about its profitability and legality.[94] On the one hand, the colonial state delegated a large part of its authority to the concessions, on the pretext that it did not have the financial means to become directly involved in African colonization. On the other hand, the several colonial state officials felt that the system of concessions was open to fraud and abuse.[95] This double link between the colonial state and the concessions, already

---

[85] Special issue "Commercial Empires in Equatorial Africa." *Economic History of Africa*, 12 (1983): 13–31.
[86] ANOM FM SG GCOG/XIV, 1 and 2.
[87] *La Dépêche coloniale*, December 23, 1903; Coquery-Vidrovitch, *Le Congo*, 1: 103.
[88] ANOM, GGAEF 8Q58.
[89] ANOM, GGAEF, 8Q59, Libreville, Rapport d'inspection de la Société du Haut-Ogooué, Année 1908.
[90] ANOM, GGAEF, 8Q59, Libreville, Inspection report.
[91] ANOM, FP, PA/16(V)/5 (Brazza mission, notes); FP/PA/16(V)/3 (criminal affairs, women).
[92] ANOM, FP, PA/16(V)/5 (mission Brazza, notes); FP/PA/16(V)/3 (criminal affairs, women). See, in particular, Bobichon, Rapport sur le portage.
[93] ANOM FM 2AFFPOL/19. Observations of the French League for the Protection of Human Rights and the Women's International League for Peace and Freedom on the system adopted by the major concessions.
[94] On these debates: Coquery-Vidrovitch, *Le Congo*; Maurice Hamelin, *Des concessions coloniales. Étude sur les modes d'aliénation des terres domaniales en Algérie et dans les colonies françaises du Congo* (Paris: Librairie nouvelle de droit et de jurisprudence Arthur Rousseau, 1898).
[95] Henri Cuvillier-Fleury, *La mise en valeur du Congo français* (Paris: Librairie de la société du recueil général des lois et des arrêts, 1904); Union Congolaise, *Les sociétés concessionnaires du Congo français depuis 1905. Situation financière, plantations, main-d'œuvre (1906–1908)* (Paris: Bernard Grasset, 1909).

11 NEO-COLONIALISM IN THE AGE OF THE WELFARE STATE 265

very important in terms of profits and taxation, becomes even more problematic in terms of labor and violence against the local population. The fact that taxes could be paid in kind and in labor, and not necessarily in cash, made it difficult to separate tax from labor; the payment of taxes through the concessionary companies therefore opened the way to the worst abuses; local workers were forced to work for the companies in order to repay their "debts" to the colonial state.[96] Violence was often used to enforce this rule.[97]

Forced labor was ultimately linked to the fiscal colonial state. The broader problem of financing public works and the relationship between tax obligations and the labor of the local population was resolved. Financial autonomy and budgetary constraints meant that labor costs had to be reduced, while at the same time the local population had to contribute in some way to the state effort. A capitation tax was introduced in the Sangha in 1894 and then extended to the whole of the Congo in 1900.[98] The justification for this tax was twofold: On the one hand, the "native Africans" were expected to develop a "taste and sense for work"; on the other hand, it was to compensate for the costs and efforts of the civilizing mission, as well as for the protection provided by the colonial state against raids by slave traders. Africans could pay either in kind or in cash; the colonial administration favored the latter system, while the concessionary companies favored the former, especially in rubber-producing regions. The companies attempted to collect the tax themselves and remit the monetary equivalent, after deducting costs, to the colonial administration.[99] The tax did not solve the problem, however, as the majority of the population refused to pay it. Village chiefs and women were taken hostage until the tax was paid; entire villages were ransacked and burned. Protests multiplied and degenerated into violence, triggering bloody reprisals and summary executions of chiefs and men.[100] As the price paid by the colonial authorities was higher than that paid by the companies, local populations escaped and left the territories under concession. This provoked further aggression and violence. The state authorities complained not only about the violence, but also about the fact that the head tax in the Congo was significantly lower than in Senegal and West Africa in general because of the actions of the companies.[101]

Debts to the colonial state were not only payable in kind; labor services could also be demanded. Workers were requisitioned mainly as porters and for road

---

[96] G. A. Nzenguet Iguemba, *Colonisation, fiscalité et mutations au Gabon, 1910–1947* (Paris: l'Harmattan, 2005).
[97] ANOM, GGAEF, 8Q58 and 8Q59.
[98] Journal officiel du Congo français, circular dated July 15, 1900.
[99] From the Ministry of Colonies to Albert Grodet, May 1901, ANOM AEF GGAEF, 8 Q, XIV-1.
[100] ANOM AEF 2H/8.
[101] See Rapport de Brazza au ministre des Colonies, Brazzaville, August 23, 1905, Fonds Mission Brazza 26.

and railroad construction. Forced recruitment, accompanied by abuse and violence, was extremely common. Contrary to official statements, the porters' caravans received almost no food; the porters fled or obtained supplies en route by looting villages. The abandonment of roadside areas was one of the most striking consequences of these policies.[102]

Abuses were rife. As early as 1888, missionaries denounced the atrocities committed by the French in the Congo. Later, Roger Casement, the British consul in Boma, wrote a report for the Foreign Office. His damning revelations reached Edmund Morel, a British journalist of French origin, who not only denounced French crimes in the press, but also founded the Congo Reform Association to demand British diplomatic action. British public opinion mobilized, and the British government lodged an official protest against France. The French government decided to set up a commission of inquiry headed by Brazza, former commander-in-chief in the Congo, which organized expeditions to the regions concerned to verify the abuses alleged in the British report. In 1900, Albert Grodet was appointed Governor General of the FEA. In his position at the FWA, Grodet had called for more justice and fewer abuses;[103] he had the same attitude in Equatorial Africa. Two scandals were denounced, one in 1903, the other in 1905. In 1903, an administrative official, Georges Toqué, allowed a black native accused of stealing cartridges to be punished by drowning. Shortly afterwards, Fernand Gaud, a native affairs officer, celebrated Bastille Day by detonating dynamite in the anus of a native prisoner. The incident was not revealed until two years later, first in *Le Petit Parisien* of February 15, 1905, then the following day in *Le Matin* and *Le Temps*.

Meanwhile, in May–June 1904, in the Bangui region, a French officer named Culard, also a native affairs agent, took fifty-eight women and ten children hostage to force local workers to stockpile rubber. It wasn't until late May that a doctor discovered the survivors, thirteen women and eight children:

> At the time of the visit, I found in the infirmary, on different days, three dying bodies with the following physical characteristics: extraordinary emaciation beyond that of any chronic disease, desiccated, ashen skin, cellular tissue without fat, slimmed muscles, flat stomachs. He is no longer able to understand, move or speak. The state of apathy and depletion suggests that the individuals were isolated in an unhealthy place and died of starvation after surviving for a relatively long period of time by occasionally consuming a little food. The bodies were silently thrown into the river.[104]

---

[102] François Zuccarelli, "Le recrutement de travailleurs sénégalais par l'État indépendant du Congo, 1884–1896," *Revue française d'histoire d'outre-mer*, XLVII, 168–9 (1960): 475–481.
[103] Roberts, *Litigants and Households*: 51.
[104] Docteur Fulconis, May 27, 1904, ANOM, fonds Brazza, 1905-1, quoted in La rapport Brazza: 25.

The administrator of Oubangui-Shari, a certain Yaeck, arrived on the scene on June 17. He immediately granted the survivors rations of rice and salted beef "on an exceptional basis," but only in exchange for "light work consisting of bringing in two small sheaves of straw each day."[105] Yaeck sent his report to the Commissary General on June 30. Culard denied having taken the women and children hostage; on the contrary, he claimed that he had found them in that condition in the forest and had sent them to Bangui out of pure humanity.[106] Gentil arrived in Bangui on August 29, but did nothing. He referred the case to the head of the legal department in Brazzaville, who concluded that there was no evidence to incriminate the agents of the administration. "There was no crime, no offense, no criminal intent."[107]

The following year, in May–June, 119 women and girls were taken hostage in Krébedjé, near Fort Sibut.[108] In reality, they had been kidnapped in retaliation for the murder of twenty-one agents of the concession company in Ouhamé-Nana. Brazza immediately reported the facts. The women were released and the case hushed up.[109]

In general, the concession companies were willing to kill to maintain order and force the local population to work. For example, the Compagnie M'poko, on the border between Congo and Oubangui-Shari,[110] had no qualms about placing armed men (about 400 European mercenaries in 1906) in every village, where they held hostages, whipped and executed people. The investigation led to the conviction of 236 people, only seventeen of them Europeans. The company was found guilty of 750 proven murders and 1,500 probable murders.[111] However, the charges against the company were dismissed by the court, and only the African militiamen were sentenced to prison terms ranging from five to twenty years of forced labor.[112]

What's worse, the archives confirm that the highest colonial authorities, up to the Minister of Colonies, were well aware of the facts. Subsequently, they all denied any knowledge of the events, and the commission of inquiry set up after the Brazza report accepted their arguments.

The use of the law was part of this policy. The Code de l'Indigénat, first adopted in Algeria in the early 1880s, was gradually extended to other

---

[105] ANOM, Rapport de Brazza au ministre des Colonies, Brazzaville, August 23, 1905, Fonds Mission Brazza 26.
[106] Culard, July 20, 1904, ANOM Fonds Mission Brazza 26.
[107] ANOM, Rapport de Brazza au ministre des Colonies, Brazzaville, August 23, 1905, Fonds Mission Brazza 26.
[108] Fort Sibut post information diary, May 14, 1905, ANOM 16/PA/V/4.
[109] Telegram of June 6, 1905, ANOM, FM GC XIX 4.
[110] ANOM FM 2A FFPOL/38.
[111] Report from Colonial Inspector Butel to the Special Commissioner, November 19, 1907, ANOM, FM 2AFFPOL/38.
[112] "Preface," *The Brazza Report*: 33.

colonies.¹¹³ The code stated that indigenous people were French subjects but not French citizens. The distinction between indigenous subjects and citizens in the colonies corresponded to the distinction between nationals and foreigners in France.¹¹⁴ The subject in the colonies and the foreigner in France both had limited rights; these two oppositions supported each other in public perception and policy. However, immigrants in France could obtain naturalization for their children: The prerogatives of blood and soil intermingled and could gradually erode status inequalities. In the colonies, this possibility was much weaker, if not non-existent, and this was the main difference between foreigners in France and natives in the colonies; in Africa, the Code de l'Indigénat took up these notions.¹¹⁵ Women were raped and chained, men were beaten and often murdered.¹¹⁶ This situation of lawlessness and persistent abuse went hand in hand with that of forced labor and disguised forms of slavery practiced by local actors, concessionary companies and the colonial state itself.

The rule of law was particularly harsh and unequal in the labor market. Colonial administrators and concession companies justified the use of coercion and criticized the "modern tendencies" then in vogue in Paris and supported by certain "sociologists" in favor of overprotection of workers. For these concession companies and administrators, there were two main reasons why such a policy could not be implemented in Africa: "the planters and bosses already have limited power over the indigenous population, and it would be absurd to give them any more."; and, on the other hand, according to this report, French entrepreneurs would face considerable economic and climatic risks and would have to contend with the indolence of Africans. In fact, "we have to multiply the constraints to teach them how to work."¹¹⁷ It is worth noting that in French Africa, natural rights were invoked at the very moment when

---

[113] ANOM FM 1AFFPOL/1703 Indigenat. FM 1AFFPOL/1700 Native customs Africa.
  A growing bibliography is available. Among others: Martine Fabre, "L'indigénat : des petites polices discriminatoires et dérogatoires," in Bernard Durand, Martine Fabre, Mamadou Badji, eds., *Le juge et l'Outre-mer*, vol. 5 (Lille: Centre d'histoire judiciaire, 2010): 273–310; Olivier Le Cour Grandemaison, *De l'indigénat* (Paris: Zone 2010); Isabelle Merle, "De la légalisation de la violence en contexte colonial. Le régime de l'indigénat en question," *Politix*, 17, 66 (2004): 137–162; Laurent Manière, "Deux conceptions de l'action judiciaire aux colonies. Magistrats et administrateurs en AOF (1887–1912)," *Clio-Thémis* 4 (2011): www.cliothemis.com/Clio-Themis-numero-4. See also Emmanuelle Saada, "Nation and Empire in the French Context," in George Steinmetz, ed., *Sociology and Empire: The Imperial Entanglements of a Discipline* (Durham and London: Duke University Press, 2013): 321–340.
[114] Patrick Weil, *Qu'est-ce qu'un Français?* (Paris: Grasset, 2007).
[115] James Lehning, *To be a Citizen: The Political Culture of the Early French Third Republic* (Ithaca: Cornell University Press, 2001). See also Pierre Rosanvallon, *La démocratie inachevée* (Paris: Gallimard 2000).
[116] ANOM, GGAEF, 8Q58 and 8Q59; GGAEF, 4(1) D 10.
[117] ANOM AEF G 1 AEF 2H/8.

they were rejected in France as a means of protecting work and the poor, which was moving from charity to the welfare state. Forms of labor inspection were introduced in the colonies only in 1932 and especially in 1936, but it was not until twenty years later, in 1952, that a colonial labor code was adopted, just as the empire was being dismantled.

For both France and Britain, however, the economic justification for the occupation of Africa remains controversial. Conventional historiography maintains that Africa was difficult to exploit until the interwar period and that its occupation was driven primarily by geopolitical considerations. For the early twentieth century, however, the question remains. New datasets show that British Africa declined in importance in its trade between the 1880s and the First World War,[118] while the reverse was true for French Africa.[119]

This can be explained in part by the fact that during this period Britain benefited from lower transportation costs (steam, Suez) as well as its dominant role on the international world markets. France, on the other hand, was slowly recovering from the terrible shock of the previous century, and although its economy was booming, it was able to benefit less than Great Britain on the international markets. Hence the greater role of Africa–France trade as a percentage of France's total international trade compared to Britain. Overall, the French Empire probably contributed less in value to France's growth than did the British Empire; and yet its administration was relatively cheap, as the army and the state bore most of its costs, while only the lowest incomes of the population were taxed.[120] Transfers from the colonies to France were relatively modest, and still significant for a part of the population (mainly linked to colonial enterprises); while France did not contribute to improving the well-being of its colonies, the gap with metropolitan France was widening steadily over time.

Conclusion Part III

The previous chapters have tested the main Western approaches to work and freedom, not in the abstract, but in terms of their implementation on the

---

[118] Gareth Austin, *Labour, Land, and Capital in Ghana: From Slavery to Free Labour in Asante, 1807-1956* (Woodbridge: Boydell & Brewer, 2005); Frankema Ewout, "Colonial Taxation and Government Spending in British Africa, 1880–1940: Maximizing Revenue or Minimizing Effort?" *Explorations in Economic History*, 48, 1 (2011): 136–149; Leigh Gardner, *Taxing Colonial Africa: The Political Economy of British Imperialism* (Oxford: Oxford University Press, 2012).

[119] Denis Cogneau, *Un empire bon marché. Histoire et économie politique de la colonisation française, XIXe–XXIe siècle* (Paris: Seuil, 2024); Frankema, Williamson, Woltjer, "An Economic Rationale for the West African Scramble?"; Denis Cogneau, Yannick Dupraz and Sandrine Mesplé-Somps, "Fiscal Capacity and Dualism in Colonial States: The French Empire 1830–1962," *The Journal of Economic History*, 81, 2 (2021): 441–480.

[120] Cogneau, *Un empire bon marché*.

ground. The limitations of these implementations, at least for workers, confirm the implicit inegalitarian perspective hidden in supposedly universal approaches to freedom, beginning with British utilitarianism. Bentham, Mill, Maine and several British officers sought an answer to slavery and unfreedom in the utilitarian principle; the result was the persistence of formal inequalities before the law, which aggravated real inequalities and discrimination in political, economic and social terms. Similar limitations influenced the notion and practice of British contractualism in the regulation of indentured immigration. Both approaches combined legal bias and market discrimination in the name of freedom.

French revolutionary ideals expressed serious limitations when confronted with slavery, not the least of which was the ultimate disregard for these principles outside of France in the colonial world. Colonial authorities in the Mascarene Islands and French Africa identified "freedom" with the right of masters to persecute workers on the one hand, and with the obligations of workers on the other.

Like the British and French, American abolitionism racialized social, legal, civil and economic inequalities between white and colored workers, while the Russian path of reconciling early industrialization, peasant and household welfare, and lack of political rights produced whatever economic growth and growing social inequalities that became extreme with the outbreak of the First World War.

The emergence of the welfare state confirmed this unresolved tension between political and social rights, for men and women, whites and blacks, the local-national worker and the colonial worker. Polanyi's great transformation in fact expressed the great divergence between the worlds of labor in the core of empires and in their peripheries.

General Conclusion and Extrapolations

Empire, labor and coercion: These three elements at the heart of this book are most often associated with the pre-capitalist, pre-modern world, while "modernity" is usually associated with the success of the nation-state, capital, wage labor and democracy. But we have shown that labor, coercion and empire are fundamental to the functioning of capitalism, certainly until the end of the nineteenth century in Western Europe, and much later in other parts of the world. Capitalism can exist without wage labor (contrary to the popular argument since Smith, Marx and Weber) or democracy (Acemoglu).

The conclusions I draw here are based on my deliberate choice to study three empires: Russian, French and British. Much remains to be done to understand how these experiences relate to those of other empires and regions of the world. No doubt different conclusions would be drawn. Focusing primarily on the United States, for example, would have revealed a form of capital-intensive capitalism that also used slave labor and where democracy remained racialized for a long time. The Portuguese Empire would have revealed a long and persistent relationship between domesticity, service and slavery, but with a massive introduction of slaves into society, while universal access to basic rights remained a chimera. The deliberate choice to study three empires – Russian, French and British – has allowed me to identify fundamental elements and avoid certain pitfalls, without claiming to be exhaustive. First of all, this choice is certainly not intended to reintroduce Eurocentrism into world history by turning the usual history of Western achievement on its head. On the contrary, it aims to challenge Eurocentrism: The break with Eurocentrism is made not only by studying non-European worlds (and certainly not by using Western criteria), but by radically problematizing "the West," its capitalism and its institutions. The coexistence of empire, forced labor and capitalism is not a contradiction, but the very mode of operation of capitalism. In fact, nation and empire, freedom and unfreedom, labor and capital were and are co-substantive. One commands the other and vice versa; one cannot even be defined without the other. If this is the case, the question is not to point out the contradictions, but to find out why coercion, labor and empire prevailed over their counterparts (wage labor, capital and the nation-state) until the end of the nineteenth century in Western Europe, and even later elsewhere in the world. The answer lies primarily in the link between the state and capitalism. If the modern state grants unequal rights and often takes the form of an empire that generates inequality, if labor is almost always subject to legal and social constraints, and if the law is a source of inequality rather than equality, this is not because unscrupulous actors have hijacked the values of Western modernity, but because the latter was built on empire, labor and coercion. From the nineteenth century to the end of the twentieth, states and institutions protected inequality and promoted coercion, not only in Russia and the United States, but also in Britain and France, and especially in their colonies. Workers had few rights. But why was this so?

To understand the reasons, I looked at the origins of aristocratic capitalism as it emerged in the mid seventeenth century. Historiography has often focused on the crisis of the seventeenth century, where Marxists like Dobb and Steensgaard see the transition from feudalism to capitalism, an argument that Braudel strongly criticized, emphasizing instead the long-term evolution of capitalism. My position is somewhere between these two interpretations. Admittedly, capitalism was already in place in the twelfth century, thanks to long-distance trade, finance and monopolies, not to mention the growing production for the market in both town and country. But the transformations of the seventeenth century changed capitalism: State-building and empire-building converged; not before empire, then (from the nineteenth century) nation (an argument put forward by Weber, Tilly and many others), but the two overlapped and fed off each other. What was new at the time was that territorial powers resorted to legal fictions to legitimize their power and social hierarchies. Titles and notarized documents legitimized the rights of landlords over their serfs and slaves, and of masters over their apprentices and workers. Ownership of human beings was as central as ownership of objects, to the point where the line between the two became increasingly blurred. Slaves were objects; servants, workers and domestic servants ceded all their time and rights to their masters. The growing importance of production over trade and services underpinned this institutional development.

These elements created a virtuous circle for the elites and a nightmare for the workers; the reason these rules and practices were so widespread and enduring was that they were made socially acceptable by the joint action of the family, the village, the guilds, the cities and the state. All demanded work with limited rights. The absence of democracy throughout the period under study was a crucial support for this social order.

Of course, there were many forms of resistance: desertion by soldiers and sailors, by slaves, but also by servants and ordinary workers. It manifested itself in acts of rebellion, defiance of conscription, resistance to the authority of village chiefs and that of the state or landowners. Nevertheless, it is clear that these forms of resistance were not very effective in the seventeenth and part of the eighteenth centuries, because institutions, norms, social concerns and economic hierarchies and logics all favored betting on the intensification of labor and coercion rather than on higher wages and the intensification of capital. And yet, in all the contexts we have studied, the mobilization of the law by working people was massive, despite the injustice of the law, despite the corruption and inequalities peculiar to the legal worlds of the time. Slaves, serfs, workers, immigrants, indentured servants, peasants, wage earners, servants and sailors persisted, sometimes for years, and saw their rights recognized only gradually. Was this irrational behavior in terms of the cost-benefit ratio? No doubt, especially in the short run. But is this a reason to ignore it, as most historical analyses have done? Those damned of labor rarely won their cause, and yet, over time, they came to the fore, taking advantage of a loophole in the existing system: competition between masters and between states and colonial powers. Everywhere, this breach produced results favorable to workers: emancipation in Russia before the official abolition of serfdom, compensation for immigrants in Mauritius and Réunion Island, protections for seafarers after centuries of coercion. These local and national stories of thousands of cases whose archives abound and of which I have only been able to give a glimpse here, make up a more general story. Admittedly, legal resistance was not equal everywhere, and until recently it benefited men more than women.

Second, workers' rights were not restricted to the same extent, and when they mobilized, they were not equally successful. One way to explain these differences is to ask, for each context, why standards and rules were set, by whom, and with what results. In Russia, it was certain tsarist elites and landowners who wanted to give the peasants a greater "voice" from the 1770s and even more so after 1830. For them, it was a matter of avoiding rural unrest, but also of regulating conflicts within noble families and between these families and other groups claiming access to landed property and its political and social privileges. Thus, the focus was not on the interests of the peasants, but rather on competition among landowners, between landowners and the state, and between rural elites and the new urban elites. Over time, however, the peasants managed to turn these norms to their advantage. Later, laws more favorable to them were enacted, encouraged by reformist ambitions: The large landowners knew the advantages they could gain by recognizing the freedom of the peasants, to the detriment of the mass of small farmers.

In the European colonies, the stakes were quite different: While in Russia it was competition between economic and political elites that led to the creation of a framework at least somewhat favorable to workers, in the colonies it was competition between colonial powers that helped these workers to appropriate the law (quite dangerously at first and for decades) and to improve the outcome of claims. The United Kingdom, for example, threatened to stop sending Indians to Réunion if French landowners did not respect labor standards.

How could these inequalities in access to justice be addressed? In Russia, France, Réunion, England, Mauritius and the AEF, indentured servants and slaves were constantly on the run, moving from estate to estate, changing masters. They escaped in the hope of a better life. How many were there?

Sources always exaggerate the number of fugitives: Russian owners, Mauritian planters, Congolese companies, Quebec colonists, as well as captains and shipowners, constantly complained about these departures and demanded compensation from the authorities and, above all, from their competitors. At every opportunity, figures were quoted, almost always contradicted by other documents. The most interesting aspect for us is not to correct or clarify these figures, but to highlight the attention paid to the absconders. It highlights the importance and complexity of the constraints and the need to negotiate them at all levels. While the desire to retain workers was paramount, the difficulty of achieving this goal was expressed everywhere, with varying degrees of force. Whether it was the Russian administration, the Mauritian police, the militias in the Congo or the French bailiffs and police, the authorities demonstrated their inefficiency in catching up with people on the run. More often than not, the aim was to make an example rather than to solve the problem. The difficulties in coordinating the administrations and the confusion caused by these cases contributed to the failure of the prosecutions.

Geography played a crucial role. In principle, it was quite difficult to escape from Réunion and Mauritius, at least more difficult than from central Russia. However, the fact that many people managed to do so confirms that the competition between planters on the one hand and between agriculture and urban society on the other was fierce, and that institutions played a full part in this game. In the Congo, too, the forest and, above all, the proximity of the territories of competing empires facilitated flight. But unlike in Russia, and even more so in Réunion and Mauritius, reprisals against captured refugees and especially against the local population were of a rare violence. Entire villages were destroyed, groups of women raped and killed, and children burned. In Mauritius, it was more often the chain that awaited the fugitive. In Russia, one might fear the knout, but more often the passport was confiscated – temporarily, as the landlord's interest in the movements and activities of his serfs often outweighed his desire to punish them.

Against this general background, the empires differed in certain respects. At the turn of the seventeenth century, Russia built its empire on the basis of a strong centralization of power, state control of markets (especially for supplying the army) and the massive use of colonial soldiers. The Russian state disarmed the landowners and acquired a monopoly on violence and taxation. The alliance between state power and the landed nobility was based on a simple exchange: colonization for serfdom. The state demanded more troops and settlers, and in return gave the anxious nobles more rights over their peasants.

In France and England, the situation was quite different: Recruitment was also centralized; however, imperial construction was not accompanied by the restoration of serfdom on the continent, but by other institutional innovations.

It was not a question of democracy or freedom, as is often claimed, but of something else. In England, then in Great Britain (officially since 1701), an alliance was formed between merchants, industrialists, landowners and the state. All acquired new rights at the expense of the masses. Servants were no longer serfs, but workers subject to ever heavier constraints. Unlike in Russia, these conditions, harsh as they were, were not comparable to those of workers in the new colonial worlds. First white emigrants, then slaves, were subjected to extreme coercion, whereas in Russia the peasant serfs who colonized the steppes enjoyed greater freedom than the serfs of central Russia. The Russian empire used the colonies to counterbalance the power of the central landowners, while the French and British empires did the opposite. Their elites in the home countries were sustained by trade and colonial slavery. In Britain, international markets and the growing number of servants complemented these mechanisms. Sugar and luxury goods fueled these markets and accompanied the expansion of slavery. The empire of sugar and slavery complemented the growth of markets and innovation; by contrast, in Russia, much of the empire was a burden, except at the opposite end of the spectrum, for wheat.

These social and political hierarchies were linked to the roles of land, capital and labor in the economic process. Not only in Russia and France, but also in Great Britain, until the mid nineteenth century, innovations were labor-intensive rather than capital-intensive. This was because capital was expensive, while labor was cheap. Labor shortages did not lead to higher wages, but to coercion. Again, conventional economists would see a contradiction: If demand for labor was so high, why did wages stagnate? The answer is that labor markets, and markets in general, don't work the way they do in neoclassical theory, they are not governed by the law of supply and demand in a situation of perfect competition. On the contrary, inequality and power drive markets. In Great Britain, the alliance between the landed aristocracy, merchants and industrialists rested on three pillars: domestic markets, slavery and the intensification of labor. The latter can be explained by the need to meet demand at a time when capital was expensive and institutional constraints on labor were strong and effective. The technical innovations so often highlighted, while not negligible, were also labor-intensive. This solution also had its limits: Labor productivity under constraint increased for much of the eighteenth century but stagnated after the Napoleonic Wars. The colonies supplemented national economic growth. The ghost acres and labor that crossed the Atlantic supported British labor-intensive growth. This process was partly financed by sugar, which played a crucial role in the eighteenth century. Cotton also made its debut in the eighteenth century, thanks to an aggressive import-substitution trade policy, particularly with Asia and Africa. In the nineteenth century, cotton made it possible to develop domestic markets as never before while absorbing the shock of the Napoleonic wars and the transition between the First and Second Industrial Revolutions.

In France, too, the alliance between the crown and the landed aristocracy prevailed. Peasants were certainly not serfs, but on the contrary, they were well integrated into commercial networks. However, unlike in Great Britain, social hierarchies were less marked by the master–worker divide than by that between town and country. Urban workers (few in number) were relatively protected, both before and after the Revolution, while rural workers (the majority of the population) were not. Another difference emerges here: Although sugar was the main colonial commodity, as in the British Empire, domestic markets did not experience the same growth. These facts help explain why the Revolution and independence of Saint-Domingue came as such a major shock to France. Unlike Great Britain, which was faced with the independence of its American colonies, France lost its assets in the Revolution without having any others. The *sans-culottes* were not proletarians, and the peasants did not dream of self-sufficiency. Both were linked to the markets, both wanted to regulate the markets, and in this they shared the ambitions of the landowners and "bourgeois" who, while extolling free competition, were in fact seeking market regulation that would benefit them. They achieved this at the expense of working people, particularly in the countryside.

France maintained slavery, albeit disguised after 1848, in its colonies for most of the nineteenth century. The alliance between land capitalism and finance capitalism continued well into the Industrial Revolution. The persistence of phenomena such as peasant-workers and multi-professional farms contributed to this longevity, as they tended to confirm rather than challenge the hierarchy of authority and the notion of labor as a service along the social chain of production. It was against this chain that the protests and resistance of the world of labor arose. However, as in previous periods, these protests were expressed more in the cities and certain industries than in the countryside and in small units of production or trade. In the French colonies, slaves, ex-slaves and new immigrants were subjected to the most extreme repression. Peasant-workers in metropolitan France and the persistence of serfdom in the colonies go hand in hand in the French imperial economy, just as landowners in France and planters in the colonies join financial rentiers in the same political and social bond.

Meanwhile, Russia entered the proto-industrial and industrial era, based on the alliance between the landed nobility, the tsar and, despite everything, the peasants. The latter were subservient to the landowners and the tsar, but at the same time indispensable to the functioning of the system. They were not alienated like American slaves, to use Orlando Patterson's language. Russian peasants were supported by their communities, challenging the rights of estate overseers and stewards, and even those of the lords. Peasants demanded not only civil rights, but above all economic rights. Indeed, serfdom became a means of redistributing the income from the peasants' growing commercial activities to the landowners. This situation led to disputes, and state elites allowed many of these disputes to continue. They also encouraged emigration and the emancipation of serfs to keep the nobility in check. Ultimately, in the Russian Empire, merchants and urban "bourgeois" were the real outcasts. In this context, the Russian Empire brought geopolitical power rather than real economic benefits. The steppes provided wheat and tea, but not sugar, and did not finance an industrial revolution. On the contrary, they strengthened the alliance between landowners, the state and peasants based on relatively commercial agriculture and an expanding proto-industry. In Russia, the empire strengthened and confirmed old economic trends and socio-political balances, rather than weakening them.

While comparative analysis highlights the similarities and differences between the three empires studied, the connections were also fundamental. Masters and servants laws, apprenticeship rules before and after the abolition of slavery, vagrancy and indentured servitude are all forms of labor regulation that circulated among the empires and were eventually transformed. If this circulation of institutions took place, it was because the three empires had more in common than is generally recognized: a labor-intensive economy sustained by legal and economic coercion, and the absence of any rights for the mass of their populations.

Equally fundamental were the links between the continent and its colonies. The highly differentiated colonial experiences of each empire (the Steppes and western regions or Siberia for Russia, the Americas, Africa and the Indian Ocean for the other two empires) influenced the regulation of labor on the continent. In Russia, the rise of serfdom in the center was directly related to imperial expansion and the relaxation of coercion in the annexed territories. Similarly, but with the opposite result (to that of Russia), indentured labor in the French and British colonies was an extension of labor inequalities in their European territories. Later, the identification of slaves and wage-earners became a social and political issue that played an important role in shaping the rights and duties of workers. French and British workers sometimes sympathized with slaves, but often contrasted their own condition ("the true slave") with that of colonial slaves. The welfare state gave sanctuary to the latter orientation.

In France and Britain, the proletarian revolution did not take place for the simple reason that real proletarians were rare in the First Industrial Revolution and enjoyed the protection of the welfare state in the second. The excluded – peasants, artisans, petty traders and women – were unable to build political and social movements capable of overthrowing capitalist regimes, at least by the turn of the century, especially as Western revolutionary movements either marginalized them or (more often) deeply divided them.

With the Second Industrial Revolution, the alliance between the landed aristocracy and the capitalist world collapsed. The old rentiers disappeared, replaced by new capitalists and financial rentiers. The extension of the right to vote in France and Britain limited political radicalism by dividing the most extreme groups into those who accepted the parliamentary game and those who rejected it. Later, the abolition of slavery and the Great Divergence led to the emergence of large-scale industrial capitalism and a reorientation of relations between the mother country and the colonies. In France and Great Britain, the Second Industrial Revolution and the emergence of the welfare state (the Great Transformation of which Polanyi speaks) provoked tensions and even revolts (long depression, crisis of small production units, political movements in support of peasants and artisans). However – and this is missing from Polanyi's argument – in addition to women, artisans and peasants, others paid the price of this new capitalism: the colonial populations, who remained excluded from the new social and political rights and benefits until decolonization.

The empires of labor did not disappear, but they transformed. By the end of the nineteenth century, they were no longer based on subordinate labor in the homeland and slavery in the colonies, but welfare on the mainland contrasted sharply with the extreme post-slavery inequality in the colonial worlds. The welfare state expressed the great divergence of labor between the homeland and the colonies. The social movements that led to the recognition of previously disregarded workers' rights gave life to national systems of social rights that went far beyond the internationalist ideals of the time.

This was not the case in Russia, where the abolition of serfdom was a top-down response to the great divergence. The abolition of serfdom was only one element in a long transition that took place without the major upheavals of the French Revolution, the Revolution of Saint-Domingue, or the American Civil War. Russia's slow development had both benefits and costs. The former included labor-intensive growth even after 1861, based on decades, if not centuries, of consolidated economic organization along the same lines. The downside was that the world of aristocracy, peasantry and proto-industry was radically incompatible with the Second Industrial Revolution. The reforms adopted after 1861, including those of Stolypin, were not aimed at promoting large-scale industrial capitalism, but rather, as always, at reconciling the landed aristocracy, the peasantry and industrialization. The impossibility of achieving this compromise was due not only to economic competition from other countries, but also, and above all, to the First World War, which put an end to seasonal migrations between town and countryside and steered technical transformations, including in industry. Changes in the peasant and proto-industrial economy came to an abrupt halt. The communist regime was initially born out of opposition to this change. However, it soon sought a different compromise between large-scale production plants like those established in the West, but using a strategy derived from the First Industrial Revolution (i.e., intensification of work and coercion). The Soviet economy, born out of opposition to large-scale transformation, became a variant. It used large production units and forced labor in its own empire, whereas in the West the welfare state and large-scale production coexisted at home, and only colonial labor was forced.

Throughout the twentieth century, the welfare state proliferated in the West, especially after 1945, to counter the rise of communism, while the USSR persisted in maintaining a war economy even in peacetime. The decline of labor-intensive manufacturing in the USSR was slow but inevitable. Beginning in the 1970s, as decolonization in the West and South came to an end, the communist world imploded. Western capitalism entered a new phase, aided by decolonization and the demise of the USSR. Neoliberalism no longer needed the welfare state, which was gradually dismantled. Business leaders decentralized their operations on a global scale, taking advantage of an available and submissive workforce. Paradoxically, the defenders of the welfare state in Europe have not hesitated to attack not only globalization but also immigration, whether from Eastern Europe or other continents. Today, capitalism is globalized and financialized, which is not the case for the defenders of workers' rights, who remain strongly nationalist. That is the difference. It is this discrepancy that allows today's informal labor empires to survive.

BIBLIOGRAPHY

Archives

Departmental Archives

Archives Charente Maritime, Ex Moreau minutes, April 19 and 25, 1664.
Archives Charente Maritime, Minutier Teuleron, 1638–1680.

Archives de la Marine, Rochefort, série R, 1 R 20, "Colons. Paiement des gages."
Archives de la Marine, Rochefort, série R, 1R 26, "Actes d'engagement, Canada, 1731–1738."

Archives départementales de la Réunion (ADR), série C*1272 (traite 1746–1753) and C 1273 (traite 1758–1765).
ADR 10M9 statistiques du travail (labor statistics).

Archives Nationales, Paris

AN C 944 to 963, Enquête sur le travail agricole et industriel prescrite par le décret du 25 mai 1848.
AN C 1157–61 (parliamentary debates).
AN C 2222, Pétition des habitants de l'ile de Saint-Martin à la chambre des deputes (Petition of the inhabitants of the French part of the island of Saint-Martin to the Chamber of Deputies), July 8, 1846.
AN C 2225, société française pour l'abolition de l'esclavage.
AN B24, gens de couleur.
AN, CC 9A/27; CC 9 A/30; CC 9C/1, gens de couleurs.
AN, F12 4476, temps de travail, pétitions.
AN Z1D, amirauté de France, minutes des jugements.

Archives Nationales T 210/2, Cul de Sac.
Archives Nationales, Marine, B3 455, folios 62 to 136.

Archives Coloniales (ANOM), Aix-en-Province

On Africa

FM 1AFFPOL/1703, Indigénat.
FM 1AFFPOL/1700, Coutumes indigènes Afrique.

FM 2AFFPOL/19, Incidents du Bas M'Bomou. Observations of the French League for the Protection of Human Rights and the Womens international League for Peace and Freedom on the system adopted by the large concessions.
FM 2AFFPOL/38, Rapport de l'inspecteur des colonies Butel au commissaire spécial, November 19, 1907.
GC XIX 4, Télégramme du June 6, 1905.
AEF (Afrique équatoriale française) 2H (travail)/8.
AEF 3D/3, Mission Fillon.
AEF, 8 Q, XIV-1, From the Ministry of Colonies to Albert Grodet, May 1901.
FM SG GCOG (Congo, Oubangui, Gabon governments) /XIV 1 and 2 recruitment of Kroumen workers.
Fonds Mission Brazza 26, Culard, July 20, 1904.
Fonds Brazza, 1905–1, Docteur Fulconis, May 27, 1904.
FP, PA/16(V)/5, mission Brazza, notes; FP/PA/16(V)/3, criminal cases, women.
Rapport de Brazza au ministre des Colonies, Brazzaville, August 23, 1905, Fonds Mission Brazza 26.
GGAEF (gouvernement général Afrique équatoriale françaises) 8Q58.
GGAEF 2H 15.
GGAEF 8Q58 and 8Q59; GGAEF 4(1) D 10.
GGAEF 8Q59, Libreville, Rapport d'inspection.
16/PA/V/4, Journal de renseignements du poste de Fort-Sibut, May 14, 1905.

On Réunion Island

FM SG/Reu (Réunion) c 379 d 3211, engagés, immigration.
FM SG/Reu c 382 d.3323, engagés, immigration.
FM SG/Reu c 383 d 3323, immigration.
FM/ SG Reu c380/d228.
FM/SG REU 380/3228, minute 7.
Gen c149 d1248.

General Series and Censuses

G1, 460, 461, Nouvelle France, recensements de 1659, 1666.
G1 497, Recensement de la population, Saint-Domingue.
SG Martinique C 33 d 289.
F 3 222, Code de la Guadeloupe.

On the Abolition of Slavery

Généralités 162 d. 1326, Comptes rendus des séances de la Commission d'abolition de l'esclavage.

B3 folio 19, dated February 11, 1671.

C 11A5 folio 54 et folio 165; also folio 106.

C 7A 47, Victor Hugues au Comité de salut public, 4 thermidor an II (July 22, 1794).
F3 236, Ordonnance du July 15, 1738.

C 4 1720–1750.
FM F/3/202, Napoléon Bonaparte, "Proclamation du Consul à tous les habitants de Saint-Domingue" (17 brumaire an X [November 8, 1802]).
1671, B 3 folio 23. Lettre de Colbert à Talon.
Noariat Valeau Saint-Fi, minute du December 28, 1791.

Archives publiques du Canada

MG1-G1, recensement de 1666.
MG 17 (archives des églises et missionnaires), A 7, 2, 3.

Bibliothèque nationale de France, section des manuscrits

Nouvelles acquisitions de France (NAF), 9328.
BN NAF 93227, Recensement de la population de la Martinique en 1660.

British Library

BL Additional Manuscripts 36/ 785, Imports of sugar.
BL Additional Manuscripts 38, 714, f. 37; 8133 c f 237, Estate Concentration, West Indies.
BL Additional Manuscripts 21254–21256, Proceeding of the Committee for the Abolition of the Slave Trade, 1787–1819.
BL MSS Brit. Emp. S 2o, E2/4, Anti-Slavery Papers, minute book of the Committee of the Anti-Slavery Society.

British Library, Indian Documents IOR

BL IOR F/4/369 several files, among which 9221; also F/4/1034, n. 28499, Traficking Nepalese children.
BL IOR L/PJ/6/376, Assam planters' complaints.
BL IOR L/PJ/6/635, Assam planters' complaints.
BL IOR L/R/5/11, Law suits, Assam.
BL IOR Mss Mar D 31 fol. 110, Sexual slavery.
BL IOR V 3244, Indigo production.
BL IOR, Bengal Judicial Consultations, P/132/21.
BL IOR, Bengal Judicial Consultations, P/132/57.
BL IOR/V/23/101, No. 37, Papers Related to Tea Cultivation in Assam, 1859–1860.
BL, IOR, Political dispatch to India, February 13, 1838, E/4/753: 909–12.

Maryland Archives Online

Proceedings and Acts of the General Assembly of Maryland, vol. 1, January 1637/8– September 1664 (Baltimore: Maryland Historical Society 1883): 553–554. Available online: https://msa.maryland.gov/megafile/msa/speccol/sc2900/sc2908/000001/000001/html/am1--533.html.

Provincial court, vol. 49, several cases. Also vols. 65 and 68.
Provincial court, vol. 57, several cases.

Mauritius National Archives (MNA)

B1B, First Immigration, Arrivals of Indian Immigrants.
H66, Planters' petitions.
RA 1955, Immigration, Police.
RA 2205, Immigration, Protectors of slaves.

Rhode House Library, Oxford, Lugard Papers, Mss. British Empire, 30-99.

REM (Rossiiskoi etnograficheskii musei, Saint-Petersburg), fond 7. Ethnographic expeditions.

RGADA (Russian Archives of Ancient Acts)

fond 89, *Turetskie dela*, delo 3.
fond 123, Krymskie dela 13, l. 53.
fond 199 (G. F. Miller).
fond 210 Belgorodskii stb 772.
fond 294, opis' 2 and 3;
fond 342, opis' 3, delo 749.
fond 407, opis' 1, delo 158.
fond 615 (krepostnye knigi mestnyjh uchrezhdenii XVI-XVIII v), opis' 1; fond 294 (Manufaktor-Kontora), opis-1-3.
fond 1287 (Sheremetev), opis' 3, chast' 1, delo 107, 117, 1745.

RGIA (Russian Imperial Archives)

fond 18, opis' 2, delo 1927, ll. 1, 3, 212-213. Peasants in textile manufactures.
fond 379 opis'1. Fugitive peasants.
fond 1088 (Sheremetev, opis' 3, 5, 10).
fond 1149, opis' 2, delo 20, 90. Illicit serfdom.
fond 1291, opis 53, delo 8, 280. Peasant migration.

Rossiiskaia Akademiia nauk. Arkhiv, fond 1714, op. 1 (A.A. Novosel'skii), delo 66, l. 123; RGADA, fond 123, opis' 3, delo 13.

TsIAM (Moscow provincial archives)

fond 14, opis' 1, delo 3266, ll. 2-38. Manufactures workers rules.
fond 54 (Moskovskoe gubernskoe upravlenie), 1783-1917, opis' 1, for example 56, 284, 966, 1509. Deistviia Nizhegorodskoi gubernskoi uchenoi arkhivnoi komissii (Proceedings of the Nizhegorod provincial archive commission) (Nizhegorod: Publications of the province), several booklets, 1890s.
fond 2354, opis' 1, delo 41, ll. 197a-99, 228. Manufactures workers rules.

The National Archives (Kew) TNA

BT (Board of Trade) 6/141.
CO (Colonial Office)1/44, ff. 142–379.
CO 140/2, 1673, census in Jamaica.
CO 167/263, Mauritius Island.
CO 318/2/115, Barbados Census 1676.
CO 318/116, Slaves apprenticeship.
CO 1/43, n. 37, Slave mortality on boats.
CO 137/19.
CO 137/32.
CO 142/31, "A List of Landholders in the Island of Jamaica," December 31, 1754.
CO 152/13; 152/14, Barbados, estate owners.
CO 167/213, 202, 266, Colony of Mauritius, annual reports, 1860–1890.
CO 167/252, Mauritius, indentured desertion.
CO 318/1 (customs).
CO 390/6: 31-2, Caribbean estates, sugar production.
CO 533/16, W. D. Ellis minute, October 12, 1906; Eastern African Protectorate, no. 8, 1906.
FO (Foreign Office)
FO 20/ 636 High Court of Admiralty, Ledgers for Goodes Soulde in ye Barbados, 1636.
FO 65/6, Russian exports.
FO 84/174, Indentured immigration, Mauritius.
FO 97/340, 341, Russian exports.

Printed Sources

BPP (British Parliamentary Papers), *Report from the Commissioners for Inquiring into the Administration and Practical Reform of the Poor Laws, 1834*, XXVIII, appendix A.
BPP 1789, 36, 646 part 4, Barbados.
BPP 1790, 29: 697–698.
BPP "Slavery in India" 1828, section 125.
BPP 1831, VI: 144. Grey C. E. and E. Ryan, "Some Observations on a Suggestion of a Code of Law," submitted September 13, 1830 to the Governor-General in Council. Bentick to Grey and Ryan, October 9, 1831.
BPP, *House of Commons Committee Reports*, 1st series, IX, 1774–1802
BPP, November 5, 1831, House of Commons, *Papers in Explanation of the Condition of the Slave Population*.
BPP 1831-2, February 16, 1832: 14.
BPP, *Return of the number, names, and ages of all persons committed to any prison in England and Wales for any offence in a union workhouse*, 1843, XLV: 343–361.
BPP, Select Committee on. District Asylums, etc.
BPP 1841, 45: 16, Petition of the inhabitants of Calcutta.

BPP1842, 30: 26
BPP 1847 (325) 39.
BPP1854, 52 (2050), Colony of Mauritius, annual report.
BPP, 1861, 44, Papers Relating to Indigo Cultivation in Bengal.
BPP 1861, 72 includes the *Papers Relating to Indigo Production in Bengal, Preliminary to Appointment of Commission, 1854-1860. Papers Relating to the Passing of Act X of 1859 (an Act to Amend the Law Relating to the Recovery of Rent in the Presidency of Fort William in Bengal)* (Calcutta: Office of the Superintendent of Government Printing, 1883).
BPP 1863, 41: 271 "Statement Exhibiting the Moral and Material Progress and Condition of India."
BPP, 1875, 704: 34 and appendices A and B. Colony of Mauritius, 1860-1885.
BPP *Return of the number of persons (inmates and casuals) committed to prison from each union workhouse (England and Wales) for the half year ending on 25 day of March 1874,* 1876 LXII: 393.
BPP 1894, 58, "Chief Commissioner to the Government of India, May 4, 1894."

Decisions of the Sovereign Council adopted between 1663 and 1760 were collected and published in: *Jugements et délibérations du Conseil Souverain de la Nouvelle-France / Législature de Québec,* 6 volumes (Québec: Imprimerie Coté et Cie, 1885-1891).

Hansard Parliamentary Debates (HPD)
1831, vol. 16.
1833 vol. 18.
1833, vol. 19.
1834, vol. 22; vol. 25.
1840, vol. 42.
1841, vol. 48.
1846, vol. 88.

Judicial Statistics, England and Wales, 1857-1875, 19 volumes (London: Home Office, 1858-1876).

La révolution française et l'abolition de l'esclavage (Paris: Edhis, 1968), 12 volumes.

Materialy po istorii Uzbeksoi, Tadzhiskoi i Turkmenskoi SSR, vol. 1 (Leningrad, Moscow: Nauka, 1932).

Materialy vysochaishe uchrezhdennoi 16 noiabria 1901 g. Komissii po issledovaniiu voprosa o dvizhenii s 1861 g. po 1901 g. blagosostoianiia sel'skogo naseleniia srednezemledel'cheskikh gubernii sravnitel'no s drugimi mestnostiami Evropeiskoi Rossii: V 3 chastiakh (Materials collected by the 1901 Commission on the study of economic development from 1861 to 1901, comparison between the central agrarian provinces and other regions of European Russia) (Saint-Petersburg: Ministry of Agriculture, 1903).

Pol'noe Sobrannye Zakonov Rossiskoi Imperii (Complete Collection of the Laws of the Russian Empire), 33 volumes (Saint-Petersburg: Tipografiia II Otdeleniia sobstvennostoi ego Imperatorskogo Velichestva Kantseliarii, 1649-1913).

Recueil des usages locaux en vigueur dans le département de la Vienne (Poitiers: Bertrand: 1865).
Recueil des usages locaux du département d'Indre-et-Loire (Tours: Guiland Verger, 1863).
Reports on the Tea and Tobacco Industries in India (London: Stationary Office, 1974).

Published Works

Abashin, Serguei N., Dimitrii Iu. Arapov and Nataliia E. Bekmakhanova, eds., *Tsentral′naia Aziia v sostave Rossiiskoi imperii* (Central Asia in the Context of the Russian Empire) (Moscow: Novoe literaturnoe obozrenie, 2008).

Abenon Lucien, Jacques Cauna and Liliane Chauleau, *Antilles 1789. La révolution aux Caraïbes* (Paris: Nathan, 2019).

Abernethy, David, *The Dynamics of Global Dominance: European Overseas Empires, 1415–1980* (New Haven: Yale University Press).

Acemoglu, Daron and James Robinson, *Economic Origins of Dictatorship and Democracy* (Cambridge: Cambridge University Press, 2005).

Acemoglu, Daron and Alexander Wolitzky, "The Economics of Labor Coercion," *Econometrica*, 79, 2 (2011): 555–600.

Acemoglu, Daron, Simon Johnson and James Robinson, "Reversal of Fortune: Geography and Institutions in the Making of the Modern World Income Distribution," *Quarterly Journal of Economics*, 117, 4 (2002): 1231–1294.

Acemoglu, Daron, Simon Johnson and James Robinson, "The Rise of Europe: Atlantic Trade, Institutional Change, and Economic Growth," *The American Economic Review*, 95, 3 (2005): 546–579.

Adelman, Jeremy, *Worldly Philosopher: The Odyssey of Albert O. Hirschman* (Princeton, NJ: Princeton University Press, 2014).

Ageron, Charles-Robert, *Les Algériens musulmans et la France, (1871–1919)* (Paris: PUF, 1968).

Ageron, Charles-Robert, *France coloniale ou parti colonial* (Paris: PUF, 1978).

Ageron, Charles-Robert, ed., *De l'Algérie française à l'Algérie algérienne* (Saint-Denis: Bouchène, 2005).

Agulhon, Maurice, *1848 ou l'apprentissage de la République (1848–1852)* (Paris: Seuil, 1992).

Akelev, Evgenii and Andrey Gornostaev, "Millions of Living Deaths: Fugitives, the Polish Border and Eighteenth Century Russian Society," *Kritika*, 24, 2 (2023): 269–297.

Ali, Shanti Sadiq, *The African Dispersal in the Deccan* (New Delhi: Orient Black Swan, 1996).

Allen, Frederick, "On the Fixed Nature of Sharecropping Contracts," *The Economic Journal*, 95 (1985): 30–48.

Allen, Richard, *Slaves, Freedmen, and Indentured Laborers in Colonial Mauritius* (New York: Cambridge University Press, 1999).

Allen, Richard, "A Serious and Alarming Daily Evil: Marronage and Its Legacy in Mauritius and the Plantation Colonial World," *Slavery and Abolition*, 25, 2 (2004): 1–17.
Allen, Richard, "Suppressing a Nefarious Traffic: Britain and the Abolition of Slave-Trading in India and the Western Indian Ocean, 1770–1830," *William and Mary Quarterly*, 66, 4 (2009): 873–894.
Allen, Richard, "Satisfying the Want for Laboring People: European Slave Trading in the Indian Ocean, 1500–1850," *Journal of World History*, 21, 1 (2010): 45–73.
Allen, Richard, *European Slave Trade in the Indian Ocean, 1500–1850* (Athens: Ohio University Press, 2015).
Allen, Richard, "Ending the History of Silence: Reconstructing European Slave Trading in the Indian Ocean," *Tempo*, 23, 2 (2017): 295–313.
Allen, Robert, *Enclosure and the Yeoman* (Oxford: Clarendon Press, 1992).
Allen, Robert, "Agriculture during the Industrial Revolution," in D. McCloskey and R. Floud, eds., *The Economic History of Britain since 1700*, vol. 1 (Cambridge: Cambridge University Press, 1994): 96–122.
Allen, Robert, "Tracking the Agricultural Revolution in England," *Economic History Review*, LII, 2 (1999): 209–235.
Allen, Robert, *Farm to Factory: A Reinterpretation of the Soviet Industrial Revolution* (Princeton, NJ: Princeton University Press, 2003).
Allen, Robert, "Pessimism Preserved: Real Wages in the British Industrial Revolution" *Oxford University Department of Economics Working Paper* 314, 2007.
Allen, Robert, *The British Industrial Revolution in Global Perspective* (Cambridge: Cambridge University Press, 2009).
Allen, Robert, *The British Industrial Revolution in Global Perspective* (Oxford: Oxford University Press, 2009).
Allen, Robert, "The High Wage Economy and the Industrial Revolution: A Restatement," *Economic History Review*, 68, 1 (2015): 1–22.
Allen, Robert and J. L. Weisdorf, "Was There an Industrious Revolution before the Industrial Revolution? An Empirical Exercise for England, 1300–1830," *Economic History Review*, 64, 3 (2011): 715–729.
Allen, Robert, Jean-Pascal Bassino, Debin Ma, Christine Moll-Murata and Jan Luiten van Zanden, "Wages, Prices, and Living Standards in China, Japan, and Europe, 1738–1925," *Economic History Review*, 64, 1 (2011): 8–38.
Alpers, Edward, "The French Slave Trade in East Africa 1721–1810," *Cahiers d'études africaines*, 10, 37 (1970): 80–124.
Alpers, Edward, *Ivory and Slaves in East Central Africa: Changing Patterns of International Trade to the Later Nineteenth Century* (Berkeley: University of California Press, 1975).
Alston, Lee and Joseph Ferrie, *Southern Paternalism and the American Welfare State: Economics, Politics, and Institutions in the South, 1865–1965* (Cambridge: Cambridge University Press, 1999).

Alston, Lee and Kyle D. Kaffman, "Competition and the Compensation of Sharecroppers by Race: A View from Plantations in the Early Twentieth Century," *Explorations in Economic History*, 38, 1 (2001): 181–194.

Amussen, Susan, *An Ordered Society: Gender and Class in Early Modern England* (Oxford: Blackwell, 1988).

Anand, Ram, *Origins and Development of the Law of the Sea* (The Hague: Martin Nijhoff, 1983).

Anderson, B. L., and David Richardson, "Market Structures and the Profits of the British African Trade in the Late Eighteenth Century. A Comment," *Journal of Economic History*, 43, 3 (1983): 713–721.

Anderson, B. L., and David Richardson, "Market Structures and the Profits of the British African Trade in the Late Eighteenth Century. A Rejoinder Rebutted," *Journal of Economic History*, 45 (1985): 705–707.

Anderson, Clare, *Legible Bodies: Race, Criminality and Colonialism in South Asia* (Oxford: Berg Publishers, 2004).

Anderson, Clare, *Subaltern Lives: Biographies of Colonialism in the Indian Ocean World, 1790–1920* (Cambridge: Cambridge University Press, 2012).

Anderson, Matthew Smith, "The Great Powers and the Russian Annexation of the Crimea, 1783–4," *The Slavonic and East European Review*, 37, 88 (1958): 17–41.

Anderson, Michael, "India 1858–1930: The Illusion of Free Labor," in Douglas Hay and Paul Craven, eds., *Masters, Servants, and Magistrates in Britain and the Empire, 1562–1955* (Chapel Hill: The University of North Carolina Press, 2004): 422–454.

Anderson, Terry and Robert Thomas, "The Growth of Population and Labor Force in the Seventeenth-Century Chesapeake," *Explorations in Economic History*, 15, 3 (1978): 209–312.

Andersson, Fredrik and Jonas Ljungberg, "Grain Market Integration in the Baltic Sea Region in the Nineteenth Century," *The Journal of Economic History*, 75, 3 (2015): 749–790.

Anisimov, Evgenii V., *Podatnaia reforma Petra I: vvedenie podushnoi podati v Rossii 1719–1728 gg* (Tax reform under Pierre I: the introduction of per capita taxation in Russia, 1719–1728), (Moscow: Nauka, 1982).

Anisimov, Evgenii V., "Remarks on the Fiscal Policy of Russian Absolutism during the First Quarter of the Eighteenth Century," *Soviet Studies in History*, 28, 1 (1989): 10–32.

Anstey, Roger, "Capitalism and Slavery: A Critique," *Economic History Review*, 21 (1968): 307–320.

Anstey, Roger, *The Atlantic Slave Trade and British Abolition* (London: Macmillan, 1975).

Ardeleanu, Constantin, "Russian British Rivalry Regarding Danube Navigation and the Origins of the Crimean War (1846–1853)," *Journal of Mediterranean Studies*, XIX, 2 (2010): 165–186.

Ardeleanu, Constantin, "The Opening and Development of the Black Sea for International Trade and Shipping, 1774–1853," *Euxeinos*, 14 (2014): 30–52.

Armitage, David, *The Ideological Origins of the British Empire* (Cambridge: Cambridge University Press, 2010).
Armitage, David and Sanjay Subrahamanyam, *The Age of Revolution in Global Context* (New York: Palgrave, 2010).
Armstrong Clegg, Hugh, Alan Fox and A. Thompson, *A History of British Trade Unions since 1889*, vol. 1 (Oxford: Clarendon Press, 1964).
Arrow, Kenneth, Henri Chenery, B. Minhas and Robert Solow, "Capital-labor Substitution and Economic Efficiency," *Review of Economics and Statistics*, 43, 1 (1961): 225–250.
Aston, Trevor and Charles Philpin, eds., *The Brenner Debate: Agrarian Class Structure and Economic Development in Pre-industrial Europe* (Cambridge: Cambridge University Press, 1985).
Atkinson, Alan, "The Free-Born Englishman Transported: Convict Rights as a Measure of Eighteenth-Century Empire," *Past and Present*, 144, 1 (1994): 88–115.
Atman, Artur, "The Russian Market in World Trade, 1500–1860," *Scandinavian Economic History Review*, 29, 3 (1981): 177–202.
Aufhauser, Keith, "The Profitability of Slavery in the British Caribbean," *Journal of Interdisciplinary History*, 5, 1 (1974): 45–46.
Austen, Ralph, "The Trans-Saharan Slave Trade: A Tentative Census," in Jan S. Hogendorn, ed., *The Uncommon Market: Essays in the Economic History of the Atlantic Slave Trade* (New York: Academic Press, 1979): 23–76.
Austen, Ralph, *African Economic History* (London: Heinemann, 1987).
Austen, Ralph, "The Nineteenth Century Islamic Slave Trade from East Africa (Swahili and Red Sea Coasts): A Tentative Census," *Slavery and Abolition*, 9 (1988): 21–44.
Austen, Ralph, "The Nineteenth Century Islamic Slave Trade from East Africa (Swahili and Red Sea Coasts): A Tentative Census," in William Gervase Clarence-Smith, ed., *The Economics of the Indian Ocean Slave Trade* (London: Frank Cass, 1989): 21–44.
Austin, Gareth, *Labour, Land, and Capital in Ghana: From Slavery to Free Labour in Asante, 1807–1956* (Woodbridge: Boydell & Brewer, 2005).
Austin, Gareth, "Reciprocal Comparison and African History: Tackling Conceptual Eurocentrism in the Study of Africa's Economic Past," *African Studies Review*, 50, 3 (2007): 1–28.
Austin, Gareth, "Factor Markets in Nieboer Conditions: Pre-Colonial West Africa, c.1500–c.1900," *Continuity and Change*, 24, 1 (2009): 23–53.
Austin, Gareth, "Slavery in Africa, 1804–1936," in David Eltis, Stanley Engerman, Seymour Drescher and David Richardson, eds., *The Cambridge World History of Slavery: Vol. 4 AD 1804–AD 2016* (Cambridge: Cambridge University Press, 2017): 174–196.
Austin, Gareth and Kaoru Sugihara, eds., *Labour-Intensive Industrialization in Global History* (London: Routledge, 2012).
Avrutin, Eugene and Stephen Norris, eds., *Racism in Russia: From the Romanovs to Putin* (London: Bloomsbury, 2022).

Bairoch, Paul, "L'économie française dans le contexte européen à la fin du XVIIIe siècle," *Revue économique*, 40, 6 (1989): 939-964.
Bairoch, Paul, *Economics and World History: Myths and Paradoxes* (Chicago: University of Chicago Press, 1993).
Baker, Bruce and Brian Kelly, eds., *After Slavery: Race, Labor, and Citizenship in the Reconstruction South* (Gainesville: University Press of Florida, 2013).
Ball, Erica, Tatiana Seijas and Terri L. Snyder, eds., *As If She Were Free: A Collective Biography of Women and Emancipation in the Americas* (Cambridge: Cambridge University Press, 2020).
Banerjee, Samanta, *Dangerous Outcast: The Prostitute in Nineteenth Century Bengal* (Calcutta: Seagull Books, 1998).
Baptist, Edward, *The Half Has Never Been Told: Slavery and the Making of American Capitalism* (New York: Basic Books, 2014).
Barcia, Manuel, *Seeds of Insurrection: Domination and Resistance on Western Cuban Plantations, 1808-1848* (Baton Rouge: Louisiana State University Press, 2008).
Bardhan, Pranab, *The Political Economy of Development in India* (New Delhi: Oxford University Press, 1984).
Barjot, Dominic, Olivier Dard, J. Garrigues, D. Musiedlak and É. Anceau, eds., *Industrie et politique en Europe occidentale et aux États-Unis (XIXe et XXe siècle)* (Paris: Presses Universitaires de la Sorbonne, 2006).
Barnsby, George, *Social Conditions in the Black Country* (Wolverhampton: Integrated Publishing Service, 1980).
Baron, Ava, "Masculinity, the Embodied Male Worker, and the Historian's Gaze," *International Labor and Working Class History*, 69, spring (2006): 143-160.
Barrett, Thomas, "Lines of Uncertainty: The Frontier of the North Caucasus," *Slavic Review*, 54, 3 (1995): 578-601.
Barrett, Thomas, *At the Edge of Empire: The Terek Cossacks and the North Caucasus Frontier, 1700-1860* (Boulder, CO: Westview Press, 1999).
Barreyre, Nicolas, *Gold and Freedom: A Spatial History of the United States after the Civil War* (Charlottesville: University of North Carolina Press, 2015).
Barry, Boubacar, *La Sénégambie du XVe au XIXe siècle; traite négrière, Islam, conquête coloniale* (Paris: L'Harmattan, 1988).
Bartlett, Roger, "Serfdom and State Power in Imperial Russia," *European History Quarterly*, 33, 1 (2003): 29-64.
Bassin, Mark, "Inventing Siberia: Visions of the Russian East in the Early Nineteenth Century," *American Historical Review*, 96, 3 (1991): 763-794.
Battisti, Michèle, ed., *La piraterie au fil de l'histoire, un défi pour l'État* (Paris: Presses de la Sorbonne, 2014).
Baudeau, Abbé, "De l'éducation nationale," *Éphémérides du citoyen*, 2, 11 (1767): 165-185.
Baum, Robert Martin, *Shrines of the Slave Trade: Diola Religion and Society in Precolonial Senegambia* (New York: Oxford University Press, 1999).
Bayly, Christopher, *The Imperial Meridian* (London: Longman, Pearson Education, 1989).

Bayly, Christopher, *The Birth of the Modern World, 1780–1914* (London: Blackwell, 2004).
Beaulieu, Alain, "L'empire colonial français et les nations amérindiennes," in Serge Joyal and Paul-André Linteau, eds., *France-Canada-Quebec* (Montréal: Presses de l'Université de Montréal): 17–38.
Beauvois, Daniel, *La bataille de la terre en Ukraine* (Lille: Presses Universitaires de Lille, 1993).
Beckels, Hilary, *White Servitude and Black Slavery in Barbados, 1627–1715* (Knoxville: University of Tennessee Press, 1989).
Becker, Seymour, *Russia's Protectorate in Central Asia, Bukhara and Khiva, 1865–1924* (London: Routledge, 2004).
Beckert, Sven, "Emancipation and Empire: Reconstructing the Worldwide Web of Cotton Production in the Age of the American Civil War," *The American Historical Review*, 109, 5 (2004): 1405–1438.
Beckert, Sven, *Empire of Cotton* (New York: Knopf, 2014).
Beckert, Sven and Seth Rockman, eds., *Slavery's Capitalism: A New History of American Economic Development* (Philadelphia: University of Pennsylvania Press, 2016).
Beckles, Hilary McD, *Natural Rebels: A Social History of Enslaved Black Women in Barbados* (New Brunswick, NJ: Rutgers University Press, 1989).
Bédard, Éric and Julien Goyette, eds., *Parole d'historiens. Anthologie des réflexions sur l'histoire au Québec* (Montréal: Les Presses de l'Université de Montréal, 2006).
Bennett, J. Harry, *Bondsmen and Bishops, Slavery and Apprenticeship on the Codrington Plantation of Barbados, 1710–1838* (Berkeley: University of California Press, 1958).
Benot, Yves, *La révolution française et la fin des colonies* (Paris: La Découverte, 2004).
Benot, Yves and Marcel Dorigny, eds., *Rétablissement de l'esclavage dans les colonies françaises* (Paris: Maisonnove et Larose, 2003).
Bentham, Jeremy, *The Works of Jeremy Bentham*, 11 volumes, John Bowring, ed. (Edinburgh: William Tait, 1838–1843).
Bentley, Gilbert, *The Evolution of National Insurance in Great Britain: The Origins of the Welfare State* (London: Joseph, 1966).
Benton, Lauren, *Law and Colonial Cultures* (Cambridge: Cambridge University Press, 2002).
Berg, Maxine and Pat Hudson, *Slavery, Capitalism, and the Industrial Revolution* (Cambridge: Polity Press, 2023).
Berg, Maxine, Felicia Gottman, Hanna Hodacs and Chris Nierstrasz, eds., *Goods from the East, 1600–1800: Trading Eurasia* (Basingstoke: Palgrave, 2015).
Berlin, Ira and Philip Morgan, eds., *Cultivation and Culture: Labor and the Shaping of Slave Life in the Americas* (Charlottesville: University Press of Virginia, 1993).
Bessière, Arnaud, "Les domestiques canadiens, ces oublié(s) de l'histoire de la Nouvelle France," *Canadian Studies*, 82 (2017): 27–45.

Bessner, Baron de "De l'esclavage des nègres," *Archives Nationales FM C/14/42.*
Betts, Raymond, *Assimilation and Association in French Colonial Theory, 1890–1914* (New York: Columbia University Press, 1961).
Bhattacharya Sabyasachi, ed., *Towards a New History of Work* (Delhi: Tulika Book, 2014).
Bidet Jacques and Jacques Textier, eds., *La crise du travail* (Paris: PUF, 1995).
Biernacki, Richard, *The Fabrication of Labor* (Berkeley: University of California Press, 1995).
Billings, Warren, ed., *The Old Dominion in the Seventeenth Century: A Documentary History of Virginia, 1606–1689* (Chapel Hill: University of North Carolina Press, 1975).
Bitis, Alexander and Janet Hartley, "The Russian Military Colonies in 1826," *The Slavonic and East European Review*, 78, 2 (2000): 323–330.
Black, Jeremy, *A Military Revolution? Military Change and European Society, 1550–1800* (Basingstoke, UK: Macmillan, 1991).
Blackburn, Robin, *The Overthrow of Colonial Slavery, 1776–1848* (London: Verso, 1988).
Blackburn, Robin, *The Making of New World Slavery* (London: Verso, 1997).
Blackstone, William, *Commentaries on the Laws of England*, 4 volumes (London: Strahan, Woodfall 1793–1795; new edition: Chicago: University of Chicago Press, 1979).
Blais, Hélène, *Mirages de la carte. L'invention de l'Algérie coloniale* (Paris: Fayard, 2014).
Blakemore, Richard, "The Politics of Piracy in the British Atlantic, 1640–1649," *International Journal of Maritime History*, 25, 2 (2013): 159–172.
Blanchard, Ian, "Le développement économique en perspective historique: l'avenir de la Russie à la lumière de son évolution à l'époque moderne (1700–1914)," in Michèle Merger and Dominique Barjot, eds., *Les enterprises et leurs réseaux: hommes, capitaux, techniques et pouvoirs xixe-xxe siècles. Mèlanges en l'honneur de François Caron* (Paris: Presse de l'Université de Paris-Sorbonne, 1998): 381–392.
Blassingame, John ed., *Slave Testimony: Two Centuries of Letters, Speeches, Interviews, and Autobiographies* (Baton Rouge: Louisiana State University, 1977).
Blum, Alain and Irina Troitskaia, "La mortalité en Russie au XVIIIe et XIXe siècles. Estimations locales à partir des Revizii," *Population*, 51 (1996): 303–328.
Blum, Jerome, *Lord and Peasant in Russia from the Ninth through the Nineteenth Century* (New York: Atheneum, 1964).
Bodenhorn, Howard, *A History of Banking in Antebellum America: Financial Markets and Economic Development in an Era of Nation-Building* (Cambridge: Cambridge University Press, 2000).
Bogdanov, Leonid, *Voennye poseleniia v Rossii* (Military colonies in Russia) (Moscow: Nauka, 1992).
Bokarev, Iurii, *Ekonomicheskie posledstviia raspada rossiiskoi imperii v rezul'tate pervoi mirovoi voiny* (The economic consequences of the collapse of the Russian empire because of WWI) (Ekaterinburg and Moscow: UMTs UPI, 2009).

Bolland, Nigel, "Systems of Domination after Slavery: The Control of Land and Labor in the British West Indies after 1838," *Comparative Studies in Society and History*, 23, 4 (1981): 591–619.

Bompard, Jean-Pierre, Thierry Magnac and Gilles Postel-Vinay, "Migrations saisonnières de main-d'oeuvre: Le cas de la France en 1860," *Annales d'Économie et de Statistique*, 19 (1990): 97–129.

Bonnassie, Pierre, *From Slavery to Feudalism* (Cambridge: Cambridge University Press, 1991).

Bontouri, Lina, *Archives in the Digital Age: Standards, Policies and Tools* (Cambridge: Chandos Publishing, 2017).

Boritt, Gabor S., ed., *Why the Civil War Came* (Oxford: Oxford University Press, 1996).

Borritt, Gabor S. and Scott Hancock, eds., *Slavery, Resistance, Freedom* (Oxford: Oxford University Press, 2007).

Borodkin, Leonid, Brigitte Granville and Carol Scott Leonard, "The Rural/Urban Wage Gap in the Industrialisation of Russia, 1884–1910," *European Review of Economic History*, 12, 1 (2008): 67–95.

Bose, Sugata, *Peasant Labour and Colonial Capital: Rural Bengal since 1770* (Cambridge: Cambridge University Press, 1993).

Bose, Sugata, *A Hundred Horizons* (Cambridge, MA: Harvard University Press, 2006).

Bosma, Ulbe, "Towards an Indian Ocean and Maritime Asia Slave Database: An Exploration of Concepts, Lessons, and Models," *Esclavages et post esclavages*, 3 (2020), https://doi.org/10.4000/slaveries.2946.

Bosma, Ulbe, *The World of Sugar* (Cambridge, MA: Belknap Press, 2023).

Bosma, Ulbe, Juan Giusti-Cordero and Roger Knights, eds., *Sugarland Revisited, Sugar Colonialism in Asia and the Americas, 1800–1940* (New York: Berghahn, 2007).

Bouche, Denise, *Les villages de liberté en Afrique noire française, 1887–1910* (The Hague: Mouton, 1968).

Bouchet, Thomas, *Un jeudi à l'Assemblée. Politique du discours et droit au travail dans la France de 1848* (Québec: Editions Nota bene, 2007).

Boutiller, Jean-Louis, "Les captifs en AOF (1903–1905)," *Bulletin de l'IFAN*, 30, série B, 2 (1968): 520.

Bradley, Keith, Paul Cartledge and David Eltis, eds., *The Cambridge World History of Slavery*, 4 volumes (Cambridge: Cambridge University Press, 2011–2021).

Brass, Tom and Marcel van der Linden, eds., *Free and Unfree Labor: The Debate Continues* (Berne: Peter Lang, 1997).

Braudel, Fernand, *Civilisation matérielle, économie et capitalisme* (Paris: Colin, 1978).

Bréard Charles, ed., *Journal du corsaire Jean Doublet, de Honfleur* (Paris: Perrin, 1887): 33–37.

Breman, Jan, *Labour Bondage in West India* (Oxford: Oxford University Press, 2007).

Breman Jan, Isabelle Guerin, and Aseem Prakash eds., *India's Unfree Workforce: Of Bondage Old and New* (New Delhi: Oxford University Press, 2009).

Brenner, Robert, "Agrarian Class Structure and Economic Development in Pre-industrial Europe," *Past and Present*, 70, 1 (1976): 30–74.
Brenner, Robert, *Merchants and Revolution: Commercial Change, Political Conflicts and London's Oversea Traders, 1550–1653* (London: Verso, 1983).
Brickell Bellows, Amanda, *American Slavery and Russian Serfdom in Post-Emancipation Imagination* (Chapel Hill: University of North Carolina Press, 2020).
Broadberry Stephen and Bishnupriya Gupta, "The Early Modern Great Divergence: Wages, Prices and Economic Development in Europe and Asia, 1500–1800," *Economic History Review*, 59, 1 (2006): 2–31.
Broadberry, Stephen, Bruce Campbell, Alexander Klein, Mark Overton and Bas van Leeuwen, *British Economic Growth, 1270–1870* (Cambridge: Cambridge University Press, 2015).
Brooks, Jeffrey, *When Russia Learned to Read* (Princeton, NJ: Princeton University Press, 1985).
Brophy, Alfred, "Slaves as Plaintiffs," *Michigan Law Review*, 115, 6 (2017): 895–914.
Brower, Daniel, *The Russian City between Tradition and Modernity, 1850–1900* (Berkeley: University of California Press, 1990).
Brower, Daniel and Susan Leyton, "Liberation through Captivity: Nikolai Shipov's Adventures in The Imperial Borderlands," *Kritika*, 6, 2 (2005): 259–279.
Brown, William Well, *Narrative of William W. Brown: An American Slave* (London: Charles Gilpin, 1949).
Brunschwig, Henri, *Noirs et blancs dans l'Afrique noire française ou comment le colonisé devient colonisateur (1870–1914)* (Paris: Flammarion, 1983).
Buchanan, Francis, *A Journey from Madras through the Countries of Mysore, Canara and Malabar* (London: Cadell and Davies, 1807).
Buggle, Johannes and Steven Nafzinger, "The Slow Road from Serfdom: Labor Coercion and Long-Run Development in the Former Russian Empire," *Bofit (Bank of Finland) Discussion Paper*, 22, 2018.
Burbank, Jane, *Russian Peasants Go to Court: Legal Culture in the Countryside, 1905–1917* (Bloomington: Indiana University Press, 2004).
Burbank, Jane and Frederick Cooper, *Empires: A World History* (Princeton, NJ: Princeton University, 2010).
Burds, Jeffrey, "The Social Control of Peasant Labor in Russia: The Response of Village Communities to Labor Migration in the Central Industrial Region, 1861–1905," in Esther Kingston-Mann and Timothy Mixter, eds., *Peasant Economy, Culture, and Politics of European Russia, 1800–1921* (Princeton: Princeton University Press, 1991): 52–100.
Burds, Jeffrey, *Peasant Dreams and Market Politics: Labor Migration and the Russian Village, 1861–1905* (Pittsburgh: University of Pittsburgh Press, 1998).
Buret, Eugène, *De la misère des classes laborieuses en France et en Angleterre* (Paris: Paulin, 1840).
Burke, Edmund, *The Works of the Right Honourable Edmunde Burke* (London: Bell, 1889).
Burnard, Trevor, *Writing the History of Global Empire* (Cambridge: Cambridge University Press, 2023).

Burnard, Trevor and John Garrigus, eds., *The Plantation Machine* (Philadelphia: University of Pennsylvania Press, 2016).
Burnard, Trevor and Giorgio Riello, "Slavery and the New History of Capitalism," *The Journal of Global History*, 15, 2 (2020): 225–244.
Bush, Barbara, *Slave Women in Caribbean Society 1650–1838* (Bloomington: Indiana University Press, 1990).
Bush, Michael, ed., *Serfdom and Slavery* (New York; London: Longman, 1996).
Bushkovitch, Paul, "Taxation, Tax Farming and Merchants in Sixteenth-Century Russia," *Slavic Review*, 37, 3 (1978): 381–398.
Butel, Paul, *Les négociants bordelais, l'Europe et les îles au XVIIIe siècle* (Paris: Aubier, 1974).
Butel, Paul, *L'économie française au XVIIIe siècle* (Paris: Sedes, 1993).
Buti, Gilbert and Philippe Hrodej, *Histoire des pirates et des corsairs. De l'antiquité à nos jours* (Paris: CNRS éditions, 2016).
Buttino, Marco, *Samarcanda* (Roma: Viella, 2015).
Cairns, John, "Blackstone in the Bayous: Inscribing Slavery in the Louisiana Digest of 1808," in Wilf Prest, ed., *Re-Interpreting Blackstone's Commentaries: A Seminal Text in National and International Contexts* (Oxford: Hart Publishing, 2014): 105–124.
Campbell, Gwyn, ed., *The Structure of Slavery in Indian Ocean Africa and Asia* (London: Frank Cass, 2004).
Campbell, Gwyn, ed., *Abolition and Its Aftermath in Indian Ocean Africa and Asia* (London: Routledge, 2005).
Campbell, Gwyn, *An Economic History of Imperial Madagascar, 1750–1895: The Rise and Fall of an Island Empire* (Cambridge: Cambridge University Press, 2005).
Campbell, Gwyn and Alessandro Stanziani, eds., *Bonded Labour and Debt in the Indian Ocean World* (London: Pickering & Chatto, 2013).
Campbell, Gwyn and Alessandro Stanziani, eds., *Debt and Slavery in the Ancient and Mediterranean Worlds* (London: Pickering & Chatto, 2013).
Campbell, Gwyn and Alessandro Stanziani, eds., *Debt and Slavery in the Indian Ocean World* (London: Pickering & Chatto, 2013).
Campbell, Gwyn, Suzanne Miers and Joseph C. Miller, eds., *Women and Slavery* (Athens: Ohio University Press, 2008).
Campbell, Mavis, *The Maroons of Jamaica 1655–1796* (Trenton: African World Press, 1990).
Canny, Nichols, ed., *The Origin of Empire: British Overseas Enterprise to the Close of the Seventeenth Century. Oxford History of the British Empire*, vol. 1 (Oxford: Oxford University Press, 1998):
Carbado, Devon and Donald Weise, *The Long Walk to Freedom: Runaway Slaves Narratives* (Boston: Beacon Press, 2012).
Carlyle, Thomas, *Occasional Discourse on the Negro Question* (first published in Fraser's Magazine for Town and Country, 1849 vol. XL, 1849, then London, 1853).
Caron, François, *Histoire économique de la France XIXe-XXe siècle* (Paris: A. Colin, 1996).

Carotenuto, Audrey, *Les résistances serviles dans la société coloniale de l'ile Bourbon, 1750-1848* (PhD thesis, Aix-Marseille, 2006).
Carr, Lois and Lorena Walsh, "The Planter's Wife: The Experience of White Women in Seventeenth-Century Maryland," *William and Mary Quarterly*, 34, 4 (1977): 542–571.
Carrey, Émile, *Recueil complet des actes du Gouvernement provisoire (février, mars, avril, mai 1848)* (Paris: A. Durand, 1848).
Carrez, Jean-Pierre, *Femmes opprimées à la Salpêtrière de Paris (1656–1791)* (Paris: Éditions Connaissances et Savoirs, 2005).
Carter, Marina, "Indian Slaves in Mauritius (1729–1834)," *Indian Historical Review*, 15, 1–2 (1988–1989): 233–247.
Carter, Marina *Servants, Sirdars and Settlers: Indians in Mauritius, 1834–1874* (Delhi: Oxford University Press, 1995).
Castel, Robert, *Les métamorphoses de la question sociale* (Paris: Fayard, 1995).
Catterall, Helene T. ed., *Judicial Cases Concerning American Slavery and the Negro*, 5 volumes (Washington: Carnegie Institution, 1926–37).
Chakraborty, Titos and Matthias von Rossum, "Slave Trade and Slavery in Asia: New Perspectives," *Journal of Social History*, 54, 1 (2020): 1–14.
Chamberlain, Muriel Evelyn, *The Scramble for Africa* (London: Routledge, 2010).
Chanok, Martin, *Law Custom and Social Order: The Colonial Experience in Malawi and Zambia* (Cambridge: Cambridge University Press, 1985).
Charter, Kathy, "Black People in England, 1660–1807," in Stephen Farrell, Melanie Unwin, and James Walvin, eds., *The British Slave Trade: Abolition, Parliament and People* (Edinburgh: Edinburgh University Press, 2007): 66–83.
Chase, Malcom, *Chartism: A New History* (Manchester: Manchester University Press, 2007).
Chatterjee, Indrani, *Gender, Slavery, and Law in Colonial India* (New Delhi: Oxford University Press, 1999).
Chatterjee, Indrani and Richard Eaton, eds., *Slavery and South Asian History* (Bloomington: Indiana University Press, 2006).
Chaudhuri, Kirti N. *The Trading World of India and the English East India Company, 1660–1760* (Cambridge: Cambridge University Press, 1978).
Cheney, Paul, *Cul de Sac* (Chicago: University of Chicago Press, 2017).
Chevaleyre, Claude, "Acting as Master and Bondservant. Considerations on Status, Identities, and the Nature of 'Bondservitude' in Late Ming China," in Alessandro Stanziani, ed., *Labour, Coercion and Economic Growth in Eurasia, 17th–20th Centuries* (Leiden: Brill, 2013): 237–272.
Chevaleyre, Claude, "Insiders by Analogy: Slaves in the Great Ming Code," *Slavery and Abolition*, 43, 3 (2022): 460–481.
Chicherin, Boris, *Sobstvennost' i gosudarstvo* (Property and the state), 2 volumes (Moscow, 1882–83; new edition, Saint Petersburg: Izdatel'stvo Russkoi Khristianskoi gumanitarnoi akademii, 2005).
Chowdhury, Benoy, *Growth of Commercial Agriculture in Bengal, 1757–1900* (Calcutta: R K Mitra, 1964).

Clapp, Elizabeth and Julie Roy Jeffrey, eds., *Women, Dissent and Anti-Slavery in Britain and America, 1790–1865* (New York: Oxford University Press, 2011).
Clarence-Smith, William Gervase, "Runaway Slaves and Social Bandits in Southern Angola, 1875–1913," *Slavery and Abolition*, 6, 3 (1985): 23–33.
Clarence-Smith, William Gervase, ed., *The Economics of the Indian Ocean Slave Trade* (London: Frank Cass, 1989).
Clark, Gregory, "Productivity Growth without Technical Change in European Agriculture before 1850," *The Journal of Economic History*, 47, 2 (June 1987): 419–432.
Clark, Gregory, "Agriculture and the Industrial Revolution,1750–1850," in Joel Mokyr, ed., *The British Industrial Revolution: An Economic Perspective* (Boulder: Westview Press, 1993): 227–266.
Clark, Gregory, "Commons Sense: Common Property Rights, Efficiency, and Institutional Change," *Journal of Economic History*, 58, 1 (1998): 73–102.
Clark, Gregory, "Farm Wages and Living Standards in the Industrial Revolution: England, 1670–1869," *Economic History Review*, 54, 3 (2001): 477–505.
Clark, Gregory, "The Agricultural Revolution and the Industrial Revolution" (University of Davis, Faculty of Economics, Working paper, 2002): https://faculty.econ.ucdavis.edu/faculty/gclark/papers/prod2002.pdf.
Clark, Gregory, "The Long March of History: Farm Wages, Population, and Economic Growth, England 1209–1869', *Economic History Review*, 60, 1 (2007): 97–135.
Clark, Gregory, Kevin H. O'Rourke and Alan M. Taylor, "Made in America? The New World, the Old, and the Industrial Revolution," *American Economic Review*, 98, 2 (2008): 523–528.
Coates, Timothy, *Convicts and Orphans, Forced and State-Sponsored Colonizers in the Portuguese Empire, 1550–1755* (Stanford: Stanford University Press, 2001).
Cobden, John, *The White Slaves of England: Compiled from Official Documents* (New York: Saxton, 1860).
Cogneau, Denis, *L'Afrique des inégalités. Où conduit l'histoire* (Paris: Éditions de la rue d'Ulm, 2006).
Cogneau, Denis, "Histoire économique de l'Afrique: renaissance ou trompe l'oeil?," *Annales HSS*, 71, 4 (2016): 879–896.
Cogneau, Denis, *Un empire bon marché. Histoire et économie politique de la colonisation française, XIXe–XXIe siècle* (Paris: Seuil, 2024).
Cogneau, Denis, Yannick Dupraz and Sandrine Mesplé-Somps, "Fiscal Capacity and Dualism in Colonial States: The French Empire 1830–1962," *The Journal of Economic History*, 81, 2 (2021): 441–480.
Cohen, William, *At Freedom's Edge: Black Mobility and the Southern White Quest for Racial Control, 1861–1915* (Baton Rouge: Louisiana State University Press, 1991).
Colas, Alejandro and Bryan Mabee, eds., *Mercenaries, Pirates, Bandits and Empires: Private Violence in Historical Context* (London: Hurst, 2011).

Colley, Linda, *Britons: Forging the Nation 1707-1837* (New Haven: Yale University Press, 1992).
Colley, Linda, "What Is Imperial History?," in David Cannadine, ed., *What Is History Now?* (London: Palgrave Macmillan, 2002): 132-147.
Colley, Linda, *Captives: Britain, Empire, and the World, c.a. 1600-1850* (New York: Anchor, 2004).
Collins, E. J. T. "Migrant Labor in British Agriculture in the Nineteenth Century," *Economic History Review*, 29, 1 (1976): 38-59.
Commons, John, *Legal Foundations of Capitalism* (London: Macmillan, 1924, new edition New Brunswick and London: Transaction Publishers, 1995).
Conchon, Anne, *La corvée des grands chemins au XVIIIe siècle* (Rennes: PUR, 2016).
Condorcet, Nicolas (under the name of Schwartz), *Réflexions sur l'esclavage des nègres* (Neufchâtel: Société typographique, 1781).
Conermann, Stephan and Gül Sen eds., *Slave and Slave Agency in the Ottoman Empire* (Bonne: V. and R. University Press, 2019).
Confino, Michael, "Servage russe, esclavage américain," *Annales ESC*, 45, 5 (1990): 1119-1141.
Conklin, Alice, *A Mission to Civilize* (Stanford: Stanford University Press, 1996).
Conrad, Alfred H. and John R. Meyer, "The Economics of Slavery in the Antebellum South," *The Journal of Political Economy*, 66, 2 (1958): 95-130.
Conrad, Robert, *The Destruction of Brazilian Slavery, 1850-1888* (Berkeley: University of California Press, 1972).
Conrad, Sebastian, *What Is Global History?* (Princeton: Princeton University Press, 2016).
Cooper, Frederick, *From Slaves to Squatters: Plantation Labor and Agriculture in Zanzibar and Coastal Kenya, 1890-1935* (New Haven and London: Yale University Press, 1980).
Cooper, Frederick, "From Free Labor to Family Allowances: Labor and African Society in Colonial Discourse," *American Ethnologist*, 16, 4 (1989): 745-765.
Cooper, Frederick, *Decolonization and African Society* (Cambridge: Cambridge University Press, 1996).
Cooper, Thomas, *Supplement to Mr Cooper's Letters on the Slave Trade* (Manchester: Wheeler, 1787).
Coornaert, Emile, *Les corporations en France* (Paris: Gallimard, 1941).
Coquery-Vidrovitch, Catherine, *Le Congo au temps des grandes compagnies concessionnaires* (Paris: EHESS, 2001).
Cordell, Dennis D. and Joel W. Gregory, eds., *African Population and Capitalism: Historical Perspectives* (Boulder: Westview Press, 1987).
Cottereau, Alain, "Les prud'hommes au xixe siècle: une expérience originale de pratique du droit," *Justices. Revue de droit processuel*, 8 (1997): 9-21.
Cottereau, Alain, "Droit et bon droit. Un droit des ouvriers instauré, puis évincé par le droit du travail, France, XIXe siècle," *Annales*, 57, 6 (2002): 1521-1557.
Cottias, Myriam, "Droit, justice et dépendance dans les Antilles françaises, 1848-1852," *Annales HSS*, 59, 3 (2004): 547-567.

Crafts, Nicolas, "Industrial Revolution in England and France: Some Thoughts on the Question: "Why Was England First?" *The Economic History Review*, 30, 3 (1977): 429–441.
Crafts, Nicolas, *British Economy during the Industrial Revolution* (Oxford: Clarendon Press, 1985).
Crafts, Nicholas, "Understanding Productivity Growth in the Industrial Revolution," *Economic History Review*, 74, 2 (2021): 309–338.
Craton, Michael, *Testing the Chains: Resistance to Slavery in the British West Indies* (Ithaca: Cornell University Press, 1982).
Craton, Michael and James Walvin, *A Jamaican Plantation: The History of Worthy Park, 1670–1970* (Toronto: University of Toronto Press, 1970).
Craven, Paul and Douglas Hay, "The Criminalization of Free Labor: Masters and Servants in Comparative Perspective," *Slavery and Abolition*, 15, 2 (1994): 71–101.
Crebouw, Yvonne, Salaires et salariés agricoles en France, des débuts de la révolution aux approches du XXe siècle (PhD thesis, Paris Sorbonne, 1986).
Crisp, Olga, "Labor and Industrialization in Russia," in *The Cambridge Economic History of Europe*, vol. 7, pt. 2, Peter Mathias and Michael Postan, eds., (Cambridge: Cambridge University Press, 1978): 308–415.
Cross, Gary ed., *Worktime and Industrialization: An International History* (Philadelphia: Temple University Press, 1988).
Cross, Gary, *A Quest for Time: The Reduction of Work in Britain and France, 1840–1940* (Berkeley: University of California Press, 1989).
Crouzet, François, *De la supériorité de l'Angleterre sur la France. L'économique et l'imaginaire* (Paris: Perrin, 1985).
Crouzet, François, ed., *Britain Ascendant: Comparative Studies in Franco-British Economic History* (Cambridge: Cambridge University Press, 1990).
Crouzet, François, *La guerre économique franco-anglaise au XVIIIe siècle* (Paris: Fayard, 2008).
Cunfer, Geoff, *On the Great Plains, Agriculture and Environment* (College Station: Texas A and M Press, 2006).
Curtin, Philip, *The Atlantic Slave Trade* (Madison: University of Wisconsin Press, 1969): 88.
Cuvillier-Fleury, Henri, *La mise en valeur du Congo français* (Paris: Librairie de la société du recueil général des lois et des arrêts, 1904).
Czap, Peter, "The Perennial Multiple-Family Household, Mishino, Russia, 1782–1858," *Journal of Family History*, 7, 1 (Spring 1982): 5–26.
Daget, Serge, *La traite des Noirs* (Rennes: Editions Ouest-France, 1990).
Daget, Serge, *La répression de la traite des noirs au XIXe siècle* (Paris: Karthala, 1997).
Darity, William, "The Number Game and the Profitability of the British Trade in Slaves," *Journal of Economic History*, 45, 3 (1985): 693–703.
Darity, William, "Profitability of the British Trade in Slaves Once Again," *Explorations in Economic History*, 26, 3 (1989): 380–384.
Darwin, John, *After Tamerlane: The Rise and Fall of Global Empires, 1400–2000* (London: Penguin Book, 2007).

Daudin, Guillaume, "Comment calculer les profits de la traite?" *Outre-mer*, 89, 336-337 (2002): 43-62.

Daudin, Guillaume, "Profitability of Slavery and Long-Distance Trading in Context: The Case of Eighteenth-Century France," *The Journal of Economic History*, 64, 1 (2004): 144-171.

Daudin, Guillaume, *Commerce et prospérité: la France au XVIIIe siècle* (Paris: PUPS, 2005).

David, Paul, Herbert Gutman, Richard Sutch, Peter Temin and Gavin Wright, eds., *Reckoning with Slavery: A Critical Study in the Quantitative History of American Negro Slavery* (Oxford: Oxford University Press, 1977).

Davies, Brian, "The Recovery of Fugitive Peasants from Muscovy's Southern Frontier: The Case of Kozlov, 1636-1640," *Russian History*, 19, 1 (1992): 29-56.

Davis, Brian, *State, Power, and Community in Early Modern Russia: The Case of Kozlov, 1635-1649* (Basingstoke, NY: Palgrave, Macmillan, 2004).

Davis, David, *Driven to the Field: Sharecropping and Southern Literature* (Charlottesville: University of Virginia Press, 2023).

Davis, David Brion, *Slavery and Human Progress* (New York: Galaxy Books, 1984).

Davis, David Brion, *The Problem of Slavery in the Age of Emancipation* (Ithaca: Cornell University Press, 1988).

Davis, Ralph, *The Industrial Revolution and British Overseas Trade* (London: Leicester University Press, 1979).

Davis, William C., *Look Away! A History of the Confederate States of America* (New York: Free Press, 2002).

de Haan, Arjan, "Migration on the Border of Free and Unfree Labor: Workers in Calcutta's Jute Industry, 1900-1990," in Jan Lucassen and Leo Lucassen, eds., *Migration, Migration History: Paradigms and New Perspectives* (Bern: Peter Lang, 1997) 197-222.

de la Fuente, Alejandro and Ariela Gross, "Concluding Thoughts: Boundary Crossing: Slavery and Freedom, Legality and Illegality, Past and Present," *Law and History Review*, 35, 1 (2017): 119-130.

de Lamennais, Félicité, *De l'esclavage moderne* (Paris: Pagnerre, 1839).

de Queirós Mattoso, Katia, *To be a Slave in Brazil, 1550-1888* (New Brunswick, NJ: Rutgers University Press, 1987).

De Vito, Christian and Anne Garritsen, eds., *Micro-Spatial Histories of Global Labour* (London: Palgrave, 2018).

De Vito, Christian, Juliane Schiele and Matthias van Rossum, "From Bondage to Precariousness? New Perspectives on Labor and Social History," *The Journal of Social History*, 54, 2 (2020): 1-19.

de Vries, Jan, *The Industrious Revolution* (Cambridge: Cambridge University Press, 2008).

de Wimpffen, Alexandre-Stanislas, *Haiti au XVIIIe siècle* (Paris: Pluchon, 1993).

Deakin, Simon, "Contrat de travail," in Alessandro Stanziani, ed., *Dictionnaire historique de l'économie-droit, XVIIIe-XXe siècles* (Paris: LGDJ, 2007): 289-298.

Deakin, Simon and Frank Wilkinson, *The Law of the Labor Market: Industrialization, Employment, and Legal Evolution* (Oxford: Oxford University Press, 2005).
Deane, Phyllis and William Alan Coale, *British Economic Growth, 1688–1959* (Cambridge: Cambridge University Press, 1962).
Debien, Gabriel, *Les engagés pour les Antilles 1634–1715* (Paris: Société de l'histoire des colonies françaises, 1952).
Debien, Gabriel, *Plantations et esclaves à Saint-Domingue* (Dakar: Université de Dakar, 1962).
Debien, Gabriel, "Le marronnage aux Antilles françaises au XVIIIe siècle," *Caribbean Studies*, 6, 3 (1966): 3–43.
Debien, Gabriel, *Les esclaves aux Antilles françaises, XVIIe-XVIIIe siècles* (Guadeloupe: Basse-Terre, Société d'histoire de la Guadeloupe, 1974).
Dechêne, Louise, *Habitants et marchands de Montréal au XVIIe siècle* (Paris: Plon, 1974).
Defoe, Daniel, *A Plan of English Commerce* (London: Rvington, 1728).
Delsalle, Pierre, *La Brouette et la navette: tisserands, paysans et fabricants dans la région de Roubaix et de Tourcoing (Ferrain, Mélantois, Pévèle), 1800–1848* (Lille: Westhoek, 1985).
Demier, Francis, "Droit au travail et organisation du travail en 1848," in Jean-Luc Mayaud, ed., *1848: Actes du 150ème anniversaire* (Paris, Créaphys, 2002): 159–184.
Dennison, Tracy, *The Institutional Framework of Russian Serfdom* (Cambridge: Cambridge University Press, 2011).
Dennison, Tracy and Steven Nafzinger, "Living Standards in Nineteenth Century Russia," *Journal of Interdisciplinary History*, 43, 3 (2013): 397–441.
Desan, Suzanne, Lynn Hunt and William Maw Nelson, *The French Revolution in Global Perspective* (Ithaca and London: Cornell University Press, 2013).
Deschamps, Hubert, *Les méthodes et les doctrines coloniales de la France du XVIe siècle à nos jours* (Paris: Colin, 1953).
Desjardin, Sergine, *Marie Major* (Montréal: Guy Saint-Jean Éditeur, 2002).
Dewerpe, Alain, "En avoir ou pas. A propos du livret ouvrier dans la France du XIXe siècle," in Alessandro Stanziani, Ed., *Le travail contraint en Asie et en Europe, XVIIe-XXe siècles* (Paris: MSH éditions, 2010): 217–240.
Dewhurst Lewis, Mary, *The Boundaries of the Republic: Migrants Rights and the Limits of Universalism in France, 1918–1940* (Stanford: Stanford University Press, 2007).
Dickens, Charles, *All The Year Round*, June 15, 1867: 585.
Diouf, Sylviane, *Slavery's Exiles: The Story of the American Maroons* (New York: New York University Press, 2014).
Dixon, Simon, *The Modernization of Russia, 1676–1825* (Cambridge: Cambridge University Press, 1999).
Dod, Charles R., *Electoral Facts 1832–1853 Impartially Stated*, ed., H. J. Hanham (London: Harvester Press, 1972).

Dokuchaev, Vasily, *Sochinenia* (Collected works) (Moscow: Gozizdat, 1961).
Dolbilov, Mikhail, *Zemel'naya sobstvennost' i ozvobozhdenie krestian'* (Land property and peasant freedom) (Moscow: Rosspen, 2002).
Domar, Evsey D., "The Causes of Slavery or Serfdom: A Hypothesis," *The Journal of Economic History*, 30, 1, (Mar., 1970): 18–32.
Domar, Evsey D. and Mark J. Machina, "On the Profitability of Russian Serfdom," *The Journal of Economic History*, 44, 4 (1984): 919–955.
Domat, Jean, *Les lois civiles dans leur ordre naturel*, first edition 1697, reproduced in OEuvres (Paris: Pierre Aubouin, 1835), vol. 1.
Doolittle, William, "Agriculture in North America on the Eve of Contact: A Reassessment," *Annals of the Association of American Geographers*, 82, 3 (1992): 386–401.
Dorigny, Marcel ed., *Les abolitions de l'esclavage* (Saint-Denis: Presses Universitaires de Vincennes, 1995).
Dorigny, Marcel, ed., *Esclavage, résistances et abolitions* (Paris: CTHS, 1999).
Dorigny, Marcel and Bernard Gainot, *La société des amis des Noirs. Contribution à l'histoire de l'abolition de l'esclavage* (Paris: Unesco, 1998).
Dorigny, Marcel and Bernard Gainot, *Atlas des esclavages* (Paris: Editions Autrement, 2006).
Douglass, Frederick, *Narrative of the Life of Frederick Douglass, an American Slave: Written by Himself* (Boston: Anti-Slavery Office, 1845).
Douglass, Frederick, *The Frederick Douglass Papers*, John Blassingame, ed., 5 volumes (New Haven, Yale University Press, 1991).
Douki, Caroline, David Feldman and Paul-André-Rosental, "Pour une histoire relationnelle du ministère du Travail en France, en Italie et au Royaume-Uni dans l'entre-deux-guerres: le transnational, le bilatéral et l'interministériel en matière de politique migratoire," in Alain Chatriot, Odile Join-Lambert and Vincent Viet, eds., *Les Politiques du Travail (1906–2006). Acteurs, institutions, réseaux* (Rennes: Presses Universitaires de Rennes): 143–159.
Drescher, Seymour, *Econocide: British Slavery in the Era of Abolition* (Pittsburgh: University of Pittsburgh Press, 1977; new edition: University of North Carolina Press, 2010).
Drescher, Seymour, *Capitalism and Antislavery: British Mobilization in Comparative Perspective* (New York: Oxford University Press, 1987).
Drescher, Seymour, *The Mighty Experiment: Free Labor versus Slavery in British Emancipation* (Oxford: Oxford University Press, 2002).
Drescher, Seymour, *Abolitions: A History of Slavery and Antislavery* (Cambridge: Cambridge University Press, 2009).
Drescher, Seymour and Stanley Engerman eds., *A Historical Guide to World Slavery* (New York: Oxford University Press, 1998).
Drescher, Seymour and Pieter Emmer, eds., *Who Abolished Slavery: Slave Revolt and Abolitionism* (New York: Berghahn, 2010).
Drouet, Pascal and Yan Brailowsky, *La bannissement et l'exil en Europe au XVIe et XVIIe siècles* (Rennes: Presses Universitaires de Rennes, 2010).

Dru Stanley, Amy, "Histories of Capitalism and Sex Difference," *Journal of the Early Republic*, 36, 2 (2016): 343–350.

Druzhinin, Nikolai M., *Gosudarstvennye krest'iane i reforma P.D. Kiseleva* (State peasants and the reform of P. D. Kiselev) (Moskow: Nauka, 1958).

Dube, Allison, "The Tree of Utility in India: Panace or Weed?," in Marin Moir, Douglas Peers and Lynn Zastoupil, eds., *J.S. Mill's Encounter with India* (Toronto: University of Toronto Press, 1999): 34–52.

Dubois, Laurent, *Les esclaves de la République. L'histoire oubliée de la première émancipation 1789-1794* (Paris: Calman-Levy, 1998).

Dubois, Laurent, *A Colony of Citizen: Revolution and Slave Emancipation in the French Caribbean, 1787-1804* (Chapel Hill: University of North Carolina Press, 2004).

Dubois, Laurent, *Avengers of the New World* (Cambridge, MA: Belknap Press, 2004).

Duby, George, *Les trois ordres ou l'imaginaire du féodalisme* (Paris: Gallimard, 1978).

Duchet, Michèle, *Anthropologie et histoire au siècle des lumières* (Paris: Albin Michel, 1971).

Dumas, Silvio, *Les Filles du roi en Nouvelle-France. Étude historique avec répertoire biographique* (Québec: Société historique de Québec, 1972).

Dunn, Richard, "The Barbados Census of 1680: Profile of the Richest Colony in English America," *William and Mary Quarterly*, 3rd series, 26, 1 (1969): 3–30.

Dunn, Richard, *Sugar and Slaves: The Rise of the Planter Class in the English West Indies, 1624-1713* (New York: Norton, 1973).

Duprat, Catherine, *Usages et pratiques de la philanthropie. Pauvreté, action sociale et lien social, à Paris, au cours du premier XIXe siècle* (Paris: Comité d'histoire de la Sécurité sociale, 1996).

Durand, Bernard, Martine Fabre, and Mamadou Badji, eds., *Le juge et l'Outre-mer*, vol. 5 (Lille: Centre d'histoire judiciaire, 2010):

Eckert, Andreas, "Regulating the Social: Social Security Social Welfare, and the State in Late Colonial Tanzania," *The Journal of African History*, 45, 3 (2004): 467–489.

Eckert, Andreas, ed., *Global Histories of Work* (Boston: De Gruyter, 2016).

Economakis, Evel G., "Patterns of Migration and Settlement in Pre-revolutionary St. Petersburg: Peasants from Iaroslav and Tver Provinces," *Russian Review*, 56, 1 (1997): 8–24.

Edwards, Bryan, *The History, Civil and Commercial of the British Colonies in the West Indies* (Edinburgh: Mundell, 1798), vol. 1: 232.

Ekama, Kate, Lisa Hellman and Matthias von Rossum eds., *Slavery and Bondage in Asia, 1550-1850: Towards a Global History of Coerced Labour* (Oldenburg: De Gruyter, 2022).

Eklöf, Stefan and Leos Müller, eds., *Persistent Piracy: Maritime Violence and State Formation in Global Historical Perspective* (Houndsmill: Palgrave Macmillan, 2014).

Eldem, Edhem and Sophia Laiou, eds., *Istanbul and the Black Sea Coast: Shipping and Trade, 1770-1920* (Istanbul: The ISIS Press, 2018).

Eltis, David, *Economic Growth and the End of the Transatlantic Slave Trade* (New York: Oxford University Press, 1987).
Eltis, David, "The Slave Economies of the Caribbean: Structure, Performance, Evolution and Significance," in F. Knight, ed., *The UNESCO General History of the Caribbean* (London: Macmillan, 1997): 104–137.
Eltis, David, *Coerced and Free Migration: Global Perspectives* (Stanford: Stanford University Press, 2002).
Eltis, David and Stanley Engerman, "The Importance of Slavery and Slave Trade to Industrializing Britain," *Journal of Economic History*, 60, 1 (2000): 123–144.
Eltis, David and David Richardson eds., *Extending the Frontiers: Essays on the New Transatlantic Slave Trade Database* (New Haven: Yale University Press, 2008).
Eltis, David, Pieter C. Emmer and Frank D. Lewis, "More than Profits? The Contribution of the Slave Trade to the Dutch Economy: Assessing Fatah-Black and Van Rossum," *Slavery & Abolition*, 37, 4 (2016): 724–735.
Eltis, David, Stephen D. Behrendt, David Richardson and Herbert S. Klein, *The Trans-Atlantic Slave Trade: A Database on CD-ROM* (Cambridge and New York: Cambridge University Press, 1999).
Eltis, David, Stanley L. Engerman, Seymour Drescher, and David Richardson, eds., *The Cambridge World History of Slavery Vol. 3, AD 1420–AD 1804* (New York: Cambridge University Press, 2011).
Emmer, Petr, *Colonialism and Migration: Indentured Labour Before and After Slavery* (Dordrecht: Martinus Nijhoff, 1986).
Emmons, Terence, *The Russian Landed Gentry and the Peasant Emancipation of 1861* (Berkeley: University of California Press, 1968).
Emmons, Terence and Wayne Vucinich, *The Zemstvos in Russia: An Experiment in Local Self-Government* (New York: Cambridge University Press, 1992).
Engel, Barbara, *Between the Fields and the City: Women, Work, and Family in Russia, 1861–1914* (New York: Cambridge University Press, 1994).
Engerman, Stanley, "The Economic Impact of the Civil War," *Explorations in Entrepreneurial History*, 3, 3 (1966): 176–199.
Engerman, Stanley, "The Slave Trade and British Capital Formation in the Eighteenth Century: A Comment on Williams Thesis," *Business History Review*, 46 (1972): 430–443.
Engerman, Stanley, "Economic Adjustment to Emancipation in the United States and the British West Indies," *The Journal of Interdisciplinary History*, 13, 2 (1982): 191–220.
Engerman, Stanley, "Europeans and the Rise and Fall of Slavery in the Americas: An Interpretation," *American Historical Review*, 98, 5 (1993): 1399–1423.
Engerman, Stanley, ed., *Terms of Labor: Slavery, Serfdom, and Free Labor* (Stanford: Stanford University Press, 1999).
Epstein, Steven, *Speaking of Slavery* (Ithaca: Cornell University Press, 2001).
Erdem, Y. Hakan, *Slavery in the Ottoman Empire and Its Demise, 1800–1909* (Basingstoke: Palgrave, Macmillan, 1996).
Esper, Thomas, "The Odnodvortsy and the Russian Nobility," *Slavonic and East European Review*, 45, 104 (1967): 124–135.

Estwick, Samuel, *Considerations on the Negroe Cause, Commonly So Called, Addressed to the Right Honourable Lord Mansfield, Lord Chief Justice of the Court of King's Bench* (London: J. Dodslay, 1773, second edition).
Etkind, Alexander, *Internal Colonization: Russia's Imperial Experience* (Cambridge: Polity Press, 2011).
Fabre, Martine, "L'indigénat: des petites polices discriminatoires et dérogatoires," in Bernard Durand, Martine Fabre and Mamadou Badji, eds., *Le juge et l'Outre-mer*, vol. 5 (Lille: Centre d'histoire judiciaire, 2010): 273–310.
Faccarello Gilbert and Philippe Steiner, *La pensée économique pendant la révolution française* (Grenoble: Presses universitaires de Grenoble, 1990).
Faillon, Etienne-Michel, *Histoire de la colonie française du Canada* (Montréal: Bibliothèque paroissiale, 1865–8).
Falk Moore, Sally, *Social Facts and Fabrications: Customary Law on Kilimanjaro, 1880–1980* (New York: Cambridge University Press, 1980).
Fall, Babacar, *Le travail forcé en AOF* (Paris: Karthala, 1993).
Fanger, Donald, "The Peasant in Literature," in Wayne S. Vucinich, ed., *The Peasant in Nineteenth-Century Russia* (Stanford: Stanford University Press, 1968): 231–262.
Farcy, Jean-Claude, *Guide des archives judiciaires et pénitentiaires, 1800–1958* (Paris: CNRS éditions, 1992).
Farcy, Jean-Claude, "Les archives méconnues de la justice civile," in Frédéric Chauvaud, and Jacques-Guy Petit, eds., *Histoire et archives. L'histoire contemporaine et les usages des archives judiciaires (1800–1939)* (Paris: Champion, 1998): 397–408.
Farcy, Jean-Claude, and Ronald Hubscher eds., *La moisson des autres* (Nice: Créaphys édition, 1996.
Farrell, Stephen, Melanie Unwin, and James Walvin, eds., *The British Slave Trade: Abolition, Parliament and People* (Edinburgh: Edinburgh University Press, 2007.
Fede, Andrew T., *Roadblocks to Freedom: Slavery and Manumission in the United States South* (New Orleans: Quid Pro Books, 2011).
Federici, Silvia, *Caliban and the Witch: Women, the Body, and Primitive Accumulation* (New York: Penguin, 2004).
Federico, Giovanni, *Feeding the World: An Economic History of Agriculture, 1800–2000* (Princeton, NJ: Princeton University Press, 2005).
Feinstein, Charles H., "Capital Formation in Great Britain," in Peter Mathias and Michael Postan, eds., *The Cambridge Economic History of Europe, vol. VII: The Industrial Economies: Capital, Labor and Enterprise* (Cambridge: Cambridge University Press, 1978): 28–94.
Feinstein, Charles H., "Pessimism Perpetuated: Real Wages and the Standard of Living in Britain during and after the Industrial Revolution," *The Journal of Economic History*, 58, 3 (1998): 625–658.
Feinstein, Charles H. and Sidney Pollard, eds., *Studies in Capital Formation in the United Kingdom, 1750–1920* (Oxford: Clarendon Press, 1988).
Feuille hebdomadaire de l'Ile Bourbon, August 30, 1848 and October 11, 1848.

Field, Donald, *The End of Serfdom: Nobility and Bureaucracy in Russia, 1855–1861* (Cambridge: Harvard University Press, 1976).
Field, Jacob, "Domestic Service, Gender, and Wages in Rural England, 1700–1860," *Economic History Review*, 66, 1 (2013): 249–272.
Fieldhouse, David, "The Economic Exploitation of Africa: Some British and French Comparisons," in Prosser Gifford and William Roger Louis, eds., *France and Britain in Africa: Imperial Rivalry and Colonial Rule* (New Haven: Yale University Press, 1971): 659–660.
Filliot, Jean-Marie, *La traite des esclaves vers les Mascaraignes au XVIIIe siècle* (Paris: Orstom, 1974).
Findlay, Ronald, "The Triangular Trade and the Atlantic Economy of the Eighteenth Century: A Simple General Equilibrium Model," *Essays in International Finance*, no. 177 (Princeton, NJ: Princeton University Press, 1990).
Findlay, Ronald and Kevin H. O'Rourke, *Power and Plenty: Trade, War, and the World Economy in the Second Millennium* (Princeton: Princeton University Press, 2007).
Finkelman, Paul, *Slavery in Courtroom: An Annotated Bibliography of American Cases* (New Jersey: The Lawbook Exchange, 1998).
Finley, Moses, *Ancient Slavery and Modern Ideology* (New York: Viking Press, 1980).
Fisher, Alan, *The Russian Annexation of the Crimea, 1772–1783* (Cambridge: Cambridge University Press, 1970).
Fisher, Alan, "Muscovy and the Black Sea Trade," *Canadian-American Slavic Studies*, 6, 4 (1972): 582–593.
Fisher, Michael, *Counterflows to Colonialism: Indian Travellers and Settlers in Britain, 1600–1857* (Delhi: Permanent Black, 2004).
Fisher, Raymond H. *The Russian Fur Trade, 1550–1700* (Berkeley: University of California Press, 1943).
Fisher, H. E. Stephan, *The Portugal Trade: A Study of Anglo-Portuguese Commerce, 1700–1770* (London: Methuen, 1971).
Florentino, Manolo and Márcia Amantino, "Runaways and *Quilombolas* in the Americas," in David Eltis, Stanley L. Engerman, Seymour Drescher and David Richardson, eds., *The Cambridge World History of Slavery Vol. 3, AD 1420–AD 1804* (New York: Cambridge University Press, 2011): 708–740.
Flory, Céline, *De l'esclavage à la liberté forcée. Histoire des travailleurs africains engagés dans la Caraïbe française au XIXe siècle* (Paris: Karthala, 2015).
Fogel, Robert, *Without Consent or Contract* (New York: Norton, 1994).
Fogel, Robert and Stanley L. Engerman, *Time on the Cross: The Economics of American Negro Slavery* (New York: Norton, 1974).
Foner, Eric, *Nothing but Freedom: Emancipation and Its Legacy* (Baton Rouge: Louisiana University Press, 1983).
Foner, Eric, *Free Soil, Free Labor, Free Men: The Ideology of the Republican Party before the Civil War* (Oxford: Oxford University Press, 1995).
Foner, Eric, *Reconstruction: Americas's Unfinished Revolution, 1863–1867* (New York: Harper, 2002, first edition 1988).
Forget, René, *Eugenie, fille du Roy*, 3 volumes (Québec: Michel Brulé, 2006–2012).

Fortunet, Françoise, "D'une république à l'autre: les conseils de prud'hommes ou l'institution d'une justice de paix de l'industrie," in Jacques Lorgnier, Renée Martinage et Jean-Pierre Royer, eds., *Justice et République(s)* (Lille: Ester Éditions, 1993): 325–335.

Fouchard, Jean, *Les marrons de la liberté* (Paris: Deschamps, 1988).

Fowler, Simon, *The Workhouse: The People, the Places, the Life Behind Doors* (Barnsley: Pen and Sword History, 2014).

Fox Genovese, Elizabeth, *Within the Plantation Household: Black and White Women of the Old South* (Chapel Hill: North Carolina University Press, 1988).

Frader, Laura, "Labor History After the Gender Turn," *International Labor and Working-Class History*, 63 (2003): 21–31.

Frankema, Ewout H. P., "Colonial Taxation and Government Spending in British Africa, 1880–1940: Maximizing Revenue or Minimizing Effort?" *Explorations in Economic History*, 48, 1 (2011): 136–149.

Frankema, Ewout H. P., Jeffrey G. Williamson and Pieter J. Woltjer, "An Economic Rationale for the West African Scramble? The Commercial Transition and the Commodity Price Boom of 1835–1885," *The Journal of Economic History*, 78, 1 (2018): 231–267.

Franklin, John Hope and Loren Schweninger, *Runaway Slaves: Rebels on the Plantation* (Oxford: Oxford University Press, 1999).

Franzmann, Tom, "Antislavery and Political Economy in the Early Victorian House of Commons: A Research Note on 'Capitalist Hegemony'," *Journal of Social History*, 27, 3 (1994): 579–593.

Fraser, Derek, *The Evolution of the British Welfare State* (4th ed.) (London: Palgrave Macmillan, 2009).

Freedland, Mark, *The Contract of Employment* (Oxford: Oxford University Press: 1976).

Freehling, William, *The Reintegration of American History: Slavery and the Civil War* (Oxford: Oxford University Press, 1994).

Freeze, Gregory, "The Soslovie (Estate) Paradigm in Russian Social History," *American Historical Review*, 91, 1(1986): 11–36.

Fridenson Patrick and Bénédicte Reynaud, eds., *La France et le temps de travail, 1814–2004* (Paris: Odile Jacob, 2005).

Frostin, Charles, "Du peuplement pénal de l'Amérique française aux XVIIe et XVIIIe siècles: hésitations et contradictions du pouvoir royal en matière de déportation," *Annales de Bretagne et des pays de l'Ouest*, 85, 1 (1978): 67–94.

Fuma, Sudel, *De l'Inde du sud à la Réunion* (Port-Louis: Graphica, 1999).

Gabaccia, Donna, ed., *The Cambridge History of Global Migrations*, 2 volumes (Cambridge: Cambridge University Press, 2023).

Galenson, David W., "Demographic Aspects of White Servitude in Colonial British America," *Annales de démographie historique*, 66, 1 (1980): 239–252.

Galenson, David W., *White Servitude in Colonial America: An Economic Analysis* (Cambridge: Cambridge University Press, 1981).

Galenson, David W. "The Rise and Fall of Indentured Servitude in the Americas: An Economic Analysis," *The Journal of Economic History*, 44, 1 (1984): 1–26.

Galenson, David W., "The Rise of Free Labor: Economic Change and the Enforcement of Service Contract in England, 1361–1875," in John James, and Mark Thomas, eds. *Capitalism in Context: Essays on Economic Development and Cultural Change in Honor of R.M. Hartwell* (Chicago: University of Chicago Press, 1994): 114–137.

Gallissot, René, "Socialisme colonial, socialisme national des pays dominés," *L'homme et la société*, 4, 174 (2009): 75–96.

Gardner, Leigh, *Taxing Colonial Africa: The Political Economy of British Imperialism* (Oxford: Oxford University Press, 2012).

Garrigus, John, "Blue and Brown: Contraband Indigo and the Rise of a Free Colored Planter Class in French Saint-Domingue," *The Americas*, 50, 2 (1993): 233–263.

Gatrell, Peter, *The Tsarist Economy, 1850–1917* (New York, St Martin's Press, 1986).

Gaudin, Corinne, *Ruling Peasants: Village and State in Late Imperial Russia* (Dekalb: Northern Illinois University Press, 2007).

Gautier, Arlette, *Les soeurs de Solitude: Femmes et esclavage aux Antilles du XVIIe au XIXe siècle* (1985; repr., Rennes: Presses Universitaires de Rennes, 2019).

Gayot, Gérard, *De la pluralité des mondes industriels. La manufacture royale des draps de Sedan, 1646–1870* (Paris: EHESS, 1995).

Geggus, David P., *Slavery, War, and Revolution: The British Occupation of Saint-Domingue, 1793–1798* (Oxford: Clarendon Press, 1982).

Geggus, David P., "Sugar and Coffee Cultivation in Saint-Domingue," in Ira Berlin, and Philip Morgan, eds., *Cultivation and Culture* (Charlottesville: University of Virginia Press, 1993): 73–98.

Geggus, David P., "Slave Society in the Sugar Plantation Zones of Saint-Domingue and the Revolution of 1791–3," *Slavery and Abolition*, 20, 2 (1999): 31–46.

Geggus, David P., *The Impact of the Haitian Revolution in the Atlantic World* (New York: Columbia University Press, 2001).

Gemery, Henry, "Markets for Migrants: English Indentured Servitude and Emigration in the Seventeenth and Eighteenth Centuries," in Petr C. Emmer, ed., *Colonialism and Migration: Indentured Labor before and after Slavery* (Dordrecht: Martin Nijhoff, 1986): 33–54.

Genicot, Louis, *Rural Communities in the Medieval West* (Baltimore: Johns Hopkins University Press, 1991).

Genovese, Eugene, *Roll, Jordan, Roll: The World the Slaves Made* (New York: Vintage Books, 1976).

Genovese, Eugene, *From Rebellion to Revolution: Afro-American Slave Revolts in the Making of the Modern World* (Baton Rouge: Louisiana State University Press, 1979).

Genovese, Eugene, *The Slaveholders' Dilemma: Freedom and Progress in Southern Conservative Thought, 1820–1860* (Columbia: University of South Carolina Press, 1992).

Gerbeau, Hubert, "The Slave Trade in the Indian Ocean: Problems Facing the Historian and Research to be Undertaken," in *The African Slave Trade from the Fifteenth to the Nineteenth Century* (Paris: UNESCO, 1979): 184–207.

Gerbeau, Hubert, "Les esclaves asiatiques des Mascareignes: Enquêtes et hypothèses," *Annuaire des pays de l'Océan Indien*, 7 (1980): 169–197.

Gerschenkron, Alexander, *Economic Backwardness in Historical Perspective* (Cambridge, MA: Harvard University Press, 1962).

Gestwa, Klaus, *Proto-Industrialisierung in Russland* (Göttingen: Vandenhoeck and Ruprecht, 1999).

Giacomini, Sonia Maria, *Mulher e escrava: Uma introdução histórica ao estudo da mulher negra no Brasil* (Petrópolis: Rio, 1988).

Giddens, Anthony, *A Contemporary Critique of Historical Materialism* (Berkeley: University of California Press, 1981).

Giddens, Anthony, *The Constitution of Society* (Berkeley: University of California Press, 1984).

Gifford, Prosser, and William Roger Louis, eds., *France and Britain in Africa: Imperial Rivalry and Colonial Rule* (New Haven: Yale University Press, 1971).

Gilles, David, "La condition juridique de la femme en Nouvelle-France: essai sur l'application de la Coutume de Paris dans un contexte colonial," *Cahiers aixois d'histoire des droits de l'outre-mer français*, Aix-en-Provence, 1, 1 (2002): 77–125.

Gilles, David, "Les filles du roi en Nouvelle-France: administrer une politique de peuplement colonial sous l'Ancien régime," in Eric Gasparini et Patrick Charlot, eds., *La femme dans l'histoire du droit et des idées politiques* (Dijon: Éditions universitaires de Dijon, 2008): 29–59.

Ginzburg, Carlo, *Clues, Myths and the Historical Method* (Baltimore: John Hopkins University Press, 2013).

Ginzburg, Carlo and Carlo Poni, "Il nome e il come. Scambio ineguale e mercato storiografico," *Quaderni storici*, 40, 1 (1979): 181–190.

de Girando, Baron, *Traité de bienfaisance publique* (Bruxelles: Société belge de librairie, 1839).

Godbout, Alain, "Familles venues de La Rochelle," *Rapport aux Archives nationales du Québec*, XLVIII, (1970): 119–126.

Godbout, Archange, *Les passagers du Saint-André. La recrue de 1659* (Montréal: Société généalogique canadienne-française, 1964).

Goetz, Rebecca Anne, *The Baptism of Early Virginia: How Christianity Created Race* (Baltimore: Johns Hopkins University Press, 2012).

Goldin, Claudia Dale, *Urban Slavery in the American South, 1820–1860: A Quantitative History*, (Chicago: University of Chicago Press, 1976).

Goldin, Claudia, and Frank Lewis, "The Economic Cost of the American Civil War: Estimates and Implications," *The Journal of Economic History*, 35, 2 (1975): 299–326.

Goldstein Sepinwall, Alyssa, *Haitian History: New Perspectives* (New York: Routledge, 2013).

Gommans, Jos, *Mughal Warfare* (London: Routledge, 2002).

Goodwin, Barry K. and Thomas J. Grennes, "Tsarist Russia and the World Wheat Market," *Explorations in Economic History*, 35, 4 (1998): 405–430.

Gornostaev, Andrey, *Peasants on the Run: State Control, Fugitives, Social and Geographic Mobility in Imperial Russia, 1649–1796* (PhD, Georgetown University, 2020).
Gorshkov, Boris, "Serfs on the Move: Peasant Seasonal Migration in Pre-reform Russia, 1800–1861," *Kritika: Explorations in Russian History*, 1, 4 (2000): 627–656.
Gottschang, Thomas and Diana Lary, *Swallows and Settlers: The Great Migration from North China to Manchuria* (Ann Arbor: University of Michigan, Center for Chinese Studies, 2000).
Govindin, Sully-Santa, *Les engagés indiens* (Saint-Denis la Réunion: Azalées, 1994).
Grant, Kevin, *A Civilized Savagery: Britain and the New Slaveries in Africa, 1884–1926* (New York: Routledge, 2006).
Grantham, George W. "Agricultural Supply during the Industrial Revolution: French Evidence and European Implications," *Journal of Economic History*, 49, 1 (1989): 43–72.
Grantham, George W. "Divisions of Labour: Agricultural Productivity and Occupational Specialization in Pre- Industrial France," *The Economic History Review*, 46, 3, (1993): 478–502.
Grantham, George W., and Mary MacKinnon eds., *Labor Market Evolution* (London and New York: Routledge, 1994).
Green, David, "Pauper Protests: Protests and Resistance in Early Nineteenth-Century London Workhouses," *Social History*, 31, 2 (May 2006): 137–159.
Green, Toby, *A Fistful of Shells* (London: Penguin, 2018).
Greene, Jack, *All Men Are Created Equal: Some Reflections on the Character of the American Revolution* (Oxford: Oxford University Press, 1976).
Greene, Jack, *Negotiated Authorities: Essays in Colonial Political and Constitutional History* (Charlottesville: University of Virginia Press, 1994).
Greene, Jack, ed., *Exclusionary Empire: English Liberty Overseas, 1600–1900* (Cambridge: Cambridge University Press, 2010).
Gregory, Paul, *Russian National Income 1885–1913* (Cambridge: Cambridge University Press, 1982).
Grenouilleau, Olivier, *Les traites négrières* (Paris: Gallimard, 2004).
Grenouilleau, Olivier, *La revolution abolitionniste* (Paris: Gallimard, 2017).
Grubb, Farley, "The Incidence of Servitude in Transatlantic Migration, 1771–1804," *Explorations in Economic History*, 22, 3 (1985): 316–339.
Grubb, Farley, "The Market for Indentured Immigrants: Evidence on the Efficiency of Forward-Labor Contracting in Philadelphia, 1745–1773," *The Journal of Economic History*, 45, 4 (Dec. 1985): 855–868.
Grubb, Farley, "The End of European Immigrant Servitude in the United States: An Economic Analysis of Market Collapse, 1772–1835," *The Journal of Economic History*, 54, 4 (1994): 794–824.
Grubb, Farley, "Does Bound Labour Have to Be Coerced Labour? The Case of Colonial Immigrant Servitude versus Craft-Apprenticeship and Life-Cycle Servitude in Husbandry," *Itinerario*, 21, 1 (1997): 28–51.

Grubb, Farley, "The Trans-Atlantic Market for British Convict Labor," *The Journal of Economic History*, 60, 1 (2000): 1–29.
Guasco, Michael, *Slaves and Englishmen: Human Bondage in the Early Modern Atlantic World* (Philadelphia: University of Pennsylvania Press, 2014).
Guha, Sumit, "Slavery, Society and the State in Western India, 1700–1800," in Chatterjee, and Eaton, eds., *Slavery and South Asian History* (Bloomington: Indiana University Press, 2006): 162–186.
Guinnane, Timothy, Ron Harris, Noemi Lamoreaux and Jean-Laurent Rosenthal, "Pouvoir et propriété dans l'entreprise," *Annales HSS*, 63, 1 (2008): 73–110.
Gullickson, Gay, "Agriculture and Cottage Industry: Redefining the Causes of Proto-Industrialization," *The Journal of Economic History*, 43, 4 (1983): 831–850.
Günes-Yagci, Zübeyde, "The Black Sea Slave Trade According to the Istanbul Port Customs Register, 1606–7," in Christopher Witzenrath, ed., *Eurasian Slavery, Ransom and Abolition in World History, 1200–1860* (Farnham: Ashgate, 2015): 207–220.
Habakkuk, Hrothgar John, "The Economic History of Modern Britain," *Journal of Economic History*, 18, 4 (1958): 486–501.
Habakkuk, Hrothgar John, *American and British Technology in the Nineteenth Century* (Cambridge: Cambridge University Press, 1962).
Hagen, William, *Ordinary Prussians: Brandenburg Junkers and Villagers, 1500–1840* (Cambridge: Cambridge University Press, 2002).
Hall, Bruce, "How Slaves Use Islam: The Letters of Enslaved Muslims Commercial Agents in the Nineteenth Century Niger Bend and Central Sahara," *The Journal of African History*, 52, 3 (2011): 279–297.
Hamelin, Maurice, *Des concessions coloniales. Étude sur les modes d'aliénation des terres domaniales en Algérie et dans les colonies françaises du Congo* (Paris: Librairie nouvelle de droit et de jurisprudence Arthur Rousseau, 1898).
Harley, Charles Knick, "British Industrialization before 1841: Evidence of Slower Growth during the Industrial Revolution," *Journal of Economic History*, 42, 2 (1982): 267–289.
Harley, Charles Knick, "Slavery, the British Atlantic Economic and the Industrial Revolution," *University of Oxford Discussion Papers in Economic History*, 113, (2013) www.nuff.ox.ac.uk/economics/history/paper113/harley113.pdf
Harley, Charles Knick, "Slavery, the British Atlantic Economy, and the Industrial Revolution," in Adrian Leonard and David Pretel, eds., *The Caribbean and the Atlantic World Economy: Circuits of Trade, Money and Knowledge, 1650–1914* (Basingstoke: Palgrave Macmillan, 2015): 161–183.
Harris, Jose, *Unemployment and Politics: A Study in English Social Policy, 1886–1914* (Oxford: Clarendon Press, 1972).
Harris, Ron, *Industrializing English Law: Entrepreneurship and Business Organization, 1720–1844* (Cambridge: Cambridge University Press, 2000).
Harvey, Mark, "Slavery, Indenture, and the Development of British Industrial Capitalism," *History Workshop Journal*, 88 (2019): 66–88.
Haudrière, Philippe, *La compagnie française des Indes* (Paris: Les Indes savantes, 2005).

Haupt, Heinz-Gerhard and Jurgen Kocka, eds., *Comparative and Trans-national History* (New York: Berghahn, 2009).

Havard, Gilles and Cécile Vidal, *Histoire de l'Amérique française* (Paris: Flammarion, 2019).

Hay, Douglas and Paul Craven, *Masters, Servants, and Magistrates in Britain and the Empire, 1562–1955* (Chapel Hill and London: The University of North Carolina Press, 2004).

Hay, Robert, *Landsman Hay: The Memoirs of Robert Hay, 1789–1847* (London: Rupert Hart-Davis, 1953).

Heers, Jacques, *Esclaves et domestiques au Moyen Age dans le monde méditerranéen* (Paris: Hachette, 1996).

Helg, Aline, *Plus jamais esclaves: De l'insoumission à la révolte, le grand récit d'une émancipation (1492–1838)* (Paris: La découverte, 2016).

Hellie, Richard, *Muscovite Society*, syllabus division (Chicago: University of Chicago Press, 1967).

Hellie, Richard "The Law Code of 1649" and "Muscovite-Western Commercial Relations," in *Readings in Russian Civilization*, Thomas Riha, ed., 2nd edition (Chicago: University of Chicago Press, 1969), 154–172.

Hellie, Richard, *Enserfment and Military Change in Muscovy* (Chicago: University of Chicago Press, 1971).

Hellie, Richard, "Recent Soviet Historiography on Medieval and Early Modern Russian Slavery," *Russian Review*, 35, 1 (1976): 1–36.

Hellie, Richard, "Reply," *Russian Review*, 36, 1 (1977): 68–75.

Hellie, Richard, *Slavery in Russia* (Chicago: University of Chicago Press, 1982).

Hellie, Richard ed., *The Muscovite Law Code (Ulozhenie) of 1649*, part. 1 (Irvine, CA: Charles Schlacks, 1988).

Hening, William Waller, *The Statutes at Large; Being a Collection of all Laws of Virginia, from the First Session of the Legislature, in the Year 1619* (New York: Bartow, 1823).

Hepple, Bob ed., *The Making of the Labor Law in Europe* (London: Mansell, 1986).

Heyberger, Laurent, *Les Corps en colonie. Faim, maladies, guerres et crises démographiques en Algérie au xixe siècle* (Toulouse: PUM, 2019).

Higginbotham, Peter, *Voices from the Workhouse* (London: The History Press, 2012).

Higgs, Robert, *Competition and Coercion: Blacks in the American Economy, 1865–1914* (Cambridge: Cambridge University Press, 1977): 18–22.

Hindle, Steven, *The State and Social Change in Early Modern England, 1550–1640* (New York: Palgrave, 2002).

Hirsch, Francine, *Empire of Nations: Ethnographic Knowledge and the Making of the Soviet Empire* (Ithaca: Cornell University Press, 2005).

Hirschman, Albert, *Exit, Voice, and Loyalty* (Cambridge, MA: Harvard University Press, 1970).

Hoare, Prince, *Memoirs of Granville Sharp, Esq.* (London: Colburn, 1828).

Hoch, Steven, "Serfs in Imperial Russia: Demographic Insights," *The Journal of Interdisciplinary History*, 13, 2 (1982): 221–246.

Hoch, Steven, *Serfdom and Social Control* (Chicago: University of Chicago Press, 1986).
Hoch, Steven, "The Banking Crisis, Peasant Reforms, and Economic Development in Russia, 1857–1861," *American Historical Review*, 96, 3 (1991): 795–820.
Hoch, Steven, "On Good Numbers and Bad: Malthus, Population Trend and Peasant Standard of Living in Late Imperial Russia," *Slavic Review*, 53, 1 (1994): 41–75.
Hoch, Steven, "Famine, Disease and Mortality Patterns in the Parish of Boshervka, Russia, 1830–1932," *Population Studies*, 52, 3 (1998): 357–368.
Hoch, Steven, and Wilson Augustine, "The Tax Censuses and the Decline of the Serf Population in Imperial Russia, 1833–1858," *Slavic Review*, 38, 3 (1979): 403–425.
Hodgson, Marshal, *Rethinking World History* (Cambridge: Cambridge University Press, 1993).
Hoedgendorn, Jan, *The Uncommon Market: Essays in the Economic History of the Atlantic Slave Trade* (New York: Academic Press, 1979).
Hoefte, Rosemarijn, "Indenture in the Long Nineteenth Century," in David Eltis, Stanley Engerman, Seymour Drescher and David Richardson, eds., *The Cambridge World History of Slavery: Vol. 4 AD 1804–AD 2016* (Cambridge: Cambridge University Press, 2017): 610–632.
Hoffman, Philip, *Growth in a Traditional Society: The French Countryside, 1450–1815* (Princeton: Princeton University Press, 1996).
Hoffman, Philip, Gilles Postel-Vinay and Jean-Laurent Rosenthal, *Priceless Markets* (Chicago: University of Chicago Press, 2000).
Hofmeester Karin and Marcel van der Linden, eds., *Handbook: Global History of Work* (Oldenburg: De Gruyter, 2018).
Holt, Thomas, *The Problem of Freedom: Race, Labor and Politics in Jamaica and Britain, 1832–1938* (Baltimore and London: Johns Hopkins University Press, 1992).
Hooker, M. B. *Legal Pluralism: An Introduction to Colonial and Neo-Colonial Laws* (Oxford: Clarendon Press, 1975).
Hopkins, Anthony, *An Economic History of West Africa* (New York: Columbia University Press, 1973).
Hopkins, Eric, "Working Hours and Conditions during the Industrial Revolution, a Re-appraisal," *Economic History Review*, 35, 1 (1982): 52–67.
Hoppit, Julian, *Britain's Political Economies: Parliament and Economic Life, 1660–1800* (Cambridge: Cambridge University Press, 2017).
Horne, Gerald, *The Counter-Revolution of 1776: Slave Resistance and the Origins of the United States of America* (New York: New York University Press, 2014).
Horrell, Sara and Jane Humphries, "Women's Labour Force Participation and the Transition to the Male-Breadwinner Family, 1790–1865," *The Economic History Review*, 48, 1 (1995): 89–117.
Horwitz, Morton, *The Transformation of American Law, 1780–1860* (Cambridge, MA: Harvard University Press, 1977).
Hosking, Geoffrey, *Russia: People and Empire, 1552–1917* (Cambridge, MA: Harvard University Press, 1997).

Howe, Anthony, *Free Trade and Liberal England, 1846-1946* (Oxford: Oxford University Press, 1997).

Huberman, Michael, *Escape from the Market: Negotiating Work in Lancashire* (Cambridge: Cambridge University Press, 1996).

Hubscher, Ronald and Jean-Claude Farcy, eds., *La moisson des autres* (Paris: Créaphys édition, 1996).

Hudson, Pat, ed., *Regions and Industries: A Perspective on the Industrial Revolution in Britain* (Cambridge: Cambridge University Press, 1989).

Hummel, Jeffrey, *Emancipating Slaves, Enslaving Free Men: A History of the American Civil War* (Chicago: Open Court, 2014).

Humphries, Jane, *Childhood and Child Labour in the British Industrial Revolution* (Cambridge: Cambridge University Press, 2011).

Hunt, Lynn, *Inventing Human Rights: A History* (New York: Norton, 2007).

Huret, Roman, *American Tax Resisters* (Cambridge, MA: Harvard University Press, 2014).

Huzzey, Richard, "Free Trade, Free Labor, and Slave Sugar in Victorian Britain," *Historical Journal*, 53, 2 (2010): 359-379.

Huzzey, Richard, *Freedom Burning: Anti-Slavery and Empire in Victorian Britain* (Ithaca and London: Cornell University Press, 2012).

Iakovlev, Aleksandr', *Kholopstvo i kholopy v moskovskom gosudarstve XVII v.* (Kholopstvo and kholopy in the Russian state, seventeenth century) (Moscow: Nauka, 1943).

Indova, Emilia I., "Rol' dvortsovoi derevni pervoi poloviny XVIII v. v formirovanii russkogo kupechestva" (The role of the village court during the first half of the eighteenth century in the formation of a Russian bourgeoisie) *Istoricheskie Zapiski*, 68 (1961): 189-210.

Indova, Emilia I., *Dvortsovoe khoziaistvo v Rossii* (The palace economy in Russia) (Moscow: Nauka, 1964).

Indova, Emilia I., "O rossiskikh manufakturakh vtoroi poloviny XVIII v," (On the Russian manufactures during the second half of the eighteenth century), *Istoricheskaia geografiia Rossii: XIX-nachalo XX v.* (Moscow: Nauka, 1975): 248-345.

Inikori, Joseph, "Market Structures and the Profits of the British African Trade in the Late Eighteenth Century," *Journal of Economic History*, 41, 4 (1981): 745-776.

Inikori, Joseph, *Africans and the Industrial Revolution in England* (Cambridge: Cambridge University Press, 2002).

Irwin, James, "Explaining the Decline in Southern per Capita Output after Emancipation," *Explorations in Economic History*, 31, 3 (1994): 336-356.

Ismard, Paulin, Benedetta Rossi and Cécile Vidal eds., *Les mondes de l'esclavage. Une histoire comparée* (Paris: Seuil, 2021).

Izmes'eva, Tatiana, *Rossiia v sisteme evropeiskogo rynka. Konets XIXe-nachalo XX v.* (Russia in the system of the European market, end of the nineteenth to the early twentieth century) (Moscow: Nauka, 1991).

Jacobs, Harriet, *Incidents in the Life of a Slave Girl: Written by Herself* (Boston: Maria Child, 1861).

Jarrige, François and Bénédicte Reynaud, "La durée du travail. La norme et ses usages en 1848," *Genèse*, 85, 4 (2011): 70–92.

Jennings, Evelyn, *Constructing the Spanish Empire in Havana* (Baton Rouge: Louisiana State University Press, 2020).

Jewsbury, George, *The Russian Annexation of Bessarbia, 1774–1828: A Study of Imperial Expansion* (New York: Columbia University Press, 1976).

Joffe, Muriel, "Autocracy, Capitalism, Empire: The Politics of Irrigation," *Russian Review*, 54, 3 (1995): 365–388.

Johnson, Walter, *River of Dark Dreams: Slavery and Empire in the Cotton Kingdom* (Cambridge, MA: Harvard University Press, 2013).

Jones, Eric, *Agriculture and Industrial Revolution* (Oxford: Oxford University Press, 1974).

Jones, Eric, *The European Miracle* (Cambridge: Cambridge University Press, 1981).

Jones, Peter, "Looking Through Different Lens: Microhistory and the Workhouse Experience in Late Nineteenth-Century London," *Journal of Social History*, 55, 4 (2022): 925–947.

Jordan, Winthrop, *White Over Black: American Attitudes Towards the Negro, 1550–1812* (Chapel Hill: The University of North Carolina Press, 2nd edition, 2012).

Journal officiel du Congo français, circular dated July 15, 1900.

Jummer, Musleem, *Les affranchis et les Indiens libres à l'île de France au XVIIIe siècle, 1721–1803* (PhD, Université de Poitiers, 1984).

Kabuzan, Vladimir M., *Izmeneniia v razmeshchenii naseleniia Rossii v XVIII-pervoi polovine XIX v.* (Changes in the rate of growth of the Russian population during the eighteenth and the first half of the nineteenth century) (Moscow: Nauka, 1971).

Kabuzan, Viktor, *Naselenie Severnogo Kavkaza v XIX-XX vekakh: etnostatisticheskoe issledovanie* (The population of North Caucasus in the nineteenth and twentieth centuries: an etnostatistical study) (St. Petersburg: BLITs, 1996).

Kahan, Arcadius, *The Plow, the Hammer and the Knout* (Chicago: University of Chicago Press, 1985).

Kaplan, Herbert, "Russia's Impact on the Industrial Revolution in Great Britain during the Second Half of the Eighteenth Century," *Forschungen zur Osteuropäischen Geschichte*, 29 (1981): 7–59.

Kaplan, Herbert, "Observations on the Value of Russia's Overseas Trade with Great Britain during the Second Half of the Eighteenth Century," *Slavic Review*, 45, 1 (1986): 85–94.

Kaplan, Steven, *La fin des corporations* (Paris: Fayard, 2001).

Kappeler, Andreas, *Rußland als Vielvölkerreich: Entstehung, Geschichte, Zerfall* (Munich: C. H. Beck, 1992).

Kappeler, Andreas, *The Russian Empire: A Multiethnic History* (London: Pearson, 2001).

Kappeler, Andreas, *Der schwierige Weg zur Nation: Beiträge zur neueren Geschichte der Ukraine* (The difficult path to nationhood: Contributions to the history of modern Ukraine) (Vienna: Böhlau, 2003).

Kappeler, Andreas, *"Great-Russians" and "Little-Russians": Russian–Ukrainian Relations and Perceptions in Historical Perspective* (Seattle: University of Washington Press, 2003).
Kappeler, Andreas, Zenon E. Kohut, Frank E. Sysyn and Mark von Hagen, eds., *Culture, Nation, and Identity: The Ukrainian–Russian Encounter, 1600–1945* (Edmonton: Canadian Institute of Ukrainian Studies Press, 2003).
Kashchenko, Serguei, *Reforma 19 Fevralia 1861 goda na severo-zapade Rossii* (The reform of 1861 in the north-west of Russia) (Moscow: Mosgosararkhiv, 1995).
Katz, William Loren, *Breaking the Chain* (New York: Atheneum, 1990).
Kessler-Harris, Alice, *Gendering Labor History* (Dekalb: University of Illinois Press, 2007).
Khodarkovsky, Michael, *Russia's Steppe Frontier* (Bloominton: Indiana University Press, 2004).
Khoroshkevich, Aleksandr', *Russkoe gosudarstvo v sisteme mezhdunarodnykh otnoshenii kontsa XV-nachala XVI v.* (The Russian state in the system of international relations in the late fifteenth and early sixteenth centuries) (Moscow: Nauka, 1980).
Khristoforov, Igor, *Sud'ba reformy: Russkoe krest'ianstvo v pravitel'stvennoi politike do i posle otmeny krepostnogo prava (1830–1890-e gg.)* (The fate of reforms: the Russian peasantry and the government policies before and after the abolition of serfdom, 1830–1890) (Moscow: Sobranie, 2011).
Kieniewicz, Stefan, *The Emancipation of the Polish Peasantry* (Chicago: Chicago University Press, 1969).
King, Charles, *The Black Sea: A History* (Oxford: Oxford University Press, 2015).
Kingston-Mann, Esther, "Marxism and Russian Rural Development: Problems of Evidence, Experience and Culture," *American Historical Review*, 86, 4 (1981): 731–752.
Kingston-Mann, Esther, *In Search of the True West* (Princeton: Princeton University Press, 1999).
Kingston-Mann, Esther, and Timothy Mixter, eds., *Peasant Economy, Culture, and Politics of European Russia, 1800–1921* (Princeton: Princeton University Press, 1991).
Kish Sklar, Kathryn and James Brewer Stewart, eds., *Sisterhood and Slavery* (New Haven: Yale University Press, 2006).
Klein, Martin, *Islam and Imperialism in Senegal: Sine-Saloum 1847–1914* (Stanford: Stanford University Press, 1968).
Klein, Martin ed., *Breaking the Chains: Slavery, Bondage and Emancipation in Modern Africa and Asia* (Madison: University of Wisconsin Press, 1993).
Klein, Martin, "Simulating the African Slave Trade," *Canadian Journal of African Studies*, 28 2 (1994): 296–299.
Klein, Martin, *Slavery and Colonial Rule in French West Africa* (Cambridge: Cambridge University Press, 1998).
Klein, Martin, "The End of Slavery in French West Africa," in Hideaki Suzuki, ed., *Abolitions as a Global Experience* (Singapore: NUS Press, 2016): 199–227.

Kolchin, Peter, *Unfree Labor: American Slavery and Russian Serfdom* (Cambridge, MA: Harvard University Press, 1987).
Kolff, Dirk, *Naukar, Rajput and Sepoy: The Ethnohistory of the Military Labour Market in Hindustan, 1450-1850* (Cambridge: Cambridge University Press, 1990).
Kolsky, Elizabeth, *Colonial Justice in British India* (Cambridge: Cambridge University Press, 2009).
Konstam, Angus, *Buccaneers, 1620-1700* (Oxford: Osprey Publishing, 2000).
Konstam, Angus, *Privateers and Pirates, 1730-1830* (Oxford: Osprey, 2001).
Konstam, Angus, *The Pirate Ship, 1660-1730* (Oxford: Osprey, 2003).
Kooiman, Dick, "Conversion from Slavery to Plantation Labor: Christian Mission in South India, Nineteenth Century," *Social Scientist*, 19, 8/9 (1991): 57-71.
Kostal, Rande W. *A Jurisprudence of Power: Victorian Empire and the Rule of Law* (Oxford: Oxford University Press, 2005).
Kotkin, Stephen, "Mongol Commonwealth? Exchange and Governance Across the Post-Mongol Space," *Kritika*, 8, 3 (2007): 487-531.
Koval'chenko, Ivan D., *Russkoe krepostnoe krest'ianstvo v pervoi polovine XIX v.* (Russian serf peasantry during the first half of the nineteenth century) (Moscow: Nauka, 1967).
Koval'chenko, Ivan D., and Leonid Milov, *Vserossiiskii agrarnyi rynok, XVIII–nachalo XX v.* (The all-Russian agrarian market, eighteenth-early twentieth centuries) (Moscow: Nauka, 1974).
Kovalaschina, Elena, "The Historical and Cultural Ideals of the Siberian Oblastnichestvo," *Sibirica*, 6, 2 (2007): 87-119.
Kozlova, Natalia, *Pobegi krest'ian v Rossii v pervoi treti XVIII veka* (Peasants on the run in Russia during the first third of the eighteenth century) (Moscow: Moskovskii universitet, 1983).
Krakovitch, Odile, "Les archives des bagnes de Cayenne et de Nouvelle-Calédonie: la sous-série colonies H aux archives nationales," *Revue d'histoire du XIXe siècle*, 1, 1 (1985): 45-51.
Kula, Witold, *An Economic Theory of the Feudal System* (London: New Left Books, 1976).
Kumar, Ashutosh, "Subaltern Mobility and Labor Contract: Indian Indenture in New World History," *Journal of World History*, 32, 1 (2021): 19-28.
Kumar, Dharma, "Colonialism, Bondage, and Caste in British India," in Martin Klein ed., *Breaking the Chains*: Slavery, Bondage, and Emancipation in Modern Africa and Asia (Madison: The University of Wisconsin Press, 1993): 112-130.
Kumar, Krishan, *Visions of Empire: How Five Imperial Regimes Shaped the World* (Princeton: Princeton University Press, 2017).
Kumar, Prakash, *Indigo Plantation and Science in Colonial India* (New York: Cambridge University Press, 2012).
Kussmaul, Ann, *Servants in Husbandry in Early Modern England* (Cambridge: Cambridge University Press, 1981).
Kussmaul, Ann, *A General View of the Rural Economy of England, 1538-1840* (Cambridge: Cambridge University Press, 1990).

La Dépêche coloniale, December 23, 1903.

Lafleur, Gerard, "Le peuplement des Antilles françaises au XVIIe siècle," *Actes des Congrès nationaux historiques et scientifiques*, 133, 6 (2012): 53–69.

Lalouette, Jacqueline, *Jean Jaurès. L'assassinat, la gloire, le souvenir* (Paris: Éditions Perrin, 2014).

Landes, David, *The Unbound Prometheus. Technological Change and Industrial Development in Western Europe since 1750 to the Present* (Cambridge: Cambridge University Press, 2003).

Landry, Yves, "Les filles du Roi émigrées au Canada au XVIIe siècle, ou un exemple de choix du conjoint en situation de déséquilibre des sexes," *Histoire, économie et société*, 11, 2 (1992): 197–216.

Landry, Yves, *Orphelines en France, pionnières au Canada: les Filles du roi au XVIIe siècle* (Montréal: Leméac, 1992).

Lara, Oruno D., *La liberté assassinée. Guadeloupe, Guyane, Martinique et La Réunion, 1848–1856* (Paris: Editions L'Harmattan, 2005).

Larin, Robert, *Brève histoire du peuplement européen en Nouvelle-France* (Québec: Éditions du septentrion, 2000).

Larson, Pier, *Oceans of Letters: Language and Creolization in an Indian Ocean Diaspora* (Cambridge: Cambridge University Press, 2009).

Lauderdale Graham, Sandra, *Caetana Says No: Women's Stories from a Brazilian Slave Society* (Cambridge: Cambridge University Press, 2002).

Lauderdale Graham, Sandra, "Writing from the Margins: Brazilian Slaves and Written Culture," *Comparative Studies in Society and History*, 49, 3 (2007): 611–636.

Le Cour Grandemaison, Olivier, *De l'indigénat* (Paris: Zone, 2010).

Le Donne, John, *Absolutism and Ruling Class: The Formation of the Russian Political Order, 1700–1825* (Oxford: Oxford University Press, 1991).

Le Glaunec, Jean-Pierre, "Resister à l'esclavage dans l'Atlantique français: aperçu historiographique, hypothèses et pistes de recherche," *Revue d'histoire de l'Amérique française*, 71, 1–2 (2017): 13–33.

Le Goff, Jacques, *Du silence à la parole. Droit du travail, société, État (1830–1985)* (Quimper: Calligrammes-La Digitale, 1985).

Lebon, André, *La politique de la France en Afrique, 1896–1898* (Paris: Plon, 1901).

Ledovskaia, Irina V. "Biudzhet russkogo pomeshchika v 40–60kh godakh XIX v" (Estate owners' budgets in the 1840s–'60s), in Akademiia Nauk SSSR, *Materialy po istorii sel'skogo khoziaistva i krest'ianstva SSSR*, vol. 8, (Moscow: Nauka, 1974): 240–245.

Lee, Robert, *The Manchurian Frontier in Ch'ing History* (Cambridge, MA: Harvard University Press, 1970).

Lee Downs, Laura, *Manufacturing Inequality: Gender Division in the French and British Metalworking Industries 1914–1939* (Ithaca: Cornell University Press, 1995).

Lefebvre, Philippe, *L'invention de la grande entreprise. Travail, hiérarchie, marché. France, fin XVIIIe-début XXe siècle* (Paris: Presses universitaires de France, 2003).

Lefeuvre, Daniel, *Pour en finir avec la repentance coloniale* (Paris: Flammarion, 2006).
Lehning, James, *To be a Citizen: The Political Culture of the Early French Third Republic* (Ithaca: Cornell University Press, 2001).
Lentz, Thierry and Pierre Branda, *Napoléon, l'esclavage et les colonies* (Paris: Fayard, 2006).
Leonard, Carol, *Agrarian Reforms in Russia* (Cambridge: Cambridge University Press, 2011).
Lequin, Yves, *Les ouvriers de la région lyonnaise* (Lyon: PUL, 1974).
Leventer, Herbert, "Comments on Richard Hellie's "Recent Soviet..."" *Russian Review*, 36, 1 (1977): 64–67.
Levine Frader, Laura, "Gender and Labor in World History," in Teresa Meade and Merry Wiesner-Hanks, eds., *A Companion to Global Gender History* (London: Wiley, 2020): https://doi.org/10.1002/9781119535812.ch2.
Lévy-Leboyer, Maurice and François Bourguignon, *L'économie française au XIXe siècle. Analyse macroéconomique* (Paris: Economica, 1985).
Lévy-Leboyer, Maurice and J.-C. Casanova, *Entre l'État et le marché. L'économie française des années 1880 à nos jours* (Paris: Gallimard, 1991).
Lewis, David Rich, *Neither Wolf nor Dog: American Indians, Environment and Agrarian Change* (New York: Oxford, Oxford University Press, 1994).
Lieven, Dominic, *Empire: The Russian Empire and Its Rivals from the Sixteenth Century to the Present* (London: Pimlico, 2003).
Lin, Man-Houng, *China Upside Down: Currency, Society and Ideologies, 1808–1956* (Cambridge, MA, Harvard University Press, 2006).
Lincoln, Margarette, *British Pirates and Society, 1680–1730* (London: Routledge, 2014).
Lindert, Peter and Jeffrey Williamson, "Revising England's Social Tables, 1688–1867," *Explorations in Economic History*, 19, 4 (1982): 385–408.
Lindert, Peter and Jeffrey Williamson, "English Workers' Living Standards during the Industrial Revolution: A New Look," *Economic History Review*, 36, 1 (1983): 1–25.
Litvak, Boris, *Russkaia derevniia v reforme 1861 goda: Chernozemnyi tsentr 1861–1895 gg* (The Russian countryside in the reform of 1861: the Central Black Earth, 1861–1895) (Moscow: Nauka, 1972).
Liu, Cuirong, Ts'ui-jung Liu, James Lee, David Sven Reher, Osamu Saito and Wang Feng, eds., *Asian Population History* (Oxford: Oxford University Press, 2001).
Lovejoy, Paul, *Transformations in Slavery* (Cambridge: Cambridge University Press, 3rd edition, 2012).
Lovejoy, Paul and Jan Hogendown, *Slow Death of Slavery: The Course of Abolition in Northern Nigeria, 1897–1936* (Cambridge: Cambridge University Press, 1993).
Lucas, Rafael, "Marronage et marronnages," *Cahiers d'histoire*, 89 (2002): 13–28.
Lucassen, Jan, ed., *Wage and Currency* (Bern: Peter Lang, 2008).
Lucassen, Jan, *The Story of Work: A New History of Humankind* (New Haven: Yale University Press, 2022).

Lucassen, Jan and Leo Lucassen eds., *Migration, Migration History, History: Old Paradigms and New Perspectives* (Bern: Peter Lang, 1997).
Lucassen, Leo, "Working Together: New Directions in Global Labour History," *Journal of Global History*, 11, 1 (2016): 66–87.
Ly, Abdoulaye, *La Compagnie du Sénégal* (Paris: Karthala, 1993).
MacFarlane, Alan, *Marriage and Love in England, 1300–1840* (Oxford: Blackwell, 1986).
Machado, Pedro, "A Forgotten Corner of the Indian Ocean: Gujarati Merchants, Portuguese Indian and the Mozambique Slave Trade, c. 1730–1830," in Gwyn Campbell, ed., *The Structure of Slavery* (London: Frank Cass, 2004): 17–36.
MacLeod, Christine, *Inventing the Industrial Revolution* (Cambridge: Cambridge University Press, 1988).
MacPherson, David, *Annals of Commerce* (Edinburgh: Nichols, 1805).
Maestri, Edmond, *Esclavage et abolition dans l'Océan Indien, 1723–1860* (Paris: L'Harmattan, 2002).
Magnac, Thierry and Gilles Postel-Vinay, "Wage Competition between Agriculture and Industry in Mid-Nineteenth Century France," *Explorations in Economic History*, 34, 1 (1997): 1–26.
Main, Gloria Lund, *Tobacco Colony: Life in Early Maryland, 1650–1720* (Princeton, NJ: Princeton University Press, 1982).
Mair, Lucille, *A Historical Study of Women in Jamaica, 1655–1844* (Barbados: University of West Indies Press, 2006).
Major, Andrea, *Slavery, Abolitionism and Empire in India, 1772–1843* (Liverpool: Liverpool University Press, 2002).
Man'kov, Arkhadii, *Razvitie krepostnogo prava v Rossii vo vtoroi polovine XVII veka* (The development of serfdom law in Russia during the second half of the seventeenth century) (Moscow and Leningrad: Akademiia nauk SSSR, 1962).
Manceron, Gilles, *Jean Jaurès vers l'anticolonialisme. Du colonialisme à l'universalisme* (Paris: Les petits matins, 2015).
Mandle, Jay, "The Plantation States as a Sub-Region of the Post-bellum South," *The Journal of Economic History*, 34, 3 (1974): 732–738.
Mandrou, Robert, "Vers les Antilles et le Canada au XVIIe siècle," *Annales ESC*, 14, 4 (1959): 667–675.
Mani, Lata, "Contentious Traditions: The Debate on Sati in Colonial India," *Cultural Critique*, 7 (1987): 119–156.
Manière, Laurent, "Deux conceptions de l'action judiciaire aux colonies. Magistrats et administrateurs en AOF (1887–1912)," *Clio-Thémis*, 4 (2011): www.cliothemis.com/Clio-Themis-numero-4.
Mann, Michael, *The Sources of Social Power, vol. 3, Global Empires and Revolutions* (Cambridge: Cambridge University Press, 2012).
Manning, Patrick, *Slavery, Colonialism and Economic Growth in Dahomey, 1640–1960* (Cambridge: Cambridge University Press, 1982).
Manning, Patrick, *Slavery and African Life: Occidental, Oriental and African Slave Trades* (Cambridge: Cambridge University Press, 1990).

Manning, Patrick, "The Slave Trade: The Formal Demography of a Global System," *Social Science History*, 14; 2 (1990): 255–279.
Manning, Patrick, *Francophone Sub-Saharan Africa* (Cambridge: Cambridge University Press, 1998).
Mantena, Karuna, *Alibis of Empire: Henri Maine and the Ends of Liberal Imperialism* (Princeton: Princeton University Press, 2010).
Mantoux, Paul, *The Industrial Revolution in the Eighteenth Century: an Outline of the Beginning of the Modern Factory System in England* (New York: Harper, 1928, French original 1906).
Marc, Bloch, "Pour une histoire comparée des sociétés européennes," *Revue de synthèse historique*, 46 (1928): 15–50.
Margoline-Plot, Eugenie, *Les pacottilles d'indiennes, la boutique et la mer* (PhD, University of Lorient, 2014).
Marinescu, Ioana, *Les prud'hommes sont-ils efficaces?* (Master's thesis: EHESS, 2002).
Marseille, Jacques, *Empire colonial et capitalisme français. Histoire d'un divorce* (Paris: Albin Michel, 1984).
Martin, Virginia, *Law and Custom in the Steppe: The Kazakhs of the Middle Horde and Russian Colonialism in the Nineteenth Century* (Richmond, Surrey: Routledge Curzon, 2001).
Marx, Karl, *Das kapital* (Italian translation, Roma: Einaudi, 1972).
Masoero, Alberto, "Autorità e territorio nella colonizzazione siberiana," *Rivista Storica Italiana*, CXV, 2 (2003): 439–486.
Mason, Cathy, ed., *The Economy of Early America: Historical Perspectives & New Directions* (University Park: Pennsylvania State University Press, 2006).
Masson, André, "L'opinion française et les problèmes coloniaux à la fin du Second Empire," *Revue française d'histoire d'outre-mer*, 51, 3–4 (1962): 366–455.
Mathieu, Jacques, *La Nouvelle-France. Les français en Amérique du Nord, XVIe–XVIIIe siècle* (Montréal: Presses de l'Université de Laval, 2001).
Matsuzato, Kimitaka, *Imperiology: From Empirical Knowledge to Discussing the Russian Empire* (Sapporo: Slavic Research Center, 2007).
Mauro, Frédéric, "French Indentured Servants for America, 1500–1800," in Petr C. Emmer, ed., *Colonialism and Migration: Indentured Labor before and after Slavery* (Dordrecht: Martin Nijhoff, 1986): 105–125.
Maxwell-Stewart, Hamish, "Convict transportation from Britain and Ireland, 1615–1870," *History Compass*, 8, 11 (2010): 1221–1242.
Mayaud, Jean-Luc, "Salariés agricoles et petite propriété dans la France du XIXe siècle," in Jean-Claude Farcy, and Ronald Hubscher, eds., *La moisson des autres* (Nice: Créaphys édition, 1996): 29–56.
Mayaud, Jean-Luc, ed., *1848: Actes du 150ème anniversaire* (Paris, Créaphys, 2002).
Mayer, Arno, *The Persistence of the Old Regime: Europe to the Great War* (London: Pantheon Books, 1981).
Mayeur, Jean-Marie, *Les débuts de la IIIe République, 1871–1898* (Paris: Seuil, 1973).
McClennan, James III, *Colonialism and Science: Saint-Domingue in the Old Regime* (Chicago: The University of Chicago Press, 2010, orig. 1992).

McCloskey, Deidre, *Bourgeois Dignity: Why Economics Can't Explain the Modern World* (Chicago: The University of Chicago Press, 2011).
McCloskey, Donald, "The Enclosure of Open Fields: Preface to a Study of Its Impact on the Efficiency of English Agriculture in the Eighteenth Century," *The Journal of Economic History*, 31, 1 (1972): 15-35.
McDaniel, W. Caleb, *Sweet Taste of Liberty: A True Story of Slavery and Restitution in America* (New York: Oxford University Press, 2019).
McDonald, Roderick A. ed., *Caribbean Accounts: Essays on the British West Indies and the Atlantic Economy* (Kingston: University of the West Indies, 1996).
McFarlane, Anthony, "Cimarrones and Palenques: Runaways and Resistance in Colonial Colombia," *Slavery and Abolition*, 6, 3 (1985): 131-151.
McKay, John, *Four Russian Serf Narratives* (Madison: Wisconsin University Press, 2009).
McKee, Helen, "From Violence to Alliance: Maroons and White Settlers in Jamaica, 1739-1795," *Slavery & Abolition*, 39, 1 (2018): 27-52, DOI: 10.1080/0144039X.2017.1341016.
McKenzie, Robert Tracy, *One South or Many? Plantation Belt and Upcountry in Civil War Era Tennessee* (New York: Cambridge University Press, 1994).
McKeown, Adam, "Global Migration, 1846-1940," *Journal of World History*, 15, 2 (2004): 155-189.
McNeill, Hector, *Observations on the Treatment of Negroes in the Island of Jamaica* (London: G.G.J. and J. Robinson, No. 25, Pater-Noster-Row, and J. Gore, 1788).
Meade, Teresa, and Merry Wiesner-Hanks, *A Companion to Global Gender History* (London: Wiley, 2020).
Mehta, Uday, *Liberalism and Empire* (Chicago: University of Chicago Press, 1999).
Meillassoux, Claude, *Anthropologie de l'esclavage* (Paris: PUF, 1986).
Melton, Edgar, "Proto-industrialization, Serf Agriculture, and Agrarian Social Structure: Two Estates in Nineteenth-century Russia," *Past and Present*, 115 (May 1987): 73-81.
Menard, Russell R., "British Migration to the Chesapeake Colonies in the Seventeenth Century," in Lois Green Carr, Philip Morgan, Jean Russo, eds., *Colonial Chesapeake Society* (Chapel Hill: Northern Illinois University Press, 1988): 99-132.
Menard, Russell R., *Migrants, Servants and Slaves: Unfree Labor in Colonial British America* (Aldershot: Ashgate, 2001).
Menard, Russell R., "The Africanization of the Workforce in English America," in Gwyn Campbell and Alessandro Stanziani, eds., *Debt and Slavery in the Mediterranean and Atlantic Worlds* (London: Pickering and Chatto, 2013): 93-104.
Merivale, Herman, *Lectures on Colonization and Colonies* (London: Orme, Brown, Green and Longmans, 1841).
Merle, Isabelle, "De la légalisation de la violence en contexte colonial. Le régime de l'indigénat en question," *Politix*, 17, 66 (2004): 137-162.
Metcalf, Thomas, *Imperial Connections* (Berkeley: University of California Press, 2007).

Mettas, Jean, *Répertoire des expéditions négrières françaises au XVIIIe siècle*, 2 volumes (Paris: Société française d'histoire d'outre mer, 1978).
Meyer, Jean, *Histoire de la France coloniale, I. Des origines à 1914* (Paris: Colin, 1991).
Midgley, Claire, *Women Against Slavery* (London: Routledge, 1992).
Miers, Suzanne and Igor Kopytoff, eds., *Slavery in Africa: Historical and Anthropological Perspectives* (Madison, WI: University of Wisconsin Press, 1977).
Miers, Suzanne and Richard Roberts, eds., *The End of Slavery in Africa* (Madison: University of Wisconsin Press, 1988).
Miglorini, Luigi Mascilli and Mirella Mafrici, eds., *Mediterraneo e Mar Nero. Due mari tra età moderna e contemporanea* (Naples: ESI, 2012).
Milewicz, Przemyslaw, "National Identification in Pre-Industrial Communities: Peasant Participation in the November Uprising in the Kingdom of Poland, 1830–1831," *Jahrbücher für Geschichte Osteuropas*, 58, 3 (2010): 321–352.
Milewski, Melissa, "From Slave to Litigant: African Americans in Court in the Postwar South, 1865–1920," *Law & History Review*, 30, 3 (2012): 723–769.
Miliukov, Paul, "Eurasianism and Europeanism in Russian History," *Festschrift für Th. G. Masaryk zum 80. Geburtstag* (Bonn: F. Cohen, 1930).
Mill, James, "Colony," in *Supplement to the Encyclopedia Britannica* (London, 1820): 31–33, reprint in G.W. Smith, ed., *John Stuart Mill's Social and Political Thought. Critical Assessments* (London: Routledge, 1998), vol. III: 498.
Mill, James, *The History of British India* (London: James Madden, 1858, first edition: 1817).
Mill, John Stuart, "Review of John Elliot Cairnes, The Slave Power," in *Westmister Review* (July 1862): 489–510.
Millar, Joseph Calder, *Slavery and Slaving in World History: A Bibliography, 1900–1996* (Armonk: M. E. Sharpe, 1999).
Millar, Joseph Calder, "Credit, Captives, Collateral and Currencies: Debt, Slavery and the Financing of the Atlantic World," in Gwyn Campbell and Alessandro Stanziani, eds., *Debt and Slavery in the Mediterranean and the Atlantic World* (London: Pickering & Chatto, 2013): 105–122.
Millar, Joseph Calder, *The Problem of Slavery as History* (New Haven: Yale University Press, 2016).
Miller, Aleksei, ed., *Rossiiskaia imperiia v sravnitel´noi perspektive: Sbornik statei* (The Russian Empire in Comparative Perspective) (Moscow: Novoe izdatel´stvo, 2004).
Miller, Alexej, *"Ukrainskij vopros" v politike vlastej v russkom obchtchestvennom mnenii (vtoraja pol. XIX v.)* (The Ukrainian question in the politics of power in the Russian social thought) (St. Petersburg: Aleteia, 2000).
Miller, Alexei and Alfred J. Rieber, eds., *Imperial Rule* (Budapest: Central European University Press, 2004).
Minard, Philippe, *La fortune du colbertisme. État et industrie dans la France des Lumières* (Paris: Fayard, 1998).

Ministère de l'industrie et du commerce, *Enquête sur les conseils de prud'hommes et les livrets d'ouvriers*, 2 volumes (Paris: Imprimerie impériale, 1869).
Ministerstvo zemledeliia, *Ezhegodnik GUZiZ* (Yearbook of the Land Colonization Commission) (St. Petersburg: Ministerstvo zemledeliia, 1908–1916).
Ministerstvo sel'skogo khoziaistva, *Obzor dejatel'nosti za...1908-1914 (Report on the activity of the ministry, 1908-1914)* (St. Petersbourg: Ministerstvo sel'skogo khoziaistva, 1909–1916).
Mintz, Sidney, *Sweetness and Power: The Place of Sugar in Modern History* (New York: Penguin Books, 1986).
Mironov, Boris, *Vnutrennyi rynok Rossii vo vtoroi polovine XVIII – pervoi polovine XIX v* (The domestic market in Russia during the second half of the eighteenth century-first half of the nineteenth century) (Leningrad: Nauka, 1981).
Mironov, Boris. "Consequences of the Price Revolution in Eighteenth-century Russia." *The Economic History Review*, 45 (1992): 457–78.
Mironov, Boris, *The Social History of the Russian Empire*, 2 volumes (Boulder, CO: Westview, 1999).
Mironov, Boris and Carol S. Leonard, "In Search of the Hidden Information: Some Issues in the Socio-Economic History of Russia in the Eighteenth and Nineteenth Centuries," *Social Science History*, 9, 4 (Autumn 1985): 339–359.
Mitchell, Brian Redman, *British Historical Statistics* (Cambridge: Cambridge University Press, 1988).
Mitchell, Charles and Jean Baker, eds., *The Civil War in Maryland Reconsidered* (Baton Rouge: Louisiana State University Press, 2021).
Mogilner, Marina, *Homo Imperii: A History of Physical Anthropology in Russia* (Lincoln: University of Nebraska Press, 2013).
Mohapatra, Prabhu, "Assam and the West Indies, 1860–1920: Immobilizing Plantation Labor," in Douglas Hay and Paul Craven, eds., *Masters, Servants, and Magistrates in Britain and the Empire, 1562–1955* (Chapel Hill: The University of North Carolina Press, 2004): 455–480.
Mohapatra, Prabhu, "From Contract to Status or How Law Shaped Labour Relations in Colonial India, 1780–1880," in Jan Breman, Isabelle Guerin, Aseem Prakash, eds., *India's Unfree Workforce: Of Bondage Old and New* (New Delhi: Oxford University Press, 2009): 96–125.
Mohapatra, Prabhu P. and Marcel van der Linden, eds., *Labour Matters: Towards Global Histories: Studies in Honour of Sabyasachi Bhattacharya* (New Delhi: Tulika, 2009).
Moir, Marin, Douglas Peers, and Lynn Zastoupil, eds., *J.S. Mill's Encounter with India* (Toronto: University of Toronto Press, 1999).
Mokyr, Joel, ed., *The Economics of the Industrial Revolution* (Totowa: Rowman and Allanheld, 1985).
Mokyr, Joel, *The Lever of Riches* (Oxford: Oxford University Press, 1990).
Montesquieu, Charles Secondat, Baron, *Esprit des lois* (Paris: Garnier, 1967, orig. 1748).
Moogk, Peter, "Emigrants from France in Canada before 1760," *The William and Mary Quarterly*, 46, 3 (1989): 463–505.

Moogk, Peter, "Reluctant Exiles: Emigrants from France to Canada before 1760," *The William and Mary Quarterly*, 46, 3 (1989): 463–505.

Moon, David, *Russian Peasants and Tsarist Legislation on the Eve of Reform, 1825–1855* (Basingstoke: Macmillan, 1992).

Moon, David, *The Russian Peasantry, 1600–1930: The World the Peasants Made* (London and New York: Addison Wesley Longman, 1999).

Moon, David, *The Plough that Broke the Steppe* (Oxford: Oxford University Press, 2013).

Moorhouse, Hallam, ed., *Letters of the English Seamen, 1587–1808* (London: Chapman & Hall, 1910).

Moreau de Saint-Méry, Médéric Elie Louis, *Lois et constitutions des colonies française de l'Amérique sous le vent de 1550 à 1685*, 6 volumes (Paris: Delabarre de Nanteuil).

Morgan, Gwenda and Peter Rushton, *Banishment in the Early Atlantic World: Convicts, Rebels, and Slaves* (London: Bloomsbury, 2013).

Morgan, Philip D., *Slave Counterpoint: Black Culture in Eighteenth-Century Chesapeake & Lowcountry* (Chapel Hill: University of North Carolina Press, 1998).

Moriceau, Jean-Marc, "Les Baccanals ou grèves des moissonneurs en pays de France, seconde moitié du XVIIIe siècle," in Jean Nicolas, ed., *Mouvements populaires et conscience sociale* (Paris: Maloine, 1985): 420–433.

Morineau, Michel, *Les faux-semblants d'un démarrage économique: agriculture et démographie en France au XVIIIe siècle* (Paris: Colin, 1971).

Morris, Henry F. and James Read, *Indirect Rule and the Search for Justice: Essays on East African Legal History* (Oxford: Clarendon Press, 1972): 112–113.

Morris, Thomas, *Southern Slavery and the Law, 1619–1860* (Chapel Hill: University of North Carolina Press, 1999).

Morrison, Alexander S., *Russian Rule in Samarkand, 1868–1910: A Comparison with British India* (Oxford: Oxford University Press, 2008).

Morrison, Michael A., *Slavery and the American West: The Eclipse of Manifest Destiny and the Coming of the Civil War* (Chapel Hill: University of North Carolina Press, 1997).

Moyn, Samuel, *The Last Utopia: Human Rights in History* (Cambridge: Belknap, 2010).

Muller, Viola, *Escape to the City: Fugitive Slaves in Antebellum Urban South* (Chapel Hill: The University of North Carolina Press, 2022).

Munro, J. Forbes, *Africa and the International Economy* (London: Rowman and Littlefield, 1976).

Nadri, Ghulam, *The Political Economy of Indigo in India, 1580–1930: A Global Perspective* (Leiden: Brill, 2016).

Nafziger, Steven, "Land Commune and Factor Market Imperfections: Micro Evidence from Late Nineteenth Century Russia," *Explorations in Economic History*, 47, 4 (2010): 381–402.

Nafziger, Steven, "Communal Property Rights and Land Redistribution in Late Imperial Russia," *The Economic History Review*, 69, 3 (2016): 773–800.

Naidu, Suresh, "Recruitment Restrictions and Labor Markets: Evidence from the Post-Bellum US South," *Journal of Labor Economics*, 28, 2 (2010): 413–445.

Naidu, Suresh, "Suffrage, Schooling, and Sorting in Post-Bellum South," NBER working paper 18129 (2012), www.nber.org/system/files/working_papers/w18129/w18129.pdf.

Naidu, Suresh and Noam Yuchtman, "How Green was my Valley? Coercive Contract Enforcement in Nineteenth Century Britain," *NBUR working papers*, 2009.

Nicolas, Jean, ed., *Mouvements populaires et conscience sociale* (Paris: Maloine, 1985).

Nieboer, Herman, *Slavery as an Industrial System: Ethnological Researches* (The Hague: Martinus Nijhof, 1900).

Nikitenko, Alexander, *Up from Serfdom: My Childhood and Youth in Russia, 1804–1824.* trans. Helen Saltz Jacobson (New Haven: Yale University Press, 2001).

Niort, Jean-François, *Le Code Noir. Idées reçues sur un texte symbolique* (Paris: Le cavalier bleu, 2015).

Noiriel, Gerard, *Les ouvriers dans la société française* (Paris: Seuil, 1986).

North, Douglass, *Structure and Change in Economic History* (New York: W. W. Norton, 1981).

North, Douglass and Barry Weingast, "Constitution and Commitment: The Evolution of Institution Governing Public Choice in Seventeenth-Century England," *The Journal of Economic History*, 49, 4 (1989): 803–832.

North, Douglass and Robert Thomas, "The Rise and Fall of the Manorial System: A Theoretical Model," *Journal of Economic History*, 31 (1971): 777–803.

North, Douglass and Robert Thomas, *The Rise of Western Civilization: a New Economic History* (Cambridge: Cambridge University Press, 1973).

Northrup, David, *Indentured Labor in the Age of Imperialism: 1834–1922* (Cambridge: Cambridge University Press, 1995).

Novak, William, *The People's Welfare: Law and Regulation in Nineteenth Century America* (Chapel Hill: University of North Carolina Press, 1996).

Novosel'skii, Aleksandr', "Otdatochnye knigi beglykh, kak istochnik dlia izucheniia narodnoi kolonizatsii na Rusi v XVII veke," (Fugitive registers as a source for studying colonization in seventeenth-century Russia) *Trudy istoriko-arkhivnogo instituta*, 2 (1946): 127–154.

Novosel'skii, Aleksei, *Bor'ba Moskovskogo gosudarstva s tatarami v pervoi polovine 17 veka* (The struggle of the Muscovite state against the Tatars in the first half of the seventeenth century) (Moscow, Leningrad: Nauka, 1948).

Nunn, Nathan, "The Long-term Effect of Africa's Slave Trades," *Quarterly Journal of Economics*, 123, 1 (2008): 139–176.

Nzenguet Iguemba, G. A., *Colonisation, fiscalité et mutations au Gabon, 1910–1947* (Paris: l'Harmattan, 2005).

O'Brien, Patrick, "Agriculture and the Industrial Revolution," *Economic History Review*, 30, 1 (1977): 166–181.

O'Brien, Patrick, "European Economic Development: The Contribution of the Periphery," *Economic History Review*, 35, 1 (1982): 1–18.

O'Brien, Patrick, "Review of *Ten Years of Debate on the Origin of the Great Divergence*," *Reviews in History* (2010): www.history.ac.uk/reviews/review/1008.
O'Brien, Patrick and Stanley Engerman, "Exports and the Growth of the British Economy from the Glorious Revolution to the Peace of Amiens," in Barbara Solow, ed., *Slavery and the Rise of the Atlantic System* (Cambridge: Cambridge University Press, 1991): 177–209.
O'Brien, Patrick and Caglar Keydar, "Les voies de passage vers la société industrielle en Grande-Bretagne et en France," *Annales ESC*, 34, 1 (1979): 1284–1303.
O'Brien, Patrick and Roland Quinault, eds., *The Industrial Revolution and British Society* (New York: Cambridge University Press, 1993).
O'Rourke, Kevin and Jeffrey Williamson, *Globalization and History: The Evolution of a Nineteenth-century Atlantic Economy* (Cambridge, MA: MIT Press, 1996).
Ochsenwald, William, *Religion, Society, and the State in Arabia: The Hijaz under the Ottoman Control* (Columbus: Ohio University Press, 1984).
Ogilvie, Sheilagh, "Whatever Is, Is Right? Economic Institutions in Pre-Industrial Europe," *Economic History Review*, 60, 4 (2007): 649–684.
Olmstead, Alan and Paul Rhode, "Cotton, Slavery and the New History of Capitalism," *Explorations in Economic History*, 67, January (2018): 1–17.
Olszak, Norbert, *Histoire du droit du travail* (Paris: PUF, 1999).
Orde Brown, G. St. J., *The African Labourer* (London, 1933 reprint Frank Cass, 1967).
Osterhammel, Jürgen, *Colonialism: A Theoretical Overview* (Princeton: Markus Wiener, 2005).
Osterhammel, Jürgen, *The Transformation of the World: A Global History of the Nineteenth Century* (Princeton, NJ: Princeton University Press, 2014).
Ostrovskii, Aleksandr' V., *Zernovoe proizvodtsvo Evropeiskoi Rossii v kontse XIX-nachala XX v.* (The production of wheat in the European Russia during the nineteenth-early twentieth centuries) (St. Petersburg: Poltorak, 2013).
Oudin-Bastide, Caroline and Philippe Steiner, *Calcul et Morale. Coûts de l'esclavage et valeur de l'émancipation, XVIIIe–XIXe siècles* (Paris: Albin Michel, 2015).
Overton, Michael, *Agricultural Revolution in England* (Cambridge: Cambridge University Press, 1996).
Pallot, Judith, *Land Reforms in Russian 1906–1917* (Oxford: Oxford University Press, 1999).
Palmer, Vernon, "The Quest to Implant the Civilian Method in Louisiana: Tracing the Origins of Judicial Methodology," *Louisiana Law Review*, 73 (2013): 793–819.
Paneiakh, Viktor M. *Kholopstvo v pervoi polovine XVII veke* (*Kholopstvo* in the first half of the seventeenth century) (Leningrad: Nauka, 1984).
Paquette, Robert. "Slave Resistance and Social History," *Journal of Social History*, 24, 3 (1991): 681–685.
Pargas, Damian and Julian Schiele, *The Palgrave Handbook of Global Slavery Through History* (Basingstoke: Palgrave, 2023).
Parthasarathi, Prasannan, *Why Europe Grew Rich and Asia Did Not: Global Economic Divergence, 1600–1850* (Cambridge: Cambridge University Press, 2011).
Patnaik, Utsa and Manjari Dingwaney, eds., *Chains of Servitude: Bondage and Slavery in India* (Madras: Sargam Books, 1985).

Paton, Diana, "Gender History, Global History, and Atlantic Slavery," *American Historical Review*, 127, 2 (2022): 726–754.
Paton, Diane and Pamela Scully, eds., *Gender and Slave Emancipation in the Atlantic World* (Durham: Duke University Press, 2005).
Patterson, Orlando, *Slavery and Social Death* (Cambridge, MA: Harvard University Press, 1985).
Peabody, Sue, *There Are No Slaves in France* (New York: Oxford University Press, 1996).
Penati, Beatrice, "The Cotton Boom and the Land Tax in Russian Turkestan, 1880s–1915," *Kritika*, 14, 4 (2013): 741–774.
Perham, Margery and Mary Bull, eds., *The Diaries of Lord Lugard* (Evanston: Northwestern University Press, 1959).
Pershin, Pavel, *Zemelonoe ustroistvo dorevoliutsionnoi dereveni* (Moscow: Gozizdat, 1928).
Peterson, Dale, *Up from Bondage: The Literature of Russian and African American Soul* (Durham, NC: Duke University Press, 2000).
Pettigrew, William A., *Freedom's Debt: Politics and the Escalation of American Slavery, 1688–1752* (Chapel Hill: University of North Carolina Press, 2012).
Pickering Paul A. and Alex Tyrrell, *The People's Bread: A History of the Anti-Corn Law League* (London and New York: Continuum, 2000).
Piketty, Thomas, *Le capital au XXIe siècle* (Paris: Seuil, 2013).
Piketty, Thomas, *Capital in the 21st Century* (Cambridge: Harvard University Press, 2014).
Piketty, Thomas, *Capital and Ideology* (Cambridge: Harvard University Press, 2020).
Piot, Charles, *Remotely Global: Village Modernity in West Africa* (Chicago: University of Chicago Press, 1999).
Pipes, Richard, "The Russian Military Colonies," *Journal of Modern History*, 22, 3 (1950): 205–219.
Plokhy, Serhii and Frank E. Sysyn, *Religion and Nation in Modern Ukraine* (Edmonton: Canadian Institute of Ukrainian Studies Press, 2003).
Polanyi, Karl, *The Great Transformation* (New York: Beacon, 1944).
Pomeranz, Kenneth, *The Great Divergence* (Princeton, NJ: Princeton University Press, 2000).
Popkin, Jeremy, *You Are All Free: The Haitian Revolution and the Abolition of Slavery* (Cambridge: Cambridge University Press, 2010).
Postan, Michael, "The Chronology of Labor Services," *Transactions of the Royal Historical Society*, 20 (1937): 169–193.
Postan, Michael, *Cambridge Economic History of Europe: Expanding Europe in the Sixteenth and Seventeenth Centuries* (Cambridge: Cambridge University Press, 1973).
Postel-Vinay, Gilles, "The Dis-integration of Traditional Labor Markets in France: From Agriculture *and* Industry to Agriculture *or* Industry," in George Grantham and Mary MacKinnon, eds., *Labor Market Evolution* (London: Routledge, 1994): 64–83.

Pothier, Robert-Joseph, *Traité du contrat de louage* (Paris: Bugnet, 1861).
Pouchepadass, Jacques, *Planteurs et paysans dans l'Inde coloniale. L'indigo du Bihar et le mouvement gandhien du Champaran (1917-8)* (Paris: L'Harmattan, 1986), English translation: *Champaran and Gandhi: Planters, Peasants and Gandhian Politics* (New Delhi: Oxford University Press, 1999).
Prakash, Gyan, "Terms of Servitude: The Colonial Discourse on Slavery and Bondage in India," in Martin Klein, ed., *Breaking the Chains: Slavery, Bondage and Emancipation in Modern Africa and Asia* (Madison: University of Wisconsin Press, 1986): 131–149.
Prakash, Gyan, *Bonded Histories: Genealogies of Labour Servitude in Colonial India* (Cambridge: Cambridge University Press, 1990).
Prakash, Om, *The Dutch East India Company and the Economy of Bengal, 1630-1720* (Princeton: Princeton University Press, 1985).
Pravilova, Ekaterina, *Zakonnost' i prava lichnosti: administrativnaia iustitsiia v Rossii, vtoraia polovina XIX v.-oktiabr' 1917* (Legality and the rights of the person: administrative justice in Russia in the second half of the nineteenth century to October 1917) (St. Petersburg: Izd-vo SZAGS, 2000).
Pravilova, Ekaterina, "Tsena Imperii: Tsentr' i Okrainy v rossiiskom biudzhete XIX-nachala XX vv." (Price of the Empire: center and periphery in the Russian budget, nineteenth-early twentieth centuries," *Ab Imperio*, 4 (2002): 115–144.
Pravilova, Ekaterina, *Finansy Imperi. Dengi i vlasti v politiki Rossii na nationaln'nykh okraninakh, 1801-1917* (Imperial finance. Money and power in the politics of Russia in the national bordelands) (Moscow: Novoe Izdatelstvo, 2006).
Prest, Wilf ed., *Re-Interpreting Blackstone's Commentaries: A Seminal Text in National and International Contexts* (Oxford: Hart Publishing, 2014).
Pretty, David, *Neither Peasant nor Proletarian. The Workers of the Ivanovo-Voznesensk Region* (PhD dissertation, Brown University, 1997).
Price, Richard ed., *Maroon Societies* (New York: Anchor Books, 1973; 3rd edn., 1996).
Price, Richard, "Maroon societies in the Americas," *Oxford Encyclopedia of Africa online*, 2020, https://doi.org/10.1093/acrefore/9780190277734.013.935.
Puckrein, Gary, *Little England: Plantation Society and Anglo-Barbadian Politics, 1626-1700* (New York: New York University Press, 1984).
Rable, George C., *The Confederate Republic: A Revolution Against Politics* (Chapel Hill: The University of North Carolina Press, 1994).
Raeff, Marc, *Siberia and the Reforms of 1822* (Seattle: University of Washington Press, 1956).
Rainbow, David, ed., *Ideologies of Race: Imperial Russia and the Soviet Union in Global Context* (Montreal: Mac Gill-Queen University Press, 2019).
Ransom, Roger and Richard Sutch, *One Kind of Freedom: The Economic Consequences of Emancipation* (New York: Cambridge University Press, 1977).
Ransom, Roger and Richard Sutch, "Capitalists without Capital: The Burden of Slavery and the Impact of Emancipation." *Agricultural History*, 62, 3 (1988): 133–160.

Rebérieux, Madeleine, *La République radicale? 1898-1914* (Paris: Seuil, 1975).
Rediker, Marcus, *Between the Devil and the Deep Blue Sea: Merchants, Seamen, Pirates, and the Anglo-American Maritime World, 1700-1750* (Cambridge: Cambridge University Press, 1987).
Rediker, Marcus, *Outlaws of the Atlantic: Sailors, Pirates, and the Motley Crews in the Age of Sail* (London: Verso, 2014).
Rediker, Marcus, Titas Chakraborty and Matthias van Rossum eds., *A Global History of Runaways: Workers, Mobility, and Capitalism, 1600-1850* (Berkeley: University of California Press, 2019).
Régent, Fréderic, *Esclavage métissage, liberté* (Paris: Grasset, 2004).
Régent Fréderic, *La France et ses esclaves* (Paris: Grasset, 2007).
Reid, Douglas, "The Decline of Saint Monday," *Past & Present*, 71, 1 (1976): 76-101.
Reid, Douglas, "Weddings, Weekdays, Work and Leisure in Urban England, 1791-1991," *Past & Present*, 153, 1 (1996): 135-163.
Reid, Joseph, "White Land, Black Labor, and Agricultural Stagnation. The Causes and Effects of Sharecropping in the Post-bellum South," *Explorations in Economic History*, 16, 1 (1979): 31-55.
Reid, Richard J. *Warfare in African History (New Approaches to African History)* (New York: Cambridge University Press, 2012).
Reis, Joao José, *Rebellion in Brazil: the Muslim Uprising of 1835 in Bahia* (Baltimore: John Hopkins University Press, 1983).
Renault, François, "L'abolition de l'esclavage au Sénégal: l'attitude de l'administration française, 1848-1905," *Revue française d'outre-mer*, 58, 1 (1971): 5-80.
Renault, François, *Libération d'esclaves et nouvelle servitude: les rachats de captifs africains pour le compte des colonies françaises après l'abolition de l'esclavage* (Abidjan: ANSOM, 1976).
Riasanovsky, Nicholas V. "The Emergence of Eurasianism," *California Slavic Studies*, 4 (1967): 39-72.
Rice, Alan and Martin Crawford, eds., *Liberating Sojourn: Frederick Douglass and Transatlantic Reform* (Athens: Ohio University Press, 1999).
Richardson, David, "Market Structures and the Profits of the British African Trade in the Late Eighteenth Century: A Comment," *Journal of Economic History*, 43, (1983): 713-721.
Richardson, David, "The Slave Trade, Sugar, and British Economic Growth, 1748-1776," *Explorations in Economic History*, 17, 4 (1987): 739-769.
Richardson, David, "Accounting for Profits in the British Trade in Slaves: Reply to William Darity," *Explorations in Economic History*, 26 (1989): 492-499.
Riello, Giorgio, *Cotton: The Fabric that Made the Modern World* (Cambridge: Cambridge University Press, 2013).
Riello, Giorgio and Thirtankar Roy, eds., *How India Clothed the World: The World of South Asian Textiles, 1500-1850* (Leiden: Brill, 2009).
Riley, Edward M., ed., *The Journal of John Harrower: An Indentured Servant in the Colony of Virginia, 1773-1776* (New York: Holt, Rinehart &Winston, 1963).

Rivers, Larry Eugene, *Rebels and Runaways: Slave Resistance in Nineteenth Century Florida* (Urbana: The University of Illinois, 2012).
Roberts, Justin, "Race and the Origin of Plantation Slavery," *Oxford Research Encyclopedia of American History*, 2016, https://doi.org/10.1093/acref ore/9780199329175.013.268, accessed April 10, 2022.
Roberts, Richard, *Warriors, Merchants and Slaves: The State and the Economy in the Middle Niger Valley, 1700–1914* (Stanford: Stanford University Press, 1987).
Roberts, Richard, *Two Worlds of Cotton: Colonialism and Regional Economy in the French Soudan, 1800–1946* (Stanford: Stanford University Press, 1996).
Roberts, Richard, "Representation, Structure and Agency: Divorce in the French Soudan during the Early Twentieth Century," *The Journal of African History*, 40, 3 (1999): 389–410.
Roberts, Richard, *Litigants and Households: African Disputes and Colonial Courts in the French Soudan, 1895–1912* (Portsmouth: Heinemann, 2005).
Robinson, Geroid T., *Rural Russia Under the Old Regime* (New York: Longmans, 1932).
Rockman, Seth, *Scraping by: Wage Labor, Slavery, and Survival in Early Baltimore* (Baltimore: Johns Hopkins University Press, 2009).
Rodet, Marie, *Les migrantes ignorées du Haut-Sénégal, 1900–1946* (Paris: Karthala, 2009).
Roediger, David R., *Towards the Abolition of Whiteness: Essays on Race, Politics, and Working Class History* (London: Verso, 1994).
Romaniello, Matthew, *Enterprising Empires: Russia and Britain in Eighteenth Century Eurasia* (Cambridge: Cambridge University Press, 2019).
Rönnbäck, Klass, "New and Old Peripheries: Britain, the Baltic, and the Americas in the Great Divergence," *Journal of Global History*, 5, 3 (2010): 373–394.
Rönnbäck, Klass, "On the Economic Importance of the Slave Plantation Complex to the British Economy During the Eighteenth Century: A Value-Added Approach," *Journal of Global History*, 13, 3 (2018): 308–327.
Rosanvallon, Pierre, *L'État en France de 1789 à nos jours* (Paris: Seuil, 1990).
Rosanvallon, Pierre, *La démocratie inachevée* (Paris: Gallimard, 2000).
Rosanvallon, Pierre, *La société des égaux* (Paris: Seuil, 2011).
Rose, Sonya and Sean Brady, "Rethinking Gender and Labor History," in John Arnold, ed., *History after Hobsbawm, Writing the Past for the 21st Century* (Oxford: Oxford University Press, 2017): 242–258.
Rosental, Paul-André, "Le BIT et la politique mondiale des migrations dans l'entre-deux-guerres," *Annales HSS*, 61, 1 (2006): 99–134.
Rotschild, Emma, *The Inner Life of Empires* (Princeton, NJ: Princeton University Press, 2011).
Rouet, Gilles, *Justice et justiciables au XIXe et XXe siècles* (Paris: Belin, 1999).
Rowlands, Marie, "Continuity and Change in an Industrializing Society: The Case of the West Midlands Industries," in Pat Hudson, ed., *Regions and Industries: A Perspective on the Industrial Revolution in Britain* (Cambridge: Cambridge University Press, 1989): 103–131.

Roy, Kaushik, *War, Culture and Society in Early Modern South Asia, 1740-1849* (Abingdon and New York: Routledge, 2011).

Roy, Thirtankar, *Traditional Industry in the Economy of Colonial India* (Cambridge: Cambridge University Press, 1999).

Roy, Thirtankar, *Rethinking Economic Change in India: Labour and Livelihood* (London: Routledge, 2005).

Roy, Thirtankar, "Labour Intensity and Industrialization in Colonial India," in Gareth Austin and Kaoru Sugihara, eds., *Labour-Intensive Industrialization in Global History* (London: Routledge, 2012): 107-121.

Roy, Tirthankar and Giorgio Riello, eds., *Global Economic History* (London: Bloomsbury, 2018).

Rozhkova, Maria, *Ekonomicheskie sviazi Rossii so Srednei Aziei: 40-60gg XIX veka* (Economic ties between Russia and Central Asia in the 40s to 60s of the nineteenth century) (Moscow: Nauka, 1963).

Rozier, Abbé, *Cours complet d'agriculture ou Dictionnaire universel d'agriculture*, vol. 8: "Domestique" (Paris: Clouzier, 1789).

Rudin, Ronald, *Faire de l'histoire au Québec* (Québec: Septentrion, 1998).

Rudolph, Richard, ed., *The European Peasant, Family, and Society: Historical Studies* (Liverpool: Liverpool University Press, 1995).

Rudolph, Robert, "Agricultural Structure and Proto-industrialization in Russia: Economic Development with Unfree Labor," *The Journal of Economic History*, 45, 1 (1985): 47-69.

Saada, Emmanuelle, "Nation and Empire in the French Context," in George Steinmetz, ed., *Sociology and Empire: The Imperial Entanglements of a Discipline* (Durham and London: Duke University Press, 2013): 321-340.

Sabel, Charles and Jonathan Zeitlin, eds., *World of Possibilities* (Cambridge: Cambridge University Press, 1997).

Sabol, Steven, *The Touch of Civilization: Comparing American and Russian Internal Colonization* (Boulder: University Press of Colorado, 2017).

Sahadeo, Jeff, *Russian Colonial Society in Tashkent, 1865-1923* (Bloomington: Indiana University Press, 2007).

Salais, Robert, Nicolas Bavarez and Benedicte Reynaud, *L'invention du chômage* (Paris: PUF, 1986).

Salber Phillips, Mark, "Rethinking Historical Distance: From Doctrine to Heuristics," *History and Theory*, 50, 4 (2011): 11-23.

Sangari, Kumkum and Sudesh Vaid, eds., *Recasting Women: Essays in Colonial History* (New Delhi: Kali for Women, 1989).

Sarkar, Sumit, *Writing Social History* (Delhi: Oxford University Press, 1997).

Sartori, Paolo, ed., *Explorations in the Social History of Modern Central Asia (Nineteenth-Early Twentieth Century)* (Leiden: Brill, 2013).

Saunders, Daniel, *Russia in the Age of Reaction and Reform, 1801-1881* (London: Longman, 1992).

Saunders, William, "Sailor Songs and Songs of the Sea," *The Musical Quarterly*, 14, 3 (1928): 236.

Say, Jean-Baptiste, *Cours d'économie politique* (Brussels: Meline, Cans et Compagnie, 1843).
Schermerhorn, Calvin, *The Business of Slavery and the Rise of American Capitalism, 1815-1860* (New Haven: Yale University Press, 2015).
Schmidt, Nelly, *Abolitionnistes de l'esclavage et réformateurs des colonies, 1820-1851. Analyses et documents* (Paris: Karthala, 2000).
Schnakenbourg, Christian, *Histoire de l'industrie sucrière en Guadeloupe aux XIXe et XXe siècles* (Paris: L'Harmattan, 2007).
Schoelcher, Victor, *Des colonies françaises. Abolition immédiate de l'esclavage* (Paris, 1842, re-edition, éditions du CTHS, 1998).
Schrader, Abby, "Unruly Felons and Civilizing Wives: Cultivating Marriage in the Siberian Exile System: 1822-1860," *Slavic Review*, 66, 2 (2007): 230-257.
Schuler, Monica, "The Recruitment of African *Indentured* Laborers for European Colonies in the Nineteenth Century," in Petr C. Emmer, ed., *Colonialism and Migration: Indentured Labor before and after Slavery* (Dordrecht: Martin Nijhoff, 1986): 125-161.
Schwartz, Stuart, "The Mocambo: Slave Resistance in Colonial Bahia," *Journal of Social History*, 3, 4 (1970): 313-333.
Schwartz, Stuart, *Slaves, Peasants, and Rebels: Reconsidering Brazilian Slavery* (Urbana and Chicago: University of Illinois Press, 1992).
Schwarz, Philip, *Twice Condemned: Slaves and the Criminal Laws of Virginia 1705-1865* (New Jersey: The Lawbrook Exchange, 1998).
Scott, James, *Weapons of the Weak: Everyday Forms of Peasant Resistance* (New Haven: Yale University Press, 1985).
Scott, James and David Lake, "The Second Face of Hegemony: Britain's Repeal of the Corn Laws and the American Walker's Tariff of 1846," *International Organization*, 43, 1 (1989): 1-29.
Scott, Rebecca, *Slave Emancipation in Cuba, 1860-1899* (Princeton, NJ: Princeton University Press, 1985).
Scott, Rebecca J., "Defining the Boundaries of Freedom in the World of Cane: Cuba, Brazil, and Louisiana after Emancipation," *The American Historical Review*, 99, 1 (1994): 70-102.
Scott, Rebecca J. and Jean M. Hébrard, *Freedom Papers: An Atlantic Odyssey in the Age of Emancipation* (Cambridge, MA: Harvard University Press, 2012).
Scott, Rebecca, Thomas Holt, Frederick Cooper and Aims Mc Guinness, *Societies after Slavery: A Selected Annoted Bibliography of Printed Sources on Cuba, Brazil, British Colonial Africa, South Africa and the British West India* (Pittsburgh: University of Pittsburgh Press, 2004).
Scott, Tom ed., *The Peasantries of Europe: From the Fourteenth to the Eighteenth Centuries* (London: Longman, 1998).
Semevskii, Vasilii, *Krest'ianskii vopros v Rossii v XVIII i pervoi polovine XIX veka* (The peasant question in Russia in the eighteenth to the first half of the nineteenth century), 2 volumes (St. Petersburg: Obshchstevennaia pol'za, 1888).

Semevskii, Vasilii, *Krest'iane v tsarstvovanie Imperatritsy Ekateriny II* (The peasantry under the reign of Catherine II), 2 volumes (Sankt-Petersburg: tipografiia F. S. Sushchinskago, 1901).

Sen, Sudipta, *Distant Sovereignty: National Imperialism and the Origin of British India* (London: Routledge, 2002).

Serbina, Ksenia N. *Krest'ianskaia zhelezodelatel'naia promyshlennost' tsentral'noi Rossii XVI-pervoi poloviny XIXe vekoi* (The peasant metallurgic home industry in Central Russia from the sixteenth to the first half of the nineteenth century) (Leningrad: Nauka, 1978).

Sewell, William, *Logics of History: Social Theory and Social Transformation* (Chicago: University of Chicago Press, 2005).

Sharma, Jayeeta, *Empire's Garden: Assam and the Making of India* (Durham: Duke University Press, 2011).

Sharp, Granville, *A Representation of the Injustice and Dangerous Tendency of Tolerating Slavery, or of Admitting the Least Claim of Private Property in the Persons of Men, in England* (London: Legaret Street, 2023, original London: 1769).

Shaw, Charles, *When I was a Child* (New edition, Churnet: Valley Books, 1998).

Sheridan, Richard, *Sugar and Slavery. An Economic History of the British West Indies, 1623–1775* (Baltimore: Johns Hopkins University Press, 1974).

Sheridan, Richard, "The Maroons of Jamaica, 1730–1830: Livelihood, Demography and Health," *Slavery and Abolition*, 6, 3 (1985): 152–172.

Sheriff, Abdul, *Slaves, Spices and Ivory* (London: J. Currey, 1987).

Shipov, Nikolai, *Istoriia moei zhizni* (Story of my life) (Moscow, Leningrad: Academia, 1933, original 1881).

Shipova, Elena, *Slovar' turkizmov v russkom iazyke* (Dictionary of Turkish in the Russian language) (Alma-Ata: Nauka, 1976).

Shlomovitz, Ralph, "Bound or Free? Black Labor in Cotton and Sugar Cane Farming, 1865–1880," *Journal of Southern History*, 50, 4 (1984): 569–596.

Shukla, Prabhat Kumar, *Indigo and the Raj: Peasant Protests in Bihar, 1780–1917* (Delhi: Pragati Publication, 1993).

Shumway, Rebecca, *The Fante and the Transatlantic Slave Trade* (Rochester, NY: University of Rochester Press, 2011).

Siegelbaum, Lewis, and Leslie Page Moch, *Broad Is My Native Land: Repertoires and Regimes of Migration in Russia's Twentieth Century* (Ithaca: Cornell University Press, 2014).

Sifneos, Evrydiki, Oksana Iurkova and Valentina Shandra eds., *Port-Cities of the Northern Shore of the Black Sea: Institutional, Economic and Social Development, Eighteenth–Early Twentieth Centuries* (Rethymnon: Black Sea History Working Papers, 2021).

Simms, James Y. Jr, "The Crisis in Russian Agriculture at the End of the Nineteenth Century: A Different View," *Slavic Review*, 36, 3 (1977): 377–398.

Simms, James Y. Jr, "The Crop Failure of 1891: Soil Exhaustion, Technological Backwardness, and Russia's Agrarian Crisis," *Slavic Review*, 41, 2 (1982): 236–250.

Sinchcombe, Arthur L., *Sugar Island Slavery in the Age of Enlightenment: The Political Economy of the Caribbean World* (Princeton, NJ: Princeton University Press, 1995).

Singha, Radhika, "Making the Domestic More Domestic: Criminal Law and the Head of the Household, 1772-1843," *Indian Economic and Social History Review*, 33, 3 (1996): 309-343.

de Sismondi, Simon, *Études sur l'économie politique* (Bruxelles: Société typographique belge, 1837).

Sivasundaram, Sujit, *Waves Across the South* (Chicago: University of Chicago Press, 2021).

Sladkovskii, Mikhail Iosifovich, *History of Economic Relations between Russia and China* (New Brunswick and London: Transaction Publishers, 2008, original 1966).

Slovar' russkogo iazika XVIII veka (Dictionary of the Russian language of the eighteenth century) (St. Petersburg: Sorokin, 1998).

Smith, Abbott Emerson, *Colonists in Bondage: White Servitude and Convict Labor in America, 1607-1776* (New York: Norton, 1947).

Smith, Adam, *An Inquiry into the Nature and Causes of the Wealth of Nations*, 1776 reproduced in: R.H. Campbell, A. Skinner, *The Glasgow Edition of the Works and Correspondence of Adam Smith*, vol. 2. (Oxford: Oxford University Press, 1976).

Smith, G. W. ed., *John Stuart Mill's Social and Political Thought: Critical Assessments* (London: Routledge, 1998).

Smith, Thomas, *De Republica Anglorum: A Discourse on the Commonwealth of England* (1583, reprint, edited by L. Alston, Cambridge: Cambridge University Press, 1906).

Snell, Keith D. M. "Agricultural Seasonal Unemployment, the Standard of Living, and Women's Work in the South and East, 1690-1860," *The Economic History Review*, 34, 3 (1981): 407-437.

Snell, Keith D. M. *Annals of the Labouring Poor: Social Change and Agrarian England 1660-1900* (Cambridge: Cambridge University Press, 1985).

Snyder, Timothy, "Ukrainians and Poles," in Dominic Lieven, ed., *The Cambridge History of Russia*, vol. 2 (Cambridge: Cambridge University Press, 2006): 165-183.

Société d'histoire des Filles du Roy, *Les filles du Roy pionnières de Montréal* (Québec: Éditions du septentrion, 2017).

Société d'histoire des Filles du Roy, *Les filles du Roy pionnières de la Côte Sud* (Québec: Éditions du septentrion, 2022).

Sokoloff, Kenneth and David Dollar, "Agricultural Seasonality and the Organization of Manufacturing in Early Industrial Economies: The Contrast Between England and the United States," *The Journal of Economic History*, 57, 2 (1997): 288-321.

Solomon, Peter ed., *Reforming Justice in Russia, 1864-1994: Power, Culture, and the Limits of Legal Order* (Armonk, NY: M. E. Sharpe, 1997).

Solow, Barbara, "Caribbean Slavery and British Growth: The Eric Williams Hypothesis," *Journal of Development Economics*, 17, 4 (1985): 99-115.

Solow, Barbara, ed., *Slavery and the Rise of the Atlantic System* (Cambridge: Cambridge University Press, 1991).

Sombart, Werner, *Der Modern Kapitalismus*, 3 volumes (München: Dunker und Humboldt, 1902).
Sonenscher, Michael, *Work and Wages* (Cambridge: Cambridge University Press, 1989).
Spencer, Jonathan, J. B. Norton and J. A. Homburg, "Biogeochemical Studies of a Native American Runoff Agroecosystem," *Geoarcheology, an International Journal*, 22, 3 (2007): 359-386.
Spieler, Miranda, *Empire and Underworld: Captivity in French Guyana* (Boston, MA: Harvard University Press, 2012).
Spieler, Miranda, *Slaves in Paris: Hidden Lives and Fugitive Histories* (Cambridge, MA: Harvard University Press, 2025).
Stanley, Amy Dru, *From Bondage to Contract: Wage Labor, Marriage and the Market in the Age of Slave Emancipation* (New York: Cambridge University Press, 1999).
Stanziani, Alessandro, *L'économie en revolution. Le cas russe, 1870-1914* (Paris: Albin Michel, 1998).
Stanziani, Alessandro, "The First World War and the Disintegration of Economic Spaces in Russia," in Judith Pallot, ed., *Transforming Peasants: Society, State, and the Peasantry, 1861-1930* (London: Macmillan, 1998): 174-194.
Stanziani, Alessandro, *Histoire de la qualité alimentaire* (Paris: Seuil, 2005).
Stanziani, Alessandro, "Free Labor-Forced Labor: An Uncertain Boundary? The Circulation of Economic Ideas between Russia and Western Europe from the Eighteenth to the Mid-nineteenth Century," *Kritika, Explorations in Russian and Eurasian History*, 9, 1 (2008): 27-52.
Stanziani, Alessandro, *Dictionnaire historique de l'économie droit* (Paris: LGDJ, 2010).
Stanziani, Alessandro, *Bâtisseurs d'Empire* (Paris: Liber, 2012).
Stanziani, Alessandro, *Rules of Exchange: French Capitalism in Comparative Perspective, Eighteenth-Twentieth Centuries* (Cambridge: Cambridge University Press, 2012).
Stanziani, Alessandro, ed., *Labor, Coercion and Economic Growth in Eurasia, Seventeenth-Twentieth Centuries* (Leiden: Brill, 2012).
Stanziani, Alessandro, "Local bondage in Global Economies. Servants, Wage Earners and Indentured Migrants in Nineteenth Century France, Great Britain and the Mascarene Islands," *Modern Asian Studies*, 47, 4 (2013): 1218-1251.
Stanziani, Alessandro, *Bondage, Labor and Rights in Eurasia, Seventeenth-Twentieth Century* (New York: Berghahn, 2014).
Stanziani, Alessandro, *After Oriental Despotism* (London: Bloomsbury, 2014).
Stanziani, Alessandro, "Comment mesurer l'efficacité des institutions ?" *Histoire et mesure*, 30, 1 (2015): 3-24.
Stanziani, Alessandro, "Slavery and Bondage in Central Asia and Russia: 14th-Nineteenth Centuries," in Christopher Witzenrath, ed., *Eurasian Slavery, Ransom and Abolition in World History, 1200-1860* (Farnham: Ashgate, 2015): 81-104.

Stanziani, Alessandro, "Runaways: A Global History," in von Rossum, Matthias and Jeannette Kamp, eds., *Desertion in the Early Modern World: A Comparative History* (London: Bloomsbury, 2016): 15–30.

Stanziani, Alessandro, *Labor on the Fringes of Empire* (New York: Palgrave, 2018).

Stanziani, Alessandro, "Labour Regime and Labour Mobility from the Seventeenth to the Twentieth Century," in Tirthankar Roy and Giorgio Riello, eds., *Global Economic History* (London: Bloomsbury, 2018): 175–195.

Stanziani, Alessandro, *Les entrelacements du monde* (Paris: CNRS Éditions, 2018).

Stanziani, Alessandro, "Serfs, Slaves or Wage Earners? The Legal Status of Labour in Russia in a Comparative Perspective," in Damian Alan Pargas and Felicia Rosu, eds., *Critical Readings on Global Slavery* (Leiden: Brill, 2018): 1044–1068.

Stanziani, Alessandro, "Russia Economic History in Global Perspective" in Matthias Middell, ed., *The Perspective of Global History* (London: Bloomsbury, 2019): 115–137.

Stanziani, Alessandro, "Russian Capitalism: Exceptionalism versus Global Labour-Intensive Path, 1700–1914," in Kaveh Yazdani and Dilip Menon, eds., *Capitalisms: Towards a Global History* (Oxford: Oxford University Press, 2020): 95–127.

Stanziani, Alessandro, *Les metamorphoses du travail contraint* (Paris: Presses de Sciences-Po, 2020).

Stanziani, Alessandro, *Eurocentrism and the Politics of Global History* (New York: Palgrave, 2020).

Stanziani, Alessandro, "Global History, Area Studies and the Idea of Europe," *Cromhos*, (2021): 1–9, DOI: 10.36253/cromohs-12562.

Stanziani, Alessandro, *Capital terre* (Paris: Payot, 2021).

Stanziani, Alessandro, *Tensions of Social History* (London: Bloomsbury, 2023).

Stanziani, Alessandro, *Les guerres du blé. Environnement, économie, géopolitique* (Paris: La découverte, 2024).

Stanziani, Alessandro and Gwyn Campbell, eds., *The Palgrave Handbook of Bondage and Human Rights in Africa and Asia*, 2 volumes (New York: Palgrave Macmillan, 2019).

Staughton, George, Benjamin Nead and Thomas McCamant, eds., *Charters to William Penn, and Laws of the Province of Pennsylvania* (Philadelphia: University of Pennsylvania Press, 1986): 1–77.

Steinberg, Marc, "Capitalist Development, the Labor Process, and the Law," *American Journal of Sociology*, 109, 2 (2003): 445–495.

Steinfeld, Robert, *The Invention of Free Labor: The Employment Relation in English and American Law and Culture, 1350–1870* (Chapel Hill: University of North Carolina Press, 1991).

Steinfeld, Robert, "Changing Legal Conceptions of Free Labor," in Engerman, Stanley, ed., *Terms of Labor: Slavery, Serfdom, and Free Labor* (Stanford: Stanford University Press, 1999): 137–167.

Steinfeld, Robert, *Coercion, Contract and Free Labor in the Nineteenth Century* (Cambridge: Cambridge University Press, 2001).

Steinmetz, George ed., *Sociology and Empire: The Imperial Entanglements of a Discipline* (Durham and London: Duke University Press, 2013): 321–340.

Steinmetz, Willibald, ed., *Private Law and Social Inequality in the Industrial Age: Comparing Legal Cultures in Britain, France, Germany, and the United States* (Oxford: Oxford University Press, 2000).

Stoler, Ann Laura, Carole McGranahan and Peter Perdu, eds., *Imperial Formations* (New York: School for Advanced Research Press, 2007).

Subrahamanyam, Sanjay, "Connected Histories. Notes Towards a Reconfiguration of Early Modern Eurasia," *Modern Asian Studies*, 31, 3 (1997): 735–762.

Sunderland, Williard, "Peasants on the Move: State Peasant Resettlement in Imperial Russia, 1805–1830," *Russian Review*, 52, 4 (1993): 472–485.

Sunderland, Williard, *Taming the Wild Field: Colonization and Empire in the Russian Steppe* (Ithaca: Cornell University Press, 2004).

Supiot, Alain, *Les sans-emplois et la loi* (Paris: Calligrammes, 1988).

Supiot, Alain, *Critique du droit du travail* (Paris: PUF, 2002 [1994]).

Suranyi, Anna, *Indentured Servitude: Unfree Labor and Citizenship in the British Colonies* (Montreal: McGill University Press, 2021).

Suranyi, Anna, "Indentured Servitude, the Right to Counsel and White Citizenship in Seventeenth-Century Chesapeake," *American Journal of Legal History*, 64, 4 (2023): 339–358.

Suzuki, Hideaki, ed., *Abolitions as a Global Experience* (Singapore: NUS Press, 2016).

Tamanaha, Brian, Caroline Sage and Michael Woolcock, eds., *Legal Pluralism and Development: Scholars and Practitioners in Dialogue* (Cambridge: Cambridge University Press, 2012).

Tarasov, Iurii, *Russkaia krest'ianskaia kolonizatsiia iuzhnogo Urala: vtoraia polovina XVIII- pervaia polovina XIX vekoi* (The Russian peasant colonization of south Urals, second half of the eighteenth century, first half of the nineteenth century) (Moscow: Gozizdat, 1984).

Tarrade, Jean, *Le commerce colonial français à la fin de l'ancien régime* (Paris: PUF, 1972).

Temin, Paul, "The Post-Bellum Recovery of the South and the Cost of Civil War," *The Journal of Economic History*, 36, 4 (1976): 898–907.

Temin, Peter, "Labor Scarcity and the Problem of American Industrial Efficiency in the 1850s," *Journal of Economic History*, 26, 3 (1966): 277–298.

Temperley, Howard, *British Antislavery, 1833–1870* (London: Longman, 1972).

Testart, Alain, *L'esclave, la dette et le pouvoir* (Paris: Editions errance, 2001).

Thelot, Claude and Olivier Marchand, *Deux siècles de travail en France* (Paris: Nathan, 1997).

Thompson, Alvin, *Flight to Freedom: African Runaways and Maroons in the Americas* (Kingston: University of the West Indies Press, 2006).

Thompson, Edward P. *The Making of the English Working Class* (London: Vintage Books, 1963).

Thompson, Edward P. "Time, Work-discipline and Industrial Capitalism," *Past and Present*, 38, 1 (1967): 56–97.

Thompson, Frances Michael, *English Landed Society in the Nineteenth Century* (London: Routledge, 1963).

Thompson, Frances Michael, "The Second Agricultural Revolution, 1815–1880," *Economic History Review*, 21, 1 (1968): 62–77.

Thompstone, Stuart, "Russian Imperialism and the Commercialization of the Central Asian Cotton Trade," *Textile History*, 26, 2 (1995): 233–57.

Thornton, John, *Warfare in Atlantic Africa, 1500–1800* (London: Routledge, 2000).

Tikhonov, Iurii, *Pomeshchic'i krest'iane v Rossii: feodal'naia renta v XVII-nachale XVIII v* (The private estates' peasants in Russia: the feudal rent in the seventeenth to early eighteenth century) (Moscow: Nauka, 1974).

Timmer, Charles, "The Turnip, the New Husbandry, and the English Agricultural Revolution," *Quarterly Journal of Economics*, LXXXIII, 3 (1969): 375–395.

Tinker, Hugh, *A New System of Slavery: The Export of Indian Labour Overseas, 1830–1920* (London: Hansib, 1974).

Tise, Larry, *Proslavery: A History of the Defense of Slavery in America, 1701–1840* (Athens: University of Georgia Press, 1987).

Tocqueville, Alexis de, *Mémoire sur le paupérisme* (Cherbourg: Mémoires de la société académique de Cherbourg, 1835).

Todd, David, *A Velvet Empire: French Informal Imperialism in the Nineteenth Century* (Princeton: Princeton University Press, 2021).

Toledano, Ehud, *Slavery and Abolition in the Ottoman Middle East* (Seattle: University of Washington Press, 1996).

Tomic, Dale, *Prelude to Emancipation: Sugar and Slavery in Martinique, 1830–1848* (Madison: University of Wisconsin Press, 1978).

Tomkins, Alannah, "Poor Law Institutions Through Working Class Eyes: Autobiography, Emotion, and Family Context, 1834–1914," *Journal of British Studies*, 60, 2 (2021): 285–309.

Tomlins, Christopher, *Freedom Bound: Law, Labor, and Civic Identity in Colonizing British America, 1580–1865* (Cambridge: Cambridge University Press, 2010).

Torre-Schaub, Marta, *Essai sur la construction juridique de la catégorie de marché* (Paris: LGDJ, 2002).

Touati, Ismet, *Le Commerce du blé entre l'Algérie et la France, xvie-xixe siècles* (Saint-Denis: Bouchêne, 2018).

Toussaint, Auguste, *Histoire de l'île Maurice* (Paris: PUF, 1974).

Treadgold, Donald, *The Great Siberian Migration: Government and Peasant in Resettlement from Emancipation to the First World War* (Princeton, NJ: Princeton University Press, 1957).

Trentmann, Frank, *Free Trade Nation: Commerce, Consumption and Civil Society in Modern Britain* (Oxford: Oxford University Press, 2008).

Trivellato, Francesca, "Is There a Future for the Italian Macrohistory in the Age of Global History?," *California Italian Studies*, 2, 1 (2011), 10.5070/C321009025.

Troinitskii, Aleksandr', *Krepostnoe naselenie v Rossii po 10 narodnoi perepisi* (The Russian serf population according to the tenth census) (St. Petersburg: Wulf, 1861): 45.

Trudel, Marcel, *Deux siècles d'esclavage au Québec, suivi du Dictionnaire des esclaves et de leurs propriétaires au Canada français* (Montréal: Hurtubise HMH, 2004).

TsSK (Tsentral'nyi Statisticheskii Komitet, *Statisticheskiya dannyya o razvodakh i nedeistvitel'nykh brakakh za 1867–1886* (Statistical data on marriages and separations, 1867–1886) (St. Petersburg: MVD, 1893).

Turley, David, *Slavery* (Malden, MA: Blackwell, 2000).

de Tussac, François-Richard, *Cri des colons contre un ouvrage de M. l'évêque et sénateur Grégoire, ayant pour titre de la littérature des nègres* (Paris: Les Marchands de nouveautés, 1810).

Tvalchrelidze, A. *Stavropol'skaia guberniia v statisticheskom, geograficheskom, istoricheskom i sel'sko-khoziaistvennom otnosheniiakh* (The province of Stavropol in statistical, geographical, historical and rural reports) (Stavropol': Tipografiia Koritskogo, 1897).

Union Congolaise, *Les sociétés concessionnaires du Congo français depuis 1905. Situation financière, plantations, main-d'oeuvre (1906–1908)* (Paris: Bernard Grasset, 1909).

Usner, Daniel, "From African Captivity to American Slavery: The Introduction of Black Laborers to Colonial Louisiana," *The Journal of Louisiana Historical Association*, 20, 1 (1979): 25–48.

Vad, Ganesh Chimanji, ed., *Selection from the Satara Raja and Peshwas' Diaries* (Pune: Deccan Vernacular Translation Society, 1902–11).

Vaillant, Jean-Baptiste, ed., *Correspondance de Napoléon Ier publiée par ordre de l'empereur Napoléon III*, 32 volumes (Paris: Imprimerie impériale, 1858).

van der Linden, Marcel ed., *Workers of the World* (Leiden: Brill, 2008).

van der Linden, Marcel, *The World Wide Web of Work* (London: UCL Press, 2023).

van Regermorter, Jean-Louis, *La Russie méridionale, la Mer Noire et le commerce international, 1774–1861* (Paris IV: PhD dissertation, 1984).

Varma, Nitin, *Coolies of Capitalism: Assam Tea and the Making of Coolie Labour* (Oldenbourg: de Gruyter, 2016).

Vatin, François, "Romantisme économique et philosophie de la misère en France dans les années 1820–1840," *Romantisme*, 133, 3 (2006): 35–47.

Velde, François and David R. Weir, "The Financial Market and Government Debt Policy in France, 1746–1793," *The Journal of Economic History*, 52, 1 (1992): 1–39.

Veneziani, Bruno, "The Evolution of the Contract of Employment," in Bob Hepple, ed., *The Making of the Labor Law in Europe* (London: Mansell, 1986): 31–72.

Verley, Patrick, *Nouvelle histoire économique de la France contemporaine*, vol. 2 (Paris: La découverte, 1995).

Verley, Patrick, *L'Échelle du monde. Essai sur l'industrialisation de l'Occident* (Paris: Gallimard, 1997).

Verlinden, Charles, "L'origine de sclavus=esclave," *Bulletin du Cange*, XVII (1942): 97–128.

Verlinden, Charles, *L'esclavage dans l'Europe médiévale* (Bruges: De Tempel, 1955).

Vernet, Thomas, ed., *Traites, esclavage et transition vers l'engagisme: Perspectives nouvelles sur les Mascareignes et le sud-ouest de l'océan Indien, 1715–1848* (Réduit: University of Mauritius, 2015).

Vidal, Cecile, *Caribbean New Orleans: Empire, Race and the Making of Slave Society* (Chapel Hill: The University of North Carolina University Press, 2019).

Vigna, Xavier and Michelle Zancarini-Fournel, "Intersections Between Labor History and Gender History," *Clio*, 38, 2 (2013): 181–208.

de Villeneuve-Bargemont, Albin, *Traité d'économie politique chrétienne ou recherches sur les paupérisme* (Paris: Paulin, 1834).

Villermé, Louis-René, *Tableau de l'état physique et moral des ouvriers employés dans les manufactures de coton, de laine et de soie* (Paris: Jule Renouard, 1840).

Villiers, Patrick, *Le commerce colonial atlantique et la guerre d'indépendance des États- Unis d'Amérique, 1778–1783: Essai d'étude quantitative* (New York: Arno Press, 1977).

Villiers, Patrick, *Marine royale, corsaires et trafic dans l'Atlantique de Louis XIV et Louis et Louis XVI* (Lille: Société dunkerquoise d'histoire et d'archéologie Septentrion, 1991).

Vink, Markus, "'The World's Oldest Trade.' Dutch Slavery and Slave Trade in the Indian Ocean in the Seventeenth Century," *Journal of World History*, 14, 2 (2003): 131–177.

Vinovskis, Maris A., ed., *Toward a Social History of the American Civil War: Explanatory Essays* (Cambridge: Cambridge University Press, 1990).

von Hagen, Mark, "Empires, Borderlands, and Diasporas: Eurasianism as an Anti-Paradigm for the Post-Soviet Era," *American Historical Review*, 109, 2 (2004): 445–468.

von Rossum, Matthias and Jeannette Kemp, eds., *Desertion in the Early Modern World: A Comparative History* (London: Bloomsbury, 2016).

Voth, Hans-Joachim, "Time and Work in Eighteenth Century London," *Journal of Economic History*, 58, 1 (1998): 29–58.

Voth, Hans-Joachim, *Time and Work in England 1750–1830* (Oxford: Oxford University Press, 2000).

Vucinich, Wayne S. ed., *The Peasant in Nineteenth-Century Russia* (Stanford: Stanford University Press, 1968).

Wagner, William, *Marriage, Property and Law in Late Imperial Russia* (Oxford: Oxford University Press, 1994).

Wahrman, Dror, *The Making of the Modern Self: Identity and Culture in Eighteenth-century England* (New Haven: Yale University Press, 2004).

Walicki, Andrzej, *The Slavophile Controversy: History of a Conservative Utopia in Nineteenth-century Russia* (New York: Oxford University Press, 1975).

Wallerstein, Immanuel, *The Modern World-System: Capitalist Agriculture and the Origins of the European World-Economy in the Sixteenth Century* (New York: Atheneum, 1974).

Walsh, Lorena, *Motives of Honor, Pleasure & Profit: Plantation Management in the Colonial Chesapeake, 1607–1763* (Chapel Hill: University of North Carolina Press, 2010).

Walvin, James, *Searching for the Invisible Man: Slaves and Plantation Life in Jamaica* (Cambridge, MA: Harvard University Press, 1978).
Wanquet, Claude, *Histoire d'une Révolution, la Réunion, 1789-1803* (Paris: Editions Laffitte, 1980-1984).
Wanquet, Claude, *La France et la première abolition de l'esclavage (1794-1802)* (Paris: Karthala, 1998).
Ward, James R., "The Profitability of Sugar Planting in the British West Indies, 1650-1834," *Economic History Review*, 31, 2 (1978): 197-213.
Ward, James R., *British West India Slavery, 1750-1834: The Process of Amelioration* (Oxford: Oxford University Press, 1988).
Warren, James Francis, *The Sulu Zone, 1768-1898: The Dynamics of External Trade, Slavery, and Ethnicity in the Transformation of a Southeast Asian Maritime State*, 2nd ed. (Singapore: Singapore University Press, 1981; reprint, Singapore: National University of Singapore, 2007).
Watson, James ed., *Asian and African Systems of Slavery* (Berkeley: University of California Press, 1980).
Webb, Sidney and Beatrice Webb, *The History of Trade Unionism*, 2nd ed. (London: Longmans, 1911).
Weil, Patrick, *Qu'est-ce qu'un Français?* (Paris: Grasset, 2007).
Weinerman, Eli, "The Polemics Between Moscow and Central Asians on the Decline of Central Asia and Tsarist Russia's Role in the History of the Region," *The Slavonic and East European Review*, 71, 3 (1993): 428-481.
Weir, Robert, "Shaftesbury's Darling: British Settlement in the Carolinas at the Close of the Seventeenth Century," in Nichols Canny, ed., *The Origin of Empire: British Overseas Enterprise to the Close of the Seventeenth Century: Oxford History of the British Empire*, vol. 1 (Oxford: Oxford University Press, 1998): 375-397.
Wells, Robert, *The Population of the British Colonies in America before 1776: A Survey of Census Data* (Princeton: Princeton University Press, 1975).
Werner, Michael and Bénédicte Zimmermann, eds., *De la comparaison à l'histoire croisée* (Paris: Seuil, 2004).
Wheatcroft, Stephen, "Crisis and Condition of the Peasantry in Late Imperial Russia," in Esther Kingston-Mann, and Timothy Mixter, eds., *Peasant Economy, Culture and Politics of European Russia, 1800-1921* (Princeton, NJ: Princeton University Press, 1991): 101-127.
Wheeler, Roxann, *The Complexion of Race: Categories of Difference in Eighteenth-Century British Culture* (Philadelphia: University of Pennsylvania Press, 2002).
Wiesner-Hanks, Merry, "World History and the History of Women, Gender, and Sexuality," *Journal of World History*, 18, 1 (2007): 53-67.
Wilbur, Elvira M. "Was Russian Peasant Agriculture Really That Impoverished? New Evidence from a Case Study From the 'Impoverished Center' at the End of the Nineteenth Century," *Journal of Economic History*, 43, 1 (1983): 137-144.
Williams, Eric, *Capitalism and Slavery* (Chapel Hill: University of North Carolina Press, 1944).

Williamson, Jeffrey, "Why Was British Growth So Slow during the Industrial Revolution?" *Journal of Economic History*, 44, 3 (1984): 687–712.
Wink, André, *Al-Hind. The Making of the Indo-Islamic World* (Leiden: Brill, 2004).
Wink, Markus, "The World's Oldest Trade. Dutch Slavery and Slave Trade in the Indian Ocean in the Seventeenth Century," *Journal of World History*, 14, 2 (2003): 131–177.
Wirtschafter, Elise Kimerling, *From Serf to Russian Soldier* (Princeton, NJ: Princeton University Press, 1990).
Wirtschafter, Elise Kimerling, "Legal Identity and the Possession of Serfs in Imperial Russia," *The Journal of Modern History*, 70, 3 (1998): 561–587.
Witzenrath, Christopher ed., *Eurasian Slavery, Ransom and Abolition in World History, 1200–1860* (Farnham: Ashgate, 2015):
Wood, Peter, *Black Majority: Negroes in Colonial South Carolina from 1670 through the Stono Rebellion* (New York: Knopf, 1974).
Woodman, Harold, "Sequel to Slavery: The New History Views the Post-bellum South," *The Journal of Southern History*, 43, 4 (1977): 523–554.
Woods, Donna, "The Operation of the Masters and Servants Act in the Black Country, 1858–1875," *Midland History*, 7 (1982): 93–115.
Worobec, Christine D. *Peasant Russia: Family and Community in the Post-Emancipation Period* (Princeton, NJ: Princeton University Press, 1991).
Wortman, Richard, *Development of a Russian Legal Consciousness* (Chicago: University of Chicago Press, 1976).
Wright, Gavin, "Slavery and the Cotton Boom," *Explorations in Economic History*, 12, 4 (1975): 439–451.
Wright, Gavin, *Old South, New South* (Baton Rouge: Lousiana State University Press, 1997).
Wright, Gavin, *Slavery and American Economic Development* (Baton Rouge: Louisiana State University Press, 2003).
Wright, Gavin, "Slavery and the Rise of Nineteenth-Century American Economy," *The Journal of Economic Perspectives*, 36, 2 (2022): 123–148.
Wrigley, Edward, *Continuity, Chance and Change: The Character of the Industrial Revolution in England* (Cambridge: Cambridge University Press, 1988).
Wrigley, Edward Anthony and Roger Schofield, *The Population History of England: A Reconstruction* (Cambridge: Cambridge University Press, 1982).
Wrigley, Edward Anthony, Robert Davies, Jim Oeppen and Roger Schofield, *English Population History from Family Reconstitution, 1580–1837* (Cambridge: Cambridge University Press, 1997).
Yaney, George, *The Urge to Mobilize: Agrarian Reform in Russia, 1861–1930* (Urbana: Illinois University Press, 1982).
Yerri, Urban, *L'Indigène dans le droit colonial français* (Paris: fondation Varenne, 2010).
Young, Arthur, *Political Essays Concerning the Present State of the British Empire* (London: Strahan and Cadell, 1772).

Young, Arthur, *General Report on Enclosures* (London: British Library, 1808).
Zahedieh, Nuala, *Capital and the Colonies: London and the Atlantic Economy, 1600–1700* (Cambridge: Cambridge University Press, 2010).
Zakharova, Lidia, ed., *Velikie reformy v Rossii, 1856–1874* (The great reforms in Russia, 1856–1874) (Moscow: Nauka, 1992).
Zakharova, Lidia and John Bushnell, eds., *The Great Reforms in Russia* (Bloomington: Indiana University Press, 1994).
Zaller, Robert, "Representative Governments: How Sure a Thing," in Maija Jansson, ed., *Realities of Representation: State Building in Early Modern Europe and America* (New York: Palgrave, 2007): 215–224.
Zemon Davis, Natalie, *The Return of Martin Guerre* (Cambridge: Harvard University Press, 1983).
Zimmermann, Andrew, *Alabama in Africa* (Princeton, NJ: Princeton University Press, 2010).
Zolotareva, Olga, *Voices of Equality: American Anti-slavery and Russian Anti-serfdom Poetry*, https://ucbcluj.org/voices-of-equality-american-anti-slavery-and-russian-anti-serfdom-poetry/.
Zuccarelli, François, "Le recrutement de travailleurs sénégalais par l'État indépendant du Congo, 1884–1896," *Revue française d'histoire d'outre-mer*, X LVII, 168–169 (1960): 475–481.
Zurndorfer, Harriet. *Change and Continuity in Chinese Local History* (Leiden: Brill, 1989).
Zürcher, Erik-Jan, ed., *Fighting for a Living: A Comparative History of Military Labour, 1500–2000* (Amsterdam: Amsterdam University Press, 2013).
Zyrianov, Pavel, *Krest'ianskaia Obshchina Evropeiskoi Rossii 1907–1914 gg* (The peasant commune in European Russia) (Moscow: Nauka, 1992).

Websites

www.slavevoyages.org/tast/assessment/estimates.faces
https://collab.iisg.nl/web/LabourRelations/
https://labour.org.uk/category/latest/press-release/digital/
https://libguides.princeton.edu/c.php?g=84552&p=542394
https://microform.digital/boa/collections/67/volumes/451/slave-trade-1641-1838
www.archives.gov/research/african-americans/slavery-records-civil.html
www.genealogie.mu/index.php/en/expertise/research/online-archives
www.nationalarchives.gov.uk/help-with-your-research/research-guides/slavery-or-slave-owners
http://bit.ly/46qGllG
www.ucl.ac.uk/lbs/project/details/
www.zwangsarbeit-archiv.de/en/index.html

INDEX

absenteeism, 67, 110, 205, 207
Algeria, 87, 209, 214, 257, 259, 267
Angola, 27, 152, 257
Antilles, 14, 27, 94, 96, 111, 177–180, 213
anti-vagrancy, 243
apprentices, 30, 55, 60, 63–64, 72, 190, 197–198, 216, 247, 272
apprenticeship, 56, 65, 85, 94, 195, 197–198, 209, 211, 243, 258, 277
aristocracy, 6, 85, 234, 249, 275–278
army, 37, 46, 50, 67, 74, 132, 134, 263–264, 269, 274
Assam, 80, 206–208
Australia, 9, 117
Azov, 48

Baltic, 6, 124–125, 130, 134, 229, 231, 234
Barbados, 14, 66, 68–69, 155–157, 159, 177, 198
beggars, 91, 101, 200
Belgium, 143, 170, 253, 256, 263
Bengal, 80–83, 199, 203, 206–207, 251
Bentham, Jeremy, 187, 199, 209, 217, 270
Bessarabia, 47, 130–131
birth rates, 126, 137, 222, 224
Black Earth, 121, 127, 221
Black Sea, 41, 48–49, 124, 130–131, 133–134, 234
Bombay, 81, 83, 199, 203–204
Bordeaux, 105–106, 173, 177–178, 180
Borneo, 250
Brazil, 7–8, 28, 152, 158, 180, 244, 251–253
Brazza, Pierre Savorgnan de, 261, 264–267
breach of contract, 56, 93, 200, 207–208, 215, 240, 243
Brittany, 92, 171

Burke, Edmund, 188
Burma, 250

Calcutta, 81–83, 203–204, 206–207, 251
Canada, 9, 49, 63, 67, 92–104, 107, 117, 130, 168, 180, 225
Cape, 77, 81, 105, 254, 257
Caribbean, 7, 10, 14, 27, 61–62, 92, 104, 106–107, 151–155, 158–160, 162, 174, 177–178, 181–182, 193–194, 202, 215, 238, 252
Carlyle, Thomas, 202
Casement, Roger, 266
caste, 78–80, 82, 84, 204
Catherine II, 48–49, 121, 132
Catholic, 42, 62, 108, 132–133, 212, 218, 260
Caucasus, 18, 28, 44, 130–131, 227–229, 231
Central Asia, 38, 40–42, 47, 78–79, 81, 125, 129–131, 228, 232, 234, 250–252
cereals, 130, 168, 259
Ceylon, 250
Chesapeake, 64, 66–69
chiefs, 40, 73, 254–255, 259, 261–262, 264–265, 272
children, 40, 42–43, 56, 60, 63, 65–66, 69–70, 72–73, 78–80, 84, 102–104, 109–110, 126, 137, 142, 146, 171, 198, 200, 226, 249, 266–268, 274
China, 8, 11, 16, 22, 37, 134–135, 165, 182, 250
Christian socialists, 196
citizenship, 8, 63, 193–194, 211, 242, 260
civilizing mission, 228, 256, 258, 260, 262, 265
coal, 247
Coastal Guinea, 257
Cobden, John, 202

345

Code, 249
Code Noir, 108–109
coercion, 1, 3, 10, 16, 19, 21, 25, 31–32, 55, 57, 72, 117, 119, 160, 201, 226, 240, 242, 245
colonists, 63, 100, 104, 106, 203, 274
common law, 59, 70, 82, 111
competition, 9, 22, 31, 91, 100, 104, 123, 134, 142, 156, 171, 182, 191, 203, 212, 237, 243, 245, 249, 253–254, 263, 273–276, 278
concession companies, 264, 267–268
concubines, 26, 82, 95, 113
Condorcet, Nicolas, 191
corn, 8, 106, 130, 141, 167, 201, 237, 239, 241
corvées, 44, 98, 100, 121, 123, 133
Cossack, 41, 47, 223
cotton, 2, 4–7, 23, 95, 125, 128, 130, 150–151, 154, 158, 164–166, 168, 172, 178, 181, 189, 195, 231–232, 235–239, 242–244, 246, 251–252, 258, 275
court, 32–33, 44–45, 51–52, 55, 65–66, 68, 74–75, 79, 88, 111–112, 185, 214–215, 222, 240, 243, 255, 267
credit, 64, 77, 80–82, 90, 128, 138, 161–162, 165, 174, 179, 181, 198, 227, 230, 232, 241, 244
Crimea, 41–42, 48, 131, 134
Cuba, 8, 17, 28, 159, 244, 251

debt, 11, 24, 64, 77, 79, 82, 161–162, 172, 201
debt bondage, 77, 79, 81–82, 84, 98, 201
Deccan, 78–79
Delaware, 65
deserters, 30, 50, 208
desertion, 30, 94, 99, 207–208, 215, 263–264, 272
Diderot, Denis, 190
domestic servants, 30–31, 42–43, 55, 66, 88, 90, 93, 99, 146, 188, 257, 272
domesticity, 3, 271
dowry, 43, 52, 81, 102–103
dubla, 79
Dutch, 16, 21–22, 68, 76–77, 81, 97, 104, 106, 117, 151–152, 155–156, 195, 210, 250

Eastern Europe, 3–4, 121, 229, 279
Egypt, 251–253

EIC (East India Company), 80–82, 84, 199–200, 207, 254
enclosures, 64, 85, 138–140, 223
engagés, 8, 29, 93–94, 108, 214
engagisme, 77
Enlightenment, 159, 190–192, 217
Ethiopia, 77–78
Eurocentrism, 12, 17, 23, 271

Faidherbe, Louis, 260
famine, 84, 126, 222, 224, 259
Fergana, 125, 251
Finland, 226, 228
food, 145, 148
foreign trade, 48, 135, 172, 179, 181
French Equatorial Africa, 258
frontier, 15, 18, 28, 42, 46, 250
fugitive, 28, 46, 74, 111
Fur, 49, 130

gender, 13–15, 66, 80, 146, 244
Georgia, 74, 240, 243–244
Germany, 9, 22, 32, 125, 196, 225, 251, 256
global labor history, 10, 13, 21
globalization, 11, 250
Gold Coast, 152, 162, 254, 257
grain, 79, 124–125, 127, 130–132, 134–135, 154, 172, 224–225, 231, 237, 259
Grodet, Albert, 265–266
Guadeloupe, 9, 92, 107–109, 113, 159, 174–175, 177–178, 192–194, 210–211, 213
guild, 190, 247
Guinea, 107, 173, 257–258
Gujarat, 79, 82

Haiti, 178, 195
hali, 79
humanitarianism, 256

indentured, 3, 8, 14–15, 23–25, 27–28, 31, 33, 62–67, 70, 85–86, 92–94, 99–100, 104–107, 110, 114–115, 155, 167–168, 173, 175, 203–204, 206–207, 209, 214–217, 235, 241–242, 251, 258, 270, 273, 277
Indian Ocean, 7, 10–11, 24–25, 75–79, 81–83, 85, 94, 107, 109, 152, 161, 173, 201, 250, 277

indigent, 59, 91
indigo, 93, 106, 175, 178, 206–207
Indonesia, 77
Industrial Revolution, 1, 4–6, 8, 12, 18–19, 60, 85, 117, 124, 136–151, 161, 164–168, 172, 225, 235, 239, 247, 276–277
industrialization, 4–6, 31–32, 67, 118, 123–124, 128, 136–137, 147–148, 164, 187, 192, 196, 225, 234, 238–239, 270, 278
industrious revolution, 137, 142, 146, 168
intermediaries, 23, 93, 97–98, 174, 178, 205
international trade, 48, 124, 133–134, 149–150, 163, 172, 176, 237, 253, 269
Ireland, 61, 101, 125, 240
irrigation, 232
Ivory Coast, 173

Jamaica, 27, 66, 73, 110, 113, 154–157, 159, 174, 177, 180, 194–195, 198, 215
Jaurès, Jean, 260
Jews, 132, 227
journeymen, 55, 247
Justice of the Peace, 88

kamīus, 82
Kenya, 29, 257
Khanate, 37, 40, 48, 125, 131
Kharkiv, 231
Kherson, 49
kholopy, 40, 42–43, 54
kidnapping, 49
krepostnoe pravo, 44
krepostnye liudy, 44

La Rochelle, 95, 97, 99, 105–106, 173
labor contracts, 248
labor inspection, 269
labor productivity, 142, 148–149, 170, 172, 182, 208, 225, 275
Lancashire, 137, 144, 197
land redistribution, 223
landlords, 45, 47, 52–53, 69, 121–123, 127, 129, 132–133, 220–221, 228, 235, 272

landowners, 1, 3, 29, 33, 37–39, 45, 47, 49–50, 53, 65, 67, 85, 96, 114–115, 122–123, 127–128, 132, 134, 157–158, 169, 176, 202–203, 205–206, 221, 223, 226, 228–230, 235, 272–276
Latin America, 11
legal pluralism, 33
legal status, 8, 15, 24, 39, 45, 51, 55, 67, 70, 99, 108–109, 112, 114, 133, 217, 248
Leroy Beaulieu, Paul, 260
livestock, 125, 139–140, 144, 154, 158
Louis Napoléon, 214
Louisiana, 6, 17, 26, 28, 75, 92–93, 104, 106, 109, 181–182, 236–237, 242–244
Lugard, Frederick, 255

Macaulay, Thomas, 200
Madagascar, 76, 78, 84, 107, 173, 203
Maine, Henri Sumner, 199, 242, 254–255, 270
Malawi, 29, 77
Malaysia, 215, 250
Malthus, Thomas, 149, 188, 222
Manchuria, 250
Marathas, 79–80, 83
maroons, 27–28, 31, 73, 110
Martinique, 92, 104, 107–109, 113, 159, 174–175, 177–178, 180, 194, 209, 211, 213
Marx, Karl, 18, 23–24, 26, 35, 136, 138, 147, 149, 176, 183, 196, 246, 271
Massachusetts, 70, 74, 242
master, 16, 55, 57, 87, 113, 258
Masters and Servants Acts, 2, 57, 72, 88, 188, 200, 240, 247, 256, 258
Mauritius, 6, 8, 12, 15, 28–29, 77, 84, 108–109, 113, 173, 192–193, 203–205, 208, 210, 214–215, 273–274
mechanization, 2, 7, 144, 146, 158, 172, 189, 231, 239, 241, 244, 246–247
Mediterranean, 24, 40, 43, 48, 64, 131, 161, 169, 192, 253
merchants, 30, 38, 83, 156, 178, 189, 222, 258
Merivale, Herman, 197
microhistory, 10, 12, 60
migrants, 89
Mill, James, 199
Mill, John Stuart, 199–201

minimum wage, 58–59, 208
monopoly, 23, 104–105, 129, 156, 159, 174, 178–179, 191, 220, 274
mortality rate, 97, 100, 155, 157, 175, 208
Mughal, 79, 84, 125, 199
mulattoes, 70
Muscovite, 39, 41–42, 45
Muslim, 28, 38, 42, 79, 83, 107, 125, 232
Mysore, 80, 83

Nantes, 96, 105–106, 108, 112, 173–174, 178, 180
Napoleonic War, 5, 167, 182, 275
nationalism, 134, 192, 233
neo-colonialism, 2
New England, 63
New France, 93, 96–98, 100–102, 104
Nigeria, 29, 257
Nogays, 40, 42
Normandy, 95–96, 171
Novorussia, 49, 227

odnovortsy, 39
Orenburg, 44, 125, 227
Ottoman Empire, 7, 11, 16, 37, 40, 42, 47–48, 125, 130–131, 135, 253

peasant commune, 54, 133, 219, 223–224
peasant-soldier, 15, 37, 43, 49–50, 72
peasantry, 126, 222, 224, 226
Peonage, 251
Persian Gulf, 77–78
pluriactivity, 4, 169, 181, 227, 244
Poland, 37, 40, 48, 130, 132, 228
Poland-Lithuania, 37, 40, 132
Polanyi, Karl, 9, 18, 58–59, 235, 246, 270, 278
pomest'e, 38–39
Poor Laws, 55, 58–60, 72, 91, 188, 197–198, 212, 247–248
Portuguese, 12, 83, 85, 101, 106–107, 152, 162, 174, 251, 257, 263, 271
profits, 2, 4–6, 8, 19, 44, 62, 68, 100, 104, 148, 152–153, 156, 158, 160, 163, 166–167, 172–173, 175–179, 181–183, 189, 191, 233–234, 238–239, 265
property, 17, 19, 22–23, 31–32, 35–36, 39–40, 44, 56, 61, 70, 72–73, 79–81, 102, 108–109, 114, 128, 138–139, 158, 176, 178, 186, 189, 193, 196, 209–210, 220, 223, 232, 237, 244, 247, 249, 259, 262, 273
proto-industry, 122, 137
prud'hommes, 87–88, 90–91, 213

Quakers, 189, 192, 202, 218
Oubangui-Chari, 258
Quebec, 93, 101–103, 181, 274
quit-rent, 121, 123, 127

Rajputs, 79–80
Raynal, Abbé de, 190
redemption, 220, 229
refugee, 262
rent, 207
rentiers, 3, 67, 114, 183, 249, 276–277
resistance, 7, 25, 27–28, 31, 59, 73–74, 110
Réunion Island, 108, 113, 158, 192, 209, 211, 214, 259, 273
rice, 197, 244
Rousseau, Jean-Jacques, 190, 264
runaway, 27, 73–74

Safavid, 125
sailor, 3–4, 25, 30, 83, 99–100, 113, 272
Saint-Domingue, 6–7, 104, 107–110, 112–113, 159, 174–175, 177–178, 180–182, 192–194, 202, 276, 278
Schoelcher, Victor, 210–213, 260
scramble for Africa, 2, 253
seasonality, 58, 144, 239, 241
Second Empire, 214, 260
Senegal, 105, 214, 258–260, 262, 265
Sepoy, 80, 207, 254–255
servants in husbandry, 63, 88–89, 145, 169
servitude, 7–9, 24, 40, 42–43, 62–68, 71–72, 77–80, 82–84, 98, 100, 104–115, 155, 175, 181, 201, 216, 240–241, 243, 249, 251, 255, 258, 277
sharecropping, 210, 243–244
Siberia, 6, 15, 41, 47, 49, 54, 129, 226, 230, 234, 250, 277
sirdars, 203, 205
Sismondi, Simon de, 209–210
Société Notre-Dame, 96

soil, 154–155, 158, 186, 221–222, 224, 228, 236, 268
soldier-colonists, 99–100
Somalia, 77–78, 257
Somerset, 111, 185–186, 240
Soslovie, 221
South Asia, 11, 16, 77–78, 80, 125, 203
Speenhamland, 58–59
stock exchange, 138
stock markets, 2
Stolypin, Petr, 223, 278
Sudan, 77, 257–258, 262
Suez, 253, 269

Tashkent, 125, 129
Tatars, 41–42, 49
tax, 37–39, 41, 43, 46, 51, 83, 98, 128, 177, 181, 229, 231, 237, 265
tea, 129, 131, 134–135, 159, 180, 206–208, 251, 277
textile, 232
Thiers, Adolphe, 212
tobacco, 93, 106
Trade Union Act, 247
Transcaucasia, 228–229
Tsar, 48, 133, 194, 220, 230
Turkestan, 125, 229, 231, 233, 251
Turkey, 253, 263

Ukraine, 6, 15, 41, 47–48, 128, 130, 132–134, 227, 229–231, 234
Ulster plantation, 62

unemployment, 89, 136, 144, 147, 212, 248
unions, 31, 60, 91, 109, 172, 182, 248–249, 256
urbanization, 169, 225
utilitarianism, 185, 217
Uzbekistan, 125

vagrancy, 58
Virginia, 32, 62, 65–66, 70–71, 74, 154, 177, 185, 237, 243–244
Volga, 47, 130, 227
Voltaire, François-Marie Arouet, 190
votchina, 38

wage, 23, 143, 149, 171, 204, 225, 236, 241–242
Wallerstein, Immanuel, 6, 124, 161, 164
war captives, 40–42, 70, 95
Webb, Sidney, 247
West Africa, 26, 29, 107, 118, 162, 254, 258–259, 261, 265, 269
wheat, 2, 6, 50, 124–125, 129–131, 134, 168, 170, 172, 201, 209, 225, 230–231, 234, 241, 247, 259, 275, 277
wine, 20, 171–172, 209, 259
woman, 52, 56, 66, 102
workhouse, 59–60, 213, 215

yields, 140–141, 149, 170, 183, 232

Zanzibar, 29, 77, 255, 257
zemstvos, 222

For EU product safety concerns, contact us at Calle de José Abascal, 56–1°, 28003 Madrid, Spain or eugpsr@cambridge.org.

www.ingramcontent.com/pod-product-compliance
Ingram Content Group UK Ltd.
Pitfield, Milton Keynes, MK11 3LW, UK
UKHW021941250126.
467337UK00021B/1078